PRINCIPLES OF
POLITICAL ECONOMY

BY

CHARLES GIDE

PROFESSEUR AU COLLEGE DE FRANCE
PROFESSEUR HONORAIRE A LA FACULTÉ DE DROIT
DE PARIS

TRANSLATED FROM THE
TWENTY-THIRD FRENCH EDITION BY
ERNEST F. ROW, B.Sc. (Econ.)

AMS PRESS
NEW YORK

Reprinted from the edition of 1924: Boston

First AMS edition published in 1971

Manufactured in the United States of America

International Standard Book Number: 0-404-02739-3

Library of Congress Catalog Card Number: 78-126685

AMS PRESS INC.
NEW YORK, N.Y. 10003

PREFACE

This book has been completely revised in order to include the changes necessitated by the great events of the last few years. I am anxious that the book should retain the character it has always had since it was first published, now many years ago. What I should like my readers to find in it is not so much a learned exposition of economic theories, or a new social programme, as a clear picture of the economic world as it actually exists — a vast world that is full of drama, for what it shows us is not the play of impassive laws, dealing out fortune or misery to individuals and nations, but the impassioned struggles on the one hand, and the brotherly assistance on the other, by which men strive to acquire the first or to avoid the second.

Whatever may be said to the contrary, economic science has not been proclaimed bankrupt by the Great War and the Russian revolution which sprang from it. It is quite otherwise; these events have for the most part confirmed and completed, through experiment on the most colossal scale that has ever been known, the essential principles of political economy as they have hitherto been taught.

In some cases, to be sure, economic phenomena have appeared on such a scale that they have, I will not say belied, but surpassed all expectation; such, for example, are the social disturbances caused by the issue of inconvertible paper money. It is probable, also, that the war has aggravated the bitterness of social inequality, and may even seem to have aroused in the workers a certain dislike of work, owing to the demoralizing contrast between the fortunes so easily acquired by some and the misery so unjustly inflicted upon others.

In any case, the war has led to an extraordinary heightening of interest in economic problems, by showing how important they are to the life of the various peoples, whether it be the older nations, clinging, half ruined, to the edge of the abyss, or those that have been newly created and are trying to find their way. Many younger members of the last generation, both in France and elsewhere, have found this book a friendly guide to the knowledge and love of these problems; my hope is that it may render the same service to the present generation.

CHARLES GIDE

PUBLISHER'S NOTE

This book is a translation of the twenty-third edition of Professor Gide's *Principes d'Économie Politique*, published in 1921, the first edition having appeared in 1883. In accordance with the plan followed in the English versions of earlier editions of the book, certain modifications and adaptations have been made, in order to render it more serviceable to American readers. In a few cases the text has been slightly abridged by the omission of details relating solely to French economic or legal procedure. But no material alterations or omissions have been made in the author's text without notice being given of them in the footnotes, and all matter for which the translator is responsible — other than statistics, etc., substituted for French ones — is placed within *square brackets*.

The translator has made some use of Dr. C. W. A. Veditz's English version of the eighth French edition, where the author had left his text unchanged. But this book may be regarded, broadly speaking, as an entirely new work.

The Appendix, which includes a brief discussion of certain topics of especial interest to American readers, has been prepared by Dr. E. A. Goldenweiser, who has made use of certain parts of the material prepared by Dr. Veditz for his translation of the eighth edition.

CONTENTS

GENERAL NOTIONS

BOOK II — CIRCULATION

BOOK III — DISTRIBUTION

PART I — THE VARIOUS MODES OF DISTRIBUTION

PART II — THE VARIOUS CLASSES OF RECIPIENTS

PRINCIPLES OF
POLITICAL ECONOMY

GENERAL NOTIONS

CHAPTER I — ECONOMIC SCIENCE

I. THE OBJECT OF POLITICAL ECONOMY

The heavenly bodies, the earth that we inhabit, the elements that it contains, as well as the animals and plants that live on its surface — in fact, all the things that constitute the material universe and all the relations that exist between them — are the subjects of a distinct group of sciences known as *the physical and natural sciences*.

But in this vast world there are other objects no less worthy of our study, namely, men themselves, living in society; in fact, they could not possibly live otherwise. The relations that unite men socially form the subject of a separate group of sciences, called *social sciences*. As there are among men many kinds of social relations — moral, legal, economic, political, religious, and, finally, linguistic relations which serve as a vehicle for all the others — so there are many distinct social sciences, known as ethics, law, political economy, politics, the science of languages, the science of religions, and so forth.

It is true that the lines of demarcation among the social sciences, which all deal ultimately with man as a member of society, cannot be drawn so sharply as those that separate sciences having dissimilar subjects, such as geology, botany, and zoölogy. Indeed, the frontiers of these sciences. especially of the three most closely related to each other, will always be more or less indefinite: how are we to study exchange, rent, money-lending, or wages, without reference to property, contract, and duty?

But though the economist, the lawyer, and the moralist often meet on the same ground, they look at things from different points of view. To *do our duty*, to *exercise our rights*, to *provide for our wants*, are three quite different aims of human activity; and it is the last of these that is the proper subject of economic science.

We may say, therefore, without trying to be more precise, that political economy has to do with only those relations of men living in society which tend to satisfy their wants and promote their welfare, so far as this welfare depends upon the possession of material objects.

At present there is a tendency to divide the science into two branches: *pure political economy*, and *social economics*.

On the one hand, *pure political economy* (sometimes called also *economics*) studies those economic relations that arise naturally among men living together, just as one would study the relations arising among any other bodies. It does not undertake to pass judgment on these relations, either from the moral or from the practical standpoint, but simply to explain what they are. Thus it claims to be an exact science, and even to be able to employ the methods of mathematics.

On the other hand, *social economics* studies rather the voluntary relations which men have established among themselves in the form of social organizations, written laws, or other institutions of any kind, with the object of improving their social conditions. It undertakes to investigate and determine the best means for achieving this end. Hence it partakes rather of the character of the moral sciences, which enquire *what ought to be*, and of the arts, which enquire *what must be done*. It is also described sometimes, especially by German economists, as *social politics*.[1]

This distinction between pure political economy and social politics is made in all special treatises in virtue of the principle of division of labour. But in a treatise written for instruction, like the present volume, it would be rather awkward than otherwise, for the separation of theory from practice would detract from the interest of the exposition. We shall therefore have to deal with social economics as well as with political economy.

The wide field of political economy must itself be subdivided, to

[1] Social economics, or social politics, should not be confused with *applied political economy*. The latter points out the best practical means of increasing the wealth of a country, such as banks, railways, monetary and commercial systems, and so forth, whereas social economics seeks especially to make men happier by providing them not only with more comfort but with more security, more independence, and more leisure. Consequently it is concerned more particularly with the working classes. These two sister sciences live in two different worlds and are scarcely even on friendly terms: one dwells in the world of business and the other in social reform committees.

Questions of applied political economy are scarcely touched on in this volume: they will be found dealt with in the author's *Political Economy* (Translated by C. H. M. Archibald; published by D. C. Heath and Company.)

make it easier for us to find our way through it.   The classical three-fold division into Production, Distribution, and Consumption is due to the French economist, Jean-Baptiste Say.   This division corresponds to the three fundamental questions: How do men produce wealth?   How do they share it among themselves?   What use do they make of it?   Then later on there was withdrawn from the immense domain of Production all that has to do with Exchange — commerce, credit, etc. — and to this part was given the name *Circulation*.   But, as we shall see, to exchange is to produce; the only difference is that this kind of production of utilities does not involve material alterations in the object exchanged, as industrial operations do.

On the other hand, most economists have dropped that part of the science which relates to Consumption, because, they say, the question of the use made of wealth is a moral one.   Such is not our opinion.   The use made of wealth, whether it be consumed or saved, is an economic act of the first importance, and one which is obviously the final cause of all the economic acts which precede it.   Political economy, it is true, has hitherto looked almost entirely at the producer, but there is some ground for thinking that the consumer is destined to play the leading rôle on the economic stage.

These divisions of our subject are regarded nowadays as somewhat out of date, and in modern books on political economy they are often replaced by other classifications which aim at presenting the facts in a more scientific form.   That plan may have its advantages, but we have not thought it expedient, in a book like this, to upset the traditional framework at the risk of bewildering the students for whom it is particularly intended.   We have thought it necessary, however, to add an introductory section concerning Wants and Value.

II. THE FORMATION OF ECONOMIC SCIENCE

It was in 1615 that political economy first received the name under which it is now known.   This was in a French book by Antoine de Montchrétien, called *Traicté de l'Œconomie Politique.*

This name has been criticised, and many others have been proposed in place of it, as being more scientific.   It would obviously be better, from a terminological point of view, if our science were described, like most sciences, by a single word, such as *economy* or *economics*, especially since the name *economy* was already in use in ancient times and one of the books of Xenophon even bears this word as a title.   But for the ancients it meant what we may call domestic economics, or household economy (οἶκος, household, and νόμος, law or rule). The qualifying adjective *political*, chosen by Montchrétien, indicated that the science had no longer to do with the economy of the household, but with that of the nation, and the name was particularly appropriate because it announced a historic revolution — the establishment of the great states of modern Europe.

But we must beware of regarding this date, which saw the baptism of political economy, as the date also of its birth. As a study of facts, political economy goes back to a far earlier date, and, as a science, which means a systematic arrangement of these facts, it is more modern.

Economic facts, or some of them at any rate, take such a prominent place in the life even of primitive man that we can well believe that they must always have engaged man's attention. Exchange was practised as early as the stone age, and the law of labour is written in the first pages of Genesis. But a fact may be familiar without furnishing material for science. On the contrary, it only arouses curiosity and provokes a desire for explanation if it is something out of the ordinary. The subtle Greek philosophers do not seem to have felt any need to explain to themselves how and why free men were exempted from the law of labour by the institution of slavery: it seemed quite natural to them. But they observed and analysed with extreme care the nature of money, the division of industry into separate trades, and the methods of acquiring property. It was first the prophets of Israel, and, at a later date, the Church Fathers and the Doctors of the Middle Ages who, inspired by the same religious spirit, were impressed by the contrast between wealth and poverty. They condemned luxury, and, in particular, the practice of lending money at interest, which they called *usura vorax.*

Yet no one ever sought for the connection between these different questions; no one dreamed of grouping them together into a single science. They counted among the accomplishments of the sage rather than of the savant. They were matters of morals, or politics, or theology, and took the form of good advice, offered either to rulers or to individuals.

The discovery of America gave the first impetus, during the sixteenth and especially the seventeenth centuries, to the formation of a true economic theory in a systematic shape; that is to say, what had been merely advice now took the form of a body of co-ordinated and logical precepts. Countries like France, Italy, and England, seeing with envious eyes how Spain was acquiring treasure from her mines in the New World, sought to discover how they too might procure gold and silver. This was precisely the title of a book published by an Italian, Antonio Serra, only two years before that of Montchrétien (1613), viz., "How to make Gold and Silver abound in Kingdoms where there are no Mines." It was believed that the means consisted in the sale abroad of manufactured products; and, with this purpose in view, efforts were made to develop foreign trade and home manufactures by a complicated and artificial system of regulations to which the name *mercantile system* has generally been applied.

A strong reaction against all these "systems" took place in France in the middle of the eighteenth century. Men's one idea was a return to "a state of nature," and a repudiation of all artificial arrangements. All the literature of the eighteenth century is impregnated with this feeling, including political science in the writings of Rousseau and Montesquieu. Montesquieu's book, *The Spirit of Laws*, begins with the immortal sentence: "Laws are the necessary relations *resulting from the nature of things*."

It was only then that economic science was really born. In 1758, one of the physicians of the French king Louis XV, named Quesnay, published *Le Tableau Économique*. A group of eminent men became his disciples, and though they only called themselves *economists* they have ever since been celebrated in history as *physiocrats*.

The physiocratic school introduced two new ideas into economic science — ideas that were diametrically opposed to the mercantile system. These were: —

(1) Belief in the existence of a "natural and essential order of human societies" — such is the title of a book written by one of the physiocrats, Mercier de la Rivière. The evidence for this order becomes obvious as soon as the fact is observed, and we cannot help conforming to it. It is useless, therefore, to devise laws, regulations, and systems: all we need do is to *let things alone (laisser faire)*. The word *physiocracy* comes from two Greek words meaning "the government of nature."

(2) The superiority of agriculture over commerce and industry. The physiocrats regarded the soil, the forces of nature, as the only source of wealth, because it alone gives a *net product*. The non-agricultural classes of society are *sterile* classes.

The first of these principles was to serve as the foundation of the whole edifice of economic science. Indeed, no facts in themselves can form the basis of a science unless we discover relations of interdependence between them — an "essential and natural order." Nor was it only a new science that was inaugurated by the physiocratic doctrines; it was also a new political system, which was to last for a century and to achieve great things under the name of the liberal policy.[1]

Unfortunately the physiocrats were less happily inspired in their exclusively rural conception of production and of wealth, as we shall see later. In this respect they were rather behind their time than in advance of it, for, though they did not know it, they were living on the eve of the establishment of the industrial and capitalist régime. This fundamental error brought their system into discredit.

The publication in 1776 of *An Inquiry into the Nature and Causes of the Wealth of Nations*, by a Scotch professor, Adam Smith, marks a decisive era in the history of political economy. It assured the unquestioned pre-eminence of the English school of economists for nearly a hundred years, and procured for its author the title, not wholly deserved, of "the father of political economy."

Adam Smith, in fact, had a vision, inspired by genius, of the economic revolution that was already on the way. Moreover, he rejects the second physiocratic principle and gives to industry its legitimate place in the production of wealth. But he confirms and develops most brilliantly the first of these principles, namely, the belief in economic laws and in *laisser faire*, at least as a rule of practical conduct.

Again, he was far superior to the physiocrats in observing facts and in profiting by the lessons of history, and he so far enlarged the field of economic science that its boundaries have scarcely been extended since his time.

Not long after Adam Smith two economists appeared simultaneously in England, whose theories, lauded by some and execrated by others, left their mark for a century upon economic science. The first was Malthus, whose famous theory of the increase of population (1803), although it concerned a subject of a somewhat special nature, was destined to create a considerable stir throughout the whole realm of economic science, and to provoke a burning controversy which rages to-day as acutely as ever. The second, Ricardo, was still more celebrated for his theory of rent (1817) — a theory which, continually extended and transformed, became the basis of economic science and even of the doctrines which replaced it.

---

[1] This policy was first applied by Turgot, a famous economist of the same period, though he did not share the errors of the physiocratic school, first as intendant of Limoges and afterwards as minister of King Louis XVI. He began by decreeing *freedom of exchange*, by abolishing internal customs duties and grain taxes; later on he decreed *freedom of labour* by abolishing corporations or guilds.

In France, at the same period, Jean-Baptiste Say published his *Treatise on Political Economy* (1803) — a book that is truly French in its clearness of exposition, its excellent arrangement, and its classification of principles, but which has not made such fruitful contributions to the development of the science as those of the great leaders we have just mentioned. However, translated into all the languages of Europe, this book was the first really popular treatise on political economy, and has served more or less as a model for the innumerable well-known manuals that have been written since then.

It was Say's book in particular that set forth clearly the character of political economy as a natural, or purely descriptive, science. Adam Smith had defined it as "proposing to enrich both the people and the sovereign," thus giving a practical aim to the study and making it an art rather than a science. But Say, amending this definition, writes: "I would rather say that the object of political economy is to make known the means by which wealth produces *itself*, distributes *itself*, and consumes *itself*," meaning thereby that in the economic sphere everything acts spontaneously, of its own motion, automatically,[1] just like the functions of respiration, circulation, and digestion, which are essential to the physical life.

From this point, political economy can be regarded as definitely established in its classical form. But it was not long before it split up into a large number of schools, whose distinctive characteristics we shall indicate in the next chapter.[2]

III. WHETHER THERE ARE NATURAL LAWS IN POLITICAL ECONOMY

When we give the name of *science* to any branch of human knowledge, our object is not simply the conferment of an honorary title. We mean that the facts with which it deals are connected by certain relations called "laws."

In some spheres of knowledge the regular connection of occurrences is so obvious as to attract the attention even of persons least accustomed to scientific speculation. A mere glance at the sky is enough to show the regular nightly progress of the stars, the monthly suc-

---

[1] This is the significant title he gives to his book: *Treatise on Political Economy; or a Simple Exposition of the Way in which Wealth Produces, Distributes, and Consumes Itself.*

[2] To supplement these brief notes, as well as those in the following chapter, see Gide and Rist's *Histoire des Doctrines Economiques depuis les Physiocrates jusqu'à nos jours.* [English translation by R. Richards, *A History of Economic Doctrines*; published by D. C. Heath and Company.]

cession of the phases of the moon, and the annual journey of the
sun through the constellations.   In the remotest days of history,
shepherds watching their flocks and sailors steering their vessels
had already discovered the periodicity of these movements, and thus
paved the way for a true science, the oldest of all sciences —
astronomy.

The phenomena that are manifested in the constitution of bodies
organized and unorganized are not so simple as this, and the uniformity of their coexistence and succession is less easy to comprehend.
Long centuries had to elapse, therefore, before the human mind,
bewildered by the complexity of things, succeeded in laying hold of
the guiding thread, in finding order and regularity in these very
facts, and thus building up the sciences of physics, chemistry, and
biology.

Little by little the idea of a permanent regularity of phenomena
has penetrated all domains, even those which at first seemed destined
to remain closed to it for ever.   Even the winds and waves, which
poets had made the emblems of inconstancy and caprice, have been
brought, in their turn, under the sway of universal law.   The great
laws which govern currents of air and of water have been discovered,
and the sciences of meteorology and oceanography have been established.

The time was bound to come when this great idea of a Natural
Order of things, after having step by step invaded like a conquering
power all other fields of human knowledge, should at last penetrate
the domain of social facts.   The honour of having first recognized
and proclaimed the existence of what they called the "natural
government of things," is due, as we have seen, to the physiocrats,
though since their time the name of *natural laws* has been preferred.

After the physiocrats, the economists set themselves the task
of discovering natural laws in political economy, and indicated a
fairly large number of them, whose existence seemed as certain as
those of the physical and natural sciences — such universal, permanent, and ineluctable laws as the law of supply and demand, the law
of division of labour, the law of rent, the law of the decreasing rate
of interest, the law of competition, Gresham's law, etc.   And not
only did they find laws everywhere; many economists, especially
of the French school, tried to prove that these laws were "good"
— harmonious and providential, as Bastiat said — meaning that
they anticipated our wants, that they arranged things much better
than we could do by our written laws, and that they even laboured
to correct our errors.

Such an apologetic conception of economic laws could not fail to evoke a strong reaction. Such, indeed, was the case; and, as always happens, the reaction went too far. About the middle of last century the German school set out to denounce this search for natural laws as an error and a ridiculous madness. It declares that the method is completely sterile, and it acknowledges no other laws — if laws they can be called — than *historical* laws, which are naturally peculiar to each race, and which are in no sense universal or ineluctable. They do not rule men, but are, on the contrary, merely the expressions of their national characters and customs: such as they are, they may provide the explanation of their collective acts.

Nevertheless, we cannot give up the idea that economic facts are governed by laws, thus throwing aside the splendid effort made during the last two hundred years to establish political economy as a science in the true sense of the word. But we may admit that some change is needed in the idea that has resulted.

First of all, we must give up attributing to these laws a "normative" character, that is to say, assimilating them to the laws enacted by legislators for the welfare of the people. If in the economic world there are natural laws analogous to those of the physical world, then they must like them be perfectly indifferent to our preoccupations, and we shall more often have to strive against them than to make use of them.

Nor must we picture these laws to ourselves as seated on thrones, whence they govern the world. We must rid them of that imperative character which marks civil and penal laws, and which is symbolized in pictures and statues by a sword.

The word *law* should suggest no other idea than that of *a constant relation between certain facts*, such that if one fact is given, the others accompany it or follow it — as, for example, the relation between the quantity of a commodity and its price, or between its price and the demand for it.

Moreover, it is exactly the same with physical laws. They also express nothing more than certain relations that are spontaneously established between things — relations which can be called necessary ones *only if certain foregoing conditions are fulfilled.* Atoms of oxygen and hydrogen are not compelled to produce water; but *if* one atom of oxygen and two of hydrogen are brought together under certain conditions of temperature, pressure, etc., they will form water. Similarly, men are not obliged to buy and sell, but *if* a man disposed to sell meets a man disposed to buy, and *if* their offers are mutually acceptable, they will necessarily conclude a bargain at a fixed price which can be determined.

Now this price is not the outcome of the vendor's free will, nor of that of the purchaser, nor of that of both together, for there is a *market rate*, as it is called — a price which is quoted on the exchanges, which is forced upon the market, and to which all buyers and sellers must conform, despite oscillations upwards and downwards. That is what is meant when we say that there is a law of prices.

Some people, however, protest against describing these things as *laws*, and profess to see nothing in them but *tendencies*, because natural laws admit of no exceptions and involve the power of exact forecast, whereas the so-called laws of economics admit of many exceptions, and any forecasts based upon them would be mere guesses, too often proved false by actual events. But this twofold objection does not seem to us well founded.

In the first place, an economic law does not admit of *exceptions*, save in the same way that natural laws do. That is to say, it acts so long as it is not counteracted by an opposite force. It is not an exception to the law of gravitation that an aeroplane leaves the earth. Neither is it an exception to the law of labour that some men have found means to free themselves from it by making other men work for them. It is a law that the demand for a commodity increases as its price goes down: nevertheless it may happen as an "exceptional case" that a fall in price diminishes the demand instead of stimulating it, as would doubtless be the case with diamonds, as soon as they were produced artificially.[1] But even in this case the law of demand would not be violated: it would only be modified by another law, the law that makes the demand for luxuries depend upon a certain degree of scarcity.

In the second place, economic laws admit of making *forecasts*, just as physical laws do. There is no question, it is true, of such forecasts as the astronomer can make when he announces a hundred years beforehand the very minute and second when an eclipse of the sun or the moon will take place. But no other sciences are as exact as this. The botanist does not always know what the outcome of his cross-breeding will be. And the weather forecasts of meteorologists, other than those of the village almanacs, scarcely cover

---

[1] And as is the case at this very moment of writing, the fall in prices having caused a cessation of demand and a general deadness of the market. But why is this? Because consumers are expecting a still greater fall, and hope to precipitate it by their refusal to buy.

more than two or three days. Yet no one doubts that wind and rain, hailstorms and tempests, are governed by natural laws. Now a commercial crisis can be foretold much further in advance than the coming of a cyclone, and the passage of a train between Lyons and Marseilles is certainly less variable than the flow of the Rhône whose banks it follows; yet one is regulated by man and the other by nature. If, in fact, our economic forecasts are always uncertain and short-dated, it must by no means be concluded that economic facts depend only on chance and fancy, but simply that the motives that determine men's actions are too numerous and too intricately tangled for us to unravel the skein. Finally, if men one day become infinitely wise, it is probable that economic forecasting will operate with as much certainty as that of the astronomers.[1]

It is true that it would be absurd to try to foretell the movements and doings of Tom, Dick, or Harry; but this is of no interest to the economist. He is not a fortune-teller. The only thing that concerns him, whether in formulating laws or in setting up institutions, is *the behaviour of men taken in the mass.*

Notice, moreover, that those so-called practical people who most vehemently deny that economists can foretell happenings in the economic world, yet never fail to employ the art of forecasting in the ordinary course of their lives, and the management of their daily business. Every one who speculates — and who is there that does not speculate? — resorts in some fashion to scientific prevision. The financier who buys shares in a railway company foresees the continuity and progressive increase of traffic along a certain line, and the high price he pays for the shares indicates, whether he wishes it or not, his firm confidence in the regularity of an economic law. Yet it is quite evident that everybody who travels or sends goods by this railway, does so only because he *wills* to do so. And the finance minister who increases the tax on alcoholic drinks or the rate of postage knows perfectly well that the consumption of alcohol and the circulation of letters are optional, and will remain so. None the less he foresees that they will diminish: he is even obliged to estimate the extent of the diminution, in order to draw up his budget.

Is it necessary, then, to say that the existence of natural laws is in

---

[1] As an argument against the existence of natural laws in social matters, the fact is adduced that many things do not take place in the way *foreseen*. But this simply proves our ignorance. Think, rather, how often things fail to happen as *willed*. Does not this prove that there are stronger forces at work in the world than the will of man?

no way incompatible with individual initiative and activity, and that, on the contrary, it is the one essential condition of their efficacy? How could man exercise any useful control over facts if they were not bound together by a chain of known and constant relations?[1]

Of course there are some facts which are entirely removed from human influence, by reason of their size or their distance. Such are the phenomena of astronomy, geology, and even meteorology. We can only submit to them in silence; our faculty of prevision would not help us to avoid collision with a comet or to escape an earthquake. But there are many other regions in which modern science is all but supreme. Most of the compounds in inorganic chemistry, and those the most important, have been produced by the savant in his laboratory. To see the stock-breeder in his cattle-shed or the gardener in his garden, ceaselessly modifying animal and vegetable forms and creating new breeds, one would imagine that living nature allows itself to be moulded with as much docility as lifeless matter. Even atmospheric phenomena are not entirely withdrawn from the sway of human industry: by appropriate methods of clearing or planting trees, as the case may be, man claims to be able to modify the rule of winds and waters, and to renew the miracle of the prophet Elijah by making the rain and the dew to fall from heaven at his pleasure!

Much more can man exert his powers over economic facts, simply because they are human facts and we have a direct hold over them.[2] No doubt man's action in this respect is confined within certain limits, as it is in the sphere of physical phenomena. Science seeks to determine what these limits are, and all men should strive to respect them, whether individually by way of private enterprise or collectively by way of legislative regulations. As Bacon's old maxim says: *Naturæ non imperatur nisi parendo* (to govern nature you must first obey her). The utopian tortures nature uselessly to get from her what she cannot give: the man of science only asks for what he knows is possible. But the realm of the "possible" is infinitely wider than the classical school imagined.

[1] It has been wittily observed by M. Espinas, in his *Sociétés Animales*, that if human activity were incompatible with a natural order among phenomena, the fact of cooking an egg would have to be regarded as a miracle.

[2] It is recognized even by determinists, even by those who deny the freedom of the will — and such cannot certainly be the case with the school that calls itself "liberal" — that man has the power to modify the order of things in which he lives. But they make this one reservation: that every such action of man is itself necessarily *predetermined* by certain causes. This, however, is a purely metaphysical question into which we need not enter.

CHAPTER II — THE VARIOUS SCHOOLS OF ECONOMIC THOUGHT

I. THE SCHOOLS FROM THE POINT OF VIEW OF METHOD

In scientific language the term "method" is used to designate the road that must be followed to lead to the discovery of truth.

The *deductive* method starts from certain general data that are admitted to be beyond dispute, and then proceeds, by way of logical reasoning, to deduce an infinite series of propositions. Geometry may be taken as a type of the sciences that employ the deductive method. Law students will readily recognize also that law itself, particularly Roman law, employs the deductive method; the Roman jurist, starting from a few principles laid down by the Twelve Tables or found in the *jus gentium*, proceeded to construct the whole of that huge monument of learning called the Pandects. This method is also called the *abstract* method, because it aims at simplifying phenomena by reducing them to the single element that one wishes to study, and setting aside all the rest.

The *inductive* method starts from the observation of certain definite facts, and bases general propositions upon them. For example, the fact that all bodies fall, leads to the law of gravitation.

There used to be much dispute — though it is somewhat forgotten to-day — as to which of these two methods is the most suitable for the purposes of economic science.

It was certainly by the deductive method that political economy was first established. The classical economists erected the columns and the framework of their splendid edifice on the foundation of a small number of principles that were either regarded as axioms or suggested by very general observations — such principles as the growth of population and the diminishing return in agriculture. And even for the construction of the whole of pure political economy they could have managed, if necessary, with one simple principle, that "in all circumstances man seeks to obtain the maximum of satisfaction with the minimum of trouble." They tried thus to simplify the object of their study by regarding man as a being who is swayed entirely by self-interest — the "economic man," the same

13

in all lands and in all ages — and by setting aside all disturbing motives.

But half a century ago the efficacy of this method began to be challenged, and the inductive method to be extolled in place of it — the method which Bacon had introduced in the physical and natural sciences some centuries earlier, and which has since yielded such marvellous results. In the economic sphere this method is nowadays called *realistic*, especially in Germany, where it is in general use. It confines itself to the patient observation of such accumulated social facts as are within our knowledge. These facts are drawn from history when they relate to the past, and from statistics and from information given by travellers when they relate to the present. The exponents of this method are known also as the *historical* school, because they maintain that history alone can enlighten us as to the actual character of social facts, by showing us how social and economic institutions arose, and how they become transformed.[1]

The result is that the twofold characteristic of universality and permanency which the classical school attributed to economic phenomena, and which it dignified with the name of "natural law," vanishes into thin air.

The method just described is undoubtedly safer than the other, since it abstains from all sweeping generalizations. But is it as fruitful? Probably not. It is in fact a delusion to suppose that the use of the purely inductive method can ever be as efficacious in the social sciences as in the physical and natural ones. There are two reasons for this.

---

[1] The historical school of political economy, like the historical school of jurisprudence founded by Savigny, first arose in Germany. It dates from the publication of Professor Roscher's *Groundwork of Political Economy* in 1843, or perhaps more truly from List's *National System of Political Economy* in 1841.

In France the historical method in the social sciences was brilliantly inaugurated at about the same time by the publication of Le Play's book on *The Workers of Europe* (1855). Since then it has been faithfully applied by the "Le Play school," which takes its name from its founder, mainly in the form of monographs concerning working-class families. Nevertheless, the use of the historical method by this school differs so much from the way it is employed by the German school that it would be a great mistake to confuse them. Le Play starts from the principle that in social matters no new inventions are possible, and searches mainly in the past for lessons and examples; the German school only looks to the past for the germ or the roots of the present. Thus the Le Play school is conservative in the matter of formulating programmes of social action, whereas the German school, on the contrary, is progressive and even radical.

It is convenient to connect with the historical or realistic method the one which has been extolled by the so-called scientific, or rather Marxian, socialists, under the name of *historical materialism* (see below).

To begin with, the observation of facts is more difficult in the social sciences, although at first sight it may seem paradoxical to declare that it is harder to observe facts that concern us so closely as these, and in regard to which we are not only spectators, but actors as well.   Yet this is the very reason why we cannot see them clearly.

In the second place, social facts are infinitely more diversified. Whoever has seen one cockchafer has seen them all; but whoever has seen one miner has seen nothing at all.   In reality, the observation of economic and social facts is a task far beyond the capacities of any single person, and one which can only be accomplished by the collective labour of thousands of men who unite the results of their observation, or of States employing for this purpose the powerful means of investigation which they have at their disposal.   Thus arises a new and distinct science called *statistics*.   For example, the simplest of all the facts that the social sciences can study is the number of persons that make up a given community.   Yet is it not evident that a single observer is absolutely powerless to ascertain this fact?   Only public authorities are in a position to undertake this task, and even so the official census returns are far from guaranteeing perfect certainty.   This is still more the case when it comes to enumerating certain specified classes, as, for instance, landowners or millionaires.

Furthermore, the mere observation of facts would never have given the marvellous results that evoke our admiration in the natural sciences, were it not for the help of a particular method of observation, practised under certain prearranged conditions and called *experiment*.   Now in the social sciences direct experiment is impossible.   The chemist, the physicist, and even the biologist (although the latter encounters greater difficulties) can always take the phenomenon that they wish to study, and subject it to artificially determined conditions which may be varied at will.   In order, for instance, to study the breathing of an animal, they can place it under the bell-jar of an air-pump, and regulate the air pressure as they please.   But the economist, even though he be also a law-giver or an omnipotent despot, does not possess this power of experiment. None the less, we constantly speak in political economy of "data drawn from experience"; we say that such and such a nation has made the experiment of a system of protection, or of the regulation of labour, and has found it work well or ill, as the case may be. But *experience* is not the same thing as scientific *experiment* — far from it![1]   This is shown by the fact that while in the course of

[1] Pierson points out, quite rightly, that most mistakes, or at least what are now regarded as mistakes, passed originally for the fruits of experience.

centuries many States have tried protection, and others free trade, the problem is scarcely nearer solution than it was in the beginning.

The form of experiment — if, indeed, we can give it that name — with which the economist should content himself is that of comparing the results accruing from different laws and different institutions. For instance, he can compare the working of a State railway system with that of one that is owned by railway companies, or examine the effect of the formation of a co-operative society upon prices.

A field of inestimable value for experiment of this kind has been opened to economists of the present day and the most distant future by the recent war, owing to the huge disturbances it has introduced into the whole economic organization of the world — such, for instance, as the total or partial suppression of the international exchanges, the total or partial abrogation of the law of supply and demand in the home market by the system of requisitions, the fixing of prices, the rationing of commodities, the issue of incredible amounts of paper money, the cessation of competition at home and abroad owing to blockade and to the establishment of monopolies, and so forth. Yet the conclusions drawn for the future from these phenomena will always be uncertain and disputable, because the conditions will never be exactly similar.

Economists of the new school often ridicule the fondness of the classical economists for using Robinson Crusoe to illustrate their arguments. Yet by so doing they were rendering homage to the experimental method, though on an imaginary basis. If we cannot put a bird under the bell-jar of an air pump we assume that it is there and imagine how it would behave. It is not so far as we think from abstraction to experiment, for they both proceed in the same manner, namely, by isolating one fact from the complex of related facts to which it belongs. Only one method actually isolates it, while the other does so only in imagination.

No matter how justified, in some respects, the ridicule may be that has been directed against the abstract man — the *economic man* of the classical school — we must nevertheless admit that there are certain general characteristics possessed by all mankind. The best proof of this may be found in history itself, which teaches that wherever human societies have been placed under analogous conditions, the same social types have been evolved. Take, for instance, the feudal system in Europe in the twelfth century and in Japan down to the nineteenth century; the successive forms of property and of marriage; the simultaneous employment of the precious metals as money; the similarity of funeral rites; and even the uniformity of fairy tales, such as that of Hop-o'-my-thumb, which, as we are told by those skilled in folklore, is found to-day, in a more or less identical form, all over the world.

We cannot, therefore, absolutely reject the employment of the abstract method and the "let us suppose," so dear to the school of Ricardo and so obnoxious to the historical school. The labyrinth of economic facts is far too complicated for us ever to be able to find our way through it by the aid of observation alone, and to disentangle those fundamental relations which form the subject-matter of the whole science. To bring light into this darkness and order into this chaos we must make our appeal for help not only to abstraction but also to imagination, that is to say, to hypothesis.

The opposition between the deductive and the inductive method is somewhat academic. In reality there is but one method, which proceeds by three stages: —

(1) To *observe* facts, without any preconceived notions, and especially those facts that at first seem the most insignificant;

(2) To *imagine* a general explanation which will enable us to connect certain groups of facts together in a relation of cause and effect: in other words, to formulate a hypothesis;

(3) To *verify* this hypothesis by finding out, if not by actual experiment then at least by observation carried out in a special manner, whether the application of the hypothesis exactly fits the facts.

This is the procedure followed even in the physical and natural sciences. All the great laws which lie at the foundation of modern sciences, from Newton's law of gravitation downwards, are only *verified hypotheses*. We may go further than this, and say that the great theories which have served as bases for the scientific discoveries of our own day — such as the existence of ether in physics, and the doctrine of evolution in the natural sciences — are only *unverified* hypotheses.[1]

The mistake of the classical school, therefore, did not consist in a too frequent use of the abstract method, but only in having too often taken the abstraction and the hypothesis for the reality. For example: after having imagined its "economic man," prompted

---

[1] As Jevons has observed in his *Principles of Science*, the method employed for the discovery of truth in the sciences is similar to that unconsciously used by those who try to find the meaning of rebuses or ciphers on the back pages of illustrated papers. In order to guess the meaning of these enigmas, we *imagine* some meaning or other. Then we observe whether this really agrees with the figures or pictures before us; if it does not, it is a hypothesis to be rejected. We then conceive another one, and so forth, until we obtain a more successful result or give it up as a bad job.

solely by self-interest — which it had a perfect right to do — its error lay in believing in the real existence of such a man, and in the existence of no one else in the economic world.

The deductive method, then, is not dead: but it lives to-day in the form of two new methods.

The first of these is the *mathematical* method. This method considers the relations which arise among men in any given circumstances as *relations of equilibrium*, like those studied in mechanics, and capable, like them, of being expressed as algebraic equations. To accomplish this, the problem must be reduced to a certain number of given conditions, excluding all the others, exactly as is done in mechanics.[1]

The second is the *psychological* method, called also the *Austrian* method, from the nationality of its most eminent representatives.[2] This school devotes its attention exclusively to the theory of value, which it makes the centre of all economic science. And as value, according to this school, is only the expression of human desires, economic science is naturally reduced to a study of human desires and the causes which intensify or diminish them, which involves a very subtle psychological analysis. Moreover, the old classical principle, revived under the name of the *hedonistic* principle (from a Greek word meaning pleasure or enjoyment) — the principle of obtaining the maximum of satisfaction with the minimum of effort — was itself entirely psychological.

It is evident that these two modern schools employ the deductive method carried to its extreme consequences. None the less we must do them the justice of conceding that they have not committed the error into which the old deductive school had fallen, of being caught in the trap of their own speculations. They do not regard their hedonistic principle, or their abstractions, as anything but the hypotheses necessary for the establishment of a pure science.

On the other hand, if the abstract method of Ricardo is thus revived in the mathematical and psychological schools, the naturalistic method of J. B. Say may also be said to live again in the *organic* school, which makes political economy an annex of natural history and biology, by assimilating human societies to living beings, each

---

[1] This method was started by Cournot in France, many years ago (*Recherches sur les principes mathématiques de la théorie des richesses*, 1838), but with no success. It was reintroduced by Jevons, Marshall, and Edgeworth in England, by Walras at Lausanne, Vilfredo Pareto and Pantaleoni in Italy, Gossen and Launhardt in Germany, and Irving Fisher in the United States.

[2] Professors Karl Menger, von Boehm-Bawerk, and Wieser.

of their institutions being regarded merely as an organ adapted to the performance of a certain function. Physiological laws are thus transformed into social laws: railways correspond to the circulatory system of arteries and veins; telegraph wires form the nervous system; the rich are the "adipose tissue" of the social organism; and the stock exchange is its heart.

But this school, which prospered for a time, has suffered a considerable decline. Many sociologists protest nowadays against the comparison of society to an organism. Herbert Spencer himself, who had developed these analogies most brilliantly in his *Principles of Sociology*, protested subsequently against all attempts to assimilate human societies to living organisms.

II. THE SCHOOLS FROM THE POINT OF VIEW OF SOLUTIONS

It is not only in the matter of method that economists are divided into a number of different schools, but still more in regard to programmes of action — what the Germans call *social politics* — the *solutions* proposed for social problems.

In contemporary economic thought we can distinguish many schools — almost as many schools as authors, in fact. But, like the colours of the spectrum, they can be reduced to three fundamental ones.

1. *The Liberal School*

The first of these schools is sometimes called the *classical* school, because all the founders of political economy belonged to it — the physiocrats, Adam Smith, Ricardo, J. B. Say, and John Stuart Mill. It is also sometimes called the *individualist* school, because it regards the individual as both the originator and the end of economic activity. Its adversaries call it, ironically, the *orthodox* school, because of the dogmatic nature of its assertions and because it excludes from the science all who regard it differently. But it has many times declared that it will accept no other title than that of the *liberal* school. Moreover, this name describes it very well, and agrees with the celebrated formula which for a long time served as its motto: *laisser faire, laisser passer;* so it will be best to give it this name exclusively.

But is it really a "school"? Against this insinuation its partisans haughtily defend themselves, claiming to represent the science itself. They give themselves, and are conceded by their opponents, the name of "economists," simply. And it is true that the beginnings of this school coincide with the origin of economic science itself.

The doctrines of the school are simple, and may be summed up in three points: —

(1) The liberal school believes in the existence of a Natural Order, in the sense that human societies are governed by *natural laws*, which we could not alter even if we wished, because they are not of our own making. Moreover, we have not the least interest in modifying them, even if we could, because they are good laws, or at any rate the best possible. The part of the economist is confined to discovering the action of these natural laws, and the duty of individuals and of governments is to strive to regulate their conduct in accordance with them.[1]

(2) The liberal school is individualist, in the sense that it regards *individual effort* as the prime and even the sole motive power of social evolution. It does not consider this as any contradiction of the doctrine of natural laws just described, for these laws, as this school conceives them, do not in any wise restrain human liberty: on the contrary, they are only the expression of relations which arise spontaneously among men living in society, wherever these men are left to themselves and are free to act according to their own interests. These individual interests, though apparently antagonistic, are in reality concordant, and a harmony is established among them which constitutes precisely the natural order of things, and is far superior to any artificial arrangement that could be devised.

(3) The rôle of the legislator, if he wishes to ensure social order and progress, must therefore be limited to developing individual initiative as much as possible, removing whatever might hinder such initiative, and only preventing individuals from injuring each other in the exertion of it. Consequently, *the intervention of authority should be reduced to the minimum* that is indispensable to the safety of all — in one word, to the policy of *laisser faire*.

---

[1] This optimistic tendency is particularly marked in the French school. It reaches its climax in Bastiat's book, *Les Harmonies économiques*, and Dunoyer's *La Liberté du Travail*, but it appears again in the writings of several more recent French economists, as, for example, in M. Paul Leroy-Beaulieu's book on the distribution of wealth, which bears this significant subtitle, *The Tendency to a Smaller Inequality of Conditions*, and in the works of M. Yves Guyot.

This tendency is much less prominent in the English school, which, on the contrary, is in some respects plainly *pessimistic*. It is notably so in the theories of Ricardo, Malthus, and even John Stuart Mill (to be noticed later on), such as the laws of population, rent, wages limited of necessity to means of subsistence, diminishing return, the stationary state, etc., but none the less this school accepts them as unavoidable necessities.

This conception certainly lacks neither simplicity nor grandeur. Whatever may be its future destiny, it possesses at least the merit of having served to establish the science of political economy; and if other doctrines must one day take its place, it will none the less remain the foundation on which they are built.

We shall certainly not reproach it, therefore, as the German school has done, with having led to nothing but a barren metaphysical doctrine of natural laws. But, by the logical development of the very principles we have just outlined, the liberal school has been driven to justify all existing economic institutions, to deny or to minimize the grievances complained of by the working classes, and even, when their sufferings could not be denied, to see in them only the inevitable consequence of general progress and a necessary sanction, as it were, of the law that bids men labour and be thrifty.[1] The result is that this school has drawn upon itself the epithet *harsh* — a title which is undoubtedly altogether improper as applied to a scientific conception, but which must be understood to mean that this conception has become hateful to the sufferers who are looking for relief. "No matter," would be the proper reply, if such indeed were the truth! But this attitude would seem to have been dictated less by a truly scientific spirit than by a settled determination to justify the existing social order. In fact, our reply ought to be as follows: —

(1) The idea that the existing economic order is a *natural* order, in the sense that it is the spontaneous outcome of natural laws and of liberty, and that therefore it is, if not all that it should be, at least *all that it can be*, does not seem to be well founded. History shows us that what we call the fundamental institutions of the social order, such as landed property and the wage-system, etc., are very often the result either of war and brutal conquest (for example, the appropriation of the soil of England and Ireland by the landlords, or that of the Polish and Baltic provinces by the Prussians, originated historically in conquest, usurpation, or confiscation); or else of laws made by certain classes of society for their own benefit (such as laws of inheritance, fiscal laws, etc.). If, therefore, the world were to be made over again, and even if it could be remade under conditions of absolute freedom, there is no proof that it would resemble the world of to-day.

(2) Even if we admit the existence of natural laws, and even if we admit, as we have done, that these laws may be defined as con-

---

[1] "It is good that there should be lower regions in society for the reception of families that misbehave. This dreadful hell is poverty!" (Dunoyer, *Liberté du Travail*.)

stant and necessary relations between certain facts, there is no ground whatever for concluding that these facts are themselves either constant or necessary. Nor does it by any means follow that our social institutions possess that fixed and definite character which the liberal school is pleased to claim for them. An economic law can just as well be revolutionary as conservative. In any case, if the supreme law of nature is the law of evolution, as contemporary science teaches, then we should have to say that natural laws, far from excluding the notion of change, always presuppose it. The liberal school regards the wage system, for instance, as a fixed and definite institution; socialists and co-operators regard it, on the contrary, as a transitory one, like the systems of slavery and serfdom which preceded it. This is not the place to argue in favour of either one view or the other, but what we can say is that natural laws may be appealed to by the second school as well as by the first. And it is the same with the question of the ownership of land.

(3) Still less is it right to conclude, even admitting the existence of natural laws, that they are necessarily good, or at least the best possible, and that therefore the best thing to be done in the interests of all is to leave them alone. The spider's web is an entirely natural fact; but this knowledge brings little consolation to the fly that is struggling in it. Now the economic world is full of spiders' webs, and there is nothing anti-scientific in bringing along a broom.

As for the *vis medicatrix naturæ*, which inspires the doctrine of *laisser faire* — the belief that nature is the best of physicians — every scientist to-day regards it as an old woman's superstition. No doubt there are forces in every living body that fight spontaneously against disease and death — otherwise all life would have disappeared from the earth, or rather it would never have appeared at all. But if we leave to nature the task of healing the sick during an epidemic, or tending the wounded after a battle, few of them will recover. It is just the same in the life of society. All that can be said is that since economic science is even less advanced than medical science, it may often be a wiser policy for governments to withhold their hand than to intervene blindly.

2. *The Socialist Schools*

The socialist school is as old as the classical school: we may even say it is older, for there were socialists long before there were economists. It was only, however, after economics had assumed a scientific character that socialism became established, by the very fact of its antagonism to the new science. As the doctrines of this school are pre-eminently of a critical nature, and show great divergencies among themselves, they are much harder to formulate than those of the preceding school. However, they may be summed up as follows:[1] —

(1) All schools of socialists regard the existing social order as evil because it confers on a small number of parasites the power of exploiting the masses by making them work for the benefit of their masters: *paucis humanum genus vivit*. Not only so, but they also regard it as anti-economic because it involves a waste of labour and of wealth.

They look forward, therefore, to a new order of things in which ownership shall no longer be a means to the attainment of an income by other people's labour. And according as these schools are more or less exacting in their demands for restrictions on the right of ownership, they can be classified as follows, in a descending scale: *communism*, which demands the suppression of all private property; *collectivism*, which only requires the suppression of property which involves the employment of wage-earners; *agrarian socialism*, which would be satisfied with the suppression of property in land, because land is a natural form of wealth; and the *co-operative* school, which aims only at the abolition of profit, without touching private property.

(2) These socialist schools are more or less *revolutionary*, without denying thereby the doctrine of evolution. They regard revolution — the sudden putting into practice of a secret and slowly matured plan — as just one of the normal forms of evolution, not only in the social sphere, but also in the biological and the geological. Earthquakes and the upheaval of mountains were one of the factors that determined the present form of the earth, and the chicken, when it leaves the egg, has to break the shell with its beak. Every birth is to some extent a revolution, and when the new society is ready to be born from the womb of the old, violence would merely play the part of a midwife.

[1] Socialism, if we leave out of consideration a long line of precursors extending as far back as Plato, is represented in the nineteenth century principally by the following exponents. In France: Saint-Simon (*Système industriel*, 1821); Fourier (*Association Domestique Agricole*, 1822); Proudhon (*Qu'est-ce que la Propriété?* 1840); in England: Owen (whose chief work, *New Views of Society*, was published in 1812); in Germany: Rodbertus (*Social Letters to Kirchmann*, 1850); Karl Marx (*Capital*, vol. i, 1867, followed by three posthumous volumes).

Down to the middle of the nineteenth century socialism was most vigorously expounded in France; but since then contemporary socialism, often called *Marxism*, has taken its distinctive physiognomy from Germany.

Modern socialists, unlike their predecessors, whom they describe as "Utopians," believe no longer that the existing social order can be changed at will.[1] It might even be said that the socialist schools are more determinist than the liberal school, in the sense that they affirm the omnipotence of environment over the individual. This was the doctrine even of Owen and Fourier, and it is affirmed by the Marxian school under the name of *historical materialism*, meaning thereby that the facts of the economic order, particularly those relating to production and the industrial arts, determine all social facts, even the most distant and the highest in the scale, such as those that belong to the political, moral, religious, and aesthetic orders. "By changing their methods of production," wrote Marx, "men change all their social relations. The hand mill will give you a feudal form of society; the steam-driven mill, a society ruled by the industrial capitalist." And on these lines they undertake to explain, by purely economic causes, the coming of Christianity or the Reformation, the Renaissance, the party strife of Guelphs and Ghibellines or whigs and tories, and anything else you please.

However, this determinism does not possess the fatalistic character that is attributed to it, for even if social evolution is determined by the substitution of steam mills for hand mills it must not be forgotten that they are both products of human industry, and that consequently the collective action of man is itself the prime factor in that evolution which gives rise to it and passes beyond it.

(3) The socialist schools aim at transforming into public services everything that falls to-day within the scope of private enterprise.

But this does not mean, as it is frequently said to mean, that socialism wants everything to be done by the State. So far is it from wishing to place everything in the hands of the State, that it desires, on the contrary, to abolish the State. The general support that it gives to legislative projects for extending the functions of the State is given merely as a temporary measure for transforming individual enterprises into collective ones. For it professes as much contempt as the liberal school does for the State of to-day — the *bourgeois* State, as it calls it — that is to say, the State as organized by politicians and employers and inspired by the same interests as the capitalists. In its plans for social reorganization it even avoids using the phrase "State ownership," and speaks instead of "socialization" or "nationalization," which means simply that every enterprise is to be conducted solely in the public interest and without

---

[1] It is true that Marxian socialism proclaims "the conquest of public powers" as a means to its end; but syndicalist socialism stands aside from all political action.

thought of profit. But these committees of management are to lose all political character, and become purely economic: they will be nothing but the administrative councils of a kind of huge co-operative society embracing the whole country. That is where pure socialism differs from *State socialism*, which we shall notice further on.

(4) Lastly, the most salient feature of socialism as it exists to-day is that it is a class socialism. That is to say, it lays it down as a fact that the interests of the wealth-possessing classes are necessarily antagonistic to those of the workers.[1] It does not deny that the bourgeois or capitalist classes have had their part to play in the formation of the existing society, but, having become parasitic, they should be eliminated. Hence the declaration of *class war* which is the fundamental principle of the socialist programme. It should be observed that this feature did not appear in the older socialism, or in French socialism in the nineteenth century. It is specifically a working-class characteristic, and it is particularly prominent in a quite modern form of socialism called *syndicalism*. As the name of this system indicates, its organ is a syndicate: now the syndicate, by its very definition, can only admit workers, and can therefore only be concerned with class socialism. The programme of this school, quite naturally, aims at the abolition of the wage system rather than of property. It scorns to employ any political means, for it has at its disposal a far more powerful weapon — that of the general strike.

It is impossible in this chapter to estimate the value of the complaints made by the socialist school against the present social order: we shall meet with them again when we come to deal with the subject of distribution. Suffice it to say here that the actual successes of socialism in every country can scarcely be explained unless it

---

[1] Among the various socialist schools the *anarchist* school is distinguished by such marked characteristics that it should be placed in a separate category. The very name "socialism" is scarcely applicable to it, for it carries individualism to an extreme, together with a horror of all regulation and all constraint. It appears rather as a kind of exaggerated liberalism (and it is willing to be called *libertarian socialism*). But, whereas the liberal school is satisfied with reducing legislation to a minimum, the libertarian school would abolish it altogether. Moreover, it rejects individual property as incompatible with the full independence of the individual, for, as it has been wittily said by M. Wilfred Monod, a Christian socialist: "Is not the right of *private* property the right to *deprive* another of it?"

It should be noted also that anarchism differs from syndicalist socialism in that its adherents have always been intellectuals rather than workers.

holds a portion of truth, and that as a *critical* doctrine it has exerted a wholesome influence on the thought and the tendencies of our time.

But as a *constructive* doctrine, as a scheme of economic organization to replace the system under which we live, it has met with no success. All the systems hitherto proposed, after having won over a few enthusiastic disciples, have been abandoned or continue to exist only as vague hopes (save only the co-operative system); and as for the so-called scientific socialism, it has refused to formulate a scheme of organization, and has even had to repudiate those which the bolder spirits had prematurely drawn up.

3. *The Reforming Schools*

Under this head we group together the various schools which, while admitting that the existing economic organization is the result of natural laws and could not be destroyed without bringing the nation to ruin, recognize none the less that it is full of injustice and waste. They are determined, therefore, to seek the means of providing a remedy.

The characteristics common to these schools are as follows: —

(1) They reject the characteristic principle of the liberal school, the doctrine of *laisser faire*, which means relying on the free play of individual interests to ensure the satisfaction of the public interest. They believe, on the contrary, that the public interest stands in great need of being safeguarded, and they seek for institutions which shall achieve this end: some find a suitable institution in the State, some in the principle of association, some in religion, and so forth.

(2) They also reject the absolute separation sought to be effected by the school of pure political economy between justice and utility, between economics, law, and morals. All these schools — State socialism, Christian socialism, juridical socialism, and "solidarism" — have a more or less *ethical* character, as it is called.

i. *State Socialism*

This school absolutely rejects all idea of natural law in the economic sphere, and even turns it to ridicule; it attaches correspondingly greater importance to the *positive laws* promulgated by the legislator, and regards them as one of the most powerful factors in social evolution. It is led therefore to extend considerably the functions of the State, and in this matter it shares none of the dislike and distrust felt by the liberal and socialist schools.

This school has exerted a great influence in recent times, not only over the minds of men, but over legislation. The great movement for *labour legislation* that dates from the last quarter of the nineteenth century; the treaties concluded between States for the international regulation of labour; the moral and often financial support given by the State to a multitude of social institutions, are in great measure due to the influence of this school. It has certainly done a great service to science in widening the narrow, factitious, deliberately simplified, and irritatingly optimistic point of view which always delighted the classical school. It has forced economic science to abandon that systematic abstention from interference to which it was wedded; and to the question, What is to be done? — the question that human misery has so long been asking — it has tried to find another answer than the barren *laisser faire*.

At first it was always the State that made the laws, and it is the laws that make justice. When it is said that laws cannot change morals — *quid leges sine moribus?* — it is enough to point to the action of the State in prohibiting absinthe, obscene literature, malthusianism, and gambling. Is it really imagined that legislation can only follow customs, and give a sanction to them? Does it not rather strive against them?

Even if the State be still badly organized, it must not be forgotten that in the course of history it has done some very great and very fine things, even if we look at the economic sphere alone — things which individual enterprise was powerless to accomplish, in putting an end to the iniquities that self-interest and the desire for profit had definitely encouraged. Such are the abolition of slavery, of serfdom, and of trade privileges, the regulation of labour, the protection of children, the making of roads, and the sanitation of cities. No doubt these reforms were first instigated by individuals: we cannot forget the part played by Wilberforce and Mrs. Beecher Stowe in getting negro slavery abolished, or that of Lord Shaftesbury in freeing the children from the factories. No doubt the State only puts itself in motion after individuals have made a start, and can act only through individual instruments — the State is always a *person*, be it hero or writer — but none the less it is by collective power that these individual good intentions manage to get realized.[1]

Here are the principal objections that are raised against State socialism: —

[1] During the war which has lately turned the world upside down, there was an enormous extension of State socialism — almost as much in liberal England as in Germany. It will be said, no doubt, that the laws of war-time are not the same as those of peace; but is the public safety anything but the public interest raised to its highest term?

It is said that the State, even when it accomplishes reforms that are good in themselves, can only do so by means of *constraint*. But, to begin with, it must be observed that constraint is inevitable in every case of collective enterprise, even in cases of voluntary association, since the minority has to bow to the will of the majority. Moreover, it is a mistake to think that the State acts always by way of constraint, prescribing one thing or forbidding another; sometimes it acts by way of *example*, as when it employs labour in its workshops and yards; more often it acts by giving *assistance*, as when it makes roads, ports, canals, or telegraphs, or subsidizes certain industries, such as railways, or institutions founded by private initiative, such as mutual aid societies, loan societies, unemployment insurance, and pension funds. Sometimes it actually establishes and puts at the disposal of its citizens such institutions as professional schools, savings banks, and insurance organizations.

Another and more practical objection to State socialism is that too often the State has shown the most deplorable incapacity in economic matters, and has also often become the instrument of parties, rather than the organ of the interests of the whole nation. This is only too true, but these defects are due less to the essential nature of the State than to its present organization.

We must not forget that the State and the municipalities, even in countries that are most advanced from a democratic point of view — we should rather say, *especially* in these countries — was organized *only for political purposes, and not by any means for the exercise of economic functions*. The latter are even made subordinate to the former: witness the influence of electioneering interests when it is a question of building a railway or reducing the staff of an arsenal! The division of labour in matters of government is still in an embryonic form; public functions are arbitrarily distributed; the power of governments is unstable; so-called universal suffrage, which too often does not even represent the will of the majority, is crudely organized; and all these circumstances render the State actually unfit for the accomplishment of economic ends. But it is reasonable to hope that when the State is constituted with a view to its new functions, it will be able to act more economically and more effectively than it has hitherto attempted to do. A beginning has been made by the establishment here and there of self-governing and reasonably competent organs of State, such as the "public offices" for food and housing.

ii. *Solidarism*

State socialism has reached its fullest development in Germany; but in France it appears rather in the shape of "solidarism."

The fact of solidarity — the mutual interdependence of mankind, so clearly demonstrated by the division of labour, by exchange, and, as regards successive generations of men, by heredity — has long been noticed. But it was regarded in the past as a natural law which did not require the assistance of individuals to work itself out, and which, moreover, could not by any means always be considered a blessing, for solidarity in evil, such as the transmission of disease by contagion or heredity, is more visible than solidarity in good. And, from the moral point of view, it seemed contrary to justice, for justice demands that each man should be responsible only for his own actions.

The desire ̠of the solidarist school, on the other hand, is that solidarity, from being merely a crude fact, should become a rule of conduct, a moral duty, even a legal obligation having legal sanction. The reason it gives is this: that since solidarity, as a natural law, has shown us clearly that all our deeds react for good or for evil upon others, and their deeds upon us, our responsibility and our risks are enormously increased. If some are poor and wretched, we ought to assist them, for two reasons: first, because we are probably in part the *authors* of their misery, by the way we have conducted our business, our investments, our purchases, or by the example we have set them; therefore, being responsible, our duty is to relieve them; secondly, because we know that we ourselves or our children are liable to become the *victims* of the misery of others: their diseases will infect us, their depravity will demoralize us; therefore it is also our interest, rightly understood, to succour them.

Human society must be transformed, then, into a sort of vast mutual aid society in which natural solidarity, corrected by each man's good will, or, in default, by legal constraint, shall become the foundation of justice, and in which every man will be called upon to assume his share of other men's burdens and to take his share also of other men's profit. And to those who are afraid that this will diminish individuality, self-help, and self-reliance, the answer must be given that individuality is asserted and developed as much in helping others as in helping oneself.[1]

Solidarism differs from socialism in maintaining what are called

---

[1] Vinet, the protestant theologian of Lausanne, has admirably said that "to give oneself, one must own oneself."

the bases of the existing social order — property, inheritance, free disposal of one's possessions — and the inequalities which result therefrom. But it mitigates these inequalities by binding the weak and the strong together with a thousand bonds of voluntary association. However, it also allows of State intervention whenever labour legislation, sanitary laws, or laws concerning adulteration tend to prevent the degradation of the masses, or even when certain kinds of compulsory insurance or thrift tend to inspire the various classes of the nation with the spirit of solidarity. It cannot be forgotten that the State is itself only the oldest and most impressive instance of solidarity among men. No doubt solidarity does not acquire its full moral value until it becomes voluntary, but solidarity imposed by law may be indispensable in preparing the ground for the growth later on of free co-operation.[1]

Solidarism, just like State socialism, has inspired most of the legislation in France of late years for the protection of labour, insurance, poor relief, and education. It has recently achieved an impressive triumph in the undertaking by the government to compensate the inhabitants of the invaded districts for all the damage caused by the war.[2]

iii. *Social Christianity*

The Christian school believes strongly in natural laws, like the classical school, and calls them *laws of providence*. Only it believes

---

[1] In a little volume by Claudio Jannet, Frédéric Passy, Stiegler, and Gide, called *Quatre Écoles d'Économie Sociale* (Geneva, 1890) will be found the programme that we drew up at that date, under the title, *L'École Nouvelle*.

[2] M. Léon Bourgeois has tried to give a legal shape to the somewhat vague concept of solidarity. Every man, he says, *is born a debtor to society* in virtue of a tacit contract — what he calls a *quasi-contract* — which is a result of the collective advantages, produced by the labour of all, of which he has his share. He should begin, therefore, by paying his debt — for example, by contributing to the insurance, the relief, and the education of his brothers, as well as by all other methods yet to be determined upon. It is only after this preliminary condition has been fulfilled that economic liberty and private property can have full sway.

The objection to this ingenious theory is that there cannot be debtors without creditors. Now it is not easy to say which members of society are to be considered creditors, and which as debtors. Or rather, should not everyone be regarded as both debtor and creditor? — in which case the debt is extinguished by "confusion." It might be thought, at first sight, that the rich are debtors and the poor creditors, for the poor are generally spoken of as "disinherited." But nothing is less certain than this, for very possibly the rich man has really given much more to society than he has received from it — some great inventor, for instance — and, conversely, the poor man may be disabled or crippled and quite incapable of giving anything in exchange for what he has received.

that the play of these laws of providence may be profoundly upset by the wrong use of human freedom, and that this is, in fact, exactly what has happened. Through the fault of man, through Adam's sin, the world is not what it ought to be, not what God would have wished it to be. Unlike the liberal school, therefore, this school is by no means optimistic: it does not regard the social order as good, nor even as tending naturally to become better. Man's duty is not to follow his own nature but to overcome it.

The catholic school goes further. It regards the proud faith in liberty, which it calls *liberalism*, as the real cause of social disorganization. It launches such vigorous criticisms against the existing organization of society — against capitalism, against profit, against interest (branding it, as in the middle ages, with the name of usury — *usura vorax*), against joint-stock companies, against free trade and all forms of internationalism, and above all against competition — that it has won for itself from liberal economists the name of *catholic socialism*. It objects strenuously, however, to this designation, and indeed, despite certain points of view which they have in common, it differs *toto orbe* from the socialist school. To begin with, it by no means proposes to abolish the fundamental institutions of the present social order — property, inheritance, and the wage system — but rather to consecrate them in the spirit of Christianity. Furthermore, it does not believe in evolution or in the spontaneous progress of mankind. As regards practical measures, it pins its faith above all to professional association, or the guild system, with a view to the continuance in a modern spirit of the old corporative rule.

It would seem as if the protestant school ought to be even further removed from socialism than the catholic, since protestantism is generally looked upon as the religion of liberalism and individualism. Yet it is just as hostile to economic liberalism so far as this liberalism is based upon faith in natural laws, for it feels even more strongly than the catholic school that nature is sin and must be striven against.[1] But to the younger school this sin has ceased to be purely individual, and has become particularly *social sin*, demanding, therefore, *social salvation*.

This school believes that the world must be radically reformed, so as to approximate to the Kingdom of God, whose coming should

---

[1] The confession of faith of the Reformed Churches of France, read in public every Sunday, says: "We acknowledge and confess that we are miserable sinners, inclined to evil, and incapable by ourselves of doing right." This is only a repetition, moreover, of the words of the apostle Paul.

be awaited and prepared for in this world by all believers.   It also denounces competition and the pursuit of profit.   It accepts the institution of property, but regards it as a *social function*.

As regards a practical programme, co-operation, with its motto, "Each for all, and all for each," is the solution which seems in general to correspond most closely to the evangelical ideal.

CHAPTER III — WANTS AND VALUE

I. THE WANTS OF MAN

The wants of man are the underlying motive of all economic activity, and consequently the starting-point of economic science. The whole of political economy could therefore be introduced into this chapter.

Every living being, in order to develop and accomplish its purposes, needs to borrow certain elements from the world around it, and, when they are lacking, the result is, first, suffering, and finally, death. From the plant, and even from the crystal, up to man, this necessity increases with the increase of individuality. Every want, so long as it is unsatisfied, gives rise in living beings to an impulse which seeks the means of satisfaction, and, as soon as it finds it, becomes a *desire*. This desire in its turn induces the *effort* necessary to obtain the object that will satisfy it.

Now because effort is always more or less painful, man sets his wits to work to get the maximum of satisfaction with the minimum of effort. This law — the law of least effort, called by economists the hedonistic principle, from the Greek ἡδονή, meaning pleasure or satisfaction — is the basis of all economic science and of industry as well, for every mechanical discovery, every improvement in organization, all economic progress, in short, derives from this principle.

But political economy is not therefore based on idleness, for the law of least effort implies not so much a distaste for effort as a wise economy of effort — that is to say, a more useful employment of time and labour. The most active men in business, just like the best trained athletes, are those who make the best application of this law.

The wants of man have several characteristics, each of which is of great importance because some great economic law is based on it. These characteristics are as follows: —

(1) Man's wants are *unlimited in number*. This feature distinguishes man from the animals, and is the mainspring of civilization in the strictest sense of the word, for to civilize a people is only to increase its wants — as we see in colonization.

33

The wants of humanity are like those of a child. At birth the
child needs nothing but a little milk and a warm covering; but little
by little he requires more varied food, more complicated garments,
and something to play with; each year gives rise to some new desire.
In primitive communities man's wants are almost all primary ones
— the physiological needs we have just mentioned; other wants
are still unknown. But the more we see the more we learn, and the
more our curiosity is awakened, the more do our desires increase and
multiply. So also we are conscious to-day of a thousand wants that
were unknown to our grandfathers: wants of comfort, hygiene,
cleanliness, education, travel, intercourse — the taste for flowers is
of quite recent date — and it is certain that our grandchildren will
feel yet new wants. If we were to discover, on another planet, beings
superior to man, we should no doubt find among them a multitude
of wants of which we in this world can have no idea.[1]

This indefinite multiplication of wants, then, has created modern
civilization and all that we call progress. This does not mean that
it makes men happier. It has often been remarked that the multiplication of desires and of desirable objects — otherwise called
wealth — has no necessary connection with the increase of happiness.

Moreover, it must be observed that even purely economic wants
are not devoid of moral value. In fact, every new want constitutes
a new social *bond*, for we can generally only satisfy our wants by the
aid of our neighbour, and this strengthens the sentiment of solidarity. The man who has no wants — the hermit — is sufficient
unto himself, which is precisely what a man should not be. As for
the working classes, we should rejoice, and not regret, that new

---

[1] It would be useful, alike from the economic and the moral point of view, if we
could draw up a hierarchy or scale of wants. But there is no standard available for
this purpose.

Perhaps, however, we should be right in thinking that the importance of wants
can be measured by the order of their appearance in history or pre-history, if sociology
could supply us with sufficiently precise information. It is obvious that the want of
food came first. That of *defence* of the individual against animals or enemies must
have followed it very closely. That explains the longstanding and terrible importance
of the need for *weapons*, which was no doubt just as great, or even greater, in the life
and work of men of the stone age as it is in the budgets of civilized countries in the
twentieth century. But the curious and unexpected thing is that the want of *ornament* came before that of clothing. This is the first of the wants that distinguish
men from animals. As Théophile Gautier has observed: "No dog ever conceived of
wearing ear-rings; but the stupid Papuans, who eat clay and earthworms, hang
coloured berries and shells in their ears." On the other hand, the need for *rapid
communication* came much later, but has increased enormously in modern times.

wants and desires continually torment them; for otherwise they would have remained in a state of eternal slavery.

(2) Wants are *limited in intensity*. This is one of the most important propositions in political economy, for on it, as we shall see, is founded the new theory of value.

Wants are limited in the sense that a certain amount of some object or other is sufficient to satisfy each of them. A man needs only a certain quantity of water to assuage his thirst.

But there is more in it than that. Every want goes on decreasing in intensity as it becomes satisfied, up to the point of *satiety.* At this point the want disappears and is replaced by disgust or even suffering.[1] To suffer thirst is the worst of torments; but so was the medieval "water torture," by which the victim was compelled to swallow excessive quantities of water.

The more natural or *physiological* a want is, the more clearly marked is its limit. It is easy to tell how many pounds of bread and how many pints of water a man needs. But the more artificial or *social* a want is, the more elastic is its limit. Certainly it is scarcely possible to say how many horses would be needed by a sportsman, how many yards of lace by a fashionable woman, how many rubies by an Indian prince, and, above all, how much money by any civilized man, before these people were fully satisfied and cried "Enough!" Nevertheless, we may say that for them too satiety is inevitable. At all events, as each new object is added to those already possessed, the resulting pleasure goes on rapidly diminishing.

It is true that in the case of money satiety is rare and almost inconceivable. This is for the very simple reason that money is the only kind of wealth which has the property of satisfying, not one definite want, but *all* possible wants; consequently it only ceases to be desired when all other wants have been met. This puts back the limit to an almost infinite distance. None the less it is evident that an *extra* half-crown does not provide a millionaire with a pleasure at all comparable to that which it procures for a beggar. Buffon, who was no economist, but a very clever man, noticed this long ago: "The poor man's half-crown," he said, "that is going to pay for something of prime necessity, and the half-crown that fills up

---

[1] This is like the well-known mathematical series which go on diminishing until they reach zero and then begin to increase below zero, but as minus quantities. The different degrees of want are the positive terms of the series; the different degrees of satiety, down to disgust, are the negative terms; between the two is zero, which is the point of indifference.

the money-bag of the rich financier, are two identical objects in the eyes of a mathematician; but, from the moral point of view, one of them is worth a sovereign and the other is not worth a farthing." Of course it is only to its rich owner that the half-crown is not worth a farthing, for its purchasing power in the market remains the same.

(3) Wants are *competitive*, which means that one want can very often be developed only at the expense of other wants which it abolishes or absorbs; and they are very often *interchangeable*, so that one can easily take the place of another, like the parts of a bicycle or a gun. Just as "one nail drives out another," according to the proverb, so one want drives out another. That fact is the basis of a very important economic law called the *law of substitution*. It has been noticed often and in various countries that the popularity of the bicycle and the motor-car has done considerable damage not only to the trade in riding-horses and to coach-building, but even — most unexpectedly — to the manufacture of pianos![1]

This law of substitution is of capital importance because it operates as a kind of safety-valve for the consumer, when the satisfaction of one want becomes too burdensome by ordinary means.

Morality and hygiene make use of this law when they endeavour to replace lower and more brutal wants by those of a higher order. Thus, to combat drunkenness, for example, temperance societies have found nothing better than opening "temperance restaurants" in which an effort is made to accustom people to drink tea or coffee. Notice also that a material want may be replaced by an intellectual want — the public-house, for example, giving way to the reading-room — or by a moral want, as when, for instance, a workman goes without a drink in order to pay his subscription to a provident fund, a trade union, or a political association.

(4) Wants are *complementary:* they generally go in company, and cannot easily be satisfied separately. What is the use of an odd shoe or an odd glove? What use is a carriage without a horse, or a motor-car without petrol? A good overcoat is not sufficient to keep out the cold: we must also have had a good dinner. The

---

[1] It is important to distinguish between the substitution of *one want for another want*, and the substitution of *one object for another object* for the satisfaction of the same want — what is called a *succedaneum*. The latter kind of substitution is less interesting. The recent war furnished numberless examples, and these on the largest scale: bread made of rye or even potatoes instead of wheat, nettles substituted for cotton as a textile fabric, cellulose used instead of cotton for explosives, saccharine in place of sugar, and all the *ersatz* commodities that enabled Germany to defy the blockade for so long.

want of food, at least among civilized men, involves the want of a large number of other things, such as tables, chairs, table-cloths, napkins, plates, glasses, knives, and forks. To obtain the maximum of satisfaction it even needs to be associated — as it is in banquets — with certain aesthetic forms of enjoyment, such as flowers, lights, glittering table appointments, beautiful clothes, and music.

(5) All wants are appeased or even extinguished for the time being when they are satisfied; but they are not long in coming to life again, and the more frequently and regularly they have been satisfied, the more peremptory do they become. And when a want has many times found the same means of satisfaction it tends to become fixed as a *habit*, which means that it can no longer submit to interruption without physiological suffering on the part of the organism, however artificial the want may be: "Habit," as the saying goes, "is second nature." This law is also of great importance, especially in relation to the question of wages. It sets the level of existence, the *standard of life*, and this standard is not easily lowered. There was a time when workmen wore neither shirts nor shoes, when they had no coffee or tobacco, when they ate neither meat nor wheaten bread; but to-day these wants are so deep-seated and ingrained that a workman would undoubtedly perish if he could no longer satisfy them and was suddenly reduced to the condition of his social equals in the days of Alfred the Great.

If we add, finally, that a habit which has been transmitted from generation to generation tends in time to become established through *heredity*, and that our senses are becoming every day more subtle and exacting, we shall understand the despotic power that may eventually be acquired by a want that originally seemed most futile and insignificant.

But if it is true that every want becomes intensified in proportion to its power of finding satisfaction, it is equally true that it disappears when it finds no means of satisfaction. It is like a fire which increases when it is supplied with fuel, and goes out when it gets none. No doubt a physiological and essential want cannot be suppressed; if it cannot obtain satisfaction from one object it will have to find another, on pain of death. But in the case of artificial and harmful wants, like the want of alcohol or opium, the best and almost the only means of suppressing them is to refuse to satisfy them at all.

II. WEALTH

Our wants and desires necessarily relate to an object outside ourselves. The remarkable property possessed by certain objects of satisfying one or other of our wants and supporting our life or increasing our well-being, is called *utility* (from the Latin word *uti*, meaning to use). And every object which has this property is called *wealth*, independently of the amount of value it possesses: a glass of water is wealth in the economic sense of the word.[1]

Of course not *all* the things around us — animals, vegetables, and unorganized bodies — possess this property. Three conditions are requisite for an object to be useful: —

(1) There must be some relation between the qualities possessed by the object and one of our wants. Bread is useful because, on the one hand, we need food, and because, on the other hand, corn contains exactly the elements best suited for our nourishment. The diamond is much sought after because it is a part of our nature, as also of that of certain animals, to take delight in looking at brilliant objects; and because the diamond possesses the property of glittering with incomparable splendour, owing to its refractive power, which is superior to that of any other known body.

It should be carefully observed that of the two terms in this relation it is the man and not the object that is by far the most important to the economist. One might be inclined to believe the contrary — to think that the anticipated satisfaction depends on the properties of things; that the utility of gold is of the same nature as its weight or its lustre or its rustlessness; that utility attaches to the objects themselves, like a quality which appeals to the senses. But this is not so; and this is proved by the fact that this correspondence between an object and our wants is not always due to nature — it may be due to social usages, to fashion, or to our own beliefs. For hundreds of years, and at the present day in some countries, men have attributed wonderful properties to certain more or less authentic relics, which have therefore been regarded as incomparable wealth. There are many mineral waters and patent medicines that are in great demand, although their curative powers are exceedingly doubtful. Then think of all the costumes that are no longer worn, the books that are no longer read, the pictures that are no longer admired, the money that is out of circulation, the

---

[1] Since the word *wealth* in everyday language means something of great value, it would perhaps be better to use the term *goods* instead, meaning "that which is good," like *bien* in French and *bona* in Latin.

remedies that no longer cure . . . what a long list we could make
of all the items of wealth whose utility has been as fleeting and short-
lived as the wants that gave rise to it! Yet, even so, if the desire
of the collector — the keenest of all desires — should chance to
fix on this dead wealth, it would acquire a new life and soon possess
a far greater value than it had during its first existence.

According to scientists and hygienic experts, alcoholic drinks have
none of the virtues attributed to them: they furnish neither strength
nor warmth. But what of that? Millions of men in all countries
unfortunately believe that they possess these utilities, and that
suffices to make them constitute wealth, and even such wealth as is
estimated in millions of pounds and from which governments themselves draw part of their revenues.

(2) The mere existence of this relation between an object and
one of our wants is not sufficient: we must be *aware* of it, or, if it
is an imaginary one, as in the examples just given, we must *believe*
in it. One of Aristotle's maxims, often repeated in the Middle
Ages, was: *Nil amatum nisi precognitum*, "nothing can be loved
(or desired) except it be first recognized."

There is probably not a single thing in the wide world around us
that could not be used to satisfy our needs, and consequently to
increase our wealth, if man's knowledge could see far enough. But
so long as they are unknown they remain as useless as the fertile
lands or precious metals discovered by astronomers, with the aid of
telescopes and spectrum analysis, on Mars and Venus. In fact
there is only a very small number of bodies that are classed as useful. For example, out of some hundreds of thousands of species
included in the animal kingdom, barely two hundred are utilized to
furnish us with food, with labour, and even with recreation. And
of plants and minerals the proportion is infinitely smaller still.

However, the number of utilities increases rapidly with the progress of science. Coal is one of the most remarkable examples.
Its employment first as domestic fuel, and then as a source of power,
is of quite recent date, and it was still more recently that we discovered how to draw out of these black lumps, as out of a conjuror's
hat, first light, in the form of gas, then all the colours, all the perfumes, all the chemist's drugs, and finally nearly all the explosives.

(3) But it is not enough even for us to know that an object has
the power of satisfying our wants: we must also be able to apply it
to that purpose. It must not only be recognized as useful: it must
be *capable of being utilized*. And this is not the case with everything. There are many forests that rot on the ground because they

cannot be exploited. Many rivers, even in France, are full of gold which cannot be economically extracted. There are vast forces lying hidden in the ebb and flow of seas, in the streams of the country-side, in molecular attraction; but we can make no use of them, at any rate in the present state of our knowledge. We know well enough that there is aluminium in the clay that makes the mud of our streets, but we have not found out how to extract it. And it is only quite recently that we have succeeded in extracting nitrogen from the inexhaustible reservoir of the air.

Now does this property of satisfying our wants and giving us enjoyment belong only to *things* (what the Roman lawyers called *res*)? Surely it belongs also to *acts* — to the doings of our fellow men, many of whom undoubtedly provide us with much enjoyment and are even *useful* to us in the economic sense of satisfying our wants directly, without the intervention of any material wealth. Thus the doctor gives us health; the teacher, knowledge; the judge, justice; the policeman, security; the writer and the artist, the highest and purest forms of enjoyment; and the servant carries out our orders. It is man himself who is most useful to man. It cannot be doubted, either, that the satisfaction thus obtained is equal or even superior to that which we get from things, and that we value it just as highly or more highly, since we pay heavily for it if necessary. In this connexion, it is true, we are more inclined to speak of *service* than of utility. But that matters little; we are always saying of some object or other — a bicycle, a pocket-knife, or a fountain pen — that "it renders us good service," just as, conversely, we say to our friends, "please make use of me," — a mere polite formula, no doubt, but one that is scientifically quite correct. And we might even say that things only render us services, just as persons do: what is called their "utility" is the same thing as "service."[1]

But if men desire wealth so much it is not only because it enables them to satisfy their wants or their whims; it is also because it gives them power over men and things. I am not speaking of the social and political influence that money gives, but of economic power — notably the power of commanding at one's pleasure the labour of hundreds and thousands of men. And for this there is no need to be a captain of industry: every capitalist exerts this power indirectly.

[1] At the same time it is a little awkward to describe a service as "wealth": that is why there used to be so much discussion of the question whether "immaterial wealth" can exist.

Such, then, are the two aspects under which wealth appears: *enjoyment-wealth* and *power-wealth.*

The possibility of enjoyment cannot exceed a certain maximum, so that if wealth yielded only enjoyment the pursuit of wealth would also be limited. It is the other aspect of wealth, the desire for command over men and things, that drives human effort beyond all assignable limits, and that has caused the rise of those American millionaires, so rightly named the "kings" of cotton, steel, or oil. Nor should it be overlooked that this desire is a nobler one than the other, though socially it may become more dangerous.

Enjoyment-wealth grows and is spent in the form of *income;* and *power-wealth* is realized in the form of capital. That is why modern socialism aims at abolishing wealth as an instrument of man's power over his fellows, while leaving it in existence as a means of enjoyment and an object of consumption. But it is not easy to separate these two functions.

III. THE DIFFERENCE BETWEEN WEALTH AND VALUE

In ordinary speech the words "wealth" and "value" are synonymous. But in political economy they bear meanings which are by no means identical, and in some respects even opposite to each other.

(1) The idea of wealth implies a relation between *man and things*, whereas value implies a *relation between things* — a relation that takes actual form in the shape of exchange, or if that is impossible, as when things are too far apart in space or time, in the shape of a statement of value.

For all good things are not equally objects of desire. We set up an order or classification among them, just as there are dishes at our table that we like best, and favourite books in our libraries. Even Robinson Crusoe on his island drew up a comparative scale of the objects he possessed, and he had to apply it when it came to taking things from the wreck, by starting with those by which he set most store.

Value, then, is a *relative* notion, like size and weight. If there were only one object in the world, it could not be called large or small, nor could we say that it had much or little value.

That is what distinguishes value from utility, for the latter exists by itself, just like the want that it satisfies. When I say that such and such a thing — a gun or a horse — *is useful,* I make a statement that is perfectly clear and definite. But if I say that a pearl *is worth*, the statement is incomplete and even meaningless: *what is it worth?* To make it intelligible we must add that it is worth so much money, or, if we are among savages, so many pieces of calico, or so many elephant tusks; that is to say, we must compare it with some other kind of wealth.

It is true that in everyday speech we say that such and such an object has "great value," without adding anything else. But the other term of the comparison is understood, though it is not expressed. We mean that the object has great value relatively to the unit of money, in which case we compare it to that other value called a coin; or else we mean that it occupies a high rank among objects of wealth, in which case we are comparing it with all other kinds of wealth considered collectively. Similarly, when we say that platinum is very heavy, without expressing any comparison, we mean either that it has a high specific gravity, comparing it with the weight of water, or else that it occupies a high place in a list of all known bodies arranged according to weight.

From this relative character of value it follows that a *simultaneous* rise or fall of values is impossible: such a statement has no meaning. Whenever we exchange or compare two things, the value of one can only be increased in proportion as the value of the other diminishes. Thus understood, the law is self-evident; it might even be called tautologous, for the exchange value of one thing is nothing but the amount of something else that it enables us to obtain. So to say that one is worth more is to say that the other is worth less. Thus when money, which enables us to obtain everything else, falls in value, we must give more of it, when we make a purchase, to obtain any other kind of goods; which is the same thing as saying that a fall in the value of money means a general rise in prices, and conversely.

It is the same with value as with weight: the relative weights of two things cannot both change at the same time, for this would mean that the two scales of the balance would rise or fall simultaneously.

(2) The idea of wealth is necessarily bound up with that of *abundance:* the more goods a man has the wealthier he is. But the idea of value, on the other hand, is bound up with that of *scarcity* — of limitation of quantity.[1] Yet does not each one of us measure his

---

[1] Ricardo was the first to call attention to this point in his chapter on the distinctive properties of wealth and value. For him the essential difference lay in the fact that value depends on difficulty of production, and wealth on ease of production.

wealth by the sum total of the values he possesses in his pocket-book or in the form of fixed property? Undoubtedly; but we know too that if the objects we possess are everywhere too abundant, their value becomes depreciated and our wealth diminishes. Consequently, if we have it in our power to make these things scarce on the market we shall not fail to do so. That law was known and acted upon by the spice-merchants of the Dutch Indies when they destroyed as much of the crop as they thought excessive; and it is to-day the reason for the existence of those associations of manufacturers, called Trusts or Cartels, which limit production on pain of a fine.

Suppose, on the other hand — to take an imaginary case — that through the progress of science and industry, all objects become as abundant as the water of the brooks or the sand of the seashore, so that men can satisfy their wants by merely drawing upon them at will. In this case it is obvious that everything will have lost all exchange value, for there can be no exchange of objects which are free to all. They will have neither more nor less value than the water of the brooks or the grains of sand themselves. And since the sum of many zeros can never make anything but zero, there will no longer be any *individual* value or wealth. In this utopian world there will be no rich men any longer, for all men will be equal in face of the valuelessness of things, just as the king and the beggar are equal before the light of the sun. But *real* wealth, in those circumstances, would be at a maximum.[1]

IV. WHAT IS VALUE?

We have just said that the word "value" implies a relation, a comparison, a preference. But why is it that one thing is worth more than another? Simple as it seems, this question has been the torment of economists for hundreds of years.

The innumerable answers that have been given to it may be grouped into two great theories which we will examine in turn: the *utility* theory, and the *labour* theory.

---

[1] J. B. Say said: "Since wealth is composed of the value of things possessed, how can a nation be wealthiest when things are at the lowest price?" And Proudhon, in his *Contradictions economiques*, defied "any serious economist" to answer this poser. But the answer is that the definition underlying the argument is inaccurate: though it is true of an individual that his wealth is made up of the sum of the values he possesses, it is not true of a nation.

1. *The Utility Theory of Value*

The first answer that suggests itself to the mind is that things ought to be more or less valuable according as they more or less completely satisfy our wants — in other words, according as they are more or less useful.

But we must be careful to notice at the outset that this kind of utility cannot be the same as utility in the common acceptation of the word. The word *useful* implies a moral judgment, the suitability of the object for satisfying certain wants which are considered good; it is generally opposed, on the one hand, to what is *harmful*, and, on the other hand, to what is *superfluous*. Thus we place the utility of corn and coal and iron in the front rank, but we object to speaking of the "utility" of pearls or lace or some old postage-stamp. Yet the value of these latter objects is far higher than that of the former. Value, therefore, has no connection with utility in the moral sense. Consequently, in its economic acceptation the term "utility" can only mean the property of satisfying any want or desire whatever, and this utility can only be measured by the intensity of that want or desire.

To avoid this perpetual misunderstanding it would be as well to replace the word "utility" by some other term. The older economists called it *value in use*, as opposed to value in exchange, or exchange value. This name described it well, and it is a pity, perhaps, that it has been abandoned. In the first edition of this book (1883) we proposed the term *desirability*, which has the double advantage of not prejudging the character of the desire as moral or immoral, reasonable or unreasonable,[1] and of clearly marking the *subjective* character of value, whereas the term *utility* inevitably suggests the idea of a quality inherent in the object, like hardness, elasticity, etc. And this is not the case; value is not created by nature.

Let us go a step further. Even with this rectification the term "utility" seems insufficient to give us the key to the riddle, for while we can recognize that a diamond has great utility or great desirability for a fashionable lady, it is obvious that water has also, not only in the Sahara, but for every one of us at all times. ᾽Άριστον μεν ὕδωρ, said the poet Pindar — "water is the best of all things" — and yet its value is generally *nil*. It is much the same with bread:

---

[1] M. Vilfredo Pareto has proposed the term *ophelimity*, a Greek word which expresses a "relation of suitability" between an object and a desire. But the word has had little more success than the one that we had proposed.

it would certainly be a great privation for every Englishman to eat his meals without bread; then how are we to explain the very small value of this object also?

That is why another conception has had to be introduced to explain value — the idea of *scarcity*. This, by itself, would not suffice to create value, for however rare a thing might be — even if it were unique — it is clear that it would have no value if it were of no use. Cherries are as scarce at the end of the season as at the beginning: nevertheless they acquire no value from the scarcity at the end of the season, because they are only desired when they are early. If I have written a tragedy, my manuscript is unique, which is the highest degree of scarcity; but it will not thereby acquire any value.[1]

It might be thought, however, that scarcity in itself creates value, if we think of the many instances of enormous prices being paid for such things as postage-stamps whose only interest lies in their being the only ones of their kind. Yet, even in these cases, it is very clear that the value depends solely on the desire of the collector who wants to have a more complete set of stamps than his rivals. The difficulty of filling gaps, and the rarity of the object, act simply as obstacles in the way of desire, like a dam thrown across a river, whose removal makes the water flow more strongly than before.[2]

But if each of these two elements is insufficient by itself, it seems that they are sufficient when combined. We thus arrive at this first explanation: that value is *scarce utility*. And some eminent economists think that we can leave it at that.

But nowadays economists of the psychological school, and especially of the school that has become famous as the Austrian school, are no longer content with this explanation. They have set themselves to dig a little deeper into this concept of value, and have come to the conclusion that utility is amply sufficient to explain value, without the necessity of adding anything else, provided only that the word "utility" is properly defined.

To understand this point, let us return to that old stumbling-block, the example of water. Water is not only useful in the ordinary sense of the word; it is also useful in the sense of "desirable." Then why has it no value?

[1] Yet utility, in the ordinary sense of the word, *i.e.* in the sense of *quality*, does determine value in the case of products of the same kind. Thus the prices in a shop of cloth, or fruit, or jewels, or motor-cars is fixed according to their quality, which means that, other things being equal, we prefer whatever will best satisfy our wants.

[2] A Mauritius postage-stamp issued in 1847 has fetched, at different sales, as much as £1200 and £1400. Why this fabulous price? Simply because the engraver had made a mistake, so that the stamp bore the words *Post Office* instead of *Post Paid*.

We must reply that the objection is groundless, for these reasons: —

(1) In the first place, it is not true that water has no monetary value. When used for irrigation or as a motive power it has value — sometimes even a very considerable one. It even has a certain value as drinking water in all towns. So it is only in reference to the jug of water on our table that we are justified in saying that water has no value: that jug, it is true, has little or no value. Now can we also say that this jug of water is *very desirable?* By no means; for if it chanced to be upset I should only have to get it filled again at the tap. A thing that can be replaced at will can never be very keenly desired — one can neither be much grieved by its absence nor rejoice much in possessing it.

Consequently, the apparent contradiction between the extreme usefulness of water and its lack of value does not really exist: it results solely from a confusion of ideas. When we speak of the great utility of water, we are thinking of water *in general*, as an indispensable factor in the life of the world; when we say that water has no value, we are thinking of the small quantity necessary to meet our individual requirements.

It is the same with bread. When we say that bread is very useful, we are thinking of the utility of bread in general to the white races of the world: that is indeed great, but so too is its total value — some £800,000,000 at least before the war, and perhaps five times as much to-day. But, as a consumer, I have no concern with the world's wheat harvest: my wants are limited to my daily bread. Now this small quantity cannot very greatly excite my desire, for I can easily replace it, though not quite so easily as I can replace the water; so the value of wheat is considerably greater than that of water.

The utility that we have to consider, then, in seeking the basis of value, is never the total utility of an object, but the utility of the small fraction that is necessary to satisfy our wants.

(2) Not only so, but we must further observe that each of these fractions has a very different degree of utility. It is important, therefore, to know which one we have in view — which of the fractions it is whose utility determines value.

Let us suppose that my daily supply of water is contained in a series of numbered buckets, arranged in a row. Bucket No. 1 has the highest degree of utility for me, for I shall use it to quench my thirst; bucket No. 2 has also a great utility, though not so great as the first, for I shall use it for cooking; bucket No. 3 has still less utility, for I shall use it for washing; No. 4 is for my horse to drink; No. 5 to water my dahlias; No. 6 to wash my kitchen floor. Bucket

No. 7 will be of no use to me at all, so I shall not take the trouble to fill it any longer. If some evil spirit, like the one conjured up by the "clumsy wizard" of a German legend, were to amuse itself by bringing me a 10th or a 20th or a 100th bucket, till I was drowned, it is obvious that these would be not only not useful but positively *harmful.* We cannot therefore say that these buckets of water are either useful or useless, but that they present a complete scale of *diminishing utilities,* ranging from infinity to zero, and even lower.

Let us stop and consider bucket No. 6, the last one which had any utility at all. Its utility was small, but none the less it was worth the trouble of drawing this bucketful from the well. Now we are able to affirm — and this is the most interesting point in the argument — that none of the other buckets can have a greater value than that determined by *the utility of this last one.* The reason is this: that, whatever happens, it is by the acquisition or the loss of this last unit that we measure our enjoyment or our privation. Suppose that bucket No. 1, which I was going to drink from, gets accidentally upset. Shall I weep and lament and say that I must die of thirst? That would be the height of lunacy, of course. It is obvious that I should not have to go without my drinking-water on that account: I should only have to sacrifice another bucketful to make up for it. Which bucket? Obviously the one that is least useful, namely, the 6th — the last one that I filled. That is why it is the last bucket that determines the value of all the rest. And as the value of this last bucket is extremely small — at any rate in our country: it would be different in an African village — that is why the value of water is extremely small. Its *final utility* is infinitesimal.

Now let us leave this numbering of buckets, which we adopted only for purposes of demonstration and which is no longer of any use, for it is evident that all the buckets are identical and interchangeable. Consequently they must all have *the same value,* and this value is precisely that which answers to the last want that is satisfied or frustrated, as the case may be.

To sum up this argument: —

Value is determined not by total utility, but only by the utility of that portion of the object of which we are in need. This utility is not the same for each unit that we possess; and it goes on diminishing, because the intensity of our want goes on diminishing as the number of units that we possess increases. Now it is the utility of the last unit possessed — the least useful portion, therefore, for it corresponds to the last want satisfied — which determines and limits the utility of all the others. That is why it is called *final utility*.[1]

This theory is based upon the law of satiety that we explained in connection with wants (see p. 35). We saw that all wants and desires cease as soon as they are satisfied, and even change to repulsion for the object that they but lately coveted. Yet it may be said, surely, that water remains useful even after we have quenched our thirst? Yes, it is useful in the physical sense that it retains thirst-quenching properties, but from an economic point of view it is no longer an object of desire to me or to anyone, for we all have enough of it, or even too much.

This theory is admirable as an accurate and subtle psychological analysis of human wants and their varying intensity.[2] Yet it only revives an older doctrine — that of Senior and the elder Walras in particular — which attributed value to scarcity, with the understanding that the scarcity applied to a desirable object, for otherwise it could not create any value at all (see p. 45 above). In reality, therefore, final utility is only the learned name for *scarce utility*. But the merit of the theory lies in the reconciliation it has effected between the two conceptions of utility and scarcity, by showing that they are inseparable, and that utility, in the economic sense of the word, is necessarily a "function," in the mathematical sense, of the quantity of the object in question.

It must nevertheless be admitted that a certain amount of verbal

[1] *Final utility* must therefore be carefully distinguished from *total utility*. The latter consists of the sum of the utilities of all the buckets of water, and is consequently always much greater than the utility of the last bucket. That is why the total utility of *water* is enormous, though the utility of *a bucket of water* is small.

The term *final* is not altogether a satisfactory one. It has been criticized for implying the idea of a diminishing series — a scheme of numbered units which is useful for demonstration purposes but does not correspond to reality. Some economists prefer the term *marginal utility*, as the Germans call it. "*Liminal*" *utility* might be better still.

[2] But it was not till the middle of the nineteenth century that the theory of final utility was first formulated. This was by a French mining engineer, Dupuit (1844), who was followed by a German named Gossen (1854). But the work of these two remained quite unknown till the theory was set up anew (1871–1873) by Jevons in England, John C. Clark in the United States, Walras in Switzerland, and Karl Menger in Austria. The fact that these authors reached practically the same conclusions, simultaneously and independently, obviously creates a presumption in favour of the truth of the theory. It has found its chief exponents in Austria — not only Menger, but Boehm-Bawerk and Wieser after him.

artifice is involved in thus reducing very complex elements to a single idea, and expressing them by a compound word. For final utility implies not only scarcity but difficulty of acquisition as well,[1] since scarcity or limitation of quantity is hardly ever an absolute fact: under modern economic conditions it is only a relative one. There is nothing in the world whose quantity is so rigidly fixed that we cannot increase it if we take enough trouble. This applies even to natural products, and still more, of course, to the products of human industry. The reason that diamonds are rare is not that nature has put into circulation a strictly limited number and then broken the mould: it is simply that a great deal of trouble or a great deal of luck is requisite to find them, and consequently the quantity in existence can only be increased with difficulty. When we say that chronometers are rare we do not mean that the world contains an insufficient number of them to meet our needs, but simply that the manufacture of a good chronometer takes a considerable time and demands special skill, so that the quantity of them is limited by the time and labour available. It would even be a bold thing to assert that the number of paintings by Raphael is absolutely fixed: for it is not impossible that some one may some day discover others of which we know nothing, in some old church or barn.

In our explanation of value, therefore, even when we base it upon utility, we cannot ignore the greater or smaller degree of difficulty involved in the production of wealth, and so true is this that a mere *possibility*, though not yet realized in practice — such as the discovery of a method of crystallizing carbon into diamonds — might be quite sufficient to bring about a lowering of value, even before it was industrially applied.

On the other hand, this theory seems better suited to a Robinson Crusoe than to men living in society and in a world of exchange. The final utility of a pair of glasses is enormous for me if I am so shortsighted that I can neither read nor walk without them. But as I know I can always replace them at any optician's if I chance to break them, their final utility cannot be greater than the four or five shillings I should have to pay for them, a sum which represents simply their cost of production.

---

[1] Some economists have held that these words, *difficulty of acquisition*, offer a complete and satisfactory explanation of value — on condition, however, that utility is understood; for nothing could be more difficult than to recover a pebble thrown to the bottom of the Atlantic, but this confers no value upon it.

2. *The Labour Theory of Value*

This theory has held a prominent place in the history of economic doctrines. Expounded for the first time by Adam Smith, though in a somewhat uncertain form, and then vigorously asserted by Ricardo, it has been accepted by economists of the most opposite schools, from optimists like Bastiat to socialists like Rodbertus and Karl Marx.

Every object, said Proudhon, *is worth what it costs.* And what it costs is not the money we pay for it, for purchase is only the transfer of a thing that already exists: it is the labour that has been expended in producing it.[1]

At first sight this theory looks very attractive. To begin with, it gives a precise, objective, and easily measured notion as the foundation of value. The mind is satisfied by the statement that such and such an object — a watch, for instance — is worth a hundred times as much as a loaf of bread because it represents a hundred times as many hours of work. The explanation is plausible: in any case it can be verified by enquiry; whereas to say that the watch is worth a hundred times as much as the loaf because its utility is a hundred times as great, is to make a comparative estimate which tells us nothing definite. Nor is this estimate made any clearer by substituting "final utility" or "desirability" for the term "utility."

Secondly, this theory answers better to the idea of justice, because it sets up a moral element — labour — as the foundation of value. And it is on this account particularly that it has attracted so many generous-minded men. Could we but succeed in proving that the value of everything owned is determined by the labour it has cost, then the problem of allotting to every man a value equal to the produce of his labour would be greatly simplified, and it would be easier to establish the social organization firmly upon a principle of justice.

At the same time it must be observed that this explanation of value has been employed for two exactly opposite purposes. The upholders of the existing economic order have used it to prove that

---

[1] We often hear it said also that *value* is determined by the cost of production, meaning by that *the sum of the prices paid for the various productive services* — wages, interest, rent, etc., — and that is how the manufacturer understands it. But in this sense the cost of production affords no explanation of value, for these constituent elements of the cost price are themselves only values, so that we are only explaining one value by means of others. All that this explanation does is to affirm a necessary relation between the value of the product and the sum of the values of its constituent elements.

all property, including the ownership of land and of capital, is in conformity with social justice, since all value is founded upon labour. But the socialists, on the other hand, have used it to prove that property is usually a spoliation of the workers, since for the most part the workers are not owners and the owners are not workers. Therefore under the existing régime, they say, property and value are indeed founded upon labour, but upon *other people's labour*, and not that of the owner. If then we wish every one to own the value created by *his own* labour, we must overturn the existing order of things.

But these considerations, whether justificatory or critical, must count for nothing in an explanation of value. There only remains then to examine the economic argument that all value involves a certain amount of labour, and that the value is measured by the quantity of that labour.

(1) Observe in the first place that this theory cannot deny that utility — the property of satisfying any of man's wants or desires — is still the fundamental condition of all value. It would be absurd, indeed, to imagine that anything could have any value at all if it was of no use, no matter how much labour it cost. But, it is said, if utility is the *condition* of value, it is not its *cause*. The utility of things is what differentiates them from each other: labour is what gives them all the common characteristic of being valuable, from an economic point of view.

But is this true of *all* things? Certainly not; there are innumerable things which have value of their own without having cost any labour, simply because they are useful and sought after. Such are mineral springs, oil springs, guano deposited by sea-birds, those sandy beaches at the mouth of the Rhône, untilled except by the sea wind, which fetch high prices for planting vineyards, and building sites in Park Lane or Fifth Avenue.

(2) Notice in the second place that if the value of a thing is determined by the labour employed in its production, then the value of everything is *necessarily unchangeable*, because the labour worked into it is past labour, and what is past cannot be changed — as Lady Macbeth said, "What's done, is done." Now every one knows, on the other hand, that the value of an object varies unceasingly from time to time, simply because it depends upon demand, or desire, and it is quite obvious that these variations are entirely independent of the labour expended in producing the object originally. Past labour is dead, whereas value is living.

To meet this argument it is replied that what makes value is not the past labour that was employed in producing the object in question, but the similar, present labour necessary under existing social conditions to replace the object: in other words, the labour of *reproducing* it; or else, as Karl Marx said, the *social labour* necessary for its production, which is measured by the average number of hours actually necessary to produce it.

Very well; but it remains none the less true that this average social labour changes but slowly with the progress of industry, and cannot therefore explain the frequent, often daily variations in the value of things, resulting from changes in supply and demand upon the market. We must say, then, that there are two kinds of value: *normal* value, determined by the labour, or rather the cost, of production; and *current* value, determined by supply and demand, that is to say, by scarcity and utility. That is how it was put by John Stuart Mill, who compared normal value to the level of the sea, and market value to the movement of the waves, constantly upsetting this level. But even so it must be recognized that this "level of the sea" is only an abstraction that is never perfectly realized; that therefore the value based upon labour is similarly only an abstract conception; and that in practice it is value based upon utility that we must take into account.

Nor is it only in fleeting variations and oscillations around a centre of gravity that current value shows itself independent of labour cost; in many cases the changes take the shape of definite divergences. Such is the case with the wine that improves in quality and increases in value as it lies in the cellar, while no change has taken place in the labour of the vine-grower who gathered the grapes or even in the social labour employed in making the wine. Such also is the case with land and houses, which may acquire increased value solely on account of their situation — that is to say, their utility — even though their original value was due to the labour of clearing the land or building the houses. On this very phenomenon is founded the celebrated economic law of *rent*. It implies, as we shall see, an excess in the selling price of an object over its labour cost. And rent exists everywhere, to a greater or less degree.

(3) Finally, this theory that value is nothing but labour seems to suggest a false idea of value by materializing it in its object, regarding it, as Karl Marx did, as "crystallized labour." Now value, as changeable as fashion, is totally unlike the unchangeable crystal. Value is only a beam of light projected on things by our desire, and as the revolving beam of this lighthouse turns hither and thither it makes the objects in the world around us leap out of the shad-

ows, to disappear again into the darkness when it is turned elsewhere: they have had value, and now they have it no longer.

We can see, then, that this labour theory of value is surrounded
on all sides by the utility theory, and cannot get free from it. Must
it therefore be dismissed in favour of its sister theory? No; for
we have already seen that the utility theory is itself insufficient
without a reference to the causes which limit the quantity of the
objects in question, and of these causes the principal one is labour.

Let us ask ourselves some questions. Why do we attach a certain
value to an object? Why is such and such a thing dear to us?[1]
We can easily see, after a little consideration, that we can give two
different and, in some respects, opposite replies: we can be attached to things either because of the *pleasure* we get from possessing
them, or because of the *pain* that their acquisition has cost us.
The deepest kind of love — maternal love — is itself made up of
these two elements.

The isolated producer, say Robinson Crusoe on his island, certainly valued his canoe not only for the services it performed for
him, but also for the enormous amount of labour that he had to put
into the building of it, and which he would have had to undergo
again to replace it if it had got wrecked.

Still more is this the case in a state of society in which almost
all goods come to us by way of exchange, where each of us can only
procure a thing by handing over something else, and where consequently every acquisition is coupled with a privation. As buyers
and consumers we think especially of the pleasure we shall obtain
from the object we wish to purchase: as sellers and producers we
think particularly of the pain and expense that will eventually be
necessary to replace the wealth that we are giving up.

Both theories, therefore, must be retained together as inseparable and complementary. No doubt the mind is generally better
satisfied by a single cause, but here, where we are dealing with exchange value, it is inevitable that value should have two aspects
and be double-faced, like Janus — one face turned towards the
buyer, the other towards the seller — one face laughing, and the
other weeping.

Yet of these two aspects of value the utility aspect seems to us
predominant, for the simple reason that consumption is the end,
and production only the means. In logic, as well as in practice,
it is the consumer who gives his orders.

[1] It is not for nothing that we use the same word *dear* to express two different senti-
ments: a thing is *dear* both when we love it, and when it costs us much.

So far as it is possible to summarize such complex notions in a few words, we can say: —

An object has more or less value according to the intensity of our desire for it.

The intensity of this desire depends on two things: (a) *The enjoyment that the object is capable of giving to those who do not possess it;* (b) *the sacrifices that will be incurred by those who possess it, if they lose it and have to replace it.*[1]

V. HOW VALUE IS MEASURED

To measure is to compare two quantities — length, volume, weight, etc. — and not only to compare them but to find out how many times one is contained in the other. For this purpose we have special instruments according to the nature of the quantity we wish to measure — foot-rule, scales, etc. Thus to measure the weights of two bodies — to weigh them — we put them into the scales of a balance. If the scales hang level it means that the weights of the two bodies are equal. If we have to put twice as much on one side as on the other, we say that one body weighs twice as much as the other.

We have also a means of measuring value — the method of *exchange*. Exchange is a kind of weighing, and it, too, is performed in a balance, only the balance is not visible; it exists in the inner consciousness of each of the exchanging parties. Each of them, in his inner consciousness, weighs what he has to give up against what he wants to obtain, and makes up his mind according as the one is lighter or heavier than the other. Moreover value, or at least exchange value, is itself a measuring, for, as we have seen, the idea of value implies a comparison or relation. This may be well expressed by saying that the exchange value of a thing is measured by *the quantity of other things for which it can be exchanged*, or, more shortly, by its *power of acquisition.*[2]

---

[1] This double law of value is already contained implicitly in the usual formula for the *law of supply and demand*. Taken in the narrow sense, this latter law expresses simply a relation between two quantities, the quantity offered and the quantity demanded (at a given price). But, in the wider sense, demand means the fact that things are more or less desired, *i.e.*, their final utility; and supply means the fact that they are more or less difficult to procure, *i.e.*, their cost of production.

[2] But we must beware of saying, as is too often said, that power of acquisition is what constitutes value. Our desire alone is what constitutes value. Power of acquisition is only an *effect* of value, just as the power of attraction of an electro-magnet is only an effect of the current that penetrates it.

If, therefore, in exchange for a hundredweight of wheat I can obtain five hundredweight of coal, I say that the value of wheat is five times as great as that of coal, or, conversely, that the value of coal is a fifth of the value of wheat; in other words, *the values of two kinds of goods are always in inverse proportion to the quantities exchanged.* The more of a thing we must give in exchange, the less is it worth, and the less we must give, the greater is its value.

It must be observed, however, that though exchange exactly measures the *relative* value of things — their differential values — it does not measure their *absolute* value — if, indeed, there is any meaning in this phrase; that is to say, it does not measure the causes which operate on value — the degree of intensity of our desires — any more than the balance measures weight, in the sense of gravity or terrestrial attraction. If we carry our balance up to the top of Mont Blanc, or even up to the moon, it will still imperturbably mark the same weight, although gravity has sensibly or enormously diminished. Similarly, exchange will indicate the same respective values, the same prices, even though there may have been considerable variations in the causes that determine these values, such as desirability, scarcity, cost of production, and so forth. For example, it might happen that the progress of human industry had facilitated the production of everything and thus created abundance; or, on the other hand, that the pressure of population had increased the demand for everything and created a shortage; but neither of these phenomena would be revealed by a variation in prices, for these causes would have operated simultaneously on both scales of the balance.

At the same time we have some instruments that enable us to recognize variations in gravity itself, and not merely in relative weight — the pendulum, for instance. Have we any similar instruments for measuring absolute value? It might be thought, perhaps, that money is just such an instrument; but no! for money, being itself only a form of value, is necessarily affected by the same causes as those which influence other forms of value. Money can no more reveal to us the causes of variation in value than the copper or brass weights that we use as standards can show us changes in gravity.

Money is only a *common measure* of all exchange values: it is nothing more than that, but that is a great deal.

To get a clear idea of size, or weight, or value, or any other quantitative notion, it is not enough to compare and measure things two by two: we must have a common measure for them all. Thus to measure length men have taken for the second term of the comparison either some part of the human body (foot, ell, cubit), or a fixed fraction of the circumference of the earth (metre). Similarly to measure weight they have adopted for comparison a fixed weight of distilled water.

The object of a common measure is to enable us to compare *two things in different places*, which cannot, of course, be compared directly; or to compare *the same thing at different times*, and ascertain whether and how much it has varied. The metre allows us to compare the height of the Laplander with that of the Patagonian, and to measure how much taller the latter is than the former. If the same standard is in use, or at least known, some thousands of years hence, it will enable us to compare the men of that day with the men of our own day, and to find out whether human stature has degenerated.

To measure value, therefore, it is not enough to compare one value with another, as is done in the case of barter; it is needful also to take the value of some one fixed thing as the second term of the comparison. But what thing are we to choose?

Every race and every age has made use of a different measure. Homer says that the armour of Diomedes was worth a hundred oxen. A Japanese would have said, until quite recently, that it was worth so many hundredweight of rice. An African negro would put its value in yards of calico, and a Canadian trapper in foxskins or otter-skins.

It is a remarkable fact, however, that the civilized races have almost all agreed in choosing as their measure of value, or standard, the value of the precious metals, gold, silver, and copper, but especially the first two. They have all made use of a little lump of gold or silver, called a sovereign, a franc, a mark, a dollar, a rouble, etc. To measure the value of any object whatever, they compare it with the value of that little weight of gold or silver that serves as the monetary unit; in other words, they see how many of these little ingots must be handed over in order to obtain the goods in question. If, for instance, ten ingots are required, the goods are said to be worth ten pounds or ten dollars or ten francs, as the case may be: that is their *price*.

The price of a thing is therefore the expression of the relation that exists between the value of the thing and the value of a certain weight of gold or silver. More briefly, it is its *value expressed in money*. And since money in every civilized land is the sole measure of value that is employed, the word "price" has come to be synonymous with the word "value."[1]

The reason why the precious metals have been chosen as a common measure of value is that they possess two particular properties that enable them to perform this function, if not perfectly, at least better than any other known object. These two properties are, first, very great value in small bulk, making them very *easy to transport;* second, a chemical immutability, which makes them *last almost indefinitely.* Thanks to the first of these properties the value of the precious metals varies less between one *place* and another than that of anything else; thanks to the second, it varies less between one *year* and another. And this double invariability in space and time is the essential condition of every good standard of measurement. We shall see later on however, that when we take account of long periods of time — not even as much as several centuries, but only one generation — this invariability is illusory. (See the section on "The History of Money," Book II, Chapter II.)

Now can we find a better measure of value than the precious metals? Several have been proposed, the principal one being *wheat.* This seems at first sight an astonishing choice, for if we consider the value of this commodity in different places or at different times we find that there are few kinds of goods whose fluctuations of value are more marked. At a given time a bushel of wheat may sell for 6s. in France, 4s. 6d. in London, and even for a shilling in certain parts of Siberia; and from year to year, according as circumstances are good or bad, the value may also vary considerably. At the moment of writing (July, 1922) the price of a bushel of wheat in England is about 7s., whereas in France last year it was about 40 francs.

To this it is replied that though the value of wheat is incomparably more variable than that of the precious metals when differences of place or only short intervals of time are considered, yet it is far more stable when longer periods are concerned. Wheat satisfies a physiological need that is permanent and varies little. No other commodity possesses to the same degree the double characteristic (1) of being almost indispensable (at least in the countries where European civilization obtains) up to a certain limit, determined by the quantity necessary to nourish a man, and (2) of being almost entirely useless beyond this limit, since no one cares to consume more than his hunger demands. Hence, despite the great and sudden fluctuations in its production, owing to the vagaries of the

[1] See Book II, Chapter I.

weather, the law of supply and demand has a constant tendency to restore its value to the level determined by physiological need; it does this, moreover, with greater effectiveness whenever production has temporarily deviated from the position of equilibrium.

It is true, therefore, that wheat does offer, so far as variations in value are concerned, virtues and defects that are *precisely opposite* to those that characterize the precious metals. But this does not qualify it for the rôle of the money material: at the most it fits it to serve as a complementary and corrective measure of value. In fact it has often been used by statisticians as a good basis for estimating the cost of living at different periods of history.

Yet another common measure that has been proposed is the *minimum wage* of an unskilled workman, a manual labourer who earns just enough to live on. This proposal is based on the assumption that the amount necessary to keep a man alive is a fixed quantity. But we need only refer to what has been said concerning the wants of man (p. 34), and to what we shall say later on as to wages, to recognize that this assumption is entirely contrary to facts.

The wisest course after all, therefore, is to fall back upon money. But we need not be at all discouraged because this measure of value leaves much to be desired. Political economy is not the only science that has to put up with imperfect instruments. The most exact sciences are often faced by the same difficulty. I have heard the great astronomer, Leverrier, say that it was of little consequence to him whether his instruments were perfectly accurate, and that he did not even strive after it: the essential point was to know the amount of the error so that it could be corrected. And that is precisely what has to be done in the case of the monetary instrument: we must learn to discover, to measure, and to correct its variations.

It remains to find out how this is to be done.

VI. HOW THE STANDARD OF VALUE IS CORRECTED — INDEX NUMBERS

Can we find any means of first *ascertaining* and then *correcting* the apparent variations that result from the variation of the standard of value? These are two distinct questions.

So far as the method of discovering variations in the value of money is concerned, it is obvious that we can only recognize them by comparison with the values of other objects. It will be no use looking at a sovereign, for it is plain that, by definition, this little lump of gold is always worth a pound; it seems even absurd to say that it may be worth more or less than this.

Suppose, however, that a list were drawn up of the prices of all commodities, without exception, at a given time — say, for instance, on the eve of the war. Suppose that a new list is drawn up to-day, and that we find, on comparing the two lists, that the prices of all these commodities, *without exception*, have become four times as great. What conclusion are we compelled to draw?

Such a phenomenon as *a general and uniform rise of prices* admits of only two possible explanations. Either we must admit that things are what they seem to be, and that all commodities have undergone a general and identical rise in price; or else we must admit that the value of one thing — money — has fallen, no alteration having taken place in the value of other commodities. Between these two explanations, common sense permits of no hesitation, even for a moment. The second explanation is as simple and clear as the first is improbable because of the extraordinary combination of circumstances that it presupposes. Is it reasonable, indeed, to imagine the existence of some cause which can act simultaneously and uniformly on the value of objects which are entirely dissimilar as regards their utility, their quantity, and the method of their production? Such a cause would have to be capable of raising the price, at the same time and in the same proportion, of wool and coal, of wheat and diamonds, of paper and wine, of land and labour, and of all other objects having no connection whatever with each other.

To prefer this latter explanation would be every bit as unreasonable as to prefer the Ptolemaic system to the Copernican, as an explanation of the movement of the heavenly bodies. This motion likewise can be explained in two ways: either by the movement of the entire vault of the sky from East to West, or, quite simply, by the movement of our earth in the opposite direction. Even if all direct proof were wanting, we could not hesitate between these two explanations. How indeed could we imagine that bodies so different in their nature and so enormously far apart as the sun, the moon, the planets, the stars, and the nebulae, could travel thus, like soldiers on parade, keeping their proper ranks and their proper distances? The very same kind of reasoning is involved in the supposition that all prices can move uniformly; it can only be reasonably explained as a kind of optical illusion, an *apparent* movement, caused by a real but opposite movement in the value of money.[1]

[1] We can draw yet another comparison from the science of astronomy. It has been found that the stars, though falsely called "fixed," really move in very divergent

This, however, is only a supposition, and is never actually realized. As a matter of fact we never find a uniform and identical rise in the prices of all commodities. Thus at this very moment, although the rise of prices above the pre-war level hardly admits of any exception, yet it is very unequal and may vary from double to a hundredfold according to the commodity or the country. This means that there are *special* causes of price variation for each commodity. At the same time the universality of the rise in prices would be inexplicable without some *general* cause underlying the special and local causes; and this general cause can only be the depreciation of money.

It is for the purpose of isolating this general cause that economists nowadays draw up tables known as Index Numbers. As it would be impracticable to include *all* commodities in these lists, they choose the principal ones; and the choice of these is a very delicate matter. The compilation of Index Numbers is an art in itself, and many chapters would be needed to set out the methods followed and the difficulties to be overcome.

If we wish to estimate changes in the cost of living we must take retail prices, for these are the only ones that affect the consumer. But for estimating variations in the value of money we must discard retail prices, because they are too irregular and vary with local conditions: they do not admit of being "quoted." So we shall take only wholesale prices, such as are quoted on commercial exchanges and in customs returns, etc. But we must choose things of the most different kinds, so as to neutralize as far as possible the causes of variation which are special to particular classes, by allowing them to counteract each other.

Having chosen our commodities, we proceed to add up the prices for each of the years we are comparing. But, before doing this, we take the average of all the prices of each commodity. Then we make a further simplification, for instead of setting down the actual figures obtained by adding these average prices, we take 100 to represent the sum of the prices for the year that serves as the basis of the comparison, and express the price-totals for each of the other years as a ratio of this 100. Suppose, for example, that the sum of the prices is £1,380 for the year 1913, and £4,140 for the year

directions. In one part of the sky they seem to approach each other; in another part they seem to diverge; the constellation Hercules in particular seems to expand. To explain this general movement we have no resource but to regard it as an optical illusion produced by the movement of our solar system towards the constellation Hercules. Attempts have even been made to measure this movement.

1920; then instead of setting down these two figures, which convey nothing to the eye, we set down 100 and 300. By thus discarding the actual figures and putting a percentage instead, we can measure the rise in prices immediately: prices have trebled themselves, though this exact rise was not apparent before. This was very nearly the actual rise in prices in England between 1914 and 1920.[1]

[1] Here are the index numbers for prices in England, covering the period of the war, taken from the *Ministry of Labour Gazette:*

1914 (July)	....	100	1918 (July)	....	205
1915 "	....	125	1919 "	....	210
1916 "	....	150	1920 "	....	252
1917 "	....	180	1920 (Nov.)	....	276

Hence the prices of 1920 represented an advance on pre-war prices of 176%. Prices, therefore, nearly trebled themselves.

We can conclude from this that money underwent an enormous depreciation. (This is easily to be explained, as we shall see later on, by the excessive issue of paper money.) But it would not be accurate to assert that this depreciation was exactly in inverse proportion to the rise in prices, namely, about 64%.

Here, for purposes of comparison, are the index numbers of certain other countries, also for the end of 1920, a date which seems to have marked the highest point in prices:

France	424
Italy (Rome)	375
United States	175

In Russia and most of the eastern countries of Europe the rise is incalculable, the value of paper money having fallen almost to nothing.

BOOK I — PRODUCTION

PART I

THE AGENTS OF PRODUCTION

In virtue of a tradition that dates back to the time of the first economists, three agents of production have always been distinguished: *Land*, *Labour*, and *Capital*. This threefold division has the advantage of being a convenient classification, and there seems to be no need to abandon it, at least in an elementary book like this.

It requires, however, some preliminary correction. Classical political economy has always shown an unfortunate tendency to place these three agents of production on an equal footing, whereas the parts they play are certainly very unequal.

Of the three, Labour is the only one that can claim to be an *agent* of production in the exact sense of the word. Man alone plays an active part; he alone takes the initiative in every productive process.

Land — or rather Nature, for we are not concerned only with the cultivated soil, but with the whole of our material environment, solid, liquid, and gaseous — plays an entirely *passive* part, and merely obeys man, generally after long resistance. Nevertheless it is indispensable to production, and not only to the production of material wealth. It might even be called the *primary* factor of production, for not only is it a necessary adjunct of labour, but it exists before labour. Man's activity could not exert itself in a vacuum; it does not proceed by uttering a creative *fiat;* it must find indispensable materials outside itself; and it is nature that supplies them.

The third agent, Capital, also plays an entirely passive part, like nature, and does not really deserve the name of "agent"; nor can it even be described as a primary factor of production, as nature can. It is only a subsidiary factor, derived from the other two, both logically and genealogically. Capital, as we shall see more precisely later on, is a product of labour and of nature, set aside for purposes of production. The most suitable name for it is that of *instrument* of production, in the widest sense of the term.

It should be observed that each of the three agents of production appeared on the economic scene at its own time. In primitive communities of hunters. fishermen, or shepherds, it was nature that supplied almost everything; then in ancient times it was joined by labour, first agricultural and afterwards industrial; while in modern societies capital has at length appeared, and dominates the other two to such an extent that the present social régime is constantly described as a *capitalist* régime.

Like all classifications this one is obviously in some respects arbitrary, and in reality the three factors or agents are often mixed up. When land has been cleared, drained, and cultivated it becomes a product of labour, and is therefore capital. Conversely, labour cannot be separated from nature: the human organs — the workman's hand, the painter's eye, the voice of the singer — are obviously natural agents.[1] And finally, man himself becomes capital when education has stored his brain with acquired knowledge and incorporated this knowledge in his actions.

[1] That is why it is nonsense to ask whether labour *alone* can produce, without the help of nature. We are tempted to answer "yes," if we think of the production of immaterial wealth, or services. But we forget that even in this case labour is never *alone*. It implies not only living organs, but an environment as well — air and sound and light, and so forth. See below, *The Productiveness of Labour.*

CHAPTER I — NATURE

The term "nature" does not signify a definite, specific factor of production, but a vague entity, the sum total of those pre-existing elements which are provided for us by the world in which we live. If man is to produce, nature must supply him with a favourable *climatic environment*, sufficiently fertile *land*, and later on with *motive power* to assist his labour. We might add *time* to this list, for our existence is conditioned by time as well as space.

I. LAND

Land supplies man with three things: (1) a place to stand on, to build his house on, and to cultivate his fields; (2) those kinds of vegetables and animals which alone can satisfy his two primary wants — food and clothing; (3) the underground minerals and fuels which feed his industries.

§ 1

In his primitive state man is content with the products that the earth spontaneously gives him. But this does not mean that he has not to work terribly hard to procure them; it only means that he cannot modify them. This is the first stage in industry — the *hunting* or *fishing* stage. It lasted, so far as we can tell, infinitely longer than the industrial periods that succeeded it — some 200,000 years, according to certain palæontologists. At the same time it is by no means true to say that hunting was the earliest form of human industry, for it presupposes the existence of weapons — bow, spear, sling, or snare. It must therefore have been preceded by a period that is now lost in the darkness of the past, when human industry was in no way different from animal industry, when man was obliged to stalk and capture his wretched prey as best he could. That was the régime of the *quest*, as it has been expressively termed, to distinguish it from the hunting stage.

However many thousand years the hunting stage lasted, it never succeeded in raising any race of people to what we should call a civilized condition. This is because it was too little productive, or rather, perhaps, too destructive, to allow a population to reach

the minimum density required by social life and industrial development.   If the population of the British Isles had to live by hunting,
even supposing we could restore the game that has now disappeared,
it would become reduced to some hundreds of thousands of men.
The number of the Red Indians was no higher than that at a time
when they ruled over a territory several times as large as the British
Isles.

With the fishing industry it is quite different.   Fishing, at least
sea fishing, has been far more effectual in keeping men alive, and
even in raising them to a relatively high level of civilization.   This
superiority of fishing over hunting is easily explained by the differences between these two modes of exploiting natural wealth:

(a) The food provided by fishing is generally more abundant and
less dependent on chance than that yielded by hunting.   Nor does
it depopulate the sea as hunting depopulates the forests, especially
when it is practised only with primitive tackle.   The result is that
it permits men to congregate in sufficient density and to settle down,
whereas the hunting tribes must be for ever wandering in search of
new hunting grounds.   In other words, fishing permits the building
of towns.   None the less, as every fisherman is necessarily a sailor,
this settled life does not exclude long ocean voyages, and it is thus
that international relations were first established; witness the Scandinavian lands and their adventurous Northmen.

(b) Fishing can scarcely be usefully pursued by men in isolation;
it is better practised by groups of men, whereas the hunter hunts
alone and strives jealously to conceal his tracks.   The boat and the
fishing-net are the outcome of collective labour and can only be used
by a group or association which can already be described as co-
operative.   The social influence of these instruments is quite different, therefore, from that of the bow or sling of the hunter; every
boat's crew learns of necessity to obey its leader, and to choose him
carefully.   In this way, also, fishing has social and political consequences that differ largely from those of hunting.

§ 2

The second stage is the *pastoral* stage.   This is a natural development of the hunting stage, with this vast difference, that man now
breeds animals instead of killing them, and thus substitutes productive for destructive exploitation.   But the greatest service rendered to man by pastoral industry is that besides providing him with
his daily food (milk, butter, and meat) and clothing (wool and
leather), it also procured him leisure, in his tent or in the field,

while idly watching his flocks. This enabled him to lay the earliest foundations of industry, in the weaving of wool; of science, in the observation of plants and stars; and of literature, in songs and heroic tales.

The pastoral industry also created the patriarchal family and, along with it, a social régime and forms of government of which traces yet survive in the laws and constitutions of modern nations. But we are not here concerned with these.

Thus the origins of civilization are bound up with the domestication of animals. This domestication, according to M. de Mortillet, dates back to some 16,000 or 18,000 years ago.

Pastoral industry, however, could draw nothing from the earth but what the earth spontaneously offered. Consequently it could only support a very limited population on a given area — a larger population than could be maintained by hunting, but a smaller one than fishing permitted; and the tribe could only exist by constantly changing its pasturage to maintain its flocks. Hence it was condemned to a nomadic life, and in this respect the pastoral régime was inferior to that of the fishing stage.

§ 3

So far we have spoken only of the exploitation of the earth for the purpose of procuring animal food. But the provision of vegetable food followed a parallel line of development.

Fruit-gathering supplied man with food long before hunting began. It corresponds to the *quest* period, but it held a far larger place among the means of existence of primitive peoples, and even continued into the earliest ages of civilization. If the oak was sacred to Jupiter, this was not only because it attracted the thunderbolt, but because it bore acorns, and the acorn was the staff of life for the peoples of Europe even in the historic period — for the Gauls, for instance. Acorn bread was eaten even in the time of Charlemagne.[1]

No doubt as soon as man had learned how to tame wild animals, he conceived the idea of taming, breeding, or cultivating wild plants. That was the birth of *agriculture*. However, it certainly did not begin with the operation of tilling the soil which is implied to-day in the word "agriculture." That operation presupposes a vast number of previous inventions — not only the plough, but the iron

---

[1] Those who have tried to eat raw acorns cannot believe that men could ever have tolerated such food. But they would hardly find wheat more appetizing if they had to eat it just as it comes from the husk! The men who lived on acorns did not eat them raw; there is no doubt that they found out how to cook them.

with which the plough is shod, and for which the bronze of the preceding age was no substitute. It presupposes also the training of the ox to submit to the yoke, for it is a curious fact that for thousands of years man knew how to make use of cattle to provide him with food and clothing, and how to employ the horse in hunting and in war, but he did not know how to make animals assist him in his work. Lastly, agriculture in its modern sense presupposes the discovery of cereal crops, beginning with barley, which seems to have been the first one to be grown. Imagination shrinks from measuring the full import of the action of the first man who was able to recognize that some of these humble grasses bore grains that were good to eat.

It seems probable, therefore, that the cultivation of cereals was preceded by a rudimentary form of horticulture or arboriculture that was already practiced by the hunting or pastoral races, although their wandering life can scarcely have been convenient for gardening. Perhaps there is some historical significance in the story in Genesis that shows us Adam cultivating the Garden of Eden and gathering the fruits of the trees before Cain became a tiller of the soil.

Agriculture, in the sense of tillage, can scarcely date back earlier than the beginning of historic times. Its birth was celebrated by ancient writers as a comparatively recent event.[1] They greeted it as the dawn of the era of civilization, which was rather unjust to the pastoral age, though the latter had been less prominent in Europe than in Asia. Wheat-growing, however, laid upon the sons of Japhet a much heavier burden of labour than the previous methods of exploiting the land, for besides the toil of ploughing there was also the labour of the mill and the kneading-trough, groaned over by so many generations of women and slaves.

But wheat has well repaid man for his labour. It has done so, first, by teaching him the law of regular work which the pastoral life had been unable to teach: "In the sweat of thy brow shalt thou eat bread"; and then by teaching him thrift as well. Since wheat is easily preserved, man was able to store it in his granaries. The granary was the first savings-bank of the human race. Thus famine, hitherto a constant menace, became much less threatening, even if it was not altogether eliminated. The two other great cereals, rice, which has sufficed for the nourishment of enormous masses of the yellow race, and maize, the national food of the New World, require less labour to turn them into food, if not to grow them, for they do

---

[1] "Ceres taught men to turn up the earth when they could no longer find acorns or arbutus berries in the sacred forest." (Virgil, *Georgics*, I. 147–9.)

not need to be made into bread.   But at the same time they have
not engendered the same virtues in those who consume them: up to
the present, at any rate, the leadership of the world has remained
with the bread-eaters.

With the coming of agriculture, nomadic life gradually ceased,
though not suddenly, for the first attempts must have quickly
exhausted the soil.   Then the city was born.   The substitution of
a partly vegetable diet for the flesh-eating of the preceding age
seems even to have had a softening influence upon manners.   Men
no longer offered bleeding victims to their gods, but consecrated
meal and unleavened bread.   No doubt agricultural peoples made
war like pastoral ones, but they fought with somewhat less ferocity,
it would appear.   Contrary to what might be expected, the sons of
Cain were gentler than the sons of Abel.

With the coming of agriculture, labour took the first place in
production, and nature, who till then had provided almost alone for
the wants of man, retired into the second rank.   We can leave her,
then, for the time being.

It must be said, however, that not even to-day have primitive
methods of exploiting the earth altogether disappeared.   There
are pastoral races still in existence in Asia and Africa, and if there
are hardly any hunting or fishing peoples left, in the full sense of
those words, yet fishing is still a very important industry, and a
means of livelihood to millions of men.   Moreover, hunting itself
is still represented by such great undertakings as that of the Hudson
Bay Company, which supplies the civilized world with furs.   But
the same process of development is apparent in these enterprises as
that which transformed the hunting peoples, at the dawn of history,
into pastoral ones.

In the case of living beings, whether animal or vegetable, industry is able to some extent to avert the fate which threatens them,
by changing its methods of procedure.   Instead of hunting, man can
breed and rear animals; instead of fishing, he can practise piscicul-
ture; instead of clearing the forest, he can replant it; in other words,
he can leave the extractive industries for the agricultural.   Thus,
for example, in Canada, now that fox-skins have come to fetch exorbitant prices owing to the extermination of the foxes, fox-breeding
has become a most profitable industry.   More than ten companies
have been formed to exploit it.   Similarly in Florida there are actually
farms for rearing crocodiles, whose skin is very valuable.   As for
the ostrich, it is well known that they are reared on a large scale in

South Africa; and some attempts have been made to rear them also in the French African colonies.[1]

II. THE LAW OF DIMINISHING RETURN

Since the area and the volume of the earth are alike limited in quantity, it is a necessary consequence that the quantity of produce that can be drawn from it is also limited. This fact has very important results.

The law of limitation is most in evidence in the extractive industries. When the mine is exhausted the miner is bound to stop, and as a rule he is obliged to stop long before that point is reached, because his work ceases to be remunerative, though it may once more become profitable when the science of metallurgy makes fresh progress.

But this law of limitation embraces all human industry, and is not to be evaded by passing from extractive to agricultural production, for even in this higher form of industry there are obstacles to be met with.

(1) To begin with, agricultural production is limited by the quantity of *mineral substances* that are indispensable to plant life. Every plot of land, even the most fertile, contains only a fixed amount of nitrogen, potash, phosphoric acid, and so forth, and every crop takes away a portion of these substances. It is true that agricultural science succeeds not only in giving back to the land the elements thus withdrawn from it, but even in enriching it by the addition of new elements. But it must be borne in mind that the sources upon which the farmer draws to enrich the soil are themselves limited, for natural manure only restores to the soil a part of what the cattle have consumed, and chemical manures are minerals (phosphates, potash, nitrates, guano, etc.) the deposits of which are scanty and quickly exhausted.

(2) Moreover, agricultural production is limited by the conditions of *space* and *time* that are indispensable to vegetable and animal life; these conditions are much more rigid and less open to modification than those of industrial production. As has been suggested

[1] The finest example among plants is that of rubber. The destructive exploitation of the forests of the Amazon and the Congo has been gradually replaced by industrial cultivation in the Dutch and British colonies of the East Indies. It is owing to this that rubber is the only raw material whose price did not rise during the war, in spite of the enormous consumption that was caused by the war.

elsewhere, the right name for this industry is *viviculture* rather than agriculture. The farmer is reduced to an almost passive part; he must look on patiently while nature performs her work according to laws which he knows but imperfectly as yet, and whose slow operation he cannot change. It takes long months for the grain that sleeps in the furrow to become transformed into an ear of corn; and it takes long years for the acorn to become an oak. Again, every plant, whether wheat or oak, requires a certain irreducible minimum of room in which to spread its roots and to breathe. Of course we can hasten the flowering of the lilac or the ripening of peaches in hot-houses, at great expense; but this kind of cultivation, which has already become an industry, is merely a luxury of the rich. The industrial worker, on the other hand, is not tied down to the inexorable succession of the seasons: summer and winter, day and night, he can stoke up his fires or drive his loom. In his furnaces and his vats he can work up the inorganic materials at his pleasure. His concern is only with physical or chemical laws, which are far less mysterious than those of organic life. The proof of this lies in the fact that these laws have been tamed, and made to obey man's commands with mechanical precision.

The limitation of agricultural production, however, is elastic and not inflexible, as is that of extractive production. The amount of produce may even be increased to an almost indefinite extent, though only at the price of an effort which goes on increasing until it ends in being out of all proportion to the amount of produce obtained. There are two ways in which this increase can be secured.

(1) We may increase our produce by an *extension* of the area under cultivation. There is no country, even among the most highly civilized, where the whole of the soil is cultivated, even if we include pasture-land and forests under this heading. Nevertheless, the amount of land that remains available for cultivation is generally of little value, and we shall not find much help in this direction towards supplying the needs of future generations. Even in relatively new countries like the United States the limitation of the extent of land is beginning to make itself felt; the areas still available are generally lacking in water and can only be cultivated by the troublesome process of "dry farming." There is not much wheat-land in the world now remaining to be cultivated, since wheat can only be grown in the temperate zone; and it seems as if we cannot expect much more bread from this source than the amount necessary for the 600 millions of men who actually consume it.

Any surplus population above that number will perhaps have to find some other kind of food.[1]

(2) The second method of increasing the produce of the soil is more *intensive* cultivation. Perhaps there is not a single piece of land of which the farmer could not, if necessary, increase the yield. Only, after a certain stage of agricultural industry has been passed, he can only do so at a *constantly increasing cost in labour*. Consequently there will be a point at which the amount of labour expended to increase the yield is greater than the value of the crop.

Suppose an acre of land produces 30 bushels of wheat, which is about the average yield in the United Kingdom, and that these 30 bushels represent 70 days' labour, or £8 in money. Then the law of diminishing return (or of a return that is not proportional to the labour expended), declares that to make this land produce twice as much wheat (*i.e.* 60 bushels) we must expend more than 140 days' labour or more than £16 in money. To double the produce, we may have to treble, to quadruple, or perhaps even to multiply a hundredfold, the amount of labour and expense.

This law is certainly borne out by the experience of every day. Ask an intelligent farmer whether his land could not produce more than it does, and he will reply: "Certainly; the wheat crop would be larger if I chose to use more manure, to dig more deeply, to clear the soil of the smallest weeds, to have the soil dug by hand, to have each grain of seed transplanted by hand if necessary, and finally to protect the harvest from insects and birds and parasitic weeds." Then ask him why he does not do all this, and he will reply that he would not get back his expenses: the extra crop would cost more than it would be worth. There is therefore in the output of any piece of land a point of equilibrium which marks the limit beyond which no one will pass. It is not that we cannot pass it if we wish to, at any cost, but that we do not wish to, because there is no advantage in doing so.

The proof of this is as follows: If it were not so, if we could increase the production of a given piece of land indefinitely, on the sole condition of increasing the labour and expense in proportion, it is obvious that the owners of the land would certainly not hesitate to do this. Instead of extending their cultivation over a more or less wide expanse of land, they would prefer to concentrate it on

---

[1] The cultivation of the *bread-fruit* tree has been considered. This grows naturally in the tropical zone, and produces much more freely than wheat. Economic evolution would thus take us back to the time when men fed on the fruit of the oak-tree. (See above, p. 66.)

the smallest possible area: this would be far more convenient. But in this event the face of the earth would be quite different from what it is. The simple fact that things are not like this at all, and that cultivation is constantly being extended to less fertile or less favourably situated land, is a sufficient proof that we cannot in reality expect more than a limited crop from a given piece of land. (See Book III, Part II, Chapter I.)

Each kind of cultivation gives its own maximum return. So it is evident that if the farmer changes his cultivation he may move the limit a step farther. An acre of land under potatoes may produce eight or ten times as much in weight as wheat. But none the less the cultivation of potatoes is subject likewise to the law of diminishing return.

We must not confuse the actual return with the monetary return. The latter does not depend only on the fertility of the land, but also on the circumstances that determine prices, and these are not subject to the law of diminishing return. There are no limits imposed by nature on a rise of prices. If, for instance, we were to grow roses instead of corn, and produce otto of roses, we might make £80 an acre; but man does not live on otto of roses.

Again, the law of diminishing return is not confined to agricultural and extractive industries, as the classical economists taught. It is a general law of production, and can be formulated thus: every increase in yield requires a more than proportional increase of power. This can be proved from the transport industry: beyond a certain point, if we wish to increase the speed of a ship by only a tenth — say, from 20 knots to 22 — we must increase the motive power by more than a quarter. If we wanted to double its speed we should have to increase the power tenfold — and even then we should not succeed.

III. MOTIVE FORCES

The work of production consists simply in changing the form or the place of matter. The resistance that matter offers to these changes by reason of its inertia is often considerable, and man's muscular power is not very great. In all times, therefore, but especially since the abolition of slavery has forbidden him to employ the strength of his fellow-men for nothing, man has tried to make up for his weakness by using certain motive forces — more properly called "energies" — that are provided by nature.

Man makes use of these natural forces by means of machinery. A machine is merely a tool, with this difference: that instead of being worked by hand it is set in motion by natural forces, such as the weight of falling water, the expansion of vapour, etc.[1]

It should be observed that the more powerful these natural forces are, the more time and trouble are required to tame them and make them serve the purposes of man. The harnessing of Niagara demands a different equipment from that needed to harness a small waterfall. And we shall see later on that it is the same even in agriculture: land that is naturally fertile costs more to clear than a sandy desert. Every employment of natural forces involves a struggle like that of Hercules against the monsters, and the energy that the victor must display is necessarily proportionate to the power of his adversary.

That is why there are still only four or five natural forces that man has been able to make use of in production: the muscular strength of *animals*, the pressure of *wind* and running *water*, the expansive power of *vapours* (especially of steam, though recently also of explosive gases), and lastly and quite recently, *electricity*, which, however, is generally only an altered form of water power or steam power. But there are numerous others, known and unknown. The waves raised by the wind on the surface of the sea, the tides that wash thousands of miles of coast twice a day, the store of heat enclosed in the centre of the earth[2] — these are truly inexhaustible reservoirs of power. And the forces that we can see are as nothing to those that we can guess at, even if it be only the energy latent in molecular combinations that radium has revealed

---

[1] This definition applies only to *power machines,* but in everyday speech the term "machine" is applied also to instruments worked by man whenever they serve to increase the rapidity of labour, as, for example, hand-looms, sewing-machines, typewriters, etc. We also call a bicycle a machine. But these would be better named *tool machines.*

Tools or implements enable man's strength to be better utilized, sometimes even by increasing it, just as power machines do, but with this defect: that *whatever is gained in power is lost in speed.* Thus with the help of a hydraulic press a child can exert a pressure that is theoretically unlimited, and Archimedes boasted, quite rightly, that with a lever and a place on which to rest it he could move the world. Yet the interesting calculation has been made that, even had he found this necessary point of support, he would only have succeeded in raising the world an infinitely small distance if he worked at it for several million years.

Now since time is a very precious factor, of which we ought to be extremely careful, the increased power obtained by the use of tools is in practice limited, whereas with power machines it is unlimited.

[2] There is a district in Tuscany where natural jets of steam (*soffioni*) issuing from the earth have been harnessed and intensified by the digging of holes; in this way several thousands of horse-power have been made available.

to us.   If we may believe the physicist, the atomic energy contained
in *a single gramme* of matter would amount to millions of horse-
power, if it could be liberated.

The domestication of various animals — the horse, ox, camel,
elephant, reindeer, Eskimo dog, etc. — supplied man with the first
natural force for carriage, draught, and tillage.   This was itself a
valuable achievement, for animals are relatively stronger than men.
A horse's strength is estimated at seven times that of a man, whereas
its food costs less than man's.   But the number of these animals is
limited, and the more so as a country becomes more populous,
for they require much space to feed in; so the motive power that
they represent is comparatively small.

The motive force of the wind and of rivers has always been used
for transport purposes, but its industrial application has until recently been almost entirely confined to turning windmill sails and
water-wheels.   The water mill, which dates from the first centuries
of the Christian era, was the first machine, properly so called, in the
sense that it was the first application of natural forces to the work
of production.

Of these two natural forces, however, the wind is generally too
weak and in any case too intermittent, while the other force, water,
though more powerful and amenable, suffers from the grave inconvenience of being localized in certain places.   It was not until
Newcomen (1705) and James Watt (1769) had made use of heat
to expand water vapour in a closed vessel, that that marvellous
instrument of modern industry, the steam-engine, was created.
And the superiority of steam from that day to this is due to the
fact that it is *artificial:* it is not created by nature, but by man.
For that very reason it possesses this inestimable advantage, that
man can use it *where* he pleases, *when* he pleases, and *as* he pleases.
It is mobile, portable, and continuous, and its pressure can be raised
to many times that of the atmosphere without any other limit in
practice than that imposed by the resistance of the vessel that contains it.

But water is now beginning to take a highly important place as a
motive force, since means have been found to convey its power for
hundreds of miles.   Moreover, it is infinitely *divisible* as well as
portable, so that water power can be made to radiate at will around
the point where nature seemed to have fixed it.   Thus the Rhône,
which used to waste its energy in grinding down pebbles, is carried
nowadays into the lofty workrooms of Lyons to drive the looms of
the silk-weavers.   Motive power is already being distributed into

the homes of the people, like water and gas, so that it can be procured by merely turning a tap or pressing a button.

The action of water is due, however, to its flow, and not to its quantity or extent. (What use could be made for motive purposes of the thousands of millions of cubic feet of water that lie at rest in such a lake as Geneva, or even in a gently-flowing stream like the Seine?) Consequently, water has been utilized mainly at its maximum gradient, that is to say, at a waterfall; and this means going up as near as possible to the sources of rivers and to the glaciers which are the reservoirs that supply them. That is the origin of the famous name "white coal," which was given to this new force more than fifty years ago (1868) by M. Bergès, an engineer of Grenoble. What he meant by it was not running water in general, as is usually thought, but simply the glacier, as a reservoir of force — the force of gravity — which is stored up in it as heat is stored up in coal: the one force is liberated by the downward flow of the water, as the other is by combustion.

By a lucky chance, which would have been regarded in olden times as the work of Providence, but which can be explained geologically, the very lands that are poorest in black coal are those that are most richly endowed by nature with white coal, and conversely. Thus in Europe, Switzerland, Northern Italy, and Scandinavia, which have not an atom of black coal, have splendid supplies of white coal, whereas England, Belgium, and Germany, so rich in mines, have but few falls and water-courses that can be utilized for motive power.[1] It is the same in America: Canada and Brazil have tremendous quantities of power in their waterfalls, but they seem to have scarcely any supplies of coal. France is pretty equally divided, for without being destitute of coal (she produces two-thirds of what she consumes) she possesses a regular army of hydraulic horses, the equivalent of eight or ten millions of horse-power, half of it in the Alps, a quarter in the Pyreneès, and the rest in the Central Plateau, the Jura, and the Vosges. Less than a million and a half of this horse-power is actually utilized, however. In this respect France is surpassed in Europe by Norway and Sweden alone. If she could utilize the whole of her water power, it would suffice to

[1] [Water power is already being used, however, in the Snowdon region for the production of aluminium by means of the electric furnace. "As there is much water power in North and Central Wales it is most likely that in the future this power, now running to waste, will be made of service and provide work for more people than can get a living in these regions at present." (J. F. Unstead, *The British Isles of To-day*, pp. 117–8.)]

free her from the annual tribute she pays to the foreigner by her purchase of twenty million tons of coal a year.

The economic superiority of white coal over black coal lies in the fact that it is not consumed by being utilized. Black coal is like a treasure that has lain buried since primeval days; we are drawing on it lavishly, and the treasure chest will soon sound hollow. White coal, on the other hand, renews itself like the rainfall; it is the sun's task to keep on drawing up the water that has finished its work, and placing it once more on the heights. The supply of power will only come to an end in the event of a general drying-up of the earth and the disappearance of the glaciers — a contingency that we are threatened with, it is true, by some learned men, but which, fortunately, is not yet proved.

The cost of installation of hydro-electric plant, such as barrages, forced conduits, turbines, dynamos, reservoirs, or artificial lakes for regulating the flow of water, is very great, but once the installation is made the running cost per horse-power is practically *nil*. In using coal, on the other hand, this cost is comparatively high, the average consumption being about $2\frac{1}{2}$ pounds of coal per horse-power per hour. That is why, in mountain villages lighted by white coal, they do not take the trouble to put out the lamps during the daytime.

But if it is true that the motive force of water is everlasting, or continually being renewed, unlike coal which is dead and fossilized, it is no less true that the quantity of water in existence is limited as that of coal is. We shall never be able to increase the number and power of water-courses, but only to make better use of them.

In default of more water power, some people have had visions of obtaining from the sun itself the power that is needed. But, even if we could succeed in doing so, the force borrowed from the sun would be limited to an even greater degree than are the other natural forces, for the sun does not shine always or everywhere. If some day the sun is used to work our factories, what a blow that will be to England — far worse than the competition of white coal! The fogs of the North Sea will be her funeral shroud, and men will have to carry on their industries and build their cities in the heart of the Sahara.

IV. THE PROBLEM OF MACHINERY

The natural forces harnessed by machinery work wonders to which we have become hardened by familiarity. Not only do they enable us to perform the same tasks as before under conditions of amazing superiority, but, more than that, they allow us to do things hitherto undreamed of. To name only two examples out of a hundred, the newspaper press and the railways, those two great factors of civilization that have so profoundly modified all the conditions of modern life — public, intellectual, and moral, as well as economic — were both of them created by the steam-engine.

The everyday use of the motor-car — and to-morrow probably it will be the aeroplane — has already had important social consequences whose full significance cannot yet be estimated. These are indeed the instruments that set men free from the bondage that the physical world imposes upon them — the bondage of distance, of time, and of gravity. And while they increase man's independence in relation to nature, they knit more closely the ties of solidarity that bind him to his fellows.

Suburban railways in large towns will be the most effectual agent in remedying the evils of overcrowding and in solving the distressing problem of working class housing.

The superiority of machinery over human labour is due both to technical and to economic causes.

The *technical* causes are these: (1) The *power* that enables matter to be raised, moved, or worked up. The Pharaohs were able, by collecting a sufficient number of workmen, to build the pyramids; and the Panama Canal might possibly have been constructed in the same fashion if a hundred years had been devoted to the task. But the combined blows of the hammers of a thousand smiths could not do what is done by the steam hammer, the hydraulic press, or the rolling mill; nor could a hundred thousand rowers propel gigantic steamers or ironclads at thirty miles an hour. — (2) *Speed.* — Man cannot follow with his hand or even with his eye the rotation of a turbine or a spindle, or the tick-tack of a boring machine or an electric riveter. — (3) The *precision* and especially the *uniformity* of the work, that makes it possible to produce interchangeable parts. The hand of the most highly skilled workman can reach a degree of precision of $\frac{1}{250}$ of an inch, but it will not succeed in making two identical parts. Machinery does this, and cannot even do otherwise; and thus all the parts of thousands of guns or bicycles are interchangeable.

The *economic* causes of the superiority of machinery over human labour may be summed up in the one word *cheapness* — the lowering of the cost of production. If we consider that one horse-power involves an average hourly consumption of only $2\frac{1}{2}$ pounds of coal (rather more in the case of small machines, and rather less in bigger ones), and that the normal cost of this amount of coal — not the present day cost! — is not more than a halfpenny, we shall realize the difference between the cost of machine labour and the workman's wages. It is true that coal is not the only expense in using machinery: there is also the cost of oil, expenses of maintenance, interest and depreciation fund on the capital represented by the machine (whose life is a fairly short one), and finally the wages of the man who works it, for machinery will not quite run by itself, though it very nearly does. Nevertheless the saving is enormous, even when everything is counted in; and it goes without saying that the more expensive hand labour becomes, the greater is the saving. So the rise of wages has been one of the most effective agents in stimulating mechanical progress; a single strike has sometimes been enough to cause the introduction of machinery into a factory. If the slave system had continued, machines would never have been invented.

Books on political economy are full of examples of the cheapness produced by machinery. The most striking instances are drawn from the transport and the printing industries: a ton of goods carried at the rate of a penny a mile, or a newspaper of four or six pages, containing as much matter as a book and sold (until recently) for a halfpenny — these are the miracles wrought by machinery.

In France at the present day, although she is far from being one of the most advanced manufacturing countries, there are fifteen millions of horse-power, each representing the strength of a score of men. As the number of men employed in industry and agriculture in France is not more than ten million, we may say that the productive power of each man is thus multiplied by 30, or, to put it more picturesquely, that each French workman has thirty slaves at his service.[1] He ought therefore to be in very much the same position as the Roman patricians, and able, like them, to accumulate all the refinements of wealth and idleness. How is it, then, that with these new servants in place of the slaves of old, the men of to-morrow. will yet be unable to live the noble life of the ancients, devoting the hours saved from material labour, like the Greeks in their Agora and the Romans in their Forum, to politics, to artistic recreations, to gymnastic exercises, or to lofty philosophical speculation — with

---

[1] [Similarly, Professor Marshall says, speaking of the English textile industries which employed nearly half a million men and more than half a million women: "The strain that is taken off human muscles in dealing even with those soft materials is shown by the fact that for every one of these million operatives there is used about one horse-power of steam, that is, about ten times as much as they would themselves exert if they were all strong men." (*Principles of Economics*, p. 342 n.)]

this difference only, that what was then the privilege of a small class will now be the rule for every one? This is, indeed, an alluring prospect. But our exultation disappears if we consider how slight is the assistance rendered by machinery in satisfying the two fundamental needs of every human society — the need of food and the need of shelter.

It is calculated that in France less than 200,000 horse-power are employed in agriculture — not even $1\frac{1}{2}\%$ of the total. Is this slow development of the use of machinery in the production of food entirely due, as is often thought, to the conservative attitude of agricultural folk, or is it not rather due to the very nature of agricultural production? This latter explanation seems to us to be the true one. Land is life's laboratory, and life has special laws of development which are peculiar to it (see above, p. 64). Moreover, most of the machines used in agriculture aim only at economizing hand labour or speeding it up, and not at increasing the quantity of produce. Threshing machines and sheep-shearing machines, like the machines that chop sugar, and those (in Chicago) that turn a pig instantaneously into sausages, add not a grain to the sum of human wealth, to the stock of corn, wool, sugar, or meat. Machines for ploughing or irrigation, however, may increase the depth and fertility of the available land.

In the matter of house-building, machinery is hardly used at all, except for cutting stones and in certain special kinds of construction.

The employment of natural forces is restricted, then, more completely than one would think, to the sphere of manufacture and transport, and it is here that it has procured all the abundance and cheapness that could be expected. It is true, however, that mechanical progress in transport reacts indirectly on food and housing, by facilitating the importation of agricultural produce, fertilizers, and building materials.

But here is another aspect of the question. If it is true that a single horse-power does the work of twenty men, each new horse-power created will enable the one man who controls it to dispense with the labour of twenty other workmen, who will be condemned to unemployment in consequence. And since each of these twenty men will strive to retain his place, it looks as if the result must be an underbidding of each other which will cause a lowering of wages.

A century ago the economist Sismondi obtained a reputation for heresy, which was better merited on other counts, by the eloquence with which he denounced machinery as the scourge of the working classes and the whole nation. He said that the invention of machines "made population superfluous," (which is the title of one of the chapters in his book, *Nouveaux Principes d'Economie Politique*). If, said he, machinery should reach such a degree of perfection that the King of England could produce all that was needed to satisfy the wants of his people by merely turning a handle, what would become of the English nation?

It is well known that the workers also were violently opposed to the introduction of mechanical processes in industry, and showed their hostility on many occasions by breaking the machines and mobbing the inventors. We need only mention the Luddite Riots in the midland counties early in last century, the burning of the Jacquard loom at Lyons about the same time, and the destruction of Papin's steamboat in 1707. Even to-day we have seen the dock labourers of Marseilles and Boulogne objecting to the installation of cranes, and the fishermen of Brittany rebelling against the employment of steamboats and revolving nets in the sardine fishery, because they think that the more fish they catch the less they will be paid — and this at a time of general food shortage!

This attitude is natural, for the workers are necessarily the first to feel the effect of the mechanical inventions that come to cut the ground from under their feet. And as they live from day to day they cannot wait till things settle down.

But, on the other hand, those economists who were out to prove that in our economic organization there can be no conflict between social interest and individual interest, were bound to deny the existence of the evils attributed to machinery, and to declare that it always provides more work and more comfort for the worker. Thus arose a controversy which once held a prominent place in the classical treatises, but which has lost much of its importance to-day.

Here are the arguments by which the classical economists sought to set aside the grievances attributed to machinery. It must be recognized, however, that they are not unanswerable.

(1) *Reduction of the cost of living.* — Every mechanical invention, it is said, results in a lowering of the cost of production and therefore of prices. Numberless instances may be cited. We have just mentioned two of them — railways and newspapers; we can also mention all articles of clothing of the ready-made kind. Consequently, it is said, even supposing that the result of the introduction of machinery is a fall in wages, yet the workman gets compensated, as a consumer, for the misfortunes he suffers as a producer.

But the workman only gets this compensation if he is a consumer of the products that he makes himself. Now such a coincidence as this is extremely rare. The mechanical manufacture of certain kinds of lace has lowered their price, but the poor woman who used to make them by hand is not in the habit of wearing them, so she gets no compensation whatever.

Even admitting that the product in question is consumed by the worker, it can only constitute a minute fraction of his consumption, and the compensation thus obtained would be ridiculously small. The woman who used to knit stockings, and who loses her wages through the invention of a knitting machine, will find little consolation in the prospect of buying her stockings more cheaply from the shop.

To make this compensation a real one, *mechanical progress would have to take place simultaneously in all branches of production*, so that the consequent fall in prices would be general and simultaneous. In this case it might be said to matter little to the workman if he receives only half his former wages, since all his expenses would also be halved. But unfortunately, as we have just pointed out, mechanical inventions are not applied in all branches of production, but only in a small number of them; and their effect is particularly slight upon those very expenses — food and housing — which occupy the chief place in the working-man's budget.

(2) *Increase in the demand for manual labour.* — Far from suppressing or restricting the demand for manual labour, machinery results, it is said, in increasing this demand. In fact every mechanical invention, simply by causing a fall in prices, must bring about correspondingly larger sales, according to the "law of demand," and consequently it always ends by bringing back the workers who have been temporarily turned out. Instead of taking work from them, it makes work for them. And there are plenty of examples to support this view. Thanks to the multiplication of books since the invention of printing, there are many more printers to-day than there were copyists in the Middle Ages. Thanks to the railways, there are many more travellers, and therefore many more workmen employed in transport than there were postilions, ostlers, and postmasters. Thanks to mechanical looms, there are many more workers employed in textile industries than there were hand-loom weavers in former days.

To this we may answer, first of all, that although an increased sale is the normal consequence of a fall in prices, this is not always the case. It is notably not so in the following cases: (*a*) Whenever a commodity satisfies only a limited want. The example of coffins has become classical, but there are many other products — such as salt, umbrellas, spectacles, and keys — the consumption of which would be only slightly increased by a fall in price. If the price of hats was halved it is not likely that we should use twice as many. As for articles of luxury, an increase in their number might even result in a diminution of consumption, by lowering their value. — (b) Whenever one industry is bound up with other industries. This is a very common case. The production of bottles and casks might become cheaper, but no more of them would be sold if there were no more wine to put into them. Similarly, the production of watch springs is limited by that of watches, the production of iron bolts by that of rails and boilers, while that of rails and boilers is limited in its turn by other causes independent of prices, such as the development of transport, mining production, and so forth.

Moreover, even admitting that a fall in prices produces a proportional or more than proportional increase in consumption, yet a certain time must elapse — perhaps several generations — before this is brought about. It takes time for the old prices to fall, especially since the manufacturers are interested in keeping them up, and old acquired habits also delay the fall. Competition wins in the end, but rival industries are not set up in a day. Still more time is needed for the fall in prices to extend the sale of these products into those new strata of society that do not quickly change their tastes and desires. If the weaver of last century, looking at his idle and superseded loom, could have known that his grandchildren would find work and higher wages to-day in splendid factories, he would no doubt have found some moral consolation in the knowledge, but it would not provide him with bread and butter.

In short, the classical argument comes to this: that though the invention of machinery may provoke crises and produce suffering, these are only temporary and right themselves spontaneously. This may certainly be admitted, but it is poor consolation, for the same could be said of all the evils in the world — they are all temporary, except death.

What we ought rather to say — though the optimist school does not like making such confessions — is that the evils complained of are not confined to machinery. *All economic progress*, whether it consists in mechanical inventions or in new methods of organizing labour, *can have no other effect than to render a certain amount of labour useless.* As the organization of our modern societies is founded on the division of labour, so that each man lives by one particular kind of work, this progress, whatever form it takes — not only mechanical invention, but all improvements in organization, like large shops, co-operative societies, trusts, and so forth — must make some one's labour useless, and rob him of his livelihood at the same time. There lies the fatal obstacle.

It is from that point of view that socialists regard things. They attribute all the evils resulting from machinery not to the machines themselves but to their *appropriation by the capitalist.* The most enlightened of the workers, the trade union leaders, understand well enough that, notwithstanding all the disturbances it brings in its train, machinery is a necessary and beneficent form of industrial evolution, and that it would be contrary to the highest interests of the working classes, as well as useless, to try to stop it. They refuse to be hostile to machinery through conservatism and hatred of new things; they are inclined, on the contrary, to extol beyond measure the miracles of social transformation that they expect from it. If the machines belonged to the community, they think, then they would have no other effect than to reduce everybody's share of toil — they would no longer rob anyone of his livelihood. Their object, therefore, is no longer to destroy the machines, but to nationalize them.

Meanwhile the workers' organizations and the employers themselves have learned to take the necessary measures to soften the shock that results from the introduction of machinery into industry: they strive to make the workers benefit by the economies effected in the cost of production, either by an increase of wages or by a reduction of their hours of work.

Nevertheless it would be a decided exaggeration to claim that complete success will be attained in this matter. The existence in all industrial countries of a surplus of manual labour — what socialists call the reserve of the industrial army — which employers can draw on when they need, and whose very existence keeps down the rate of wages, can hardly be explained except by the continued action of mechanical inventions and other forms of industrial progress, tending constantly to reduce the number of human arms that are needed.

All we can reasonably hope for the future is that the grievous after-effects of mechanical inventions will tend to grow less. It is plain enough, indeed, that the introduction of a new machine into an industry that is already carried on by mechanical means does not now provoke a rebellion like that caused by the first mechanical loom among the hand-weavers, any more than the discovery of a new gold mine that pours its produce into a huge existing stock, provokes a disturbance of prices like that which followed the dis-covery of the first mines in the New World. In the economic de-velopment of humanity, history shows us sudden and convulsive changes, followed by long periods when things are in a more or less stationary condition. So it is quite possible that the great economic transformation of our own time will be followed by a long period of rest, or at least of very slow progress, like the peaceful course — peaceful from an economic standpoint — of the periods that have gone before.

CHAPTER II — LABOUR

I. THE PART PLAYED BY LABOUR IN PRODUCTION

To accomplish its purposes, and principally to satisfy the needs of its existence, every living being must perform a certain amount of work. The seed itself works to raise the crust of hardened earth that covers it, so as to come through and breathe the air and light. The oyster, fastened to its bed, opens and closes its shell to draw food from the water that surrounds it. The spider spins its web; the fox and the wolf go in search of prey. Nor is man exempt from this universal law: he also must make persevering efforts in order to satisfy his needs. In plants this effort is unconscious; in animals it is instinctive; in man it has become a deliberate act, and is called *labour*.

But are there not some kinds of wealth that man can obtain without labour — wealth that nature generously bestows upon him? That is a difficult question.

First of all it must be observed that there is not one single object among those that are called *products* that does not in some measure presuppose the intervention of labour. The very etymology of the word *product*, from *productum*, "drawn forth," shows this. For how could anything have been thus drawn forth, except by the hand of man? If fruits are to serve for the satisfaction of our wants, man must yet take the trouble to gather them — even those that nature herself gives us, such as the bread-fruit, bananas, dates, and all the crustaceans and shell-fish that the Italians call "sea fruit." And fruit-picking is certainly a kind of labour which may become very troublesome.

It must also be noticed that people seldom realize what a considerable part labour plays even in the creation of those products that are often very inaccurately described as "natural." They are inclined to think, for instance, that everything that grows on the earth — cereals, vegetables, and fruit — is due to the generosity of the earth, *magna parens frugum*.[1] As a matter of fact, most of the plants that supply man with food have been, if not created, yet so

[1] Xenophon saw things more truly when he said: "The gods sell us all kinds of goods at the price of our labour."

modified by cultivation and by the labour of hundreds of generations
that botanists have so far been unable to discover their original
types. Wheat, maize, lentils, and beans have nowhere been discovered in a wild state. Even the kinds that are found growing
wild are extraordinarily different from their cultivated relatives.
They have had first to be brought from the four corners of the earth,
and then subjected to centuries of acclimatization.[1] Between the
sour berries of the wild vine and our bunches of grapes, between the
succulent fruits and vegetables of our gardens and orchards and the
tough roots and bitter and sometimes poisonous berries of the wild
varieties, the difference is so great that these fruits and vegetables
might well be regarded as artificial products, actually created by the
industry of man. This is proved by the fact that if the unceasing
labour of cultivation is relaxed for a few years, these products swiftly
degenerate, as it is called — which simply means that they go back
to the wild state and lose all the properties with which human industry has endowed them.

Now there are certain observations to be made even about those
forms of wealth which are not "products" because they exist before
any act of production takes place. Such are the earth, in the first
place, and all the organic and inorganic substances with which it
supplies us: the bubbling spring of water or petroleum, the growing
forest, the natural grass land, the stone quarry, the coal or metal
mine, the waterfall that turns the mill-wheel or the turbine, the
guano bed deposited by sea-birds, the fishery teeming with fish,
shell-fish, or coral. Of these things it must be said:

(1) That this natural wealth does not exist as wealth, that is to
say, as useful and valuable objects, until human intelligence has
discovered its existence, and especially its *utility* — the properties
which make it fit to satisfy some one or other of our wants (see
above, p. 38).

(2) That this natural wealth cannot be utilized — cannot serve
to satisfy human wants — until it has been subjected to a certain
amount of labour. Virgin soil cannot be utilized until it has been
cleared; a mineral spring is useless until the water is collected and
bottled; mushrooms and shell-fish must be gathered or caught —
a more or less laborious process — and must certainly also receive
some preparation in the way of cooking.

Yet, after doing labour the justice of recognizing that it is never

---

[1] The potato comes from Chile, the tomato from Peru, the peach from Persia, the
cherry from Asia Minor, etc.; and how different they are from their rude ancestors!
The origin of many others is unknown, because the original species have disappeared.

entirely absent when wealth is created — even so-called natural wealth, — we must not conclude that the *value* of this wealth is proportional to the amount of labour expended on it. This view we have already explained and criticized. When, for instance, somewhere in the Caucasus or America, an oil-well worth millions is discovered by a lucky boring, it would be absurd to contend that this stream of gold is the produce of labour.

II. HOW LABOUR PRODUCES

We must distinguish three varieties of labour:

(1) *Bodily* labour, which is generally, but not necessarily, manual labour, is indispensable for the production of all material wealth, for, as we have just said, the raw material of all wealth must always be transformed, or at any rate extracted. And in this transformation the hand of man is the initial agent, though not the only one.[1]

The wonderful and infinitely various actions proceeding from this hand are almost miraculous. Yet man has no fairy's fingers. His hands and his limbs are nothing but muscular force directed by intelligence, so they can only produce the same effect as any other motive force, namely, a change of place.[2]

This movement or change of place may be either a *change in the position of the object itself*, or a *change in the position of its constituent parts*. In the latter case we say that the object has undergone a "transformation," or change of form; but every transformation is really only a displacement. The exquisite shapes assumed by clay under the hand of the potter or the sculptor, the rich and ingenious patterns wrought by the fingers of the lace-maker, are only the effects produced by the displacement of particles of clay or threads of textile material. All that man's labour can do is to move, separate, invert, superpose, and arrange — movements, all of them. Take the production of bread, for example. Consider the various actions involved: ploughing, sowing, reaping, winnowing, grinding, sifting, kneading, putting into the oven — and you will see that they all represent nothing but various movements or displacements imposed upon matter. But as regards the actual transformations that take place in the constitution of the bodies dealt with, modifying

[1] Though man has less muscular strength than animals, he generally has more dexterity, and he owes this especially (as the word itself indicates, coming from *dextra*, the right hand) to that marvellous organ, the hand, with the thumb placed opposite to the fingers.

[2] The work of nature also probably consists ultimately in movement; but this is a matter for the physicist.

their physical or chemical properties and thereby assisting in production — the mysterious development of a plant out of a seed;
the fermentation that turns a sugary syrup into alcohol; the chemical
reactions that make iron and carbon into steel — these have nothing
to do with manual labour. All that man does is to put the materials
in the right place: the seed in the ground, the grapes in the vat,
the ore in the blast furnace; and nature does the rest.

When we consider how feeble is this motive power of man, and how
limited is its field of action, we shall be the more astonished that it
has been sufficient to transform the world. Nor must it be thought
that man knows by the light of nature how to use his hands for
working: it has required centuries of apprenticeship, and muc.
still remains to be learned.[1]

Immaterial products, or services (see above, p. 87), do not generally involve manual labour, but they always involve *bodily* l. bour,
that is to say, the work of other organs than the hand. For barrister:
teachers, and actors this organ is the voice; for doctors, sailors,
artists, and writers it is the eyesight; for the country postman it is
the legs. But physical fatigue may be just as great in these cases
as in manual labour.

(2) The labour of *invention* is purely intellectual, but it is no less
indispensable to production than manual labour, for every single
thing utilized by man, and every single productive process must
have been invented. It is owing to invention that the inheritance
of mankind is extended every day by some new conquest. From
the clay that makes the mud of our streets, industry produces that
solid, light, and glittering metal that we call aluminium; and the
worthless residue of coal is converted by industry into perfumes
and into colours more splendid than Tyrian purple. Yet, even so,
the list of things that we know how to utilize is short indeed, compared with the immense number of things of which we make no use.
Out of the 140,000 known varieties of the vegetable kingdom, less
than 300 are cultivated; and out of the hundreds of thousands of
species in the animal kingdom there are barely 200 that we have
learned to utilize.[2] And even among the mammals, our nearest
relations, there are hardly a score that we utilize, whether for food,
for labour, or for company. In the inorganic world the proportion
is no more favourable. But the catalogue of our riches grows longer
every day, and there is every reason to believe that if our knowledge

---

[1] According to the American engineer, Taylor, man does not even yet know how to
work. For the Taylor method, see my *Political Economy*.

[2] De Candolle, *Origine des plantes cultivées*, p. 366.

were perfect there would not be a single blade of grass or grain of sand in the whole wide world for which we had not discovered some use.

Nor is it only wealth that has to be discovered; it is also the way to transform and utilize it. That is to say, manual labour itself in all its forms — each movement of a weaver's fingers or a blacksmith's arm — has had to be invented by the first craftsman. And it must not be thought that in this domain invention ever completely stops: it is involved in the humblest labour, preventing it from crystallizing into routine. Invention, in the economic sense of the word, is not the brain-wave of a man of genius,[1] but simply the adapting of new means to any end whatever. According to Hobson, the mechanical loom as it exists to-day is the accumulated result of 800 small and detailed inventions.

It should be noted that every invention, once made, is privileged to serve for an indefinite number of productive acts — or rather, reproductive acts. It is just this that makes it so difficult for the legislator to protect the property rights of inventors.

(3) Finally, every productive undertaking, whenever it is carried on collectively and not in isolation, requires the labour of *organization and direction*. This is itself a very effective form of labour, the importance of which increases as industry in our modern societies becomes conducted on an increasingly large scale. It is one of the best known and most important characteristics of labour that its efficiency is increased by combination, in the sense that three workers working together can produce more than three times the produce of one. But this is by no means the same as saying that increasing the number of units in the group is sufficient to obtain a more than proportionally larger product. When we harness ten or twelve horses together, the resulting power is far from being superior, or even equal, to the sum of their individual forces. In every undertaking there is an *optimum* number of workers, relatively to the given conditions, neither more nor less. Collective labour, therefore, can only be superior to individual labour in so far as it is organized and commanded. Moreover, you will scarcely find anyone nowadays, even among manual workers, who thinks that this kind of labour — the labour of the industrial leader — is worth less than the labour of execution.

---

[1] If we think of Buffon's statement that "genius is prolonged patience," and remember the lives of the great inventors, we shall be more inclined to recognize that invention is only one form of labour.

III. THE EVOLUTION OF IDEAS CONCERNING THE PRODUCTIVENESS OF LABOUR

The history of this term "productive" is an interesting one. Applied at first to one particular kind of labour, it has gradually been extended in its application, and is now bestowed indiscriminately on all kinds. It is interesting also to follow the succession of economic doctrines on this subject.

(1) The physiocrats confined the term "productive" to *agricultural* labour (including hunting and fishing), and denied it to all other labour, even that of manufacturing. The reason given for this discrimination was not only that these agricultural industries supply the materials of all wealth — materials which other industries merely work up, which is quite true, — but especially that these industries are the only ones in which nature works in conjunction with man — that nature alone can create a "net product," which is not true.

(2) The definition of the physiocrats was unquestionably too narrow. The raw materials supplied to us by the agricultural and extractive industries are generally altogether unfit for our consumption, and have to undergo numerous modifications which constitute the precise task of the *manufacturing* industries. The latter are therefore the indispensable complement of the former, and without them the productive process is as incomplete as a play with the third act suppressed. Of what use is the ore at the mouth of the mine, unless it is to be taken on to the smelting-house first, and then to the forge? Of what use is the wheat before it has passed through the hands of the miller and the baker? Without the labour of the weaver, flax would be as useless as the nettle. What right have we, then, to refuse these labours the title "productive," since without them these kinds of wealth would be useless to us — would not even be wealth at all?

As for the contention that extractive and agricultural industries *create* wealth, while manufacturing industry only *transforms* it, this also is a mistake. The farmer creates nothing, any more than the manufacturer. All that he too does is to transform the simple substances drawn from the soil and the air. He makes wheat out of water, potash, silica, phosphates, and nitrates, exactly as the soap-maker makes soap out of soda and fat.

Ever since the time of Adam Smith, therefore, no economist has hesitated to extend the term "productive" to include the labour of manufacture. At the same time there is a certain portion of

truth in the physiocratic doctrine, and this must be retained.   This
is the fact that agriculture occupies the front rank among the various
kinds of labour, simply because food takes the first place among our
various needs; agriculture cannot with impunity be sacrificed or
neglected, as belligerent countries have learned from bitter experience.

(3) With regard to the labour of *transport* there has been more
hesitation, because transport seems to make no change in the object
transported.   Is not a package of goods the same at the arrival
station as it was at the station of departure?   In that fact, it was
said, lay a characteristic difference between transport and manufacture.

This distinction is scarcely philosophical, for every displacement
involves an essential modification of the thing displaced.   Strictly
speaking it is even the only modification that we can make in matter,
as we have already seen (p. 87).   Besides, if we consider that displacement is not a sufficiently essential modification to entitle it to
be called productive, then we must refuse to call the extractive
industries productive.   For what difference is there between the
work of the miner who transports coal or ore from the bottom of
the shaft to the surface, and that of the carman who transports it
from the mine to the factory — unless we contend that displacement
is productive when it takes place vertically and not when it takes
place horizontally?   Is it necessary to observe, then, that just as
manufacturing industry is the indispensable complement of agricultural and extractive industries, so the transport industry is the
indispensable complement of these preceding ones?   What would
be the use of stripping off the bark of the cinchona or tapping the
rubber trees in the forests of Brazil, of digging guano on the islands
of Peru, of hunting for elephants' tusks in South Africa, if there
were no carriers and sailors to transport these products to the places
where they could be utilized?   Of what use to a landowner is the
finest crop in the world, if he cannot transport it for want of roads?

The late war, by cutting or hindering communications between the
belligerents and the rest of the world, revealed the productive nature
of transport in a terrible fashion, for the stoppage of transport was
enough to bring great countries to the verge of famine.   It was even
possible to see populations suffering from the lack of certain kinds
of wealth which yet existed in superabundance in their own countries,
but which could not be transported owing either to the congestion
or to the absence of railways.   Notable examples of this were wheat
in Russia, coal in Germany, and butter in Switzerland.

(4) With regard to *commerce*, hesitation was still more prolonged.

There is no doubt that the productive character of commercial operations can be justified by the simple fact that commerce is historically and logically inseparable from transport, and that the separation between them, as we shall see further on, came only at a late period. Even to-day merchants are still the real directors of transport: the carrying industries only execute their orders. Therefore, and since we have admitted that transport is an act of production, it seems that we must say the same of commerce.

But commerce does more than transport goods. Its business is to *store* them, and this is to some extent transporting them in time, as it were. It often also makes them undergo certain *transformations:* this is the case with the baker, the pastry-cook, the tailor, and the druggist — so much so, indeed, that statisticians are doubtful whether to class these people as manufacturers or merchants. But even among merchants properly so called, the wine merchant decants and dilutes and mixes his wines, the grocer roasts his coffee, and so on. So if we wanted to separate the trading from the manufacturing class we should not know where to draw the dividing line.

But the problem becomes harder when we are faced by a purely commercial action, in the definite legal sense of buying in order to sell again — such as dealings on the Stock Exchange, for instance — and still more in the case of the transfer of property without any change of place, such as the sale of real estate. Here the operation has become completely dematerialized, and those who hold that wealth can only be material (see above, p. 38) ought logically therefore to refuse to call such actions productive. But those who believe, as we do, that wealth consists of everything which meets our needs and gives us satisfaction, will not hesitate to call any operation an act of production if it makes the ownership of an object pass from the hands of one who can make no use of it, into the hands of one who both can and will. Why should it not be called productive, since the whole secret of production is *the making useful of something useless?* (See Book II, Chapter I.)

(5) Finally, it is the labour that consists only in services rendered, such as the *liberal professions*, that has given rise to the keenest discussion. It may seem strange, for example, to apply the term "productive" to the labour of the teacher of the piano, or of the surgeon who amputates a leg. Where are their products? Where is the wealth that they have created?

It is sufficient, however, to notice two things: (*a*) that if they do not create any material wealth they none the less create utilities, in the form of services rendered; and that utility, not the material substance to which it may be attached, is the end and object of production; (b) that in the social organism, thanks to the law of division of labour to be explained later, there is such mutual dependence among all the labours of men that they cannot be separated, and immaterial services are an indispensable condition of the production of all material wealth.

Take, for example, the production of bread. No doubt we shall put in the front rank the manual labour of the ploughmen, sowers, reapers, carters, millers, and bakers. But it is obvious that the labour of the farmer or landowner, even if he never puts his hand to the plough, is no less useful in the production of wheat than that of the shepherd in the production of wool, even if he never shears a sheep himself. Nor can we ignore the labour of the engineer who plans the irrigation system, or the architect who puts up the farm buildings and barns. It would even be ungracious to forget the labour of the inventors, from some Triptolemus or other who invented the plough, down to his successors who discovered the different kinds of cereals, or manures, or the rotation of crops, or the methods of intensive cultivation.

Must we stop there? We might, undoubtedly; and it is here that many economists draw the line of demarcation between those kinds of labour which ought to be called productive because they add new utility to something, and the labour that consists solely in services rendered. But is the labour requisite for the production of wheat confined to agriculture? What about the labour of the policeman who keeps the thieves away, the lawyer who prosecutes them, the magistrate who sentences them, the soldier who protects the crops against hostile armies which are worse than thieves? Do not these also contribute to the production of wheat? And what is to be said of the labour of those who trained the farmer himself and his employees — the instructor who taught them the first principles of agriculture or the means of acquiring them, and the doctor who keeps them fit? Is it a matter of indifference, then, even from the point of view of wheat production alone, that the workers should be well taught and healthy, that they should enjoy order and security and the benefits of good government and good laws? Should we set aside, as having no bearing on the production of wheat, even such alien labours as those of authors, poets, and artists? Perhaps the taste for farming might be usefully developed in a community by those novelists who depict scenes of rural life, or the poets who

celebrate the delights of field labour, and teach us to repeat, with
the author of the *Georgics:*

> "O fortunatos nimium sua si bona norint
> Agricolas!"

Where, then, are we to stop? We see the circle of productive
labour stretching away even to the utmost bounds of society, like
the concentric rings that spread over the surface of the water from
the central point that we have touched, and becoming lost in the
distance. The various kinds of labour we have just considered do
not certainly contribute in the same way to the production of wheat:
some act directly, and others indirectly; but we can at all events
affirm that none of them could be eliminated, from the labour of
the ploughman up to that of the King, without causing the cultivation of wheat to suffer.

It must not be inferred, however, that all the kinds of labour we
have just passed in review are equally important in the economic
world. They are all necessary, but each one in its proper place.
A country that had as many barristers as ploughmen, for instance,
would be on the way to ruin.

The truth is that though every profession may be useful within
the limits of the need that it satisfies, it becomes harmful beyond
that limit, for then it degenerates into parasitism. What is wanted
is *a right proportion between the effective strength of each professional
group and the importance of the need that it has to satisfy.* Unfortunately this exact balance is far from being maintained in our
civilized societies. Thus agricultural labour is becoming more and
more neglected. That is a universal fact, and one that is as deplorable as it is universal. It is not so deplorable from the point of
view of productiveness — for manual labour in agriculture may be
replaced to some extent by machinery — as from that of the physical
and moral health of the population, and even from the standpoint
of political stability. France is still better off in this respect than
most other countries, but this is simply because industry is relatively
less developed there than elsewhere.

Again, when workers leave the land to enter factories there may
be a gain in total production, apart from the drawbacks in other
respects; but it is not the same when they leave agricultural labour
to go in search of "a soft job" — and such is too frequently the
case. We see the number of persons engaged in petty trade or in
government employment increasing every day, and there is certainly
some ground for the complaints that are made of the increase in

the number of these middlemen and officials, as well as the exorbitant tribute that is levied by both these classes on the product of the labour of the whole community.

IV. HARDSHIP AS A CONSTITUENT ELEMENT OF LABOUR

It is an indisputable fact that man will hardly ever work of his own accord, but only under the pressure of external causes, such as, in the case of children, punishments, prizes, and the instinct of emulation; and, for men, need, desire of gain, ambition, and professional distinction. Most men work with ardour only to hasten the time when they will be able to give up working. It must be concluded, therefore, that all productive labour involves a certain amount of *hardship*. This is a law of capital importance in political economy. If labour did not involve hardship, then, we may say, all economic phenomena would be different from what they are: neither slavery nor machinery, for instance, would ever have existed, since their only object is to dispense with a certain amount of labour.

But why is labour painful? It is not easy to say, although every one feels that it is so. Labour, after all, is only a form of human activity, and activity is by no means painful in itself. To act is to live, and absolute inaction is such atrocious torture that when it is too prolonged, as in solitary imprisonment, it either kills the prisoner or drives him mad.

Is it because labour always involves a certain amount of *effort*, and man is naturally an idle animal? This is not a sufficient explanation, for many forms of exercise that are regarded as pleasures — such as mountain-climbing, rowing, cycling, motoring, flying, and all kinds of games — demand more intense effort than work does, and yet many men are passionately devoted to them.

In games, however, the effort is voluntary and free: it seeks and finds satisfaction in itself alone; it is an end in itself. In work, on the other hand, the effort is imposed by the necessity of attaining a certain end, the satisfaction of some want. It is only the *antecedent condition of subsequent enjoyment*, — a "task," as it is called, — and that is why it is painful. Between a boating man who rows for pleasure and a boatman who rows for his living, between an Alpine climber and the guide who accompanies him, between a girl who spends the night at a ball and a dancer who figures in a ballet, I can see only one difference: the first rows, climbs, or dances with the sole object of rowing, climbing, or dancing, while the others do so to earn their living. But this difference is enough to cause the same forms of activity to be regarded by some as pleasures and by others as hardships. Thus Candide, Voltaire's hero, enjoyed cultivating his garden; but he would have disliked it if he had had to grow vegetables and go to market with them. The tourist who walks along a road merely for the sake of the walk finds pleasure in it, but the postman who tramps it morning and evening for a special purpose, always finds it long and wearisome. Now for almost the whole of the human race, labour is only the path they are compelled to follow by the necessity of earning a living: they work to live, and not for pleasure.

What proves that the painfulness of labour is due to its being compulsory, is that the hardship varies directly with the amount of constraint and inversely with the amount of freedom. It reached its maximum in the case of the Roman slave fastened to the hand-mill or chained to the bench of a galley; and it is still heavy for the wage-earner who has to earn his daily bread. It is felt at its lowest point by the peasant who tills his own land as a labour of love; by the chairman of a trust, directing a battle for thousands of millions of dollars, like a general commanding an army corps; and by the artist who conceives an idea and embodies it in marble or on canvas.

From this point it is but a step to the conclusion that work might be completely freed from its painful character under a social system in which the pressure of hunger and misery was no longer felt. And the majority of socialists have taken that step. *Attractive labour* was to be the central feature of the society that Fourier proposed to organize. He declared that the painfulness of work is simply due to the faulty organization of our modern societies. "If Louis XVI," said he, "could take delight in making locks, why could not all men likewise work for the pleasure of it?"

It must be admitted, indeed, that work will grow less and less painful as men become richer and more independent, because it will then more and more lose its character of a task imposed upon us by necessity, and become a free activity instead. Yet even if the law of labour should cease to be economically inevitable, it would remain a moral law, imposing upon us the duty of solidarity. Work, by its very definition, could only become a game when it *ceased to be productive of wealth.*

At present, however, every man who works is under the influence of two opposing forces: on one side there is the *desire to procure some kind of enjoyment,* and, on the other side, the *desire to avoid the hardship that the labour inflicts upon him.*   According as either of these motives outweighs the other, he will continue his work or abandon it.

As Jevons has ingeniously observed, the hardship endured by the worker goes on continually increasing as the work continues, whereas his expected satisfaction goes on continually diminishing as the most urgent of his needs begin to be met.   Take the case of a worker drawing buckets of water from a well.   His fatigue increases with each fresh bucket that he has to fill, while, on the other hand, the utility of each successive bucket diminishes (see p. 46).   At which bucket will he stop?   That depends to a certain extent on his power of resistance to fatigue, but chiefly on the scale of his wants.   The Eskimo, who has no use for water except to quench his thirst, will stop at the first or second bucket; but the Dutchman, who feels the need of cleaning his house from top to bottom, will perhaps have to draw fifty buckets before he thinks he has enough.

In the same way the soldier, who has to carry all his baggage on his back, is obliged, before putting any new object in his pack, to set up a psychological balance between the additional enjoyment this object will give him, and the additional hardship entailed upon him by the extra weight.   It is evident that this hardship goes on increasing as his knapsack fills, while the additional utility goes on diminishing, so that ultimately he is bound to reach a last object, as it were — the xth object — which will have to be abandoned, much to his regret, because it would *cost more than it is worth.*

If the stimulus of future wants is added to the stimulus of actually existing ones — if, for instance, in a land where water is scarce, the worker plans to fill a tank in anticipation of a drought — then productive activity may be increased to a marvellous extent.   But this faculty of weighing an immediate hardship against a distant satisfaction — the faculty of *foresight* — belongs only to civilized races, and even to the well-to-do classes among them.   The savage and the poor are alike improvident.

CHAPTER III — CAPITAL

I. WHAT IS CAPITAL?

As we have already observed (p. 62), it is not easy to see at first what this third agent of production is doing here, and why it has the honour of appearing in the same rank as the other two. Is it not an intruder? For if labour and nature seem quite distinct from the wealth that they produce, it is not the same with what is called capital, this being itself only the product of labour and nature. If capital in its turn has the power of giving birth to wealth, it can only do so with the aid of its parents. Is not this a kind of economic incest, or at least a confusion of terms?

Yet it is really quite simple. For to say that capital is one of the necessary factors of production is merely to state the fact that *no wealth can be produced without the help of other pre-existing wealth.* And there we have an economic fact whose importance certainly cannot be exaggerated. Just as no fire can be lighted, at least in ordinary conditions, without a lighted match, torch, or tinder-box; just as no living being can be produced without the presence of a portion of pre-existing living matter — germ, cell, or protoplasm; so also no wealth can be produced, in normal economic conditions, without the presence of a portion of pre-existing wealth, which plays the part of a *fuse.* As a name must be given to this pre-existing wealth with such a characteristic function, we call it *capital.*

Of all the innumerable writers who have told us tales of Robinson Crusoes, and have proposed to show us man by himself at grips with the necessities of existence, there is not a single one who has not been careful to provide his hero with a few implements or provisions saved from the wreck. They knew quite well that without this precaution they would have had to end their story at the second page, for the existence of their hero could not be prolonged farther than that. Yet had not all these Crusoes their own labour and the treasures of a fertile, though virgin, nature from which to obtain a living? Yes; but something still was lacking, and as they could not do without it, the author had to manage somehow or other to procure it for them. This indispensable "something" was *capital.*

But there is no need to go in search of a Robinson Crusoe to become convinced of the utility of capital. In the midst of our civilized

98

societies the situation is no different. There is no harder problem to solve, in the actual world we live in, than how to acquire something when we possess nothing. Take the case of a labourer, a man without means: what can he do to produce the necessaries of existence — to earn his living, as we call it? A very little reflection will show us that there is no kind of productive industry that he can undertake — not even that of a poacher, for he would need a gun or at any rate a snaring wire; nor even that of a rag-collector, for in that case he would need a basket and a hook.[1] He would be as wretched, as helpless, and as sure to die of starvation as a Robinson Crusoe who had saved nothing from the wreck, were he not enabled, by the wage-system, to enter the service of a capitalist who would provide him, on certain conditions, with the raw material and the implements necessary for production.

Animals, no doubt, have to be content with what nature and their own labour give them for the satisfaction of their wants, and primitive man was necessarily in the same case. It is evident enough that the *first* capital of the human race must have been formed without the aid of any other capital, just as — to go back to our former analogy — the first fire must have been lighted without a previous fire, and the first living cell must have sprung from the inanimate world in conditions which will certainly never be reproduced. In the same way, therefore, it must once have happened on the earth that man, more destitute than Crusoe on his island, solved the difficult problem of producing the first wealth without the aid of pre-existing wealth. It must have been with the help of his hands alone that man put in motion the mighty wheel of human industry.

But, when this wheel was once started, the hardest step was over, and the slightest push was enough to give it a constantly increasing speed. The first stone picked up at his feet, the flint from which man's ape-like ancestors struck fire, served at the beginning as an assistant in the creation of other assistants in rather more favourable conditions, and these in their turn helped to create yet others. The power of production increases in a geometric ratio, in proportion to the quantity of wealth already acquired. But it is well known that though a geometric series increases after a certain point with enormous rapidity, the increase at the beginning is slow. So our

---

[1] Intellectual production is no exception to this rule. The professions of the lawyer, doctor, civil servant, etc., presuppose the existence and utilization of a certain amount of previous wealth, not only in the form of instruments of labour, like libraries, laboratories, medical instruments, carriages, and suitable clothes, but especially in the shape of money advanced during the years of study and preparation

modern societies, living on the accumulated wealth of a thousand generations, make light of the task of multiplying wealth in all its forms; but they should not forget how slow and perilous it must have been, at the beginning, to accumulate the first wealth, and how many centuries must have passed over the earliest human societies, during the dark ages of cut flints and polished flints, before the first capital was formed. Many must assuredly have died of poverty during this terrible period. It has been given only to a small and select number of races to pass safely through it, and to rise to the rank of really capitalist societies: *ad augusta per angusta.*

But let us define more precisely the nature of the service rendered by capital. It is a twofold one. The first service is of a technical description: capital appears here as an *instrument*, in the widest sense of the word, from the flint tool to the most complicated of machines or such works as the Suez Canal and, in the future, the Channel Tunnel. It is wealth that has no direct utility — it can satisfy none of man's wants — but it serves to produce other wealth which is destined for consumption. It is an *intermediate* wealth, as Boehm-Bawerk, the Austrian economist, neatly puts it. How this instrument is employed makes up the science of technology, which is outside our province here.

The other service rendered by capital is of an economic order. Capital takes the shape of an *advance*, enabling us to *await* the outcome of a productive operation. This advance may consist of actual supplies of food, or, as is more usual in the modern world, of money, or even of credit instruments. Every productive operation takes time, and waiting is a hardship, just as effort is. Even nature takes time to ripen fruit and to mature the wine in the bottles; and it is the same with man's labour.

As a general rule, the more productive an operation is, the longer is this period of waiting. When man lives from hand to mouth, the labour of making a living — by hunting, fishing, or picking wild fruits — only occupies a few hours. But in the case of agricultural labour and industrial enterprises the interval between the first tilling of the ground and the harvest, or between the setting up of the looms and the sale of the completed fabric, may run to years. The time taken by all labour is longer than it seems, because we forget that we must add the time taken in producing the implements made on purpose for a particular piece of work. And it is just there that the delays are longest. Thirty-five years elapsed between the day when de Lesseps drove the first pick-axe into the site of the Panama Canal and the day when the first ship passed through it.

The conception of capital is closely bound up, therefore, with that of duration of time; and this is so not only in the sphere of production but also in that of distribution, for we speak of interest as "the price of time."

The question, What is capital? seems to give rise to the further question, What is *income?* But income is sufficiently defined by the definition we have already given of capital: all that is not capital, in fact, is income — every product, that is to say, which is intended to procure for us an immediate satisfaction. The cow and its milk, the loom and the cloth, the share certificate and the coupons to be detached from it, are illustrations of capital and income respectively.

Income, therefore is a stream that flows unceasingly, like the water issuing from a spring. The flow is generally measured for the period of a year, so that we speak of an annual income; but it is really a continuous stream.

By living in society, however, we have lost the habit of regarding income as consisting of concrete, consumable objects or products in kind. It appears to us only in the shape of money, that is to say, the means of buying these objects of consumption. When we say that a person has an income of £500 a year, we mean that he has the power of buying and consuming goods annually up to the value expressed by that figure. It is the value of the income that measures the value of capital: it must be so, since capital has no other utility than that of its produce. All value that is described as capital — rent, shares, or even land — is merely the value of the net income capitalized, or multiplied by a certain figure called the rate of income — a figure that varies according to laws which we shall have to study.

Income may be turned into capital whenever it is invested, or employed in a productive operation, instead of being consumed. Fortunately, that is what happens to a large part of income in all progressive countries. Can capital, conversely, be turned into income? Not if it is instrumental capital, as in the examples mentioned above; but if it takes the form of provisions or money it can be turned into income — do we not speak of living on our capital?[1] But this consumption will not last long, for it will stop as soon as the capital is consumed.

[1] Capital can be consumed indirectly, or *realized,* as it is called, even if it takes the form of factories, mines, or flocks, by selling it or mortgaging it — exchanging it for money and spending the latter. But this means finding a buyer or lender willing to make the exchange, and that is why, in a time like the late war, a country can only make money out of its capital if it can find buyers or lenders abroad.

Finally, the notion of income extends much farther than that of capital, for land and labour also produce income. We shall have to deal with these when we come to the subject of distribution.

II. WEALTH WHICH IS CAPITAL AND WEALTH WHICH IS NOT CAPITAL

In taking an inventory of a private fortune, as in a case of inheritance, for instance, we distinguish three classes of goods:

(1) *Immovable goods*, like land and houses;

(2) *Capital*, called also transferable securities, such as stocks and shares, claims on companies or the State or individuals, etc.;

(3) *Movable goods*, used in our everyday life: furniture, clothing, books, ornaments, plate, wines, everything that figures in our fire insurance policies, and also money.

These three classes correspond, in fact, to differences marked out by the nature of things. In the first two classes are the goods that produce income, and the third includes this income itself in the concrete shape of goods intended to procure us enjoyment, called *consumption goods*.

Some kinds of goods, however, are difficult to classify: houses, for instance. In the eyes of a lawyer, a house is immovable or real property, like land; but to the economist it is only a product. It matters little that it is fixed in the earth — so are railway lines. Where, then, are we to put houses? In the second class, as capital, or in the third, along with objects of consumption? In our opinion they should go in this third class, at any rate if they are dwelling-houses, for evidently factories, farms, and shops should be classed with capital. But if the house has no other purpose than to give us lodging, to shelter us from cold and rain like a cloak or an umbrella or a bed, and even in so far as it provides us with the comfort of a home, and the moral and material enjoyments covered by that term, then it satisfies our immediate wants. A house is the box in which we keep everything that meets our daily needs. The fact that it lasts a long time signifies nothing, for it lasts no longer, and perhaps even not so long, as many of the things it contains, such as plate, bronzes, money, and even some kinds of furniture.[1]

---

[1] I ought to state, however, that this distinction is keenly disputed. Many economists think that a house is always capital, even when it is only used as a dwelling, because it always produces an income in the shape of shelter, comfort, and services rendered. But, at that rate, the armchair I sit in must also be capital producing income, since it, too, renders me a service. Some economists, indeed, would go even as far as that.

There are many other kinds of goods besides houses whose proper classification is a matter of discussion. The lines of demarcation between the three categories are not very clearly defined.

First there is the distinction between land and capital. Land is undoubtedly not a product but the mother of all wealth, whereas capital is only a product of labour and of land itself. But when we look at land as it has been made by the labour of a thousand generations — land cleared, cultivated, manured, irrigated, and drained — land which has become garden mould, as much altered by man's hand as the potter's clay — in this condition must we not describe land as capital?

No! All we must say is that it has absorbed **an** enormous quantity of capital. But this capital, through being invested in the earth and digested by it, as it were, has lost the character of capital and obeys henceforth the same laws as land — the law of diminishing return, for instance. The term capital should be restricted simply to the buildings erected on the soil and the implements they contain, together with the live stock.[1]

Here is another difficulty. Between consumption goods, intended for the immediate satisfaction of our wants, and capital, serving only to produce consumption goods, the distinction seems clear enough; yet in reality it is not so. It must be observed, in fact, that many things possess compound properties, and serve a double purpose, so that they sit astride the boundary line, as it were, and can be placed in the first or second category according to which of these properties is utilized. An egg is at the same time a seed and a food. It is capital, then, if we utilize its germinative properties by hatching it, but it is an object of consumption if we utilize its edible properties by cooking it for breakfast. Coal is capital when used to drive a locomotive, and an object of consumption when used to warm one's feet. A motor-car may be indispensable to a doctor, in which case it is capital, but it may also be used merely for joy-riding.

[1] If nature must not be confounded with capital, the same can be said of labour, which is evidently a primary factor, distinct from its produce. Yet labour, like land, may also be improved by previous labour: that is just what education does. Several economists therefore call *acquired knowledge* capital — such knowledge, for instance, as is authenticated in the liberal professions or the public service by diplomas. But here, too, we must insist on the distinction between labour and capital. It is true that this knowledge may be a source of income, but this income will none the less be the fruit of labour. The knowledge, to be sure, can only have been acquired, and the diplomas obtained, with the help of a certain amount of money capital, but that is another question.

But here is quite another difficulty! There are no goods whatever, even those which by their very nature can serve only for personal consumption and gratification, which cannot be sold, lent, or let on hire, and thereby bring in an income or profit to their owner. Now the fact of bringing in an income has become nowadays the characteristic mark of capital. It must therefore be recognized that there is not a single kind of goods which cannot become capital if the owner, instead of using it to satisfy his own personal needs, turns it into an instrument of profit. Not only can a motor-car, a sea-side villa, or a fancy-dress costume be *let on hire*, and thereby become capital, but anything we eat or drink, any article of adornment or amusement, may become what is called "stock in trade," which is just capital.

In short, we find all consumption goods pouring in a crowd into the category of capital, by way of sale or hire, and our classification vanishes into thin air!

We must retain it, however; but we must introduce a new and essential distinction — between *productive* capital and *lucrative* capital. Productive capital is that which by its nature can serve only for the production of new wealth, and is made simply for that purpose. Of this character are all implements, machines, and engineering plant. Lucrative capital is wealth which by its nature can serve only for consumption, but which can bring in an income by being sold, lent, or let on hire by its owner, like the examples mentioned above. This kind of capital produces nothing, therefore, from the social point of view, for it makes no addition whatever to the total amount of wealth in existence, but from the individual point of view it produces a great deal, for it may yield enormous profits.

It should be noticed that what is called capital in everyday speech, in opposition to immovable property, — namely, all the *transferable securities* represented by government stock, bonds or shares, mortgage deeds, and so forth — is generally only lucrative capital, in the sense that it brings in no other income than that which is drawn from the purse of the debtor or the tax-payer.

There are some distinctions to be drawn, however. A *government stock* certificate generally represents only a consumption loan, most often for war expenses or other government needs — except in rare cases where the State has borrowed money to execute public works or create a national industry. Consequently the income it provides is not the price of a product or an economic service, but a claim upon the income of the debtor — in this particular case, upon the incomes of the tax-payers.

It is the same with *bonds* or *debentures*, such as those issued by towns, railways, loan societies, etc., which are merely notes of hand or mortgages.

But with *shares* it is not the same. These always represent a loan made to some industrial organization with a view to a productive undertaking, and the dividends they carry are paid out of the produce of this undertaking. Mining or railway shares are only documents representing concrete capital in the shape of mine-shafts, galleries, coal-buckets, rails, locomotives, and so on. Only care must be taken in drawing up an inventory of a country's wealth, not to count these things as capital twice over — once as actual, concrete capital, and once more as a share certificate which merely represents it: one is the real capital, the other only its shadow.

What are we to say about money, whether in coin or notes? Are we to regard it as capital or consumption goods? And, if we call it capital, will it be productive capital or lucrative capital? The question does not admit of any precise answer, because money is anything you like: that is precisely its characteristic — to serve for all purposes. It can procure us immediate gratification when it is in our purse; or serve for production when it is paid out to workmen in the shape of wages; or provide for our future wants when it is stored up in a cash-box in the form of savings. Moreover, if the coins are worn as a necklace, as sequins are worn by eastern women, then money becomes simply an ornament. It is the destination of money, therefore, which alone determines its classification. If, however, we look not to individuals but to society, we shall see that we must class money with productive capital, as a necessary instrument and vehicle of exchange, along with waggons, weights and measures, and so forth.

III. THE MEANING OF PRODUCTIVENESS OF CAPITAL

The part played by capital in production gives rise to unfortunate misconceptions. When we say that all capital yields an income we imagine that it yields it in the same way that a tree brings forth fruit or a hen lays eggs. We regard *income*, therefore, as a product formed exclusively by capital and issuing from it, and we are led to think that capital which does not yield any income is afflicted by some congenital disease.[1]

[1] Interest was called τόκος in Greek, meaning "the bringing forth of children," and the same word appears in the legal term for compound interest: "anatocism."

What helps to propagate this false idea is the fact that most forms of capital take the shape of stocks, bonds, or share certificates, from which, according to the time-honoured formula, we *detach the coupons* which represent the income.   For six months or a year, according to the nature of the document, the coupon goes on growing; when the appointed day arrives, it is ripe; it can then be plucked, and we actually tear it off or cut it off, just as we remove a fruit from the branch.

But the resemblance goes further than that.   Just as when the fruit or the seed is gathered we can sow it again and grow a fresh plant that will yield more fruit, or just as when the egg is laid we can hatch it out and make it produce a chick that will give us more eggs — so also, by investing this coupon, we can create fresh capital that will yield us new interest coupons.   Thus we can see capital increasing and multiplying in accordance with the same laws as those that control the multiplication of the animal and vegetable species. But the law of compound interest, as it is called, is even more marvellous than the multiplication of herrings or microbes.   For a single halfpenny, invested at compound interest on the first day of the Christian era, would have yielded by now a value equal to that of some thousands of millions of globes of solid gold as large as the earth.   That is an arithmetical calculation which has become famous.

Now we must wipe out the whole of this fanciful picture which has so strongly aroused — and not without reason — the wrath of the socialists.   This mysterious kind of productive and generative power attributed to capital as part of its nature, is a pure chimera. Notwithstanding the popular saying, money produces no offspring, nor capital either.   Not only has a bag of coins never produced a single new coin, as Aristotle remarked long ago, but a bale of wool has never produced a single fresh tuft, nor has a plough ever brought forth little ploughs.   And though it is true — as Bentham said, thinking to refute Aristotle — that a flock of ewes will produce sheep, that is assuredly not because the flock is capital, but simply because it consists of animals, and nature has endowed living beings with the power of producing individuals like themselves.   Capital, in the form of raw materials, implements, or provisions, is absolutely inert until it is animated or fertilized by labour.

It is true that labour also, as we have already seen (p. 62), is sterile under existing economic conditions without the aid of capital. We might be tempted to conclude, therefore, that they are both equally fertile apart, and become creative as soon as they are combined, so that their respective shares in production are as indistinguishable as those of the sexes in the production of offspring. But they must not be put on the same footing, for capital, as we have seen (p. 62), is itself only the product of labour. To say that labour is barren without the aid of capital, simply means that *present labour* can only produce with the collaboration of *past labour*. A plough and its team of horses, in the hands of a ploughman, enables him to produce much more corn than the labour of his hands alone. And it is this extra amount of corn that constitutes the so-called income of capital. None the less, it does not come from the plough, but from *the man aided by the plough*. The plough itself, too, comes from the labour of a man present or past. Those who see nothing in a plough but capital, may be reminded of the charming notion of M. Alfred Fouillée, that the inventor of the plough labours unseen by the ploughman's side.

Yet there are many people who do nothing, and live on the produce of their capital. We say that they have independent means. How, then, is this to be explained, if capital is not productive by itself? Quite simply. If the person of independent means, — the *rentier*, as he is called — does not live on the produce of his labour, since by hypothesis he does not work at all, it is because he lives on the produce of the labour of somebody else — somebody who makes use of his capital. For he has *invested* his capital, which means that he has lent it to others who utilize it. Whenever, therefore, he receives a coupon it must be inferred that somewhere, near by or at a distance, there are men unseen, *who work with this borrowed capital, and whose labour has produced the interest, profits, or dividends received by the rentier.* The interest coupons on mining shares stand for the value of the tons of coal extracted by the labour of the miners, and those on railway shares represent the result of the labour of the engine-drivers, railwaymen, station-masters, and pointsmen who have co-operated in the transport industry. This is what is sometimes called "making one's capital work"; and Rodbertus observes that the true view of the position has been so far upset that we commonly speak of the capitalists as "giving work" to the workers and enabling them to live, whereas in reality it is the workers who give capital its income, and enable the independent capitalist to live.

It is the same even when the capital in the hands of the borrower has been dissipated or consumed unproductively. In that case the interest received by the lender is no longer the produce of the labour of the borrower, but always that of someone else who must be sought for farther off. For instance, the coupons of government stock do not generally represent wealth produced by the labour or industry of the State, for the State is in the habit of spending unproductively the greater part of the capital lent to it.   They represent, instead, the produce of the labour of all the inhabitants of the country, which has been poured every year into the treasury in the shape of taxes, and passes thence into the hands of the stock-holders.   So too when a young spendthrift borrows money to squander, the interest that he pays to the money-lender certainly does not represent the produce of his own labour, but perhaps that of his tenants, or, if the loan has to be repaid out of his future inheritance, the produce of his father's labour.   And long after the spendthrift has squandered the borrowed capital, or after it has vanished in smoke on the battle-field, it will remain just the same, as a form of lucrative capital, that is to say, as a credit instrument in the hands of the money-lender or the government stock-holder.

It must be concluded, then, that the so-called product of capital is never anything but the product of labour, sometimes of the labour of its owner, but very often, in our societies, the product of another man's labour.   It does not necessarily follow that payments made for the use of capital always involve parasitism, as socialists too hastily declare.   The charge is often true, but the fact of living on another man's labour does not in itself by any means imply exploitation, for we are each of us called upon, under a social order based upon division of labour and exchange, to live on other people's labour.   It is a case of mutual dependence or reciprocity.   It only degenerates into exploitation if the service rendered, or the loan received, does not admit of reciprocity.   We must know, therefore, whether the capital lent to the borrower by the capitalist *rentier* has procured for the former the advantage of making his labour more productive — an advantage balanced by the interest he pays — or whether this service could not have been rendered to him by other means.   But this question must be left for the chapters on Interest and Profit.

IV.   FIXED CAPITAL AND CIRCULATING CAPITAL

Capital is not eternal.   As a rule it is not even very long-lived, because it gets destroyed by the very act of production, whether this act be instantaneous or constantly repeated.[1]   But according as its

[1] John Stuart Mill explained the often-noticed but mysterious fact of the rapidity with which countries recover from the ravages of war or some great disaster, by reference to this law of the continual renewing of capital.   "The growth of capital,"

life is longer or shorter, it can serve for a larger or smaller number of acts of production.

But capital acquires unlimited durability when, instead of remaining in its natural, concrete shape, it changes to the abstract form of *value*, for then it becomes constantly renewed by repayment or redemption.   Such is the case, for example, with capital lent to a borrower who has to pay interest for ever, as when a loan is made to the State as a *perpetual annuity*, or when the money lent has to be returned at a fixed date, thus allowing it to be lent afresh, and so on indefinitely.   Again, it may take the form of value put into industry or commerce by its owner, so as to bring in not only an income but also an increased value sufficient to replace it in case of loss. Hence arise those mythological comparisons so often applied to capital, such as the metamorphoses of Proteus, or the phœnix rising reborn from its ashes.

The name *circulating* capital is given to capital which can only be used once because it disappears in the very act of production — for instance, the corn that is sown, the manure that is dug into the soil, the coal that is burned, the cotton that is spun; and *fixed* capital is the name given to that which can be used for several acts of production, ranging from the most perishable implements, like a needle or a sack, up to the most durable, such as tunnels or canals, although these latter themselves can only remain in existence if they are maintained, or continually being remade.[1]

There is a great advantage to production in employing very durable capital.   However great, in fact, may be the labour required to set it up, and however slight may be the labour expected to be saved each year by its assistance, sooner or later a time must necessarily come when the labour saved is equal to the labour expended.   When

he says, "is similar to the growth of population.   Every individual who is born, dies . . . .   An enemy lays waste a country by fire and sword, and destroys or carries away nearly all the moveable wealth existing in it: all the inhabitants are ruined, and yet in a few years after, everything is much as it was before . . . .   There is nothing at all wonderful in the matter   What the enemy have destroyed, would have been destroyed in a little time by the inhabitants themselves."   (*Principles of Political Economy*, Bk. I, Chap. V, §§ 6, 7.)

The recent war will give the economists of to-day a splendid opportunity of seeing whether Mill's law is true.

[1] Some economists, however, adopt a different criterion to distinguish fixed from circulating capital: the former is that which cannot be separated from productive enterprise, and the latter is that which only yields a profit by being *exchanged*.   These two classifications do not coincide at all: thus, coal burnt in an engine would be fixed capital according to this definition, whereas it is circulating capital according to the definition in the text.

that moment has arrived, the capital will be *redeemed*, which means that henceforth the labour saved will constitute a net gain to society. From that point, for as long as the capital lasts, the services it renders will be rendered for nothing. So the progress of civilization tends constantly to replace short-lived capital by that which is more durable.

The earliest groupings of population took place on the heights, as we see even to-day in the villages of the Kabylie district of Algeria. It was the women who supplied the need for water by fetching it in pitchers from the spring and climbing back to the village. I saw this myself in my childhood in the little town where I was born; and it is no light task if you multiply it by the number of water-carriers and the number of journeys they have to make. Where is the capital in this case? It is the pitcher, and it is fixed capital just the same, even though it often gets broken.

But now someone sets up a pump to raise the water from the spring to the village, or, better still, if circumstances permit, they build an aqueduct by which the water will flow of itself according to the gradient. The building of the aqueduct will represent per-haps a million or ten million times the labour employed in making and renewing the pitchers, but for a thousand years or more it will eliminate all the labour used in bringing up water. The saving will be incalculable.[1]

At the same time there are two points that must not be forgotten:

(1) The formation of fixed capital requires an immediate sacrifice in the shape of a large amount of labour or expense, whereas the remuneration that is expected to result from it, in the shape of labour abolished or expense saved, is postponed — and, as a rule, *the more lasting the capital the longer is this remuneration delayed.* If the construction of a ship canal, like the Panama Canal, for instance, is to cost a hundred million pounds, which is not to be repaid for 99 years, we must then weigh the immediate sacrifice of a hundred millions against a remuneration for which we must wait a century. Now such a balancing of alternatives requires a high degree of fore-sight and boldness, and a resolute faith in the future — qualities which are only to be found in combination in highly civilized com-munities. That is why fixed capital is rarely employed by peoples

---

[1] In 1913 the city of Los Angeles, in California, started building an aqueduct 258 miles long. It has taken nine years to build, and has cost $25,000,000. But it supplies some 3,500 million cubic feet of water per day. Reckoning interest and depreciation at $1,500,000, the price of a cubic foot of water works out at something like $\frac{1}{2000}$ of a cent, *plus* the cost of maintenance.

whose social condition is backward, and whose political organization is lacking in stability. All the wealth of such peoples takes the form of articles of consumption or circulating capital. Consider India or Persia, for instance, where you still find all the treasures of the Arabian Nights, but no railways, roads, mines, or machines.

(2) Finally, it must be pointed out, to the disadvantage of fixed capital, that if its durability is too great it *runs the risk of becoming useless*. Consequently, great prudence is required in looking ahead, as we have just said. The material durability of capital, in fact, is not everything: what really matters is its continued utility. And though we can count on the first, up to a certain point, we can never absolutely count on the second. Utility, as we know, is unstable; and what seems the most firmly established may vanish after a certain time. We cannot imagine that the utility of water and of the aqueduct that conveys it can ever disappear; yet the great aqueduct called the Pont du Gard, built by the Romans for the town of Nîmes, is nothing now but a magnificent and useless ruin. This is because the water of the Rhône has been brought to Nîmes. When we drive a tunnel or dig a canal we have no guarantee that traffic will not take some other route after a century or two. Now if the capital sunk in the tunnel is not redeemed by the time this change takes place, a great deal of labour will have been expended uselessly. It is prudent, therefore, in view of our uncertainty about the future, not to build for eternity. From this point of view the use of too lasting a form of capital may be a dangerous operation.

This reservation holds good even of lucrative capital. Neither an individual nor a bank will ever agree to advance capital which cannot be redeemed or repaid in less than two hundred years. Why is this? Because results that can only appear after such a long time do not come within the range of human foresight. In fact, it might be laid down as a rule that any employment of capital which does not look like paying for itself in the course of three generations, should in practice be avoided.

V. HOW CAPITAL IS FORMED

Popular wisdom and the majority of economists also would say that capital is formed *by saving*. But what does this mean? For we know, and have repeated many times, that all capital is a *product*, and, like all products, can only be formed by the two primary agents of production, labour and nature. We need but glance at all imaginable kinds of capital — tools, machines, works of art, materials of every kind — to see that they can have had no other origin than this.

But what, then, is this new character appearing on the scene? Is *saving* a third primary agent of production that we have forgotten? Some economists, and notably the English economist Senior, have declared that it is. He called saving *abstinence*, so as to give it a more definite personality (and also in order to get special terms for it when the time for distribution should come). Moreover, in enumerating the three primary agents of production he, quite logically, replaced capital by its cause, and said that the three agents were nature, labour, and abstinence. And the same classification ought to be adopted by all who still hold that capital is the fruit of saving.

But this would be unreasonable. It is inconceivable how anything whatever could be *produced* by a purely negative act; whether we call it abstinence or saving, in either case it is simply an abstention. It is all very well for Montaigne to say that he "knows no action more active and brave than this inaction"; that may be true from a moral point of view, but it does not explain how this inaction can create even a pin. Production is a positive act, not a negative one.

What is meant, then, by the statement that capital is created by saving? Simply this: that if wealth were consumed as soon as it was formed, capital would never exist. It is obvious, indeed, that if the poultry farmer left no eggs in the nest to be hatched, there would never be any chickens. Nevertheless, if a child asked you where chickens come from, and you told him that the only way to get chickens was to abstain from eating eggs, he would be right in regarding this answer as a piece of good advice, to be sure, but as a foolish explanation.

Now the reasoning which makes saving the original cause of the formation of capital is analogous to that. It amounts to saying that non-destruction is one of the causes of production. Let us say simply that saving is a *condition* of the formation of capital, in the sense that if the wealth produced is consumed from day to day to satisfy our immediate needs, then evidently there will be none left available for making advances and for obtaining time for making implements, for instance. Let us say that if man, like the ant and other animals, had not the power of foreseeing his future wants, all wealth would certainly be consumed or wasted from day to day, as it is among certain savage tribes. Consequently, capital would never have been formed, and civilization itself, the child of leisure, would never have been born. Let us go still further, and say that foresight, sobriety, and other moral virtues are indispensable conditions, if not of the original formation of capital, yet at any rate of its preservation — nothing more so. But the economists who make saving the efficient cause of capital, do so, unconsciously or consciously, from the desire to justify the payment of interest on capital as the remuneration for this act of abstinence.

In short, the birth of capital always presupposes an excess of wealth produced over wealth consumed, but this excess may be obtained in two ways: production may exceed wants, or consumption may be restricted and brought below the level of wants. The term "saving," and especially the term "abstinence," do not apply at all to the first of these two cases, which is fortunately by far the more common; historically, it is in that way alone that capital has been formed.

Can we mention a single instance of wealth created by abstinence? The first flint axe belonging to quaternary man was cut by extra labour, as the result of a lucky day's hunting that brought him a larger supply of food than usual and thus gave him a day's freedom to create this first bit of capital. Is it to be supposed that, in order to pass from the hunting stage to the agricultural stage, races of people must have first saved a whole year's supply of provisions? Nothing is less probable. They simply domesticated their cattle, which became their first capital and gave them the leisure necessary for undertaking longer forms of labour, as well as giving them security for the morrow. But, as Bagehot very pertinently enquires, how does a herd of cattle represent any saving whatever? Has its possession entailed any privations on the part of the owner? Quite the reverse, for thanks to the milk and meat he has been better fed, and thanks to the wool and leather he has been better clothed.

And to-day, as in the days of the pastoral peoples, great undertakings are carried out not with past wealth but with present wealth.

But, it may be asked, even admitting that capital in the form of implements is only the product of labour, must not capital in the form of stock at least be regarded as the result of saving? No; this inference does not seem to us necessary if we admit, what we have tried to prove, that the provision of a stock results not from privation but from an excess of production — a lucky day's hunting, or a superabundant crop.

What suggested and gained credit for the idea of saving as the mother of capital, was the use of money as almost the sole form of wealth. In fact, if we go back to the origin of all money-capital we shall see a certain number of coins *set aside* — shut up in a safe or a money-box, or taken to the savings-bank. So we have got into the habit of looking at capital only in the shape of an investment, for we certainly only invest what is surplus to our needs, and consequently every loan or investment presupposes an excess of income over expenditure — and therefore a saving. And the conclusion has been drawn that all true capital, production capital, must have had the same origin. But that is where the mistake lies.

We have no intention, to be sure, of questioning the importance of saving. But though saving plays a considerable part in consumption, under which head we shall meet with it again, it must not be placed among the factors of production. Everything must be put in its right place. Saving only affects production when it leads to *investment*, that is to say, when the money saved is returned to production to be consumed there in the shape of capital.

PART II

THE ORGANIZATION OF PRODUCTION

CHAPTER I — HOW PRODUCTION IS REGULATED

I. BUSINESS MANAGEMENT AND COST OF PRODUCTION

We have just studied separately each of the factors or agents of production. But we have also seen that they can do nothing separately. If they are to act, then, they must be brought together into one man's hands, or at least under the same management. How is this conjunction brought about?

It is possible for the same person to provide all three factors at once: he can provide the labour by working himself, and the land and capital because he owns them. The peasant who tills his own land with his own hands and with the help of his own horse and plough, is the typical form of this first method of production. He is called the *independent producer*.

As a rule, however, the same individual does not combine all three agents of production. One man may have land and his own muscular strength, but no capital: such is the peasant who borrows on mortgage. Another will have his own labour and capital, but has to rent his land: that is the tenant farmer, or the tradesman who rents his shop. Others may have land and capital, but be unable or unwilling to provide the labour themselves: they will engage workmen.

We may even imagine a case in which the producer can himself provide neither labour, capital, nor natural agents, but has to borrow them all. Such undertakings as mines, railways, or the Suez Canal, are carried out in this way, the projectors obtaining the land (surface or underground) on a long lease, the capital by loans and the issue of shares, and the labour by the employment of thousands of workers.

Now whenever all or some of the means of production have to be borrowed by the man who takes the lead in production, he is

called the *entrepreneur*. His business, which is of the first importance, is to combine all the elements of production so as to obtain
the best possible result.

The *entrepreneur* is therefore the pivot on which the whole of
the economic mechanism turns. On him converge all the factors of
production; and from him also, as we shall see, proceeds all the income. For what is called income, under the various names of
interest, dividends, rents of every kind, wages, and salaries, is
simply the price paid for the hire of capital, land, and labour, or
any other productive services. The *entrepreneur*, therefore, is
both the great employer and the great distributor.

We have learned from our study of the factors of production that
to produce any kind of wealth whatever, it is necessary to consume
a certain amount of pre-existing wealth. Now the sum total of this
wealth is what is called, in the language of economists, the *cost of
production*. But there are two costs of production which must be
carefully distinguished: one social, and the other individual.

The *social*, or what we might also call the *real*, cost of production
is made up of three elements: (1) land – the larger or smaller area
of ground which must be occupied; (2) labour — the sum total,
larger or smaller, of the human efforts that must be employed;
(3) capital — the larger or smaller amount of wealth that must be
consumed; and since this capital itself is a function of time (see
above, p. 101), it may be said shortly that social cost of production
is summed up in the three elements, effort, space, and time.

The *individual*, or relative, cost of production — better described
as the *net cost* — is the price that the *entrepreneur* has to pay to
obtain each of the factors of production: rent, which is the hiring
price of the site he occupies; wages, the price of the labour he employs; and interest, the hiring price of the capital he borrows, or,
more briefly, the price of time.

Take, for example, the exploitation of an iron mine. The *entrepreneur* sets down as expenses of production:

(1) The hiring price of the land he occupies, in the shape of the
rent paid to the owner — a very high one in England, but a trifling
one in France (though made up for by a share levied by the State);

(2) The wages he pays to the workmen he engages;

(3) The interest and depreciation fund on the capital he has
borrowed.

Even when the *entrepreneur* is the owner of the land and capital
employed, this calculation remains the same, for if his accounts are
properly kept he must set down among his expenses of production

the interest on the capital he has invested in the undertaking, and also on that with which he bought the land. The undertaking must pay *him* the hiring price of the productive services, just as it would pay it to others.

It is evident, however, that each of these items, representing an expenditure, or *expense*, as it is called, for the *entrepreneur*, represents an income for other people — for the workman, the capitalist, and the landowner — who are directly or unconsciously his collaborators. Consequently it would be a huge error in calculation to think that the sum of the values paid out by the *entrepreneur* represents the sum of the values actually consumed by the act of production. These latter values, fortunately, are very much less.[1]

If we pass from a primary industry, such as we have taken as an example, to transformative industries, and follow the raw material — iron ore, in this case — into the hands of the iron-master, the maker of ploughs or sewing needles, etc., it is evident that the original cost of production goes on growing like a snowball from the superimposed layers of production expenses. These, however, are always the same: namely, the hiring prices of labour, capital, and land — call them wages, interest, and rent.[2]

The *entrepreneur* draws a balance, then, between the sum of the values destroyed and the value created; he naturally only goes on so long as he foresees that the second will be greater than the first. He makes a kind of exchange, exchanging *what is* against *what will be*. He may make a mistake in his reckoning; if so, it is accidental, and so much the worse for him.

---

[1] This mistake has been constantly made lately in estimating the cost of the war. War can be compared to a vast business undertaking — though not a productive one! — in which the State is the *entrepreneur*. The cost of production to the French as a belligerent State rose to more than eight thousand million pounds, in the sense that that was the sum total of its expenditure. But that was not the cost of production to the country — fortunately! — for the greater part of this expenditure (purchases from contractors, army pay, separation allowances, etc., etc.) was received by those to whom it was due, and even enriched a goodly number of them.

The cost of the war to the nation — the real cost — is another matter. It is the sum of all the wealth actually destroyed — houses bombarded, factories pillaged, ships sunk, and, above all, raw materials and stocks swallowed up in unproductive consumption. These losses enter partly into the public expenditure mentioned above, but for the most part they are outside it, and make up what is called the reparations account.

[2] That is why we must not place *the cost of raw material* among the expenses of production (as examination candidates never fail to do if they are asked for the component elements of cost of production); for obviously the cost of raw material must in its turn be split up into the three primary elements indicated above.

We often hear it said, and it has even been taught by great economists, that value is determined by cost of production. We must understand what this means. If it means that the value of the product is equal to the sum of the values consumed to produce it, it is a truism, just like saying that the whole is equal to the sum of its parts. But if it means that the cost of production is the cause of value, in the sense that every product is worth more or less *because it has cost more or less*, the statement is unfounded. We might just as well say, and with even greater reason, that the cost of production is determined by the value of the object we wish to produce. In fact, the first business of the *entrepreneur*, before undertaking the production of something new, is to find out at what price he will be able to sell it, and then to arrange things so as not to expend more to produce it than it will be worth. This is more important still in the case of an article already quoted on the market. Anyone wanting to undertake the business of coal-mining says to himself: "As coal is worth so much a ton in this district, I must see if I can extract it at a more remunerative price, so that it leaves me a margin of profit." If he has made his calculations badly, and is obliged to spend more for extracting it than the coal will be worth, his folly will not have the effect of increasing the value of coal by a farthing. It will have the effect of ruining him and making him close the mine — that is all.

Still, is it not evident that as a matter of fact and for almost all the things we can see, the selling price does tend to approach the cost price, or at least to follow its variations, just as if there were some necessary bond of dependence between them? This is true; but the phenomenon can be explained in the simplest fashion. What we have here is not a relation of cause and effect, but the action of an outside cause — competition — tending always, like a sort of atmospheric pressure, to bring together *the cost of production and the value of the product, and even to make them coincide;* and this force increases as the divergence between these two values tends to increase. It is easy, indeed, to understand that as soon as the cost price and the selling price draw apart from each other, leaving an increasing margin of profit, all the competitors rush to produce the article in question, and, by multiplying the produce, soon bring about a lowering of its value or price. It might even be asserted that under a system of perfectly free competition, this coincidence between price and cost of production would be perfectly realized. That is one of the most important laws of political economy, because it automatically regulates production, as we shall see in the next section.

In actual fact, however, this coincidence is never realized, because competition never acts perfectly. As we shall see, there is hardly a business which does not enjoy a more or less definite monopoly, arising either from situation, or from patent rights, or from protective duties, or from an open or tacit alliance that enables entrepreneurs to keep the selling price above the cost price and thus realize a profit.[1]

But then, it may perhaps be asked, if the value of everything tends to coincide with its cost of production, is not all the toil of the human race a foolish business, exactly like the labour of the daughters of Danaus, who had to fill a bottomless cask? For if each act of production merely reproduces old values that have been destroyed, in the form of new values, where is the advantage? This contradiction, however, is an apparent one only, resulting from confusion between individual and social cost of production — a distinction that we made a few pages back.

The law just mentioned, which tends continually to reduce the value of the product to the value of its component elements, or the total expenses of production, applies only to the individual cost of production — the money cost, or cost price. If it should happen, owing to competition, that the value of the product leaves nothing to the entrepreneur over and above his expenses of production — leaves him no produce, in other words, — it would be an annoying result for him, but the business would be remunerative all the same for all the collaborators whose services had been paid for. It may even happen that they gain a great deal when the entrepreneur loses. The first Panama Canal undertaking — that of de Lesseps — lost all its capital, but gains of millions of pounds were made by a large number of people — engineers and bankers, not to mention the newspaper men.

But if we look at the social cost of production, then it is not true

---

[1] It may happen that the value of certain products falls *below the cost of production,* without putting a stop to production. This is when the cost price of an article gets gradually lower as a result of industrial progress. In this case competition tends to reduce the price, not to the level of the old cost of production, but to that of the new cost, otherwise called the cost of *reproduction.*

The same thing occurs when the capital engaged in the business can no longer be set free, as, for instance, in mines or railways. In this case, even when the business no longer covers the interest and depreciation of this first-established capital, it may continue all the same, so long as it brings in a little more than the expenses of exploitation.

to say that the wealth produced does not generally exceed the wealth consumed, but quite the reverse.   It is the nature of every productive operation to create more utilities than it destroys — to leave a *net product*, as it is called, not only in agriculture, as the physiocrats taught, but in all forms of production.   It must be so, for how could civilization have developed, how could humanity have risen above animality, if production did not normally leave a net product, serving to enlarge its consumption and to increase its capital?   It is obvious that man could never have founded a family or a city if he never reaped more corn than he consumed as food and as seed.

II.   THE AUTOMATIC REGULATION OF PRODUCTION

A state of health in the social organism, as in all living bodies, consists in a proper balance or equilibrium between production and consumption.   Not to produce enough is an evil, for then a certain set of wants remains unsatisfied.   To produce too much is another evil, less than the first, undoubtedly, but none the less real.   Every excess of production, indeed, necessarily involves not only a waste of wealth, but, above all, a loss of power, and therefore useless hardship.

When each man produces for himself what he means to consume, like Robinson Crusoe on his island, or rather like man in the first stage of domestic industry — the ancient family, or the medieval corporation — this equilibrium is easily maintained.   Each of us individually, or each little group, is able more or less to foresee its own wants, and although its forecast may not be infallible, it can regulate its production accordingly.

The problem becomes more difficult as soon as the producer produces no longer for himself and his family, but for another — for a customer — for it is evidently harder for us to foresee another man's wants than our own.   Yet even under a system of division of labour and exchange, the equilibrium between production and wants is not too difficult to maintain so long as the producer works *to order*, or at least so long as the habits of each customer are known and his consumption is easy to foresee.   The baker and the pastry-cook can pretty accurately calculate the number of loaves and cakes that they will have to supply every day.

But the problem becomes really difficult in an economic system like ours, where the market has grown enormous, production has become frenzied, and the producer no longer waits for the orders of the consumer, properly so called, but obeys the commands of merchants, middlemen, and speculators, who themselves take the lead, buying and selling *for the account*, and anticipating the wants of the public.

However, it was precisely at the commencement of this new régime that the legislator, with a boldness that would have been foolhardy if it had been conscious, made a clean sweep of all the old regulative system, and decided that production should henceforth know no rule but freedom. It was the French Revolution, by the famous law of the 17th March, 1791, that abolished the corporative or guild system in France, under which an individual could only take up a trade when he had fulfilled certain conditions. Thus was proclaimed *the freedom of labour*, the right of every individual to produce what seemed to him best. This reform, greeted by a chorus of acclamations, was quickly imitated throughout the rest of Europe.[1]

But did not this freedom of each man to produce what he pleased lead to anarchy in production, by adding a fresh element of uncertainty to that already caused by the anticipation of future wants? That is what was asserted by the socialists, especially during the first half of the nineteenth century. Economists, on the contrary, generally exulted in the sight of the order and balance that reigned in production.

The fact is that it is almost miraculous at first sight to see how hundreds of millions of men, without any mutual agreement, can each find every day what he needs — at least if he is able to pay for it. What Providence or what hidden force is it, then, that thus controls the production of wealth from day to day, so that there is neither too much of it nor too little?

The explanation offered by economists is very simple. They say that production is regulated in the surest, quickest, and simplest manner by the *law of supply and demand*, in the following fashion.

If a particular branch of industry happens to be insufficiently provided with labour and capital, the want that it is designed to satisfy is not fully met, and its produce therefore acquires a higher value. Greater profits are realized by the producers, and particularly by the *entrepreneur*, who is the principal agent of production and the first to profit by the rise in prices. Then other producers — capitalists or workers — engage in this branch of production, attracted by these abnormally high profits. The production of the commodity in question increases, therefore, until the quantity produced rises to the level of the quantity demanded.

[1] [In England the guild system had fallen considerably into disuse since the sixteenth century, being gradually replaced by the "domestic system" of industry.]

Whenever, on the other hand, some commodity has been produced in greater quantity than is needed, its value must fall. This fall reduces the income of the producers, and the profits of the *entrepreneur* in particular, for it is he who bears the first brunt of all changes. So he withdraws from a course of production in which he experiences disappointment and loss, and the production of the commodity slackens off until the quantity produced falls to the level of the quantity consumed.

Such is the beautifully harmonious and spontaneous organization of production that has been so often celebrated, especially by Bastiat. It is a kind of mechanism that works automatically — far superior, it is said, to any system of artificial regulation, however ingenious.

This regulative law is indisputable as a tendency; but many conditions are necessary if it is actually to operate — conditions which are only rarely fulfilled.

First of all, supply must answer instantaneously to demand. The agents of production must be assumed to be perfectly mobile, and to move with the speed of electricity from points where they are superabundant to points where they are insufficient. There must be a single world market, or at least markets that are closely united, like vessels communicating with each other, so that, if equilibrium is disturbed, it may be restored almost instantaneously.

Now, even if we admit that the economic world is tending towards such a state of affairs as this, it must be acknowledged that it is still far from having attained it. In fact, all agricultural and industrial production presupposes the employment of capital that is engaged for a longer or shorter period of time (see the section on *Fixed Capital and Circulating Capital*), and such capital, by the very fact that it has become "fixed," has ceased to be mobile. The French vine-growers are being told that they are producing too much wine and must make "something else"; and it is probable, indeed, that the law of supply and demand — if it is only the competition of Algerian wines — will sooner or later compel them to do so. But what is to be done with the millions of pounds of capital buried in the ground in the shape of vine plantations and cellars?

Nor is this all. Even when the law of supply and demand is in full operation, it is by no means "harmonious" in the sense intended by Bastiat, for we must not forget that value has no relation to utility in the common and "normative" sense of the word. It distributes production and professions not in accordance with man's true needs, but according to his desires and the price he is willing and able to pay for their satisfaction (see above, p. 121).

It follows, then that the most useful functions, such as that of agriculture, tend to be neglected, while the most unproductive, such as that of town shopkeepers, for instance, not to mention the numerous parasitic public officials, are absurdly multiplied. Need we recall the fact that the number of retailers of alcoholic drinks in France reaches the incredible figure of nearly 470,000 — say about 1 to every 24 adult men — while the number of agricultural labourers is continually growing smaller?[1]

The numbers engaged in other vocations, such as the medical profession, would be sufficient if they were better distributed. But they are almost all concentrated in towns, where many of them, through lack of clients, are reduced to the worst expedients for obtaining a living, and there remains but an inadequate number for the rural population. Thus the distribution of doctors in Paris shows very plainly that their number is not proportionate to the number of the sick but to the rate of profit. In the wealthy districts there is one doctor to every 100 or 130 inhabitants, while in the poorer quarters there is only one to every 3,000 or 6,000, and in one district there is one doctor for 17,772 inhabitants![2] That is how free competition adapts services to needs. No one certainly will say that the poor have less need of doctors than the rich![3]

Finally, it must not be forgotten that "demand" does not come directly from the consumers, but from the middlemen, merchants, and speculators;[4] and that it is a demand founded less upon real and present wants than upon wants which perhaps will not be realized. It will not be surprising, therefore, if there is overproduction, or, conversely, if production remains below the level of wants. That is what we shall see before long in the chapter on *Crises*.

[1] [In England and Wales there were 105,630 licensed premises in 1920 — say about 1 to every 95 adult men.]

[2] [Compare the following figures showing the number of doctors in certain English towns and London districts (from the *Medical Directory* for 1914): Brighton and Hove, 235 (1 in 738 of the population); Bournemouth 190 (1 in 414); Ilford (190) 43; Wigan, 42 (1 in 2,123 of the population); London, Harley-street, 297; Wimpole-street, 167; Hampstead, 169; Bethnal Green, 28; Bermondsey, 28.]

[3] In connection with an epidemic of smallpox that broke out in Brittany in January 1893, the newspapers remarked the fact that not one doctor was to be found within a radius of nine miles.

[4] It must not be concluded, as is sometimes a little too hastily done, that speculation — the anticipation of future events — is necessarily an evil. On the contrary, the speculator who buys when he foresees a shortage and sells when he foresees abundance may exercise a very beneficent regulative influence. But speculation very often makes mistakes, especially when it is turned into a game.

III. COMPETITION

The law of supply and demand requires two conditions to enable
it to function completely. These are: (1) freedom for every man
to produce and to sell what he thinks best; (2) freedom for every
man to sell at the price he thinks best, or at least at the price he can
get. When these conditions are fulfilled we say that there is *free
competition*. Competition, then, appears as the great regulator of
the whole economic mechanism of modern society.

It used to be the rule in treatises on political economy to recognize
the following virtues as belonging to competition:

(1) It stimulates *progress* by the emulation it arouses among
competing industries, and by the elimination of routine methods
in industry;

(2) It promotes *cheapness*, to the great advantage of all, and
especially of the poorer classes;

(3) It brings about a *progressive equalization of conditions*, by
reducing the rate of profits, wages, rent, interest, etc., to the same
level.

The virtues of competition are summed up by Bastiat in this
lyrical description: "It is the most progressive, the most equalizing,
the most conducive to the common welfare, of all the laws to which
Providence has entrusted the progress of human societies." And
the blessings of competition are made more apparent by contrasting
it with the system of monopoly, under which the public is delivered
over to the discretion of a single individual. Competition, it is
said, means democracy in the economic realm, whereas monopoly
is autocracy.

The socialists of the first half of the nineteenth century took the
opposite view, and denounced competition as the cause of all social
evils, because they regarded association as the solution of the social
problem.

We must certainly not fail to recognize the services rendered by
competition to the public welfare: it protects the consumer against
exploitation at the hands of merchants and producers. But how
does it do this? Simply by setting in opposition to each other the
interests of these producers — just in the same way as the interests
of small nations may be safeguarded by the jealous rivalry of the
greater powers. But such a safeguard is as precarious in the economic
sphere as in the political, and may well be replaced by a higher form
of organization.

Competition makes the consumer pay too dearly for this protection. In fact, if we look more closely at the three virtues attributed to it, we shall see how easily each of them may degenerate into a vice. This is because competition, as we have just shown, has a double aspect: it involves both freedom of labour and a struggle for existence. Consider these points:

(1) It is true that competition may stimulate production by arousing a spirit of rivalry among producers. But it also stimulates deterioration in the *quality* of the produce. In order to keep up the struggle, each competitor strives to substitute raw materials of inferior quality and a lower price, for those that are better and consequently more expensive. The result is that among the signs of progress one of the most remarkable is undoubtedly the adulteration of commodities. It has become a veritable art, laying every scientific discovery under contribution.[1] Some kinds of trade, such as the grocery trade, and some manufactures, such as those of artificial manures and preserves, have become so notorious in this respect as to necessitate legislative interference. If the competitive system shows a great advance on the guild system from the point of view of industrial enterprise, the same cannot be said of it from the point of view of the quality of the goods produced.

Nor is it only the product that deteriorates. There is also, if I may venture to say so, a deterioration in the producer, which too often results from competition. If competition assures victory to the strongest and the cleverest, it may very well happen that it eliminates the most scrupulous, or rather that it compels him to "do at Rome as the Romans do." Examples of this are the tradesman who is unwilling to adulterate his goods, or who would like to close his shop on Sunday, and the manufacturer who does not want to reduce his employees' wages or increase the length of their day's work.

(2) It is true that competition has the effect of lowering prices, when it is "free," as the economists say, meaning when merchants and manufacturers are simple enough to contend with each other for customers and to undersell each other. But those times are past, at any rate in the home market. Among the tradesmen of a town or the manufacturers in an industry there is always a tacit understanding to sell at the same price. In trade and industry on a large scale this understanding nowadays takes the form of a writ-

---

[1] Examples are innumerable. Drinkable wine can now be made without grapes, jam without fruit or sugar, butter without milk, milk without a cow, even eggs without a hen. So too flour is made with a large proportion of talc, and silk fabrics containing only 5% silk and 95% mineral matter!

ten agreement — the famous *cartel* or *trust* (see below). Sometimes, moreover, and notably in the liberal professions (those of
lawyers, doctors, and chemists), this understanding that one will
not charge a client less than one's competitor — who in this case is
called a colleague or a brother —becomes a professional rule of honour.

It is only in international commerce that competition retains its
beneficent effects, for combination is difficult between producers in
different countries. But none the less it is tending to become international.

Not only is it the case that competition does not always lower
prices, but it frequently happens, paradoxical as the statement may
seem, that it raises them, by increasing the cost of production.
The most striking example is that of a new railway competing with
one that already exists between two towns. It is clear that the
traffic, which will remain the same with two lines as it was with one,
will have to support a double cost of establishment and maintenance.
Another excellent example is the bread-making business. The
number of bakers in each town is ridiculously excessive. Each of
them, selling less bread owing to competition, is compelled to make
up for it by raising the price or tampering with the weight. And
so, as M. de Foville wittily puts it, the competition of the traders
makes prices rise just as the competition of the trees in the forest
makes them rise to the sky in their struggle for air and light.[1] It
was not the same under the guild system, where the number of
dealers in each trade was limited.

(3) It is true, in the third place, that competition may exercise
an equalizing influence on fortunes, by levelling down profits that
exceed the common standard. Yet which is the country in which
the inequality of wealth is greatest — the country that has given
birth to that portentous phenomenon, the millionaire? It is the
very country where competition is most feverish, where everyone
hustles around in the hunt for dollars, and where the good old French
maxim: "Each for himself and God for us all," has been replaced
by the American saying: "The devil take the hindmost."

Competition only makes profits equal when the competitors are
equal in ability — that is to say, when it involves the previous ex-

---

[1] There were 3,050 bakers' shops in Paris in 1911 — 1 to every 900 inhabitants, or,
say, 1 to every 200 or 300 households. So the average sale of bread by each of them
did not exceed about 1,000 pounds a day. It might easily be increased tenfold, and
then the general expenses charged on each loaf would be reduced by nine-tenths.
Such is the case in the great co-operative bakeries, like the Edinburgh one, which bakes
20,000 loaves a day.

istence of the system it is thought to create. When competition takes place between those who are unequal — between the strong and the weak, — it can only aggravate this original inequality. So we cannot count on competition to realize distributive justice.

Finally, even assuming, as is done in pure economics, that a society might exist under such conditions that competition could take place without restraint, and could assure to everyone the maximum of satisfaction at the minimum price, it would scarcely be desirable, from the social and moral point of view, that this assumption should be capable of realization. For this would mean the rule of absolute individualism — each for himself. Society would be nothing but a sale-room, like the floor of the Stock Exchange, with everyone shouting his price. The social ideal is not to be discovered there. We must seek it rather in a co-operative system, organized with a view to the satisfaction of wants, and not to the pursuit of profit.[1]

IV. OVERPRODUCTION AND THE LAW OF OUTLETS

To judge from the state of poverty to which the vast majority of men are condemned, it would look as if production must still be far behind human wants, and as if the great business of life must be to stimulate it to the greatest possible extent. And yet, strangely enough, the fear that haunts manufacturers and business men, and that is most often on their lips, is the fear of overproduction, of a general excess of products, of what is called a *general glut*. How can this be?

Economists themselves have never shared this apprehension. To them the danger of general overproduction seems entirely imaginary and absurd. They do not deny, to be sure, that in certain branches of industry, or even in many of them, production may chance to exceed demand, owing to miscalculation. But they deny altogether that *general* overproduction can really exist, and they attribute the fear of it to a mere optical illusion whose cause is easily understood. It is because the producers whose products are over-abundant on the market and therefore sell badly, make a great outcry,

---

[1] See our discussion on *Competition and Co-operation* in the book called *Le Coopératisme.*

There are moral and philosophical arguments, besides the economic ones, for the belief that *co-operation* is destined more and more to supplant *competition*. And even in the domain of biology a new school is beginning to teach that association and mutual assistance are just as powerful a factor as the struggle for existence in the progress and improvement of species.

whereas those whose products are scarce and consequently sell well, remain silent. Hence we hear of nothing but overproduction, and we end by imagining that it is universal.

But that is not all. The opinion of economists is that, given a state of congestion in any one branch of production, the most effective remedy for the evil is just to stimulate a corresponding increase in the other branches. The crisis that results from abundance can only be cured by abundance, conformably to the motto of a famous school of medicine: *similia similibus*, "like cures like." Thus it is to the interest of all producers that production should be as abundant and varied as possible. This theory is known as *the law of outlets*. It was first formulated by J. B. Say, who was very proud of it, and said that "it would change the policy of the whole world." It can be expressed as follows: *The greater the variety and abundance of other products, the more outlets will be found for each product.*

To understand this theory we must first leave money out of consideration and suppose that products are exchanged directly for products, as under the system of barter. Suppose, for example, that a trader arrives at one of the great markets of Central Africa — in the Soudan or on the Congo. Is it not to his interest to find the market as well stocked as possible with numerous and various products? Of course it is not to his interest to meet with a large quantity of the very goods that he can offer himself — guns, for instance. But he wants to find as much as possible of all other kinds of things — ivory, gums, gold-dust, ground-nuts, and so forth. Every new kind of merchandise that appears on the market constitutes an investment or an *outlet* for his own goods; so the more there is of it, the better for him. As J. B. Say well expresses it: "What most favours the sale of one commodity, is the production of another."

The same thing happens, we are told, under the system of buying and selling. The greater the resources of other people, the better chance there is for each of us to find a sale for his own products, and the more they have produced the greater will be their resources. The best thing we can wish, then, for a producer who has produced *too much* of anything, is that other producers also may have done the same: the superabundance of some commodities will correct the superabundance of others. Has England produced too much calico this year? Well, if India has had the good fortune to produce too much wheat, the calico will be disposed of far more easily.

Again, let us suppose that industry, thanks to a prodigious increase in mechanical power, throws on the market an enormous quantity of goods, but that agricultural production has not kept pace with manufacture — agricultural produce has only increased to a very slight extent. Then the value of agricultural produce goes up, compared with the value of manufactured goods, and consumers, having to spend more on food-stuffs, have not sufficient means to buy many manufactured articles. But if, on the contrary, agricultural production keeps pace with mechanical production, then the balance is restored. The consumer, spending less on food, will have no difficulty in absorbing the excess of manufactured goods.

In short, then, the outlet theory simply goes to prove that an excess of production is never an evil *if the increase takes place simultaneously and proportionally in all branches of production.* In this case, in fact, the relations between the quantities exchanged are not altered, so the economic equilibrium is not disturbed.

This, indeed, is indisputable; but we must go a step further in our hypothesis. We must assume that money, the instrument of exchange, also shares in the general overproduction, for if the quantity of money were to remain the same, the result would be that its rate of exchange with other products would necessarily be altered. Its comparative scarcity would confer a greater purchasing power upon it, which means that there would be a general fall in prices. But supposing that the production of money increases in the same proportion as everything else, then there would be no change in values or prices and no external sign would reveal to the public that they were rolling in abundance.

As a matter of pure theory, therefore, the law of outlets is perfectly well founded. But in actual fact an increase in production never takes place under the conditions set forth in that theory. There is not one chance in a million of seeing an equal and simultaneous increase in all branches of production. Such increases take place by fits and starts, by intermittent and local spurts.

Generally, too, they take place only in the case of manufactured products, where wants are already abundantly provided for, and where overproduction means rather a waste of labour and capital. They very rarely occur in agriculture or house-building, where, on the contrary, they would be welcome, because in this direction wants are still very far from being completely satisfied.

That is why the law of outlets, though true in principle, does not prevent those incessant disturbances of equilibrium in exchange which provoke *crises*. And that is also why producers seek nowadays to prevent these disturbances by commercial understandings (trusts or cartels) which are one of the most characteristic features

of our time.   These we shall study later on.   Their essential character is that of a mutual engagement, entered into by producers in
one branch of industry, not to produce more than a certain amount,
which is fixed according to the state of the market.

V. CRISES

A crisis, as the word indicates with sufficient clearness, is a sudden
disturbance of economic equilibrium.   But it can be studied under
two very different and even opposite aspects.

Crises may appear as a kind of disease of the economic organism,
showing symptoms similar to those of the numberless ills by which
man is afflicted.   Some are periodic in character; others, on the other
hand, are irregular.   Some are short and violent, like attacks of
fever; they manifest themselves in the same way by a great rise of
temperature followed by sudden depression.   Others are slow, like
anæmia, as M. de Laveleye says.   Some are confined to one particular country; others are epidemic, travelling round the world,
like cholera.

But these comparisons assume that the crisis is a *pathological*
phenomenon.   Should we not, however, regard it rather as a *physiological* one — as a manifestation that has nothing abnormal about
it, and that is quite compatible with a state of perfect health?   May
it not be rather the outcome of exuberant vitality — a crisis of
growth — a function, and perhaps even a necessary condition, of
economic progress?   And if crises are destined ever to disappear,
would not their disappearance be rather the melancholy symptom of
a society engulfed in the quicksands of the "stationary state"?

Thus there emerge two conceptions of crises, one pessimistic and
the other optimistic; and this difference of opinion as to their nature
necessarily involves differences of opinion as to the way to explain
them and the means of averting them.

(1) *Symptoms.* — The economic phenomena that distinguish crises
are always more or less the same, so that their diagnosis is not difficult.   The only differences are that they are more or less accentuated.
If we had to enumerate them all, they would make a long list, for
as scarcely any economic relations remain altogether unaffected by
the disruptive effects of a crisis, almost any of them could be taken,
if desired, as the sign indicating its existence.[1]

---

[1] In France a commission has been set up by the government, since 1908, to investigate and publish "the signs of economic crises," with the object of avoiding or
mitigating unemployment.

The first sign that reveals crises is their *periodicity*. They have been seen to follow each other, at least during the nineteenth century, with the majestic regularity of the ocean swell, each wave extending over about ten or a dozen years, five or six in an upward direction, and five or six more downward. The same alternation is undoubtedly to be found more or less in all economic phenomena — price movements, wages, rates of interest — and even also in natural phenomena such as barometric variations, the rise and fall of waters, the advance and retreat of glaciers. Rhythm is the law of the world. There is nothing very mysterious in that. It is even impossible for it to be otherwise. Whenever any variation is confined within certain limits, which is usually the case, there is necessarily an oscillation between the extreme points. But in the case of crises there is something impressive about this regularity of movement, and it was the desire to explain it that led to the first enquiries into their causes.

Another distinguishing feature of crises is their *epidemic* character. It frequently happens that there is excessive or insufficient production in such and such an industry. That is, in fact, the way in which most crises start. But they only become crises when the disturbance travels from one industry to another and from one country to another, and this points to the action of some general cause, as to which economists are not in agreement.

But besides these general features, here are the three particular signs by which crises are preceded and announced:

(*a*) *A rise of prices*, giving evidence of activity of consumption, abundance of ready money, and credit facilities;

(*b*) *A rise in the value of transferable securities*, especially shares, signifying activity in business undertakings and an increase of profits and dividends;

(*c*) *A rise in wages*, implying activity in the labour market, and an increased demand for labour.

But what actually constitutes the crisis is this: that at a given moment, by some mysterious cause, all these movements change their direction, and the upward trend suddenly becomes a downward one. Then we get symptoms opposite to those just indicated:

(*a*) *A fall in prices*, betraying a decrease in consumption, scarcity of money, and the disappearance of credit;

(*b*) *A fall in the value of securities*, revealing the sinking of profits and dividends, and the failure of the most hazardous business enterprises — a fall which is accompanied by a rise in the rate of discount;

(*c*) *A fall in wages*, marking the stoppage of production, the cessation of demand for labour, and the imminence of unemployment.

The moment of the crisis is marked by this passage from a state of activity to one of depression — a moment which can sometimes be determined with such precision that the day, and almost the hour, can be indicated. At other times, however, it is spread out over a longer period and leaves a certain amount of doubt even as to the year.

(2) *Causes.* — Jevons was the first to notice that, during the nineteenth century, crises followed each other at approximately regular intervals of ten years. The dates were as follows:

1815	1857
1827	1866
1836	1873
1847	1882

And if Jevons had lived longer — he died in 1882 — how pleased he would have been to see the last two crises of the century appear just at the predicted times, one in 1890, and the other in 1900! Can such regularity be attributed to chance, or does it not rather suggest the idea of some astronomical cycle? In fact it was towards the heavens that Jevons lifted his eyes in search of an explanation, and he thought he had found it in the periodicity of the spots on the sun. But what connexion could he establish between sun-spots and crises? Just this: that these variations in the intensity of the sun's radiance reacted on the earth in the form of good and bad harvests, which, in their turn, determined the crises. Nothing, it will be seen, was lacking to this cosmic romance.

But it is only a romance. And even in the matter of the ten-yearly periodicity of crises the twentieth century has refuted the supposed law, for the first crisis came in 1907.

The astronomical explanation of crises having been abandoned, it remains to find another. Economists have not been at a loss: they have provided innumerable explanations. In 1895 a German author named Bergmann counted 230 of them, and others have been found since. Their number might even be called infinite. For, given the complexity and mutual dependence of all economic phenomena, it is enough that one of them should be interfered with — as if it were one of the wheels of a watch — for the whole mechanism to be thrown out of gear; or, if we prefer a physiological analogy, the injury of one organ is enough to make the whole organism suffer.

However, the search for causes can be limited and defined by observing that a crisis is not any disturbance whatever, but one that has certain definite characteristics. Consequently the cause we are seeking must be one that will explain these characteristics, and particularly the periodicity of the phenomenon.

(a) The explanation by *overproduction* is the one that is naturally suggested by the sight of the progress of mechanical industry. Sooner or later there must come a day when this mass of products thrown upon the market exceeds the capacity for consumption and can no longer be absorbed. So it is got rid of by a general collapse of prices. The manufacturers, to avoid the necessity of selling at a loss, try to obtain money from the bankers or by the sale of securities, and this results in a rise in the rate of discount and a fall in the value of securities, so that money becomes scarce, precisely in consequence of the superabundance of goods. Such manufacturers as cannot manage to procure money, become bankrupt. Here, then, we find what seems a sufficient explanation of all the features of a crisis, as enumerated above.

The periodicity of the crisis is also explained on this hypothesis, for it is easy to understand that this alternating movement by which production outruns consumption, and then at a given moment stops out of breath, while consumption, proceeding at a uniform pace, catches it up and outdistances it in its turn, proceeds of necessity in a rhythmical fashion. In fact, a certain amount of time is needed after each collapse, for industry to make good its losses, build up its reserves afresh, and renew its plant with a view to satisfying new wants.

Yet this explanation meets with several serious objections, and notably this one: it is incomprehensible why crises should be heralded by a rise in prices, if they are due to overproduction. It is true that the fall, and even collapse, of prices appears in the downward period of the crisis, after the saturation point has been reached. But why does it not show itself before that moment, and as soon as production begins to be excessive? Are we to reply that it is because production is itself outstripped by the rising tide of consumption? But in that case it is no longer overproduction that is the cause of the crisis: we must call it rather over-consumption.

(b) The explanation by *under-consumption* is one that appeals by preference to the minds of those who look at the wretchedness resulting from the existing economic state of things — to socialists, or socializers, like Sismondi. They do not deny that crises are occasionally caused by overproduction due to the greed of capitalists who, to make up for the fall in profits, try to get it back, as they say, in the matter of quantity. But the fundamental cause is the insufficiency of the resources of the great mass of consumers of the working class — the wage-earners — who have not the means of buying back the produce of their own labour. Nor must it be said, by way of setting aside this doctrine, that the wants of man are infinite or indefinitely elastic, for in order to dispose of an article it is not enough to find people who desire it; you must also find those who have the means of acquiring it. Now the increase in the incomes of the mass of the population has not kept pace with the increase in manufacturing production. These two causes — each the converse of the other, but tending to the same result — go on continually increasing in intensity: on the one hand, the growing need of the manufacturers to extend their production as much as possible; on the other hand, the growing number of wage-earners and the insufficiency of their wages. Consequently, when the balance is once disturbed, instead of automatically righting itself, as it has done hitherto, it will become more and more unstable, and crises will become more and more severe, until the time comes when they will bury the capitalist system under its own ruins. That system is thus destined to perish by the very consequences it has itself given birth to.

This explanation, however, seems to fit the facts no better than the preceding one, for just as that one seemed in contradiction to the general rise of prices, so this one seems to be refuted by the rise in wages which generally precedes a crisis. Why does the impossibility of the purchase by the working classes, with their wages, of the produce of their own labour, manifest itself just at the end of the period in which those classes have earned most, and when, therefore, their power of consumption has been increased? It is comprehensible that under-consumption exists as a chronic evil, and that it is a sufficient explanation of misery and poverty; but it is difficult to see why it should show itself in the shape of a crisis at a given moment and at regularly recurring intervals.

Moreover, even admitting the theory underlying this explanation, namely, that the wage-earning class receives less and less of the produce of its own labour and thus becomes more and more robbed by the possessing class, we cannot see why the result should be a *general* insufficiency of consumption, for why would not the robbers consume as much as the robbed? It is not likely that their appetites would be less. Of course they will consume different things: there will be less consumption of prime necessaries and more of luxuries; but this should be altogether to the advantage of industry, which generally makes more out of the latter than out of the former.

(c) Economists, therefore, are in general agreement nowadays on a third explanation. They find the cause of crises in *over-capitalization* rather than in overproduction. Although this theory itself takes many different forms, the following are its commonest features.

If industry had only to adapt production to wants from day to day, it would be easy enough. Even if it did not exactly succeed, a crisis would not be the result, any more than a crisis occurs when a pastry-cook finds himself with a surplus of cakes at the end of the day, through having misjudged the wants of his customers. But large-scale industry cannot be content with day-to-day production: it must anticipate wants and, in order to be able to meet them, it must create a long time beforehand all the necessary means of manufacture and transport, such as factories, machinery, mines, trucks, ships, etc. — and that takes time. Meanwhile people's wants increase, they grow impatient, and prices rise. Then when the means of production are at last ready to come into action, they suddenly pour out floods of products on to the market. Observe, too, that these floods cannot now be stopped at will, for when capital has once been invested as fixed capital it can no longer be set free; it has to continue working even when the market has become saturated, and even when it is working at a loss. It will easily be understood, therefore, why the fall in prices may end in a complete collapse. It will not end until a certain number of new businesses have become bankrupt or have given up the struggle, or until the fall in prices has had its usual effect of increasing consumption, so that the excess is gradually absorbed.

It can be understood, also, why crises are separated by fairly regular intervals. The length of these periods is just that which is necessary for the fresh building-up of the capital destroyed by the crisis. And this theory perfectly explains, too, why crises are phenomena that accompany the capitalist system, and more especially the system of large-scale industry.

Moreover, we can understand better now why even those who are not engaged in business — people of independent means and the general public — are actors in the crisis, helping to precipitate it, and bearing the consequences. What, in point of fact, do we see on these occasions? Here is a period of prosperity: harvests are good, there is no fear of war, industry progresses, everything goes well. Then we see the prices of all shares going up — copper mines, coal mines, rubber shares, banks, railways. Every small share-holder turns over his bill-case and everyone asks those whom he thinks well-informed: "Tell me what is going to rise." He runs little risk of going wrong, for everything rises. Everywhere new businesses are being started, new rubber plantations are made, watercourses are exploited, picture palaces are opened, and even old-established businesses increase their capital by fresh issues of stock.

Then comes the day when all these businesses begin to compete with each other. An ominous crash occurs: one of them has gone under. Immediately there is a panic, and just as, not long before, the more prices rose the more eager were the buyers, so now, the more they fall the more eager are the holders to sell. There are few capitalists who manage to get out in time, as it is called. By degrees all those securities that represented so much anticipated income and the "capitalization of so many hopes," as M. Seligman eloquently says, sink down, even before it can be known whether overproduction has really taken place.[1]

(3) *Remedies.* — To begin with, is there any occasion to seek for remedies? Here we get back to the question proposed at the opening of this section. If the crisis is only a physiological phenomenon — a normal rhythmic movement, like the pulsation of the economic organism — then we can only let it be. But if it is to be regarded as a pathological trouble, then indeed the search for a remedy is plainly indicated. Now it seems to follow from an examination of

[1] Why should there not be crises of *underproduction* (*i.e.*, shortage) as well as of overproduction? Cannot the equilibrium between production and consumption be disturbed as well by deficient as by excessive production? It even seems that such crises should be feared the most, for, after all, an excess of production, which means abundance, cannot be an evil in itself. It becomes so only in consequence of some fault in the economic structure, whereas insufficient production must involve misery and, eventually, death.

It is true that dearths and even famines have held a prominent and terrible place in the history of all races, and when we thought them definitely eliminated, at least in Europe, we have just seen them reappear in all their horror as a result of war.

Nevertheless we are right in not placing dearths in the category of crises, for they possess neither the essential characteristic of periodicity nor any of the other symp-toms that we have enumerated. There is the rise in prices, to be sure; but this ap-pears in exactly opposite conditions, since here it is only the consequence and outcome of the deficit, whereas the classical type of crisis is preceded by the rise in prices and the fall only follows it.

the causes that we have just been glancing at — whichever one seems the best founded — that they all involve a certain amount of disorder and some troublesome consequences which we should attempt to avert.

But the remedy will obviously depend on the cause that is assigned. If we believe it to be overproduction, we must set ourselves to limit this production: as, for instance, by the institution of cartels and trusts (see below), which, by regulating production, would prevent the excessive rise of prices and consequently their fall also, or would at least act as a parachute for them, as it has been picturesquely said. Or an alternative remedy would be simply to set up a co-operative system, under which production would be organized only with a view to wants and not with a view to profit, and there would therefore be no stimulus to overproduction of an excessive and purely speculative kind.

If we find the cause of a crisis in the fact that the working classes have not the means of increasing their consumption as rapidly as production increases, then we must seek for the remedy in the establishment of a socialist régime which shall assure to the worker the whole of the produce of his labour.

If we regard over-capitalization as the cause of crises we shall have to count on the banks, which are the great and almost the only credit providers. It will devolve upon them to intervene at the right moment, either by raising the rate of discount to contract credit (see chapter on *Banks*) when they see that the rapidity of circulation is increasing to a disquieting extent, or, on the other hand, when the crisis is imminent, by hastening to the rescue of the houses that will be the first to succumb, and whose fall will precipitate the general crash. Legislation, too, can perhaps exercise preventive action, either by controlling the issue of shares in new undertakings, or by regulating dealings on a time basis.

If this last explanation is the true one, however, the remedy is more doubtful, for the evil is more psychological than economic. It is rather a question of education, a case for teaching the public not to believe that because a share goes up they must buy it, and that because it goes down they must sell it. This lesson teaches itself, in the sense that a bad sale, a fall in prices, the difficulty of pro-curing money, and the spectacle of failures, by frightening pro-ducers, cannot fail to check overproduction. Only, this remedy ceases to act as soon as the chilling effect of the shower-bath has ceased. Perhaps the most efficacious remedy would simply be a knowledge of crises sufficiently accurate to enable their return at a definite time to be foreseen.   For it is permissible to believe that a crisis foreseen and to some extent discounted, would thereby be either averted or at least much weakened.   Yet we must not trust to that, for it often happens that the fear of an evil has the precise effect of producing that evil!   The Great War might probably have been avoided if everyone had not foolishly said that it was inevitable.

CHAPTER II — ASSOCIATION IN PRODUCTION

I. SUCCESSIVE FORMS OF ASSOCIATION IN PRODUCTION

"To-day, Good Friday," wrote Fourier in 1818, "I have discovered the secret of universal association." This was a vain boast, for although he set forth the principle of association with remarkable vigour, he certainly did not discover it. Association is not the kind of phenomenon that requires discovery: it is patent to all eyes. It is probably the most general of all the laws that govern the universe, since it is manifested not only in the relations of men living in society, but also in those that unite worlds into solar systems, and molecules or cells into unorganized or organized bodies. It is seen even in the logical relations that enable us to think. Wild animals obey the laws of association, and some of these animal societies — those of bees, ants, and beavers — have been and will remain for men an inexhaustible source of instruction and admiration.

Association is employed for all purposes, but we are only concerned here with association with a view to production, taking the word "association" not in the legal sense of a society bound together by contract, but in the economic sense of any grouping of individuals working for a common end. Association in this sense is necessary for men in all kinds of work that are too great for one man's strength, even if it be merely the lifting of a weight, and also in such kinds of work as must necessarily be performed together because of their complementary nature, such as the work of the sower and the harrower who covers up the seed, the reaper and the man who binds the sheaves, the driver and the fireman on the same locomotive.

Association among men has passed through three stages:

(1) First of all it was *instinctive*, just like that of the animals. It is not only for fighting that men group themselves instinctively, but also for work and for play; they like working alone no more than they like playing alone.

The most natural and evidently the first form of association was that of man and wife, parents and children. It will perhaps be said

139

that there is nothing economic about this, and that it is caused solely by the sex instinct and the maternal instinct. Yet marriage as a permanent union, and in any case the *household*, was originally essentially an economic association. When you asked the North American Indians why they married, they replied, "Because our wives go and fetch wood and water and food, and carry all our baggage." It was most probably this economic aspect that made the family a permanent institution in a way that the sex instinct or the parental instinct could not possibly have done.

(2) Association next became *coercive*, first in the shape of slavery. Slavery must be regarded, in fact, as a mere enlargement of the primitive family, determined by economic causes — the need to form a more powerful association. (The Latin term *familia* includes slaves, and the slave himself was called *familiaris*.) Nor is there anything surprising, at a time when wives themselves were often obtained by conquest — witness the rape of the Sabines — in the fact that conquest served also to introduce workers from outside into the family. They very often ended by becoming adopted members of the family, as we can see in the accounts written by travellers in Morocco not long ago, as well as in the old Greek tragedies.

It was this compulsory co-operation that enabled the men of old, yoked together in hundreds and moving in time to a brass instrument beaten by a sort of band-master, as we see in the Egyptian bas-reliefs, to build the Pyramids, or to row their galleys with three or four tiers of oars.

With the introduction of *serfage*, association became less strictly coercive, at least to the extent that the personal relations between master and workman became milder. But, on the other hand, the bond between the worker and the land grew tighter, for the characteristic feature of serfage is that the serf was attached to the soil.

Association still kept its semi-coercive character under the *corporative* or *guild system*. It was compulsory in the sense that no one could engage in work without belonging to the corporation or guild connected with that kind of work, and without conforming to the rules imposed by the guild, or later on by the government. But in this case the obligation constituted a privilege rather than a form of servitude. It was an advantage and an honour to be admitted into the trade association that was called a guild. A candidate was only admitted after serving a long apprenticeship and undergoing a test of his ability by executing a "masterpiece." Later on, the masterpiece was replaced by the payment of dues, which grew heavier and heavier, and technical ability was less necessary for admission than money, favour, or relationship to one of the masters. Thus was dug the first ditch between master and work-man — a ditch that was gradually to widen into a gulf. The workers, called *companions* or *varlets*, saw the path to mastership closed to them — the path, that is to say, to independent production, — and were condemned to remain simple wage-earners for ever.[1] Then it was that the guilds, which had become exclusively associations of masters, were opposed by associations composed entirely of workers. These were the earliest labour organizations, and they played a great part in the history of the working classes.

(3) Thus the course of development which seemed in the Middle Ages as if it was going to unite capital and labour in the same asso-ciation, came to an end. None the less, it resulted in a new form of association — the one we have studied in the preceding chapter under the name of *business:* a larger or smaller grouping of individ-uals, of whom one, the employer, supplies the capital, the tools, and the land, while the others, called wage-earners, furnish the labour.

This system has done wonders in the matter of the production of wealth; but as a form of association it cannot be regarded as a mark of progress. On the contrary, it marks a step backward. The workers have not the very slightest feeling that they are associated in a common task with the employer and the shareholders, nor have they any longer any desire to be so associated. For, instead of will-ing agreement, this system has created a fierce conflict which is nothing else than what is called the social problem.

Not only is there no longer a contract of association between workers and employer, in the definite legal sense of the term, involv-ing participation in profits and losses, in the work of direction, and in responsibility, but it is scarcely possible to distinguish even the appearance of any mutual agreement whatever for the hire of ser-vices. In fact, the so-called contract for labour is only an engage-ment or enlistment of it.

We shall see later on, however, that legislation is tending nowa-days to give the wage system the character of a reciprocal contract by calling on the workers to share in the drafting of "workshop

[1] It would be incorrect, however, to think that the guild system ever included all the workers under its rule. It has been very well shown by M. Hauser (*Ouvriers du temps passé*) that such a generalization is very much exaggerated; but he seems in his turn to go to the other extreme when he declares that in the Middle Ages, "free labour was the most usual system."

regulations," and by awarding damages in cases of breach of agreement. Moreover, the parties concerned — employers and workmen — are also tending to give the system some of the characteristics of association, by such institutions as the collective contract, profit-sharing, and co-partnership, to be dealt with later in the chapter on *Wage-Earners*.

II. ASSOCIATION AMONG WORKERS

Since the actual contract in business is only a bastard form of association — an association in fact but not in law, and compulsory rather than voluntary, — may we not hope that it will give place to a free and complete form of association, in which everyone will realize clearly that he is sharing in a collective undertaking in which he desires to co-operate?

It is not impossible, of course; for that form of association is realized already in the *workers' associations for production*, or *associations for co-operative production*, which have been formed with the object of doing without the employer, so that the workers become their own masters and keep for themselves the produce of their own labour.

France is looked upon as the birthplace of this kind of institution, and rightly so, for it was there that the first workers' association for production was founded, in 1834, by a political writer named Buchez. But it was not till after the revolution of 1848 that any great activity took place in this direction. It is not for nothing that this date coincides with that of the advent of universal suffrage: the one institution meant republicanism in the domain of government, and the other meant republicanism in the workshop. More than two hundred societies of this kind were then founded in France, and particularly in Paris; but they all died except three or four which are still in existence to-day. There was a revival of activity in 1866–67, and of late years their number has rapidly increased, so that there are now about a thousand. Some of these societies have been very successful and have become important firms. Yet the whole lot together count hardly more than 50,000 members, and the total amount of their business does not reach £4,000,000. It is small-scale industry.[1]

The obstacles met with by co-operative societies for production

[1] ["A number of English experiments in co-operative production were made in cotton manufacturing between 1850 and 1860. But the difficulties consequent upon the American Civil War ruined most of these enterprises, nor have they subsequently been revived on any large scale." (Hadley, *Economics*, p. 380.)]

are very numerous and account only too well for their lack of success.

(1) The first is their *lack of capital*. We know that if we could eliminate the capitalist from the business of production we could never eliminate capital; and large-scale industry requires nowadays even more and more capital. How is this to be provided by simple working men? A halfpenny at a time, deducted from their daily savings? That can be done, and is actually done in some businesses on a small scale, but only at the cost of heroic sacrifices: it cannot be counted on in a general way. Or are the capitalists to be asked for it? They will hardly be eager to invest their money in such uncertain undertakings. Nor, on the other hand, are the workers disposed to seek aid from the capitalists, since their object is simply to get rid of them.

However, we shall not regard this difficulty as insuperable. If workers' associations are solidly organized and have once established their reputation, they will find means of borrowing all the capital that they require, either by setting up a common bank — there is one already in France — or by applying to the co-operative credit societies or the consumers' co-operative societies, both of which have considerable amounts of capital to dispose of.

(2) The second obstacle is the *lack of customers*. Workers' associations are not generally well enough equipped to produce cheaply and for popular consumption on a large scale. Nor, on the other hand, have they generally a name or mark that is sufficiently well-known to attract rich customers. In France, fortunately for them, they have found customers in the shape of the State and the municipalities, and it is owing to their orders that many of the French societies are able to exist.

(3) The third obstacle is the *lack of economic education* among the working classes. This has hitherto led to three results. In the first place it has made it almost impossible to find among the workers men capable of directing an industrial undertaking. Secondly, even if such men have been found, they have not been chosen and retained as managers, their very superiority becoming too often a reason for their exclusion. Finally, even when the workmen have accepted the leadership of these men, they have not had the widsom to assure them a share in the produce proportional to the services they perform, for the superiority of intellectual over manual labour is not yet sufficiently understood. None the less, great progress has been made: there are some associations that keep their managers

for life, pay them well, and even show no feeling of jealousy when they receive public honours or keep a motor-car.

(4) The fourth and last stumbling-block is that these associations tend too often to *set up afresh the same institutions that they proposed to eliminate*, namely, the system of master and wage-earners. As soon as ever they succeed there is a great temptation to close their ranks, to refuse all new members, and to engage wage-earning workers; they thus become societies of small employers. That is the main charge brought against this institution by socialists, and it must be admitted that it is well founded. On the other hand, to ask workmen who came in at the beginning and who have succeeded by dint of privations and perseverance in founding a prosperous business, to admit on an equal footing those who came in at the eleventh hour, is certainly to demand from them a rare measure of disinterestedness. Yet here, also, education is advancing, and these deviations from true co-operative principles are becoming increasingly rare.

The creation of associations for production may be very much facilitated in the following ways.

(1) By the system of profit-sharing, when the employer is willing to pave the way for his abdication by so arranging the sharing of profits that his workmen become his partners during his lifetime and his successors after his death. The most famous examples of this method are furnished by M. Godin in the *Familistère* at Guise, and by Mme. Boucicaut in the case of the Paris shops called the *Bon Marché*.

(2) By the action of trade unions. Several co-operative productive associations in France owe their origin to trade unions. In this case, they do not set to work all the members of the organization simultaneously, because they have neither enough capital nor enough markets for this, but only those workmen in the union who ask for work, and who are taken in turn.

This trade union assistance, however, is tending to diminish, for the unions are becoming more and more hostile to the co-operative productive association. They regard it now merely as a source of weakness to the syndicalist movement. As soon as workmen join a productive association, they say, they forget their class interests and think only of their co-operative interests: they seek only to make profits and, in case of a strike, to save their funds, becoming thus infected by the spirit of capitalism.

(3) By consumers' co-operative associations. When these are sufficiently developed and united into federations, they can give support to co-operative productive societies by lending them the

capital they need, and by providing regular *customers* for the purchase of their products — two of the very things they require to make them succeed. This is what is done by consumers' co-operative societies in England.[1]

III. ASSOCIATION OF CAPITAL

If free association has hitherto scarcely come into operation in the case of labour, it is quite otherwise with capital. Capital, in the shape of money or securities, enjoys a freedom and ease of movement that labour cannot possess, and this mobility is enormously increased by the development of credit. If workers or landed proprietors are to co-operate in a productive enterprise, it must be in the place where they are, and can therefore only include persons living in the same district. Labour cannot be transferred without the person of the labourer, and he is not easily uprooted from the spot where he has always lived; while as for the land, that is quite immovable. Capital alone has the wings of an eagle, and can fly from the ends of the earth to any place where there is some profit to be made.

Whenever a business assumes considerable proportions — and this, as we have seen already, is the general tendency — the *entrepreneur* can no longer procure the necessary labour by himself. So a number of capitalists combine to provide the requisite capital, and the business is constituted as a *joint-stock company*. This system was invented in Holland in the eighteenth century, and has become extraordinarily common in our own day.

The characteristic of this kind of society is that the capital required by the business is divided into small parts — generally 500 francs (£20) in France,[2] and a pound in England, — which are called *shares*, or portions of ownership in the company.[3] Thus a company with a capital of a million pounds will issue a million shares of

---

[1] [We have omitted from this section a certain amount of detail relating to the working of co-operative production in France. Consumers' co-operative societies are dealt with later on in, Book IV, Chapter I, Section III.]

[2] Only a quarter of this need be deposited, for the company to be legally constituted. And in the case of so-called "co-operative" societies the value of the share may be as low as 25 francs (£1) and the deposit merely a tenth of that sum.

[3] Legally, a share is not a portion of the joint-ownership of the capital of the company, for this capital is not the joint property of the members or shareholders: it belongs to the company itself, which is legally a person, quite apart from the person of any or all of its members. But that is merely a legal fiction devised to facilitate the administration of the company; in reality, the company's capital is collective property.

£1 each.   Each man will then take as many as he pleases, according
to his means or the degree of confidence that he has in the undertaking; he may take a single share if he likes.   It goes without
saying that he will only receive a part of the profits of the undertaking proportional to the number of his shares: this part is called
a *dividend*.   But what particularly attracts the shareholder is that
his liability and his risk are also limited to the amount of the shares
he holds — which marks an essential difference between this and
other associations.   In England the word *limited* is imposed by
law upon the titles of joint-stock companies.   This dilution ot the
risk to an infinitesimal dose has made possible the most hazardous
enterprises.   Railways would never have been built, the Suez
Canal would never have been dug, nor would the Channel Tunnel
be possible, if limited liability companies had never been invented.
For no capitalist could find the millions necessary for such undertakings, whereas when the risk is divided into an infinite number of
parts it ceases to frighten even those whose purses are very light.
In fact, only a few people were ruined by such a huge collapse as
that of the Panama undertaking, to which £52,000,000 was subscribed almost entirely by small capitalists.[1]

These companies have other methods of attracting capitalists,
large and small, besides that of ordinary shares.   To the prudent
ones who desire primarily a safe investment and a regular income they
offer *debentures*, which differ from ordinary shares (though they are
generally of the same value) in giving the right to a fixed income
called *interest*, which is always paid, whether the year's working is
successful or the reverse.   The debenture-holder is therefore a true
creditor, who runs no risks unless the company becomes insolvent,
and even in this case he gets paid before the shareholder.   Conversely, if a capitalist is of a more adventurous disposition, most
companies offer him *founder's shares*, giving him a right to a share in

---

[1] We are far removed, therefore, from the days of Adam Smith, who said of this form
of business: "The only trades which it seems possible for a joint stock company to
carry on successfully . . . are those, of which all the operations are capable of being
reduced to what is called a routine, or to such a uniformity of method as admits of
little or no variation.   Of this kind is, first, the banking trade; secondly, the trade of
insurance . . . . thirdly, the making and maintaining a navigable cut or canal;
and, fourthly, the similar trade of bringing water for the supply of a great city."
(*Wealth of Nations*, Book V, Chap. I.)

What is there nowadays that is not done by the joint-stock method?   Not long
ago the Melbourne papers announced the formation of a company to exploit the
magnificent voice of a young Australian singer.   They had her trained, and £1 shares
were being quoted some years later at £3, 10s.

the profits only beyond a certain figure, and only after the ordinary shareholders have been paid. These, therefore, only suit those who have a firm and lasting faith in the future of the business.

These joint-stock companies have developed so enormously everywhere that they are tending to become the normal mode of production. Thousands of them are formed every year, and to-day they represent thousands of millions of capital. They are not all new undertakings, of course; for many of them were started as individual enterprises, and found it advantageous to turn themselves into companies.

A company generally possesses another distinguishing characteristic: it is *anonymous*. This means that it is not an association of persons, like the labour associations or co-operative societies of the preceding section, but an association of capital. Of course the capital has owners, but they do not count; their names may be known, if they are inscribed on the shares, but if they are "bearer" shares, as is becoming more and more common, the anonymity is complete. This is the last word in capitalist association — no longer an association of men, but one of money-bags.

Yet of course there must be someone to direct the business. There is a small body of directors, with a chairman at their head, but even their liability does not extend beyond the amounts of their holdings, except in case of serious faults. They are the representative government of the company, elected by the general meeting of the shareholders, and only bound to render an account of their charge once a year. No other effective control can be exercised by the shareholders.

It is not only in the production of wealth that a revolution has been effected by the joint-stock system, enabling huge enterprises to be undertaken by the concentration of capital. The same thing is happening in the sphere of distribution, by an operation which looks at first sight like the opposite of the one just described — the division of the ownership of capital into an infinite number of parts. But we shall meet with this again in dealing with Distribution.

From the worker's point of view, businesses run by companies generally offer more favourable conditions of labour, both in the matter of wages and in security of employment and welfare organizations. Trade-unionists and socialists themselves willingly acknowledge their superiority, and even regard the conditions prevailing in them as more favourable to their propaganda and to the development of solidarity among workers.

Legislation has generally shown itself very favourable in all countries to associations of capital — much more so than to associations of labour or any other kind of association. Thus whereas in France societies of a commercial nature have always held a prominent place in legislation and the legal code, "non-profit-making" associations have been either definitely forbidden or tolerated at the pleasure of the government. It was not until 1884, as we shall see elsewhere, that the professional associations, abolished at the Revolution, were restored under the name of "syndicates," nor was it until 1901, 112 years after the Declaration of the Rights of Man, and 32 years after the establishment of the third republic, that the right of association was recognized for every citizen, and even then only with numerous restrictions concerning the powers of acquisition possessed by these associations.[1]

Capitalist societies, on the other hand, have been able to increase their wealth without limit, and the legislator has not regarded them, at any rate up to the present, as a danger to the State. But to-day the point of view has somewhat changed, and a period of restrictions for joint-stock companies is probably about to open.

These restrictions will be inspired by a fourfold purpose:

(1) *Safeguarding the public*, which allows itself to be led into temptation by the inducement of a profit that is always promised, not always realized, and subject to a very limited amount of risk. The ease with which the most extravagant undertakings can find credulous and enthusiastic subscribers as soon as the shares are issued, has long been observed and is illustrated, comically or tragically, every day. Even in the case of genuinely productive enterprises the public is very often cheated by the over-valuation of the actual capital.

(2) *Safeguarding the shareholders*, and the debenture-holders as well, both of whom, and especially the latter, are handed over to the tender mercies of the directors. This, however, is a matter of commercial law.[2]

---

[1] [Similarly in England it was only after a long struggle that the right of combination was at length conceded to the workers. By Acts of 1799 and 1800 all combinations were declared illegal, and this prohibition applied in theory to associations of employers as well as of workers. These laws were repealed in 1824, though the right of association was somewhat modified in the following year. The growth of the trade union movement (corresponding to the French "syndicates") led to further concessions in 1867, 1871, and 1876.]

[2] Debenture-holders are simply creditors of the company, and creditors for a very long term, for their repayment is spread over a period of half a century or more. Nor have they any control over the company, nor any regular meeting where their opinions can be voiced.

(3) *Safeguarding the workers.* — By a recent French law[1] companies are invited to establish "labour shares," to participate in profits and management on the same footing as capital shares. This new kind of company remains optional at present. But other projected laws are pending to impose this form of workers' participation on all companies engaged in public services — mines, railways, tramways, etc.

(4) *Safeguarding the State.* — There are many ways of doing this. The object of some is to curb the power of the companies lest they should become States within the State. Others aim at preventing foreign capitalists from getting a footing and laying hands on the national wealth by the formation of companies calling themselves "national." Others, again, are directed against bearer securities, and would only permit the issue of shares bearing the owner's name, the object being, first, to prevent the evasion of taxes, and, secondly, to enable foreign capital to be distinguished from native capital.

We cannot here discuss these points. They are mainly legal questions, and readers must be referred to special works on the subject. We will only observe that since joint-stock companies are by their nature adapted to hazardous and speculative undertakings, there is a risk of removing the very reason for their existence if they are subjected to a too rigorous control.

Some economists believe that the anonymous kind of company will become not only the typical form in all business, but will extend into every sphere of human activity, and notably into that of the public services. But that we do not desire. Anonymity — *the association of capital alone*, and not of individuals — removes all sense of responsibility, and though irresponsibility is a source of strength from the economic point of view, it is a mark of inferiority from the moral one.

[1] [For fuller particulars see the section on *Profit-Sharing and Copartnership* in Book III, Part II, Chapter III.]

CHAPTER III — THE DIVISION OF LABOUR

I. HISTORY OF THE DIVISION OF LABOUR

If the labour that has to be performed is of quite a simple kind, such as digging the ground, lifting a weight, rowing a boat, or cutting wood, then the work does not lend itself to any division at all: everyone performs the same movements on his own account. This we might call simple co-operation.

But if the operation is in the least degree complex and comprises various movements, there is everything to be gained by splitting up what looks like a simple task when looked at as a whole. This is called *division of labour;* it might also be called co-ordinated co-operation.

Adam Smith begins his classic work with an exposition of the division of labour, showing thereby the supreme importance that is to be attached to it.[1] And since the days of this great man the scope of this law has been continually extending, not only from the economic, but also from the social, moral, and even philosophical standpoint. It stretches far beyond the walls of the workshop where Adam Smith first admired it.

The division of labour, by its very definition, presupposes association. But this association is not necessarily deliberate, nor even conscious: it may operate even without the knowledge of those who are taking part in it. It may be spontaneous and automatic. It is just that which gives it the character of a natural law.

Division of labour is one of those rare economic phenomena — like saving — which are found among certain kinds of animals.

We must distinguish several forms of division of labour, corresponding to the successive stages of economic development.

(1) In the first stage — that of domestic economy — it exists only in a rudimentary state: every member of the community does a little of everything, and this "everything" is not very varied.

---

[1] The vocational division of labour, and its social utility, had, however, been remarked on even in antiquity. Thus in the *Republic* Plato makes Socrates say: "Things are made better and more easily when each man does what suits him best, and is freed from all other cares." And the celebrated fable related by Menenius Agrippa to the revolting plebeians conveys the same truth.

Even here, however, division of labour appears already in the form imposed by nature — that of the differentiation of the *sexes*.

But this primitive division of labour is far from corresponding to what we should nowadays regard as the aptitudes proper to each sex: namely, muscular work for men, and household duties for women. It was quite different from this. The man undertook the nobler kinds of work, such as fighting, hunting, and looking after the cattle, and the woman did the more menial tasks — not only housekeeping and weaving, but the labour of transport, like a veritable beast of burden, and even the labour of cultivation. *Cura agrorum feminis delegata*, "the care of the fields is left to the women," said Tacitus, speaking of the Germans. And we see the same thing even to-day among all the native tribes of Africa. Woman was the first slave, and her first emancipation came from the introduction of real slavery — the enslaving of captives, — for it freed her from the crushing toil of turning the millstone and grinding the corn.[1]

(2) Next, under the system of domestic economy, certain kinds of work began to be specialized — notably that of the blacksmith, the most venerated task of all. It is the only trade, moreover, that was practised on Olympus, by that somewhat boorish figure, Vulcan. And since these first craftsmen could not obtain sufficient employment in a single family, they would go from one to another, working for anyone who wanted them.

This is the second phase of the division of labour — *vocational* division, or division into trades. At the same time, trades in the proper sense of the term were not formed until the wandering workman settled down and set up a shop.

Was this vocational division of labour due originally to the natural aptitudes of individuals? Possibly it was in the case of free workers. But it must not be forgotten that these free workers were rare. The slave had only to do what his master told him. And even for free men it seems more probable that tasks were assigned to each

---

[1] According to Bücher, the man's business was to procure animal food, first by hunting and later on by looking after the herds, while the woman procured the vegetable food, first by gathering fruit and later on by agriculture. Not along ago, in certain Arab tribes, women might have been seen harnessed to the plough along with an ass or a camel. This division of tasks does not seem to have arisen at all from any special aptitude on the part of either men or women, but to have been entirely religious in its origin. Even in our own day, in the Breton island of Sein, says M. le Goffic, "the field of human labour is thus divided: the sea to the men, the land to the women."

In any case the restriction of women to household tasks seems to have been a somewhat late development, dating perhaps from ancient Greek times.

one for social, political, or religious reasons — witness the caste system — and that professional aptitude only came afterwards, through practice and hereditary transmission.

The division of labour in its vocational form no longer necessitates association, for it means that the craftsman is separated from the primitive community and works on his own account. But it involves *exchange* instead, for obviously the specialist workman could do nothing with the produce of his labour if he had to keep it for himself: trade implies a shop, and sale implies customers.

The result is such a difference between the two systems that it would be better, perhaps, not to call them by the same name. Instead of speaking here of the division of labour, we should rather call it the "specialization" of labour.

Under the system of corporations or guilds the separation of trades becomes more marked, because each trade guild does only one kind of work, and the regulations themselves are jealously careful that everyone shall stick to his own special branch. The same industry is subdivided either into *diverging branches* (the wood trade being divided among carpenters, joiners, wheelwrights, etc.), or into *successive divisions* (the rough wood passing from the woodcutter to the sawyer, etc.), and each branch forms a special trade. These subdivisions and ramifications go on continually, parallel with the multiplication of wants, each new want giving rise to a new trade.[1]

(3) But there comes a day when the trade turns into a manufacture — when the craftsman has become a capitalist, and employs wage-earners. This is the third phase — the *technical* division of labour. All industrial labour, as we have already seen (see above, p. 87), is ultimately a series of movements. The complex movement is split up into a number of movements, each one as simple as possible, and each one is entrusted to a different workman, so that each has but one thing to do and that always the same thing. It was this kind of division of labour that struck Adam Smith for the first time when he saw the manufacture of pins, and inspired that admirable passage that is everywhere quoted.[2]

It should be observed that this kind of division of labour differs from the preceding kinds, which are natural and spontaneous, in having been invented or contrived, like all the movements of labour.

---

[1] This growing complexity in the division of labour might be represented by a diagram in the shape of a genealogical tree. The *successive* tasks in one industry would be inscribed in the vertical columns, and the *collateral* ones in the horizontal divisions.

[2] [*Wealth of Nations*, Book I, Chapter I, third paragraph.]

With division of labour in the factory we leave the realm of exchange, for there is no question of exchange when all operations are carried on in the same building, or at any rate under the same management. We get back to co-operation instead, as under the system of household economy or the *familia* of Roman slaves. All the workmen who take part in these tasks, each in his own department, cannot but see and know that they are co-operating in the same work, which is not the case with men practising different trades, except by a mental effort.

(4) Lastly, when division of labour was thus elaborated in manufacturing processes, it was also extended by the development of transport and international exchange, so that we reach the fourth phase — that of *international* division of labour — whereby each nation devotes itself more particularly to the production of those commodities that seem best suited to its soil, its climate, and the peculiar qualities of its people. Thus England specializes in coal and cotton goods; the United States in machinery; France in articles of luxury; Germany in chemical products; Brazil in coffee; Australia in wool; and so forth (see section on *Protection*).

To tell the truth, the term "division of labour" is a little exaggerated here; it is only in a metaphorical sense that the whole world is regarded as a workshop in which each race has its own special task. It would be more accurate to call it the *localization of labour* (see below, p. 165).

II.   CONDITIONS OF THE DIVISION OF LABOUR

The greater the number of the separate tasks into which labour may be split up, the more perfect is the technical division of labour. But the number of workers will necessarily have to be proportionate to the number of these distinct operations.[1] Now it is clear that the number of workmen that a manufacturer can employ depends on the extent of his business. Similarly, in the case of vocational division of labour, an artisan or tradesman can only specialize in the production or distribution of any one article to the extent that

[1] It would be a great mistake to suppose that we could carry out the division of labour by employing a single workman for each distinct operation: many more than that are usually required. Suppose that the making of a needle involves three operations: one for the head, one for the point, and one for the eye. Suppose it takes 10 seconds to make each point, 20 for the head, and 30 to pierce the eye. It is evident that two head-makers and three eye-piercers will be needed to keep pace with one point-maker. It is therefore necessary to have not three but six workmen altogether; otherwise the first one will remain idle for part of the day.

he can count on a sufficient number of customers. We can therefore formulate this law — one of those rare laws that are undisputed
— that the division of labour varies directly with *the extent of the
market*.

It is for this reason, as has often been remarked, that division of
labour hardly exists outside large centres of population, and is unknown in the country or the village. There you will find mixed up
in the same shop, groceries, pork, children's toys, stationery, and
draper's goods — all the articles which in a large town would be dealt
with by as many different tradesmen.[1] The reason is obvious:
the village shopkeeper must engage in all trades for the very good
reason that one alone would not suffice to procure him a living.

On the other hand, when an industry succeeds in getting the whole
world for its market, it can not only specialize in the production of
certain articles that meet only a very limited want, because the immense number of consumers makes up for the smallness of the
need, but it can extend the technical division of labour to its extreme
limits, even in this specialized line. That is one of the reasons for
the enormous power of large-scale industries and trusts, and it also
explains why every country attaches so much importance to securing
a large export trade. This export trade, by enabling its industries
to carry out the division of labour to the greatest possible extent,
will secure for it the industrial superiority that necessarily follows.

A second condition is generally indicated as being indispensable
to the division of labour. This is the *continuity of labour*. If labour
is intermittent, in fact, since the workman cannot be left idle during
the intervals, he must be occupied with other things and cannot
therefore confine himself to a single occupation. That is one reason
why agriculture lends itself so little to the division of labour, as we
shall see later on. This condition, however, is less imperative than
the preceding one, for a man can easily devote himself to different
kinds of work, without losing the benefits of specialization, if they
are not simultaneous but successive, and if they take fairly long
periods of time. We might even say, on the contrary, that such a
method forms a useful corrective for some of the drawbacks of continuous division of labour.

---

[1] It might seem at first sight as if large stores like Harrod's or Selfridge's were in
the same position, for they sell every kind of goods. But in reality they are nothing
of the kind, for each department is specialized and constitutes, as it were, an independent shop.

III. ADVANTAGES AND DISADVANTAGES OF DIVISION OF LABOUR

Division of labour increases the productive power of labour to an extent that surpasses imagination.   This is easily explained in the case of vocational division of labour.

(1) It creates a diversity of tasks, all different from the point of view of difficulty and of the strength or attention they require. This enables us to *fit each task to the individual capacities of the workmen.*   Under a system in which division of labour was unknown, each man would have to produce *according to his wants;* where such division exists, each produces *according to his aptitude.*   We can thus utilize each man's natural aptitudes, and avoid the waste of strength that results when everyone alike, whether strong or weak, ignorant or intelligent, has to perform the same work.   We can avoid wasting the labour of the strongest or the most efficient on tasks too easy for them, and, conversely, wasting the labour of the weakest or the most ignorant on tasks beyond their powers.

(2) *The constant repetition of the same task* gives every man a truly marvellous amount of dexterity, just as sustained and persevering application to labour of an intellectual kind develops his mental faculties and consequently his productive power to an extraordinary degree.   Nowadays doctors, lawyers, painters, novelists, and scientists, all *specialize.*   Each one finds it to his advantage to confine himself to a little corner of human knowledge, so that he can explore it more thoroughly and get more out of-it.

But as far as division of labour in the workshop is concerned, the reason for its power of increasing the product is not so obvious, for it is not easy to see why ten men together should be able to produce more than ten men apart.   If one man can only lift a load of two hundredweight, we cannot think that ten men together will lift more than 20 hundredweight — on the contrary, part of the collective effort will be wasted.

This is because we are dealing here with simple co-operation, which merely adds one unit of strength to another.   But complex co-operation does really multiply man's strength, for the following reasons.

(a) The most complicated piece of work can be split up into *a series of very simple movements*, which are almost mechanical, and therefore very easy to execute.   This facilitates production to an extraordinary extent (see p. 152).

By this means we may even reach such simple movements that human intervention is no longer necessary for their execution —

a machine can do them.   And it is, in fact, through this process of technical analysis that tasks which seemed at first sight extremely complicated, have come to be performed by machinery.[1]

(b) The continuity of labour results in a *saving of time*.   A workman who often changes his work will lose each time not only the interval occupied in passing from one operation to the other, but in particular the time necessary for *getting started*.   As it was admirably expressed by Karl Marx, division of labour "closes the pores" of the day's work.

Over against these advantages it has long been customary to set the following serious drawbacks, and to denounce them.

(a) The *degradation* of the workman, who is reduced to a purely mechanical rôle through the repetition of the same simple movement, so that all apprenticeship is rendered useless.   Time after time has Lemontey's saying been repeated: "It is a sad confession for a man to make that during his whole life he has never made anything but the eighteenth part of a pin."   And a more illustrious man than Lemontey, the very man who first showed the importance and the advantages of division of labour — Adam Smith — used still harsher terms when he said: "The man whose whole life is spent in performing a few simple operations . . . . generally becomes as stupid and ignorant as it is possible for a human creature to become."[2]

(b) The extreme *dependence* of the workman, who becomes incapable of doing anything but the particular and special operation to which he has become accustomed, and who is therefore always liable to dismissal or unemployment.   Just as the parts of a commodity that he makes are of no value except when put together into a whole, so the workman himself is only of value as a cog in the great industrial machine;   separated from it, he runs the risk of being good for nothing.

At the time when these arguments were formulated they had considerable weight;   but they are somewhat out of date at the present day.

(1) To begin with, there are no longer any workmen who spend their lives in making the eighteenth part of a pin, because pins nowadays are made by machinery.   It is true, however, that other instances can be cited, even if Adam Smith's famous example has become obsolete.   Thus the manufacture of boots and shoes may involve 72 different operations, and that of watches, more than 300.

---

[1] The invention of the principal machines — for weaving, spinning, and so forth — took place exactly at the highest point reached by division of labour in manufacture.

[2] [*Wealth of Nations*, Bk. V, Chap. I]

But for all that, this division of labour in these much-divided industries affects machines rather than men, each machine being allotted one particular operation, while the man has nothing to do but to guide it. In fact, as soon as a technical operation has become simplified to the point of being purely mechanical, the worker is quickly replaced by a machine, for in such a case it is always economical to make this substitution. Now looking after a machine is often a tiring kind of work — not because of any muscular effort involved, but owing to the nervous tension it demands, — but it is not, as a rule, degrading. The machine of the present day is not like the machine employed at the beginning of the era of mechanical industry, which could be run by any worker, man, woman, or child: it is an instrument of precision, and may be compared to a thoroughbred horse that can only be ridden by an experienced horseman.

No doubt there are still many degrading occupations, but this is not because the manual labour attaching to them is divided; it is because there are many kinds of work which, though necessary, will unfortunately be always unenjoyable, owing to their very nature. The work of the road-sweeper, or the dock labourer, or the stone-breaker by the roadside, is not divided at all: is it any more recreative than that of a workman who is always making bolts?

(2) Again, the use of machinery has resulted in a limitation of the hours of labour, and this gives the workman leisure for the recreation of body and mind. So if there is perhaps more monotony than there used to be in his daily work, there is less in his life, which is richer and more varied. Now it has been remarked by Roscher that if it is true that variety is one condition of happiness, it must be sought for not so much in labour as in the part of life that lies outside the hours of labour.

The specialist workman of to-day has fifty or sixty hours of freedom a week at his disposal, not including his hours of sleep, and he can employ them in all manner of ways in his domestic, political, trade union, religious, and intellectual life; he can read the papers, go to the pictures, to a concert, to church — too often, indeed, he goes to the public house. He leads an infinitely richer and more varied life than did the workman of bygone days, or even than the rural labourer of to-day, who yet is not subjected to the division of labour.

Vocational instruction is another corrective of division of labour, by enabling the workman to understand and pass beyond the fractional task that devolves upon him, by integrating that task in the collective work of which it forms a part, and by making the work-man conscious of his share as a co-operator in the completed work.

It should be observed that the criticisms mentioned above are levelled only against the *technical* division of labour, while the *vocational* division, through specialization of functions, trades, and studies, has rarely laid itself open to the same complaints. Yet there is no lack of specialized trades as narrow and wretched as the minutely divided tasks of the workshop. The typist who taps on a machine has a scarcely less monotonous task than the workman who hammers the heads of pins. And what is to be said of the hours spent by the heads of the State in signing their names?

It is just here, in our opinion, that there is most cause for anxiety. It should not be regarded as a very desirable ideal that every man in a nation should be a man of one trade only, so that he bears in mind and body the indelible mark of his professional work. Some harm must result therefrom, we believe, to the complete development of the human personality, and even to social progress; for society would be threatened in this case with a stereotyped system like the caste system. We are much inclined to agree with M. Espinas that "the capacity for isolation is only a very inferior characteristic of individuality," or even to go farther and call it a characteristic proper to the savage; and the "noble savage" is assuredly not the ideal type of humanity to-day, as he was for the writers of the eighteenth century. But, all the same, the capacity for changing one's trade or profession is a mark of strength and superiority in men. Most of the men who have reached the highest positions in the United States have practised a score of trades in the course of their life. It is the mark of a dynamic and progressive society to be able to utilize all its members for a number of purposes, and the only means of attaining this end is to maintain, alongside of and above the vocational instruction necessary to turn out good workmen, the general culture that produces *men* — the culture that is so well described by that fine old academic term, "the humanities."

It is to be feared also that vocational specialization does not altogether accomplish the moral end expected of it — that of developing solidarity and altruism by teaching individuals that they cannot do without each other, any more than the organs of the body can, and that they ought to put into practice the fable of the Blind Man and the Paralytic:

"I'll walk for you, and you must see for me."

On the contrary, vocational division of labour has a tendency to create a corporate feeling which is almost always in conflict with the general interest. Therein lies a grave social danger. Society as a whole is, as it were, besieged by the harsh demands of professional organizations — those of agriculturalists, manufacturers, civil servants, the nautical interest, miners, and so forth. So alive are the workers themselves to this danger, so far as it concerns them, that they have tried to draw together and subordinate the corporate interests of each trade in larger organizations like the General Labour Confederation of France.

CHAPTER IV — THE CONCENTRATION OF PRODUCTION

I. THE STAGES OF INDUSTRIAL EVOLUTION

We saw in the first chapter of Part II how the balance between wants and production is maintained — and sometimes broken. But we must now place ourselves at the dynamic instead of the static point of view, and see how production is able to follow the continually upward movement of wants. To accomplish this, it has had to pass through various forms.

The German historical school, among its other merits, may claim that of having discovered and distinguished the successive types of industrial evolution. Six of these may be fairly clearly distinguished. They are as follows:

(1) *Family or home industry.* — This system prevails not only in primitive societies but even in those of antiquity, and extends down through the days "when good King Arthur ruled this land" into the first period of the Middle Ages. People are divided into small and economically independent groups, sufficient unto themselves, and producing hardly anything but what they consume. Exchange and division of labour exist only in a rudimentary form (*History of the Division of Labour*, above).

Each group consists of a family. This term, however, must be taken in a far wider sense than it now possesses. Not only was the patriarchal family much more numerous than our modern families, but it was even artificially enlarged by outside elements — slaves, and, later on, serfs — which were incorporated with it. Slaves were legally described in Rome by the term *familia*. To this same economic period belong the villa of the wealthy Roman landowner with his army of slaves engaged in all kinds of trades, the manor or lordship of the feudal baron with his serfs, and the monastery with its vast estates, supplying all intellectual needs by means of its copyists and illuminators of manuscripts. Traces of the survival of domestic industry may still be found in our villages and small country towns, where bread-making, pork-butchering, jam-making, and laundry-work are carried on "at home."

(2) *The travelling workman.* — In the system of home industry

a certain amount of division of labour is already to be found. A day arrives when some of the members of the family, as we saw in the last chapter, detach themselves from the group, like ripe fruit, and become specialist workmen, or craftsmen. But having neither capital nor business premises, or, at the most, only some indispensable tools, they go and offer their services from door to door. They work, therefore, on the consumer's premises and with the raw material that he provides — at the farm smithy, for instance, and with the iron supplied to them, if they are blacksmiths, or, if they are tailors, with the cloth that the customer provides. This is what German economists call the *hired labour* stage. These craftsmen, however, are not yet "wage-earners" in the modern sense of the word, for they work for the public and not for a master.

This method of working has not disappeared. Not only is it still practised on a large scale in eastern countries, especially in Russia, but we meet with it in our own country districts, where it is practised by the mender of kettles, the grinder of knives and scissors, etc., and even in our towns, where the dressmaker, the cook, and the professor of music or languages, still go from house to house.

(3) *The trade or craft.* — The travelling workman one day settles down. He gives up being a hawker, and instead of going to his customer's house he waits for the customer to come and find him. He is already a capitalist on a small scale, for he produces with tools and materials that belong to him; he has become what was called, under the guild system, a *master*. Yet still he hardly employs any paid labour, but only that of the members of his own family or of apprentices.

This new phase is closely connected with the growth of towns, and it is particularly characteristic of the Middle Ages. The artisan or craftsman works only for the little market of the town where he dwells, and reserves it for himself with jealous care. He associates himself, for mutual assistance and defence, with other workers in the same trade as his own, and together they constitute those corporations or guilds that play so important a part in the economic history of the Middle Ages.

(4) *Business enterprise.* — The craftsman played a splendid part from the political as well as from the economic point of view, as we can see by recalling the heroic struggles for freedom made by the town communities of the Middle Ages. But he found his influence diminish as the town market grew larger and became by degrees a national market — or, in other words, when the great modern States were formed. He found himself faced by the competition of

merchants coming from other places, and even from abroad, on the occasion of the great fairs. Then he tried to sell beyond the limits of the town; but for that he had to resort to an intermediary. It was this intermediary who was in time to play the leading part on the economic stage, but he appeared at the beginning only as a merchant and not as a manufacturer.

As soon as ever the craftsman took the *entrepreneur* for his principal (and before long for his only) customer, and as soon as he lost touch with the public, he lost his independence: he had a master. His dependence increased when this same merchant furnished him with the raw material necessary to his industry, and sometimes even leased to him the instruments of his labour. Then, having no longer either free ownership, or raw material, or the produce of his labour, or (sometimes) any tools, the craftsman lost all the characteristics of an independent producer. He had already become merely a wage-earner, and the *entrepreneur* had become the "master."

The tragic development summarized in these few lines occupied several centuries. In England, in the textile trade, it was not completed till the eighteenth century. The system still obtains in the silk-weaving industry of Lyons, where the weavers own their looms, it is true, but receive the silk from their masters, weave it at home, and hand over the completed fabric to the master — who is wrongly called a *manufacturer*, for he is really only a *merchant*.[1]

This is not to say that every craftsman has disappeared in modern times. Every one knows that in the largest towns as well as in the villages there are still many of these small independent producers who work directly for their customers — locksmiths, painters, watch-makers, tinsmiths, electricians, and so forth — but who are small merchants rather than manufacturers. They hardly do more than put together the parts they have bought, or carry out small repairs in our homes, generally under the most burdensome and anti-economic conditions.

(5) *Manufacture.* — The craftsman, though robbed of all the attributes of an independent producer, still worked in his own home, and this preserved for him a certain amount of independence, giving him at least the free use of his time and control over his own labour. But this privilege he was destined to lose. In fact, the intermediary, or *entrepreneur*, lost no time in gathering together the workers scattered about in the same locality. He obtained various advantages from this plan, and notably that of being able to establish a skilful division of labour among them, so as to multiply their pro-

---

[1] [The system survives also in England, particularly in the clothing trades.]

ductive power while lowering the cost of production (see above). Another important advantage was that this plan enabled him to use the steam-engine. There you have the intermediary turned manufacturer. But this manufacturer had to be a big capitalist, for his precise function was to provide all the workers in his employment with the capital that was indispensable to production. So this fifth phase could only begin when large quantities of capital had been amassed in the hands of the great merchants.

This transformation began to take place in about the sixteenth century. The more perfect organization of manufacturing industry did not succeed without a struggle in eliminating guild industry and conquering the markets that were closed to it by the guild regulations. In France nothing less than State intervention was required — notably under Sully and Colbert — to create manufactures with special privileges, some of which, such as the Gobelin tapestry manufacture and the Sèvres porcelain works, have remained State industries to this day. Government intervention was not necessary in England, because her exportation to the colonies and to foreign countries sufficed to enable the new manufactures to be established and to break down the walls of the guild organization.

Manufacture possessed already all the marks of modern business enterprise from the economic point of view — the separation between master and man, between capitalist and proletarian. But from the technical point of view it had not yet acquired its characteristic feature — the use of machinery. *Manufacture*, indeed, as the name indicates, is really hand labour. Still, it was already employing machines. Looms were already complicated machines, but they were worked entirely by human strength, and this prevented production from extending beyond fairly narrow limits.

(6) *The factory system.* — But at the end of the eighteenth century motive power appeared in the form of the steam-engine, and manufacture became a matter of machinery.[1] And so we reach the typical form of modern industry, and the last phase of its development — except for those that are yet to come.

The employment of the steam-engine has resulted in the accumulation of masses of workers in the same spot in ever-increasing numbers, night labour, regulation of an almost military character, the employment of women and children, and a difficulty in slackening or stopping production in case of a falling-off in demand, leading to overproduction and crises.

[1] M. Vandervelde suggests that the term *machinofacture* should be used, in distinction from *manufacture*.

Here, then, this rapid historical sketch must end. With the coming of the factory system we reach the existing economic order of things — what socialists call the *capitalist régime*, not only because this type of business involves a greater and greater accumulation of capital, but because it involves, according to them, a separation or cleavage of society into two strata that grow more and more opposed to each other. These are the proletariat beneath, whose labour is its only means of livelihood, and, above this, a crowd of large and small capitalists who hire the labour of millions of men to whom they pay wages, employing them at their pleasure, and naturally keeping the profits for themselves.

II. CHARACTERISTICS OF MODERN INDUSTRY

These may be summed up as follows:

(1) The use of capital and manual skill *in large quantities*, the proportions of these two factors varying very considerably in different industries. In such an undertaking as the Suez Canal the proportion of labour (for towage, dredging, and pilotage) is insignificant in comparison with the capital required at the beginning and even with the exploitation capital.

(2) Increasing *specialization* of industry, through the application of the law of division of labour (see above). A manufacturer who devotes himself entirely to the production of a single article is naturally in a better position to improve his methods of production so that they become more and more perfect. Thus not only does watch-making constitute a special industry, but within this industry some workers will be engaged on watches, others on cuckoo clocks, and others again on alarm clocks; and in the department of watches themselves, one manufacturer will confine himself to watches of great accuracy, and another to cheap machine-made watches. So also in commerce, in large towns there will be one shop solely for bronze goods, another for baskets, another for trunks and travelling accessories, and so forth.

(3) *Standardization* in production, or production *in sets* — the reproduction of thousands of objects of a uniform character, resulting in a great saving both in manufacture and in the case of repairs; being identical, the different pieces are also interchangeable. If, for instance, some American motor-car factories can sell their cars at much lower prices than French factories, it is because they only turn out one model while each French firm turns out eight or ten.[1]

---

[1] Thus it is that if the Ford works can sell their cars at a price that "defies all com-

It is the same with the English ship-building yards: they build ships in sets, and this enables them not only to build them cheaply but to deliver them quickly, whereas the French ship-yards turn out only a few ships, and these all of different types according to the individual tastes of their customers.

(3) The *localization* of industries has nothing to do with their specialization, or even with their concentration, though it may lead to a certain amount of confusion with both these aspects of industrial development.

It would seem to be to the interest of similar, and therefore competing, industries to get as far away as possible from each other, so as not to have to fight for the same customers.   Yet just as in our towns we still find old streets bearing such names as Shoe Lane, Bread Street, Ironmonger Lane, and Milk Street, showing that craftsmen and merchants were once grouped according to their trades, so to-day we see certain industries attached to certain districts.   Thus in France we have the silk trade of Lyons, the woollen manufacture of Roubaix, and the watch-making of the Jura; and in England the Lancashire cotton towns, the woollen trade of the West Riding of Yorkshire, the silk industry of Macclesfield and Coventry, and so forth.

What are the causes, then, that counteract the centrifugal influences of competition and determine the localization of industries?

The commonest cause is the *proximity of raw material* or of *motive power*.   It stands to reason that a sardine-tinning factory can only be set up at a port owing to the difficulty of transporting and preserving the fish, and that metal works must be as near as possible to the deposits of ore or of coal, owing to the cost of transporting these heavy materials.[2]   The localization of industries is scarcely influenced at all by the proximity of labour, and not at all by that of capital, owing to the mobility of these factors of production.   Hydro-electric factories are set up on water-courses and at the foot of waterfalls.

Ease of transport may attract an industry to the banks of a river or to a sea-port.

peti+ion," as the saying goes, it is not only because they sell upwards of 5,000 cars a day, but especially because they are *all of the same model*.

This superiority of standardization — of a single model for every kind of manufacture — is fully recognized by French manufacturers, but its carrying out in the home market is difficult by reason of the vanity of the French consumer, who desires to be different from his fellows — which is not the least tiresome of the various forms of individualism.

[2] These works used to be attracted towards the coal, but now that the smelters have learned how to use less coal, they tend rather to approach the ore deposits.

Some influence is exerted also by *climatic conditions.* Lancashire is said to owe its superiority in spinning to the dampness of its air, which enables finer threads of cotton to be obtained than are easily obtained elsewhere. In the same way the superiority of certain German beers is due to the natural qualities of the water of that country.

But it must be admitted that in the majority of cases we cannot discover the reasons why an industry has been developed in one place rather than in another. The creation of an industry is due most often to *individual initiative,* and we can sometimes fix the date and follow the history thereof. Yet this initiative only becomes general when it finds a favourable environment, just as the seed chance-sown by the wind can only germinate and multiply if it lights on a favourable soil and atmospheric conditions suited to its nature. Certainly there was no predestination determining that the little town of Saint-Claude, in the French Jura, should specialize in diamond-cutting and the manufacture of pipes, for the raw materials of these industries had to be brought from abroad. But these industries, once established, were supported by the natural qualities and habits of life of the highland population.

As for the centrifugal influence of competition, this only affects sales on the spot and by retail, and even there it may be neutralized by a certain community of interests and wants, constituting precisely what are called corporate interests, so that even in this case the force of attraction may overcome the force of repulsion.

(5) Simultaneously with this marked tendency to specialization, and by what seems at first sight to be a development in the opposite direction, more and more factories nowadays are annexing all industries that are closely related to their own. This is called the *integration of industry.* It proceeds in an upward, downward, or lateral direction, according as the annexation applies to undertakings that supply the raw material, those that transform the manufactured article, or those that do similar work. The Krupp Company, besides its workshops at Essen, where they make guns, armour-plate, and everything that is made of steel, also owns and works iron-mines and coal-mines, naval dockyards, and gas-works for its own consumption. The American oil trust manufactures its own wooden or iron barrels, its gigantic pumps, and its tank-trucks, and it owns a whole fleet for transport purposes. So a chocolate factory will have a carpenter's shop for making its packing-cases, a paper-mill and a printing-works for making its boxes and labels,

and perhaps even cocoa plantations and ships to bring the raw material from abroad.

The utilization of by-products is one of the most interesting forms of integration. Thus a wool spinning mill will have a chemical factory for dealing with the substances extracted from the grease of the wool, and even a soap factory to turn these fatty substances into soap. So too a whole series of different industries will be created by a gas-works to make use of all the by-products derived from the distillation of the coal — coke, dyes, perfumes, explosives, and drugs.

Integration is no enemy to specialization. Each separate workshop in the factory, like each department in a large store, is specialized, and retains its technical independence. In a large shop or store you have a silk department, a linen department, a carpet department, and so on, each with its own staff and its own special buyers. These special departments, however, instead of being dispersed in different hands, are grouped under one management and mutually support each other. Integration of production is merely a higher degree of specialization, or what we might call co-operative specialization.

Co-operative societies also furnish a remarkable example of simultaneous concentration and integration, in countries where they have reached a high stage of development. Societies that are simply retail shops combine to form powerful federations for purchasing wholesale; these federations then begin to manufacture the goods that they sell in their shops, and even to start agricultural undertakings for the production of the necessary food-stuffs for the consumption of their members.

The characteristics just enumerated are particularly those of large-scale industrial production, but they are not all to be found in large-scale commerce or agriculture. The first one alone — the concentration of capital and labour — is common to all forms of large-scale production, but machinery is useless in large stores and occupies only a small place on large farms.

Specialization is very common in agriculture in the form of "monoculture" — the specialization of certain regions in the production of early vegetables, flowers, butter, and particularly wine, — but this is scarcely distinguishable from localization.

III. THE LAW OF CONCENTRATION

We have just seen that, in order to provide for growing wants and to supply a market that is constantly widening, production tends to develop from the humblest individual or family systems up to the great business enterprise with its thousands of workers and its millions of capital. This tendency to concentrate the maximum of productive power on one spot is called *the law of concentration*.

Great importance is attached to this law by economists and socialists alike — it is one of the rare points on which these two are in agreement. They consider it to be abundantly proved, and think that it is destined more and more to rule the economic world. Why is this?

In the first place, it is because of the economic superiority of large-scale production. By grouping together all the agents of production — labour, capital, natural agents, and site — it succeeds in making better use of them: that is to say, in obtaining the same quantity of wealth at less expense, or, what comes to the same thing, in producing more at the same expense. It is not surprising, therefore, that the superiority due to this saving in the cost of production enables big establishments to compete successfully with small ones, and seems as if it must gradually eliminate them.

The advantages that lead to the tendency to produce on a large scale are as follows:

(a) *Economy of labour.* — This means the possibility of establishing a more perfect division of labour, and a better use of time. In a small shop the time of each assistant often remains unoccupied. Take for instance a hundred business houses, each employing ten assistants. Combine them into one establishment, and each employee, being able now to work continuously, can do twice or three times as much work, and therefore takes the place of two or three workers.

(b) *Economy of space.* — To obtain a hundred times more room in a shop or a factory it is not necessary to occupy an area a hundred times as large, or to employ a hundred times as much building material. Geometry tells us that when the volumes of two cubes are as 1 to 1,000, their surfaces are as 1 to 100; and it is the surface alone that is expensive. Moreover, apart from mathematics, experience shows that the cost of a building or the rent paid for the hire of it does not increase in proportion to the area occupied.

(c) *Economy of capital.* — A powerful steam-engine consumes far less coal, relatively, than a weaker one, because it makes better use of the power: the difference may even be as much as ten to one. It is much more economical to use a big ship than one of small tonnage: it means a lower cost of production per ton, less space wasted in loading, a smaller crew to be paid, and so forth. And the by-products of manufacture can only be economically utilized when large quantities are being dealt with, because otherwise they only exist in minute proportions.

A large shop can carry on with a very small amount of cash in hand, relatively to the amount of business done, for three reasons: first, because it buys its goods in large quantities, or even has them made to order, and so has to pay out less money in procuring them; secondly, because these goods only remain in stock a few days, instead of for months or years as in the case of a small shop, and consequently the money paid out comes back much more quickly (£100 of capital is equivalent to £1,000 if it can be renewed ten times as quickly); and, lastly, because big businesses can get the capital they require more cheaply than small ones, for, having more credit, they generally pay a lower rate of interest.

If we enquire into the effects of the law of concentration from the social point of view — either upon the consumers or upon the workers — we must affirm that, on the whole, they are favourable. As a rule it gives consumers the benefits of cheapness and speedy satisfaction of their wants, while the workers obtain higher and more stable wages, and healthier and less uncomfortable conditions of work — advantages that small-scale industry cannot give. The time is past when factories could be called "capitalist prisons."

Trade unions favour large-scale industry for another reason also: because they regard it as the most favourable environment for the development of syndicalism and even socialism, for by gathering workmen together in huge masses and by their working together it helps to create "class consciousness" in the working population.

A beginner might imagine that socialists would be hostile to large-scale industry because it necessarily tends to extend the wage-system by progressively absorbing all who produce on their own account — small artisans, small shopkeepers, small landowners, all *independent producers* — and turning them into proletarians reduced to hiring out their services to large businesses managed by big capitalists or joint-stock companies.

But the fact is quite otherwise. It is owing to this resulting increase of proletarianism that the law of concentration is so dear to the hearts of Marxian socialists, and it is for this reason that until quite recently they made it the corner-stone of their doctrine. It is because they think that when the law of concentration has gathered all the instruments of production into the hands of a few individuals and reduced the whole mass of independent producers to the position of wage-earners, the capitalist edifice will then be like a pyramid resting on its apex — the slightest push will overturn it. All that will be needed then will be to expropriate the property of those few big capitalists for the general benefit, without having to make any other change in the organization of production. Even trusts are welcomed by collectivists because they regard them as the first step on the royal road that leads directly to collectivism.

Moreover, socialists have a great admiration for large-scale industry because of its power of organizing large numbers, its domination over natural forces, and the wealth it has succeeded in creating; they profess a sovereign contempt for small-scale production and individual enterprise. "Such a system," says Karl Marx, "excludes concentration, co-operation on a large scale, machinery, the skilful domination of man over nature, harmony and unity in the purposes, the means, and the efforts of collective activity. It is compatible only with a narrowly confined state of production and society. To perpetuate the system of isolated production would be to decree mediocrity in all things."

If large-scale industry, however, has met with the almost unanimous approval of socialists and economists, yet the opposite system still has its champions, particularly in the "traditionalist" schools; but it finds them also among co-operators, and we are not among those who wish to see it perish.

We may observe, indeed, that the system of small-scale industry — we are not speaking of home industry, which is merely an extension of the wage system — is more favourable to a fair distribution of wealth, and therefore to social peace. By reason of its extreme simplicity it prevents most of the conflicts that arise nowadays between the different classes of participators, and notably between labour and capital. It does not bring about the rule of absolute equality — which is scarcely to be desired — but it recognizes no other inequality than what results from the inequality of the land and instruments of production employed, or from the good and evil chances that are intimately bound up with all human affairs.

Even from the point of view of production, small-scale industry is not so feeble and out-of-date as it is supposed to be. Independent producers may combine and adopt some of the processes of large-scale production and the division of labour, without sacrificing their independence, their initiative, their responsibility, or their personal interest, all of which are powerful incentives to production, and always liable to be somewhat enfeebled by collective enterprise. What the great manufacturers do in their commercial agreements or trusts (to be dealt with presently), why could not the smaller ones do also in the various kinds of co-operative associations for purchase, sale, production, or credit — associations that enable the countryman and the artisan to obtain some of the advantages of large-scale production? The law of concentration does not necessarily involve the destruction of the small producer, any more than, in the political sphere, it ought to involve the suppression of small states. It should aim at federating them.

These, however, are *à priori* judgments and forecasts, dictated, perhaps, by individual opinions and hopes: what do the facts say?

They say nothing very clearly. Statistics can always be turned against their users; every school finds in them more or less what it is looking for. What seems indisputable, however, is this: that the number of businesses is tending on the whole to increase rather than to diminish. None the less we must be in no hurry to conclude that the law of concentration is being disproved by facts; we must examine the figures more closely.

To begin with, there is nothing surprising in the fact that the number of businesses regularly increases in every progressive society. We have seen that one of the signs of economic progress is the multiplication of wants. Now each new want gives rise to a new industry. There is nothing there that contradicts the law of concentration.

But if, instead of counting up all the businesses together, we look at each kind of industry separately, then the foreseen result appears clearly, namely, *the progressive diminution of the number of establishments*, along with an *increase in the total production*. This double movement is particularly marked in certain industries and commercial undertakings, such as mines, metallurgical works, maritime transport, banks, and the trade in fancy articles.

The law of concentration appears just the same if, without thus discriminating between different industries, and taking only the total figures, we set against the number of establishments the number of workpeople employed, the amount of capital engaged, and the value of the produce. We see then that for each establishment there is a greater number of wage-earners, a greater amount of capital, and a greater production.[1]

[1] [In the United States a periodical return is made of figures relating to industrial production. The following are the figures for 1899, 1914, and 1919:

	Number of Establishments	Number of Workpeople	Capital (millions of dollars)	Production (millions of dollars)
1899	207,514	4,712,000	9,076	10,657
1914	275,791	7,036,000	21,486	24,517
1919	289,768	9,103,200	44,678	62,910

This represents an average for each establishment of:

On the other hand, even in businesses that lend themselves best to concentration, development in the direction of large-scale production seems to be limited. Great stores like the Louvre and the Bon Marché in Paris seem to have reached a stationary state during the last few years. The growth of social organizations, like that of living organisms, appears to be confined by nature within certain limits. And, without insisting on this biological analogy, we can give an economic reason for this: namely, that beyond a certain limit the proportion of general expenses increases instead of diminishing, and thus the economy of large-scale production disappears. It is not in the least that the economic causes indicated above are inaccurate, but that they com   o be counterbalanced by other causes operating in an opposite direction, such as the cost of publicity and supervision, loss through waste, and so forth.[1]

We reach the conclusion, then, that if the law of concentration is to be regarded as true and as confirmed by facts, this is by no means to say that it should reach the extreme limit of a single colossal establishment that had absorbed all the rest.

The law of concentration as expounded by Karl Marx is a pure myth. He held that it ought to result in the general expropriation of all the small producers by the large ones, these latter becoming gradually less numerous until they in their turn are ripe for social expropriation. But this doctrine is sufficiently discredited to-day, even among Marxian socialists.

Moreover, there is a certain amount of confusion in this discussion as to the meaning of the word "concentration," for it may be taken in a technical sense, referring to a mode of production, or in an economic sense, referring to a method of appropriation. And concentration of *businesses* is a different thing from concentration of *fortunes*.

Finally, there seems to be a kind of division of labour between large-scale and small-scale industry, each having its own particular

	Workpeople	Capital	Production
1899	23	$43,737	$51,356
1914	25	77,907	88,869
1919	31	154,186	217,104

Although, therefore, during this period of twenty years the average number of workpeople has increased less than 50 per cent (in consequence, no doubt, of the employment of machinery), the figures expressing capital and production have about quadrupled].

[1] "In any country in any given condition of industrial development there is for each industry a size of business where the maximum net economy is reached, and beyond which, unless supported by a legal or a natural basis of monopoly, it cannot grow." (Hobson, *Modern Capitalism*, V. 15.)

sphere. It is only in certain industries that concentration makes great strides — in mining, land and sea transport, banking, metallurgical industries, and to a smaller extent in textile industries. It does not develop at all in agriculture, whatever may be said to the contrary. Certain new industries, such as photography, electrical trades, and cycle and motor manufactures, have given rise to a large number of small subsidiary industries for providing accessories and repairs. In the primeval forest the older trees do not always stifle the younger ones beneath them: sometimes they give them protection.

In this chapter we are dealing with the law of concentration only in the first of the two senses mentioned above. The question of the concentration of fortunes will be treated of later on, when we come to the subject of Distribution. Now it is particularly in the second sense of the word that the Marxians have expounded the law of concentration. They regard large-scale business as an octopus with a thousand tentacles but only one head — which it will be easy to cut off when the right moment arrives. But even if it had only one head from the point of view of business management it would not follow that it had only one from the point of view of the ownership of the capital. The concentration of industries in the form of great companies does not necessarily mean the creation of a set of millionaires, for the capital of these companies may be divided among a multitude of owners, in the form of shares. The system should be regarded as a hydra rather than an octopus — the Lernean hydra that had *as many heads as arms*, which made the task of Hercules so hard.

IV. CARTELS AND TRUSTS

We have already seen (p. 145) how the association of capital takes place in the form of joint-stock companies. We come now to a somewhat different kind of association, and one which is particularly characteristic of large-scale production. We are not concerned here with a single business financed by shareholders who are capitalists but not producers, as in the case of joint-stock companies, but with associations formed by *several businesses* (which may or may not themselves be companies). These are the *Trusts* and the *Cartels*, as they are called in the countries where they originated — the United States and Germany.

The *cartel* (charter, or contract), which may be defined as a *producers' syndicate* or *commercial agreement*, is the simplest form of association among producers. It arose from a reaction on the part of producers against the ruinous competition that was going on among them, particularly in the production of homogeneous goods where rivalry was impossible in the matter of quality, so that manufacturers had no other means of attracting customers than that of lowering the price. This competition was bound to end in a glut in the market, and a crisis, with all the disturbances we have already described (p. 133). The institution of the cartel, therefore, is inspired to some extent by a social interest and not entirely by a professional one.

The cartel is a contract, or, more correctly, a treaty of alliance between producers, who are on an equal footing and preserve their entire independence except as regards the special points that constitute the object of the agreement. It leaves each business its individuality and confines itself to grouping the businesses with a view to their selling their products under the best possible conditions. With this object it employs methods that vary in different cases but which all have the same end: to prevent competition, or at any rate to regulate it. The means adopted are:

(1) The delimitation of zones to be reserved for each of the parties to the agreement, so that each one acquires a regional monopoly.[1]

(2) The fixing of a maximum limit of production for each member, which he must not exceed.

(3) The fixing of a selling price to which all must conform. This tariff suppresses competition in the matter of price, but tends to replace it by competition for superiority of quality, which is an improvement. As conditions of production are very unequal, however, as between one business and another, this equalization of prices may create unfair inequalities of position.

(4) Each of these methods having proved of very little effect, despite the guarantees and fines imposed to enforce them, a fourth method was devised. This is the suppression of direct sale to a customer on the part of the members, the cartel being placed between the producer and the public as a compulsory intermediary. It is the cartel that buys their produce from the associated producers — the quantities for each one and the prices to be paid being fixed in advance, — and that is responsible for selling it on the best terms. Sometimes the cartel even undertakes to supply its members with the raw material used in their manufactures. By this means it becomes a kind of co-operative productive association.

Cartels have developed most extensively in Germany, especially

[1] In various Swiss towns — at Bâle, for instance — each brewery has its reserved district. so that it is very difficult for the consumer to procure the beer that he likes.

in coal-mining, and also in certain semi-agricultural industries, like the production of alcohol and sugar. There used to be more than 500 of them, and they rendered the greatest services to Germany during the war. It was owing to their organization that the industrial mobilization was able to be carried out without trouble, that the State was able to obtain the necessary supplies, and that prices could be maintained at a level that was generally lower, in spite of the blockade, than in the other belligerent countries.

With the *trust*,[1] which is more or less peculiar to the United States, we advance further on the path of concentration. The agreement or understanding develops into a fusion. Like the cartels, trusts are of various kinds, because, as we shall see, they were pursued by the American laws and compelled to flee from one refuge to another. The following three forms have followed each other:

(1) The first was scarcely different from the cartel; it was an understanding between large manufacturers or great companies with a view to regulating prices. But these understandings, described rather as *pools*, were badly hit after 1890 by the Sherman Act, which forbade "any contract, any combination, in the shape of a trust or otherwise, and any conspiracy with the object of restricting or monopolizing trade."

(2) Then followed the system of *consolidation*, as it was called, by which all the associated businesses gave up their independence and became merged into one. With this object the value of each factory was determined, and this value was paid to its owner in the shape of shares in the new society or trust. The directors of the latter therefore held everything in their hands and ruled this collection of businesses at their pleasure, suppressing, if necessary, those which seemed in a less satisfactory position. But laws were passed to prevent this form of monopolization also.

(3) At length the system was evolved which is most commonly in use to-day. Each business retains its nominal and legal independence, but this is in actual fact suppressed by the formation of a separate association to which are allotted the majority of the shares of each of the businesses. This dominating association, being all-powerful in the administration of each factory, is actually so in the administration of the whole group also. These governing associations are themselves most often under the control of big financiers,

---

[1] The term *trust* is a very old English word meaning *confidence*. The representatives of philanthropic foundations are called *trustees;* similarly the directors of trusts are those to whom the interests of all are entrusted.

who are called "kings" — the oil king, the steel king, the railway king, and so forth.

The trust differs from the cartel not only by reason of the closer bond that unites the members and even fuses them together, but also because it is a productive and not merely a commercial organization. It has been said that the Standard Oil Trust at the time of its dissolution was the most complete organization that the world had ever known, next to that of the Roman Catholic Church! The trust pushes to the extreme limit the characteristic features of large-scale industry, such as concentration, localization, and integration,[1] as it also carries to an extreme the abuses of the joint-stock company system, such as the over-capitalization of shares.[2]

Twenty years ago very few people had even heard of trusts, and we did not think it necessary to mention them in the earlier editions of this book. But they have become the most typical phenomenon in contemporary economic progress. Even the careless public is astounded by their increasing numbers, and especially by the gigantic proportions they have already reached.[3] Oil, steel, meat, whisky, tobacco, railways, maritime transport, wire, cigarettes — all are controlled by trusts. They resemble a monstrous breed of animals suddenly engendered by a capitalist age, and contemplated with equal curiosity by socialists and economists of the liberal school, although they regard them with opposite feelings. The former welcome them as the last word in capitalist concentration, after which nothing remains but collectivism; the latter are disturbed by this paradoxical result of free competition, but remain faithful to the hope that in spite of everything the same freedom which gave them birth will suffice to slay them or to render them harmless. For the rest, it has not yet been determined whether the good exceeds the evil in this movement, or whether the reverse is the case.

Two weighty arguments can be adduced in favour of the trusts:

[1] Thus the steel trust is not content with grouping the iron-works together; it includes also iron mines, and even the railways and canals that convey the ore.

[2] *Over-capitalization*, or the issue of shares at an increased rate, finds a pretext here in the anticipation of the profits expected to result simply from the creation of a monopoly.

[3] The Standard Oil Trust was the oldest and the most famous of all. Formed in 1872 by the amalgamation of 29 companies, it distributed annually from 390 to 400 million dollars in dividends on an original capital which did not exceed 100 million dollars.

The United States Steel Company, founded in 1901 to amalgamate 15 metallurgical companies, of which the most important was Carnegie's, also distributes enormous dividends, which were tremendously increased by the war.

(1) *The economy they effect in cost of production*, which is the true criterion of economic progress.

One of the most remarkable examples of reduction of the expenses of production, and one that only trusts can accomplish, is the system of pipe-lines laid down by the Oil Trust over some 83,000 miles, to convey the oil to the consumer from the places where it is produced, without having recourse to the railways.

Mention might also be made of the elimination, or at all events the diminution in number, of commercial travellers, and of expenses of publicity or advertising — in a word, of all the expense that competition involves, and that becomes useless as soon as an industry acquires a monopoly and no longer needs to run after customers, but waits for them instead: in this case it is useless to go to the expense of being eloquent. This saving alone may amount to millions of pounds.

We can add also the elimination of badly situated factories and the localization of production in the most favourable places. Notice that the cartels, or simple business understandings, are powerless to achieve these results.

(2) The maintenance of *equilibrium between production and consumption*, which the system of free competition has shown itself unable to accomplish; and consequently the elimination of crises and stability of prices. Moreover, the advocates of trusts deny that they have raised prices and quote numerous instances of progressive diminution. The policy of the trusts aims just as much at preventing an excessive rise as at preventing a fall. Besides, they say, even if the price were increased a little, the consumers would still find a compensating advantage in its stability. Generally, too, the trusts look after the quality of the products and scorn the wretched shifts of the small trader who tries to pass off bad stuff for good. The refineries of the Oil Trust are submitted to the most rigorous control. And, finally, their workpeople and employees are generally very well paid.

But the opponents of trusts have no lack of arguments either.

To begin with, it might be thought, *à priori*, very improbable, in the economic as well as in the political sphere, that a power without any counterpoise should not abuse its opportunities, or at least put them at the service of its own interests.

Admitting that the trusts have not always raised prices, and even admitting that they have enabled the consumer to benefit to some slight extent by the economies effected in the cost of production, it is certain that they have used the bulk of this saving to enrich the shareholders and to accumulate fabulous fortunes in the hands of some of them. It is the trusts that have created the hitherto unknown class of millionaires and even multi-millionaires. The modern economic era will be characterized by the appearance of these industrial mammoths, as the prehistoric ages were marked by that of the mastodon and the dinothere.

Not only have they not arrived at allowing the consumer to benefit by the lowering of the cost of production, but in some cases they have exploited him to such an extent as to provoke a general boycott.

They tend to create actual monopolies by ferociously crushing out all competition, and this not only by superior organization and lowering of cost, which would be legitimate and beneficial, but by acts of piracy — either by selling at a loss wherever a competitor shows himself,[1] or else by demanding favourable treatment from the railway companies, which is contrary to the law.

Finally, from the political point of view, the appearance of these giants, armed with all the power of corruption that unlimited wealth confers upon them, threatens to pervert the springs of government, especially in democratic societies.

Is there any way in which the economic advantages of trusts could be retained while making them powerless for evil? Such, in fact, is the somewhat contradictory problem that economists and governments are striving to solve — so far without success, for how can you prevent half a dozen big manufacturers from coming to an understanding, forming associations, or buying out competitors?

Economists of the liberal school say that if the system of protection could be eliminated, then the trusts, which have hitherto grown in the shelter of customs barriers, would be sufficiently checkmated by international competition. In support of this view they quote England, where trusts are less developed than elsewhere. But there is no ground for thinking that in the United States or Germany the trusts or cartels would be the first to succumb to foreign competition.

It seems more likely, on the contrary, that they would bear the blow much better than would weaker undertakings. The effect of general free trade would probably be not the suppression of the trusts, but their transformation from national, as they are now, to

---

[1] The following is quoted by M. Martin Saint-Léon from the report of an official enquiry into the Oil Trust. The chairman of the commission said to the vice-president of the Trust: "Is it your rule to keep your prices below cost until your rival disappears?" and the answer was, "Yes."

international — and this would certainly not make them less formidable, but very much the reverse! The Oil Trust is already international.

In conclusion, cartels and trusts may be regarded as a method of organization superior to the so-called "natural" system of free competition, not only from the technical, but also from the social point of view, on this twofold condition: (1) That they proceed by way of agreement rather than by absorption, thus realizing a form of development like that which is desirable in the political domain — federation but not centralization; (2) that they are counterbalanced by a parallel organization of consumers, in the form of consumers' co-operative associations; co-operative purchasing federations are real consumers' trusts.

V. STATE AND MUNICIPAL BUSINESS UNDERTAKINGS

Having dealt with businesses of an individual kind and those undertaken by associations, we shall find it convenient to speak now of businesses organized by the State, by municipalities, and by public authorities in general.

The State as *entrepreneur* is not exactly a new phenomenon, for some of the national manufactures of France date back to Colbert's time.[1] But the development of State enterprise, and still more that of municipal enterprise, is characteristic of the present epoch. This is due to the following causes:

(1) A *fiscal* cause — the need for finding new resources to meet expenses that are constantly growing, without crushing the taxpayer. There is no doubt that this cause operates with much greater intensity as a result of the war, now that States will have to face such budgets as were never imagined before. Given, on the one hand, the impossibility of raising the necessary millions by a tax on income without ending with total confiscation, and, on the other hand, the irritation aroused by all taxes on consumption because they add to the cost of living which is already high, no other alternative will remain to the State but to try to earn the indispensable millions itself, by turning manufacturer and merchant.

(2) A *social* cause — hostility to capitalism, and the idea that the profits and dividends of the great companies have been stolen from the people and should be restored to them. The surest means to

[1] [*Colbert* (1619–1683) was Louis XIV's famous finance minister and one of the greatest exponents of the Mercantile System.]

this end is surely that the nation itself, represented by the State or the municipality, should undertake profit-making enterprises. This tendency, however, may take very different forms — it may be that of State socialism, which is inspired by no spirit of socialism or collectivism in the true sense of those words (the Prussian State, for example); or it may be that of syndicalist socialism.[1]

What are the industries that are specially marked out by their nature to become State or municipal enterprises?

To begin with, it goes without saying that the most suitable for nationalization are those that represent a general or national interest, such as the coinage of money, the post office, and the railways. But the list gradually lengthens in proportion as economic interests assume a national character, and so one is led to add mining, hydraulic power, merchant shipping, insurance, banking, and perhaps even, as in war-time, the importation of corn and coal.

The list would include also, from the fiscal point of view, those industries which seem to give large and easily visible profits, such as sugar and oil refining, fire insurance, the importation of coffee, and the sale of alcohol and tobacco.[2]

For municipalization, those businesses are more particularly indicated which meet a need common to all the inhabitants of the town — a uniform need that demands the same satisfaction in every case, or at least admits of few inequalities, so that a single selling price is possible, or one with only two or three variants.

As a typical instance of a business that fulfils these conditions we may cite the supply of water. Water meets a universal need — one that is even physically and morally obligatory, of daily recurrence, and absolutely equalitarian; and, though the installation of the service may involve great expense, its exploitation is as simple as possible. So everyone here is agreed.

But there are other services which, though they do not fulfil the conditions so completely, get more or less near to it, and notably

---

[1] In the programme of the (French) General Labour Confederation (commonly known as the C. G. T.), the formula "industrialized nationalization" is used, to avoid all confusion with *étatisation* or state ownership — to distinguish the *nation* from the *State*.

[2] In France, besides the great fiscal monopolies of tobacco, matches, gunpowder, and the Post Office, the State has a few industries of slight importance: Sèvres porcelain, Goeblin tapestries, national printing works, stud farms, hydropathic establishments at watering-places, etc. Among the advertisements at every railway-station in Paris we find announcements of "State Pastilles," showing that the State has even turned druggist! [State enterprise in England and America is, of course, far less developed than this.]

the urban and suburban transport service — metropolitan trams and railways. This service also meets a need common to all the inhabitants of the town, a daily need, and one that is so urgent that all city life is paralyzed if the service stops. Its importance is great from the hygienic as well as the economic point of view, for it is the only thing that enables workers to dwell outside the towns. Finally, it only involves a tariff of two classes.

The same considerations apply to lighting. In fact there is no longer any controversy over these services, nor over those that concern the public health, such as baths, burials, disinfection, markets, and slaughterhouses. But it is different when towns undertake the building of houses for the working population. Opposition then becomes rampant! Yet the building of cheap and healthy houses answers well to the kind of need indicated above, for there is nothing more important than housing for the health not only of the tenants themselves but of all the inhabitants of the town. The same may be said of the milk supply, which is so useful a service in the struggle against infant mortality.

But then, what about necessary foods, like bread and meat? If the needs of the population are inadequately met, either in the matter of quality or in that of price, why not allow the municipalities the right to open bakeries and butchers' shops? This power, however, was refused to them until the war showed the necessity of it in cases where consumers were being exploited by the local tradesmen.

Admitting that these various businesses might be nationalized or municipalized, another question arises: should the State or the municipalities run them as monopolies, or place them under a system of free competition?

The answer obviously depends on the object in view. If this object is entirely fiscal — to increase the income of the State or the town so as to supplement the taxes or rates, — then they should have recourse to a monopoly, because that is the only system that enables prices to be raised with no other limit than that fixed by the purchasing power of the consumers. Thus in France the State used to sell tobacco at five times the cost price![1]

But if fiscal considerations are set aside or relegated to the second place, and if the essential object is the service of the public, as is generally the case with municipal undertakings, then the question must be decided by the nature of the undertaking.

In the case of water supply, trams, and gas, it would be anti-

[1] Since the war the profit has fallen from 80% to 50%, though the yield has trebled itself and approaches sixty million pounds.

economic and often physically impossible to lay down several competing tram lines or gas or water pipes in the same street, so there
the system of monopoly is indicated.   At the same time this monopoly may be limited to one fixed quarter or section of the town, and
consequently need not exclude similar, and, up to a certain point,
competing, undertakings.

But if the business is one of those that have hitherto been competitive — such as the baker's and the butcher's businesses — it
is better for the municipal business to be placed under the same
system.   In this case, to be sure, it cannot expect anything but the
normal profits, and that only on condition — one that will not often
be fulfilled! — that it is run as economically as its rivals.   But it may
render consumers the very great service of moderating prices by its
very existence, and of breaking up those tacit coalitions that are
always formed between tradesmen in the same locality.   Its action
will be much more effective than price regulation.

It is well known that this development in the direction of State
ownership has aroused the sharpest criticism from economists of
the liberal school, and that the incapacity shown by public authorities — in France more than elsewhere — has only too often justified
them.   For the principle involved we must refer to what was said
about State socialism at the beginning of the book (see p. 26).

But there are some irresistible movements which cannot be stopped
by criticism or even by defeat, and we believe the tendency to
nationalization to be one of these, for reasons we have just indicated.
But, to prevent the abuses we have pointed out, these nationalized
businesses must be given a purely economic character and freed from
all admixture of politics, by conforming to the following rules:

(a) State and municipal undertakings must be given an independent organization, a special budget, a distinct personality, and
an administrative board drawn from outside the municipal council
(or at any rate with a minority of municipal councillors, and with
a rule forbidding them and their near relations to be employed in any
municipal undertaking).   Moreover, the same rules as to the keeping of accounts must be imposed on them as on private businesses.[1]

(b) A place on the administrative board must be given to representatives of the consumers on the one hand, and of the employees
on the other, so as to give these State undertakings the character of
true co-operative societies, both of production and consumption.

---

[1] Italy has accomplished this by instituting *enti autonomi*, which are independent
bodies composed of delegates elected by the municipality, by the public utility and
relief services, and by the consumers' societies, each of these elements being represented in proportion to the capital it furnishes.

This will perhaps be sufficient to prevent their hardening into officialism.

(c) These undertakings, whether national or municipal, must be subject to the ordinary law, exactly like private individuals. This is an essential condition, without which the extension of the economic activities of the State would become the most intolerable tyranny. This liability is already recognized in the case of State railways, but it is generally refused in the case of the postal, telegraph, and telephone services. It is an abuse of power to allow the governing State to cover the industrial State by saying that they are one: they must be kept entirely distinct.

From the fiscal point of view the advantages of nationalization are questionable. There is undoubtedly a certain measure of incompatibility between the two objects: the procuring of resources for the State, on the one hand, and the satisfaction of the wants of the consumer in the most economical fashion possible on the other.

This latter object is certainly the essential one: a State undertaking should not have for its ideal the making of profits, but the satisfaction of wants. As regards services that are useful to everyone, or at least to the great majority of citizens, and consumption that is both necessary and desirable, the tendency will probably be even towards supplying them free. But for services that only affect a minority, and for objects of luxury consumption, it will be to the advantage of all to maintain high prices that yield a profit. There would be no harm in charging more to tobacco smokers or consumers of alcoholic drinks, so as to supply all the citizens at less than cost price with water, transport, light, and perhaps even fuel and motive power.

This programme, it should be observed, — the organization of production and exchange with a view to wants instead of profits, — is much like that of consumers' co-operative societies. That is why those who believe, as we do, in the future of these societies, cannot be opposed in principle to municipalization. For this is really only a form of co-operative association that aims at providing at the lowest possible cost for the most necessary and general wants of all the inhabitants of a given town. We also believe that municipalities will tend more and more to make use of consumers' societies, and to hand over to them the task of organizing commercial undertakings.[1] The war will have had the very important result of teaching them how closely they are related.

[1] This is what the Bolshevist government has done on a gigantic scale in Russia.

BOOK II

CIRCULATION

Circulation is not an end in itself, for wealth does not circulate for the sake of circulating. *Exchange* and *credit*, which form the two essential parts of the circulation of wealth, and which, moreover, as we shall see, are really the same thing, are only methods of *organizing labour*, having absolutely the same object as association and division of labour, namely, to facilitate production.

Yet in most books on political economy a special section is devoted to circulation, not only because this classification suits the distinction commonly drawn between *commerce* and *industry*, but particularly because these new methods of organizing labour really lead us into a different realm. Wealth has now been created: the next step is to transfer it. It will not again change its *form:* it will only change its *owner.* It will no longer be subjected to *technical* changes, but it will become the object of *contracts.*

Nevertheless it must not be concluded that we are leaving the domain of political economy for that of law. It is the economic, and not the legal, aspects of exchange that we have to study. We are not concerned to determine the rights or obligations that result from sales or commercial operations, but to enquire into the utility, or the increased value, that results from them for the exchanging parties and for the nation at large.

CHAPTER I — EXCHANGE

I. HISTORY OF EXCHANGE

Exchange occupies an exceedingly important place in modern life. To obtain some idea of it we need only remember that nearly all wealth is produced only for the purpose of being exchanged. Take the wheat in the granaries, the clothes at the dressmaker's, the shoes at the shoemaker's, the jewels at the jeweller's, the bread at the baker's, and ask yourself what part of all this wealth is destined by the producer for his own consumption. The answer is, very little or none at all. These things are only *merchandise* — objects intended for sale, as the name itself implies. Our industry, our skill, and our talents are also most frequently applied to satisfy not our own wants, but those of *others*. It rarely happens that barristers, doctors, and solicitors have to work for themselves, pleading their own causes, healing their own ailments, or drawing up their own documents. They, too, regard these services only from the point of view of exchange. That is why, when we estimate our wealth, we do not estimate it according to its utility for *us*, but solely according to its exchange value — its utility for *others*.

It must not be supposed, however, that it has always been thus. Exchange is not as simple a process as association or division of labour, which are so natural that even some kinds of animals know how to practise them. Far from being instinctive, exchange seems originally to have been antipathetic to human nature. Primitive man regarded the product of his labour as almost a part of himself. Hence arose the curiously solemn formalities by which every transfer of property was originally surrounded (such, for instance, as the *mancipatio* of Roman law). Strangely enough, giving seems to have been practised before exchange, and it is even thought that giving gave rise to exchange through the fiction of a reciprocal gift.

At first sight it might be supposed that exchange must have preceded division of labour, for each individual, historically speaking, could only have specialized in a single task when he knew he could obtain from others the wherewithal to satisfy his other needs; and that is just what Adam Smith says. Yet the truth seems rather to be the reverse of this. Division of labour came before exchange, for it could very well be practised, even without exchange, in the family or tribal community, whereas it is scarcely possible to conceive of exchange functioning without division of labour — without a certain amount of specialized production.

In the first phase of industrial organization — that of the family — there evidently could be no place for exchange, as each group formed an independent, self-sufficing organism. It was by the labour of its members and its slaves, and later on by the compulsory work of its serfs, that the family, tribe, manor, or monastery provided for the satisfaction of its wants. Exchange took place only in the case of certain foreign products brought in by foreign merchants.

In the second phase — that of corporative or guild industry — exchange appears at the same time as the separation of trades, and the *market* becomes the central place in the city.[1] There producers and consumers who are inhabitants of the same town, meet together. Merchants from without are excluded, or at any rate can only enter under certain rigorous conditions.

In the third phase — the manufacturing stage — the market becomes *national* instead of local, and it is then that exchange and commerce really begin. It has been observed that the rise of national markets coincides with the formation of the great modern States, as well as with the substitution of national for urban fortifications. This goes to prove that evolution, whether it be economic, political, or military, everywhere follows parallel lines.

The market becomes still wider by becoming colonial, as happened when the great trading companies were formed, which played so prominent a part in economic history — such as the East India Company.

Then finally, in the fourth phase — that of machinery and railways — the market becomes truly a *world* market, and commerce takes those great strides that have so profoundly modified the economic relations of our old Europe, and have made this question of international trade one of the most important problems of our time.

---

[1] By *market*, in the economic sense of the term, must be understood not merely a single place or locality, but any area in which the movement of goods and communication between buyers and sellers are rapid enough for a single price to be established. The extent of the market varies, therefore, according to the nature of the goods: any one country constitutes practically one market for wheat, and the whole world is one market for gold.

II. THE DIVISION OF BARTER INTO SALE AND PURCHASE

When exchange is carried on directly, goods against goods, it is called *barter*. But this is the most inconvenient and often even the most impracticable of operations. In fact, for barter to be successfully effected, the possessor of an object must seek for a person who *wants to obtain that object* and is *prepared to give him just the very object he himself wants* — a double coincidence that is very difficult to bring about. Nor is this all: even if this lucky meeting can be accomplished, the two objects to be exchanged *must be of equal value*, that is to say, they must satisfy wants that are equal and opposite to each other. This makes a third improbability.[1]

The invention of a *third commodity* to serve as a go-between removes these difficulties. It evidently involves a previous tacit understanding, among men living in society, that each will agree to accept this third commodity in exchange for his goods. Once this understanding is reached, exchange readily takes place. Suppose that silver be chosen for this purpose. Then in exchange for the goods that I have produced and that I wish to dispose of, I shall willingly accept a certain quantity of silver, even though I have no immediate use for it. This is because I know that when I wish to acquire anything I want, I shall only have to offer its possessor this silver, and he will accept it for the same reason that led me to accept it.

It is clear that by this means every exchange transaction can be split up into two distinct operations. Instead of exchanging my commodity A for your commodity B, I exchange A for silver, and then exchange this silver for B. The first of these operations is called *sale*, and the second, *purchase* — at least when the intermediate commodity takes the form of money, properly so called. This seems therefore to be a more complicated rather than a simpler method. But the shortest path is not always a straight line, and

---

[1] Lieut. Cameron, who travelled in Africa in 1884, tells us how he had to go to work to obtain a boat: "Syde's agent wished to be paid in ivory, of which I had none . . . So I gave Mohammed ibn Gharib the requisite amount of wire, upon which he handed over cloth to Mohammed ibn Salib, who, in his turn, gave Syde ibn Habib's agent the wished-for ivory. Then he allowed me to have the boat." (V. L. Cameron, *Across Africa*, pp. 183–4.)

Barter is still more difficult in the case of exchanging services. The Bâle Missionary Almanac for 1907 tells us that at Godthaab, in Greenland, among the Eskimos, there is a paper run by the missionaries to which the subscription is one *wild goose* per quarter or one *seal* per year.

this ingenious détour does away with an incalculable amount of trouble and labour.

What makes barter impracticable, in fact, is this — as we have already explained: that a producer, Primus, has to meet with another person, Secundus, who is prepared both (a) to acquire the thing that Primus wishes to dispose of; and (b) to hand over the very thing that Primus wishes to obtain. Henceforth, with the introduction of an intermediate commodity, the producer still has to find someone who will take his goods, but at least he does not have to expect this "someone" to give him the very goods he himself is in need of. He may want something that is obtainable from somebody else, at another time, and in a different place. The *inseparability of these two operations* is what makes them so difficult. Once the tie that unites them is broken, each of them separately becomes simple enough, for it is not very hard to find someone who wants your goods, and it is still easier to find someone else who is prepared to sell you the goods that you want.

It should be observed that in exchange in the form of barter the estimation of value is very uncertain, and this gives rise to exploitation of the worst kind. In trading with the natives of Africa, if you give the negro guns or calico in exchange for rubber or ivory, the purchasing commodity is counted at four times its value, and the value of the produce bought is halved, so that the European gets eight times as much as he gives. That, however, is a fair rate: in many cases the ratio is 1 to 100. The introduction of money is a blessing in this respect: it has been an instrument of justice and morality.[1]

It must not be forgotten, however, that although these two operations are henceforth separated, they nevertheless continue to form a whole, and that the one cannot be imagined without the other. In our everyday life we are too much inclined to look upon sale and purchase as independent and self-sufficing processes. But that is a mistake. *Every purchase implies a previous sale*, for before being able to buy we must previously have exchanged something for money — our labour, our services, or something we have produced. Conversely, *every sale implies a future purchase*, for if we exchange our produce for money it is only in order later on to exchange this money for other goods. What else could we do with it?

---

[1] All philanthropists who have denounced the frightful exploitation of the negroes in the Congo region have indicated as one of the most effective reforms the abolition of payment in kind and the introduction of money, both in paying for goods bought from the natives and for the payment of taxes by the natives.

Still, since money can be kept for an indefinite time without being used, a very long interval may elapse — a matter of years, perhaps, or even several generations — between the sale and the purchase that complements it. But in thought these two operations must be brought together, and then we shall see that in spite of the intervention of a medium of exchange and the resulting complications, man can only live, in our civilized societies as well as in primitive ones, by exchanging his produce or his services, present or past, for other produce or services, present or past. If we join up the two ends of the chain we shall always find an exchange of commodities, which is barter.

The intermediate commodity that divides barter into sale and purchase is called *money*. It plays a tremendous part in economic science, as it does in actual life, and we shall have to devote several chapters to it.

III. EXCHANGE VALUE OR PRICE

The old economists, beginning even with Aristotle, and Adam Smith at a later date, drew a distinction between two kinds of value, which they called, respectively, *value in use* and *value in exchange* (or exchange value). They showed also that these two values may be quite different from each other. Thus the value in use of a pair of spectacles is incalculably great to a short-sighted scientist, but their exchange value is very small, whereas diamond ear-rings, whose exchange value may be very considerable, have for him an infinitesimal value in use.

Why this difference? Because value in use is determined solely by the wants and desires and the personal valuation of a particular individual. It has no other foundation than the *subjective utility* of the object to that individual. It varies according to his needs or fancies, and has no general character and no social importance. Exchange value is more stable, because it is determined by the wants and desires of all the inhabitants of a country, or even of the whole world, who have the wish and the means to acquire the object. The value of a family portrait to me may be great, but that gives it no exchange value if it is a mere daub. On the other hand, if it is a Van Dyck or a Rembrandt it will have a worldwide exchange value determined by the desire of all lovers of pictures.

It might be better, therefore, to call value in use *individual value*, and exchange value *social value*, for the latter only appears when there are several persons in the market — at least two, and generally thousands.

It is evident that exchange value occupies an incomparably larger place than value in use in the life and activities of men living in society.   For though value in use may exist without exchange value, the converse does not hold good.   All exchange value necessarily implies value in use, for exchange is itself a very common and important "use" of wealth to its possessor.   And even apart from the possibility of selling it, the possession of a valuable object is a source of great satisfaction.   In the example just given it is not unlikely that the owner of a portrait of an unknown person by Rembrandt would set more store by it than by a portrait of his own grandfather.

In current speech exchange value is generally confused with *price*.   They are not the same thing, however, for we have already seen (p. 56) that price is only one of a thousand possible ways of expressing value.   Value is a relation between any two things whatever: price is a relation *in which one of the two terms is always money*.   It is not necessarily metallic, coined money, or paper money, however, for in Africa, where calico or beads are used for money, the value of goods expressed in them is their price just the same.   In every case the word "price" implies a common measure — a standard adopted for purposes of comparison.

We must now consider what are the conditions that must be satisfied by exchange value, or current price.   They may be formulated as follows:

(1) In the same market, at any given moment, for similar goods, there can be only *a single price*.   This is what Jevons called *the law of indifference*, meaning that whenever it is a matter of complete indifference whether we acquire one or another of several objects because they are identical — or, in other words, when we have no reason for preferring one thing to another, — we shall not be willing to pay more for one than for the other.

At first we might think otherwise.   For here in the market are five men selling wheat, with five sacks, and each demanding a different price, while here, on the other hand, are five buyers, each assigning a different value to the wheat that he wants.   Why should there not be as many different prices as there are pairs of buyers and sellers, the buyer who is prepared to pay most agreeing with the most exacting seller, while the buyer whose wants are least urgent makes a bargain with the seller who is most accommodating in the matter of price?   The reason is that no buyer, however anxious to buy, will consent to pay more than his competitors; and no seller, no matter how easy-going, will consent to sell his wheat at a lower price than his colleagues. So both sides wait till the market price gets settled.

This single price in the market at a given moment is what is called the *current price*.[1] This current price is published in the commercial papers that deal with each important commodity — corn, coal, cotton, wool, copper, and so forth. It is *quoted* on the various produce exchanges just as the prices of shares and government securities are quoted on the Stock Exchange, and serves as the basis of all commercial dealings.

(2) This single price must be one that *makes the quantity of goods offered coincide with the quantity demanded.*

The necessity for this is sufficiently obvious, for it would be absurd to imagine that there could be more sacks of wheat sold than there are bought — for the two lots are the same.

But this coincidence is not reached all at once. It is only attained as the result of a series of oscillations on the part of the quantities offered and demanded, corresponding to oscillations in the price. As soon as equilibrium is established, the current price emerges. Here are our five wheat sellers in the market, with the five buyers in front of them; but they are asking 58s. At this price, a couple of the buyers withdraw in dismay, and only three are left. The five sellers, seeing that their wheat is likely to be left on their hands, make a lower offer in order to attract the three buyers — they go down to 56s. But at this price one of the buyers who had fled comes back, and the four of them are now disposed to take four sacks. If the five sellers have all made up their minds to sell at any price, they will have to resign themselves to lowering it still further — say to 54s. — in order to recall the last and most timid buyer, and to make the demand rise to the level of the supply — that is to say, to five sacks. But it is possible that one of the sellers may prefer to take his sack home again rather than go below 56s. In that case,

---

[1] Two exchanging parties are all that is required to effect an exchange, but they are not enough to establish a current price: for this there must be competition between the sellers on one side and the buyers on the other. Suppose a schoolboy wants his companion's cake, and is prepared to give him his marbles for it. How many will he give? We cannot say; he will give all he has got, if he has not had any dinner! That would be the bargain made by Esau and Jacob. But if there are several boys ready to give up their cakes, and several prepared to hand over their marbles, then, and then only, will a current price be established.

That is why when rare objects are sold, and there is only one seller and perhaps only one collector present, there is no law of prices — the object is "priceless," as we very appropriately say — which means that in this case the price depends entirely on the wealth of the buyer and the cleverness of the seller.

56s. will remain the market price, for at that price there will be four sacks sold, and four sacks bought. Each demand will have found its counterpart, and the requisite coincidence is effected.

(3) The market price must be one that *satisfies the largest possible number of pairs of sellers and buyers* present in the market.

Let us imagine the sellers and buyers — call them S and B — facing each other in the corn exchange, and let us set down in order the figures that express their demands, numbering the sellers downwards from the one who asks the highest price to the one who will be content with the lowest, and the buyers upwards from the most close-fisted to the most open-handed:

S1 asks 58 shillings.			B1 offers 54 shillings.		
S2	"	57	"	B2	"	55	"
S3	"	56	"	B3	"	56	"
S4	"	55	"	B4	"	57	"
S5	"	54	"	B5	"	58	"

Suppose that S1 opens the ball by asking 58s. At this price there is only one buyer, B5, who is inclined to close with him, for none of the other four wants to pay so high a price. So at this price only one bargain would be made, and only one sack sold, whereas there are four other sellers anxious to sell, even at a lower price. However, B5 himself will not be such a fool as to give 58s. if he can get the wheat for less. So he will wait until the other and less grasping sellers have made their demands. Then comes S2, who only asks 57s. This price brings up another buyer, B4. That makes two buyers prepared to deal, but, on the other hand, there are still three who do not wish to pay so much.

At length S3 comes along and asks only 56s. To that price B3 responds in his turn, making three buyers out of five, which is a majority, and since there are just three sellers disposed to be content with this price, there will be three pairs out of five who are satisfied. No other price would satisfy so many of them, so that is the price that will rule the market and become the current price. It will not go lower. If, indeed, S4 were to come forward and say he would be content with 55s., what would happen? Of course the first three sellers would refuse to deal at that price and would retire. There would remain only two sellers faced by four buyers, and it would be impossible to complete the business.

So 56s. is the price adhered to. What will happen, then, to the two most grasping corn-dealers, S1 and S2, and the two most close-fisted buyers, B1 and B2? Either they will all accept the price 56s., or else, if they are unwilling to moderate their claims, they will just withdraw from the market, and take no part in fixing the price.[1]

We are bound to admire the ingenuity and truth that underlie this psychological analysis of the mechanism of exchange. But it must be regarded merely as a framework that includes facts of great complexity. As a matter of fact, uniformity of price is never actually realized, even in a market like the Stock Exchange which best fulfils the conditions laid down by theory.

IV. THE LAW OF SUPPLY AND DEMAND

Formerly, in the classical treatises on political economy, everything that relates to value and price was explained by a formula that was very simple and very clear, at any rate in appearance. It was said that *exchange value varies directly with demand and inversely with supply.*

This formula is now quite discredited — rather too much so, perhaps. The following objections may certainly be raised against it:

(1) In its claims to mathematical accuracy it is contrary to facts. A *halving* of the supply does not necessarily *double* the price: the price might be more or less than doubled, according to the greater or less urgency of the need to be met by the diminished supply.[2]

(2) It mistakes the effect for the cause. If an increase in the demand raises the price, it is evident that the rise in price will in turn diminish the demand; and if an increase in the supply lowers the price, it is evident that the lower price will tend in its turn to restrict the supply. In other words, instead of saying that prices are regulated by supply and demand, we could just as well say that

[1] At first sight we might be tempted to think that the first to meet and come to terms would be the seller who is most anxious to sell and the buyer who is keenest on buying — as if it were a question of marriage. But we must bear in mind that it is just because the one is anxious to sell, and the other to buy, *at any price*, that the price remains unsettled. In the example in the text, one asks 54s., but would like to get more, while the other offers 58s., but would prefer, if possible, to give less. So they remain undecided until the less eager sellers and buyers have drawn their respective prices together, as it were. Of the three sellers who have found purchasers, S3 was the least eager to sell, for his was the highest demand; and of the three buyers who have obtained what they wanted, B3 was the least eager to buy, because his offer was the lowest   Now it is perfectly logical that *the price should be fixed by the two parties who are least anxious to deal, because it is they whose opposing claims stand the best chance of being met.* These two parties are called by the Austrian school of economists the *marginal pair.*

[2] During the war we have seen price variations out of all proportion to the scarcity of the supply. The price of wine, for instance, rose from 1s. to 4s. a gallon, though the supply hardly varied at all.

supply and demand are regulated by price. Take any kind of securities selling on the Stock Exchange, for example 3% government bonds, and suppose them to be selling at £100. Every day a certain amount of these bonds are offered for sale, and a certain amount are demanded. Suppose that at the opening of the Stock Exchange there is a demand for twice as much of these bonds as there is offered for sale. Does anyone imagine that the price will rise to £200? Yet that is just what ought to take place if the formula were true. In reality, the price quoted for these bonds may not rise even £1, for the simple reason that the majority of people who would buy at £100 withdraw as soon as the price rises above this point. And while the demand for bonds diminishes as the price rises, the supply, at the same time and for the same reason, increases. A time must come, therefore, when the decreasing demand and the increasing supply are equal, and at that point equilibrium is again set up. But a rise of a shilling or two is generally sufficient to cause this result.

(3) The formula attributes no intelligible meaning to the words *supply* and *demand*. The term *supply* may, to be sure, mean the quantity of merchandise, the stock existing on the market, although in many cases a purely imaginary scarcity (such as the fear of a bad harvest) may produce the same effect. But what are we to understand by *demand?* The quantity in demand is indeterminate, since it depends entirely on the exchange value or price of the object. At a halfpenny a bottle, the demand for champagne would be almost unlimited; at £5 a bottle there would be hardly any demand at all. So we are moving in a vicious circle.

To get out of this circle economists have given up the vain attempt to discover whether price is determined by supply and demand, or the other way about, and set themselves simply to define the relations that obtain between these various facts. This kind of analysis has been carried out most thoroughly by present-day economists.

To begin with, it has been established by experience that *whenever prices rise, demand diminishes* until a certain price is reached at which it ceases altogether.[1]

---

[1] This theorem seems to have been disproved by facts since the war, for though prices rose enormously there was no apparent falling-off in demand, and for many objects demand even increased. But there is no real contradiction here. The formula in the text must be understood, like every economic law, with the proviso, *other things being equal* — that is to say, assuming that the purchasing power of the consumer remains the same. Now such was not the case, for the means at the disposal of the majority of consumers increased enormously since the war, as a result of the increase in the supply of money in the shape of bank-notes and Treasury notes, and the consequent rise in wages and profits. But as soon as the issue of paper money

This law can be graphically represented in a very simple manner. Draw a horizontal line, and mark off at equal distances along it the prices of any commodity, using the figures 1, 2, 3, 4, ... etc. to represent the price in any unit — pounds, francs, or dollars. Represent the quantity demanded at the price of 1 unit by a vertical line of any length *a* (for instance, the number of pounds or yards or gallons demanded at the price of £1), and then draw other vertical lines on the same scale showing the quantities demanded at the other prices.   These lines will be seen to get smaller and smaller till they reach zero.[1] Now join the tops of these vertical lines by another line. This line will fall more or less rapidly, and will always end by disappearing in the horizontal line, thus showing in a striking manner how demand varies in relation to price. It is called a *demand curve*.

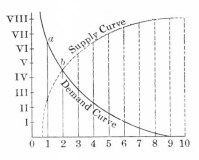

It is not for nothing that we call it a *curve*. It would be highly improbable that it should be a straight line like the side of a triangle, for that would mean that the demand varied exactly in proportion to the price, which scarcely ever happens. As a rule, demand decreases faster than the price rises, for the simple reason that the rich are far less numerous than the poor, so that a slight rise of price is sufficient to make the commodity inaccessible to the masses. This fact gives a concave form to the curve.   But its form varies with each particular commodity. For some, the curve descends very rapidly (or rises rapidly, if we look at the converse process), notably for articles of luxury. Thus if the price of motor-cars were halved, the number of buyers might possibly increase tenfold. In that case the curve would have a much steeper gradient than in our figure — a most precipitous slope, indeed. On the other hand there are commodities for which the demand falls only very slightly in spite of a rise of price; this is notably the case with objects of prime necessity. Thus the consumption of bread would hardly diminish at all even if the price were doubled, for the ordinary ration

ceased to increase — in 1920 — the law of demand immediately resumed its sway: the consumer "struck," and the fall in prices began — although, to tell the truth, it is impossible to say exactly which of these two proceedings started the other.

[1] In all such graphs the vertical lines are called *ordinates* and the horizontal ones *abscissae*.

is essential; and we should scarcely consume any more if the price were halved, for we eat it rather from necessity than for pleasure.

The curve, therefore, is sometimes concave, sometimes convex, and sometimes irregular — rising and falling in leaps. No two of them are alike, so that a well-trained economist can say from merely looking at a demand curve, with nothing else to guide him: "That is coal," or, "That is wheat."

Each commodity, then, might have its diagrammatic portrait, its distinctive mark or label, like the finger-print of a criminal who has passed through the anthropometrical department, or, if we prefer a nobler comparison, like the lines in the solar spectrum by which the physicist can recognize each of the elements.

And now, what about supply? Naturally it varies in the opposite way. *With each rise in price, the amount offered increases,* and a "supply curve" can be drawn which will present features similar to those of the demand curve. It will even be much more variable still, for does not supply depend ultimately upon production? According, therefore, as we are dealing with an article whose production is strictly limited (like works of art, or famous vintages of wine), or with an industry subject to a diminishing return (that is to say, one in which the cost of production increases more than the amount of the product, like agricultural produce), or, on the contrary, with one in which the more we produce the more the cost of production diminishes (which is the case with most industrial products) — the upward rise of the supply curve will be more or less bold or restrained as the case may be.[1]

Now place these two curves, the demand curve and the supply curve, one on top of the other, as in the figure given on page 195. The curves will necessarily cross, since they move in opposite directions, and the point of intersection is of capital importance, for it marks the exact psychological moment at which the quantities offered and demanded are equal, so that exchange takes place, as it were, instantaneously, like a chemical combination. If from this point, marked *b* in the figure, a perpendicular be dropped to the base line where the prices are marked, it will point, like the needle of a balance, to the current or market price — £2.

"And after that," the sceptics will say, "what does all that teach

---

[1] Supply generally begins by increasing rapidly when the price rises, but, having reached a certain limit, it slackens, no matter what the increase in price may be, because production gets out of breath, as it were, and cannot keep up. This movement of supply is shown in the figure above as a rapidly rising curve at first, and then a gentle slope approaching the horizontal.

us? Will all these curves enable us to foretell a rise in coffee or bread?" — Alas! no; but it is something at any rate to find neat and accurate formulas to express notions that were a bit sketchy before.

So far we have assumed the existence of any number of sellers and buyers, which is exactly what is meant by a system of free competition. But if we suppose that there is only one seller or only one buyer, obviously the whole situation is changed. This second case is what is called a system of monopoly.

It must not be imagined that under a system of monopoly the price is subject to no rule but the pleasure of the monopolist, for even under this system there is a law of prices, just as under the system of competition. For the seller is obliged, in his own interest, to fix a price that shall ensure him a maximum sale.

However, the price will generally be higher under a monopoly system than under a competitive one, because if the monopolist has no interest in fixing a price that will prevent his selling, he has still less interest in fixing it at the lowest possible point. He will choose the price that yields him the maximum net profit, even if he has to allow part of his merchandise to be lost or systematically destroyed.

Competition, on the contrary, ensures the minimum price — the price that is closest to the cost of production — because the sellers, in their anxiety to dispose of their goods, contend for customers, and undersell each other with that object, hoping that the increased number of buyers will make up for the decrease in profits. This is not always true, however, for we have seen above (p. 126) that too great an increase in the number of producers or sellers may result in raising the cost of production and consequently the price as well.

On the other hand, it is evidently to the interest of the monopolist to reduce the cost price, and in this he may succeed better than a competitive system does. We have cited some remarkable instances of this in dealing with trusts.[1]

V. THE QUANTITY THEORY OF PRICE

Price, as we have already seen (p. 56), is only one way of expressing value. It is value measured in money, or, in other words, it is the

---

[1] The distinction between competition and monopoly is never an absolute one, for they are both very rarely found in a pure state. We almost always meet with an intermediate condition of things, more or less closely approaching one or other of the extremes. There is no petty tradesman without his petty monopoly, if it be only that of being established at a certain street corner; and every monopolist has to submit to a certain amount of competition — even the French government, with its tobacco monopoly, has to put up with the competition of smuggled tobacco.

quantity of money that must be given in exchange for any commodity or any service in order to obtain it. It is evident that the greater the value of an object the greater will be the quantity of money that must be given to acquire it, or, what comes to the same thing, the smaller will be the quantity of the object that can be obtained with a given sum of money.

Price, therefore, like value itself, is merely a relation or ratio between two things. Now we know that if we change one of the two terms of a ratio, we necessarily change the ratio itself. If the length of a yard were to become to-morrow only half what it is to-day, owing to the shrinking of the standard that regulates it, it is obvious that we should think that a change had taken place in the dimensions of all objects that were not directly under our eyes, and whose measurements we were reading, for where we expected to find a yard we should henceforth find two. Yet in reality nothing of the kind would have taken place: it would be merely an optical illusion produced by the shrinking of the unit of measurement.

Similarly, if gold and silver were to lose half their value, in consequence of some much less miraculous cause, such as their superabundance, for instance, then it is clear that the price of all objects — that is to say, their value expressed in money — would appear to us to have doubled. And in this case we could not correct the error by looking at the objects, or touching them, for in matters of value we can learn nothing from our senses.

We can therefore formulate this law: *every variation in the value of money produces an inversely proportional variation in prices.*

It would be incorrect, however, to turn the formula round and say that every variation in the price of any object whatever necessarily implies an inverse variation in the value of money, for this variation in the price may also be caused by something in the object itself — for instance, in the case of wheat, a rise of price may be caused by a deficient harvest.

Consequently, whenever we are faced by a rise or a fall in prices, there are two kinds of causes to be studied: (1) those which affect the value of the particular commodity called "money"; (2) those which affect the value of any commodity that is on the market.

The specific causes that act on the value of goods are incapable of classification, for every commodity is subject to innumerable influences that are peculiar to itself. Every event, political and moral as well as economic, has an effect on prices. If there is a rise in wheat, or rubber, or house-rent, or pictures by old masters, each of these kinds of wealth must be separately investigated to discover the causes which have affected its value, and these causes will have no necessary connection with each other.

But if we look at the other term of the ratio — money — we can formulate general propositions that will apply to all cases, since money is the common denominator of all prices.

Now there are four causes of variation in the value of money. Three of these act in the same direction and the fourth inversely.

(a) The main element that affects the value of money is the *quantity* of it. We may therefore lay down this second law, corresponding to the one just enunciated: *every variation in the quantity of money produces a directly proportional variation in prices.* If the quantity of money is doubled, therefore, we must conclude from this formula that, other things being equal, prices will be doubled. Why is this? Because money is subject to the general law that every commodity depreciates in value when it is abundant, and appreciates when it is scarce. If, then, the number of coins is doubled, each of them will lose half its value, which means that two of them will have to be given instead of one, in order to obtain any object.

This can be proved in another way, for exchange is not a simple comparing of two things, like weighing, and money is not only an instrument of measurement; it is also an instrument of acquisition: all demand operates by means of it. We can say, therefore, that if everyone comes to possess twice as much money, the demand for every product will be doubled, and the doubling of the demand will cause a doubling of the price.

This law, which is called the *quantity theory* of money, and the discovery of which is one of Ricardo's titles to fame, is nowadays very much discredited.

That is the fate of all the so-called classical theories. They begin by being admired, but it is soon discovered that they are not sufficiently close to the truth, but only rough approximations. Then the critical economist comes along and shows them to be totally inaccurate. Such was the fate of the famous theory of supply and demand (see above, p. 193). Yet there was something valuable in it — so much, indeed, that we can scarcely do without it in current speech. And it is the same with the quantity theory of money. No doubt, if we take it in an absolute sense, and declare, as we have just done, that prices are doubled whenever the value of money is doubled, we run the risk of being contradicted by facts, for the quantity of money is only one of the factors that operate on prices: there are others also, as we shall see shortly. But it cannot be denied that it is at all events one of these factors, and even the most important of them. The economist has every right, just as the scientific experimenter has, to look at only one of the causes of a phenomenon, and neglect all the rest. So, to restore their truth to the formulas we have just enunciated, we have only to add the saving clause, "other things being equal." And that is how they were understood by the classical economists who first formulated them. They were not so blind as to fail to see that other causes also acted on money — not to mention those that act on commodities in general — and that they might neutralize each other.

It is a universally recognized fact that wherever money is superabundant, prices are very high. In every gold-mining region everything is paid for at fabulous prices. In the same way, whenever in the course of history the quantity of the precious metals has been suddenly increased, there has been a marked rise in prices. This happened, for instance, in the sixteenth century, after the discovery of America, a period when the rise in prices astounded contemporary observers the more because they could not account for it; and again in the middle of the nineteenth century, after the discovery of the Californian and Australian mines. The last example is the great and universal rise of prices that preceded the war and followed on the discovery of the Transvaal mines. Moreover, it is the same when there is a superabundance of paper money, as we shall see later.

(b) *The greater or smaller rapidity of circulation* of money is equivalent to a variation in its quantity, and consequently produces the same effect. It is evident that if a railway company can run its trucks twice as many miles in a day, it comes to the same thing as if it had twice as many of them. That is why a steamship is three times as useful as a sailing ship of the same tonnage. Similarly, therefore, if a piece of gold can be used for three times as many exchange transactions in a day, it is the same as if it was three pieces, and its value is reduced accordingly.

The rapidity of circulation of money depends in its turn on the density of the population. At the end of the day a given coin has passed through many more hands in a large town than in the country. For this reason the purchasing power of money is lower in towns than in the country, and prices are therefore higher. They would be higher still if this cause of depreciation, due to rapidity of circulation, were not partly compensated by the multiplicity of exchange transactions, as we shall see in paragraph (d).

But, of course, money that is stored away and does not circulate at all has no effect on prices. Money only affects prices in so far as it is an instrument of demand.

(c) The third cause is the *extent to which modes of credit have been elaborated*. These enable us to dispense with money, and consequently make it less useful and less in demand.

As far as bank-notes and inconvertible paper money are concerned, their issue is equivalent to an increase in the amount of metallic money, and ought in consequence to result in depreciation and a rise in prices. It must not be forgotten, however, that the quantity of money shut up in the banks must be deducted from the value of this paper money, and that notes can only take the place of money in circulation (see below, Chapter VI).

But it is above all by the system of cheques and book credits that credit takes the place of money. Without these powerful auxiliaries money would have been insufficient, despite the discovery of new gold mines, to meet the general increase in the needs of commerce, and we should very probably have seen an opposite movement to the one we have hitherto seen, namely, a marked rise in the value of money and a consequent fall in prices.

(d) *The greater or smaller activity of exchange* (sales, loans, discounts, wage-payments, etc.) also affects the value of money, but in a direction opposite to the three preceding causes. That is to say, the greater the number of the transactions that have to be made, the more is money in demand, and consequently the more its value rises. And since this is generally the case in all countries, there is a force residing in this increase of demand for money that tends to raise its value, or at least to prevent its depreciation, even when its quantity increases; to increase its final utility; and to provide it, as it were, with a parachute.

This question of the causes of variations in prices was being keenly discussed even before the war, owing to the great rise in prices that took place in all countries during the later years of the nineteenth century. It gave rise to innumerable enquiries in the papers and discussions on the part of learned societies. The rise after the year 1896 — the year that marked the starting-point of the ascending curve — varied from 30% to 40%, according to the country, and the majority of economists ascribed it to the enormous increase in the output of the gold mines. This output had, in fact, increased fivefold between 1883 and 1912.

But the rise in prices before the war was as nothing to the astounding rise due to the war — a rise that has varied in different countries from 150% to 1,000%, and has even gone higher than that. Can this teach us anything as to the quantity theory? Can it be explained by an increase in the quantity of money? — Certainly not, if we are referring to gold, or even silver. For the gold disappeared completely from circulation, hiding itself in the vaults of the various State banks as if it had gone back into the mine, while silver and copper grew scarce and insufficient to meet the need. But, on the other hand, the quantity of paper money increased enormously, and, since it is now the only kind of money in circulation, does it not sufficiently explain the rise in prices?

The increase of paper money undoubtedly had a great effect on prices, by multiplying purchasing power and consequently *demand*. But yet it was not the sole cause. Other and still more powerful causes operated to reduce *supply:* scarcity, or even destruction, of existing stocks; difficulty, or even impossibility, of replacing them owing to shortage of labour; lack of means of transport and consequent enormous rise in freights; and so forth.[1]

Price variations cause great disturbances in social conditions. Assuming that cheapness is the usual sign of abundance, should we not be right in thinking that low prices are the ideal to be desired and high ones a danger to be feared? This is not so, however. On the contrary, we see a rise awaited and greeted like economic fine weather, while a fall is as depressing as the rain. The man who speculates on a rise is regarded with an indulgent eye, while the one who speculates on a fall is scorned like a bird of ill omen.

This apparent contradiction is easily explained by the fact that a rise benefits traders, manufacturers, and landowners, and indirectly the workers, whose wages sooner or later follow the rise of prices — in one word, all who make up the *active* part of the population, — whereas a fall benefits only the silent mass of consumers.

Yet a rise or fall in prices is only a sign of activity or abundance when it results from causes affecting commodities. When it arises from scarcity or abundance of money it implies no change in production. It might even be thought that in this latter case it must make absolutely no difference, being purely nominal. But it is not so. No doubt price variations, so far as they result entirely from variations in the monetary standard, make little difference to those

---

[1] If the rise in prices since the war had been due entirely to an excess of paper money, then evidently the country that issued most paper should have experienced the greatest rise. Now this was not the case. Of all the belligerent countries it was France that (next to Russia) issued most notes: the amount increased sevenfold, from 5,800 million francs in July 1914 to 38,000 million francs in 1919. Yet it was not in France that the rise of prices was greatest. It may even be remarked that while the issue of notes did not increase, and even diminished a little, after 1919, it was precisely from that date to the end of 1920 that the rise in prices was most rapid.

who buy with one hand and sell again with the other, but they have important consequences for long-period creditors, and particularly for annuitants who have to receive a fixed sum of money for a large number of years or even for life; and they are important in the opposite way to debtors who have to pay such a fixed sum, among whom the greatest of all is the State. It is plain that the depreciation of money is as disastrous to the first of these classes as it is advantageous to the second.

These disturbances of price, whether for good or for evil, are on the whole unfair, since they alter the conditions laid down in contracts for loans and other payments. It would be desirable, therefore, if some means could be found of avoiding them. This can be attempted in two different ways: either by regulating the quantity of (metallic or paper) money according to need — a proceeding called the *stabilization* of money, which is too complicated to be described here; — or by dealing with the commodities instead, which is the essential function of cartels, as we have already explained (p. 177).

VI. ADVANTAGES ARISING FROM EXCHANGE

The following are the advantages that arise from exchange:

(1) Exchange enables us *to make the best use of wealth which would otherwise remain useless.*

Without exchange, what would England do with its coal, the Transvaal with its gold, Tunis with its phosphates, or Brazil with its coffee and cinchona? In analyzing the conception of wealth, we found that the indispensable condition for any object whatever to count as wealth was its capacity for being utilized (p. 38). Now in order that this may be effected, the wealth must be conveyed by means of exchange to the person who is to use it — the quinine to the fever patient, the phosphates to the farmer, the coal to the manufacturer. Suppose that exchange were everywhere abolished to-morrow, by a universal decree, and that all persons and all countries were compelled to keep for themselves all the wealth that they produced. What an enormous quantity of wealth would thus be smitten into uselessness at a single blow, and fit only to be left to rot where it stands! Not only must we say that without exchange the greater part of wealth would remain useless, but we must add that in that case it would never have been produced. Exchange, therefore, increases utility, and often even creates it.

We must regard exchange as the last of the series of productive acts that begins with invention (which is likewise an immaterial act) and continues throughout the whole range of agricultural, manufacturing, and transport operations, bringing the products step by step to their final destination, in the hands of those who will use them. Change of *form*, change of *place*, change of *ownership* — all three are equally indispensable to the attainment of the final result.

It is true that there are certain exchange and credit transactions which can hardly be said to be acts of production, such as the sale of houses, the sale of transferable securities on the Stock Exchange, running into millions of pounds, and that of pictures or furniture in the sale-room. For what difference does it make to production whether such and such a share or bond, picture or house, belongs to Peter or to Paul? These sales are purely legal transfers, of interest to the lawyer but not to the economist. We are only concerned here with transfers of the other kind — those that are connected with production.

Still, even in the case of the sale or hire, either of definite products or of land and capital, we are right in saying that though they do not constitute acts of commerce, they may yet be regarded as *creators of utility*, and therefore as productive, in the sense that the thing sold or hired always acquires more final utility (p. 92) by the very act of sale or hire, since it is evidently desired more by the buyer or borrower than by the seller or lender, for otherwise the seller would not have sold and the lender would not have lent.

(2) Exchange enables us *to make the best use of persons themselves and those of their productive powers which would otherwise remain idle*.

Observe, indeed, that if there were no exchange, each man would have to produce everything that was needful to satisfy his own wants. If his wants were ten in number, he would have to engage in ten different trades. No matter whether he did this well or ill, he would be obliged to regulate his production *not by his aptitudes but by his wants*. With the introduction of exchange the situation is completely altered. Everyone henceforth is sure of being able to obtain by exchange whatever he needs, so he devotes himself solely to the task that he can perform best. Henceforth he regulates his production *not by his wants but by his aptitudes or his means*. Before the era of exchange, everyone in the world had to produce what he needed most: now everyone devotes himself solely to producing what he can most easily produce. That is an important and marvellous simplification.

It may be said that the advantages just described are much like those afforded by division of labour; and, in fact, they are the same, but very greatly increased and multiplied. Without exchange, association and division of labour would of necessity require ·a previous agreement among those who were to work together: they would all have to agree to co-operate in the common task. But exchange *does away with the necessity for this previous agreement*, and thus enables the division of labour to extend beyond the narrow circle of the workshop or the family community and spread over the whole area of a vast country and even to the uttermost ends of the earth. Henceforth each man, near at hand or far off, will produce according to his natural or acquired aptitudes, and according to the natural properties of the region which he inhabits. He can devote himself entirely to one kind of work, and always put the same product on the market, with the certainty that owing to the ingenious mechanism of trade and transport he can obtain in exchange whatever other product he needs. It has often been observed that the things that each one of us consumes in a day are the combined result of the toil of hundreds or perhaps thousands of workers, united to one another by an invisible but very real bond of association.[1]

Exchange would be almost impossible if it had not created for itself certain indispensable instruments. These are:

(1) Professional agents called *merchants* or *traders*, to serve as intermediaries between producers and consumers;

(2) Meeting-places called *markets* to enable the owners of different objects to get into touch with each other;

(3) Instruments called *weights and measures*, to measure the quantities exchanged;

(4) *Means of transport*, to facilitate and accelerate the transfer of merchandise;

(5) An intermediate commodity called *money*, for the splitting-up of barter into sale and purchase.

Here we shall only study the last and most important of these instruments of exchange.

---

[1] It is said that Mr. Carnegie, the American millionaire, at a splendid banquet which he gave to the members of the Pan-American Congress in 1890, remarked with some pride: "Almost the whole world has contributed to the menu which is going to be put before you." Doubtless this was true: but the really wonderful thing is that a poor man could say exactly the same of *his* dinner. As M. de Laveleye has well said: "The poorest workman consumes the products of the two hemispheres. The wool for his clothes comes from Australia, the rice in his soup from India, the wheat in his bread from Illinois, the oil in his lamp from Pennsylvania, and his coffee from Java." (*Éléments d'Économie politique*, p. 198.)

CHAPTER II — METALLIC MONEY

I. HISTORY OF MONEY

It is not in virtue of any express agreement or social contract that certain objects have become *mediums of exchange*, but in consequence of certain advantages which forced them upon men's choice and marked them out for the performance of this high function.

The difficulties of barter (see above, p. 188) obliged men to choose an intermediate commodity to play a part in every act of exchange. They naturally chose the one that was most familiar to them and most commonly used — first of all the wild produce of nature, and later on articles which they had made. The cowrie shells of the coast tribes of Africa, and the cocoanuts and coloured feathers of the South Sea Islands, must have preceded, ethnographically if not chronologically, the arrow-heads of cut flint that are already industrial products.

In patriarchal societies this intermediate commodity was naturally their one and only form of wealth — cattle, whether buffalo, ox, or sheep, — and most Indo-European languages, even the Basque, have left us the memory of this primitive kind of money in the name they give to it.[1] The same fact is recalled by the figure stamped on some ancient coins, such as the bull's head at Athens.

Many other commodities, in different circumstances and in different lands, have played the part of this intermediate commodity — rice in Japan, bricks of tea in Central Asia, furs or blankets in the Hudson Bay Territory, calico or bars of salt in Central Africa. But among them all there is one class of objects that attracted man's attention very early and quickly superseded everything else in all societies that were in any way civilized. These were the precious metals: gold, silver, and copper.

Owing to their chemical properties that make them comparatively incapable of change, these are the only metals that are found in nature in a pure state — gold more so than silver, and silver more than copper. Consequently they were known and used by man before his metallurgical knowledge enabled him to know and use

---

[1] The chief example is the Latin word *pecunia*, which originally meant a herd of cattle. In Homer all values are reckoned in oxen — the value of the armour of Diomede and Glaucus, for instance. Hence arose the Greek phrase, "to put an ox on his tongue," meaning to bribe someone to keep silence.

other metals, such as iron. It is remarkable that the ancient legend of four ages — of gold, of silver, of copper, and of iron — arranges these four metals in the precise order in which they became known to man.[1] Their physical properties also — lustre, colour, and malleability — helped to make them much sought after in early times, both for ornament and for industrial purposes, and would be sufficient justification for the important part they have played in all ages and among all races.

These natural properties produce certain economic consequences of the highest importance, which give to the precious metals a very marked superiority over all other commodities. They are as follows:

(1) *Ease of transport.* — No other object is so valuable in proportion to its weight. The weight that a man can carry on his back is about 65 pounds. Now 65 pounds of coal would be worth about 9d.; the same weight of wheat, about 6s.; of wool, 25s. to 30s.; of copper, £2 to £4; of ivory, £30; of raw silk, £60; of silver (at par), £120; and of fine gold, £4,000 (at pre-war prices).

This characteristic is of enormous importance — much more so than would appear at first sight, for this reason. It is plain that if we could do away with the difficulty of transport for any commodity; if we could endow it with the capacity of being everywhere at once; if the whole world could be made into a single market for it; then the result would be that its value would be exactly the same everywhere. Suppose that such a commodity cost less in one country than in another. People would immediately come and transfer it from the first country to the second; and as transport, on our hypothesis, would present no difficulties and cost nothing, the slightest difference in value would suffice to make the operation profitable. Equilibrium, once destroyed, would therefore be instantly restored, just as the level of a liquid is instantly restored if its molecules are perfectly fluid.

Now as the precious metals are of all commodities, except precious stones, those which have the greatest value in the smallest volume, they are also the commodities whose transport is easiest and whose value will therefore most quickly recover its normal level. For 1% of its value, freight and insurance included, a cargo of gold or silver can be transported from one end of the world to the other, whereas the same weight of wheat or coal would cost 20%, 30%, or perhaps 100% of its value, according to the distance. Gold

[1] Gold, in fact, generally appears in nature in a pure state, while silver is always found in combination, as an ore. That is why, in Homer, silver and copper are more valuable, because more scarce, than gold.

rushes with the speed of the wind to the markets where its value is greatest.

It might seem to follow from this that the value of the precious metals ought to be the same, within 1% at any rate, all over the world. This, however, would be an exaggeration. On the contrary, their value is certainly not the same everywhere, and it is naturally lowest in places where they are produced. This explains the incredibly high prices reported so often from mining districts where gold issues from the earth like a spring — Australia half a century ago, and the Transvaal and the Klondyke more recently. None the less, the value of these metals may be considered as fulfilling quite satisfactorily the first requirement of a good measure of value — invariability from place to place.

(2) *Unlimited durability.* — In virtue of chemical properties that make them proof against almost any combination with air, water, or any other substance, gold and silver may be preserved without alteration. There is no other kind of wealth of which this can be said: animal and vegetable products decay, and even some metals, like iron, oxidize and crumble into dust.

This characteristic is almost as important as the first. It has the same effect in regard to *time* as the other has in regard to *place* — that is to say, invariability of value, at least relatively, from one period of time to another. Because of their durability, in virtue of which the same particles of metal may be coined and recoined for century after century, the precious metals are accumulated little by little into a mass of imposing size — something like four thousand million pounds-worth to-day, of which more than half is held by the United States, France, Russia, Germany, and England. Into this mass the supply produced every year is poured, as into a reservoir that is always growing larger, so that occasional variations tend to make less and less difference. In a rapid torrent the smallest increases in volume make enormous changes in the general level, but the greatest increases in the volume of the Rhône only raise the level of Lake Geneva a very few inches. Similarly the river of gold that pours into the world's treasury, whatever increases take place in its volume, can only raise its level very slowly. Thus, although the increase in the production of gold has been enormous in the last five and twenty years — the annual production having risen from £20,000,000 to more than £80,000,000, — yet this production represents only a small fraction of the existing stock of the two metals. Moreover, the whole of this annual supply of gold does not go to swell the stock of money — very far from it: a large part, between a third and a half, is diverted to industrial uses and to be hoarded in Eastern lands, so that the annual increase in the stock of money is scarcely £60,000,000, which represents a rate of increase of less than 3% on the total of at least 2,400 millions (counting gold alone).

How different is the case with wheat, for example. It does not last, but is consumed the first time it is used. When each new harvest comes along, the granaries are almost empty. If the wheat crop one year were doubled throughout the world, the total stock would be doubled likewise, and the fall in price would be terrible.

At the same time, variations in the output of the precious metals do, in the long run, become perceptible, for even at the small rate of increase of 3% the total stock would be doubled in thirty years. So although the value of these metals offers a sufficient guarantee of stability when only short periods of time are taken into account, it is far from doing so to the same extent when we consider longer periods. Hence arise certain serious disadvantages to which we shall have to return later.

(3) *Identity of quality.* — As the precious metals are what chemists call elements, they are always identical with themselves. An experienced merchant can distinguish Odessa wheat from California wheat, or a tuft of wool from an Australian sheep from one grown on the back of a Spanish merino; but the cleverest goldsmith, or the chemist equipped with the most powerful reagents, can find no difference between Australian gold and gold from the Ural Mountains. There is no need of "samples" here.

(4) *Difficulty of counterfeiting.* — The precious metals can be recognized at once by the eye, the ear, and the touch, owing to their distinctive colour, metallic ring, and weight. They are thus easily distinguished from all other substances, and even from other metals.[1]

(5) *Perfect divisibility.* — This must be understood not only in the mechanical sense — gold and silver being, in fact, extraordinarily ductile and malleable — but also in the economic sense. Divide an ingot into a hundred pieces, and you make no change whatever in its value. The value of each piece is exactly proportional to its weight, and the value of all the pieces together is exactly equal to that of the original ingot.[2]

[1] Nickel coins may be taken for silver ones from their appearance, but the difference is clearly apparent to the sense of touch.

[2] Precious stones are superior to the precious metals in the first of these five properties — great value in small bulk, — but in all other respects they compare very unfavourably with them. They are very variable in quality, they are capable of being successfully counterfeited, and, above all, they cannot be divided without losing practically the whole of their value.

It is one thing to use the precious metals as an instrument of exchange, and another thing to use them as money, in the strict sense of the term. Progress from the one to the other is marked by three distinct stages.

(1) The precious metals were first used in the form of crude ingots. In every exchange transaction, therefore, these ingots had to be first *weighed* and then *assayed*. The legal forms of ancient Roman law, such as *mancipatio* and its accompanying *libripens*, retained the symbolism of the time when the instrument of exchange — silver or bronze — was weighed. And in China, where coined money was not employed, the merchants could have been seen, until recently, carrying their scales and touchstone at their girdle.

(2) When men grew tired of having to carry out this double process every time they made an exchange, it occurred to them to use shaped ingots, whose weight and fineness were determined beforehand and certified, if necessary, by some official seal or stamp. The lawgiver who first conceived this ingenious plan may claim the glory of having really invented money. For thereafter the ingots were no longer *weighed* but *counted*, and that is the characteristic of money. It seems likely that it was a king of Lydia, a successor of Gyges, who coined the first money, about 700 to 650 B.C. Specimens of his coins may still be seen in the British Museum. They are made neither of gold nor of silver, but of an alloy of these two metals which the Greeks called "electron," and instead of being round they are egg-shaped or bean-shaped, and bear no marks except a few strokes and three indentations. In China also, until quite recently, the ingots often bore the mark of certain business houses, intended to certify their weight and fineness.

(3) One step yet remained to be taken. Not only was the shape of the cubical or irregular ingot somewhat inconvenient, but also, in spite of the stamp, nothing was easier than to "clip" it without detection. It was still necessary to weigh it, therefore, to make sure that it was intact. To remedy these practical drawbacks men were led to adopt the form of coined money that is familiar now to all civilized peoples — little discs covered on both sides and on the edge with raised impressions, so that no one can file them or tamper with them without leaving visible traces on the design.

Thus was reached the typical coin or piece of money in the proper sense of the word, and for hundreds of years it has not been appreciably modified. We can adopt for it the definition given by Jevons: "*Coins are ingots of which the weight and fineness are guaranteed by*

*the government, and certified by the integrity of designs impressed on
the surfaces of the metal."*

This is certainly one of the inventions that stand in the front rank
in the history of civilization — not in the same rank as the invention
of the alphabet, but not far behind it. Imagine what would be the
state of commerce and industry — not to mention economic science
— if there were no means of measuring value! We should live like
savages under a system of barter. Before accepting an order, every
manufacturer and every exporter has to calculate his cost price and
his selling price, and a farthing more or a farthing less per unit of
product may make all the difference for him between fortune and
ruin.

Nor is it only a question of profit: it is also a question of justice.
It is not for nothing that the allegorical figure of Justice always carries a pair of scales. The exploitation of which the negroes of Africa
are victims when they sell their rubber or their ground-nuts, is very
largely due to the absence of money, which conceals it. It is a fact
well known to colonials that as soon as money begins to be employed
in sales, the condition of the natives is very much improved.

II.   FUNCTIONS OF MONEY

We have just said that money as a measure of value is one of the
finest instruments of civilization. But what about money as a form
of wealth? Does it merit a place apart, an exceptional position,
among all the kinds of wealth? — That is another question.

The answer given by common opinion is quite definite. In every
age and in every place, except among savages, money has occupied
an exceptional place in the thoughts and desires of men.

It would be interesting to trace through history the various manifestations of this idea that confounds gold with wealth. We find
it in the attempts of the alchemists of the Middle Ages to change
other metals into gold and thus to discover what they called the
philosopher's stone, thinking far more of an economic revolution
than of a chemical discovery. We find it again in the enthusiasm
that was aroused in the Old World by the arrival of the first galleons
from America, and that led men to imagine that in that Eldorado
was to be found the end of all their misery. We find it in the complicated "systems" attempted by all governments during the sixteenth and seventeenth centuries, to attract specie into countries
that possessed ncne, and to prevent its export from those that had

it. And even to-day we see the same notion at work in the anxiety with which statesmen and financiers watch the import and export of specie which is caused by variations in the export and import of merchandise. The celebrated financier, John Law, declared even at the beginning of the eighteenth century that an increase in the amount of coin added to the value of a country.

But if we ask the economists if money is an exceptional kind of wealth, the answer will be very different. We may even say that it was by protesting against the popular idea — which the economists regarded as a prejudice — that political economy first revealed its existence. The science had scarcely been born, and was still in its infancy, when it affirmed through the lips of Boisguillebert (1697) that "it is very certain that money is not a good in itself, and that its quantity has nothing to do with the opulence of a country." Since then, every economist has treated money with utter disdain, declaring it to be merely a commodity like any other commodity, and even very inferior to others, as being itself incapable of directly satisfying any want or procuring us any enjoyment. Consequently, they say, it is *the only commodity of which it can be said that its abundance or scarcity is a matter of complete indifference.* If there are few coins in a country, each of them will have a greater purchasing power: if there are many, the purchasing power of each will be smaller; so what difference does it make?

These two opinions, however contradictory in appearance, are very easily reconciled. The public is right from the *individual* point of view — the only one in which it is interested. The economists are right if we ignore individuals, for the utility of money is not the same for society as it is for them.

For individuals, money has not one but three distinct utilities:

(1) It is *the only direct instrument of acquisition.* Every piece of money must be regarded as an order drawn on the total stock of existing wealth, and giving the bearer the right to claim a part of this wealth up to the value indicated on the coin.[1]

Money may take the place of every other kind of wealth because

---

[1] Coins are orders that are superior to other credit instruments because they carry their own guarantee with them: their value is assured, in part at least, by the value of the metal they contain. "If you know how to read, with the eyes of the mind, the inscription which a coin bears, you will clearly distinguish the words: 'Give to the bearer a service equivalent to that which he has given to society, a value that is disclosed, proved, and measured by the value that I myself contain.'" (Bastiat, *Maudit argent.*) At the same time we must make some demur to the optimistic assumption that every piece of money really represents a *service rendered.*

its possession is enough to procure for us anything that we want. It is like Aladdin's lamp: the genii are enlisted in its service.

It is clearly our individual interest to have as many of these "orders" as possible, and the more we have the richer we are. Of course we know well that, in themselves, they can neither satisfy hunger nor quench thirst. Men have never been stupid enough to imagine that, and, long before it was pointed out by economists, ancient legend had taught the same truth with its picture of King Midas dying of hunger in the midst of the food that his avarice had turned into gold. But, none the less, we all regard these orders as infinitely more convenient than any other form of wealth, and we are perfectly right in doing so.

In fact, given the present organization of society, we know that anyone who desires to obtain an object that he has not actually produced (which is the case with the vast majority of us), can get it only by means of a double process, which consists in, *first*, exchanging the produce of his labour, or his labour itself, for money, and *secondly*, exchanging this money for the object he wishes to acquire. These two operations are called, respectively, *selling* and *buying*.

Now the second of these operations, buying or purchase, is very simple: with money it is always easy to procure what one wants. But the other operation, that of selling, is much more difficult: it is not always easy to procure money with just any object, even one of great value. So the owner of money is much more favourably situated than the owner of goods, for, to satisfy his wants, he has only one very easy step to take, whereas the man who owns goods has to take two steps, one of which is often a very difficult one. It has been well said that a particular commodity answers only to a *special and definite want*, while money meets *any want whatever*, at our own choice. The owner of even a very useful commodity may not know what to do with it. But the owner of money is never at a loss: he can always find someone to accept it, and if by any chance he cannot use it at once, he can always keep it till a more favourable opportunity appears, which is not always possible with other kinds of wealth.

(2) Money has another very important quality, besides that of being the only direct instrument of acquisition. It is *the only instrument for the discharge of debts*. No other kind of wealth enjoys this privilege, for law, as well as custom, recognizes no other method of payment than that of money. Everyone in the commercial or industrial world is always a debtor for larger or smaller amounts, and it would be no use for the merchant or manufacturer to possess

a stock of goods even exceeding the amount of his debts, if he has no money. (It has happened more than once in cases of bankruptcy that the assets were greater than the liabilities, when everything was included.) If he cannot meet his liabilities at the appointed date with that special form of wealth which consists in coined money, he is made bankrupt. Is it surprising, therefore, that men should attach so much importance to a commodity on the possession of which their credit and their honour may at any moment depend?

Money, then, is an instrument of freedom. And besides freeing men from the bondage of debt, we may use the word "freedom" in the wider sense, and say that it frees them also from the original debt that all the sons of Adam seemed to have contracted — the obligation to work.

(3) Money has yet a third part to play — that of *storing and preserving value* until the time when it is needed. This is the part it plays whenever it is hoarded. It is true that what determines this use of money is not so much its character as coin, as the fact that it is a precious metal. In former times it was not only money that was hoarded, but gold and silver vessels and ornaments, and even precious stones as well. But it is more convenient to hoard coins than plate or jewels.

Every individual, therefore, has good grounds for thinking himself more or less rich according to the amount of money he possesses. But if, instead of considering the position of an individual, we look at the mass of individuals that make up society, we get a different point of view. Here it is that the economists' thesis — that the amount of money is a matter of indifference — is verified. It matters little to me, indeed, if the quantity of money in my possession is multiplied by ten, *if it is just the same for everyone else.* In such an event I shall be no wealthier, because wealth is purely relative, and I shall not be able to procure any greater amount of satisfaction than before, since the total amount of wealth on which these "orders" are drawn has not increased. Henceforth each "order" will give me a claim to a share only one-tenth as great as before; each piece of money will have only a tenth of its former purchasing power; or, in other words, all prices will be ten times as high, — and my position will be unchanged.

But let us go a step further and look at countries *in their relations with each other.* Then it will appear that countries, like individuals, have an interest in being well provided with money. If the quantity of money in this country were to be multiplied by ten, this would make no change in the position of Englishmen in relation to each other, supposing that the increase is the same for them all. But it would make a great difference to this country in relation to other countries, and economists have sometimes been wrong in seeming to deny so obvious a fact, in their fight against the mercantile system. It is true enough that money would depreciate here, owing to its very abundance; but it would keep intact its purchasing power in foreign markets. We should employ it in the purchase of foreign goods, and so it might procure for us an increase of satisfaction proportional to the increase in its amount.

The thesis of the economists that the abundance or scarcity of money is a matter of indifference only becomes absolutely true, therefore, when we consider neither individuals nor even countries, but *the whole human race*. Then, indeed, coined gold and silver has no other utility than as an instrument of measurement. A sufficient quantity is required for the needs of exchange, and neither more nor less than that. As these needs go on increasing progressively, it is as well that the quantity of money should increase correspondingly, and it is even desirable, as we shall see in the next section, that it should increase rather faster than the needs. But it is certain that the discovery of gold mines a hundred times richer than those now existing would not benefit man at all. Such an event would even be disagreeable rather than otherwise, for gold would then be worth no more than copper; so we should have to load our pockets with as cumbrous a kind of money as that which Lycurgus sought to force upon the Spartans.

III. VARIATIONS IN THE PRODUCTION OF GOLD AND SILVER AND THEIR EFFECTS

Gold seems to have been abundant in ancient times, at least relatively to economic needs, which were limited, and relatively also to silver. In Greece the relative values of the two metals were approximately 1 to 10; under the Roman Empire the value of silver and prices do not seem to have been very different from what they are to-day.

But after the invasions of the Teutonic barbarians the accumulated treasures disappeared, and gold and silver became very scarce. Their scarcity, and consequently their value, seems to have reached its highest point in the time of Charlemagne, which means that prices were then at their lowest. A shilling at that time was equivalent to a modern (pre-war) pound.

The production of the precious metals increased enormously as a result of the discovery of America. There was a veritable flood of specie, and prices rose fivefold in the course of the sixteenth century.

Then production slackened again when the stocks accumulated by the natives were exhausted, and it was necessary to exploit the mines. In the course of the three following centuries the average annual output did not exceed £1,200,000. It increased after the beginning of the nineteenth century, but is was not until after 1850, when the Californian and Australian goldfields were discovered, that the average production exceeded £24,000,000. Then it slackened again with the exhaustion of these mines, but took an unprecedented flight in the last years of the century owing to the exploitation of the mines of the Transvaal and the Klondyke. In 1912 the production of gold alone amounted to nearly a hundred million pounds. Since the war it has again slackened, and in 1919 it fell to about £76,000,000.

The production of silver has fluctuated in very much the same way, though the variations have not been parallel. And if we draw a diagram to show the production of these two metals and the movement of prices for the last thousand years, we shall notice that the movements of the two curves more or less correspond, which seems an indisputable proof of the quantity theory (see above, p. 196).

Will it be the same in the future? It is to be expected that it will. Gold and silver are not so scarce as it is thought: they exist everywhere — in minute quantities, to be sure, but improvements in metallurgy are continually lowering the point below which the extraction of the metal from the ore ceases to be remunerative. It is probable, therefore, that the metals will become increasingly plentiful, and increasingly less valuable in consequence. We should be justified in concluding, then, that in so far as gold and silver remain the monetary standards, the rise in prices will be continuous and unlimited.

But at this very moment we are in the presence of a monetary revolution which is removing gold from circulation and replacing it by bank-notes. During the war, the substitution of paper for metallic money was complete, the gold remaining buried in the vaults of the great banks or being exported in small quantities for making payments abroad, and that not only in belligerent countries but even in neutral ones as well.

The use of gold being thus more and more restricted through the competition of paper money, the paradoxical result followed that while the prices of everything, and notably of all other metals, increased threefold or even fivefold, *the value of gold diminished.* How can we tell, it will be asked, whether gold has changed its value, since there is only itself by which to measure it? We can tell by comparing its value with that of other commodities, or with that of silver. Or we can say, if this makes it any clearer, that the price of an ingot of gold expressed in bank-notes has risen much less than the price of coal, wheat, iron, or anything else. And the price of an ounce of gold expressed in ounces of silver, which had risen as high as 30, fell again nearly to the par price, 15.[1]

It is precisely this fall in the value of gold that has been one of the main causes of the diminution in its output that we noticed just above.

This does not mean, however, that gold will not continue to play an important monetary part and even increase its importance, for by ceasing to be a national form of money it will become an international one. If it is no longer employed in payments between individuals it will be used for payments between nations.

Will this substitution of paper for metallic money result in an acceleration of the secular depreciation of money and the rise of prices that we have just mentioned? To judge from existing facts, which show us a greater rise in prices in five years than took place before in five centuries, the answer must be in the affirmative. But perhaps this reply would be too hasty, for it would be easier, at least for a prudent government, to stabilize prices with paper money whose issue is regulated at will, than with money whose production depends on the chance discovery of mines. In other words, artificial money lends itself better to regulation than natural money (see below, Chapter IV).

The depreciation of the monetary standard is a phenomenon of considerable social importance, and one whose effects must be regarded, on the whole, as beneficial. To begin with, its ordinary result is a rise in prices. Now a rise in prices is a useful stimulus to production; it keeps the spirit of enterprise on the alert; it encourages a rise of wages; it acts as a tonic; it is a symptom of sound economic health. It is true that if these fortunate effects are intelligible enough when the rise in prices is due to an increase in commercial activity and in demand, it ought not to be the same when it bears no relation to the movement of business and is simply

[1] In France the price of a kilogramme of gold rose to 10,000 or 11,000 francs, while its normal pre-war value was 3,100 francs; so its price was trebled. But the price of other commodities rose much higher than this, for the index number rose to over 400, which means a fourfold increase (see above, p. 61).

caused, as in the case we are considering, by the depreciation of money. But this does not matter: appearance has here the virtues of reality.

Such has been the case in Europe since the war. We have lamented the dearness of everything, but the high prices have acted as a stimulus befitting a time when a mighty effort is required from every country to set industry on its feet again. This became plain as soon as the fall began, at the end of 1920, for it acted like a shower of cold water.

Moreover, a fall in the value of money is favourable to debtors, since they can discharge their liabilities by paying a smaller value than they received. To repeat a famous phrase that was applied to the discovery of the mines of the New World, depreciation means a new way to pay old debts. It acts like a fall in the rate of interest, or, still more, like an automatic redemption of capital.[1]

It is true that depreciation is just as prejudicial to the interests of the consumer and the creditor as it is favourable to those of the producer and the debtor. But the injury it does them is itself a benefit. As far as the consumer is concerned, he can make up for the increase in his expenses by the increased value of his produce if he is an independent producer, or by his rise in wages if he is a wage-earner. If he consumes without producing anything, so much the worse for him: he is justly punished by the rise in prices. As for the creditor, if he has given credit for short periods, as is customary in commerce, then the depreciation of money does not sensibly affect him. If his credit is for a long period or perpetual, if it is based on investments in government securities, landed property, railway bonds or municipal loans, etc., then he simply belongs to the class of unproductive consumers, and it is good for him to be reminded by the continual reduction in his income that he is playing the part of a parasite and that, if he wants to keep his social position or to hand it on to his children, he will do well to play a more active part, or at least to teach his children to do so. A great French

---

[1] The position of countries that borrowed hundreds of millions during the war is, from this point of view, singularly disquieting. If the depreciation of money continues and increases, it will trouble them as governments, but as debtors they will be bound to rejoice, since their load of debt will be lightened accordingly. If the currency fell to a tenth of its former value, then the interest on the various public debts would represent only one-tenth of its nominal amount. If, on the other hand, as we hope and try to accomplish, the value of the paper note gets back to par, then the State, which borrowed in depreciated money, will have to pay back twice or three times what it received, which will be an overwhelming burden. This is a contingency that is never mentioned!

financier, Laffitte, who was certainly no socialist, said long ago, speaking of the man of independent means: "He must either work or reduce his wants.   The capitalist's part is that of an idler: his task should be to economize, and it is none too heavy a one."

Moreover, these *rentiers* have the less reason for complaint because, if they are sensible, they have plenty of means of avoiding this penalty and counteracting the effects of the fall in the value of money.   They can do this either by purchasing securities *below par* — below the price at which the debtor has promised to redeem them — and thus profiting by their increase in value; or else by investing part of their fortune in the *shares* of industrial companies, whose price rises with the rise in the price of the produce, unlike bonds and other securities.

Those who suffer most from the continued depreciation of money are corporations, such as charitable foundations, scientific societies, public institutions, social organizations, etc., which cannot produce anything, since they are not profit-making bodies, and cannot often invest their funds in anything but government securities, so that their income gradually melts away.   Yet even for them it is not altogether bad that they should have to renew their life by fresh acts of generosity instead of depending always on the charity of the dead.

IV. CONDITIONS THAT GOOD MONEY MUST FULFIL

All legal money should have a metallic value strictly equal to its nominal value.   This is the ruling principle in this matter.[1]

Money, as we know, has three functions: it is an instrument of acquisition or purchase, an instrument for the payment of debts, and a means of hoarding wealth.   All three functions spring from custom, but they ought to receive the sanction of law.   In fact, only the law can compel a creditor or a seller to receive a particular kind of money by way of payment.   This is the privilege that makes money what is called *legal tender*.   Nor is there any security in saving except in so far as the money that is stored away retains this privilege.   But the privilege assumes the fulfilment of the condition indicated above.   Here, let us say, is a sovereign.   By stamping on this coin the device that represents a pound, the Government

[1] The expositions here and in the next chapter on Monetary Systems have lost much of their interest owing to the disappearance of metallic money from circulation, but they are of great theoretical importance none the less.   Besides, this disappearance may be only temporary.

intends to certify that it is really worth a pound, and that everyone can accept it with perfect confidence. If the coin does not possess the value attributed to it, the Government is guilty of actual fraud. During many centuries, unfortunately, rulers have shown few scruples in this respect; but to-day it is a matter of dignity and good faith in which a government would scarcely dare to be found at fault.

Every piece of money, therefore, must be regarded from two points of view: *as a coin, it has a fixed value, which is marked upon its face*; *as an ingot, its value is identical with the market price of the metal it contains* — for there are markets and price quotations for gold and silver, as well as for wheat and cotton.

Whenever these two values coincide — whenever, for instance, the little lump of metal weighing 123.27447 grains, 11/12 fine, which constitutes a sovereign, has a market value of £1 (corresponding to a price of £3, 17s. 10½d. per ounce[1]) — we say that the money is good, or, in technical language, that it is *standard* money. It remains to enquire how this perfect coincidence is established and maintained.

First case. — If the value of the ingot exceeds the value of the coin — if, for instance, a coin that is legally worth a sovereign contains a guinea's-worth of gold, — then the money is said to be *heavy* or over weight. This is a good fault, but it is a fault all the same; and, as we shall see presently, it may prove a serious inconvenience. At the same time there is no need for great anxiety about this contingency, for the following reasons: first, because governments are rarely likely to coin heavy money; if they do so it can only be through ignorance, for it obviously involves them in loss; to make sovereigns each containing a guinea's-worth of gold would be as ruinous a business as for a manufacturer to make rails at £5 a ton with steel that is worth 5 guineas; — and, secondly, because even if the coin were over weight, owing to certain circumstances to be dealt with later, such as a rise in the price of gold after it had been coined, it could not long remain so. In fact, as soon as people knew that the gold in a sovereign was worth a guinea, everyone would rush to realize this profit by treating the money as merchandise — selling it by weight, and continuing this process until the coins had completely disappeared. We shall see later that in bimetallic monetary systems this situation occurs fairly often.

Second case. — If the value of the ingot is lower than that of the coin — if, for instance, a coin that is legally worth a sovereign con-

[1] This refers to an ounce of gold ¹¹⁄₁₂ fine, *i.e.*, eleven parts gold to one part copper; the price of *pure* gold is of course proportionally higher.

tains only nineteen shillingsworth of gold, — then the money is said
to be *light*. This contingency is much more to be feared than the
other, because, unlike the opposite case, it is one that naturally
offers a temptation to governments. To coin sovereigns with gold
that is only worth nineteen shillings is an alluring proposition for
an impecunious and not too scrupulous government, and many of
them have, as a matter of fact, succumbed to the temptation: in
England the proceedings in this respect of Henry VIII and Edward
VI's Council of Regency are sufficiently notorious. Perhaps it will
be asked, What harm is there in it? The harm lies in this: that
the country will gradually be flooded with debased and false coin;
and once such money has got into circulation it never gets removed
by natural forces as over-weight money does. On the contrary it
remains in circulation, and, as we shall see when we come to *Gresham's Law*, it is one of the hardest of tasks to get rid of it.

To maintain the identity of metallic value and nominal or face
value, it is the rule in every good monetary system — and this is a
principle of vital importance — to allow anyone who wishes to turn
metal into money the right of doing so (not, of course, on his own
account, but at the Mint). This is what is called the system of
free coinage. As long as coinage is free, the equivalence of metallic
value and face value is assured, for if the face value of a coin chanced
to exceed the metallic value, everyone would hasten to reap the
profit that would result from the manufacture of coins. Everyone
would buy gold and take it to the Mint to be made into money,
until equality of value was again established by the scarcity of un-
coined gold and the abundance of coined gold.

It should be possible for good money to be melted down without
any loss of value. That is why our picturesque phrase says that
good money will stand the "ordeal by fire" — a relic of medieval
days, when the justice of a claim was settled by this method. Here
we may apply the economic axiom that whenever two objects can
be transformed into each other at will they must necessarily be of
equal value.

In all countries, however, there are certain kinds of coin which
do not fulfil the requirement just described — that is to say, their
intrinsic or metallic value is less than their legal or face value. These
coins are known as *token* money. They are generally coins of small
value, made of copper or silver; they are not used for large payments but only for what is called *small change*. In these circumstances the legislator can, without inconvenience, relax the rigour
of monetary principles. But, by abandoning the principle of iden-

tity of value, he has also to sacrifice the qualities of good or standard money. That is to say: (1) *he must refuse to make token money legal tender* — no one must be compelled to receive it in payment;[1] and (2) *he must suspend the right of free coinage in the case of token money*, as otherwise everyone would get silver or copper converted into coin, so as to gain the difference between its metallic value and its legal value. The government reserves to itself the right of issuing such quantities of token money as it thinks necessary.

V. GRESHAM'S LAW

Wherever two kinds of money are in circulation together, the bad money always drives out the good.

This formula expresses one of the most celebrated laws in political economy, bearing the name of the great Elizabethan merchant who is said to have discovered it three centuries ago. But long before Gresham's time, Aristophanes had noted the curious fact that men prefer bad money to good.

What gives this law at first sight the appearance of a paradox, is that it seems to say that bad money is *always* preferred to good. This seems absurd. The whole of economic science is based on the postulate that in all circumstances men prefer the product that is of better quality and that best meets their needs, and the facts of everyday life confirm this. Of two fruits we prefer the best-flavoured, and of two watches the one that goes best. Why, then, should we act differently in the case of money?

But we do not by any means act differently! We behave the same towards money as towards other kinds of wealth: we prefer the good if we are to *keep it for ourselves*, but if we are to give it to our creditors and tradesmen, why should we choose the good if the bad will serve our turn just as well — that is to say, if they are bound to accept it in payment? Gresham's law is no anomaly, therefore, but an application of the hedonistic principle that lies at the base of all political economy: the principle of giving least so as to obtain most.

It is generally in the case of two kinds of money that are both legal tender, or can serve as such, that Gresham's law comes into play. It should be observed, however, that it applies even in the case of counterfeit coin and money that is out of circulation, in the sense that nine people out of ten, being unfortunate enough to find such money in their purses, are anxious above all things to pass it

---

[1] Thus copper coins are legal tender only up to a limited amount.

on, so that the more doubtful its genuineness the faster it circulates. It is like a game of hunt-the-slipper, where an object is passed rapidly from one to another to avoid being caught.

This explains why bad money remains in circulation, but it is less easy to explain why good money disappears. What happens to it?

Well, we make use of it where we cannot make use of the bad money. This happens in these three cases, which are the three outlets by which good money departs: hoarding, payments abroad, and sale by weight.

(1) *Hoarding*. When people want to put money aside and reserve it in case of need, they are sure to conform this time to the ordinary rule, and are not foolish enough to choose the bad coins. They choose the best, because they are keeping them for themselves and it is the good money that offers them most security. They hoard gold in preference to silver, and silver in preference to paper money. And the banks do the same, seeking to increase their supply of gold and putting the silver back into circulation. In this way a certain amount of the good money may disappear from circulation. This first kind of disappearance, however, is only a temporary one.

(2) *Payments abroad* are more important in their effect. For although we have the legal right to use bad money as well as good in paying our debts to our fellow-countrymen, this alternative fails us when we have to pay for purchases abroad. Our foreign creditor, being in no way bound to take our money, will accept it only for the weight of fine metal it contains — that is to say, for its real or metallic value. We cannot think of sending him light-weight coin, therefore. The conclusion that is forced upon us is that we must keep this latter for home trade, where it does as well as the other, and keep the good money for our foreign trade. There lies a second and more important cause of the disappearance of good money.[1]

It was thus that the gold money of the belligerent States — or at least all that they could dispose of without depleting too much the stocks held by their note-issuing banks — found its way during the war into neutral countries.

(3) The third cause that makes good money disappear very rapidly is its *sale by weight*. This looks a very strange proceeding, and one whose utility is not obvious. Yet in reality it is a very simple matter. As soon as the value of gold rises so that the metallic

---

[1] M. Paul Leroy-Beaulieu puts it very well when he says that "*local* money drives out *universal* money."

value of a gold coin is greater than its legal value — as soon as it is *worth more as metal than as money*, — it is plainly to the interest of the owner to use it as metal instead of as money. It is therefore withdrawn from circulation and sent to the market for precious metals. If the value of bronze were to rise considerably, surely many bronze objects — bells, cannon, statues, and so forth — would be melted down to realize the value of the metal they contained? Or ·again, when spirits of wine rises very much in price, a great deal of wine is sent to the distilleries to be converted into spirit. Similarly, when the value of a precious metal rises, coins made out of it cease to be money and become goods, which their owners are eager to realize by selling them to the merchants, who melt them down either for industrial purposes or to send them as raw material to foreign mints.[1]

That is how Gresham's Law operates. Let us see now in what cases it operates. There are three such cases:

(1) Whenever *worn* money is in circulation along with *newly-coined* money. It was exactly in these circumstances that the action of the law was observed by Sir Thomas Gresham. New coins had been made, in Elizabeth's reign, to replace those in circulation, which were completely worn out, more by clipping than by legitimate wear and tear. But it was noted with dismay that the new coins quickly disappeared, while the old ones swarmed more abundantly than ever.[2]

It is important, therefore, that a government should undertake frequent recoinages, so as to keep its money always fresh and new. Otherwise it will later on find great difficulty in replacing the old money by the new; and great watchfulness is needed, since money wears out rapidly.

(2) Whenever *depreciated paper money* circulates along with *metallic money*. It is in this case that Gresham's Law was most strikingly illustrated by the war. As soon as the paper money began to be issued the gold very largely disappeared, and was only reluctantly drawn from its hiding-places in response to the patriotic appeals of the various governments.

---

[1] It was to prevent this flight of metallic money that during the war all the belligerent nations, including England, prohibited the export of gold, in ingots as well as coin. Yet this measure did not prevent gold and silver coins from being bought and melted down to be smuggled abroad.

[2] In the case noted by Aristophanes the opposite process occurred: the new money drove out the old. But this was because the situation was reversed: the new money was worse than the old; it was coined, he says, out of less fine metal.

(3) Whenever *light* money circulates along with *standard* money, and even when *standard* money circulates along with *heavy* money. In this case the lighter money drives out the other. This is the most interesting of the three cases. It appears in almost every country that has adopted a combined gold and silver currency. But an examination of this case would lead us into the question of monometallism and bimetallism, which we shall deal with in the next chapter.

Note. — For an account of the experience of the United States and its monetary system see the Appendix.

CHAPTER III — MONETARY SYSTEMS

I. THE MAKING OF A MONETARY SYSTEM

The first thing to be done in making a monetary system is to choose the monetary *unit* that is to give its name to the money of the country. In the case of measures of length, capacity, or weight, there are certain data that serve to guide us, such as the human limbs, or the weight that a man can carry; but in the matter of a measure of value the choice is more arbitrary: are we to say, for instance, that the unit is to be the value represented by the mean daily minimum consumption? But that involves a further difficulty, for by reason of the gradual depreciation of money owing to the law already noticed, such a primitive kind of unit diminishes more and more in value until it becomes insufficient.

That is why the monetary unit varies from one country to another, from the English pound that is worth just over 25 francs, to the Brazilian *reis* that is worth (at par) about 1/400 of a franc — a difference between the two extremes of 1 to 10,000.

The earliest French monetary unit was the pound, so called because originally, in the time of Charlemagne (742–814), it represented *an actual pound weight* of silver. The pound at that time was equal to 408 grammes, nearly 82 times the weight of the modern franc (5 grammes) into which the pound gradually changed. This descent from 408 grammes to 5 grammes was caused entirely by a continual series of emissions of lighter and lighter money: each king made a slight reduction in the weight of the old pound, while trying at the same time to keep up its old legal value.

The history of the English pound is very much the same, but somewhat more honourable to the English government, for, starting from the same point as the French pound, it stopped in its descent at the value of 25 francs — its modern (pre-war) value.

The franc, in its turn, became in process of time too small a unit to act as a measure of value. Its submultiples are of very little use, except to waste an enormous amount of clerks' time.

The American dollar, equivalent to 5.18 francs or 4.11 shillings, seems to be the monetary unit that best answers the needs of economic life. It stands about midway in the scale, and admits equally well of the coining of multiples like the five-dollar piece and of submultiples like the cent. It is also the unit that has been most often copied by other countries and that stands the best chance of being adopted as the international unit, if the oft-cherished project of an international monetary system is ever realized.

Once the unit is chosen, a sufficient number of multiples and sub-multiples must be set up to cover all degrees in the scale of values. It is obviously best to arrange them on a decimal system, for this very much simplifies all calculations of prices.

Every monetary system ought to include a sufficient number of coins to correspond to the various degrees in the scale of values, and hence to the needs of everyday payments. Thus in the English system there are eleven coins of different values, ranging from the farthing to the sovereign. But this results in a great complication, namely, the necessity of having recourse to different metals — gold, silver, and copper or other metals. In fact, if only one metal were used, it would be necessary, in view of the imperative rule that in every sound monetary system the weight of each coin must be proportional to its value (see above, p. 219), to coin multiples and submultiples that would be too big or too small to be conveniently circulated. We could not think of employing only gold: the half-sovereign is quite small enough, and a gold penny, weighing half a grain, would be impossibly small. Still less could we imagine ourselves using only copper, unless we transport ourselves to the days of the Roman *as*, for a sovereign made of copper would have to weigh something like thirty pounds! Even silver by itself would not do, although it would be less inconvenient on account of its interme-diate value. The five-shilling piece is already too large, and the threepenny piece too small, to be commonly employed. It is a matter of real necessity, therefore, to make use of at least three metals at once.

But by using several different metals we overcome one difficulty only to be faced by another that is even more serious. For the coins minted out of these different metals must obey the law that we have already stated: their weight must be exactly proportional to their value. Now there is a natural scale of relative values among these metals, but it bears no relation to the decimal system. We should have to assign fractional weights, therefore, to the multiples and submultiples.[1]

---

[1] Thus if the value of gold when the system is established is $15\frac{1}{2}$ times that of silver, and the (silver) franc weighs 5 grammes, then the gold franc would have to weigh $(5 \div 15\frac{1}{2})$ grammes, which is .3226 gramme. This would be too small a coin to be of any use, but it would correspond to a weight of 3.226 grammes for the gold 10-franc piece, and 6.452 grammes for the 20-franc piece.

This, of course, is only a minor inconvenience: the general public pays no attention to the weight of coins, and does not mind if the weights are fractional. But what is more serious is that the value of these metals varies at different times, so that when the weight of a coin is once fixed its value may come to disagree with that weight; one of the two sets of coins — either the gold or the silver — becomes too heavy; Gresham's Law comes into play; and we are faced by all the difficulties that have made the term *bimetallism* so notorious, as we shall see in the next section.

So far as coins of lower denominations are concerned — copper coins, and even silver ones — the difficulty can be avoided by deliberately rejecting the principle of agreement between weight and value — that is to say, by giving them an arbitrarily chosen weight. But in that case we must cease to allow them to be legal tender and reduce them to the rank of token money. But we cannot treat gold coins in this unceremonious fashion.

II. DIFFICULTIES IN THE WORKING OF A BIMETALLIC SYSTEM

We have just said that in any monetary system coins of different metals must be employed. But this does not mean that they must all rank as legal tender, with the two attributes mentioned above: compulsory acceptance, and free coinage. Some of the coins may well be reduced to the inferior rank of subsidiary or token money, current only below a certain amount, and only coined at the pleasure of the State. That is the case everywhere with copper and nickel coins. But what is to be done about silver? Is silver to be legal tender as well as gold? That is the question that used to be known as the question of "the single or double standard," and that is more correctly described nowadays as the question of *monometallism or bimetallism*.

If the right of being legal tender is conferred upon only one of the two metals — gold, for example, — then there is no difficulty. Silver money is relegated, like copper, to the rank of token money; a purely conventional value is attributed to it, but no one is compelled to receive it in payment of debts. Gold money is the only money that is legally current — the only one also for which perfect equivalence must be maintained between its legal and its intrinsic value.[1]

If we wish to make *two* kinds of money legal tender at the same time,

---

[1] [This is, of course, the normal currency system.]

the position becomes far more complicated. To get a better understanding of these difficulties let us take the French system, which may be regarded, especially from the point of view of its origin, as a typical bimetallic system. We will go back to the starting-point of that system (the law of the 28th March, 1803).

The monetary unit was the ancient pound transformed into the franc. It was a silver coin, so silver was taken as the standard or legal money. At that period no one thought of contesting its right to this privilege. But the government could do no less than to confer the same privilege upon gold.

For the sake of clearness we will take two similar coins that still exist in the French monetary system, — the silver five-franc piece and the gold five-franc piece. We wish them both to be legal tender, so they must both have a metallic value exactly equal to their legal value. That, as we have seen, is a condition *sine qua non*. There is no difficulty in fulfilling this condition in the case of the silver five-franc piece. At the period we are dealing with, silver was worth 200 francs per kilogramme, so an ingot weighing 25 grammes was worth exactly 5 francs. Consequently, we must make our five-franc piece weigh 25 grammes and, so far as that goes, the required condition is satisfied.

But what weight are we to give to the gold five-franc piece? A kilogramme of gold (9/10 fine) was worth 3,100 silver francs. If, therefore, we coin a kilogramme of gold into 620 pieces, each will be worth exactly 5 francs (because $620 \times 5 = 3,100$) and each will weigh 1.613 gramme; here, too, the condition is fulfilled.

Now let us take these two coins and put them in the two scales of a balance. We shall find that *to balance the silver five-franc piece we must put in the other scale* $15\frac{1}{2}$ *gold five-franc pieces.* This proves that the operation was properly performed. The kilogramme of gold was worth at that time just $15\frac{1}{2}$ times as much as the kilogramme of silver (3,100 francs against 200 francs). So we must stick to this ratio of $15\frac{1}{2}$ to 1, the legal ratio between the values of the precious metals — as celebrated in political economy as the famous geometrical ratio between the diameter and circumference of a circle, $\pi = 3.1416$.

So far, therefore, everything is going smoothly. But wait a bit! In 1847 the gold mines of California were discovered, and, in 1851, those of Australia. The annual production of gold increased fourfold. Silver, on the other hand, grew scarce, owing to the development of trade with India, which absorbed large quantities of it. The result was that the relative values of the two metals altered: to obtain a kilogramme of gold it was no longer necessary to give

15½ kilogrammes of silver, as before: 15 was enough. This is the same as saying that gold had lost more than 3% of its value. Thereafter it is clear that these little ingots of gold called coins must have undergone a corresponding depreciation: the gold five-franc piece came to be worth only 4.84 francs.

Twenty years later, in 1871, a change took place in the opposite direction. The annual production of gold decreased by a half, in consequence of the exhaustion of the Californian and Australian mines. At the same time the output of silver increased by a half, owing to the discovery of mines in Western America. Moreover, Germany just then adopted a gold standard, demonetized its silver, and poured on to the market the thalers she no longer required. Once more the relative values of the two metals changed, but this time in the opposite way: in the bullion market a kilogramme of gold would purchase not only 15½ kilogrammes of silver but 16, 17, 18, and even as much as 20 kilogrammes. This means that the silver had lost more than a quarter of its value, relatively to gold. Obviously each ingot of silver constituting a silver coin suffered a proportional depreciation: so the silver five-franc piece became really worth only 3.8 francs.

What is to be done, then? If we wish to maintain the standard character of both kinds of money — that is to say, an exact equivalence between their intrinsic and their legal value, must we be continually recoining now one and now the other, to make their weight agree with the varying values of the two metals? That seems to be the conclusion to which we are driven.[1] But this is not practicable. We shall see in the next section what expedient is adopted.

III. HOW BIMETALLIST COUNTRIES COME TO HAVE REALLY ONLY ONE MONEY

Every bimetallic system, as we have just seen, suffers from the serious inconvenience of never being able to maintain, for both metals

---

[1] Strictly speaking it would not be necessary to vary the weight of *both* moneys, but only of one of them, taking the other (always the same one) as the unit. For instance, if the five-gramme silver franc were taken as the unit, the weight of the gold coins could be altered, sometimes above and sometimes below the legal weight according to the changes in the value of gold. But even with this simplification the plan would be scarcely more practicable.

Another solution of the problem would be to keep the weight of the gold coins unchanged, and to erase from them the inscription that declares their legal value, leaving their value to oscillate freely according to the law of supply and demand. The value of the piastre used to vary thus in some countries — quite recently, for instance, in Indo-China.

at once, that equivalence between intrinsic and legal value that should characterize all good money. One of the two will always be too heavy or too light, according to the changes in the relative value of the two metals.

It might be thought, perhaps, that this drawback is more theoretical than practical. "What does it matter," it will be said, "if the legal value of our gold or silver coins is slightly higher or lower than their real value? No one pays any attention to the matter, and in any case no one suffers by it."

That is a mistake; the situation involves a very real inconvenience — and, more than that, an actual danger, for this reason: the lighter of the two moneys will gradually drive the heavier out of circulation, so that every country that nominally has a double standard finds itself, as a matter of fact, in the peculiar position of *never keeping in circulation more than one of its two kinds of money, and that one the worse of the two.* A periodical ebb and flow carries away the metal that rises in value and brings back the one that falls. This is simply and solely an application of Gresham's Law that we have already studied, but the history of the French monetary system since the middle of last century has offered an extraordinary proof of it.

When, under the second Empire (1852–1870), gold fell in value, owing to circumstances indicated in the last section, the French silver money began to disappear and to be replaced by gold money — those beautiful "napoleons" that people were little accustomed to, and that were admired and welcomed by the courtiers as signs of the wealth and brilliance of the new reign. In reality, however, they were only so abundant because they were coined out of a depreciated metal.

This replacement of one metal by another is very easily explained. If a London banker wanted silver to send to India, he tried to buy it in the cheapest market, for silver and gold are traded in like any other commodities. Since gold had fallen 3%, he could only obtain 15 kilogrammes of silver with 1 kilogramme of gold. But by sending his kilogramme of gold to the Paris Mint he could have it coined into 3,100 francs, and then exchange these 3,100 gold francs at any bank or shop for 3,100 silver francs, which weighed exactly $15\frac{1}{2}$ kilogrammes (3,100 × 5 grammes = 15,500 grammes). He would manage in the end, therefore, to obtain $15\frac{1}{2}$ kilogrammes of silver with his kilogramme of gold.

It is easy to see that this kind of business led to the export of a certain amount of silver money from France, and its replacement by an equal quantity of gold money. It was merely the operation of Gresham's Law — the substitution of light money for heavy money. Whole shiploads of French silver coins were transported to India. They were bought for their weight of silver, to be sold to the mints at Bombay and Madras for conversion into rupees. During this period these Indian mints turned into rupees more than two thousand million francs of French money.

It was not long before there was a veritable famine of silver money in France. In olden times, prohibitive measures would certainly have been resorted to, in order to stop its flight, and perhaps penalties would have been inflicted on those who exported silver money. But economic science, by pointing out the cause of the trouble, made it possible to apply a far more efficacious remedy. Silver money was disappearing because it was too heavy; it was sufficient, therefore, to weaken it by diminishing its weight or merely reducing the proportion of fine metal it contained. This was certain to clip its wings and restrain its flight. This step was taken jointly by France, Italy, Belgium, and Switzerland, by the Agreement of the 23rd December, 1865.[1] The standard of fineness for all silver coins, *except five-franc pieces*, was lowered from 900/1000 to 835/1000, which lowered their value by rather more than 7%. *All these coins, therefore, became, and have remained, token money.* According to the invariable principles that prevail in this matter, they have lost their character of legal money and have only been received since then as subsidiary money or "change."[2] Why was an exception made in favour of the five-franc piece? It was demanded by France, out of respect for the bimetallic principle, for to turn all silver coins into token money would have been to abandon silver money entirely as legal tender. It would have meant adopting frankly a gold monometallist system, as in England, and such a revolution in the monetary system terrified the French government. So the five-franc piece was retained with its former weight and fineness and its character of legal money. It naturally continued to leave the country, but it could be dispensed with more easily than the smaller change; and, if necessary, it could be replaced by the gold five-franc piece.

[1] This is what is called the *Latin Union*, though it included neither Spain nor Portugal. Greece joined it shortly after. It was originally agreed that the coins of each of these five countries should be allowed to circulate in all of them, but this right of free circulation was withdrawn by one country after another as soon as variations in the rates of exchange between them gave rise to speculation in these moneys.

[2] Up to 50 francs between individuals, and 100 francs in the government treasuries. They are received without limit, as a matter of fact, in this latter case, for the State can hardly refuse to accept money it has itself issued.

After 1871, as we have seen, an opposite change occurred in the respective values of the two metals, and the French monetary system was again thrown out of order, this time in the opposite direction. It was the gold money that became too heavy, and consequently began to emigrate; the silver became too light and began to increase in circulation. The operations explained above were renewed, but in the opposite direction. To avoid all obscurity on this essential point we will go over the explanation again.

A Paris banker procured 3,100 gold francs, either in twenty-franc or ten-franc pieces, no matter which. That makes exactly a kilogramme of gold. He put the money in a bag and sent it off to London. In the London bullion market 20 kilogrammes of silver could be obtained with a kilogramme of gold, so he bought 20 kilogrammes of silver, and had it sent back to Paris and turned into coin at the Mint. As the Mint coined a kilogramme of silver into 40 five-franc pieces (200 francs), it handed our banker $20 \times 200 = 4,000$ francs, in five-franc pieces. His gross profit was 900 francs. Deduct the cost of transport, seigniorage, etc., and also the premium necessary for obtaining gold coins, since they had become scarce, and the operation was none the less a very profitable one. It is plain, too, that for France this business resulted in a decrease of gold money and an increase of silver money. If repeated indefinitely, the inevitable result would have been the entire substitution of silver money for gold money in circulation.

The nations belonging to the Latin Union (which Greece had joined in the meantime) had, therefore, to take concerted measures for averting this new danger. Just as in 1865 they had stopped the flight of silver money by lowering its fineness, so now they could have arrested the departure of the gold money by the same means or by diminishing its weight. But the frequent recoinage, first of one money and then of another, would have ended in the disorganization of the whole monetary system, so it was thought better to resort to a simpler but cruder proceeding — the cutting of the Gordian Knot. *By the Agreement of the 5th November*, 1878, *the coinage of silver money was suspended.*[1] Henceforward the kind of transactions described above became impossible: there was no longer any profit to be made from buying silver abroad, for it could no longer be converted into money in France.

This measure succeeded completely, too, in preserving for France

---

[1] At least for five-franc pieces, the only silver legal tender money. Each State reserved to itself the right to coin small silver pieces in fixed quantities, determined by the size of its population. The number has considerably increased since the war.

her fine stock of metallic gold, which had not yet been perceptibly encroached upon.　But, as may well be imagined, this Agreement by which silver was excluded from a market of nearly eighty million people and its sale proportionally restricted, had the effect of hastening its depreciation; in other words, it aggravated the evil.　Silver, which until then had scarcely lost more than 10% or 12% of its value, fell lower and lower till it reached 77 francs per kilogramme in 1903, a price that represented less than $\frac{2}{5}$ of its legal value (200 francs) and corresponded to a ratio of 1 to 40 between the values of the two metals.　In other words, the five-franc piece was worth only two francs, and the franc, by reason of its diminished fineness, about 36 centimes.

In these circumstances the free coinage of silver has not been resumed, and no one can tell whether it ever will be.　We may say, therefore, that although the countries of the Latin Union are still legally under a system of bimetallism, they have in reality practically adopted gold monometallism.　*Of all their silver coins only one is still legal tender, and that is the very one that is no longer coined!*

V.　WHETHER IT IS ADVISABLE TO ADOPT MONOMETALLISM

After the foregoing explanation there seems to be no room for hesitation.　The monometallist system is infinitely simpler, and avoids all the difficulties that we have just enumerated.　Then why not adopt it?

Most countries have already done so: first England (1816), then Portugal (1854), Germany (1873), the Scandinavian States (1875), Finland (1878), Roumania (1890), Austria (1892), Russia (1897), Japan (1897), and Peru (1901).　And even in those States that are still nominally bimetallist, such as those of the Latin Union (France, Italy, Belgium, Switzerland, and Greece), Spain, the United States, and India, gold is in reality the only standard money.　Even in Asia, where silver monometallism used to prevail — which caused Léon Say to remark that the yellow metal was sought after by the white races and the white metal by the yellow ones — gold has more and more taken the place of silver.

Still, bimetallism has not yet entirely lost the game.　It still has advocates among economists.　Here is the main argument in its favour, and in our opinion it is not wanting in force.

We know that every variation in the value of money results immediately in a variation in prices in the opposite direction (see above,

p. 198). Now when there is only one kind of money, these variations are liable to be frequent and sudden, to derange the entire organization of commerce, and to provoke incessant crises. If, on the other hand, we use two kinds of money as measures of value, then *a sort of compensatory action is set up between them*, which is very favourable to the stability of prices, and consequently also to the prosperity of trade, for in business it is stability above all that has to be considered. The explanation of this compensatory action is rather subtle, but it is easy at any rate to obtain some idea of it.

It must be observed, to begin with, that the variations of value in the two metals will necessarily be mutually dependent, as if there were only one. This is merely a special case of the law of substitution (see p. 36), by which whenever one product is able to take the place of another in consumption, their values are necessarily equal. If electricity is a perfect substitute for gas for lighting purposes, and conversely, then the price of the one is bound to be determined by that of the other. Now there is no more perfect example of substitution than that of the silver franc for the gold franc (and conversely) under a true bimetallic system — that is to say, when the coinage of both metals is free. So far, therefore, as one can be used indifferently in place of the other, one cannot be worth either more or less than the other.

If this be admitted, it must be remembered that the cause of the superiority of the precious metals as the measure of values lies in the fact that their variations in quantity are small compared with the total amount in existence (see above, p. 208). Now the greater the stock of metal and the more numerous the sources from which it is fed, the better will this condition be fulfilled. When it is made up of two metals it is a double stock to begin with; and, moreover, the variations in it will be less perceptible, since it is unlikely that the same causes will operate to bring about an increased output of *both* metals. In the same way a·river rises less suddenly and dangerously when its tributaries are more numerous, and when they rise in regions more distant and more different in geology and climate. From this point of view it is better that our metallic reservoir should be fed by two tributaries of different origin — gold and silver — than by one alone. If there were three or four sources, its level would be still more stable, so that theoretically *polymetallism* would be even better than bimetallism. In fact, if gold had been the only metal, the discovery of the Californian and Australian mines would have caused the utmost disturbance through an enormous rise in prices, and such might have been the effect of the discoveries in the Transvaal and the Klondike. The exhaustion of these mines would cause a yet more formidable disturbance in the opposite direction. It hardly matters whether prices are high or low: what does matter a great deal is that prices should not suddenly fluctuate between high and low. The ideal of a good monetary system is *stability of prices.*

Not only are bimetallists unwilling to abandon their system, but they would also like to convert the gold monometallist countries, and they claim that none of the difficulties that are feared would arise if bimetallism were established by international agreement among all the great nations, on a basis of $15\frac{1}{2}$ to 1 or any other fixed ratio.

This assertion seems outrageous to economists of the classical school. It cannot rest, they say, with the will of any government, or even of all governments combined, to fix the value of gold and silver *ne varietur*, any more than the relative values of oxen and sheep, or of wheat and oats. The value of things is determined solely by the law of supply and demand, and is wholly beyond the scope of legislative control. The precious metals, they assert, are no exception to this rule.

This argument appears to us to involve too sweeping a generalization. Gold and silver are not commodities that can be compared to oxen or sheep or any other kind of goods, for this reason: that their main use, as we have seen, is to be made into money. When, therefore, we speak of the demand for the precious metals we mean almost exclusively the demand made by the mints of a dozen great nations. Now there is nothing absurd in thinking that if these dozen buyers agreed in fixing the prices of the two metals, they could, in fact, succeed. If they declared that they would all buy gold at 3,100 francs per kilogramme, and silver at 200 francs, it is highly probable that they would impose this price on the market.

It would be absurd, they say, to decree that an ox should always be worth ten sheep, or that a bushel of wheat should always be worth two bushels of oats. It certainly would, for the market for these commodities is an immense one, and their price is determined by the wants of each one of us — by the wants of millions of consumers. But if in the whole world there were only a dozen persons who consumed beef or mutton, it would probably rest with them to fix the price, in concert among themselves, either at the ratio of 1 to 10, or on any other basis that they desired. A similar result has very often been obtained, in spite of far less favourable conditions, by the commercial coalitions already described under the name of cartels and trusts.

Of course this line of argument must not be carried to absurd extremes. It is plainly not in the power of governments, even if they were unanimous, to decree that the ratio between gold and silver should henceforth be equality, and still less that it should be reversed and that an ounce of silver should in future be worth $15\frac{1}{2}$ ounces of gold! Such a decree would be inoperative, because the industrial use of the precious metals, though of less importance than their use as money — it absorbs about half the annual production, none the less — would suffice to prevent the choice of an extravagant ratio like those just indicated. All the governments in the world could never make silver worth as much as gold; men and women would never pay the same price for a silver ring as for a gold one — unless silver were to become as rare as platinum.

But within reasonable limits we have no hesitation in believing that an international agreement would be efficacious in fixing the relative values of the two metals, and consequently in eliminating the principal disadvantage of bimetallism — namely, the disappearance by flight of one of the two metals. Whither, indeed, could it fly, if in all countries it were subjected to the same law?

Is such an international agreement practically possible, however? That is another question. It does not appear so, for each country makes it a point of honour to adopt a gold standard. The English government in particular, whose aid would be indispensable in reestablishing bimetallism, has always set its face against it.

Since the war the position of the bimetallists has been strengthened in one way, because the value of silver has risen considerably, almost to the old ratio of 1 to $15\frac{1}{2}$. Consequently there is less fear now of the disturbances that arise from Gresham's Law.[1]

On the other hand, the question of bimetallism has lost much of its interest because the return to metallic money (gold or silver) looks very far off, not only (and inevitably) in the countries that were at war, but in neutral ones as well. The gold remains in the vaults of the banks, and is only used in the settlement of debts and transactions abroad. It seems to be reserved henceforth for the double part of a security for the issue of bank-notes and an international form of money, while paper money remains the only national currency. Here, then, we must speak of paper money.

[1] Silver has risen in price, like all other metals, and from about 2s. an ounce, the price to which it fell in 1902, it rose to 17s. 6d. in 1919. At the same time it must not be forgotten that this rise was due for the most part to the depreciation of the paper note, for the price is expressed in terms of [French] paper money [converted into sterling at the pre-war rate of exchange]. If the price were given in terms of gold, silver would not appear to have risen beyond 4s. 6d. or 5s. In 1920–21, however, it again fell considerably and became worth only about 3s.

CHAPTER IV — PAPER MONEY

I. WHETHER METALLIC MONEY CAN BE REPLACED BY PAPER MONEY

No one knows who invented paper money. It was known in China from times immemorial, and Marco Polo, the fourteenth century traveller, brought back an account of it. And among the many kinds of money used in ancient times, if we find no record of paper money we at least hear of leather money, of purely conventional value. This was called *obsidional* money, or siege money, because it was generally issued in besieged towns, as a substitute for the metallic money that was wanting.

If we did not already know from daily experience that paper money can be substituted for metallic money, we should find it hard to believe, and the question at the head of this section would seem absurd. In the case of bank-notes there is no mystery about the matter. The bank-note is only a symbol standing for an equal value of gold or securities lying at the bank, and though most people in whose hands they circulate are ignorant or careless of the fact, it is easily comprehensible that they are accepted as money. But in the case of *inconvertible* paper money — pieces of paper issued by the State with no promise of repayment (at least not at any fixed date), and with no backing of gold or silver or securities — some surprise is quite justifiable.

We certainly could not replace wheat or coal or any other kind of wealth by mere slips of paper bearing the words "One Hundred Bushels of Wheat," or "One Hundred Tons of Coal." Such scraps of paper could never feed us or warm us. And even if we used coins merely to hang round our necks, as girls do in the East with their gold and silver sequins, it is plain that many-coloured pieces of paper could not take their place.

But we know that money is unlike other forms of wealth, and that its utility in our civilized societies is of a quite immaterial kind. A piece of money is nothing but an "order" that gives us the right to claim, under certain conditions, a portion of the existing stock of wealth (see p. 212). Now a slip of paper can play the part of an "order" just as well as a piece of metal, and even much better, so far as ease of circulation is concerned. The honour of having perfectly understood and demonstrated this possibility is due to the financier Law, although his premature experiments led France into bankruptcy. But the best proof lies in the fact that the use of paper money is becoming more and more general. Why should it not, indeed? If these scraps of white or coloured paper can be invested by law and general agreement with the property of enabling us to pay for our purchases, our debts, and our taxes, why should they not circulate just as well as white or yellow coins? For these coins are only used for the same purpose.

It may even be observed that the prospect or the certainty of repayment at a longer or shorter date has scarcely any weight with the general public, however much it may have for the financier; for what difference does it make to a man who receives paper money to know that he will be able to exchange it, at some unknown date, for gold or silver? No one intends to keep it until that time arrives. It is enough to know that if you accept it you can pass it on to someone else who will accept it likewise. Its circulation is a reciprocal act of faith.

It is a remarkable fact with what facility the most economically backward populations accept the substitution of purely conventional money for money that is genuine merchandise. It is to be presumed that many of the primitive forms of money, such as cowrie shells, were conventional ones, for they hardly had any value as food, and still less, among the tribes that employed them, as objects to be hoarded. At any rate, experience has constantly shown — even recently among the native tribes of Morocco — the eagerness with which paper is accepted, after some hesitation, in place of the heavy silver coins with which men have always been familiar. And the history of all wars, especially the late great war, furnishes many proofs of this interesting psychological fact — interesting because it shows the part played by faith in human affairs, and even in men's notions of wealth. In most French towns the people themselves demanded the issue of paper money to remedy the shortage of small (metallic) change. The dirtiest of paper notes were accepted everywhere as eagerly as gold napoleons, and the fine gold money was carried with the greatest readiness imaginable to the Bank of France to be exchanged for notes. More than two thousand million francs (£80,000,000) were thus brought voluntarily. Not only did paper money circulate without any difficulty, but people started to hoard it in place of gold, which is the highest honour that could be accorded to it!

Again, the circulation of a conventional sort of money is less surprising if we consider that the value of metallic money itself is to
a large extent conventional, for when we are told (as the text-books
often tell us) that all good gold or silver money has an intrinsic value
equal to its nominal value, we must not be led astray by that word
intrinsic. If the little lump of gold that is made into a sovereign
has really a commercial value of one pound, it is largely because it
is useful for making into a sovereign or any other gold coin. If
it served only for making jewellery or gilding picture-frames it would
certainly not be worth a pound: it might not even be worth five
shillings.

The other idea, however, is an illusion that is cherished by many
economists — or, at any rate, one against which they do not sufficiently warn their readers. Most of them seem to assert that the
impression stamped by the State on the pieces of gold and silver
simply declares their real value, like the labels that tradesmen attach to their goods. But the declaration that the piece of gold
weighing 123.27447 grains is worth a pound is not merely *declar-
atory* of value: it is partly *attributive* of value. It is because the
will of the legislator — ratifying, if you like, the free choice of mankind — has raised gold and silver to the supreme dignity of becoming
money, that these metals have acquired the chief part of their value.
But if ever gold or silver money were to be demonetized, its possessor
would find only a very much depreciated security in his hands.

There is nothing in this that is peculiar to money. Human choice
always plays a certain part in conferring exchange value upon any
object whatever, but if this choice is determined by *natural* causes,
the resulting value will be partly natural and partly conventional.
Wheat itself is only valuable because the majority of civilized men
have adopted it, among other cereals, for food, and no doubt if
custom were to substitute for it some other kind of food, its value
would disappear. Yet no one would think of calling the value of
wheat "conventional." It is the same with the precious metals.
There was nothing arbitrary about human choice when it was directed upon these metals: it was dictated by the very real qualities
they possess — qualities that we have already enumerated. The
sole difference is that it is easier to replace the precious metals as
money than to find a substitute for wheat as food.

It must be acknowledged, however, that there will always be important differences between the value of metallic money and that
of paper money. They are as follows:

(1) As paper money has only the value that the law confers

upon it, it cannot pass beyond the boundaries of the region that is subject to that law. It cannot be employed, therefore, in settling international exchange operations. The value of metallic money, on the contrary, is practically the same in every civilized country, since it depends on the value of the metal itself. It can therefore circulate everywhere, as bullion if not as coin. That is why metallic money is essentially the *international money*, whereas paper money is essentially a *national* one.[1]

(2) Paper money has no commercial value, as it rests entirely on the will of the legislator, and the law that created it can likewise abolish it. If paper money is demonetized by law, nothing is left in the hands of its owner but a worthless scrap of paper: when its legal value is lost, all is lost. It is not altogether the same with metallic money. Besides its legal value, this has also a natural value — much less, to be sure, than its nominal value, as we have just said, but none the less a *commercial value* that it owes to the physical properties of the metal of which it is made; and these are far from being common and unimportant. Consequently, even if metallic money is demonetized by law, the owner of the coins does not lose everything. No doubt if gold and silver were demonetized *by all countries*, metallic money would lose the greater part of its value, because its chief market, the various national mints, would be closed to it. This is proved by the fact that silver has suffered a considerable fall in value merely through the demonetization of silver money by several countries. All the same, even on this extreme supposition, the precious metals would still preserve a certain amount of utility, since they could be employed for industrial purposes; and as these industrial uses would become more important and more numerous the greater the fall in the value of the metal, the fall might not be as great as is imagined. Suppose the metal were to lose two-thirds or three-quarters of its value. A certain value would still remain in the hands of the owner of the coins — a value of which the law could not deprive him, and which would probably be greater than that of any other commodity that could be chosen as legal money, after it had been demonetized.

(3) Finally, the value of paper money is generally more variable than that of metallic money. This is because its quantity

---

[1] Yet a Bank of England note, it will be said, is generally accepted on the Continent. But in this case it is accepted not as money but as a credit instrument — that is to say, with the intention of sending it back to England *to be cashed*. The traveller discharges his debt to his landlord with it, but his country's liability is not liquidated, for the note will have to be paid for eventually in goods or securities.

depends on the will of men, while the quantity of metallic money depends only on natural causes, such as the discovery of new mines. One is issued by governments, and the other by nature. It is therefore in the power of a thriftless legislator to depreciate paper money by issuing it in excessive quantities — an occurrence which is only too common, — whereas it is not in the power of any government *to depreciate metallic money by an excessive coinage of it.*

It is true that the discovery of exceptionally rich mines may flood the world suddenly with a considerable quantity of the precious metals, and consequently lower the value of metallic money. But these variations in the quantity of gold and silver never cause the same rude disturbances as variations in the quantity of paper money, because they extend over the whole area of the civilized world. The precious metals are everywhere sought after and accepted, so if they are overabundant in one country, they quickly flow of their own accord into others, whereas sudden increases in the supply of paper money may become disastrous, since such money is always restricted to one country, which forms, as it were, a closed reservoir, beyond which it cannot flow.

Such, then, are the disadvantages which make paper money a more dangerous instrument to handle than metallic money. They are far, however, from justifying the curses denounced against it, as when it is said that "it is the greatest scourge of nations: it is in the moral sphere what plague is in the physical."[1] At this rate all Europe is plague-stricken to-day. It must even be observed that these dangers might be mitigated and almost completely eliminated if we could imagine an international agreement concluded between all civilized nations, by which they all agreed:

(1) To give legal currency to the same paper money;

(2) Not to increase its quantity, or to increase it only to an extent fixed upon beforehand — for instance, in proportion to the increase in the population of each country.

In this case the value of the paper money, though always conventional — artificial, if you like — would none the less be as broad-based and more stable than that of metallic money itself, simply because it would be founded on the unanimous consent of the peoples of the various countries. For though it is true, as we have said, that one is issued by nature and the other by governments, it must be remembered that nature is always blind, whereas there is always a possibility that a syndicate of States might be enlightened! To-

---

[1] These words, often attributed to Napoleon, are really those of one of his ministers, M. de Montalivet (Circular of the 10th October, 1810).

day, as we shall see, there are sufficient means of information available to enable the issue of paper money to be regulated according to the need for currency. Then, as its quantity would be determined by scientific forecasts and not by mere chance, its value should be less subject to variation. The money of the future will probably be of this kind.

Besides, the fact that paper money is artificial is by no means a mark of inferiority, but quite the reverse. The chronometer is an artificial instrument for measuring time, whereas the sun is a natural one. But that does not prevent the former from being far superior to the latter for this purpose. It is even a characteristic of progress to substitute artificial instruments for natural ones: to replace the club by the rifle, the horse by the locomotive, the sunlight by the electric lamp, and the heat of the sun by artificial heat.

II. WHETHER THE CREATION OF PAPER MONEY IS EQUIVALENT TO THE CREATION OF WEALTH

The men who first conceived the idea of making paper money flattered themselves that they were thereby increasing the general wealth, just as if they had discovered a gold mine or found the philosopher's stone dreamed of by the alchemists, which would transmute other metals into gold.

In this shape the notion was evidently absurd, for it assumed that wealth could be created out of nothing. Yet the idea has been ridiculed too much, for it is perfectly true that the issue of paper money can to some extent increase the wealth of a nation. How can it do this? Adam Smith was the first to explain it. He showed that the metallic money circulating in a country is unproductive capital, and that the substitution of paper money, by making this capital available, enables it to be utilized and applied to productive purposes. Using a simile that has become very famous, he said that it was just as if means had been found of travelling in the air, whereby the whole surface of the earth that was taken up by roads could be restored to cultivation and production.[1]

Adam Smith's ingenious comparison, however, leaves some obscurity in our minds. We can see readily enough that when roads

[1] ["The gold and silver money which circulates in any country may very properly be compared to a highway . . . . The judicious operations of banking, by providing, if I may be allowed so violent a metaphor, a sort of waggon-way through the air, enable the country to convert, as it were, a great part of its highways into good pastures and cornfields, and thereby to increase very considerably the annual produce of its land and labour." (*Wealth of Nations*, Book II, Chapter II.)]

and railways are no longer required, the land they occupy may be cleared and given up to cultivation and production. (This would mean something like a million acres in France alone.) But it is not so easy to see what can be done with metallic money when means have been found of dispensing with it. Is it to be melted down and made into gold and silver plate and ear-rings? The gain in that case would be very slight. No; it would be used in making purchases or investments abroad, either in buying railway shares or other securities, land, or ships, or in renewing industrial or agricultural plant — investments which, in one way or another, would increase the income of the country. Money employed at home can furnish an income to individuals, but not to the nation.

This is the same thing as is done by families that possess plate or jewels of considerable value, when they replace them by imitation metal or imitation stones and invest the capital obtained by realizing the genuine articles, so as to increase their income. Or it is like the action of those prudent individuals who, knowing that money brings in nothing so long as it lies in their pocket or their cash-box, are careful to keep by them only just as much as is necessary, and invest all the rest. The richest folk are often those who have least money by them. The thrifty peasant has some secret drawer full of gold and silver coins, but the millionaire has nothing but a cheque-book with which to pay his tradesmen. Nations can do the same. While France was employing some three or four hundred million pounds-worth of metallic money, England, more experienced in the use of credit devices, was content with a hundred and twenty million. Yet England was certainly no poorer than France on that account, but quite the reverse.

When, therefore, the question is asked, "Is it in the power of a government, or even of the banks, really to increase the wealth of a country by issuing paper money?" the answer must not be an absolute negative. As a matter of fact the thing is feasible, but *only up to the total amount of the metallic money in existence.* If England's £120,000,000 of cash were replaced by an equal amount of notes, England's wealth would be increased by £120,000,000 — but not by a farthing more.

It must be observed, however, that though the gain just mentioned might be realized by some countries, it could not be realized *by all countries at once.* One country may utilize its stock of metal productively by selling it abroad, but if every country wished to do the same it is obvious that none of them would succeed. In that case the gold or silver coins offered by all countries seeking to get rid of them, would retain only their industrial value, and even that would be very much depreciated owing to the increase in the supply. It would be different if means were found of doing without roads: then *all countries at once* might benefit equally from the new utility of the land that used to be employed for transport and that had become available for cultivation. In this respect Adam Smith's picturesque simile fails somewhat, in our opinion.

Yet it remains true in the sense that even supposing metallic money to be replaced everywhere by paper money, the human race would henceforth save all the labour that it is obliged to employ in maintaining its stock of metal — in filling up the gaps made every day by wear and tear and accidental loss, and especially in keeping the supply at the level required by the needs of commerce and an ever-growing population. This labour is no small matter. The extraction of gold and silver from the mines, and its smelting, transport, and coinage, demand the labour of hundreds of thousands of workmen. Do away with the necessity for employing the precious metals, and all this labour will become available for new production, and the productive power of humanity will be to that extent increased.

Summing up, then, we see that the answer to the question at the head of this section is very different from that which used to be given. We must no longer say that paper money increases the wealth of a country *to the extent that it increases its stock of money*, but, on the contrary, *to the extent that it enables it to be diminished.*

III. THE EXCESSIVE ISSUE OF PAPER MONEY AND THE SIGNS BY WHICH IT IS INDICATED

We have estimated the *economic* advantages that may result to a country from the issue of paper money. But they concern only the economist, and they are never the motive that decides a government to issue it. The end that governments have in view is a simpler and more practical one — it is the *financial* advantage that accrues. When a government finds itself short of money, the creation of paper money is a very convenient method of paying its contractors and officials and meeting all its expenses, *without having to borrow, and consequently without having to pay interest.* When a government is in this situation it may be imagined that its credit is not very good, and that if it needs money, either it will find no lenders, or else the rate of interest will be very high. That is why so many States have had recourse to the issue of paper money, and on the whole there has been no particular harm in it when they have had the sense not to exceed the amount required by the needs of the country — an amount which is represented by the quantity of metallic money in circulation. But unfortunately there is a great temptation for an embarrassed government to overstep the fatal limit. Many have yielded to it, and some, but not all, have ended in bankruptcy.

The grievous history of the French *assignats*[1] is well known. They were secured on the confiscated property of the *émigrés* and the church, but they were issued in quantities enormously greater than the value of that property, up to the extravagant figure of forty thousand million francs — probably twenty times the amount of the metallic money in existence at that period. Even if the issue had consisted of good gold and silver coins it would have resulted in considerable depreciation, since it would have been twenty times as much as was needed. So it can be imagined what must have been the depreciation of mere paper money. A pair of boots cost 4,700 francs, a ream of paper 450 francs, and the subscription to the *Journal Officiel* 1,000 francs.[2]

However, in the existing state of economic knowledge, a government that exceeds the limit is altogether without excuse. There are certain signs, familiar to the economist and the financier, that reveal the danger even at a distance, and give surer indications of it than those the pilot draws from the beacon and the sounding-lead.

(1) The first of these signs is the *premium on gold*. As soon as paper money has been issued in quantities too great for the needs of a community, it begins to be depreciated, in accordance with the universal law of value; and the first effect of this depreciation — the first sign that reveals it, even though the general public may not be aware of it — is that metallic money commands a premium. This means that its value stands out above the level of the depreciating monetary instrument, as rocks emerge above the retreating tide. Bankers and money-changers begin to seek for it to send

---

[1] [The paper currency of the French Revolutionists, issued in 1789, abolished in 1797.]

[2] These fantastic prices are far exceeded in Russia at the present time: bread, 250 roubles a pound; sugar, 900 roubles a pound; butter, 1,500 roubles a pound; boots, 30,000 to 50,000 roubles a pair; a suit of clothes, 50,000 to 100,000 roubles, and so forth. And the rouble, at par, was worth 2.66 francs, or about 2s. 1½d. The cause here is the same as in the case of the *assignats*. Even in Germany the issue of notes had reached 13,000 milliards of marks by the middle of 1923. These fantastic figures, however, represent only a small and continually diminishing value in gold, for in cases of inflation a critical point is always reached at which the depreciation of the notes proceeds faster than the increase in their number. From that point onwards, the more notes that are issued the greater is the *shortage of money*.

abroad in the form of bullion, and they pay a small premium to obtain it. That is the time for financiers to keep their eyes open!

(2) The second sign is the *flight of metallic money*. However slight the depreciation of paper money may be, if it is not immediately remedied by the withdrawal of the surplus paper but is allowed to continue and increase, then the little metallic money still remaining will disappear. This phenomenon is very characteristic: it has shown itself in every country where the paper money system has been abused. It has taken place for a long time in every country of South America, notwithstanding that these are gold and silver mining countries, and it is the same to-day in the countries that were lately at war. We explained the phenomenon in detail in connexion with Gresham's Law, so we need not do so again (see pp. 222).

(3) The third sign is a *rise in the rate of exchange*. We have not yet spoken of the foreign exchanges, but it is easy to understand that claims on foreign countries — bills of exchange or cheques — are the subject of extensive dealing in all the commercial centres of the world. They have a market price like other commodities, and this is called the *rate of exchange*. These claims on foreign countries are always payable in gold, since gold is the international money. A bill of exchange on London is therefore regarded in foreign countries as equivalent to gold, and consequently, when gold is at a premium the bill of exchange benefits by the same rise in price.

(4) The fourth sign is a *rise in prices*. This only appears at a later stage, and shows that the evil has already become serious and that the permissible limit has been greatly exceeded. It must not be thought that the merchant raises his prices as soon as the paper money begins to depreciate. He ignores it, just as the public does, and they only begin to realize that depreciation has taken place when it is revealed by the rise of prices. What really starts the rise is the abundance of paper notes, which pour into everybody's hands and enable everyone to increase his demand for goods. The evil, which had been latent until then, bursts forth and is revealed to all.

It must be observed, however, that the old prices remain unchanged for those who can pay in metallic money, if, indeed, there is any of it left. Hence we get the curious spectacle of *a duplication of prices:* each commodity henceforth has two prices, one payable in metallic money and the other in paper, and the difference between them is the exact measure of the depreciation of the latter. But the phenomenon, though a strange one, is only temporary, for the gold, disappearing from circulation as soon as ever the depreciated paper money appears, can no longer be used in making purchases.

As soon, therefore, as a government notices these premonitory signs — the flight of gold, the premium paid for it, and the rise in the rate of exchange, — its first duty is absolutely to forbid the issue of any more paper money: the limit has already been reached. If it has had the misfortune to overstep this limit, and sees the appearance of those dangerous symptoms, a rise in prices and a duplication of prices, it must reverse its engines and destroy all the paper money that returns to the public treasury, until it has got back to the right amount. But it is not always possible to apply this heroic remedy. In fact, to stop the issue of paper money, a government would have to be able to resort to other means of procuring money — by borrowing, for instance; and to be able to make up for the excess of paper it would have to have a surplus of revenue over expenditure. It is because these conditions could not be fulfilled during the war, in most of the belligerent States, that the issue of paper money continued, notwithstanding the rise in prices and in the rate of exchange.

Although these premonitory signs that we have just described are of great value to governments, they are also extremely disagreeable, for the simple reason that they give information to the public as well, and involve the risk of causing disquiet. Consequently, governments strive to prevent their appearance. That is why an emergency law has been made in France since the war, forbidding, on pain of heavy penalties, the export of metallic money at a premium — what is called *agio* — and even all dealings of the same kind.[1] It is illegal, therefore, to offer or receive more than a hundred francs in bank-notes for a hundred francs in gold. Such transactions being forbidden, there is no premium on gold — at least no apparent one, — and no duplication of prices. It is true that the law cannot prevent a rise in the rate of exchange or in prices, but the general public does not worry about the rate of exchange, or is even ignorant of the rise, while as for the rise in prices, it attributes this to any other cause than the depreciation of paper money.

[1] Law of the 12th February, 1916. It has been put into force on many occasions, but has not succeeded in preventing either the secret business of melting down metallic money or its illegal export.

Perhaps it would have been wiser not to attempt to interfere with the free play of economic factors, such as we have just indicated, and to allow a premium on gold and the duplication of prices. The gold price would then have remained the true price, and it would have made it easier to return to it some day.

CHAPTER V — INTERNATIONAL TRADE

I. ADVANTAGES OF INTERNATIONAL TRADE

Exchange is not so necessary for nations as it is for individuals. It is only in a novel that individuals can be imagined playing the part of Robinson Crusoe, but a nation — even if it be quite a small one — has sufficient resources to live on its own supplies, receiving nothing from abroad. The great war, however, and the blockade imposed by it on several countries, demonstrated with tragic clearness that the cessation of international trade involves such privations that it could not be continued for long without destroying a part of the population.

It is to be observed that, contrary to current opinion as created by protectionists, it is purchases, or imports, and not exports, that a nation finds most difficulty in dispensing with.

As far as natural wealth is concerned, this is very unevenly distributed over the earth, partly through climatic differences and partly owing to differences in mineral deposits. Even a country as fortunately placed as France can draw from her own soil neither cotton, nor copper, nor oranges, nor tea, nor coffee, and can only produce coal, wool, silk, timber, etc., in insufficient quantities. Other countries are at still greater disadvantage: Italy and Switzerland have no coal and scarcely any iron; England has no wine and no plums for her national pudding.

Several European countries, moreover, have reached such a density of population that they can no longer feed their inhabitants. Thus Belgium, England, and Germany have to obtain from Russia and the two Americas a portion of their daily bread.[1]

In the matter of manufactured goods, there is obviously no natural necessity that prevents a nation from making anything whatever. But here, too, there are inequalities, such as the proximity of raw materials and natural forces, the racial and psychological character

[1] It is well known that importation was almost completely stopped for Central and Eastern Europe during and since the war, and that in spite of the strictest rationing those districts have been unable to avoid famine and its consequences. The famine is not yet over.

France herself is obliged, except in good years, to import about a million tons of wheat annually, to supplement her own food supply. [England imported wheat and flour in 1920 to the value of nearly £170,000,000.]

of the population, and the position obtained by the development of certain industries either owing to historical causes or to chance; and these inequalities enable a particular country to produce much more economically, and therefore more cheaply, than others. These other countries, therefore, that are less advantageously situated, find it to their interest to purchase these products instead of trying to produce them themselves under much harder conditions. France, for instance, can easily make motor-cars herself, and does make very fine ones, and agricultural machines likewise. But she cannot make them as economically as the United States, whose great factories are equipped for manufacturing them by the hundred thousand. In the same way England can supply France with ships, and Germany can provide her with chemical products and dye-stuffs, more cheaply than France can manufacture these things herself.

In cases like this, the advantage of importation consists in the *economy of labour* realized by the importing country. It is measured by the difference between the price paid for the imported goods and the cost of producing them on the spot. If an American car represents 500 days' labour in America, while here it would take 1000 days to make, it is plain that if we can buy it at its value — that is to say, by giving in exchange goods costing only 500 days' labour here (or say 600 days, to allow for profit and cost of transport), or their equivalent in money — then we shall have gained the difference (say 400 days' labour).

That kind of advantage is the one that the classical theory of international trade places in the front rank. Bastiat formulated it in these words: "The obtaining of an equal satisfaction with less effort." Such, indeed, is just the advantage obtained from exchange between individuals, as we have already explained (p. 204): it is like an extension of division of labour.

Exportation, unlike importation, is never a necessity — a question of life or death — for a nation. If we may venture to say so, it is a kind of luxury. Yet it is always exportation and never importation that is the object of commercial policy in every country. All the efforts of governments are directed to developing exports and keeping out imports. How is such a contradiction to be explained? The reason is this: that the advantages of importation, whether they consist in increased satisfaction or in economy, affect only the consumers, and each of them only on a small scale, so that they are lost in the crowd, as it were, whereas the advantages resulting from exportation benefit the producers. Now men are far more eager in the pursuit of profit than in realizing economies.

Innumerable articles and even books were published during the war with a view to studying the means of increasing exports — export banks, export societies, foreign agencies, commercial instruction, and so forth — whereas I am not aware that anything was published dealing with the development of importation, unless it were concerned with the special case of importation from the French colonies. And it was asserted that France's economic recovery after the war would depend on the development of her export trade. The advantages of exportation must, therefore, be very alluring. What are these advantages?

(1) To begin with, it must be admitted that the policy of national expansion is furthered more by exportation than by importation: the latter is the *passive* side of commerce, whereas exportation is the *active* side. More initiative is required, and a more highly developed commercial sense, to open up new markets than to attract imports, just as, among individuals, it is certainly harder to sell than to buy. Every industry that is in a position to export, proves, by that very ability, that it no longer needs protection, that it is free, that it can go out alone into the world, and that it has risen from the ranks of national industries to become an international one.

The export of products is one form of propaganda, just like language, ideas, and fashions, and like them it obtains for itself "clients," not only in the commercial sense, as "customers," but also in the older, political sense of the word.

(2) Secondly, exportation, being a form of sale, involves payment, and therefore the entrance of gold into the exporting country. That is the advantage by which economists of old were particularly impressed: abundant exports were equivalent, in their view, to the possession of gold mines — that object of so much desire. Besides, even at the present day, exportation is the sole means by which ex-belligerent countries, swamped with paper money, can reconstitute their stocks of gold, or at any rate procure bills on foreign countries with which to pay their debts and raise the value of their paper money.

(3) Thirdly, for countries that dispose of certain natural or artificial products in quantities superior to their own needs, exportation has the further advantage of utilizing this surplus, which would otherwise remain useless and valueless. Without exportation, what would Brazil do with its coffee, Tunis with its phosphates, Australia with its wool, the Transvaal with its gold, England with its coal, or France, in time to come, with its iron?

(4) Lastly, and most important of all, exportation is the only

means by which a country can pay for its necessary imports, for, as may easily be understood, it cannot do so with its gold, even when it has any; and everyone knows that at the present time the countries of Europe have none — at any rate those countries that took part in the war. Consequently they can depend only on their exports to pay for everything that they need for their economic reconstruction (see below).

II. WHAT IS MEANT BY THE BALANCE OF TRADE

The *balance of trade* is the difference between the value of imports and that of exports. If we examine the statistics of exports and imports for every country, we shall see that this balance leans sometimes to the side of imports, and sometimes to the side of exports; but the first case, an excess of imports, is much the commonest.

Take France, for example. French imports during the thirty years before the war, with one single exception, always exceeded her exports. The imports averaged rather more than eight thousand million francs (£320,000,000), while the exports were less than seven thousand million (£280,000,000) — an annual deficit, if we can call it so, of more than £40,000,000 (in 1913 it was £65,320,000).[1]

Are we to conclude from these figures that France had to pay more than £40,000,000 in money to foreigners every year? This is not likely, for it would be easy to see from the most casual observation that there was no perceptible decrease in the amount of money in circulation. In fact there was even an increase. The same customhouses that record the exports and imports of goods, record also the entry and departure of the precious metals; and the figures for the same period show that every year more metal came in than went out, either in money or ingots. The difference in 1913 amounted to £24,760,000.

In the case of England, the figures are still more surprising. There the annual excess of imports over exports was regularly more than £200,000,000.[2] This means that six months would have sufficed

---

[1] These figures refer to *special commerce*. The term *general commerce* includes all goods that enter or leave a country, even if they are only passing through it. *Special commerce* includes only goods produced within the country, or intended for consumption there: it does not include goods that pass through the country, or that remain there temporarily. Special commerce is therefore necessarily less extensive than general commerce: in the case of France the difference amounts to several thousand million francs. In some countries it is greater still — in Switzerland, for instance — owing to their geographical situation.

[2] [This figure is a little too high: the average excess of imports during the ten years before the war was £144,000,000.]

to drain away all the money in the country, for the monetary stock in England was scarcely more than £120,000,000. Yet nothing of the kind took place; on the contrary, just as in France, the imports of money ordinarily exceeded the exports.

What is the answer to the riddle, then? Simply this: to find out whether a country will export or import money we must take into account not only the difference between its exports and imports of goods, as the general public usually does, but the *balance of its credits and debts*. Now the balance of indebtedness (as it is called) is not the same thing as the balance of trade. Exports certainly constitute one form of credit abroad, and even the principal one, but there are many other claims that may also be paid in gold. Similarly imports constitute the principal debt to be paid abroad, but they are not the only one.

What, then, are these international credits and debts that are distinct from imports and exports, and that are so appropriately named *invisible* imports and exports? There are many of them, but the principal ones are as follows:

(1) The *cost of transport* of exported goods, *i.e.*, freight and insurance. — If the exporting country itself undertakes the transport of the goods, which is not always the case, it acquires a claim on other countries which will certainly not be counted among its exports, since it arises only after the goods have left the home port and are on the way to their destination. A country like England has enormous claims on foreign countries under this heading: they were estimated by the Board of Trade before the war at more than £80,000,000 a year and they rose during the war to three times this amount. Not only does England transport almost the whole of her own goods, but she also carries the bulk of the goods of other countries; and naturally she does not do this for nothing.

France, on the other hand, had a debt under this heading estimated at twelve to sixteen million pounds. In fact she conveyed in her own ships less than half her sea-borne exports and hardly more than a quarter of her imports.

(2) *Interest on capital invested abroad.* — Rich countries invest abroad a great part of their savings, and on this account have to receive very considerable sums every year from foreign countries, in the shape of dividend coupons for stock, shares, or debentures, or even farm rents and profits of industrial or commercial enterprises. The amount of English capital invested abroad was estimated before the war at about £4,000,000,000, of which £2,400,000,000 was invested in India and the Colonies, and £1,600,000,000 in foreign

countries. This represents an annual tribute of £160,000,000 to
£250,000,000 levied by England on foreign countries and her own
colonies under this heading. India and the Australian colonies have
negotiated almost the whole of their loans on the London market,
and, besides that, very many undertakings all over the world are
directed or financed by the English. They have acquired lands in
the United States whose area is estimated at twenty million acres
— equal to the area of Ireland.

France used also to have considerable claims abroad under this
head. They were estimated before the war at £1,600,000,000, and
represented therefore an annual income of about £80,000,000.
Since the war, of course, the claims of both these countries abroad
have very much diminished, and so far as France is concerned they
are almost counterbalanced by debts contracted abroad, chiefly
with the United States (see below).

On the other hand, Spain, Turkey, Egypt, India, and the South
American republics appear under this heading as debtors instead
of creditors. It should be observed, however, that when these debtor
countries issue a loan, and so long as this loan is not fully subscribed,
the position is reversed: they become creditors for the time being
of the countries that have to send them funds, and the latter become
their debtors. Thus every year France makes new investments
abroad, and has therefore to send money away; and this must be
deducted from what she receives as interest on her old investments.

(3) *Expenses incurred by foreigners* living in the country. — As
the money spent by these foreigners is not the produce of their labour,
but is drawn from their land or from capital invested at home, all
countries frequented by wealthy foreigners are continually receiving
money in this way. The amount is estimated at £14,000,000 for
Italy, and £8,000,000 for Switzerland. In the case of France it
must be at least £16,000,000, for a large number of foreigners of
independent means reside in Paris and at places like Nice, Pau,
etc.

The United States, England, and Russia, on the other hand, were
debtors on this account to the amount of millions of pounds. It is,
as it were, the price paid for the boarding expenses of the natives of
these countries when they go for a holiday abroad.

(4) *Remittances sent to emigrants.* — Italy's total under this
head used to amount to £18,000,000 a year, after deducting the
comparatively small sums taken by the emigrants themselves on
their departure; and Hungary's total was put at £8,000,000.

Conversely, the total amount paid by the United States to Europe in the shape of postal orders and cheques sent by emigrants, was estimated at nearly 270 million dollars.

(5) *Bankers' commissions*, when bankers extend their business to foreign countries. — Financial centres like London, Paris, and Berlin receive orders and transact business for the whole world.   As this is not done for nothing, they become creditors in this way for considerable anounts.

(6) The *sale of ships*. — Purchased ships do not appear on the custom-house registers, either as imports or exports.   England builds ships for all other countries, and is therefore creditor on this account for an enormous amount, whereas France in this respect is rather a debtor.

It will be seen that in international relations the claims that result from exports and the debts due to imports are only parts of a much larger whole.   Consequently the balance of trade, properly so called, may be favourable or unfavourable without the general balance of indebtedness being so.   No doubt the debts and credits that result from the operations of commerce are the most important, but none the less, as we have just seen, the others also may reach considerable proportions.   The forty millions or so that Italy receives from her visitors and her emigrants has contributed in no small way to the amelioration of her financial situation.

If we could know with sufficient accuracy the amount of the claims and debts of every country — including, of course, its imports and exports — we could say what was the balance remaining to its credit or debit.   We should then see, (1) that the quantity of money coming in or going out each year is equal to that balance; and (2) that the credit and debit balances counterbalance each other if we reckon them for a sufficient period of years, which means that claims and debts automatically balance each other.   We must now explain how this is accomplished.

III.   THE TENDENCY OF INTERNATIONAL TRADE TO BECOME BARTER

What is the bond that everywhere unites imports and exports together?   Why is it that we never see a country selling abroad without also purchasing abroad, or *vice versa?*   That kind of thing is common enough among individuals.   The person of independent means, for instance, is always buying but never selling, for he has nothing to sell — neither products nor services, — whereas the peasant who lives on the land grows rich from it by selling the surplus crop that he does not consume, and buys hardly anything.   This situation may continue indefinitely in the case of an individual, because the amount of money that he withdraws from the market by his sales, or puts into it by his purchases, is negligible in comparison with the existing stock of money. But in the case of business transactions running into millions of pounds, the quantity of money in any country is quite insufficient. If France, for example, were only an importer, and had to pay in money the 300 or 350 millions that her imports are worth, she would not have a farthing left at the end of the first year, for her entire stock of gold money, which alone would be available for payments abroad, is far less than this amount. For England it would be still worse, for her imports amount to £800,000,-000, and her monetary stock is only about £120,000,000. It would be gone in a couple of months!

Purchases made abroad in the shape of imports, therefore, are scarcely ever paid for in money, but by means of bills of exchange or similar credit instruments. But whence come these bills of exchange? What is their origin? Each one of them represents a sale abroad — an export — and they are much better than money, because the stock of money becomes exhausted, whereas this source is continually being renewed.

There is only one way, then, in which a country can pay for its imports — at any rate for a regular flow of imports, — and that is by paying for them in exports.[1] What will happen if a country has nothing to sell, and therefore has to pay in money? In this case the disappearance of the money will give it an enormously increased value, conformably to the law of supply and demand, which means that there will be an enormous fall in the prices of everything. Now it is plain that as soon as everything falls to a lower price in this country than abroad, no one will be foolish enough to continue to purchase abroad what he can obtain much cheaper at home. We do not see goods passing from places where they are dear to places where they are cheap, any more than we see rivers flowing uphill. In this case, therefore, importation will cease altogether. Hence arises the following law: a country can only import in so far as it can also export, and in proportion to the amount of its exportation.

Very well! We can understand now that a country cannot always play the part of an importer, for want of a sufficient supply of money. But why can it not go on exporting indefinitely, without any counter-

[1] It is the same with all debts owing abroad — not only those due to imports but also those resulting from a war indemnity, for instance. These can only be paid in goods, *i.e.*, in exports. That is what makes the settlement of the German indemnity so difficult, and what the general public finds it so hard to understand.

balancing imports? For precisely the same reasons as we have just indicated. First, because if one country were always to export and never to import, other countries would have to accept the converse rôle, and import without exporting. Now we have just explained why they could not do this, even if they wanted to. Secondly, even supposing that one country could find means, by force or fraud, of exporting without importing, what would happen? It would accumulate such a quantity of money that it would depreciate enormously, and the result would be a general rise of prices, which would necessarily put a stop to all exportation. How, indeed, could goods find purchasers abroad if they were much more expensive at home than abroad? If France had to receive each year in money the price of her exports — £280,000,000 — her monetary stock would be doubled in a year. What could she do with this mass of depreciated money, except to get rid of it by using it for making purchases abroad — in other words, by importation?

This, then, is the interaction which takes place. If there is an excess of imports, then money flows out; this causes a fall in prices, which at the same time puts a stop to importation and encourages foreigners to buy, *i.e.*, stimulates exportation. If there is an excess of exports, then money flows in; this causes a rise of prices, which at the same time puts a stop to the purchases of foreigners (*i.e.*, to exportation), and stimulates purchases abroad, *i.e.*, importation.

To sum up, there is an automatic action in the balance of indebtedness which causes it to resume its position of equilibrium when it is disturbed, the variations in the value of money operating like the regulator of a steam-engine, that tends always to bring back the speed of the machine to a uniform rate. The flow of goods can never continue in one direction, any more than the tide can; sooner or later it turns, and after having brought the money in, it carries it out again.

Ricardo expressed this in a very striking formula when he said that *international trade always tends to take the form of barter*, just as among savages, except, of course, that more elaborate methods are employed, for exchanges are not made "in kind" — goods are not directly exchanged for goods — but by setting against each other credit instruments that represent the goods themselves.

Experience, moreover, has shown that whenever a country's imports have largely increased, owing to a commercial treaty or any other cause, there has never failed to be a corresponding increase in its exports. Whenever, on the other hand, a country manages, by means of a protective tariff, to diminish its imports, it must expect to see a proportional decrease in its exports.

This theory certainly finds confirmation in facts, for statistics show that money plays only a very slender part in the settlement of international indebtedness — about 6% or 7%. It must therefore be admitted that the balance of indebtedness regulates itself, and that debts and claims tend to balance each other. This is what disciples of Bastiat would call an "economic harmony."[1] Nowadays, however, we are less emphatic about it, and willing to own that it is troublesome for a country to have, not an unfavourable balance of trade, which really means nothing, but a balance of indebtedness that makes it a debtor to foreign countries.

A decrease in the monetary stock of a country, in fact, means impoverishment — relatively, at any rate, to other countries, — and the fall in prices, even if it is a remedy, is none the less an evil also. All producers know something of this, for they see their profits diminishing, and so also do the workers, for a fall in prices is always followed by a fall in wages.

On the other hand, the existence of a debit balance, even apart from these consequences, is generally a sign of an unpleasant state of affairs: it indicates either that a country can no longer satisfy its own wants and pay with its labour for what it demands from abroad, or else that it has to pay tribute to its absentee citizens who consume their incomes away from home. And the worst thing happens when a country, having no money with which to pay this eternal debit balance, *borrows the wherewithal to liquidate it*, like the spendthrift who goes on renewing the bills he has given every time they fall due.[2]

[1] It is different when one country has a system of paper money and has no gold to send abroad. In this case it is obvious that the self-acting mechanism explained in the text can no longer operate. Such a country can import goods indefinitely without any resultant fall in prices: on the contrary, prices will rise, owing to the increasing inflation of the paper money. Such is the position of France to-day.

But if in this case equilibrium cannot be restored by the outflow of money and the fall of prices, it necessarily tends to be restored in another way: by the depreciation of money at home compared with money abroad. That is what is called a rise in the rate of exchange (see below). The consequence of this rise is that the purchase of foreign products becomes more and more burdensome, and the sale of goods abroad more and more profitable. Thus France's exports have increased rapidly in spite of the disorganization of her industries, and the difference between her exports and imports, which was terrible, is diminishing every year. In fact in the early months of 1921 the exports were already in excess of the imports.

[2] Such, unfortunately, is the situation of France at the present time; but the war is an excuse for it. Moreover, the position of many other European countries is far worse.

IV. PROTECTION

Protectionists no longer believe that money is the most desirable form of wealth, nor do they make it their chief aim to increase the stock of money, although they are still obsessed by the notion of an unfavourable balance of trade (see the preceding section). They are not hostile to the development of international trade, and they prove this by the efforts that they make everywhere to get hold of it. But they think that exchange between nations cannot be left to regulate itself by a policy of *laisser faire*, as exchange between individuals can. In the case of individuals we may allow the free play of competition and the law of supply and demand: if private interests are sacrificed to the general interest, so much the worse for them. But we cannot run the risk of seeing our country ruined or enslaved by the economic predominance of rival nations. Commercial policy ought to be directed by national interest, or by what an Italian minister during the war called "sacred egoism." What is called the protectionist system, therefore, would be better named the *nationalist system*.

The principal arguments of the protectionists are as follows:[1]

(1) *Economic Independence.*

If international trade be left uncontrolled, those nations that have been endowed by nature or by their historical development with an economic superiority in certain branches of production, will progressively monopolize the entire world market, as the great trading houses do with the national markets. The less favoured nations will then have to content themselves with the industries in which they are not subject to rivalry, and will end by being reduced to the position of mere clients. Supposing that they can themselves find some branch of industry in which they are economically superior, they will have to resort to that.

But if it is acknowledged that specialization in one kind of work is fatal to the physical, intellectual, and moral development even of individuals (see p. 156), what is to be said about such specialization in the case of a whole nation? Are we to take as our ideal a world in which France should produce only wine and ladies' hats, England only cotton goods, Germany only chemical products, the United States only machinery, China only tea, Australia only wool, Russia only wheat, Switzerland only clocks, and Greece only currants? A country in which this plan was carried to the extreme limit, so that all men worked at the same trade, would be nothing but a shape-

[1] Add to these the argument already expounded (p. 252), that all importation imposes a debt, and a very large one, upon the purchasing country.

less and unorganized mass. Biology teaches us that the development of an organized being and its position in the scale of life are in proportion to the variety and multiplicity of its functions and the differentiation of the organs that perform them. It is precisely the same with a nation: if it wants to rise to a deeper and richer life it must strive to *multiply within itself all forms of social activity*, and all its energies, and must beware, therefore, lest foreign competition should come and destroy these activities, one after the other.

Moreover, if a nation allows itself to be restricted to one speciality, what will become of it in time of war? Did not the late war show clearly the danger incurred by a country that forgets how to be self-sufficing, and has to demand the necessaries of life from neighbouring lands, which may be friends to-day and enemies to-morrow? Such a country is bound to be defeated, whatever its military superiority may be.[1]

(2) *National Labour.*

For free-traders the essential advantage of international trade lies in the fact that it enables each of the exchanging countries to save a part of the labour that it would have to provide if it wished to produce a given commodity itself (see p. 250). But where free-traders see a *saving of labour* and rejoice at it, protectionists see a *suppression of labour*, and are grieved by it. In fact, given our existing social organization based on the division of labour, we cannot save a certain amount of labour without *rendering useless a certain kind of workers.* The Chinese silk trade is advantageous to French consumers, since it enables them to obtain silk with less expense and less labour: but the farmers and workers of the Cevennes region, who used to live by the silk industry, find themselves to some extent driven out of their livelihood. At the present time motor-car manufacturers and paper-makers declare that if American cars and German paper are allowed to enter France freely, they will have no choice but to close their works and discharge their workmen.

(3) *The Fiscal Argument.*

Customs duties are the best of all taxes, because *it is the foreigner who pays them.* A country should not hesitate to resort to them, therefore, since they have the advantage not only of protecting its industries, but also of procuring fiscal resources which cost its citizens nothing.[2]

---

[1] "The customs tariff is one of the conditions of France's independence," said the French Minister of Commerce (M. David) in the Senate, 11 March, 1910; and since the war this argument has impressed public opinion with invincible force.

[2] The French protectionist leader, M. Méline, said in the Chamber (28 February, 1898): "It is the foreigner who pays the customs duties."

How much stronger is this argument to-day, when the tax-payers are bowed beneath the weight of incredible taxation! France had hoped that her allies would undertake to pay part of her war expenses, but they have not felt themselves able to do so. But she can at any rate make them share these expenses by paying duties on the goods she imports from them!

The arguments just outlined are certainly not wanting in force, since they have converted almost all countries to a protectionist policy. But it is not hard to convert men, collectively or individually, to a system that suits their interests. Now the strength of the protectionist system lies in the fact that it gives obvious satisfaction to the interests of the industrial and agricultural producers, who constitute, economically and politically, the active and governing part of the population — at all events up to the present.

Free-traders, on the other hand, have to struggle against all private interests because they look at things not only from an international standpoint but from the standpoint of the general and higher interests of each nation.

Let us see first what reply we can make to the protectionist arguments.

(1) So far as economic independence goes, it must be recognized that diversity of tasks is necessary to progress, as well as diversity of social conditions. We even admit willingly that we must not let things take their own course, as free-traders are perhaps too much inclined to do, by accepting the fatalist notion of a natural division of labour among nations, determined by the physical conditions of the soil and subsoil, or by the so-called innate aptitudes of the people. We must recognize, on the contrary, that apart from certain cases of localization of industry, determined by force of circumstances, what are called the natural superiorities of a country are generally only acquired superiorities that have started from lucky strokes of initiative, and often even from chance causes, but which have gradually taken root by constant practice and been extended by imitation. We may say if we please that France has a natural superiority in the production of wine, or Germany in the manufacture of dyes, because they are derived from coal, but we can hardly see what natural necessity, what decree of Providence, can have made the Parisian milliner specialize in ladies' hats, or the Munich brewers in beer. Still less can we see any reason for the specialization in cotton and woollen goods in one place or another. It is never too late for a country — even for an old country — to try new ways and endeavour

to do as well as others. It only remains to find out whether the imposition of customs duties is the best way to stimulate national activity. And this is not at all certain.

In a celebrated German work, List, the precursor, if not the founder, of the so-called national system of political economy, said that each nation has to pass through a series of stages — agricultural, industrial, and commercial, — and that protection is indispensable at the critical period of transition from the first stage to the second. In his system, therefore, he would not protect agriculture, but only industry, and that only during its infancy and until it was fully developed. He therefore approved of England for having made her trade free. List would to-day be regarded rather as a free-trader. His system was that of protection for the safeguarding of infant industries.

But in practice it is not easy to fix the point at which this guardianship ought to cease. Interested industries will find that the moment is never the right one, and are not ashamed to claim the benefits of perpetual infancy.

What we hear of to-day is rather *compensatory duties*. If a foreign country — say America, for instance — can produce wheat at 7s. a hundredweight, owing to the natural resources of a still virgin country, or because her budget is not encumbered by the heavy consequences of the past, whereas the French farmer can only produce it at 10s. on an average, then, it is said, it is only fair that a compensatory import duty of 3s. should be imposed on American wheat to equalize the cost, just as is done on the race-course when jockeys are not equal in weight.

Put in that way the neo-protectionist doctrine looks equitable. But when a demand is made for the establishment of equality in competition by means of compensatory duties, we still have to discover on which side the inferiority lies — which scale of the balance falls. The Frenchman says that the compensatory duty should be levied against the American, because he has the natural resources — a soil not yet exhausted by twenty centuries of cultivation, and a lighter budget. But the Americans say that compensation should be made against the French, because the French are enabled by their lower wages, their longer working day, and the lower value of money in Europe, to produce at very much lower prices.

What are we to conclude, then? Which side is wrong? Who really needs protection? Are the young to be protected against the old, or the old against the young? The weak against the strong, or the strong against the weak? And what is to be thought of an

argument that can be used indifferently in support of two contradictory theses?[1]

We must remember, on the other hand, that if it is dangerous for
a country, as for a workman, to specialize in one kind of work, it
would be no less foolish a policy to undertake to do everything, and,
with this object, to make it a rule to do without the foreigner "at
any price" — even at the cost of incurring useless effort and an
infinite amount of sacrifice oneself. Now it is to be feared that the
effect of the war has been to drive all countries — belligerents and
even neutrals as well — along this path, owing to the obsession of
the blockade and the privations they had to suffer. England is
already preparing to reverse her policy of the last fifty years, and to
put into cultivation again the corn-land that she had turned into
pasture. Nor is it only the production of food-stuffs and raw materials that each country is striving to keep to itself. It is all the
"key industries" as well — those that are held to be indispensable
to the carrying-on of other industries, like the dye industry, for
example, of which Germany has hitherto had almost the monopoly.
Now considering the thoroughgoing character of modern wars,
involving the mobilization of all products as well as of all men,
there are scarcely any industries that can be said to be useless for
national defence. The result is that every industry must be protected in order to guarantee the independence of one's country.

An entirely different lesson might, perhaps, be drawn from the
war: namely, the powerlessness of a blockade, on either side, to
obtain the expected decision. In any case, the freedom of the
seas[2] would be a surer method of preventing the return of such
privations than useless and burdensome attempts at setting up water-
tight barriers between different countries — a system that merely
means an indefinite continuance of blockade conditions after the
war.

(2) As for the argument that free trade means the suppression of
labour, or at any rate its diminution or displacement, the fact can

---

[1] As far as inequality of taxation goes, the argument for compensatory duties is
based on the idea that customs duties fall on the foreign producer. But if, as we have
seen, they are generally reflected back on the consumer in the shape of a rise in price,
we can appreciate the irony of this so-called compensation, which, while claiming to
make the combatants equal, really lays a double load on the shoulders of the one who
is already most heavily burdened!

[2] Meaning the abolition of the right of capture of ships and their cargoes in time of
war — that is to say, the application to private property on the seas of the same rule
of law as is admitted nowadays for private property on land.

no longer be disputed. But it is exactly the same argument as was used against machinery and against all industrial progress. It is evident that every invention — every organization that enables a greater degree of satisfaction to be obtained with less effort, which is precisely the object of economic activity — necessarily renders useless a certain kind of workers.[1]

But we must reply to the protectionists, as to the machine-breakers and the opponents of co-operation and large shops, that this disadvantage is compensated by the fall in prices that is effected by this very saving of labour. Now protective duties, by retaining this useless labour, tend to raise the cost of living, or at any rate to prevent its falling. The majority of the articles that are most widely consumed — those that interest the working classes — are cheaper in free-trade countries like England and Belgium than in France.

How could it be otherwise? It goes without saying that the trader who imports goods will have to add to their original value the amount of the duties paid by him at the custom-house, exactly as he has to add the cost of transport and insurance. And yet, if this addition to the price affected only imported products it would be a small matter. But it reacts on all home production, so that the public has to pay out of its own pocket ten times as much as the State receives, in the form of additions to the price.

Protectionists reply that the rise of prices is not a necessary consequence of import duties, for why not admit that the foreign seller will pay them? That is indeed possible. The duty imposed on his products gives the seller his choice between *restricting his sales* and *sacrificing something on the price*, so that, all things considered, it is possible that his interest may lead him to choose the second alternative, and pay all or part of the duty. But it must be observed that two preliminary conditions must be fulfilled if the foreign producer is to submit to this course: the first is that the cost price must be such as to make it possible; the second is that there must be no means of selling the goods in another market.

But such cases are exceptional, and the thing to be noted is that when they do occur the result is *entirely contrary to the intentions of protectionists*, who have no right, therefore, to adduce them in sup-

---

[1] This reduced demand for labour may, however, be only temporary, (a) because the lowering of prices resulting from free trade itself will bring about an *increase in consumption*, and consequently an increase in production: for example, a fall in the price of motor-cars or silk goods will lead us to consume more of them; (b) because the lowering of prices, by diminishing the amount spent by consumers on a given article, may enable them to *transfer the money thus saved to other objects, or to invest it.*

port of their system. It is obvious enough that when manufacturers or farmers demand protective duties from public authorities, it is because they consider their selling prices inadequate, or because they are afraid to see them lowered. Consequently, the duties they demand have no other object than to cause a rise of prices, or, what comes to the same thing, to prevent an expected fall. And if the government were to say: "We will give you the duties you ask for, but we warn you that they will not make prices go up," there is no doubt that the interested parties would reply: "If that is the case you can keep your protective duties, for we have no use for them."

The rise of prices is therefore always the object, if not always the result, of protection. So true is this that in times of famine the government hastens to *suspend the duty*. Since the beginning of the war every State has been eager to decree the free entry of cereals and other commodities, so as to stop the rise of prices, if possible. In the face of such facts, how can it be honestly maintained that customs duties have no effect on prices?

(3) As for the fiscal argument, what we have just said is a sufficient reply to that. It could only be well founded if it could be established that customs duties are paid by the foreigner. That may happen in exceptional cases, but it is absurd to regard it as the general rule. It would indeed be highly convenient if a country could obtain the money it needs by taking it out of the foreigner's pocket. Moreover, if this really took place, each State would certainly adopt the same method, and no one would be any better off.

Finally, free-traders do not criticize customs duties as fiscal duties. What they do call attention to — and rightly so — is that the fiscal aim is not only distinct from the protective aim but is incompatible with it. If a duty is protective, its only object can be to reduce importation, and thereby to dry up the very source of fiscal revenue. If, on the other hand, the duty is a fiscal one, it will behoove the treasury, like any merchant fixing his prices, to find what tariff will yield the maximum profit when multiplied by the amount of imports.[1]

Would it not be possible to establish a protectionist system without customs duties? Certainly it would; and there are several

---

[1] There are two methods of assessing customs duties: (*a*) *ad valorem*, when the duty is so much per cent. on the value of the imported goods, this value being generally settled by the bill of lading, though sometimes estimated by the customs officers; (*b*) *specific*, when the duty is assessed beforehand according to the nature of the goods — so much for each article, like selling prices in a shop. This means the setting up of a huge catalogue in which the tariff for each kind of goods must be searched for.

ways of doing it, the best known being that of a *premium or bounty on production* — a sum of money granted by the State to the producer, on certain conditions.

This form of protection seems far superior to customs duties, at any rate from the theoretical point of view. In fact, scarcely any of the criticisms levelled against customs duties are applicable to premiums on production, for the following reasons: (a) they place no obstacle in the way of foreign trade, but permit importation to be fully developed, by allowing foreign products to enter freely; (b) it is easy to pay them to the proper person, whereas customs duties involve an expensive administration and give rise to a powerful and demoralizing industry called smuggling; (c) they do no harm to consumers, for they do not raise the price of the goods; (d) they in no way hinder production, for they neither enhance the price of raw materials nor increase the cost of production; on the contrary, they may be so graduated as to stimulate the development of the protected industry. In this way, bounties granted to merchant shipping are greater or less according as the vessels are sailing ships or steamships, are made of wood or of steel, and according to their speed. So, too, the bounties on silk-spinning established by the French in 1891 are made proportionate to the completeness of the plant. And in the same way the bounties on sugar have helped to develop the cultivation of beet as well as the production of sugar.

Unfortunately, however, this system often provokes retaliatory duties on the part of other States. It has also this fatal defect, that bounties figure as *expenditure* in the government's budget, whereas customs duties appear as *receipts*. Now since States are generally hard up — especially nowadays! — they are naturally more inclined to receive money than to pay it away.

But, to tell the truth, that is really an advantage rather than a drawback, for it would no longer be possible to make the tax-payers believe that protection enriches them: they would know exactly what it costs.

V. FREE TRADE

After refuting the arguments of protectionists in the manner just described, free-traders then take the offensive and bring many charges against the system of protection.

(1) They complain, first, that it is a retrograde system, opposed to the economic development that is characterized by the successive extension of the market, which is first domestic, then urban, then national, and should eventually become world-wide. External

custom-houses are a survival of the internal ones that used to exist between the provinces of a single country (they were abolished in France at the Revolution), and they arise from the same cause. Every producer is anxious to get rid of his rivals; he had to give up this idea, so far as his fellow-citizens were concerned, as soon as national unity was accomplished and the law became the same for everybody; but the treatment can still be applied to foreign competitors, so he takes advantage of it. These obstacles placed in the way of international trade with the sole object of satisfying private interests, will disappear as the others did, but meanwhile they have the same troublesome effects as internal custom-houses had: they are barriers that impede the traffic. For it must not be forgotten that to dam up the flow of imports is to dam up also the flow of exports (see above, p. 257), and consequently to counteract all the efforts made to facilitate communication, such as tunnelling through mountains, cutting canals through isthmuses, covering the seas with steamships and the ocean bed with telegraphic cables, organizing exhibitions and international fairs, setting up monetary conventions, and so forth. What greater folly can be imagined than to start by spending millions on driving tunnels through the Alps or building bridges over the Channel, and then to station customs officers at each end to stop the goods or hold them to ransom? The French have spent thousands of millions of francs on the Seine, the Rhône, and the Gironde, and their canals and harbours, so as to reduce by a few centimes the cost of transport of goods imported from abroad by these routes — but at the same time they raise the price of the goods 20% or 30% by means of customs duties![1]

(2) Protection not only injures the consumer — that goes without saying, — but it also injures the producer himself, first by raising the cost of his raw materials and plant,[2] and then by lulling him to

[1] "A twenty per cent. duty is like a bad road; a fifty per cent. like a broad, deep and rapid river, without any proper facilities for crossing; a seventy-five per cent. like a swamp flanking such a river on both sides; while a hundred per cent. duty such as has been levied upon steel rails, blankets, and window-glass, is as a band of robbers, who strip the merchant of nearly all he possesses, and make him not a little grateful that he escapes with his life." (David A. Wells, *A Primer of Tariff Reform*, pp. 8, 9.) See also Bastiat's equally ingenious pamphlets on this subject.

Not long ago we read an article in a Paris paper by a member of the Senate, extolling the blessings produced by the blockade during the war, and drawing this conclusion: "The greater the difficulties of trade, the more will human ingenuity take advantage of the resources of the earth." That, at least, is protectionist logic!

[2] So true is this that in the interests of certain industries it has been found necessary to modify the duty by means of *temporary admission*. This is the system by which

sleep, as it were, in the security of a position guaranteed against foreign competition.

Prince Bismarck once referred in a speech to the pike that are placed in carp-ponds to keep the carp on the alert and prevent them getting too fond of the mud. This comparison would be very appropriate here. If it be desirable that a country should keep its position as a great industrial and commercial power — which is precisely the protectionist aim — it must be compelled constantly to renew its plant and its industrial processes, and to be continually eliminating those parts of its organization that are worn out or obsolete.

(3) From the point of view of *distribution*, protective duties give rise to injustice, for their effect is to guarantee a minimum income to the owners of the protected goods. This is paid to them by the consumers in the shape of the addition to the price, as we have just seen, and the privilege is the more striking in that the law refuses, apart from some rare exceptions, to guarantee to wage-earners the minimum wage that they also demand. It is not without reason that free-traders reproach protection with being the socialism of the rich.

(4) Finally, if we leave the economic sphere for the realm of international politics, we shall find protection to have been one of the most formidable causes of war, not only in the past but still more in our own day. The very language of protection is filled with words and figures borrowed from warfare: protectionists talk only of tariff wars, of the invasion of foreign goods, of the conquest of foreign markets. When a country has been brought up on the idea that it can only enrich or even support its population by obtaining foreign outlets, it is strongly tempted to get them by force if it cannot succeed by gentler means. And what must happen is this: that when a country finds itself shut out from the markets of neighbouring lands, it goes in search of outlets across the seas that it deems indispensable to its industries or its population, so that protection appears as a factor in colonial policy, and this in its turn produces fresh conflicts. Without going into details that are outside the scope of this book, we cannot doubt that colonial rivalries counted for

raw materials destined for exportation in the form of manufactured goods, are exempted from paying duty. When they are at length exported they will have to compete with foreign products in the international market. In order to avoid the obvious risk of fraud, the importer is obliged to sign an undertaking to pay the duty, under penalty of a heavy fine, if these raw materials, converted into manufactured goods, are not exported within a certain time.

much in the state of tension that preceded and prepared the way for the late war.[1]

VI. COMMERCIAL TREATIES

If we had to choose between the two systems just described, protection and free trade, we should not hesitate about preferring the second, for we hold with Bastiat that in case of doubt it is the consumer's interest that should rule.

Yet the system of free trade after the English or "Manchester" pattern does not seem to us to realize the ideal to be aimed at in international relations. It is even tainted, in our opinion, with an almost fatal defect: it relies, for the attainment of the welfare of all, upon *laisser faire* — upon the faith that all the individual acts of exchange between the inhabitants of all lands must unconsciously combine to promote the welfare of all. Now in the course of this book we have tried on many occasions to show the weakness of this optimistic conclusion, especially in the case of the advantages of competition.

If, therefore, we object to the protectionist system, it is because its object is to realize for every nation the principle of "each for himself and by himself," and because the ends aimed at by each country are necessarily antagonistic, each trying to enter its neighbour's market and to keep its neighbours out of its own. But are we to conclude that free trade approaches nearer to the co-operative ideal, "each for all"? It may be doubted. When we studied the subject of internal trade we had to own that, though born under favourable auspices — freedom of labour and freedom of exchange — it ended too often in a struggle for existence among producers, and dearer goods or deterioration in their quality for consumers, so that the system of free commercial competition had to be gradually replaced by that of commercial agreements and co-operative associations. There is every reason to fear, then, that the same system of free competition extended to international trade may have the same results. In short, free trade, as expressed in the formula "*laisser faire, laisser passer*," is only one aspect of the struggle for profit, just like absolute protection itself. Among nations as among individuals we should seek to establish relations that are

[1] It will be recalled that among President Wilson's famous "Fourteen Points," one of them (the 3d) was as follows: "The removal, so far as possible, of all economic barriers and the establishment of an equality of trade conditions among all the nations consenting to the peace and associating themselves for its maintenance." But in the Covenant of the League of Nations (Article 23 of the Treaty of Versailles) this clause was passed only in an unrecognizable form and without any real force.

neither antagonistic, like those of the nationalist-protectionist system, nor competitive, like those of the free trade system, but which are truly co-operative.

On the other hand, while admitting that free trade ought to provoke fewer political conflicts between nations than protection, it would be extravagant to expect the abolition of war to follow from its adoption, as its protagonists assert.[1] The fight for outlets that characterizes this system does not look like an agent of pacification: the merchants of Manchester must not be confounded with the "pioneers" of Rochdale. Nor is it apparent that England has waged many less wars than protectionist countries.

As a means of putting an end to war, no better method has been discovered than the setting up of the League of Nations. Similarly, if we wish to abolish commercial wars, or to reduce them to a minimum, what better means can be found than to bind nations together by contracts, called *treaties?* These treaties, drawn up at first by pairs of nations and then made universal, will tend to consitute a *commercial union,* either European or world-wide in its scope. That is the co-operative system that ought to replace both the nationalist system, called protection, and the competitive system, called free trade. It will not allow any country to close its markets jealously, nor to try to conquer foreign markets, but it will aim at utilizing the resources of each country in the interests of each and all.

This treaty system also enables both the antagonistic systems to be satisfied. To free-traders it offers the following advantages:

(1) It ensures the *stability* of tariffs during a long period of time (generally ten years), which is very favourable to commercial operations. It is true that, conversely, it binds the contracting countries and takes from them the opportunity of modifying their tariffs according to circumstances; but this bond should be regarded as a benefit and not an evil, for, because of it, merchants can calculate and fix their prices for a reasonably long period.

(2) It establishes solidarity or mutual dependence among all countries, even those that are not parties to the agreement, in virtue of the "most favoured nation" clause, which is usually inserted in all these treaties. By this clause *every concession made by one country to another is extended automatically to all countries with which it has already made treaties.*

(3) It leads gradually to a more and more liberal régime, owing to the reciprocal concessions obtained by the contracting parties

[1] This theory is especially emphasized in a recent book called *Pax Economica,* by Henri Lambert, a great Belgian manufacturer.

from each other each time a treaty is renewed, whereas experience shows that the system of protection, when once established, tends to increase and extend, as each industry in turn demands its share.

On the other hand, commercial treaties permit of satisfaction being given to some of the demands of protectionists:

(1) They set up the principle of *reciprocity* — what is called *fair trade*, as distinguished from *free trade* — in the following ways: (*a*) by offering an open door to countries that open theirs, and *vice versa;* (*b*) by giving a means of defence against an aggressive policy on the part of the foreigner, when he tries to force open our door by subsidizing his manufacturers or adopting the practice of *dumping*.

Dumping was a frequently-discussed question before the war, and has become even more prominent since, because it is looked upon as an economic weapon peculiar to Germany and as formidable as poison gas. The English word applied to this proceeding[1] shows, however, that it is not a German invention. But it is true that the Germans have been able to use it better than any other country, thanks to the skilful organization of their cartels. As soon as these associations of producers acquire a quasi-monopoly of the market, it is to their interest that prices should not fall owing to overproduction, and to avoid this they may find it advantageous to pour away their surplus produce abroad, even at a loss. At the same time, the dangers of this form of competition have been exaggerated, for it can only be an exceptional mode of procedure, and it may even give the importing country the advantage of getting a good bargain — as the tradesman says when he tries to tempt a customer.

(2) They permit of the fostering of *acquired situations* and the safeguarding of industries whose ruin would cause too great a disturbance, either from the political and social or from the economic point of view. They also permit of a *differentiation* of duties, taking account of differences of position among different countries and of the industries in each of them that seem more or less threatened by competition, whereas a general customs tariff is necessarily uniform and can admit of no increase or reduction of duty according to the country from which the goods come, for this would be an act of hostility. For instance, if France considers that merchant shipping ought to be maintained at any price, as a means of national defence, or the wine-growing industry, because of the huge capital engaged in it and the amount of wages it distributes, then commercial treaties enable her to support these industries.

[1] [Professor Gide uses the English word "dumping."]

Such, then, are the advantages that arise from the system of commercial treaties. Unfortunately French policy shows little favour to this method, and this is one of the causes that have placed France's international commerce behind that of her rivals. But if England at length forms her huge Empire into a customs union, and if the United States on their side succeed, as they have tried to do in various pan-American congresses, in establishing a customs union including all the republics of America, then, in face of these two "Zollverein," each occupying a third of the world, the creation of a commercial union embracing all the States of the European continent would seem to be indicated. But unfortunately this has not been made easier by the war.[1]

VII. HISTORY OF INTERNATIONAL TRADE

During ancient and medieval times international trade was less general than it is to-day. It was in the hands of a few small nations who held a monopoly of commerce and transport owing to their maritime situation — Tyre and Carthage in ancient times, the Italian republics and the Hansa towns in the Middle Ages, and Holland at the beginning of the modern period. Other nations played a purely passive part; they welcomed foreign traders, just as the African negroes receive Moslem or European merchants to-day, with a certain amount of good will, since they brought them goods they could not produce for themselves; they even tried to attract them, by granting them privileges when necessary. But, in exchange for the protection they granted these traders, they made them pay certain duties which were a kind of share in their profits, just as little African kings still levy tribute on the caravans that pass through their territories. Customs duties, therefore, — if we may already give them this name, — were originally entirely *fiscal* and in no way protective. What, indeed, could they protect, when there were no national industries?

In the sixteenth century, however, a change took place, for two reasons:

(1) Because international commerce developed to an extent unknown before when the great ocean routes of the world were opened. International competition had been out of the question when scarcely anything was transported except articles of luxury: the purple of Tyre, the brocades of Venice, Toledo sword blades, and spices from the East. But it began to make itself felt as soon as trade was suffi-

---

[1] [We have omitted a portion of this last paragraph, and also a footnote, dealing entirely with French tariff history.]

ciently well equipped for the transport of articles of general consumption, such as the cloth of Flanders

(2) Because the great States of modern Europe were formed at this time, and one of their concerns was to adopt a national policy — that is to say, to make international trade serve for the aggrandizement of their wealth and power.

Then it was that there arose a collection of theories and an entire body of policy that is known as the *mercantile system*. This system was somewhat misrepresented in the classical treatises. It was said that the mercantilists believed that money was the only true wealth, and that consequently a country could only grow rich by procuring it; and that when a country had no chance of possessing gold and silver mines, its only means of obtaining money was to sell as much as possible to other countries that possessed money, and thus to draw it from them by degrees. If, on the other hand, a country was foolish enough to buy abroad, it thereby got robbed of its money. Therefore, to export as much as possible, and to import as little as possible — in short, to aim always at having a favourable balance of trade, — was the whole conclusion of the mercantile system.

The doctrine does not seem as childish as it is said to be if we take into consideration its date, at a time when gold and silver were more scarce, perhaps, than they have been at any other period; when the growing needs of trade and industry — not to mention the government needs of the new-born States — were creating a veritable famine of money; and when men were beginning with difficulty to invent those modes of credit that were one day to permit of a more economical use of money. If the discovery of the mines of the New World dazzled men's eyes and inspired them with covetousness, it was not without reason, for it came just at the psychological moment — Bastiat would have said the providential moment.

The mercantilists were the precursors of those who are called nowadays "national economists." They founded the first national manufactures, and they sought to attract good workmen, who seemed to them a form of wealth no less precious than gold. But, above all, they conceived the idea of employing customs duties to avert foreign competition and develop national industry: with them these duties lost their *fiscal* character and became *protective*. With Cromwell in England and Colbert in France this logically coherent system reached its fullest development. It may be summed up under three heads:

(1) The discouragement of the importation of manufactured goods by protective duties;

(2) The encouragement, on the other hand, of the importation of

food-stuffs, raw materials, and anything useful in manufacture, by means of a reduction of these duties;

(3) The stimulation of the exportation of the produce of the country, by encouraging manufacture or by means of bounties.

This system, generally known as *Colbertism*, ruled without dispute until the coming of the "economists." The physiocrats mercilessly demolished the theories of mercantilism, and set up in the opposite camp the standard of *laisser faire, laisser passer*. They fought no less vigorously for the freedom of trade against the protectionist system, than for the freedom of labour against the guild system. But the French Revolution, which led to the triumph of their doctrine in the matter of freedom of labour, did nothing of the kind with freedom of trade. And the twenty years of European war that followed were scarcely a fitting preparation for the coming of free trade.

In England, however, the ideas started by Adam Smith had matured. Moreover, the land system as established in the British Isles was sufficient in itself to discredit the protectionist system, for it was a particularly odious spectacle to see the English lords, owners by right of conquest of almost all the land in the kingdom, keeping out foreign corn in order to sell their own at a higher price, and profiting by the growing needs of the population to collect higher and higher rents. The House of Lords was therefore in a poor position to resist the movement of indignation let loose by the Anti-Corn Law League, and in 1846, after the striking conversion of Sir Robert Peel, it was obliged to give in. Once the duty on corn was abolished, the rest of the protectionist edifice collapsed, including Cromwell's famous Navigation Act, to which the maritime greatness of England was attributed.

In France, a league founded by Bastiat in 1846, and modelled on the English Anti-Corn Law League, came to nothing because French social conditions were quite different from those of England. But the Emperor Napoleon III, whose policy was founded upon an alliance with England, and whose instincts were democratic, took advantage of the autocratic power that he possessed to sign a treaty of commerce with the British government without consulting the Chamber of Deputies. This famous treaty of 1860, in no way answering to the wishes of the country, had none the less a remarkable influence in Europe, and was followed immediately by the conclusion of similar treaties between all the powers of Europe, so that it was everywhere held to mark the end of the long rule of protection and the beginning of an era of real free trade.

The reign of free trade, however, was not destined to be a long one. To begin with, the United States had remained outside the movement. They had always been protectionist — even from birth, it might be said. In fact, the chief cause of their revolt against the mother country had been that they were not permitted by her to manufacture "even a horse-shoe." It was natural, therefore, that their first anxiety should be to get possession of their industrial independence. But protective duties, very moderate at first, went on increasing periodically, and always with some new object. First it was to protect their infant industries: it was that which inspired the system of List. Then after 1866 it was to pay the expenses of the great civil war. Later on this reason disappeared, and when the greater part of their debt was paid, the United States did not know what to do with the money drawn from their customs duties, so to make use of it they distributed some forty million pounds in pensions to so-called war invalids. But then a new argument was discovered for increasing customs duties — the need to defend the high wages of America against the low prices and wages of Europe. Since then, American tariffs have simply grown bigger and bigger.

Germany had paved the way for its political union since 1833, by setting up a customs union between the various German States. When the free trade period came along, she joined the movement wholeheartedly. But when her political unity was accomplished she conceived an ambition to become a great industrial power, and turned completely round in the direction of independent protectionism. It may even be said that it was Germany, along with Austria, that started the protectionist reaction, in 1879, that was quickly to win over the whole of Europe. And more recently still (1892–1894), when she had achieved this first object, and had to seek for outlets abroad, she adopted a mixed system of commercial treaties which started a new Zollverein embracing the whole of central Europe. The defeat of 1918 has put an end to this dream for the time being.

As for France, as soon as she was able to free herself, in 1892, from the commercial treaties concluded by Napoleon III, she became protectionist again. Since then she has merely moved more emphatically in the same direction, even to the extent of increasing her customs duties in 1910.

Finally, even England herself, the classic land of free trade, has begun to waver. The new protectionism first appeared there in the shape of imperialism. That is to say, it was inspired particularly by a political motive — that of uniting by bonds of self-interest the nations that make up the immense British Empire. With this end it would be necessary for the colonies, themselves for the most part strongly protectionist, to concede reductions of duties to the products of the mother country, and conversely for England to grant privileges to colonial products, which implies the imposition of duties on foreign products. But other forces are impelling England, like other countries, into the protectionist path, even more than imperialist ambitions. Among them is the need for obtaining resources to meet the enormously increased expenses caused by the war and by social legislation. If these are not obtained from the customs they must be demanded from the rich, and such, indeed, is the programme of the liberal[1] party. Naturally, however, the manufacturers and landowners prefer protective duties, and, to win over the working classes, they offer them as a remedy for unemployment.

So in Europe at the present day there are hardly more than a few small countries — Holland, Norway, and Denmark — that have remained faithful to free trade because their area is too limited for them to be self-sufficing. Everywhere else, even in Switzerland, customs barriers have been raised and tariff wars have taken the place of commercial treaties.

What influence has the great war had upon international trade? It began by almost wiping it out, through the action of the double blockade: the blockade of the central empires by the fleets of the Entente powers, and the blockade of the Entente powers by the submarines of Germany. But in consequence of the frantic rise in prices it was found that international trade increased enormously when expressed in value, while the quantity of goods carried diminished.[2]

[1] [In the widest sense of this word, of course, including particularly the extreme left.]

[2] Here are the (approximate) comparative figures for three great powers in 1913 and 1920 (in millions sterling):

	France	England	United States
1913	610	1,410	870
1920	2,310	3,280	2,770

As this increase was due solely to the rise in prices, and as this rise was enormously different in each of the three countries, it would be idle to make any comparison of the progress of trade in these countries. What is particularly noticeable is the upsetting of the balance of trade: a huge excess of imports in the case of France and England, and a huge excess of exports from the United States. In France during the six years 1915–20 the excess of imports amounted to nearly £4,000,000,000 (£960,000,000 for the year 1919 alone). Fortunately the economic laws we have already explained, and which were temporarily put out of action, have begun to operate again, and equilibrium was again established in 1921. [In the case of England the excess of imports for the same six years amounted to nearly £3,700,000,000.] The United States, on

It is somewhat difficult to find arguments in favour of protection or free trade in the disturbances created by a state of war. In fact they lend themselves to opposite interpretations. It may be said that since the belligerent States hastened to abolish the duties on food-stuffs at the beginning of the war (France abolished her corn duties on the 31st July, 1914, the eve of mobilization, and Germany in September), this proves that they expected a fall in price to follow the abolition, and that therefore it incontestably refutes the doctrine that customs duties are paid by the foreigner. But, conversely, protectionists have not failed to make use of the fact that all these States were nearly brought to destruction through lack of means of subsistence, and to draw the conclusion that it is necessary for every country to make itself independent of the foreigner (see above).

It is difficult, also, to pick out guiding principles for post-war commercial policy. All that can be said is that such policy will be cruelly torn between opposing ends: on the one hand, the need for each country to press on its exportation and to open up markets in friendly and even in neutral countries; and, on the other hand, the necessity for each country to obtain resources for its depleted exchequer, and its desire to assure its commercial independence in the interests of national defence.

the other hand, benefited during these six years by an excess of exports amounting to 17,334 million dollars — say £3,500,000,000 at par.

CHAPTER VI — CREDIT

I. HOW CREDIT IS SIMPLY AN EXTENSION OF EXCHANGE

Credit is only an enlargement of exchange — exchange in time instead of in space. It may be defined as *the exchange of present wealth for future wealth.*

For example: a wool spinner sells wool to a cloth manufacturer. But the latter has not the wherewithal to pay for it — he has no present wealth to give in exchange for the wealth that is delivered to him. But that makes no difference: the manufacturer gives in exchange the future wealth that he proposes to create out of this wool — that is to say, an equivalent value to be taken out of the value of the cloth when it is made.

Here the fact of exchange is perfectly clear: it is a real sale. The only way in which it differs from an ordinary sale is that it is a *credit* transaction and not a cash one. But this difference, which seems of little importance, has weighty consequences. It is no small thing to draw the future into the scope of our contracts.

Here is another form of credit in which the act of exchange is less easy to detect, although it is actually there. A farmer, having no wheat to sow, borrows some from his neighbour — that is to say, he engages to give it back after the next harvest. Of course he will not give back the same wheat, for he will have used that to sow his field, but he will give different wheat, drawn from his own harvest. The Roman lawyers well expressed it when they said that in cases of loan the thing was transferred in full ownership (they called it *mutuum*, because it made mine, *meum*, become thine, *tuum*) and that it was the same, conversely, with the similar thing given back when the time for payment arrived. If instead of wheat we imagine the loan to consist of a sum of money, which is the object usually borrowed nowadays, it is no less obvious that here there is still an exchange of present wealth for future wealth.[1]

---

[1] In the case of an object that the borrower has to return just as it is — such as a house or land, where the loan is called a lease — the definition we have given is no longer applicable. This is not exchange but *hire*, and it is no longer *credit*, in the proper sense of the term. I could hardly say that the landlord who lets me lodgings gives me credit, especially when he makes me pay the rent in advance, which is the rule for small lets!

Now these two operations — *sales on credit*, and *loans* — are the two essential forms of credit.

The essential characteristics of credit, therefore, are (1) the *consumption* of the article sold or lent; (2) the *expectation* of the new article that is to take its place.   For whereas the man who lets a house or farm knows that it will be restored to him, and does not lose sight of it for an instant when it is in the hands of the borrower, the man who lends a thing for consumption knows that it is taken from him irrevocably.   The sack of borrowed wheat will have to pass through the mill to become flour, or be buried in the furrow until the harvest.   The sack of borrowed crowns, whatever use they are to be put to, will have to be emptied down to the last coin in expectation of the future money that the borrower hopes to make.   Now that is a terrible position, for the borrower as well as for the lender, for this is what results:

(*a*) First consider the lender.   He is exposed to considerable risk.   No doubt he counts on receiving an equivalent amount of wealth to replace what he has lent, but this wealth is *not yet in existence*.   It will have to be produced for this purpose, and whatever is future is by that very fact uncertain.   Legislators have striven to guarantee the lender against all danger, and the precautions they have devised with this object constitute one of the most important branches of civil law: guarantee, liability, mortgages, etc.

When the debt is secured by the delivery of goods of at least equivalent value, movable or immovable (there need be no actual delivery of immovable goods, and sometimes not even of movable goods), then the maximum security is obtained and the credit is said to be *real*, meaning that the claim applies to a thing (*res*).   Yet even in this case the security is not absolute, for the immovable goods mortgaged or the object given in pledge may lose their value.   So a certain amount of confidence — an act of faith — is always required on the part of the. lender, and that is exactly why the name "credit" is reserved for this particular kind of loan, for by its etymological origin it implies an act of faith (Lat. *credere*, to believe, or trust). And credit is more and more called upon to justify its fine name, because, as we shall see, *real* credit — that which is guaranteed by a pledge or mortgage — gives place more and more to *personal* credit, which, in the shape of current banking accounts or mutual credit societies, is founded entirely upon the word of the borrower.   It will be said, no doubt, that this is a return to the past — to the days of ancient Rome, when the creditor had likewise no other security than the person of the debtor.   But the difference between the two is great, for then it was the very body of the debtor that served as a pledge — a body which could be imprisoned, whipped, and perhaps even cut into pieces (*partes secanto*, as the Law of the XII Tables had it) — whereas nowadays the only pledge of personal credit is the honour of the debtor, his moral and not his physical person.

(*b*) Secondly, consider the borrower. His obligation does not consist, like that of the tenant of a house or farm, simply in having to keep the thing lent and to maintain it in good order till he restores it at the appointed date. After he has made use of it — that is to say, destroyed it — he has to labour to build up an equivalent for it, with which to settle his debt on the day it falls due. *He must therefore take great care to employ this wealth in a productive manner.* If he is unwise enough to use it unproductively, for personal consumption, or if by ill chance he fails to produce an amount of wealth at least equivalent to that which he has borrowed, that means ruin. In fact, the history of all countries at all times is a veritable martyrology of borrowers ruined by credit.

Credit, then, is an infinitely more dangerous mode of production than those we have hitherto considered. It can only be of use in societies where economic education is highly developed.

II. CREDIT INSTRUMENTS

Credit really only comes into existence as a mode of production when the future wealth that is its real object is to some extent realized — although it does not exist — and enters into commerce in the form of *negotiable instruments*. The invention of these marked a real economic revolution, which may be assigned to the thirteenth century. It must be understood in the following way.

At the beginning, credit was not regarded as wealth, for it had no reference to a material object, nor to any wealth at all: it was a purely personal bond between creditor and debtor. In the significant words of the commentators, the obligation adhered to the body of the debtor — *ossibus haeret*. If the debtor failed to pay, the creditor could not seize his goods: there was nothing that he could seize except the very body of the debtor, and that is why, as we have just remarked, he could imprison it or even cut it into pieces. In these circumstances, the idea of *transferable* credit claims — the possibility of putting such a power into the hands of anyone else — could not possibly be entertained.

But the Roman lawyers soon took a great step forward, and credit claims came to be regarded as goods (*bona*). Then by means of ingenious devices they were made transferable (by what was called *novatio* and *litis contestatio*). This transfer of credits, however, always remained more difficult than the transfer of material goods, and even to-day, according to the French Civil Code, the transfer of credit instruments involves somewhat complicated formalities — especially the notification to the debtor.

But commercial law, as has often been noticed, always advances more rapidly than civil law, and serves it as a pioneer. So, in the Middle Ages, it made an admirable double invention — that of representing a credit claim by a written document — a *bill of exchange* or a *promissory note*.

A bill of exchange is a document by which a creditor conveys to his debtor an *order to pay*, not to himself, the "drawer" of the bill, but to *a third person*, generally in another place or another country. For this reason bills of exchange have always been used mainly for settling transactions at a distance — between different towns or different countries.

If a merchant of Venice owed a merchant of Amsterdam a thousand ducats, instead of sending the ducats in coin (which was hardly a convenient proceeding in those days), he would hand them over to one of his brother merchants in Venice, who had a claim on Amsterdam. The latter would give him in exchange a letter ordering his correspondent in Amsterdam to pay a thousand ducats to whoever presented the letter to him. So the merchant of Venice would merely send his Dutch creditor the letter instead of the money, and thus settle his debt. It is the same nowadays. Originally, however, this letter or bill could only be used by the one who had drawn it. It was not till later on, in the fifteenth century, that the idea arose of making it negotiable by a mere note written on the back of it, called an *endorsement*.

The effect of the endorsement is not merely to make the settlement of transactions marvellously simple and to enable payment to be made without the use of money by the mere transfer of the bill. It also strengthens the value of the bill, because each of those into whose hands it passes, and who affixes his signature to the back of it, becomes severally responsible for the debt that it represents. The proverb that declares that "a rolling stone gathers no moss," is very much at fault here: the rolling bill is like a snowball, and grows big with added guarantees. It is therefore a perfect credit instrument.

Although the endorsement, however, gives additional ease of circulation to the bill, it also creates an obstacle, not so much by the slight formality of having to affix a signature, as by the liability it involves. Let us go a step further: let us eliminate the endorsement itself, and create credit instruments that shall be transferable simply from hand to hand like pieces of money — bearer securities, cheques, and bank-notes.

That brings us to the last stage. Henceforth huge masses of wealth — not exactly fictitious wealth, but future wealth, which is quite different — are added to the mass of existing wealth, and circulate in the form of negotiable or "bearer" instruments. These documents are the object of an enormous trade that would in former days have appeared inconceivable, and the merchants who specialize in this trade are called bankers.

The creation of instruments representing capital is not only useful in facilitating sales, loans, and payments. It has a more curious and apparently an almost miraculous effect: it is equivalent to a *duplication of capital*, allowing two people to use it at once.

This is an enormous advantage, for if it is very advantageous for the purchaser, buying on credit, to keep his money at his own disposal for a certain time, it is, conversely, very disadvantageous for the seller to be compelled to go without it for the same period. A manufacturer has to make purchases and pay wages every day. He can only get along on condition of renewing his necessary capital from day to day by the sale of his goods. But if he sells them on credit — that is to say, without being paid for them — it looks as if it must become impossible for him to carry on.

What is to be done? It cannot be possible, it would seem, for the same capital to be at the disposal of two different persons, the lender and the borrower, *at the same time*. Yet such is actually the case; and it is the negotiable credit instrument that solves the apparently insoluble problem. In exchange for the capital that he gives up, the lender or the man who sells on credit receives a document — a piece of paper in the form of a promissory note, or bill of exchange, or what not — representing a value which can be sold, like all other values. If he wishes to resume his capital, nothing could be simpler: all that is needed is for him to sell, or *negotiate*, as it is called, this document.

Of course there is no magic about this proceeding, and the operation has a natural explanation, as we shall see in the next section.

III. WHETHER CREDIT CAN CREATE CAPITAL

Credit has acquired such importance in modern society that we are tempted to ascribe miraculous powers to it. Speaking constantly of great fortunes founded on credit, and recognizing that the most extensive enterprises of modern industry are built upon a basis of credit, we are invincibly persuaded that credit is an agent of production and that it can create wealth quite as well as land or labour.

But this is a complete illusion.   Credit is not an *agent* of production: it is a particular *mode* of production (which is a very different thing), just like exchange, and just like division of labour.   It consists, as we have seen, in the transfer of wealth or capital from one person to another; but to transfer is not to create.   Credit can no more create wealth than exchange can create goods.   As John Stuart Mill has admirably put it: "Credit being only permission to use the capital of another person, the means of production cannot be increased by it, but only transferred."

What serves to foster this illusion is the existence of credit instruments.   We have seen that all capital that is lent is represented in the hands of the lender by a negotiable instrument of the same value. Hence it seems as though the act of lending has the miraculous effect of making *two* capitals out of one.   The old capital of £1000 which has been transferred to the borrower, and the new capital represented by a note for £1000 in the hands of the lender — do not these two make £2000?

From the subjective point of view this paper note is, in fact, capital: it is capital for me, but not for the country as a whole.   It is evident, indeed, that I can only negotiate it if someone is willing to give me in exchange for it the capital that he possesses either in money or goods.   The document is not capital in itself therefore, but it merely gives me the *possibility of obtaining other capital in place of that which I have relinquished.*   It is obvious, moreover, that whatever may be the use that I wish to make of the value represented by this piece of paper — whether I want to use it to pay my expenses, or for production — I can only do this by converting it into those objects of consumption or instruments of production that are already in existence on the market.   It is by means of this real wealth that I shall carry on production or support life, and not by means of scraps of paper.[1]

_____

[1] Léon Say, in his preface to Goschen's *Theory of the Foreign Exchanges*, says: "This absolute representation of property in the form of an instrument has dissipated

If every credit instrument — every debt — was actually wealth, then every Frenchman would simply have to lend his wealth to his neighbour, in order to double the wealth of the country at one stroke, raising it, say, from ten thousand millions to twenty thousand millions!

May we not at any rate say that these instruments represent *future wealth?* Certainly; but it is precisely because the wealth is future that we cannot count it. We shall be able to count it when it is born. Until then there will always be this marked difference between present and future wealth, that the first exists and the second does not! We cannot produce and we cannot live from wealth that is merely expected. We might just as well reckon, in taking a census of population, all those members of society who are to be born during the next twenty years.

But though credit cannot be called productive in the sense of creating capital, it yet renders important services to production by enabling us to *utilize existing capital to the best possible advantage.* In fact, if capital could not be transferred from one person to another, and if everyone were reduced to the necessity of employing what he possessed himself, an enormous amount of capital would remain unemployed. In all civilized societies there are many persons who cannot make use of their own capital. Among them are the following:

(*a*) Those who have *too much* capital. As soon as a man's fortune exceeds a certain sum, it is no easy matter for him to make use of it by his own ability alone, apart from the fact that in such cases he is scarcely disposed, as a rule, to take the necessary pains to employ it.

(*b*) Those who have *not enough.* Workmen, peasants, and servants, who have saved small sums of money, are unable to employ these small savings productively. Yet these small amounts may add up to millions when they are all put together.

(*c*) Those who are unable, owing to *age, sex,* or *occupation,* to employ their capital themselves in industrial undertakings. Such are children, women, and members of the liberal professions — lawyers, doctors, soldiers, clergymen, civil servants, and officials of every kind.

all the difficulties that used to hinder the maturing and transmission of rights. To-day, by means of a French bill on England, an English bill on Canada, a Dutch bill on the Indies, and *vice versa,* we can send factories and railways and, in fact, anything that can be owned. The thing itself remains motionless, but its image is conveyed unceasingly from place to place. It is like the play of mirrors sending reflections to the ends of the earth. The mirror is tilted, and the reflection strikes higher or lower, to the right, or to the left. The object itself is in one place, but it is made use of everywhere: whoever has the reflection, has the object."

On the other hand there is no lack of people in the world — captains of industry, inventors, agriculturists, and even workmen — who could make good use of capital if they had it; but unfortunately they have not got it.

If, therefore, capital can be transferred, by means of credit, from those who cannot or will not make use of it to those who are in a position to employ it productively, this transference will be of great benefit to both parties and to the country as a whole. In every country there are millions of pounds of capital that are thus withdrawn from sterile hoarding or from unproductive consumption, and made fruitful by means of credit. It has been well said that credit possesses the virtue of transforming *latent* capital into *active* capital. In short, credit plays the same part in relation to capital as exchange does in relation to wealth. We have already seen that exchange, by transferring wealth from one producer to another, does not create it, but enables it to be better utilized, and also promotes the better employment of natural resources and the labour of producers.

IV. HOW CREDIT ENABLES US TO DISPENSE WITH MONEY

That credit enables us to *postpone* payment is obvious enough, and follows from its definition; but it is not equally clear that it enables us to *abolish* payment; for sooner or later, it will be said, when the date of payment arrives, the debtor will surely have to pay up? But no; even that will not be necessary.

Suppose that every sale, instead of being paid for in money, is paid for by the creation of a credit instrument — a cheque or bill of exchange — and that these instruments are thrown upon the market and pass from hand to hand by successive transfers. The result will necessarily be that most of them end by meeting and cancelling each other, either by *compensation* or by *confusion*, as the lawyers put it.

Suppose that there are three countries, or three persons, whom we will call A, B, and C. Suppose that A is a debtor to B, and that B is a debtor for the same amount to C, who in his turn is a debtor to A. Is it not evident, then, that instead of passing the sum of money owed by these three debtors to their three creditors round the whole circle — making A pay £1000 to B, who then pays £1000 to C, who finally hands back the money to A, from whom it came in the first place — it is simpler to settle the whole business without paying a farthing?

But of course it will be said that it is highly improbable that *C* will be debtor to *A* in this convenient fashion, so as to close the circle, as it were. This is true; but if *C* is not a debtor to *A*, he will perhaps be a debtor to *D*, or *E*, or *F*, or *G*, or *H*, so that the credit instrument chances ultimately to reach someone who is *A*'s debtor, and then the problem is solved. The more persons there are taking part in the game, the larger the circle will be, and obviously *the more chance there will be of closing the circle*, of buckling the strap, so to speak. Besides, there are intermediate agents whose express business it is to turn these chances into realities. These are the bankers, in whose hands the cheques and bills of exchange of *A*, *B*, *C*, etc., will eventually collect.

It was in international trade — in exchanges between one country and another — that merchants first had recourse to credit to enable them to dispense with money. The dangers and difficulties of transporting large sums of money over great distances inspired the Lombards, as we have said, with the idea of the *bill of exchange*, whose principal use was to avoid the conveyance of money from place to place and making many payments, one in each place. But if the transport of money was eliminated, payment was not. There was still one step to be taken to reach that end. Suppose that each of two places, say London and Paris, had drawn a bill of exchange on the other. Then each place was debtor and creditor for the same amount, and it is plain that these two debts could be extinguished by the method of payment called *compensation;* and if the amounts were unequal, compensation could take place none the less, up to the amount of the smaller of the two sums. All that would be necessary would be for the intermediate agents, the bankers, to undertake to balance the account.

But for these ingenious devices, in fact, international commerce would have been quite impossible. As we have already shown, the money that actually travels from one country to another represents only a very small fraction of the value of the goods exchanged.

But it is not only in international relations that credit instruments are able to take the place of money and make it unnecessary. It is the same among the inhabitants of a single town or a single country. In this case it is the cheque that is chiefly employed for the purpose (see below, p. 295).

Could not the cheque itself be replaced by simple booking operations? Suppose that all the inhabitants of a country open accounts in a single bank,[1] whose duty it is to receive all income for each of

[1] Or in the Post Office, where everybody is necessarily a customer. The postal cheque system was started first in Austria in 1883, and more recently in France.

its customers by entering it to their *credit*, and to make all their payments by entering them to their *debit*. At the end of the year the bank would send each customer his account, which would show a balance in favour either of the bank or the customer. This balance would be carried on to the next year, either to the debit of the customer (in the first case), or to his credit (in the second case), and so forth. It is evident that if this system were made universal, all transactions could in theory be settled by a mere process of book settlement — by what is called the *clearing system*. Then we should no longer see that army of collecting clerks, with bags attached to them by chains, who go about collecting cheques, and occasionally get murdered on the way!

By entirely doing away with the instrument of exchange,[1] however, such a system would tend, as Jevons observed, to take us back to barter — to the direct exchange of goods for goods. This phenomenon is similar to that which tends to eliminate the merchant and bring producer and consumer into touch with each other by means of co-operative societies.[2] In fact there is a curious resemblance between the ingenious and complicated proceedings that constitute the last word in economic progress, and the primitive operations of societies still in a state of barbarism. Nor is it the first time that we have noticed in the historical development of races that peculiar mode of advance of the human mind, which seems to return almost to its starting-point when it has reached the end of its progress, describing not exactly one of those great circles that so vividly impressed the imagination of Vico, but rather a curve that rises in an upward spiral.

We saw in the last chapter that international trade tends automatically to take the form of barter, the tendency being always for

---

[1] The abolition of money as an instrument of exchange would not necessarily involve its abolition as a standard or measure of value. But gold money would no doubt serve this purpose only potentially, remaining shut up in the vaults of the banks, like the Imperial Standard Yard, which is immured at the Houses of Parliament, or the bar of platinum that is kept with scrupulous care in Paris as the standard meter.

[2] Many other equally curious instances of this can be found in the other social sciences. Thus there is a tendency for the verbal formalism of primitive legislation to reappear in modern legislation, in the shape of formulas entered in registers and creating rights; direct government by the citizens of ancient cities reappears in the *referendum* of modern constitutions; compulsory military service for all citizens takes us back to the system that preceded the formation of standing armies; and so forth — not to mention the many curious revivals of ancient warfare in the weapons, helmets, war chariots, etc., of the late war.

exports to balance imports.   And do we not also arrive at a kind of barter on the hypothesis that we have just worked out — the supposition that all the inhabitants of a country are customers of a single bank?   Such a social system, in which there would be no need of money, could only take effect because everyone would pay for the products or services he consumed with his own products or his own services.

It is also a kind of barter that is practised in that wonderful institution called the *Clearing House* (see below, p. 297), for those huge bundles of cheques and bills that are exchanged and set off against each other every day are merely symbols that stand for the piles of boxes, bales, and barrels actually exchanged.   To anyone who can look behind the scenes, the Clearing House appears as a great market, like those of the African tribes or of the vanished cities of the past, with this one difference, that instead of an actual exchange of goods we have an exchange of the credit instruments that stand for them.

Money thus tends to become a pure abstraction.   Yet how far we are from the crude system of barter, despite this superficial resemblance!   For money, and the wealth it stands for, appears everywhere in its different forms — metal, paper, and instrument of credit — though dematerialized and, as it were, sublimated.

CHAPTER VII — BANKS[1]

I. FUNCTIONS AND HISTORY OF BANKS

We have seen that the exchange of commodities is almost impossible without the aid of certain intermediaries, called merchants or traders. In the same way, trade in capital would be impossible without the assistance of intermediaries called *bankers*.

The history of banking is closely connected with the history of trade since the Middle Ages, and each great bank that has been established marks a new stage in commercial development. The first banks were those of the rich Italian republics, Venice (?1400) and Genoa (1407). Commercial pre-eminence passed thence to Holland, and we see the appearance of the famous Bank of Amsterdam (1609), soon followed by those of Hamburg and Rotterdam. Finally the establishment of the Bank of England, in 1694, shows how England was about to succeed to the commercial supremacy of the world. The Bank of France came much later — not till the beginning of the nineteenth century. But in 1716 Law had founded a remarkable bank that was in advance of the time, but was famous mainly for its sorry end.

Bankers were originally merely dealers in money — *money-changers*, as they would be called to-day. In London, in the seventeenth century, the goldsmiths played this part. But while money-changers nowadays do a very insignificant business, being found only in frontier towns or at railway stations, where foreigners need to change their money, in the Middle Ages it was a very different matter. The enormous variety of moneys (for each feudal lord had the right to coin money), and the frequency of secret debasement or counterfeiting, often committed by the sovereign himself, gave great importance to these banks, where anyone could obtain good money on payment of a premium.

Bankers are traders, just like other traders. While others deal in merchandise, bankers deal in circulating capital represented by credit instruments or cash. Other merchants buy in order to sell again, and make their profit by buying as cheap as possible and selling as dear as possible. Bankers borrow in order to lend again,

---

[1] See Appendix for an account of American banks.

and make their profit by borrowing as cheaply as possible and lending at the highest rate possible.   But it is easy to understand that
these traders exercise an economic function of the highest importance,
for no goods are as important as money, at least in modern times,
and those who hold the money have the power to dispense fortune
or ruin — according as they grant money or withhold it — or at
least to render the merchant and manufacturer powerless.   In
business, the suppression of credit means death.

Such, then, are the two fundamental operations of banking:
borrowing and lending.   And since borrowing is generally performed
by means of *deposits* and lending by the method of *discount*, banks
are frequently described as "banks of deposit and discount."

But besides these two fundamental operations, banks perform
many others.   Thus there is the loan made simply on the honour of
the borrower, which consists in his opening a credit, generally in the
form of a *current account*.   The account is a debtor when the customer
draws more than he pays in, and a creditor when he pays in more
than he draws.   At the same time, this method of "open" lending,
as it is called, is very dangerous, and offers no real security.   As it
requires a very accurate estimate on the part of the bank manager
of what each of his customers *is worth*, some banks refuse to undertake it.   It is forbidden by the regulations of the Bank of France.

Secondly, there is the method of *advancing money on securities*,
which is a loan made in return for the pledging of transferable securities deposited by the borrower.   These securities ought always to
represent a sum greater than the amount of the loan, so as to cover
the risk of depreciation.

Thirdly, there is the method of *carrying over*, which is also a loan
on securities, but a short-dated one.   It is for the benefit of those
who have bought securities on the Stock Exchange, are not in a position to pay for them on the appointed day, and wish therefore to
"carry over" the payment for their purchase till the following month.

Fourthly, there is the financing of *industrial companies* — a sharing
in the creation of businesses, either by advancing capital or by subscribing shares — a speculative operation not generally undertaken
by the great French banks, but one that is practised on a large scale
by the German banks and has contributed not a little to the industrial
progress of their country.

And, fifthly, there is the method of *mortgage*.   This is a special
operation that is incompatible with those just enumerated, and
that should be reserved for special establishments.   (See my
Political Economy for mortgage loan societies.)

Finally, banks are not limited to borrowing in order to lend again. They also perform various services for their customers, whether these be traders, States, or private individuals.

To capitalists they render the service of *keeping their securities* and receiving the dividends, which is a great convenience for them, and they also facilitate the employment of their savings by recommending good investments. This is a source of considerable profit to the banker, not because of the very slight charge he makes, but because in this way he becomes the steward of his customers' wealth. He controls the sale of their securities and the reinvestment of the proceeds.

Another service that banks render to their customers is that of facilitating their payments to their tradesmen and other creditors by providing them with books of cheques payable out of their account, and with *letters of credit* on foreign banks, when they travel abroad.

To States and great companies they render the service of bringing their loans to the notice of their customers. As they do not do this for nothing (far from it!), and as these operations sometimes run into millions, this is a most profitable business for the banks.

It is not necessary that one bank should carry on all the business just described. The law of specialization and division of labour applies in banking as in other branches of commerce. Some of these operations, it may even be said, are incompatible with the others. Thus banks of deposit cannot undertake the financing of industrial companies, or even the discounting of long-dated bills, such as those drawn by an exporter on his customers in distant countries, or any kind of lending that involves a more or less permanent immobilization of capital, not to mention loans on land; for such banks must always keep their funds available for repayment on demand. So special banks are required for assisting in the creation of business undertakings and for developing the export trade.

The law of concentration, as it is called, makes its action felt in banking no less than in other forms of commerce. It is natural that the same movement that has led to the establishment of large shops should lead also to that of large banks. This is very apparent in France, where during the last thirty years several banking establishments in the form of joint-stock companies — notably the three whose names are so well known: the *Crédit Lyonnais*, the *Société Générale*, and the *Comptoir d'Escompte* — have extended their branches over the whole country and subjected the local banks, which are generally private undertakings, to overwhelming competition. The same movement has taken place on a far larger scale in other countries.[1]

The local banks, however, do not completely disappear, because they are better able than the larger credit establishments to assist and develop local industries. If their funds are insufficient for this, they can combine and form federations. Such a tendency was apparent before the war, and will no doubt be accentuated now.

II. DEPOSITS

The banker's first task is to procure capital. How is this to be done? He can, of course, to begin with, use his own capital, if he has enough of it, and that is what most provincial bankers do. If the bank is constituted as a joint-stock company, then its capital is made up of the shares subscribed by all the shareholders, and may amount to millions of pounds. The bank can use this capital for its operations, and some great banks do this, but it is the exception rather than the rule. Great banks, at least discount banks, do not generally employ their own capital, whether privately owned or subscribed by shareholders, for the purposes of their banking operations. It appears only as a guarantee fund.[2] Why is this? Because this capital is too expensive. It would have to be entered in the books at the current rate of interest, 5% or 6%, and consequently the bank could not lend it, except at a higher rate, without loss. The banker must therefore conduct his business with the *money of the public*, and he borrows it for that purpose. There is a cutting saying in a comedy which declares that "business means dealing in other people's money"; but in banking at any rate this is the bare economic truth: it is the very essence of the banker's trade.

Moreover, the interests of trade require that it should be so; and not only the interests of the banker, for, as we have just said, if the banker employed only his own capital or that of his shareholders, he could not discount bills at so low a rate as 3%, as is often done.

But how will the banker borrow this money? He will not borrow as States or towns or industrial companies do — borrowing capital that the owners wish to invest for a long period, in the form of bonds

[1] [Compare the corresponding movement in England, by which most of the local banks have been gradually absorbed by the five great banking companies.]

[2] Most great banks invest their own capital either in real estate or in securities, as a reserve or guarantee fund for their customers. Such is the case, for instance, with the Bank of France.

or shares. This method requires a higher rate of interest than the banker can afford if he is to make a profit. What he asks the public for is the circulating or floating capital that everyone has in his pocket or his cash-box. In every country there is a large amount of capital in this form — capital that is not yet fixed, which does nothing and produces nothing, but merely waits for employment. The banker says to the public: "Entrust that capital to me until you have found a use for it. I will save you the trouble of taking care of it, and will give it back to you when you need it, on demand. That in itself is a service I will perform for you. But, besides that, I will pay you a little interest on it — say 1% or 2%.[1] That is at any rate more than the money will produce for you, for in your possession it brings in nothing at all. Finally, I will render you yet a third service, for I will be your treasurer, and pay your tradespeople in accordance with your instructions, which will be a great convenience to you." That is what is called a *deposit*.[2]

When these offers are heard and understood by the public, bankers can thus obtain a large amount of capital on very easy terms. Deposits are therefore the source of a bank's life: it is by them that banks are fed, and by them that they, in their turn, feed industry with circulating capital.

Still, if it were necessary to wait for the public to bring along its available money, as is done, for instance, in savings banks, the amount of the deposits would remain somewhat limited. Deposits must become automatic if the source or spring we have spoken of is to flow abundantly. How, then, are they to become automatic? They can only become so when capitalists, even the smallest of them, make a habit of depositing all their wealth with the banks and entrusting them with the duty of drawing the income from it. Then their account grows by itself, every time dividends are payable, by the amount of the coupons attached to the securities. In countries

[1] It may even pay no interest. Some banks, such as the Bank of England and the Bank of France, pay no interest on deposits, considering that the safe keeping of the money is a sufficient service to depositors. And the fact that they none the less receive enormous sums on deposit proves that they are right. Furthermore, it was formerly the rule for those old deposit banks already mentioned to charge depositors for the keeping of their money, because in those days the banks did not invest the money deposited with them, and made no profit out of it.

[2] The word *deposit* must not be taken here in the legal sense. Strictly speaking, a deposit is something sacred which the depositor must never withdraw, whereas a deposit of money in the bank is a kind of loan that the banker has every intention of utilizing and that he accepts only for that purpose. It is different in the case of a deposit of *securities*, which the owner leaves with his banker for him to take care of and to draw the income. In this case the banker cannot dispose of them.

like England and America where this habit exists, all idle money is drained from circulation and pumped in by the banks where it can be usefully employed.

But there are some countries, on the other hand, where having a banker is a luxury reserved for millionaires. Such was the case till recently in France, and it is so to some extent even to-day. The small capitalist likes to keep his securities himself; he only feels that he owns them if he can see them, and in spite of the trouble of standing in a queue before the cashier's desk he prefers to draw his dividends himself. A personal fortune deposited in a bank, of which he only gets news every six months in a balance sheet, is an abstract form of property that does not appeal to him. And since he keeps the papers and draws the dividends, it follows of necessity that he also keeps the money they yield in his own drawer or cash-box. So instead of a productive deposit you have unproductive hoarding.[1]

Since a deposit represents a debt of which payment may be demanded at any moment, it is obviously a dangerous business for the bank, for if it wants to make the deposited money bear fruit, it runs the risk of not having it in its possession when the depositor comes to claim it.[2]

But this risk is certainly not a sufficient reason for preventing banks from utilizing the capital deposited with them, and compelling them to keep it intact as a true "deposit," as the old banks of Venice and Amsterdam did. Everyone would be worse off if this stringent method were enforced.

In the first place, the depositors themselves would suffer, for it is evident that if the bank had to keep their money in its vaults without using it, it would certainly not be able to pay them any interest. On the contrary, it would have to charge them with the expense of keeping it safe — which is precisely what the old banks used to do.

Secondly, the country also would suffer, for the social function performed by banks is that of collecting the capital that would remain unproductive as pocket money or as a reserve fund, and converting it into an active and productive form. Now it would ob-

---

[1] Since the war, however, the French *rentier* has altered his habits in this respect, and has learned to make use of banks. So the amount of deposits has increased more than threefold, and new banks are being opened at every street corner.

[2] The risk involved in the repayment of deposits is even more dangerous than in the case of bank-notes, because the repayment of deposits is certain: it is certain that sooner or later the deposit will be claimed from the bank, whereas it is by no means certain or even probable that the repayment of a bank-note will be demanded. Most notes circulate until they are worn out without ever being brought to the bank for payment, and a great number never come back at all.

viously be impossible for them to do this if they could not use their deposits.

Consequently banks do not hesitate to employ the sums of money entrusted to them. They merely take care to retain always a certain cash *reserve* to meet any demands that may arise. It is impossible to establish *a priori* any fixed proportion between the amount of this reserve and that of the deposits. The less the bank's credit and the greater the number of its large deposits, the more considerable should be its reserve, and it ought above all to strengthen its reserve in times of commercial crisis, and when State bonds and other securities are about to be issued — in short, whenever it foresees that depositors will need their money.[1]

III. CHEQUES

When a depositor wishes to withdraw his money, what does he do? If he likes, he can simply go to the bank and receive it; but when the "credit habit" has been acquired there is a different mode of procedure. He obtains a *cheque-book* from the bank — a book containing a certain number of leaves and counterfoils printed with the requisite form in which he can insert the sum that he wishes to withdraw or to pay to someone else. Here he will write his own name if he wishes to draw the money himself, or the name of the payee, as the case may be, or even no name at all, if the cheque is a "bearer" cheque — that is to say, payable to anyone who holds it.

The invention of this simple little instrument of credit has effected nothing less than a revolution in economic matters. It tends, indeed, to make money unnecessary, as we have shown above (p. 286). For what purpose do we actually need money? Simply to pay our expenses. But cheques are precisely the most convenient method of paying all expenses, for all that is needed is to write a sum of money and a name on a slip of paper, tear it out of the cheque-book, and send it to one's creditor or tradesman, or as a subscription to some charitable society, or to the tax-collector, and so forth. In England and America the habit of using cheques is so widespread that a rich man never has any money on him or in his house. There

---

[1] To lessen the risk involved in taking deposits, most banks grant a higher rate of interest to depositors who are prepared to deposit their money for a certain minimum period — six or twelve months, or even five years.

On the day when war was declared in 1914 the government thought it was its duty to decree a *moratorium*, or a postponement of repayment. This measure was intended to prevent a panic, but it was an unfortunate step to take, for it risked destroying credit in order to save the banks. Moreover, the banks would have stood the shock well enough, and there would have been no panic.

is an oft-repeated anecdote that relates how some robbers plundered a millionaire, and were balked by finding on him only 27 cents, besides the inevitable cheque-book.

In France, however, though cheques are freely employed in business, they are very little used to-day in the payment of everyday expenses, and the efforts made to educate the public in this respect, especially since the war, have not yet had any considerable effect.

The reason for this is that cheques certainly have their drawbacks, though these are easily remedied.

(1) To begin with, anyone who receives a cheque has to take the trouble to go to the bank to cash it, and is it not natural that he should prefer to be paid directly by his debtor? That is certainly the case in France, and it is one of the chief obstacles to the extension of the cheque system. But it is not the case in a country where everyone has a current account at a bank — the man who receives a cheque as well as the man who sends it. In this case the creditor or tradesman who receives a cheque does not take the trouble to cash it, but sends it to his bank, which undertakes to cash it and to place the amount to the customer's credit.

(2) Secondly, a cheque may be lost or stolen. That, indeed, is a risk it shares with the bank-note, but there is a means of guarding against it which is not possible in the case of the bank-note. This is the method of the *crossed cheque* — a cheque having two parallel lines drawn obliquely across it. Not only can this cheque be paid only at a bank, like all cheques, but the money can *only be received by a banker* — by the banker who is expressly named between the lines of the crossing; or, if the drawer has not inserted his name, then the creditor who receives the cheque will insert the name of his own banker; but, however it is done, the cheque can only be presented to the debtor bank by another bank. Now the curious thing is that the banker whose name appears on the cheque never receives the amount of it in money; he always uses it in settling his accounts with his fellow-bankers. The crossed cheque, therefore, can only be used for payments by the method of compensation. So it has been humorously defined as a cheque that is intended never to be paid. A German law of 1908 even allows the drawer absolutely to forbid the payment of a cheque in cash, by marking it "payable by compensation," or "to be carried to account." The advantage of this kind of cheque is that it cannot be used by anyone except the banker whose name it bears: consequently it matters little if it be stolen or lost, for the wrongful owner would not know what to do with it — unless we suppose the thief to be in league with the banker who is

to receive the cheque, and that he has the effrontery to induce him to place it to his credit! But even in this case the fraud would be quickly discovered.[1]

(3) Lastly, and above all, there is the risk that the cheque may not be paid on presentation because the drawer has dishonestly neglected to deposit sufficient funds to meet it, or has withdrawn them before the presentation of the cheque.

What can be done to avert or mitigate this danger? The law must punish as a fraud the act of drawing a cheque without having sufficiently *provided* for it, as the legal term goes. That is what the legislator has decided to do in France, but only by the recent law of the 22nd June, 1917. The war, in fact, has made it imperatively necessary to try to reduce to a minimum the number of notes in circulation, and consequently to increase the use of cheques with that object.[2]

But what is particularly required is a standard of public morality sufficiently high for the act of remitting an uncovered cheque to be regarded as a dishonourable one, entirely discreditable to the man who is guilty of it. That is why the extension of the cheque system in any country should be considered a mark of economic education and advanced public morality.[3]

A good many conditions must be fulfilled, therefore, if the cheque system is to become universal in any country, but the one primary and essential condition is the habit of depositing money in the bank. In this case alone can the cheque bring about the economic revolution to which we have referred — namely, the elimination of cash payments. This revolution is already on the way in England and America. All the bankers in these countries are debtors and creditors of each other for enormous sums, and so their London and New York agents have nothing to do but to balance their accounts. That is done every day when they meet together in the *Clearing House.* This is an institution of long standing in England, for it dates from 1773. Transactions are settled there, by the simple

[1] There is a tendency nowadays for cheques to take the place of bills of exchange. This is unfortunate, for it means the suppression of an admirable instrument of credit which enabled the manufacturer to renew his capital continually.

[2] [The mere drawing of a cheque without having provided for it does not appear to be an offence in English law.]

[3] The extension of the cheque system among persons not given to reflexion may, however, become a dangerous stimulus to expenditure, for when any fancy can be gratified by the mere signing of a slip of paper it is easy to yield to the temptation. The sight of the money that is paid away is a restraining influence that is absent in this case.

method of compensation, which amounted before the war to nearly sixteen thousand million pounds a year, and in 1920 to over 39 thousand millions[1] — more than a hundred millions a day. Metallic money, and even notes, appear only as an insignificant balance. It is plain that the value of all this paper money rests ultimately on a metallic basis. But every day this foundation becomes narrower and narrower, relatively to the enormous edifice of credit built upon it. It is, as has been said, like a growing pyramid standing on its apex, or a top revolving with dizzy speed on a motionless metal point, and in such conditions equilibrium seems terribly unstable. For once the top ceases to revolve, it falls!

IV. DISCOUNT

When this capital has once been borrowed by the bank at a low rate, the next step is to turn it to account by lending it to the public.

But how is this to be done? We have just seen that the banker cannot lend it for long periods, in the form of mortgages, for instance, or in financing industrial undertakings,[2] for he must not forget that this capital is only deposited with him, and he may be compelled to refund it at a moment's notice. Consequently he can lend it only for short periods, so that he is not deprived of it for long, but keeps it to some extent within reach and under his own eye.

Can we find any loan transactions that fulfil these conditions? There is one that fulfils them admirably. When a merchant sells his goods, according to trade custom he allows the purchaser a certain amount of time in which to pay. If, therefore, he is in need of money before the time for payment arrives, he must have recourse to his banker. The latter advances him the sum due for his goods, deducting a small amount which constitutes his profit, and gets in return the merchant's bill of exchange on the purchaser. The banker keeps this bill until the date when it falls due, and then collects it from the debtor. He thus recovers the capital which he has advanced.

This transaction is called *discounting*. It is a form of loan, for it is obvious that the banker who, in exchange for a bill of exchange for £1000 payable in three months, advances £985 to the merchant while waiting to receive £1000 from the debtor when the bill falls due, is in reality lending his money for three months at the rate of

[1] [The figure given by the author is "over 28 thousand millions"; but this is too low — the actual total for 1920 was £39,018,903,000.]

[2] Cheques are not discounted, as they are payable at once, or after a short interval. Consequently the substitution of cheques for bills of exchange, to which we have already referred, would have the unfortunate effect of abolishing this credit operation.

6%, or even rather more. These loans are always for short periods, for bills of exchange negotiated by bankers are not only payable as a rule in three months at the outside, but that period is a maximum one which is not often reached. Traders do not always need to negotiate their bills the very day after they have sold their goods; they may keep them for a time, and may not even need to negotiate them till just before they fall due. At the Bank of France, for instance, though the maximum legal period of delay is 90 days, in practice it is much less, and the average time during which bills remain is scarcely more than three weeks. So it is only for a very short time that the banker is deprived of the money deposited with him, since every pound returns to the bank after a short interval.

It will be apparent that if demands for the repayment of deposits are spread over a period of three or four weeks, this will enable the banker to be always in a position to meet them, owing to the return of the money he advances. Now it is very unlikely that demands for repayment of deposits will be as frequent as this, at any rate in normal circumstances. It would be difficult, therefore, to find a loan transaction that is better suited to the requirements of the deposit system. No doubt if all depositors conspired to claim their money on the same day the banker would be unable to meet their demands, for his money — or rather, *their* money — would be travelling all over the world. It would certainly not be slow in coming back, but there is always this difference between the capital borrowed by the bank in the shape of deposits and that which it lends by the method of discount, that the first can be claimed *immediately*, while the second can only be demanded *after a certain lapse of time*. And this difference may, at any given moment, involve the failure of the bank.

It remains to be added that not only is discounting a convenient method of lending, but that it is also extremely safe, on account of the joint liability of all the cosignatories. In fact there is not merely a single debtor — the *drawee*, as he is called — but always at least two, for in default of the drawee, the *drawer* is liable. Moreover, if he passes the bill of exchange on to a third person, this person also becomes liable in case of non-payment. So the position is the same as if the debtor had as many sureties as there are holders of the bill, including the one who issued it. Consequently, the more a bill circulates the more signatures it bears — sometimes it needs an additional sheet of paper to take them — and the better is its value guaranteed.[1]

[1] [A dozen lines dealing with the procedure of the Bank of France have been omitted from this section.]

V. THE FOREIGN EXCHANGES

The word "exchanges," which used to frighten examination candidates, has become familiar to everybody since the war, as it has
been so constantly heard.   It may be defined as *the art of settling
debts between two countries without the use of money.*

The portfolios of all great banking houses, at least of those that
transact business abroad, are crammed with bundles of bills of
exchange and cheques payable in all the great financial centres of
the world — London, New York, Milan, and so forth.   They represent values amounting to thousands of millions of pounds, and are
the object of a very active trade.   They go by the generic name of
paper.

The bankers who own these things and deal in them are evidently
only intermediaries or middlemen.   We must ask, therefore, from
whom they buy this commodity, this paper, and to whom they sell it.

From whom do they buy it?   From those who produce it — all
those who from any cause are creditors of foreigners, but especially
those *English merchants who have sold goods abroad,* and who, as a
result of these sales, have drawn bills of exchange on their debtors
in Paris or New York, or have received cheques on Paris or New
York from them in payment.

To whom do the bankers sell this paper?   To all who need it —
and there are plenty of them.   This paper is eagerly sought after
by all those who have payments to make in foreign countries, and
especially by *English merchants who have purchased goods abroad.*
The reason is this: in law every claim is payable in the creditor's
country.   Anyone, therefore, who has bought goods in America is
obliged to send the amount of the purchase price in dollars to his
creditor's country — which is not a convenient proceeding, nor even
always a possible one, for the debtor may happen to be in a country
where American money is not obtainable.   But if he can manage to
procure paper payable in dollars on the exchange of the country
where his creditor lives — bills on New York — he will send that
instead, and that will provide him with a more convenient and less
costly way of paying his debt.   This method is called *making a
remittance.*[1]

[1] It will be easily understood that the debtor in need of a draft cannot always find
one payable exactly where his debt is due, especially in the case of a place with which
his country has few business relations — say Algiers, for instance.   But such a slight
hindrance will not worry him.   He will buy a draft on Paris, and send it to his Algerian creditor, who will use it to pay for his purchases in France, or in any case will
find no difficulty in getting it discounted.

This double exchange operation is called *arbitrage.*   Its object is not only to facilitate

It seems as if this paper ought to be sold, or negotiated, at a price that is always equal to the sum of money that it represents. A bill of exchange or a cheque for £100 ought surely to be worth exactly £100 — neither more nor less. Yet this is not the case. It goes without saying, in the first place, that the degree of confidence that can be placed in the signature of the debtor, and the period of time that must elapse before the date of payment, may affect the value of the bill. But apart from these self-evident causes of variation, even supposing that the paper is perfectly reliable and payable at sight, still its value will vary from day to day according to changes in supply and demand, like the value of any other commodity. These variations constitute what is called the *rate of exchange*, which is quoted in the newspapers like the Stock Exchange quotations.

It is easy to understand what is meant by supply and demand as applied to commercial securities. Suppose that our credits abroad, due either to our exports or to any other cause, amount to five hundred million pounds. Suppose, further, that our debts abroad, due to our imports, or our borrowings, or any other cause, amount to a thousand millions. In this case it is clear that there will not be enough paper for those who want it, since the total supply will not exceed five hundred millions. All those, therefore, who require these bills in order to pay their debts will bid against each other, and foreign bills will rise in value; that is to say, a bill for £1000 payable at New York, Paris, or Berlin, instead of selling for £1000, will sell for, say, £1005. Such paper is, as the term goes, *above par:* it *rises to a premium.*[1]

payment by compensation, as in the case just mentioned, nor is it only a resource for debtors in difficult circumstances. It constitutes a special and very profitable branch of commerce, which consists in buying exchange where it is cheap, *so as to sell it again where it is dear.* Arbitrage brokers spend their time at the telephone, enquiring for the rate of exchange between different places.

Arbitrage has the interesting effect of extending facilities for payment by compensation to all countries. Which are the countries where paper on foreign places is dear? Those in which debts exceed credits, and which, therefore, can only settle their accounts by way of compensation. But by means of the paper that the arbitrage brokers try to procure abroad — and which they will obtain from places in the opposite situation, where the claims are greater than the debts, for only there will they find paper cheap — they will be able to restore the equilibrium and settle the whole of the country's debts by compensation. And the result of this intercourse between all the markets is that paper on any country whatever sells everywhere at very much the same price.

[1] The calculation is really more complicated than this, because in most cases — in practically every case where England is concerned — the currencies of the debtor and creditor countries are different. We must first ascertain the *par value* of the foreign money compared with the English pound — that is to say, its value according to

Conversely, if our credits abroad amount to a thousand million pounds, while our debts abroad are only five hundred millions, it is obvious that paper will be superabundant, since there will be a thousand millions of it available, and the payment of our debts will absorb only five hundred millions. Many bills, therefore, will find no purchasers and will only be able to be utilized by sending them abroad for collection. Hence the bankers will strive to get rid of them by selling them even below their face value. Thus a bill for £1000 on Paris will sell perhaps for £995: it will fall *below par*.

Whenever in any country paper payable abroad is quoted above par, the exchanges are said to be *unfavourable* to that country. What is meant by this expression? For it must be observed that if the rate of exchange is unfavourable to buyers, it must, conversely, be favourable to sellers. This is true; but what the term really means is that in these circumstances the rate of exchange indicates that the claims which this country has against foreign countries are not sufficient to counterbalance our debts abroad, and that consequently we shall have to *send a certain amount of money abroad* to make up the difference. The rise of the rate of exchange, otherwise called dearness of paper payable abroad, is therefore an infallible premonitory sign of an export of coin, and it is for this reason that we speak of an "unfavourable exchange." Conversely, whenever in this country foreign paper is quoted below par, the exchanges are said to be *favourable*. The process of reasoning in this case is just the same: a fall in the price of foreign exchange indicates that when all reckonings are made the balance of accounts will be to our credit, and we must therefore expect the arrival of coin from abroad.

We must not, of course, attach too much importance to these words "favourable" and "unfavourable." We know that for a nation to have to send money abroad or to receive it from other countries constitutes neither a great danger nor a great advantage, for its wealth does not depend on the amount of money it possesses. But from the bankers' point of view this situation is of very great importance, for if money has to be sent abroad it is from their funds that it will be taken. All the premonitory signs, therefore, are of capital importance to bankers, who have their eyes constantly fixed on the rate of exchange. This rate is quoted in all the papers,

the weight of gold it contains. Thus the franc is worth 9½d., the dollar 4s. 2d., the mark 11¾d., the rouble 2s. 1½d., and so forth. In exchange quotations a conventional unit is taken, for the sake of simplicity: a pound in England, and 100 marks, or 100 crowns, or 100 pesetas, as the case may be, in other countries. Then, by comparing the rate of exchange with the value of the monetary unit at par, we can see and measure at a glance the extent of the deviation from the par value. (See below, p. 304.)

especially to-day when so much interest is taken in it. Exchange quotations may well take their place alongside of the weather report, and might even be represented graphically, like the meteorological observations, by a curve showing the variations in the rate. This would be very appropriate, since the exchanges are the barometer of finance. Like the actual barometer, they indicate rain and fine weather; but we must be careful to read them in the opposite direction. When the barometer rises, it means fine weather, and when it falls, it means rain; but when the rate of exchange rises — that is to say, the price of bills payable abroad — it means bad .weather, because it means that gold is going to leave the country. When, on the other hand, the exchanges are low, we may expect sunshine, for the gleam of gold is forecasted!

It must be observed, however, that variations in the price of exchange are confined to much narrower limits than those of ordinary goods. In normal times this price can never be quoted very much above or very much below par.

Why, indeed, does a merchant who owes money abroad seek bills of exchange? Simply to save the expense of sending coin and changing his money into foreign money. But it is very obvious that if the premium that he has to pay to obtain a bill is higher than the cost of sending and converting coin (which is not, on the whole, very great), he will have no reason for buying a bill. Moreover, the merchant who is a creditor of foreigners, or the banker who acts as his intermediary, only negotiates these bills of exchange so as to anticipate the date of payment. He will not consent to sell them at a price much lower than their real value, but will rather wait patiently until the debtor sends him the money, as he is bound to do.

In short, then, since dealings in paper have no other object than to save the cost of transporting coin from one country to another, it will easily be understood that such dealings must lose all justification as soon as they become more burdensome than the operation of sending coin — that is to say, as soon as the variations in the price of exchange, above or below par, exceed the cost of sending coin. Now this cost, even including insurance, is very small: consequently, fluctuations in the price of exchange are also very small.[1]

The term *gold point* is given to the rate of exchange at which it

[1] At the same time, in the case of a very distant place, or one with which communication is not easy, the cost of sending specie becomes much greater, and variations in the price of bills of exchange may also be much more marked. It is clear that a merchant who had to make payments at Pekin or Khartoum would think himself very lucky if he found bills on these places, even if he had to buy them much above their nominal value. But such cases are of little importance.

becomes more economical for a debtor to send coin than to buy bills of exchange. This *gold point* is very important to the banker, for it marks the moment at which the export of gold becomes profitable, and so he must expect this gold to be sought for at the bank, in the shape of demands for the payment of bank-notes.[1]

In normal times these variations are not only of slight extent but they also tend to correct themselves. In fact, as soon as bills on foreign countries are at a premium, the result is an extra profit for all who have them to sell — that is, for exporters. So this state of affairs is a great stimulus to exportation. But the increase in exports will result in a reversal of the balance of trade, making it favourable; and in this way equilibrium tends to be automatically restored, as we have already seen. If bills on foreign countries are below par, the same process takes place, but in the opposite direction.

All this, however, is ancient history at the present moment, for since the war we have seen the rate of exchange fluctuating everywhere in an extraordinary fashion, and without any tendency towards the restoration of equilibrium. Thus, at the moment of writing, the rate of exchange on Paris whose par value is 25f. 22½c. to the pound, is quoted at 56f. 82½c.; exchange on Brussels, with the same par value, is quoted at 60f. 35c.; exchange on Italy (par value 25.22½ lire to the pound) is quoted at 102¾ lire, and so forth. This means that bills on foreign countries are worth to-day in our money only a half or a quarter of their old value. And, conversely, since if one scale of a balance rises the other must fall just as far, it means that in Paris, Brussels, and Rome, the pound is worth about 45s., 50s., and 82s. respectively.[2]

The causes of this phenomenon, which is upsetting international relations so profoundly, are numerous. Three of them are:

(1) The depreciation of paper money, already described. This has been enormous in Russia, Austria, and Germany, and has also occurred, though to a smaller extent, in France, Italy, and Belgium.

---

[1] There are necessarily two gold points, corresponding, as it were, to the two poles: one above par, marking the moment when specie goes out, and one below par, marking its point of entry.

[2] Exchange on the countries of Eastern and Central Europe (Germany, Austria, and Russia) is even more favourable to England, for the mark, the crown, and the rouble have fallen far lower than the franc and the lira. Thus 100 marks, which used to be worth nearly £5 at par, are quoted to-day at about 4d.; 100 Austrian crowns (par value £4. 3s. 4d.) are to-day worth about two-thirds of a penny; and the rouble, having lost all its value, is not even quoted at all.

[The examples and figures in this section differ from the author's, as he naturally uses French exchange rates, which are less favourable than British or American.]

(2) The disturbance of equilibrium in the balance of trade and the balance of indebtedness, as explained at the beginning of this section. One reason why the exchanges are so unfavourable to France and other countries is that their debts to foreign countries, and especially to the United States and England, have increased enormously, partly because of loans contracted to pay war expenses and partly owing to their imports of food stuffs and raw materials.

(3) Speculation.[1] Bank-notes are sought after by financiers hoping for a rise in the value of the franc or the mark, and thrown back on the market when they are afraid of a further fall.

Why cannot equilibrium be restored to-day as in normal times? Because nearly all the means of settling these debts are wanting. France, for instance, cannot send gold, since she has not enough even to cover her enormous issue of bank-notes; nor can she send goods, for owing to the depletion of her stocks, and shortage of raw materials and labour, she can scarcely produce enough for home consumption, and certainly has no surplus for exportation.

VI. BANK–NOTES

The interest of a banker, like that of every other merchant, lies in increasing the extent of his transactions as far as possible. Twice as much business means twice as much profit. How, then, can a banker extend his operations?

If he could create capital out of nothing, in the form of coin, instead of having to wait patiently until the public is willing to entrust it to him, this would certainly be a most advantageous proceeding so far as he is concerned. Indeed, since it was several centuries before the public got into the habit of bringing their money for deposit, bankers conceived the ingenious idea of creating the capital they needed, without waiting for it, by issuing simple promises to pay — *bank-notes*. And experience has shown that the idea was a good one.[2] It has succeeded admirably.

In exchange for the commercial paper which is presented for discount, the banks can therefore give their notes instead of gold or silver. But it may seem surprising that the public should accept

[1] The main cause of exchange variations since the war has been the depreciation of paper money and the unbridled speculation which has resulted from it. When the mark or the crown fluctuates by hundreds of points in the course of a day, it becomes a mere gambling instrument, like the roulette ball at Monte Carlo; men gamble on the chances of recovery or bankruptcy of the country in question.

[2] This ingenious invention is attributed to Palmstruch, the founder of the Bank of Stockholm, in 1656. But the financier, Law, was the first to issue bank notes on a large scale (1721), though his system ended in disaster.

this arrangement. Here, for instance, is a business man who comes to the bank to get a bill of exchange for £100 discounted, and he receives in return for it a bank-note for £100 — in other words, he simply receives another credit instrument. "What use is this to me?" he may ask; "I want money, not instruments of credit. If I only get credit in exchange for credit, I might just as well have kept the bill I had to start with!" But if he reflects a moment he will see that although the bank-note is only another credit instrument, like the bill of exchange, it yet represents an infinitely more convenient kind of credit, since it is equivalent to money. It is superior to other credit instruments, and especially to bills of exchange, for the following reasons:

(1) It is *transferable to bearer*, just like a piece of money, whereas a bill of exchange is subject to the formality and the liabilities of endorsement.

(2) It is *payable at sight* — that is to say, at any time one pleases. This is proclaimed in black and white on every bank-note, even to-day, whereas commercial paper is payable only at a specified date.

(3) It *always remains payable*, whereas other credit instruments lose that privilege after a certain period of time.

(4) It is *for a round sum*, in agreement with the monetary system of the country — £5, £10, £20, £50, and so on — whereas other credit instruments, being the result of commercial transactions, generally have a fractional value.

(5) It is *issued and signed by a well-known bank*, whose name is familiar to everybody, even to the general public who are ignorant of business matters, such as the Bank of England or the Bank of France, whereas the signatories to a bill of exchange are generally known only to those who have business relations with them.

All these considerations lead the public to accept a bank-note as if it were ready money, since it can always be exchanged for money.

It is true that the bank-note is inferior to the bill of exchange in one important respect — that it yields no interest. But even this is rather a mark of superiority, for if the bank-note yielded interest its value would fluctuate, like that of a bill of exchange, according to the nearness or distance of the date of payment. Now that is just what it must not do. A bank-note is not capital, as long as it is in circulation: it is money. What is important, therefore, is that its value should be as invariable as that of money.

But if the fact that a bank-note yields no interest is no drawback to the holder of it, it is a very great advantage to the bank. For it can thus obtain capital on far more advantageous terms than in the form of ordinary loans or even deposits, since these generally cost 1% or 2%, as we have seen, whereas the bank-note costs nothing but the expense of manufacture, which is very slight.

At the same time, if the issue of bank-notes is of great benefit to the banks, it goes without saying that it may also give rise to serious dangers. In fact, the amount of notes in circulation, which may at any moment be presented for payment, represents a debt that is payable on demand, just like a deposit. Consequently, the bank is exposed to a twofold peril: it may be called upon at the same time to *repay its deposits* and to *repay its notes*.

If the necessity for a cash reserve exists even when the bank has to meet only the demand for the repayment of its deposits, it is still more urgent when it adds the debt resulting from its note circulation to that which results from its deposits payable on demand. Hence we can understand why the law of several countries compels banks, when they wish to issue notes, to keep always a certain reserve.[1] When there is no such law, prudence enjoins the same thing.

VII. DIFFERENCES BETWEEN BANK–NOTES AND PAPER MONEY

In an earlier chapter (Book II, Chapter IV) we studied paper money and explained why and within what limits it can take the place of metallic money.

Paper money properly so called is paper which not only has no specie behind it, but which does not represent any promise to pay, at least at any definite date. It is generally issued by a State for the simple reason that it has no other resources, so in these circumstances it cannot make any promise to pay it back in gold or silver. It is as well to confine the name "paper money" to this kind of currency.[2]

Upon what, then, does its value depend, since it rests neither on a metallic basis nor on credit? Simply on the currency conferred upon it by law — on the fact that it performs the functions of money, and that there is no other money to take its place, so that it cannot be dispensed with.

This kind of paper money is current in many countries in the form

---

[1] See Section IX, below.

[2] [The French language draws a convenient distinction, which English does not, between *monnaie de papier* and *papier-monnaie*, the latter being the kind described in this paragraph. We might distinguish the two kinds as *convertible* and *inconvertible* paper money respectively.]

of Government or Treasury notes, and the war gave birth to many varieties of it.

The bank-note, when issued in normal circumstances, differs from paper money in three particulars:

(a) The bank-note is always repayable — always *convertible into gold or silver* at the pleasure of the bearer, whereas paper money is not. The latter has all the appearance of a promise to pay a certain sum, and as a matter of fact we may hope that the State will one day be more fortunately situated and able to cash its notes; but this more or less distant prospect can scarcely affect those who receive the notes, for they have no intention of keeping them till then.

(b) Bank-notes are issued *in the course of commercial transactions,* and only to the extent required by these transactions, generally for a value equal to that of the bills of exchange presented for discount; whereas paper money is issued by the government for the purpose of meeting its expenses, and hence its issue has no other limits and no other check than the financial necessities of the moment.

(c) Lastly, as their name indicates, bank-notes are issued *by a bank* — that is to say, by a private undertaking whose main object is to carry on commercial operations and whose principal care is to safeguard its credit. Paper money, on the other hand, is always issued by the State, and even if the State cares for the public interest it does not always find that a sufficient check.

But if such are the normal characteristics of bank-notes so long as they remain "fiduciary money," they may happen, in exceptional circumstances, to assume the character of paper money, properly so called.

Bank-notes may belong to the category of representative money, if the reserve fund that guarantees them is equal to the value of the notes issued. This occurred in France ten years ago, and in England it is the rule. There the amount of notes issued may only exceed the amount of the metallic reserve by a relatively small margin, which is itself covered by safe securities; and this rule was kept even during the war.

But, on the other hand, the bank-note may enter the category of conventional paper money — paper money properly so called. We must distinguish several phases in this unfortunate transformation.

It may happen, to begin with, that the bank-note acquires *forced circulation*, which means that it ceases to be convertible, at any rate for a time. This has happened very often, in times of crisis, to the notes of nearly all the great banks. Care must be taken not to confuse legal tender with forced circulation. A note is legal tender *when creditors or sellers cannot refuse to accept it in payment.* It has forced circulation *when the holder cannot demand its repayment in money at the bank.* Forced circulation always presupposes legal tender, but the converse is not by any means true. Bank-notes have always been legal tender in France, but they had no forced circulation until the war. Everyone was bound to accept them, but everyone could have them converted into gold at the Bank of France, just as he pleased. To-day forced circulation is the rule in almost every country except England.

At the same time, even in the case of forced circulation, there still remain the two other differences between bank-notes and paper money that we have just indicated, and especially the second one: namely, that the quantity issued is not indefinite and arbitrarily fixed, but is regulated by the needs of trade. This is a very important source of security.

But it is possible that this guarantee may also disappear — the bank-note may not only acquire forced circulation, but may be issued with the sole object of making advances to the State to enable it to pay its expenses, instead of being issued in the course of commercial transactions. Such is the position in many countries to-day. The governments, being in need of money, say to the banks: "Make us notes for as many millions as we shall choose, and lend them to us, and we will exempt you from the obligation to repay them by giving them forced circulation." In this case the issue of notes has no other limit than the needs of the State, and so the bank-note, it must be confessed, bears a strong resemblance to paper money.

Yet, even then, it differs from true paper money or State notes, and the difference lies in the personality of the issuer. This by itself is enough to make the bank-note much less liable to depreciation than true paper money. Experience has proved this so abundantly that States have generally given up the direct issue of paper money and have had recourse to the banks instead. The public, indeed, thinks that the banks will resist as long as possible any excessive issue that is urged upon them, for that means ruin for them, and it believes (not, alas, without reason) that the solicitude of a financial company that has to look after its own interests, is more watchful and tenacious than that of a government or finance minister who has only the public interest to consider.

Since the bank-note is the equivalent of money, its superabundance has the same effect on prices as a superabundance of metallic money (see above, p. 199). That is the phenomenon visible to-day throughout the world, and known as *inflation*. No doubt it would be incorrect to regard the unlimited issue of bank-notes as the sole cause of the enormous rise in prices, for there are many other causes. Yet if we draw the curves of prices and note issue, they will be found to run almost parallel. The public attributes the rise simply to the scarcity of products and the difficulties of transport, which is true enough in itself, and fails to perceive the hidden cause — the depreciation of paper money — particularly since governments strive to conceal or to deny it, so as to keep the credit of the note intact. Nevertheless it becomes difficult to hide this cause when the rise in prices gets beyond a certain point.

Inflation, then, appears as the gravest evil from which Europe is suffering, and all financiers, statesmen, and economists are striving to find a remedy for it. It seems a very simple matter: surely you have only to bring down the number of notes in circulation to its pre-war figure? But to destroy the millions of notes issued in excess would mean that the banks would first have to repay them, and that would involve the repayment by the States of the millions they have borrowed from the banks. Of course they have expressly promised to do this as speedily as possible, but they need so many millions for other purposes — if only, as in France, for the restoration of the devastated regions — that it is doubtful whether much will remain to repay the banks.[1]

Moreover, even if this repayment were feasible it would be very dangerous, for this sudden rarefaction or deflation of money would cause a fall in prices and a terrible crisis. It could only be accomplished by degrees.

VIII. RAISING THE RATE OF DISCOUNT

There is a case in which banks run the risk of having to pay a great quantity of their notes. This is when it is necessary to make heavy payments abroad. As these payments cannot be made in notes, but only in coin, the debtors have to appeal to the Bank to convert their notes into cash.

If, in consequence of a bad harvest, we have to buy a couple of million tons of wheat abroad, that means that a sum of, say, £40,000,000 must be sent to America, and the Bank must reckon on the greater

---

[1] [So far as repayment to the banks is concerned, this paragraph applies in particular to France. The position in England is different, since here the State itself has undertaken the issue of currency notes instead of delegating it to the Bank of England. But the evil effects of inflation are of course the same in either case.]

part, if not the whole, of this sum being drawn from its supplies. The vaults of the Bank, as we have seen, are the reservoir in which most of the floating capital of the country comes to be accumulated in the form of coin, and the only one that can be drawn upon in case of emergency. That is a situation that may become dangerous to the Bank if its reserve, and especially its gold reserve, is not very large. Fortunately it receives early warning of the situation by an even surer indication than the barometer gives to the sailor — namely, the rise of the rate of exchange to the critical point, the *gold point* (see p. 304). If, in fact, the exchanges become unfavourable — if foreign paper is negotiated above par — the Bank must draw the conclusion that debtors having payments to make abroad are too numerous, much more numerous than those who have payments to receive, and that consequently, since everything cannot be settled by the method of compensation, the balance must be sent abroad in cash.

Even without supposing a rise in the rate of exchange, the progressive increase in the amount of commercial paper, coinciding with a decrease in the amount of the cash reserve, indicates a disquieting situation.

When the danger is thus foreseen, the Bank proceeds to take precautionary measures. To guard against the contingency of having to make too heavy payments it must take the necessary steps either to increase its cash reserve or to diminish the number of its notes in circulation.

It is not exactly in the power of the Bank to increase its cash reserve, but it does rest with it to put no more notes into circulation — that is to say, to *make no more loans to the public*, either in the form of advances or in the form of discount; and since it is by these two operations that the bank puts its notes into circulation, it is plain that its object will be perfectly attained by this means. For, on the one hand, when the issue of notes is stopped, the quantity already in circulation will no longer increase; and, on the other hand, as the commercial bills in the Bank's portfolio successively fall due, they bring back to the Bank every day a considerable quantity either of notes (thus diminishing the number in circulation) or of coin (thus increasing the reserve).

The quantity of notes in circulation may be compared to a stream of water in a set of pipes, entering by one tap and issuing by another, so that it is constantly renewed. The flow of notes enters into circulation by being issued by the method of discount, and, having circulated, enters the bank again in the form of collections and deposits. Now if the bank turns off the "issue" tap and leaves the other one open, obviously the circulation will soon dry up completely.[1]

Nevertheless, the complete cessation of all advances and of all discounting business that we have just supposed, would be too stringent a measure. It would provoke a terrible crisis in the country by suppressing all business operations and all profits. But the Bank may bring about the same result in a less violent manner by merely restricting the amount of its advances and its discount business. To accomplish this it is sufficient either to raise the rate of discount, or to be more particular about accepting paper that is offered for discount, especially by refusing bills whose date of payment is too distant, or that bear signatures which do not seem sufficiently reliable.

Undoubtedly such a measure, even when applied with moderation, is scarcely agreeable to business men — and the less so because it makes it harder for them to obtain cash at the very moment when they need it most. The method has even been accused of provoking crises, and we can readily believe it. It is a heroic remedy, but for that very reason it is the right one in the circumstances, and a prudent bank must not hesitate to resort to it to defend its reserve. Its efficacy has been abundantly proved by experience.

Not only, moreover, does this method have happy results for the bank, by warding off the blow that threatens it, but it has beneficial effects on the country itself by modifying its economic situation in a favourable direction. Suppose that this country is threatened with having to make large payments abroad. A rise in the rate of

---

[1] Suppose, for example, that the Bank has on hand a million pounds' worth of commercial paper, that it has a cash reserve of a million pounds, and that it has notes in circulation to the value of two million pounds.

In these circumstances it is evident that if, as the result of a panic of some sort, all the holders of notes came to the Bank and demanded their immediate redemption in specie, the Bank would be unable to comply. But as soon as the Bank has reason to fear such an eventuality, all it will have to do is to cease discounting bills. This is what will happen then: the bills of exchange in the Bank's portfolio fall due one after the other, so that the sum of a million pounds returns in ninety days at the outside, and on an average much sooner than this (see p. 299). What will the situation have become by that time? If this million has been paid in cash, the bank will now have two millions in cash, which is just the amount of its notes in circulation. There is therefore no cause for alarm. If the million has been paid in notes, that leaves only a million notes in circulation, which is just the amount of the cash reserve; so there is still no cause for alarm. If the million has been paid half in cash and half in notes, then the Bank will have £1,500,000 in its cash reserve, and the same amount of notes in circulation, and in this case too there is nothing to fear. It is the same with any other imaginable combination of circumstances.

discount, effected at the right time, reverses the situation by making the country a creditor of foreign countries for considerable sums, and thus gives rise to an influx of money from abroad, or at least prevents the outflow of its own supply of money.

What takes place, in fact, is this. The first result of a rise in the rate of discount is a *depreciation of all commercial paper*. A bill of exchange for £100 which sold for £97[1] when the rate was 3%, will only be negotiated for £93 when the rate has risen to 7%. This is a depreciation of more than 4%. Henceforth the bankers of all countries, and especially those who transact arbitrage business,[2] will not fail to purchase this paper here, because it can be bought here at a low price. They will thus become our debtors to the extent of the sums they devote to these purchases.

The second result is the *depreciation of all stock exchange* securities. Every financier knows that the stock exchange is greatly affected by the rate of discount, and that a rise in the rate almost always entails a fall in the value of stocks. This is because stock exchange securities — especially those that are called *international* because they are quoted on the principal stock exchanges of Europe — are often employed by business men, or at least by bankers, in place of commercial paper,[3] to pay their debts abroad. As soon as they see that they cannot get money for their commercial paper, or that they can only do so at a heavy loss, they prefer to get funds by selling whatever stocks or securities they possess. Hence these also fall in value, following the movement of commercial paper. But just as the fall in the value of paper attracted the demand of foreign bankers, so the fall in the value of stock exchange securities gives rise to increased purchases of them by foreign capitalists, and thus the country becomes the creditor of foreign nations to the extent of the considerable sums they devote to these purchases.

Finally, if the rise in the rate of discount is great and sufficiently prolonged, it will produce a third result — *a fall in the price of all commodities*. We have just said that business men in need of money begin to obtain it by negotiating their commercial paper, and that

---

[1] To make the problem simpler, we assume that the discount is calculated for a period of one year.

[2] See above, p. 300.

[3] If you have a payment to make in Paris, for example, the simplest plan, no doubt, is to obtain commercial paper payable in Paris; but you can equally well use Italian Debt coupons, Lombard Railway debentures, Ottoman Bank bonds, Transvaal or Rio Tinto mining shares, and so forth, which are also payable in Paris. These things constitute a real international money and are continually used in that capacity (we are speaking, of course, from a pre-war point of view).

if this resource fails or becomes too costly, they fall back on any stock exchange securities that they may possess. But finally, if they have come to the end of their resources, they must, in order to get money, sell or "realize" the goods they have in stock. Hence arises a general fall in prices. But this fall, again, produces the same effects, and on a larger scale — that is to say, it stimulates purchases from abroad, and thereby increases our exports and makes us a creditor of foreign countries.

All these effects can be summed up by saying that *a rise in the rate of discount creates an artificial scarcity of money,*[1] *and thereby produces a general fall in values of all kinds.* This is undoubtedly an evil. But it also gives rise, as a consequence, to *considerable demand from abroad and consequently to the importation* of money. This is a good thing, and precisely the remedy that fits the situation.

It must not be thought that the war, although the most terrible of crises, caused an enormous rise in the rate of discount. For it must not be forgotten that the banks of all countries are sufficiently secured by their exemption from liability to cash their notes, as well as by the embargo on the export of gold. They have no need, therefore, to safeguard their reserves by having recourse to the defensive measure of raising the rate of discount. However, a rise in that rate would have had the good effect of diminishing inflation, and thereby indirectly diminishing the rise of prices, and it is a pity that the banks did not apply the brake more strongly.

IX. THE ORGANIZATION OF BANKS

The question of the freedom of banks, as it is called, used to hold an important place in treatises on political economy. It includes two different questions, and it is important that these should not be confused.

1. *Monopoly or Competition*

The first question is this: Is it better to have only one bank endowed with the privilege of issuing notes, or to leave this power to be exercised by all banks under certain conditions?

On this point there is scarcely any discussion now. If free competition can render great services in the case of goods, it is different in the case of the issue of national money, which is what bank-

---

[1] We call this scarcity *artificial,* but it corresponds all the same to a reality, or at least to a contingency that tends to be realized, namely, the flight of money to foreign countries. The evil is cured by a similar evil: it is the method of the homœopathic school of medicine — *similia similibus.*

notes are.   It even seems as if this function ought to be a privilege reserved for a State bank, just like the right of coining money.   So the general tendency is to confine the privilege of issuing notes, if not to a State bank in the strict sense of the term,[1] at all events to a bank which is placed under State control, like the Bank of France.

Even when the monopoly of issuing notes is not legally established, and when the right of issue is assigned to several banks, as in the United States and even in England, there is a tendency towards monopoly in actual practice.   Although the right of issue is still exercised in the United States by more than 7,000 local banks (which are none the less called *national banks*), it has been confined in practice, since 1913, to twelve great federal banks.   In England, when the banks that have kept the right of issue cease to exist — for banks are not immortal, any more than men — or when for any reason they give up their right of issue, they are not replaced, and the Bank of England succeeds to their privilege.[2]

As may well be imagined, this tendency towards monopoly is not regarded with favour by economists of the liberal school, especially if the monopoly is exercised by a State bank, properly so called. If it were merely a question of the issue of notes, if the State bank were to be simply a factory for manufacturing notes, like a mint, then they would readily accept it.   But the socialist or radical-socialist advocates of State banks have no intention of reducing them to the position of mere offices for the issue of notes.   They want to "go the whole hog."   They want State banks for the very purpose of fighting against what they call the financial oligarchy.   They want them to have a cash reserve to be used as a State war chest, and with the power over the whole movement of business that is given by the right to fix the rate of discount.   So here again we meet with the well-known arguments against the unsuitability of the State for the exercise of industrial functions, and especially of the very delicate function of a controller of credit.

What the opponents of State banks say is this:

(1) That a State bank would necessarily bring political considerations into its business, far more than commercial ones, and that it would never refuse to discount the paper of influential friends of the government but would often refuse that of its opponents.

---

[1] A "private" bank is one whose capital is provided entirely by shareholders, and which therefore belongs to them and is governed by them.   If, on the contrary, a part or the whole of the capital is provided by the State, the bank is partly or wholly a State bank.

[2] [See footnote to p. 323, below.]

(2) That it would be forced to get credit with the public by financing all movements of social reform.

(3) That it would never be able to refuse to lend to the State, and that consequently it would be at the mercy of the State, and induced to make ill-advised note issues ending in the depreciation of the note.

(4) That if the State and the bank were one, the credit of the State would be far from benefiting the credit of the bank. On the contrary, in times of crisis, the credit of the bank would suffer from the shock to the State.

(5) Lastly, that in case of an unsuccessful war, the victor, who has hitherto respected private banks,[1] would have no reason to respect a State bank and would regard it as lawful prize.

If the monopoly is entrusted to a *private bank*, as is the case in England and France, these arguments do not apply, even if the bank is controlled by the State. But the liberal school has certain criticisms to make against this system as well. The monopoly of one bank, even if it is confined to the issue of notes, puts the competing banks, in fact, into a position of unfair inequality, for it confers upon the note-issuing bank the right of discounting bills with notes that cost nothing. Thus in France the monopoly of note-issue has given the Bank of France such pre-eminence that it has made all other banks its vassals. The Bank of France is congratulated on having always kept its rate of discount at a more moderate level than other banks. But there is no great merit in that, since the discounting is done with notes that cost the Bank nothing but the cost of paper and engraving.

This is true — so runs the reply of the advocates of monopoly, — but the Bank of France renders a great service to the other banks in freeing them from the duty of keeping any cash. For these banks, instead of keeping a supply of idle money, procure it from the Bank of France when they need it, and so the Bank of France acts as their treasurer. It is the banker's bank.[2] And it needs an enormous reserve to enable it to play this part. This leaves it only a small margin for the issue of notes, and therefore for any exceptional profit, especially if we take into account the numerous charges imposed by the State as the price of this privilege. Moreover, the right of issuing notes arouses little jealousy abroad, as is shown by the fact

[1] Thus Germany respected the branch offices of the Bank of France during the war of 1870–71.

[2] [The Bank of England holds a similar position in relation to the other English banks. For an account of the U. S. Federal Reserve banks, see Appendix.]

that many banks in Germany and England that still enjoy the privilege, are voluntarily abandoning it.

To sum up, then, the monopoly of note issue conferred upon a single bank — a private bank, but under State control — seems to be the best solution, at any rate in practice. This ideal is realized in the organization of the Bank of France, which has been put to the proof for a hundred years and has come triumphantly through many political and economic crises.

2. *Regulation or Freedom of Issue*

Here we have a different question. The freedom of banks, in the sense of free competition between them, is one thing; freedom in the sense of freedom to issue notes at their own discretion is another. Not only does the first not necessarily imply the second, but we might even say that where freedom of competition exists among banks the regulation of their note issues is most stringent — as we shall see in the case of the United States — and where monopoly is most completely realized the control of note issues is the lightest, as we shall see in the case of France. This apparent contradiction is easily explained, for it is obvious that the greater the number of note-issuing banks the more dangerous it is to give them a loose rein.

In the palmy days of the liberal doctrine — that is to say, in the middle of the nineteenth century — it was an admitted principle that all legal regulation of issue was useless because freedom, here as elsewhere, was perfectly sufficient. That is what is called the *banking principle*, as distinguished from the *currency principle*, to be considered shortly, according to which the circulation of notes should be determined entirely by the quantity of cash held by the bank. The contest between these two principles is famous in economic history, and occupied a large place among the controversies of the first half of the nineteenth century.

Let us examine the thesis of the *banking principle* — that of freedom of issue. What is the danger to be feared from *laisser faire?* An excessive issue of notes? This danger is imaginary, it is said; the mere play of economic laws will confine the issue within reasonable limits, even if the banks wish to exceed them, for the following reasons:

(1) To begin with, bank-notes are only issued in the course of banking operations — that is to say, in discounting and making advances on securities. If a bank-note, therefore, is to enter into circulation, it is not enough for the bank to wish it to do so: there must also be someone disposed to borrow. So it is the needs of the public

and not by any means the desires of the bank that control the issue of notes. *The quantity of notes that a bank will issue will depend on the amount of commercial paper offered for discount,* and the amount of this paper will itself depend on the state of business.

(2) Secondly, bank-notes only enter into circulation for a short time; they return to the bank a few weeks after they have been issued. Here is a note for £100 issued in exchange for a bill of exchange. But in a few weeks — in 90 days at the outside, — when the bank collects the bill, the £100 note will return. It will not be the same note, but what does that matter? As many as go out, just so many come back.

"What the flood took, returns upon the ebb."

(3) Finally, even admitting that the bank can issue an excessive quantity of notes, it would be impossible for it to keep them in circulation, for if notes are issued in too abundant quantities they will necessarily depreciate, and *as soon as they depreciate, to however slight an extent, the holders will hasten to bring them back to the bank* to demand payment. It would be useless, therefore, for the bank to try to flood the public with notes, for it could never succeed, but would instead be flooded with them itself.

This is one of those arguments that are incontestable in theory but dangerous when applied in actual practice.

It is true that the quantity of notes issued depends on the demand of business men and not on the will of the bank. It must be observed, however, that if an unscrupulous bank aims only at attracting customers, it can always, if it lowers its rate of discount sufficiently, imprudently increase the number of its customers by taking them away from other banks, and thus increase also the amount of its note issue.

Again, it is true that the notes issued in excessive quantities by this imprudent bank will return for payment as soon as they become depreciated. But depreciation does not make itself felt instantaneously: it will not be felt for several weeks, perhaps. And if during this time the bank has continued to throw into circulation an excessive number of notes, when they at length return it will be too late. The bank will no longer be in a position to pay them, and will be drowned by the returning tide that we spoke of before. It is true that the bank will be the first to be punished for its imprudence by insolvency. But what is the use of that? Our business should be to prevent the crisis and not to punish the authors of it.

Absolute freedom of issue assumes, therefore, as a preliminary condition, that banks should be prudent. And if this prudence can be counted on in the case of a single great bank that has proved itself, it would be unwise to take it for granted as applying to all banks.

That is why the system of absolute freedom, without any regulation as to the issue of notes, is not in force anywhere.

The systems of regulation that have been employed in different countries may be classed under four heads:

(1) *Limitation of the amount of notes in circulation to the amount of the reserve.* In this case the bank-note becomes merely representative money to take the place of gold. It offers complete security, but, on the other hand, it has scarcely any utility, except that of taking up less room in the pocket than gold and saving the wear and tear of metallic coin. The bank thus ceases to be a credit establishment: it is no longer a bank, but simply a strong-room — a mere treasury that serves for making payments and keeping a reserve of money for contingencies. Consequently this system is not applied anywhere in its full rigour, and we only mention it for logical completeness.

(2) The second process consists in fixing either a certain *margin* or a certain *ratio between the amount of the reserve and that of the notes in circulation.*

A margin — that is to say, the difference between the reserve and the circulation, or the uncovered balance, as it is called — is fixed *ne varietur*. This is the rule adopted for the Bank of England, as we shall see later.

A ratio, or fixed proportion established once for all, is generally one-third. But it is purely empirical, and the figure varies in different countries.

The system of the ratio is somewhat more elastic than that of the margin. But they both lead to the same result: at a certain moment they make all discounting and even all payment of notes impossible, and consequently create the danger that they seek to prevent. Suppose the reserve stands at five millions and the number of notes at fifteen millions: the bank is just within the prescribed limits. But at this point it cannot pay a single note more without causing its reserve to fall below one-third of the amount of notes — for 4 is not a third of 14. So the rule has to be suspended, even under this system.

(3) The third method consists in simply fixing a *maximum for the issue of notes, without fixing any minimum for the reserve.* This is the system that is applied to the Bank of France. The maximum was fixed before the war at 6,800 million francs (say £270,000,000).

But there is no fixed minimum for the reserve, even in normal times. Although all examination candidates persist in declaring that the reserve has to be one-third of the amount of notes, this is not the case at all, and the Bank might allow its reserve to fall to zero. To tell the truth, there is some excuse for disbelieving in the existence of such a system. For it is obvious that a maximum note issue is absolutely useless as a guarantee of payment of the notes if no minimum is fixed for the reserve. It must be acknowledged, however, that notwithstanding this paradoxical system — a maximum for note issues, but no minimum for the reserve — the Bank of France in normal times has always had the prudence to keep its reserve at an excessively large ratio to its circulation rather than otherwise, and this fact is obviously the strongest argument that can be adduced in favour of the principle of freedom — the banking principle.

(4) A fourth system consists in obliging the banks to *secure their note issues by means of reliable instruments of value*, representing a value at least equal to that of the notes.

If the securities chosen to serve as guarantees are government bonds, as was the rule in the United States until 1913, this is a bad system, for it is not in the power of a bank to realize them immediately. But if these safe securities that have to serve as cover for the bank-notes might be bills of exchange — that is to say, short-dated securities, — as is now permitted by the American law of 1913, then these might be regarded as a real guarantee, though insufficient in themselves. It should be observed, however, that such a condition is not, properly speaking, a method of regulation: it is merely a return to the system of freedom, for the characteristic feature of the banking principle, as we have just said, is simply that the issue of notes is sufficiently regulated by the discounting of bills of exchange.

To sum up, it must not be hoped that any conceivable system can absolutely guarantee the payment of notes. Banks, indeed, are and must be *credit* institutions. If we wish to use credit we must put up with its inconveniences: to try to combine the advantages of credit with those of ready money is like trying to square the circle, for the one excludes the other.

At the same time there is reason to think that a bank that occupies a unique position in the country, strong in its traditions and its majesty, and realizing its responsibility, will use all necessary prudence in the issue of its notes. Experience has confirmed this view in the case of most of the great banks, and especially in the case of the Bank of France, whose organization has been put to the proof for more than a century and has come triumphantly through many political and economic storms. It seems, then, if we rely on the teaching of experience, that the best solution is a monopoly of note issue entrusted to a private bank, under State control, but with the minimum of regulation.

X. THE GREAT BANKS OF ISSUE

We cannot examine the banks of issue of every country (see my *Political Economy*), but we cannot neglect to study the working of the two that support the whole edifice of credit in France and England.

1. *The Bank of France*[1]

The Bank of France is a century younger than its great sister, the Bank of England, having been born on the 13th February, 1800. It was created by Napoleon, and remains, along with the Civil Code, the greatest of the civil monuments he has left.

The Bank of France is not a State bank, as is sometimes thought. It is a private bank, constituted, like every joint-stock company, with capital provided by the shareholders, and governed by a board of directors elected by the shareholders. Since 1806, however, its independence has been seriously impaired by the nomination by the State of its governor and two deputy governors.

The Bank's right to issue notes dates only from 1803, and the privilege is accompanied by certain conditions. These are as follows:

(1) The Bank may only discount bills of exchange that bear three signatures (to guard against all risk of insolvency), and that are drawn for 90 days at the most.

(2) None of its customers, except the State, may overdraw their accounts. The Bank may make advances to anyone, however, on certain kinds of securities, or on bullion.

(3) It may not pay any interest on deposits.

Such are the statutory regulations. But there are two more stringent ones that were added later:

(4) A maximum is now assigned to the issue of notes, which was free until 1870. This maximum has been constantly raised since that date. From 1,800 million francs in 1870 it rose step by step to

[1] [This section is somewhat abridged, by the omission of details of little interest to the American reader.]

6,800 millions before the war, and since the war it has reached 43,000 millions (say, £1,700,000,000).[1]

(5) The State has imposed various contributions upon the Bank, including a permanent loan of 200 million francs (£8,000,000) without interest, and a share in its profits in the form of a royalty calculated upon the note circulation and the rate of discount. This amounted before the war to some 15 millions (£600,000) a year, and is now more than double this figure.

This monopoly of the Bank of France, like all monopolies, has had to meet many attacks, and has given rise to acute controversy. But the Bank renders very great services to the State. In cases of emergency it puts at the disposal of the government not only the bullion stored in its vaults but also an almost unlimited supply of notes, issued according to the needs of the State. During the war it lent the enormous sum of 27 thousand million francs (£1,080,000,000) to the State, besides nearly four thousand millions (£160,000,000) to its allies. This advance was made at a rate of less than 1%, when the State was borrowing from the public at 6%, thus making a saving of more than £40,000,000 in interest.

The Bank of France also renders a service to the other banks. Instead of competing with them, it exempts them from the duty of keeping a gold reserve, and thus enables them to make use of all the funds at their disposal. When these banks need money they simply get the Bank of France to *re-discount* the bills they have themselves discounted. All they need, therefore, to be prepared for any contingency, is to have a sufficient supply of paper that fulfils the conditions necessary for it to be discounted by the Bank of France.

Thus the great credit establishments are free to devote themselves entirely to the profitable business of discounting, subscribing loans, and so forth, without any great anxiety about repayment. They have all the advantages of the banking business and hardly any of its liabilities.

2. *The Bank of England*

The constitution of the Bank of England differs in many respects from that of the Bank of France.

---

[1] Since the war the ratio between note circulation and reserve has naturally altered considerably. The return for the 7th September, 1922 gives the following figures:

Notes in circulation............................ 36,959 million francs
Gold in hand.................................. 3,584 ” ”
Silver ”   .... 286 ” ”
Proportion between bullion and note circulation, 15.75%.

(a) It is entirely a private bank, belonging only to its shareholders, and as such it is self-governed, except as mentioned below. It is therefore completely independent of the State.[1]

(b) It has a less absolute monopoly of issue than the Bank of France. It is only in London that it has the exclusive privilege of issuing notes: there are provincial banks which also issue notes. At the same time the number of banks with the right of issue is *rigorously limited*, and since 1844, the date of Sir Robert Peel's famous Bank Charter Act, those that disappear may no longer be replaced. Their number, which was 279 at that date, grows smaller every year, so that the Bank of England, which already enjoys a virtual monopoly, will soon be invested with a monopoly in law, as the legal heir to all deceased provincial banks.[2]

(c) It is subjected to a far more rigorous control in the matter of note issue and cash reserve. The amount of notes issued must never exceed the sum of the amounts of the reserve and the capital. This capital, however, only consists for the most part of a credit on the State that is not available and cannot be utilized. It is better to say more simply that the note issue may only exceed the cash reserve by a fixed amount, which is now £18,450,000 — a poor margin, it is obvious, for such a bank as the Bank of England.

With a view to ensuring the keeping of this rule, the Bank is divided into two distinct departments: the *Banking Department*, which undertakes the ordinary banking business of deposits and discounts, but may not issue any notes; and the *Issue Department*, which issues notes but does no other business. The Issue Department delivers its notes to the Banking Department simply in accordance with the needs of the latter; and when it has handed over £18,450,000-worth it can deliver no more except in exchange for coin or bullion.[3]

This automatic limitation of issue gives rise, precisely in times of crisis, to such great inconvenience that on three separate occasions

---

[1] ["The Bank of England is only a state bank in the sense that it is the bank with which the government keeps its accounts. The issue department, however, may be considered as in effect a government office, like the mint." (Nicholson, *Elements of Political Economy*, p. 293.)]

[2] Whenever one of the other note-issuing banks comes to an end [or relinquishes its right of issue] the Bank of England may increase its note issue up to two-thirds of that of the bank that has disappeared, but it must deposit an equivalent sum in securities. [The monopoly of the Bank of England became complete in 1921, when the last provincial bank of issue forfeited its privilege.]

[3] [The working of the Bank of England is shown most clearly by a study of the *Bank Return* that is issued every week in accordance with the terms of the Bank

already — in 1847, in 1857, and in 1866 — it has been necessary to suspend the law and allow the Bank to overstep the fatal limit.[1]

On the day of the declaration of war in 1914, the Government had an anxious time. There was a run on the Bank and the reserve fell on the 4th August to below £10,000,000. Ought the Act to be suspended? Everything was ready for that step. But the Government heroically refused. They preferred to have recourse to a different method: they had notes issued by the State — currency notes, or Treasury notes, for £1 and 10s. — repayable not in gold but in bank-notes. And at the same time they prohibited the export of gold. The panic subsided without its becoming necessary to resort to forced circulation, and to this day England is the only one of the ex-belligerent countries — at least in Europe — where the bank-note is still convertible into gold.[2]

Charter Act. The following is the Return for the week ending November 1, 1922.

Issue Department

Notes issued.........£144,052,400		Govt. Debt..............	£ 11,015,100
		Other securities.........	7,434,900
		Gold coin and bullion	125,602,400
		Silver bullion...........	
	£144,052,400		£144,052,400

Banking Department

Capital...............£ 14,553,000		Govt. Securities.........	£ 50,664,553
Rest................	3,128,144	Other securities.........	68,189,891
Public deposits*	15,034,269	Notes.................	20,893,560
Other deposits........	108,844,733	Gold and silver coin......	1,832,922
Seven-day and other bills	20,780		
	£141,580,926		£141,580,926

The first part of this table shows plainly how the total note issue is covered to the extent of £18,450,000 by documentary securities, and the rest by gold coin and bullion. For every note issued in excess of this £18,450,000 (which is the amount to which the original £14,000,000 has grown since 1844 by the lapsed issues of provincial banks) the corresponding value in specie must be deposited in the Issue Department. A certain proportion of this specie reserve (one-fifth) may consist of silver, this provision having been made in view of the trade with India.]

* Including Exchequer, Savings Banks, Commissioners of National Debt, and Dividend Accounts.

[1] [This necessity for the suspension of the Bank Charter Act in times of crisis has given rise to the saying that the Act is of no use until it is suspended. But it does not at all follow that the principle of limitation is unsound because it has to be removed in cases of emergency. "In fact," says Professor Nicholson, "it may be said that in this country we have a constitutional elastic limit for the issue of notes." (*Elements of Political Economy*, p. 308.) But the whole question has given rise to endless controversy, both before and since the passing of the Act of 1844.]

[2] That is, in principle. In practice it is not convertible, but no one has any interest in changing bank-notes into gold, for what use would it be, since it is forbidden either to export the gold or to melt it down?

BOOK III — DISTRIBUTION

PART I

THE VARIOUS MODES OF DISTRIBUTION

CHAPTER I — THE PRESENT MODE

I. THE INEQUALITY OF WEALTH

In all ages the poor have been many and the rich have been few — *paucis humanum genus vivit* — and that not only in poor societies, as is natural, but in the wealthiest ones as well.   Wealth, therefore, is very unequally distributed — we cannot yet say "unfairly," for that is the very question we have to investigate.

We can at least say, however, that the inequality of wealth has provoked bitter complaints in every age: the quarrel between the rich and the poor is as old as the world.

It might have been hoped that this quarrel would grow less intense as the wealth of nations increased.   But it has not been so, for if the general level rises it does not follow that the distance between rich and poor grows less, — quite the reverse.   The number of paupers diminishes, it is true;   far more men reach a position of comfort than formerly;   but the heights of fortune are continually being overtopped by yet dizzier heights.   Between the wages of an agricultural labourer and the dividends of a millionaire trust king there is a bigger difference than between the income of a serf and that of a feudal baron.

If we represent the different ranges of income — such as they appear, for instance, in income tax statistics — by horizontal oblongs whose length is proportional to the number of persons included in each, and place them one over the other, we shall get a figure resembling a pyramid — or rather an arrow-head, or a top — whose base represents the poorer classes and the apex the rich.   If the base of the pyramid is wide in proportion to its height, this shows that the inequality of incomes is not very great — which is the case in France, — and the greater the inequality of incomes the greater will be the distance from base to summit. If the inequality is extreme, the top of the figure takes the shape of a needle.[1]

The following table[2] illustrates this point. It shows the number of persons in England assessed to super-tax for the year 1918–19, classified according to the income on which they were assessed. The third column contains the quotient of the second figure divided by the first — that is to say, the average income per head.

Class	Number of Persons	Total Incomes Assessed £	Average Income Per Head £
£ 2,500–£ 5,000	39,680	136,334,000	3,436
£ 5,000–£ 10,000	15,330	105,500,000	6,882
£10,000–£ 15,000	4,450	54,320,000	12,207
£15,000–£ 20,000	1,750	30,280,000	17,303
£20,000–£ 25,000	910	20,290,000	22,297
£25,000–£ 30,000	595	16,250,000	27,311
£30,000–£ 40,000	575	19,720,000	34,296
£40,000–£ 50,000	320	14,180,000	44,313
£50,000–£ 75,000	305	18,300,000	60,000
£75,000–£100,000	135	11,680,000	86,667
over £100,000	150	30,000,000	200,000

Here the inequality of wealth is obvious at a glance, although the table only includes those whose income exceeds £2,500 a year. It does not include those who are "disinherited": there are many others who have nothing at all.

But, it will be said, what does it matter if inequality of wealth increases, so long as there is an increase in the general well-being? What difference does it make that the rich grow richer, so long as there are fewer who are poor? Only envy can find grounds for complaint in this. The important thing is that all should advance, but not that all should advance at the same pace.

Nor do people fail to add that this social inequality is not only inevitable but in some respects beneficial. It is inevitable, in that it results from the many other inequalities — physical, mental, and

[1] M. Vilfredo Pareto thinks he has found the mathematical equation for this figure — what he calls the *income curve*. And from a comparison of the statistics of different countries now and in the past, he thinks he can draw the conclusion that the form of this curve is almost invariable, the same in all places and at all times, even "for countries whose economic conditions are as different as those of England, Ireland, Germany, the Italian cities (in the Middle Ages), and even Peru (in the eighteenth century)." It would appear, then, not only that inequality of wealth is a universal law, but also that the range of inequality is not susceptible of any appreciable change.

[2] [Substituted for Professor Gide's illustration, which is drawn from French sources and relates to succession, in the absence of exact income statistics. For data upon the United States, see Appendix.]

moral — which nature has created between different individuals, and of which the inequality of wealth is to some extent only a corollary. It is beneficial because, so long at least as human societies are in a state of comparative poverty, the inequality of wealth acts as a stimulus to production to an even greater extent than want. It keeps all men on the alert, from the top to the bottom of the social ladder, by giving them a constant prospect of advancement. It gives full scope to individual initiative by concentrating powerful capital in the hands of those who are most bold. It endows the works of man with fruitful variety, thanks to the infinite series of wants and resources that it establishes among them.

Yet, for as long as these old arguments have been repeated, they do not seem to have succeeded in reconciling the masses to the inequality of wealth. In fact, it is far less readily accepted nowadays than it used to be; and this is easily explained.

To begin with, this inequality is almost the only one that continues at a time when *the other inequalities that used to distinguish man from man have disappeared one after another.* The laws have recognized civil equality; the growing diffusion of education is even tending to produce a measure of intellectual equality. Inequality of wealth alone remains and increases, and whereas it was once concealed behind greater inequalities, it now stands out in the foreground and concentrates all the anger upon itself.

In the second place, economic inequalities are far more pervasive than the older forms of inequality: their social effects are more extensive, both for good and for evil. They may even be said to dominate and, as it were, to have absorbed all other inequalities — those of nobility, power, intelligence, and eloquence — in the sense that nowadays these latter forces can scarcely exist without the support and assistance of wealth.

The possession of wealth modifies the conditions of life for those on whom its favours or its rigours are bestowed, far more than it used to do. No doubt in the days of Charlemagne, just as to-day among the Arabs of southern Algeria, no gulf of hatred was dug between fellow-citizens by the inequality between rich and poor. That is because wealth, and the pleasures that it could procure, were scarce and little varied. To-day, on the contrary, wealth and the pleasures it brings are enormously multiplied, so that the rich can fill both hands at the shops in Vanity Fair, while the poor can merely look covetously through the windows.

Nor does inequality of fortune involve only inequality of enjoyment or of power. Statistics show that life is three times as long, on an average, among the rich as among the poor,[1] so that, by the cruel irony of fate, the smaller a man's share of wealth, the greater the tribute he has to pay to sickness and death. Worse still, the poorer the man, the greater the tribute he has to pay to vice and crime, for statistics show also — what *a priori* reasoning could have foretold — that the criminality of the poorer classes is greater than that of the well-to-do. Consequently, modern science has burst like a soap bubble that axiom of commonplace morality that health and virtue are the companions of poverty. The poor have no longer even that consolation.

Finally, the inequality of wealth appears to be in no way natural, but much rather *artificial* — the result of a certain kind of social organization, of certain economic institutions, such as property and inheritance, created and maintained by those who profit by them.

If with some immaterial dynamometer we could measure the intellectual or moral inequalities that exist among men, we should probably find that they very rarely coincide with inequalities of wealth. This is not to say that wealth is not often due to certain qualities of initiative, boldness, and perseverance — such qualities as make men conquerors and victors over fortune, — but it is a matter of common observation that fortune seems in no way proportional to the merits or the virtues of men. Still less does it seem proportional to the amount of trouble taken, for it seems, on the contrary, as was bitterly remarked by John Stuart Mill, that the scale of remuneration goes on falling in proportion as the work becomes harder and more painful, until a point is reached where the hardest toil is scarcely sufficient to provide the necessaries of existence.

Yet, however little flattering to human nature this observation may be, public opinion more readily accepts those inequalities of

---

[1] According to statistics for the city of Paris for 1912, the death rate varies in different quarters of the city in a ratio of more than 4 to 1. Thus:

| Porte Dauphine | 7.9 per 1000 | Père-Lachaise | 23.7 per 1000 |
| Champs-Elysées | 9.0 per 1000 | Salpêtrière | 33.5 per 1000 |

Anyone who knows the different quarters of Paris will find this comparison sufficiently clear and startling.

[The figures for the London Metropolitan Boroughs, however, are somewhat less striking, and their correlation with inequalities of wealth is less marked. At the two ends of the scale we find:

| Woolwich | 10.6 per 1000 | Bermondsey | 21.4 per 1000 |
| Hampstead | 12.3 per 1000 | Finsbury | 21.6 per 1000] |

The inequality is even worse in the case of infant mortality.

In statistics of suicide, although the causes are numerous and varied, poverty always appears in the front rank, without a rival.

fortune that are due entirely to chance than those that are the reward of talent or even of work. This is because these merits and talents are themselves inequalities, envied or disputed, on which the new inequality, that of wealth, becomes grafted. If the gifts of chance are those that arouse least jealousy, it is because they are the only ones to which everyone alike can lay equal claim.

It is to be observed that people are not usually jealous of the winners of lottery prizes, and that their good fortune is rather greeted with a kindly welcome. The reason for this is that everyone knows that the chances in the lottery are the same for all, and the primitive sense of justice of the man in the street is satisfied: he allows Fortune her bandage so long as she has also her wheel. But when he looks at the distribution of wealth, there seems to be something wrong with the wheel that turns up the winning numbers.

What is to be aimed at, then, is not so much equality of fortunes as *equality of chances*, ensuring that each shall have the same possibility of making his fortune.

In fact, if the inequality is personal and temporary it is not an evil; the unfortunate thing is its permanent character — the formation of social classes placed one upon the other and as unchangeable as geological strata. For then the inequality of wealth has none of those stimulating effects, from the economic point of view, that we have just indicated and that might indeed be expected of it. When it becomes a class inequality it discourages those at the bottom of the scale by depriving them of all chance to rise, while it lulls to sleep those who are securely placed in a definite position at the top. It breaks the bond of mutual social dependence by digging a gulf between Dives and Lazarus that can never be bridged. It renders idle alike the hands of those who are too poor, for they have no chance of producing anything, and of those who are too rich, for they no longer feel any need to produce. It gives birth to the two evils of idleness on the one hand and pauperism on the other, and thus produces two classes of parasites, one at each end of the social scale.

The great war, among so many other tragic results, will have had the effect of still further aggravating this inequality. We have already heard much of the "new rich," but now there will be no lack of "new poor" — including not only all those whom the war has ruined, but all those also who, with the same income as before, are crushed between the rise of prices on the one hand and the enormous increase of taxation on the other.

Yet all these consequences of inequality are not sufficient ground for condemning it, for the real question is not whether some have more than others, but whether the excess *has been taken from the others*. This is the question to which the theory of distribution endeavours to give a reply. Let us suspend our judgment, therefore, for the present.

II. THE WEALTH OF NATIONS

The extreme inequality of wealth, then, appears as a social evil whose causes must be investigated, so that it may, if possible, be remedied. But we must cherish no illusions as to the results that would follow from a better distribution of wealth, supposing such to be possible. Indeed, when the total to be divided is small, the most ingenious arrangements can never make the individual shares large. Now in the case of modern communities, even those that figure in the front rank, we should speak rather of the poverty of nations than of "the wealth of nations."

The following table shows the capital and income (in millions sterling) of a number of countries before the war, and the capital and income per head of the population (in pounds sterling):

	Total Capital	Capital per head	Total Income	Income per head
United States	38,880	380	7,200	72
Germany	17,600	264	2,000	32
England	16,000	360	2,200	50
France	11,200	280	1,320	36
Italy	4,000	116	480	14
Belgium	1,800	256	200	28

From this table[1] it can be seen how small the share of each individual would be on the basis of an equal distribution. It would be better, certainly, to reckon the amounts per household instead of per head, as children do not enjoy independent incomes. For this purpose the figures per head need only to be multiplied by 4 or 5. This would give approximately £140 to £160 as the average income of a French or German family (on a basis of equal distribution), £220 to £320 for an English or American family, and £60 for an Italian family.

It will be said, no doubt, that an income of, say, £200 a year (in pre-war money) would be adequate for the majority of the inhabitants of these countries. Arithmetically this is beyond dispute, and it is a great mistake for books written in justification of the existing economic order to try to dispute it. We will merely say that a so-

---

[1] [We omit Professor Gide's account of the method adopted to obtain these figures, as it differs from the English method. The latter is described in Smart's *Distribution of Income* (Macmillan).]

ciety whose population had to subsist on this average income would have to renounce all expenditure on luxuries, and, of course, all the progress to which luxury gives rise (see below, Book IV, Chap. I, § V). And if it limits its desires to this modest competence, which is scarcely more than King Henry's[1] famous "fowl in the pot," it could undoubtedly obtain it by more economical methods than a social revolution.

The individual share would be smaller still if, instead of dividing all fortunes without exception, as we have supposed in the calculations given above, we were to *divide only the fortunes of the rich*, which is the ideal of popular socialism. In that case the portions would be ridiculously small. If we could flatten out Mont Blanc and spread its material over the whole area of France, we should only raise the level of the soil by about six inches. Similarly, if all incomes in the United Kingdom above £10,000 a year were divided equally among all the inhabitants, they would not provide £5 a head. This result, disconcerting as it may be at first sight, is explained by the *relatively small number of the rich*.

Are we to conclude from the slenderness of the national wealth and the impossibility of giving a large share to everyone that the question of distribution is of little importance? Quite the contrary; for it is precisely in cases of insufficiency that distributive justice is most imperatively necessary — we know something of this from our experiences of food rationing! — and it is in times of abundance that the question of distribution may be ignored. But the conclusion that must be drawn from the figures given above is this: that if we wish to make a marked improvement in the condition of everyone, middle classes as well as wage-earners, it is to production that our efforts must be directed. That is where modern socialism differs, as we shall see, from the older form. Distribution is rather a legal or judicial question, but the economic problem of to-morrow is how to increase production to a maximum.

Yet it must not be forgotten that production is to a large extent dependent on distribution, in the sense that if the latter is unjust, the former cannot be abundant. Labour can only be fruitful if the labourer knows that he will gather the fruit. And perhaps that is the very reason why our modern societies are not richer than they are.

[1] [Henry IV, or Henry of Navarre, king of France from 1589 to 1610, wnose idea. was that every peasant should be able to have his fowl in the pot every Sunday.]

III. HOW THE DISTRIBUTION OF WEALTH IS EFFECTED

If everyone produced independently, like Robinson Crusoe on his island, everyone would keep for himself whatever he had made, and the question of distribution would not even arise. The rule *cuique suum*, "to each man his own," would naturally be applied.

But such a system, in which, by hypothesis, there would be no exchange and no division of labour, is incompatible with any kind of social life. Even among savages who live by hunting and fishing it is never entirely realized. And in modern societies we should all be very disagreeably surprised if an attempt were made to put it into practice — if, for instance, the baker or the shoemaker were told, "You have produced so many loaves, or so many pairs of shoes. Very well; keep them; that will be your share." It is plain that what we each of us demand is not the produce of our labour in kind, but its fair equivalent. Now is this demand satisfied in our modern societies?

In every civilized society each individual, by the sale of his goods or the hiring-out of his services, is continually pouring *values* into the stream of circulation; and he is also continually drawing out *other values*, in the shape of various kinds of income. Each of us puts on the market what he possesses — the landowner his crops, the house-owner his houses, the capitalist his capital, the manufacturer the produce of his factory — and the man who owns neither land nor capital offers his arms or his brains. Naturally, each tries to sell his products or to hire out his services at the best possible price; but this does not rest with him, for the products and services sell on the market at the price fixed by the law of supply and demand, which means, if we go back to the explanation of value already given (p. 194), that they sell at a higher or lower price according as the desire of the public for them is more or less intense. Consequently it is the public — the consumer — who fixes the share that we receive, by the price that he assigns to our products or services and that he consents to pay us. And it is these shares, under the various names of *wages*, *salaries*, *rent*, *interest*, or *profits* on the sale of goods, that constitute our income.

In short, therefore, it is the law of supply and demand that determines the distribution of wealth.

Economists of the optimist school, however, are prepared to carry the discussion even into the sphere of justice. Is not the law of supply and demand, they say, which determines the equivalence of the values exchanged — is not this law the very machinery by which everyone is enabled to withdraw from the total mass a sum of values equivalent to those he has put into it? And is not this equivalence thus measured in the most impartial and least arbitrary manner, since exchange on the market is a free contract? No doubt the values that each one receives are very unequal; but is it not in conformity with justice, as well as with social utility, that the most desirable and the rarest kinds of wealth — those that meet the most pressing needs of society and are yet insufficient in quantity to satisfy those needs — should be paid for at the highest price? Is not commutative justice also distributive justice? We can only estimate the value of services rendered by the price that society assigns to them. If the public assigns a high price to my products and a low one to yours, does it not in this way exactly measure the degree of importance and of social utility that it attributes to our respective products or labour? But the public, it will be said, is not a good judge. Who, then, can be a better judge than the consumer? After all, if everyone is remunerated by the value of what he has produced, it may be said that he is remunerated *according to the services he has rendered* to society.

Moreover, these inequalities find a limiting influence in competition. Competition always tends to correct the injustice involved in such a system, for if such and such a product or service happens to be quoted at an excessive price, a crowd of rivals, anxious to profit by this piece of luck, immediately rush into the same industry or profession and quickly bring back the value to the level of the cost of production, by increasing the supply of these products or services. Ultimately, that is to say, the value of everything *tends to be determined by the trouble and expense it has cost.* What better rule than this could be imagined for determining distribution?

From the practical point of view also, it is said, the existing system of distribution is incomparably superior to any other system that can be imagined, because *it goes by itself* — it works automatically. The law of supply and demand does away with the intervention of any authority; it is not for the legislator to hand each one his share — like a mother dividing a cake among her children — for each one gives himself his share. Authority has only to intervene to prevent his taking the share of someone else.

That, then, is the classical doctrine. But how can the mode of distribution be a just one if the law of supply and demand is the sole distributor of fortune? It is a natural law, if you like, but precisely because it is *natural*, it is *amoral* — as far removed from any concern with morality or justice as any other natural law, such as the circulation of the blood, which makes all hearts beat alike, for good and for evil, or the rotation of the earth, which, as the Gospel says, "maketh the sun to rise on the evil and on the good."

There is no kind of work — if I may venture to give it that name — that has ever been more highly paid than that of boxing: it may bring in as much as £4,000 a minute. If we ask why this kind of work is paid a hundred thousand times more than that of the plough-man, the school of Bastiat could only reply: "Because the first renders society a service a hundred thousand times as great as the second; and the *proof* of this is that society is willing to pay a hundred thousand times as much for it."

Very well; but if this is so we must no longer talk about social justice, for the services that are indispensable to existence, from manual toil up to the labour of inventors who have died of poverty, have scarcely any exchange value, whereas such acts as merely require certain natural gifts or favourable circumstances, and that provide a small number of wealthy people with the most fleeting and perhaps even the most immoral enjoyment, are sought after at a high price and make the fortunes of those who can perform them.

Moreover, competition can scarcely be relied on to correct these inequalities and to bring each man's remuneration to a rate that corresponds more closely to the trouble or merit involved. For it is precisely upon the commonest kinds of work and service that competition acts, depreciating them still further, whereas luxuries and rarities, the so-called noble services, are always more or less monopolies, even by their very nature.

It should be observed that people who come into the market to exchange their products or services, do so under extraordinarily unequal conditions. The chances of fortune, the winning tickets, are only accessible to those who can lay down their stake — who have already acquired some property, — and their chances of gain are proportional to the value of the stake. Between the workman who has nothing to offer but his arms — a commodity that is supera-bundant on the market, and therefore of little value — and the capitalist who brings along his money-bags, or the landowner, urban or agricultural, who brings land that is indispensable to existence, there is a vast difference in the possibilities of making a fortune. Many favourable opportunities for making profitable investments, many bits of information from financiers and rulers, are offered to the rich capitalist and denied to the small *rentier*, and still more to the wage-earner.

It is obvious, then, that inequalities of remuneration result most of all from inequalities in men's original shares of property. The distribution of income is necessarily predetermined by the appropriation of land and capital. It is not sufficient to declare that "each draws out the equivalent of what he has put in." We must still discover where each has obtained that which he puts in. Why do some come on to the market, or rather into the world, provided for even from birth, and almost sure of the lion's share from the very beginning?

By whom, then, have they been endowed? By their own labour? By law? Or by force? That is the question we must now examine.

We must remember, again, that if this system really possesses the vaunted superiority of "going by itself," it is certainly not true that it made itself. If it goes by itself it is because the machinery is by this time well established. But when it had to be started — when individual ownership had to be created, with all its attributes of rent and interest and so forth — it required centuries of conquests, a hundred revolutions, a thousand laws, and all the might of kings, nobles, or parliaments. And, to tell the truth, this transformation still goes on without ceasing, so that it would be very hard to discover how much of the so-called natural order remains underneath the existing economic order.

IV. HOW PROPERTY IS ACQUIRED

The subject of property does not occupy a great place in books on political economy. There are many such books, and most important ones, especially in other countries than France, where it is not even mentioned in the table of contents. This is because it is held to belong to legal rather than to economic science. This is true; but yet, if the right of property is the basis of all other rights — at least of real rights, — then it must also play a large part in political economy, for it is the necessary precondition of exchange, and therefore the central point of the whole mechanism of distribution, as we have just seen.

What, then, is meant by property?

The use of things almost always implies their possession. To use bread, we must eat it; to use clothes, we must wear them; to use a house, we must dwell in it; to use the earth, we must cultivate it. But possession does not of necessity involve ownership: we may enjoy a thing by right of usufruct, as a borrower or tenant, and so forth, without owning it. Ownership or property, therefore, only appears when appropriation is distinguished from the mere personal utilization of wealth. We only own a thing when we have the right to keep it without making use of it, but preventing anyone else from touching it. The right of property is the right to do what we like with a thing, including the right to do nothing with it: a right without limits and without conditions — the *jus abutendi*. Such, at least, is the legal conception of the right of individual property, as it was cast in bronze by the Roman lawyers.

How is the right of property acquired? By *labour*, of course, it will be said; for we can scarcely imagine such a formidable right being conferred upon man by an act of creation, in the form of production *ex nihilo*. That, indeed, is just how economists understand and justify the right of property. But lawyers are very far from doing the same!

It is a fact well worthy of remark, though not often noticed, that neither in the text of the Roman law nor even in the articles of the French civil code, though born of the Revolution, does labour appear among the various modes of acquisition of property that they enumerate. So far as the past is concerned, this is intelligible, for in ancient times labour could not serve as a mode of acquiring property since it was almost always slave labour — in other words, the worker was himself the property of his master. But what about the present day? Well, even to-day labour *by itself* never constitutes a legal title to property: the characteristic feature of the "labour contract," as it is called, is that the wage-earning labourer has no rights to exercise over the produce of his labour. It is the man who sets him to work — the employer — who acquires and keeps the ownership of the product (see the chapter on *Wage-Earners*, below). And even when the worker who produces independently — peasant or artisan — has the right of property in his produce it is not by any means because it is the fruit of his labour, but because he is the owner of the land or the raw material, and his property rights extend to all that is added to these, by way of improvement.

What, then, are the modes of acquisition of property that are formulated in law? — The only ones that law is concerned with, or at any rate the ones that are of most importance, are purchase, gift, and succession (either testamentary or intestate). But all these modes are concerned with the transmission of property — that is to say, with property that passes from one person to another. None of them shows us, therefore, the foundation of property, since they all assume it to be already in existence. What we want to see is property at its birth: we want to know how it originally came into being.

Now besides these modes of *derivative* acquisition the lawyers do indeed enumerate certain modes of original acquisition; but the Code is as laconic about these as it is prolix about the others. Yet even in our old societies the birth of property surely ought not to be a rare occurrence, since new wealth is continually being created.

The lawyers indicate three original modes of occupation, but these may be summed up in one: namely, actual possession becoming transformed into a right.

To begin with, it is *occupation* that appears as the primary fact from which all property right is derived. It must be observed, moreover, that though there may seem to be little morality about this, yet so far as it involves taking possession of wealth that belongs to no one, the fact of occupation constitutes a right that is morally superior to the right of conquest, which involves the expulsion of the weak by the strong.[1]

Accession or *incorporation* is a mode of acquisition founded on the rule that the accessory follows the principal. In this way the owner of the soil obtains not only all that is detached from it in the shape of fruits and crops (with the exception, in some legal systems, of the produce of the subsoil) but also the buildings and plantations that have been raised on his land by the labour of another. And it is in virtue of the same principle that the ownership of the object manufactured by the workman is assigned to the capitalist who supplied the raw material. Accession, therefore, is only a kind of extension of the right of occupation and can only possess the same qualities.

But these two modes of acquisition only occupy a few articles in the French civil code. A larger amount of space is devoted to the third, which is *prescription* (or *usucapion*,[2] as it was called in Roman law). This assigns the ownership of anything to the man who has possessed it for a certain time — and even without the need for any lapse of time, in the case of a transferable object. Prescription, in the case of real property, does away with the need for going back to the original fact of occupation, which would be impossible to verify; and in the case of products, it does away with the need for verifying

---

[1] Originally, however, the right of occupation is only the same thing as the right of conquest, and in ancient societies men did not fear to call it by its proper name. The typical form of quiritarian property in Rome was that which was acquired *sub hasta*, under the spear. And an old Greek song says: "My wealth is my spear, my sword, and my buckler, the defence of my body; with them do I plough, and reap, and gather in the harvest of my vines." (Quoted by Guiraud, *La propriété en Grèce*, p. 127).

[2] [Also called *usucaption*.]

whether there has been accession or not. In fact, therefore, prescription is to-day the sole legal basis of property, so far as its origin
is concerned. Now there is nothing more in that, by its very definition, than a crude fact destitute of all moral value. What prescription does away with is precisely the need to discover whether property really originated in labour and saving: from the legal point of
view it covers all original sins.

If the lawyers are satisfied, then, it is easy to understand that
economists and moralists are not, and that they have striven to find
a more solid foundation for the right of property than the mere fact
of possession — namely, the labour of the producer.[1] But unfortunately it is not easy to prove that such is really the case.

Anyone who tried to use this criterion in actual practice would
be strangely deceived. Make a list of your inherited possessions.
"Is this house the product of your labour?" "No; it came to me
from my parents." — "Are these fields and this forest the product
of your labour?" "No; they are not the product of anybody's
labour." — "These goods that fill your shops, or these crops stored
in your granaries, are they the product of your labour?" "No;
they are the product of the labour of my workmen." — "Well, then
. . . . ?"

Another foundation has therefore been sought for in *social utility*.
This is the fortress in which the defenders of individual property
have had to take refuge, and so far it has held out against all attack.
It is true that many cases can be adduced in which the owner's
interest goes counter to the general interest — the classical example
is the forest that the owner's interest impels him to cut down, while
the nation s interest is to keep it; and there are many others. But
this does not matter, for there are many more cases, and more serious
ones, where, conversely, dilapidation and sterilization can be attributed to the absence of individual ownership. On the whole,
history and facts show us that individual property has up to the
present been the best means, and even the essential condition, of
the utilization of wealth, and the most active stimulus to production.

Only, if that is the reason for the existence of the right of property, it follows that the individual is no longer an owner in his own

---

[1] Attempts have also been made to find a foundation in *natural right*. But what does
this mean, except that property is an indispensable condition of personal independence,
since he who possesses nothing is compelled to put himself at another's service in order
to live? Hence there is no more revolutionary theory than this, for if property is a
natural right, what are we to say to all those who have been deprived of it and who
demand it?

interest, but in the interest of all. Property is no longer "private property," but becomes a *public function*, in the loftiest and most literal sense of the term. No longer, therefore, will it be absolute, in the old Roman sense of the word, but only to the extent that sovereignty over things and the right to dispose of them freely, are indispensable to the best utilization of them. It may vary according to circumstances and surroundings. We may admit the right of absolute ownership to be useful in some cases — for instance, in the case of a pioneer in a new country (like the *dominium ex jure Quiritium* of the Roman peasant) — but we may also acknowledge that this absolute character ought to be relaxed in the case of the ownership of a factory, a mine, a railway, a forest, or a waterfall. Certain conditions may be imposed on the owner, if only the obligation to cultivate his land.[1] And the right of expropriation in the interests of public utility, etc., will be more readily admitted.

We must now see what are the *objects* to which the right of property may apply; what *persons* may exercise it; and what are the *powers* that it confers.

V. THE KINDS OF WEALTH TO WHICH PROPERTY RIGHTS MAY APPLY

At the present day all forms of wealth may be the object of individual property rights, with the single exception of those which by their very nature are incapable of appropriation, like the sea and the great rivers. And, as a matter of fact, in all the countries of Europe almost all wealth is appropriated. But it has not always been so. There was a time, on the contrary, when the sphere of individual property was infinitely small.

At the beginning it applied only to certain kinds of wealth, and these were at first precisely those that have long ceased to be the object of property rights in all civilized countries — namely, slaves and women. It embraced also objects of direct personal use, such as jewels, arms, and horses, the individual ownership of which was evidenced by the custom of burying them with their owner in his tomb; often, indeed, his slaves and his wives were treated in the same way!

Then property came to include houses — not yet as individual property, but as family property — because the house was the home,

---

[1] During the war the obligation to cultivate land — and especially to grow wheat — was expressly imposed upon the landowner by law. As we shall see later, the law of France provides for the forfeiture of property rights in mines in case of their not being exploited. [This is not the case in England.]

the resting-place of the household gods, and these gods belonged to the family.

Still later, it extended to a portion of the land, first to the land in which were the tombs of the ancestors, for these ancestors also were a kind of family property. But, despite this first step, individual ownership of land, the most important and almost the only wealth of the ancients, was established very slowly. Yet the time is not far distant now when individual ownership will have covered the whole earth and all that it bears on its surface. To-day only the lofty mountains and a portion of the forests still maintain a precarious independence.

In course of time each kind of property has in turn assumed special importance: among pastoral peoples it was cattle; under the feudal system it was land; when the era of the steam-engine arrived, it was coal-mines. Individual ownership has even been extended in our own times to include new objects, unknown to the ancients. Of these the principal kinds are the following:

(1) *Transferable securities* — shares in property, or simply credit claims, generally in the shape of credit instruments — pieces of paper that can be slipped into a pocket-book, and that constitute nowadays the most convenient and desirable form of wealth. Thanks to these, property has been torn up out of the soil and has taken wings: more than this, it has become as it were dematerialized. The owner no longer sees it or touches it, but none the less he laughs at governments that try to seize it. It may be estimated that something like half the total fortune of a civilized country takes this form.

(2) *Immaterial wealth*, the ownership of which is still not properly established and defined. Each kind would require a chapter to itself: we must be content with merely enumerating them:

(a) Industrial property, in the shape of *patent rights*.

(b) Property in *trade marks*.

(c) Property in a *business connection*, or *goodwill*.

(d) *Literary* property.

It is possible that in the future individual property may take still other forms of which we have at present no idea.

The conception of property, then, appears as evolving under the influence of two opposite, but logically interdependent, causes: extension in regard to its object, and limitation in regard to its duration and attributes.

VI. THE PERSONS WHO MAY ACQUIRE PROPERTY

We have just seen that the *object* of property rights goes on continually extending and varying. Is it the same with the *subject* of these rights — with the classes of persons who may acquire them and become property owners? Yes, it is.

· Originally, their number was very limited: there was no true owner but the sovereign, and, later on, the head of the family. In any case slaves and foreigners, and sometimes women, were excluded. To-day not only is the right of holding property recognized as belonging to every human being, but it has even been extended to fictitious persons, called *artificial persons*, moral persons, or bodies corporate.

Legal personality — that is to say, the capacity to receive and possess goods — was first attributed to the gods, in the person of the colleges of priests attached to their temples, and later on to the Christian churches and religious communities. The extension of this form of property, and the storms it aroused in the course of history, are well known.

States, cities, parishes, and great public services such as charitable foundations, hospitals, schools, and so forth, have all been invested with the right to hold property.

Associations — even private ones — have also become property owners. But they have not obtained this right without resistance on the part of the State. The right to possess has been accorded most readily to associations of an economic character, to those that are called "companies," and that seek industrial or commercial profit. But, contrary to what one would have thought, the right was long refused (especially in France) to non-profit-making associations — those that aim at higher and more disinterested objects. And at this very moment it is only granted them grudgingly. For this old antipathy for what is called *mortmain*, or the dead hand, there is first of all an economic cause — the idea that wealth owned by a community will be badly administered, or in any case withdrawn from circulation and from trade for an indefinite period. But there is a still more important political cause, in the fear of seeing these associations become powerful enough to stand up against the State and take its place in the performance of the great social services.[1]

This dread of *mortmain*, that dates from very early days, appears to us to be out of date. If public utility is the real basis of property,

---

[1] [We omit a short account of the French law on the subject.]

as we have just shown, then surely it could nowhere be more legit-
imately placed than in the hands of those "artificial persons" which
represent all that is most disinterested — education, public health,
poor relief, mutual dependence, the rights of man and the rights of
nations, science, religion, peace, the Red Cross and similar organizations, or even pleasure and recreation in the form of innumerable
arts and sports.   To these, then, it would be impossible to give too
large a share.   They are, as it were, a salvation from the abuses of
individual property.   It is very much to be desired that a portion
of wealth should be withdrawn from individual interests and devoted to altruistic purposes.   The economic objection that this
means driving wealth out of circulation may have some weight in
the case of land, but none in the case of houses or securities.   Let
legislators be content, therefore, with limiting the right of corporate
bodies to hold property to cases where land is concerned — this,
existing only in limited quantity, might possibly even be reserved
for living persons, — but in the case of all other values given to artificial persons, there is no economic reason for fixing any other limits
than those that result from the object aimed at by the association
or foundation.

Finally, the right of holding property has been given not only to
associations but also to works — we might even say, to ideas.   That
is what is called a *foundation*, or endowment.   It is sufficient that a
man should have wished to make himself useful after his death, and
have provided sufficient funds for the work to be carried on, for him
to be able to live perpetually, to possess, and even to grow rich by
new acquisitions.   The will of the dead man lives a second life,
incarnated in the foundation that he has established.   Yet here the
law of France is even more rigorous than in the case of associations.

As a matter of fact there is an essential difference between the moral
or artificial personality attributed to a foundation and that attributed
to an association.   For the latter is still a kind of living being that
is constantly being renewed and that dies as soon as its usefulness is
ended.   But a foundation is rather a dead man who survives, em-
balmed and immovable, incapable of changing and adapting itself
to inevitable vicissitudes, and hence there necessarily arrives a day
when it crumbles into dust.   A foundation for the worship of Jupiter
cannot last when there are no more altars to Jupiter, and foundations
for saying masses would necessarily lapse in a country that passed
from catholicism to protestantism.

VII. THE ATTRIBUTES OF PROPERTY RIGHT:
INHERITANCE

"The right of property," says Article 544 of the Napoleonic code, "is the right to enjoy and to dispose of things *in the most absolute manner.*" Although this definition has ceased to be entirely true, because the right of property is subjected nowadays to continually increasing restrictions, it brings out clearly the nature of property as an absolute right — absolute in two senses: (1) in that it embraces the whole of the satisfactions that can be obtained from a thing, including even the stupid satisfaction of destroying it;[1] (2) in that it is not limited in time, or only at least by the durability of its object. *Perpetuity* and *free disposal*, then, are the two characteristics of the right of property.

§ 1

When the right of property applies to goods which perish when consumed, or whose length of life is very short, its perpetuity is of no great economic interest, since it cannot be actually realized. But when the wealth appropriated is by its nature everlasting, or at least very long-lived, then the right of property, expanding along with its object, appears in all its greatness and with all its consequences.

How numerous are these objects that last for ever? First there is land, whose length of life has no other term than that of the planet that bears us, or at least of the geological cycles that mould its surface. And that is exactly why landed property has always been of an exceptional kind; we shall have to devote a special chapter to it. Houses have not the same character of perpetuity, considered as buildings, but they share in it at least so far as concerns the ground on which they are built. Works of art, especially those carved in marble or cast in bronze, may also aspire to immortality; and it is the same with metallic money. Nevertheless in the case of these kinds of wealth, and especially the last, the perpetuity of the right of property is deprived of almost all its importance in practice (except in the matter of hoarding) by the frequency of exchange, which brings them back every moment into the whirlpool of circulation.

But if the object of the right of property is sometimes perpetual, the subject is not — unless it is an artificial person. The owner dies. That is a critical moment for the right of property. What is to

---

[1] An owner, however, may not set fire to his house. There we find a first restriction on property right — one that is due to the risk to which the fire would expose the man's neighbours.

become of it? Since the right does not die, it must pass to some other holder. Who is this to be? Is it to be the one designated by the dead man? Very well; although, as we shall see directly, that is a right that has not been admitted without some hesitation. But if the dead man has not designated anyone, who is to succeed him then? The law says, "his nearest relatives." But what is the reason for this intestate devolution, as it is called?

It has been sought to justify it on the following grounds:

(a) As *a reasonable interpretation of the wishes of the dead man when he has expressed none.* Is it not natural to think that in the case of near relatives — children, husband or wife, father, mother, or even brother or sister — if the deceased had wished to disinherit them he would have said so definitely? If he has said nothing, should it not be presumed that he wished to leave his possessions to them?

Very good — so far as the nearest relatives go; but when it comes to a distant one, the dead man's silence cannot be interpreted as a presumed wish and a definite designation.

(b) As an application of the *alimentary obligation*, consecrated by nature and by all legislation in regard to certain relatives — children, parents, and husband and wife. Surely it is a duty towards those to whom we have given life, those from whom we have received it, and those with whom we have shared it.

No doubt there are such obligations which death cannot extinguish; but none the less the reason is inadequate, for if inheritance had no other foundation than the alimentary obligation it ought not to exceed the limits of an alimentary allowance.

There is no sound argument, therefore, in favour of succession *ab intestato*, at any rate in the collateral line. It is a survival from the days when property still existed only in the family form.

Yet even from the family point of view this kind of succession cannot be said to be useful in strengthening the family, especially when it goes counter to the express wishes of the head of the family. So true is this that the LePlay School, which aims at making the family the basis of the social order, expressly demands that testamentary freedom should be granted to the head of the family, or at least that the portion reserved for heirs of the blood should be very much restricted.

From the economic point of view it must be admitted that this mode of succession has an ill effect rather than a stimulating one. It either releases the children from all need for effort, by ensuring to them their paternal heritage without their having done anything to deserve it, or else, by making some distant cousin succeed to the property of an uncle in America, it turns the legal devolution of estates into a lottery.

Many economists, therefore, and even those who are not socialists, are desirous nowadays of abolishing succession *ab intestato*, at least in the collateral line. In France it was settled by a law of 1917, due to the war and budget necessities, to abolish it beyond the sixth degree of relationship, thus confining it to near relatives.

§ 2

The other essential attribute of the right of property, as we have said, is the right of *free disposal*. We have just quoted the definition in the French civil code: "The right to enjoy and to dispose of things in the most absolute manner." In this definition, as all law students know, the one essential attribute of the right of property is the right of disposal — the *jus abutendi*, as the Roman law more forcibly expressed it. Where this attribute is wanting, you have only the right of usufruct. But this right to dispose of a thing at one's pleasure has not always been in existence. Property only gradually enlarged itself thus. In this respect it went through the same progressive development as in regard to its object. And the title of the Romans to fame, from the legal point of view, is simply that they gave to property this sovereign character which it had not previously enjoyed — and which, too, it is now beginning to lose, under the influence of new ideas.

So far as can be conjectured, the following is the order in which property became successively invested with its essential attributes:

(a) The first right was probably that of *making use* of the goods — exploiting them by the labour of free wage-earners. That is the attribute that has had the most serious social consequences, because it gave rise to the "noble" class — the class of those who are freed from the toil of working for their daily bread and enabled to devote their lives partly to leisure and partly to such occupations as confer power and influence — *otium cum dignitate* — such as politics, letters, and art.

(b) The right of *giving* seems to have been one of the most ancient modes of disposal of wealth — at least for transferable objects, — and to have preceded even the right to sell (see p. 185). In fact, if the owner has the right to consume a thing for the satisfaction of his own needs, why should he not have the right to let another man consume it? If he may destroy it, why should he not be able to give it? Is it not the noblest and most enviable privilege belonging to the right of property to be able to share its benefits with others?

(c) The right of *selling* and *letting on hire* seem only to have appeared much later — at least so far as landed property is concerned. Aristotle declared, in the fourth century B.C., that this is a necessary attribute of the right of property, but he does not seem to say that it was generally recognized as such in his day. Indeed, there are many reasons why it should not have been. To begin with, so long as property exists in the family form and under the seal of religious consecration — which was the character of ancient property — alienation is impossible because it is an impious act on the part of any member of the family. Moreover, division of labour and exchange were not yet in existence, each family being self-sufficient; and movable wealth was scarce, and everyone kept it, sometimes even until it was buried with him in the tomb, so that in these circumstances sale could only be an exceptional and abnormal act. Consequently, when it begins to appear, we find it surrounded by extraordinary formalities: it is a sort of public event. Thus the *mancipatio* had to take place before five witnesses, representing the five classes of the Roman people.

(d) The right of *bequest* — that is to say, the right of disposing of one's goods after death by means of a will — is the culmination of the right of property, since it prolongs this right beyond death. It is not in any way an application or an extension of the right of succession, as might be imagined. On the contrary, the right of disposing of one's possessions at death, far from being connected with succession *ab intestato*, has always been found in conflict with it (see above, p. 344). There has been a struggle between two conceptions — that of supreme individual ownership progressively extended till it includes testamentary freedom, and that of the ancient family ownership, the family property being retained, each head of the family receiving it in turn as a trust, and being obliged to transmit it to the succeeding generation, It is thought that even at Rome, where individual ownership developed with such vigour, a father had no right of bequest previous to the Law of the XII Tables (450 B.C.). The testamentary act was surrounded with solemnity; it had to be performed by taking to witness (*testamentum*) the people assembled in their tribes, thus borrowing the sacred form used in the promulgation of laws — *uti pater legassit, ita jus esto*, said the Law of the XII Tables (*legassit*, has made a law!). All this shows clearly enough that the act was not an everyday performance. The law nowadays has singularly lowered the dignity of this right by allowing a will to be made by a *holograph* instrument, as it is called — a simple document without any other formality than the date and signature.[1]

This conflict ended in some countries, such as the United States, in the complete victory of individual ownership in the shape of absolute testamentary freedom. But it was not the same everywhere, and in France under the rule of the Napoleonic code testamentary freedom is limited,[2] to the benefit of certain heirs to whom the law assures a minimum portion of which the testator cannot deprive them. Fathers of families, it is true, generally use their freedom reasonably enough, and rarely disappoint the hopes of their natural heirs — in other words, testamentary succession only confirms the results of succession *ab intestato*. In France it very rarely happens that a father uses even the limited power that the law allows him to dispose of the "disposable portion" of his property. It is only when there are no children, husband or wife, or near relations that the testamentary right has free scope, and it must be acknowledged that it is not always used in an intelligent manner. This right of bequest is a formidable one, in that it enables an individual to make a perpetual settlement without the possibility of any reconsideration of the decision. There are few men who are capable of exercising so high a function as this.

It is indisputable, however, that a man's power to dispose of his wealth not only during his life but even after his death is a powerful stimulus, if not to production — for bachelors are no less anxious to get rich than married men, — yet at any rate to saving. There are many men in the world — to the honour of the human race be it said — who work and save less for themselves than for others. If you compel them to think only of themselves, they will work less and spend more. In this case much wealth will be selfishly squandered in unproductive consumption, and many years will be withdrawn from productive labour by premature retirement.

But though property, through the attributes just enumerated, has given an impetus to the production of wealth, and thereby to civilization, which undoubtedly nothing could have replaced, it is far from being the case that the same benefits can be attributed to it so far as the distribution of wealth is concerned. Although it is

---

[1] [This is the simplest, but not the only kind of will permitted by French law; in England, of course, the signatures of witnesses are also ordinarily required.]

[2] [In England there is absolute testamentary freedom: every man is allowed to dispose of his property, of whatever kind, in whatever way he pleases.]

the foundation of the social order, as it is said, this right of property becomes the cause of profound but inevitable disturbances.

To begin with, ownership of a product becomes transformed, if only by the right of exchange, into ownership of the *value* of that product. In the same way, property is subjected to all the fluctuations of supply and demand, all chances, fortunate and unfortunate, all the tricks of fortune and luck, and takes on that unstable and uncertain form that characterizes wealth in modern societies. And even supposing that it originates in the individual labour or saving of its first author, it will often be difficult to discover the original title amid the transformations wrought by exchange.

The power to lend, to lease, or to rent property has created the class of *rentiers* — those, that is to say, who are able to live on the income of their capital or land, which is made use of by another man's labour, without needing to work themselves. Besides this, it cannot fail to give rise to many conflicts — between creditors and debtors, between rural landowners and farmers, and between urban landowners and their tenants. In the first two cases the conflict has been of great importance in economic history, and even in political history; the third case is more recent, but looks like being no less violent.

The right to make use of property creates a division of society into two classes, wage-earners and employers — the former working in the service of others, and the latter, in appearance at least, appropriating the fruits of their labour. It thus prepares the way for the struggle between labour and capital.

Finally, by its attribute of perpetuity, the right of property necessarily outlives the original owner and passes to his heirs, who will be unable to show the same personal title to it. Many men will find themselves owners of wealth that they have not themselves produced, but which may be presumed to have been the produce of the labour of their ancestors in a more or less distant past — a presumption not readily admitted by the "disinherited."

CHAPTER II — THE SOCIALIST MODES

I. THE SOCIALIST SYSTEMS

Since the existing mode of distribution seems in several respects to conform so little to the idea of justice, and even to be unsatisfactory from the point of view of social utility, it is natural that men should in all ages have been in search of a better one. Thus arose all the socialist systems.

We have already spoken of socialism when we described the programmes of the different schools.[1]

It was the inequality of wealth, whose glaring manifestations we have already described, that most strongly impressed the plain man at the beginning. That is why socialism in its primitive forms aimed only at establishing an equality of shares: it was communistic socialism.

This childish mode of distribution seems to have prevailed in the very remote past, for all the ancient lawgivers whose names have been handed down to us in history or legend — Minos, Lycurgus, Romulus — appeared to have adopted an equal division of the land, if not among individuals, at any rate among families. And since this original equality was necessarily destroyed in the course of a few generations, it had to be established afresh by new divisions. Such a system as this was possible in primitive communities comprising only a small number of citizens and having only one kind of wealth — land. But it had very little chance of coming to life again in the decrees of the Russian Bolshevists. Yet some trace of this naïve idea remains at the bottom of all socialist systems. For they all take it for granted that there is more than enough wealth for everyone's needs, and that if there are any who are poor it is simply because their share has been taken from them by the rich. All that is necessary, therefore, is to take back what the rich have unjustly seized, either by expropriation, as the revolutionary socialists maintain, or by progressive taxation, as is advocated by the more moderate reformers. Such, at any rate, is certainly the popular feeling.

Nevertheless it was quickly seen that inequality of wealth is only

[1] See what has been said already in the Introduction, Chapter II.

an effect, and that we must go back to the cause, which is the right of property.

But though all modern schools of socialism have this in common, that they wish to modify the system of individual ownership, they differ from each other as to the more or less absolute character of these modifications.

The majority of socialists, even those who nowadays call themselves *communists*, are content to demand the limitation of the right of private property, either in the matter of its object or in regard to its attributes.

As regards the first, they allow the right of private property to all wealth that serves only for consumption — for the satisfaction of personal wants, — and only demand the abolition, or, to use the right term, the "socialization," of goods that serve for production, namely, capital and land. Yet a part even of these might remain subject to private ownership, as we shall see.

As regards the second form of limitation, they demand the abolition either of inheritance, or of lending at interest, or of all profit-making enterprise.

The socialist schools differ also as to the means they wish to employ to carry out their programme; these range over the whole scale, from the most violent to the most moderate. The chief methods advocated are as follows:

(1) *Expropriation*, immediate or deferred, either by decree, as the result of a successful revolution, as in the case of the Bolshevists of Russia; or even by a law voted in proper form as the result of elections giving a majority to the socialist party — what is called the conquest of public powers.

This expropriation might be carried out either without indemnity, or with an indemnity, like those that are actually paid "in the interests of public utility." It is thought by revolutionaries that landowners and capitalists would not be justified in demanding an indemnity when they were merely being deprived of the privilege they have enjoyed for hundreds of years of exploiting the workers and consumers. But the moderates reply that since property has been established under the guarantee of the law — that is to say, of the national will — it is the duty of a community to respect engagements entered into in the past. At the same time it could not suit even moderate collectivists to pay these indemnities as they are paid in existing cases of expropriation, in the form of *capital* to replace the property of the expropriated owner, and to be *invested* to produce an equal or greater income, for in this case the economic situation would not be changed at all: capitalist producers would simply have been replaced by capitalist *rentiers*. Instead of this, the indemnity would be paid in the shape of *consumption goods* that would disappear when used, like the money that a spendthrift keeps in his cash-box without investing it, and on which he draws according to his needs until the cash-box is empty. Consequently, when these goods were all spent, their owner would be left to fall back into the ranks of the mere proletarians who have nothing to live on but their labour.

(2) The gradual socialization of property by the *abolition of the right of inheritance*, whether testamentary or *ab intestato*. This might be deferred to the second or third transmission of property, to make the transition easier, or it might even disinherit only future heirs, who are not yet born when the expropriation law is passed. Thus no living person would be despoiled, and as for those who are not yet in existence, what right would they have to complain? No one can have a right that was acquired before his birth.

(3) A *progressive tax*, either on income, capital, or succession, at such a rate as to bring about actual expropriation. Nor are we far from this now, if we consider that as a result of the war the interest on loans represents in several countries a charge of more than two-thirds on very large private incomes.

II. THE PRINCIPLES OF DISTRIBUTIVE JUSTICE

Suppose the end attained and property abolished. It remains to find out what is to replace it. We have seen (p. 332) that in existing society every one is remunerated by the value created, but that as these values are determined by the law of supply and demand, in which chance plays a large part, we cannot find there a principle of distributive justice, though economists think they have discovered it in the equivocal formula, *to each according to the services he has rendered.* We must therefore seek some other principle of distribution. Three of them have been proposed.

1. To each according to his needs.

This principle assumes that wealth is superabundant, or else that each of the guests seated at the common table will help himself with discretion, like well-bred people at a *table d'hôte*. But unfortunately the first and even the second of these hypotheses are purely utopian. Without denying this fact, communist socialists reply that if wealth is now insufficient the fault lies simply with the property system, but that under a communist régime wealth would multiply so abundantly that it could be freely drawn upon, like water from a spring, and piled up in heaps.

There is nothing to justify these fancies. Everything leads us to believe, on the contrary, that the amount of wealth will always be inadequate for our needs or our desires, especially since, in virtue of a psychological law that is everywhere proved to be true (see p. 34), these desires increase in proportion to the facilities that we discover for satisfying them. The piling-up of wealth, then, is impossible, and it is rationing that must be enforced. Now though the war taught us to practise this system, it has not given us a taste for it.

Another thing that we learned during the war was the amount of regulation and control and the number of penalties required to make this equalitarian system work, and the amount of fraud to which it gave rise.

None the less, the communist system has not infrequently been tried, and it would be incorrect to say that it has always failed. But the experiments that have been made confirm what has just been said: that where communism seems capable of realization it is under conditions that are the very reverse of the ideal of absolute freedom.

In the first place, communism has only been practised in *small communities*, not exceeding a few hundred or a thousand members. This is generally admitted by communists themselves, for Fourier fixed upon 1500 as the maximum number of persons for his phalanstery; Owen made it between 500 and 2000; and for the anarchists the basis of the communist organization is the self-governing *commune*, with the State abolished.[1] The reason for this is very simple: as the number of members increases, the smaller becomes the interest of each of them in the success of the society. When it is very small, each one can hope to benefit to an appreciable extent by his personal efforts, but in a communist society embracing, say, all Frenchmen, each member would be interested only to the extent of $\frac{1}{39,000,000}$ th, which would be too minute a fraction to stimulate anyone's zeal.

On the other hand, if a communist nation were to be divided into as many societies as there are parishes, then there would be rich communes and poor ones, and personal inequality would be replaced by group inequality.

Secondly, these communities must be subjected to *a very severe*

---

[1] All the communist communities in the United States have only a very small number of members. This was one reason for thinking that a communist system would not be feasible in such a vast country as Russia.

discipline.[1] It is easy, indeed, to see beforehand that community of life and equality of treatment must be incompatible with any encroachment on the part of individuals seeking to consume more than their share, and with any desire for freedom to neglect their task. And experience confirms this view, for all establishments in which community of life prevails — convents, barracks, and schools — are also those in which obedience is strictly required. It is even noticeable that in all cases of comparative success it is almost always the religious sentiment carried to the extreme of fanaticism that has alone been powerful enough to maintain in these communities the discipline indispensable to their existence. All the communist societies of the United States except that of the Icarians, which has made no progress, are religious sects, and the Jesuit republics in Paraguay[2] — the one great example of communism that can be cited, for its extent and length of life — constituted a veritable theocracy.

Finally, all these communities have remained poor, or at any rate the conditions of life among their members is not appreciably better than those of the average inhabitants of the country where they live, so that the piling up of wealth seems somewhat ironical: on the contrary, a rigid economy is imposed upon them. This is not to say, however, that there may not be some perfectly happy people in these communities, and some increase in the number of these lay monasteries is not improbable.

2. To each according to his capacity.

Saint-Simon[3] — a socialist, if you like, but one whose socialism was of an aristocratic and capitalist kind — was very far from wishing to do away with manufacturers, great employers, and even bankers. On the contrary, he wished to confer upon them the government of

[1] The history of the republic of Icaria is most instructive on this point. New members strove continually to escape from a rule that they found intolerable, and Cabet struggled vainly to obtain dictatorial power in the interest of the community. See the Rules of the Icarian Colony (1856): "Art. 4. Be prompted by devotion to the community . . . . Art. 16. Bind yourself to perform the work assigned to you by the management . . . . Art. 26. Have no preferences or dislikes in the matter of food . . . . Art. 27. Bear with resignation the discomforts and inconveniences of life in common . . . . Art. 37. Submit to discipline, etc., etc."

[Étienne Cabet (1788–1856) was a French writer, the author of a utopian romance called *Voyage en Icarie.* He founded a communist society in America — the Icarian Colony referred to above. It is not now in existence.]

[2] ["This social system was of short duration, being prematurely destroyed by diplomatic arrangements and foreign force." (Mill, *Principles of Political Economy,* Book II, Chap. I, § 4.)]

[3] [1760–1825, see Mill, *loc. cit.*]

society, under the control of a chamber of learned men.[1]   The Saint-
Simonian school did not take exception to inequality, but it wished
to replace artificial inequality by the inequality due to individual
merit.   And this is the meaning of their celebrated formula: "To
each according to his capacity; to each capacity according to the
work it accomplishes."

But the difficulty is to find the means of measuring capacity, and
even of estimating the value of each man's work.   Is the judge to
be appointed by goverment nomination, by examination or competition, by election or co-optation?   All these methods have
proved so defective when tried that from sheer discouragement the
question has arisen whether drawing lots would not be as good a
plan, as in the case of choosing a jury.

Moreover, even supposing that we could discover an infallible
criterion of talent, is it quite certain that such a system of distribution
according to capacity would be most conformable to justice?   It
might well be maintained, on the contrary, that intellectual superiority ought no more to be a title to wealth than physical superiority.   It already constitutes a privilege that is enviable enough in
itself, and need not be still further intensified by the addition of a
new privilege — the right of demanding a larger share of material
wealth.[2]

3. To each according to his work.

The principle of distribution advocated by contemporary schools
of socialism is, *to each according to his work*.   But this principle is
subject to two very different interpretations, according as the word
"work" is taken to mean the amount of *trouble taken* — the effort
employed — or the *result obtained* — the work accomplished.

By collectivists and working man socialists the principle is generally
understood in the first sense.   In Marxian socialism this principle
of distribution is perfectly logical, for it is bound up with the Marxian
theory which makes work the sole foundation of value.[3]   But if, as
we have pointed out, and as almost all economists believe nowadays,
labour is only one of the elements of value, and if the real basis
of value is final utility or desirability (p. 47), then the Marxian

[1] Saint-Simonism has sprung to life again since the war.   It has for its organ a
review, which has taken the name of the old Saint-Simonian journal, *Le Producteur*,
and in which business men, technical experts, and intellectuals collaborate.

[2] In the words of M. Renouvier: "According to public opinion, it would seem that
the cleverest and most intelligent man is a kind of natural creditor to ordinary mortals.
But therein lie serious errors against the moral law." (*Morale*, Vol. II.)

[3] "The quantity of labour is measured by the time it takes."   The labour that
makes up the substance and the value of goods is equal or indistinguishable labour
— *the expenditure of the same amount of energy*. (Karl Marx, *Das Capital*.)

system of distribution no longer squares with reality. Value will not allow itself to be bound on the bed of Procrustes where it is sought to place it. I might indeed receive in exchange for my labour a number of tickets or orders equal to the number of hours that I have put in; but no one could guarantee that in exchange for these tickets I could obtain products representing the same number of hours of labour, for no one could ever prevent a scarce object from being worth more than an abundant one, even if it cost the same number of hours of labour.

Besides, is it in accordance with social justice that each should be rewarded in proportion to the amount of trouble taken — to the number of hours and minutes measured by the clock? Is it not rather a case for repeating with Molière's *Misanthrope:*

"Time, my good sir, is quite beside the point"?

But if the principle, "to each according to his work" is taken in the second sense — to each according to the results of his work, so much the better for the man who succeeds, and so much the worse for him who fails! — then it is quite a different matter. Such a principle may be accepted as the best from the point of view of social usefulness, but from the point of view of justice it can scarcely be regarded as other than a makeshift. A justice that looks only to results, independently of efforts and intentions, is no justice in the higher sense of the word. We may even say that the principle thus interpreted is scarcely different from the one that already governs the distribution of wealth, in the existing economic order of things, for on the whole everyone receives as his share the value of the products or services that he can put into the market, as this value is determined by exchange. Many socialists, however, would be content with this, for it would be a step forward at any rate if we could eliminate or at least mitigate the thing that vitiates the existing system — namely, the excessive influence of good and evil luck, by which success is determined — and bring back all the independent social opportunities of individual effort (see p. 329).

Having given these general explanations, we must now set forth briefly the characteristics of the chief contemporary schools of socialism.

III. COLLECTIVISM

Collectivism differs from communism in not demanding the general abolition of individual property, and even claiming to strengthen it by making personal labour its basis.[1] But with this object it

[1] Collectivism is of fairly recent date. It was Pecqueur (1838) and Vidal (1846)

desires to restrict property to *products* and to abolish it so far as it applies to the *instruments of production*. And even in the matter of wealth that serves for production, collectivism does not demand at present that all which is employed productively should be held in common. It requires this *only for those goods which are exploited collectively — that is to say, by means of wage-earning workers*. Thus the land cultivated by the peasant, the fisherman's boat, and the artisan's stall, although instruments of production, would not be socialized but would remain individual property, because they are still under the régime of individual production, for as long as they remain so.[1] It is only capital and land exploited by labour, then, whether by individual *entrepreneurs* or by joint-stock companies, that are to be withdrawn from private ownership and *socialized*. But what are we to understand by this last word?

It is usually said — sometimes even in books — that to "socialize" means to place everything in the hands of the State. But this is not so; socialization does not mean State ownership.[2] The State as it exists to-day — the government, as it is called — representing the owning or *bourgeois* class, is to be replaced by a purely economic government, resembling the administrative council of the federations of consumers' co-operative societies: it will be simply the central organ of organized labour.

in France who first drew the distinction between instruments of production and objects of consumption which is the characteristic feature of the system. The first aggressive statement of the doctrine was made by Marx and Engels, in 1847, in their *Manifesto of the Communist Party*. It was Karl Marx, in his famous book *Das Capital* (of which the first volume was published in 1867 and two others after his death by his companion Engels), who gave the doctrine its critical form by providing it with all the weapons it employs in its attack upon the existing organization of society.

Although collectivism is often called Marxism from the name of its most illustrious theorist, yet all collectivists are not Marxians: in fact we find them dissenting more and more from Marxism.

[1] It is owing to this distinction that the collectivists seek in their programmes to reassure the small producers and peasants who would have been frightened by the prospect of a general expropriation. By confining expropriation *for the time being* to owners who employ paid labour — that is to say, to the rich — they reassure the others, but they neglect to add that their turn will come later on.

It is just this distinction that has been applied in the decree of expropriation issued by the Russian revolutionists, but only after the failure of their attempts at a general socialization of the land.

Moreover we know (p. 107) that collectivists do not regard the instruments of production as capital so long as they are in the hands of the workers. They are logical in making this distinction, therefore.

[2] In the earlier part of this volume (p. 24) and in every edition of this book we have warned our readers against this very common mistake.

But without stopping to define what the collectivist State will be, let us merely ask what it will do with the means of production when they are freed from individual appropriation. How will land and capital be exploited by the new State. Information on this point, though essential, is not very precise nor even very concordant. Even the "scientific" socialists generally refuse it, because they consider that all forecasts and anticipations of what will happen after the Revolution should be left to the writers of social novels. Nevertheless we may conclude from the criticisms levelled at existing business methods, both capitalist and governmental, that the exploitation of land and capital is to be entrusted to the workers themselves, organized in federations.

To distinguish itself from all the other socialist systems that have preceded it, collectivism calls itself *scientific socialism* — meaning thereby that it claims to be a demonstration rather than a system. It does not set up a desirable ideal of justice and fraternity; it does not proclaim what *ought to be;* it claims to say what *is.* The programme we have just described — socialization of the instruments of production — is not a solution arrived at by an effort of the imagination, like Fourier's visions: it is offered as the system that economic evolution itself is in process of realizing, and that will force itself upon modern communities either to-morrow or the next day[1] — peacefully, if they yield to it, and by force if they resist: *volentem ducunt, nolentem trahunt.* And this is how they prove it:

In former times, ownership was an individual matter because production was so too. There was harmony between the mode of production and the mode of distribution. The small workshop of the Middle Ages is an instance. But to-day, as a consequence of the development of industry, commerce, and ownership on a large scale,— that is to say, by the law of concentration of business undertakings — individual production is every day disappearing to make way for collective production. Witness the great factories, the mining industry, and the railway companies.

But distribution, on the other hand, continues to be based on individual ownership. Between the system of production and that of distribution, therefore, there is an antinomy, a sort of fissure that goes on growing larger and that may at any moment cause a rupture of equilibrium and the destruction of the existing capitalist régime.

Collectivists are reproached with wishing to expropriate the rich. But, they reply, whither is *laisser faire* leading us? To an approach-

[1] This conception of an evolution entirely determined by economic necessities is called *historical materialism.*

ing social state in which *all small producers will have been expropriated by the large ones.* Then "class consciousness" will awaken
— that is to say, the realization by the proletarians of their rights
and their power — and what will be the result? It will be this:
the expropriated having become almost the whole population of
the country, and the expropriators, by the very success of their
labours at concentration, being only a handful, there will necessarily
come a day when, either by force or simply by the legal conquest
of public power, the expropriators will in their turn be expropriated for the benefit of all — for the benefit of society, or of the nation.
Then harmony will again be established between production and
distribution, and the logic of evolution will be satisfied — the logic
that demands that *a collective mode of appropriation should correspond to a collective mode of production.*

Collectivism may therefore be summed up thus: its object is
the *progressive socialization of the instruments of production;* and
its method is *class warfare* — workers against capitalists and the
working class against the *bourgeois.*[1]

Now, in the first place, this proud claim of collectivism to be an
anticipation of economic evolution, as inevitable as destiny, cannot
be accepted. The supposed historical law on which all collectivism
is based — namely, the gradual transformation of all individual production into collective production — is only a generalization that
is far from covering all the facts and is even contradicted by many
of them. In agriculture, for instance, despite the affirmations of
collectivists, we can find no decisive proof of this evolution. On
the contrary, we see the land being more and more divided and the
size of the farm growing smaller and smaller, as the density of the
population increases and intensive cultivation develops. The share-
holding system has not been applied to landed property, save in
altogether exceptional cases. Nor can we say even in the case of
manufacture that small-scale industry is disappearing before large-
scale, for it is developing at least as much as the latter. There is
nothing to prove, therefore, that this general expropriation of individual producers for the benefit of a small number of collective
undertakings when these are ready to capture the nation, will ever
take place. Thus "the logic of evolution" is wanting — and this
upsets in its turn the logic of collectivism.

[1] This phrase, "class warfare," does not *necessarily* imply an armed struggle and
civil war, any more than the strife of parties, of churches, or of tongues. But it does
imply the final elimination of the capitalist class.

Again, the opposition between a mode of production that is becoming collective and a mode of distribution that remains individual, is an antithesis that is more apparent than real. In reality, the two are becoming transformed on parallel lines. In business enterprises on the joint-stock system, which is becoming increasingly general, it is not only production that is becoming collective, but property as well, for the latter is distributed among a multitude of shareholders who are generally more numerous even than the workmen employed by the company.

This separation or cleavage of society into two superimposed layers, the one growing more and more numerous and poorer, the other more and more wealthy and less numerous, together with an increasingly violent opposition of interests between the two sections — all this is merely a rough and ready sketch of a social system that is far more complex. There are not two classes in society but a large number, and their interests are so closely interwoven that the gigantic duel described as "class warfare" takes the shape in reality of a large number of separate conflicts.

The result is that the power of resistance of the possessing classes to ultimate expropriation — that is to say, to the socialization of their possessions — is not growing weaker, as the collectivists affirm: it seems rather to go on increasing. The millions of smaller folk — employees and servants, workers in town and country alike — who have bought government stock, municipal bonds, or even railway shares, are as tenacious of their property as the peasant is of his land — and their number is increasing every day.[1] They would naturally ask nothing better than to add to their small holdings a share of the property of the rich if it was a matter of equal distribution, but they would not be inclined to give up what they have, however little it may be, in exchange for a useless, indeterminate, collective draft on the national capital.

But setting aside the question whether collectivism would be simply an application of a natural law of economic development, it remains to see what its results would be, regarded as a practical solution of the problem of distribution. Now in this respect it lays itself open to many criticisms.

(1) Given the kind of wealth that would be left in private ownership — namely, personal consumption goods — the result would be

---

[1] The war has increased the number of stock-holders to an incredible extent, and particularly of small stock-holders, for the most numerous subscribers to loans are not the great capitalists. There can scarcely be anyone who does not hold some portion of the millions of stock issued by the various governments during the war.

that the right of property would be reduced to that one of its attributes which is most individualist. The so-called owner could
neither sell nor lend his share, nor could he use it to set anyone else
to work: he could only eat it, keep it, or perhaps give it away —
in any case he would be forbidden to put it to any other use than an
unproductive use.[1] No doubt the attributes that would be cut off
are those that enabled property, in many cases, to become an instrument of exploitation; but they are also those that made it an
incomparable instrument of production.

(2) It is not only all productive employment of wealth in business
that would be stopped: it is also all formation of new capital by
saving. For even supposing that some workers continued to save
a portion of their income in the form of labour coupons, they could
not think of investing it, for this would be strictly forbidden. They
would only be allowed to hoard it unproductively and without any
social utility. Could they even lend it to the nation? Gratuitously,
perhaps; but there would be little inducement to do that. And
since the national capital would still have to be maintained and increased, what source would be substituted for private saving? Public saving, we are told. The nation would do what all financial
organizations do to-day — it would deduct 10% or 20% from its
income to be set aside as a reserve fund. Very good! only we should
have to assume this government to be unlike all those that had
preceded it: it would have to be economical and thrifty — in short,
when once it had become collectivist, it would have to acquire all
the virtues of the *bourgeois*.

(3) The suppression of individual property — or, where it nominally continued, the suppression of the right of free disposal —
could not fail to bring in its train innumerable restrictions on individual freedom, if only to prevent individuals from trying to
make use of their mutilated property. Under the existing system
there are some individuals at least, not only among the rich but also
among the poor, who are independent producers and make their
way in freedom. Under a collectivist régime they would no longer
exist: the only producers would be those who produced for the nation
and under the nation's orders. They would not be called wage-
earners, or even officials, because each of these liberated proletarians
would be regarded as his own master and as working on his own

---

[1] Could he even use it to set *himself* to work independently? Perhaps he could —
provisionally, and so long as there were any independent producers; but logically he
could not, for all individual production ought ultimately to be replaced by social production.

account. Very well; but this is merely a question of terms.[1] In the consumers' co-operative society, that is often pointed out to us as an anticipation on a small scale of the great collectivist society of the future, the workers and employees regard themselves simply as wage-earners, and even go on strike occasionally.

IV. SYNDICALISM

Syndicalism is not so much a doctrine as a movement; or, if it is to be regarded as a doctrine, it should be classed along with pragmatism — the fashionable modern philosophy that seeks for truth in practical action. Attempts have been made to present syndicalism as a deduction from, and a realization of, the Marxian doctrine — as a kind of neo-Marxism; — but, if it is so, it is quite an unconscious one so far as the syndicalists are concerned, for very few of them certainly have read Karl Marx, and it is the intellectuals who have pointed out this relationship. In many respects it is rather from anarchism that the militant syndicalists have drawn their inspiration. The essential features of resemblance and difference between the two schools, however, are as follows.

(1) Syndicalism is exclusively a *workman's* socialism. It is in this respect that it may be regarded as derived from Marxism, for, as we have already seen, the strength of Marxian socialism — or social democracy, as the Germans call it — lies in its having made itself the organ of the demands of the working classes. On the other hand, syndicalism differs in this respect from anarchism, for the latter was rather a speculative and political doctrine, and drew its recruits from intellectual circles. But syndicalism differs also from Marxism in taking no interest in theories about the evolution of property: its motto is *the abolition of the wage-system.*

(2) The foundation of the syndicalist system, as its name indicates, is the syndicate. The reason is simply this: as the syndicate, by its very definition and also by its legal constitution, is a professional association that admits none but workers in the same trade, all *bourgeois* and political socialist elements are forcibly excluded from it. None the less, the isolated syndicate is too much impregnated by

[1] The question of the remuneration of labour (if we must not call it wages) under the collectivist system seems difficult to solve. Attempts have often been made (see the works of Thompson, Owen, Rodbertus, etc., and especially Georges Renard, *Le Régime socialiste*) to find a mechanical method of automatically ensuring a distribution proportional to labour. But for an *automatic* mechanism we can scarcely imagine any other than the law of supply and demand. And the new Marxism itself recognizes this nowadays.

selfishly corporate interests to represent the general interests of the working class. The direction of the movement must therefore be in the hands of federations of syndicates, and, still better, in those of the general confederation of all the syndicates — the celebrated C. G. T. (*Confédération Générale du Travail*).[1]

By means of propaganda, of the strike weapon, and even of *sabotage*, if necessary — though working class opinion is much divided on the subject of this last method of warfare — syndicalism aims at making the position of the employer untenable, so that the employing system shall be destroyed or shall abolish itself — as will happen when the employer finds that business no longer brings him anything but trouble and loss. Then the game will be won, and, say the syndicalist manifestoes, "the syndicate, which is to-day an organization for resistance, will in future be the unit for production and distribution, and the foundation of social reorganization." Then all profits, rents, and benefits will belong to labour, save for the needful deduction for the common wants.

But the elimination of all industrial leaders, employers, landowners, and capitalists, and their replacement by administrative committees, the organs of the workmen's syndicates, is just the kind of thing to awaken the liveliest apprehensions among those who have some experience of the low standard of economic education among the working classes; and this has been recognized by more than one syndicalist leader. There is reason to believe that the many complaints made against State business undertakings would apply even more forcibly here.

This programme is founded on the assumption that the working class is everything, because by its labour it is the sole producer of wealth. Now this foundation is only a sound one if the labour theory of value is admitted to be correct. If, on the contrary, it is held to be incorrect, or at least incomplete and containing only a part of the truth — and such is the opinion of most economists to-day (see pp. 43–54) — then syndicalism is wrong as to the omnipotence of labour, and cannot aspire to solve the social problem by itself. In fact, all the industrial progress and all the vast increase of wealth during the past century have been due to the initiative and the invention of those business leaders and intellectuals whom it is intended to eliminate as parasites. Will it be any different in the future? It is not impossible; yet if this elimination must take place,

---

[1] The C. G. T. has now split into two sections, a rival General Confederation having been formed by the extremists, calling themselves communists, as a result of the Russian revolution.

it may be expected that the result of the war will be to postpone it rather than to hasten it; for the necessity of rebuilding the ruins and replacing the immense amount of wealth that has been destroyed, will be too urgent for it to be possible first to eliminate those by whom this wealth was created.

V. CO–OPERATION

The necessities of practical life, more powerful than systems, have given rise spontaneously in different countries to a whole crop of associations, infinitely varied in their nature, each kind being adapted to one special end, but all alike in the possession of certain general characteristics now to be described. Thus in England there are consumers' co-operative societies; in France, co-operative societies for production; in Germany, co-operative credit societies; in Denmark, rural co-operative societies; in the United States, co-operative building societies, and so forth. All these associations have already begun, although at present to a limited extent, to carry out several of the most important requirements of socialism; and meanwhile, what is not to be despised, they have procured a very real improvement in the conditions of life of those who have made trial of them.

The war, which seemed as if it must bring them to ruin, has on the contrary given them a tremendous impetus — especially consumers' societies. This is to be explained in part by the rise in prices and the scarcity of commodities, which have made these societies into havens of refuge for consumers. But more than that: governments and municipalities in many cases have had to have recourse to them, because they have shown that they practise a superior mode of distribution, and the only one that could ensure what government regulation had been powerless to realize — namely, a fair price.

But is co-operation really to be classed among the socialist systems — even if we change its name to co-operat*ism*? It does not appear so at first sight, since none of the various forms of association just enumerated aims at abolishing property or even at adopting a new principle of distribution. They are sober and sensible associations, legally constituted as joint-stock companies, and their object seems therefore to be not to abolish individual ownership but to *make it universal*, by making it accessible to all by means of interest coupons. They make no war on capital; on the contrary, they greatly value its services, seek for it, and almost always remunerate its services by paying interest on it.

It is owing to this social pacifism that socialists refused for a long time to recognize co-operation as a member of their family, looking upon it as a *bourgeois* institution, disguised in order to lead true socialists astray.   But, as we shall see presently, they have now abandoned this mistaken opinion.

(1) In fact, though it is true that co-operative societies have no desire to abolish property or capital, yet they all aim at depriving it of its *directorship* in production, and, at the same time, at taking from it the portion that it deducts on the very ground of that directing power.   Their object is the *abolition of profit* — whether their rules forbid the making of any profit, or whether they place it in a reserve fund.   And even those societies that do make profits restore them to their members in proportion to the amount of their purchases (or of their labour, in the case of co-operative societies for production), but never in proportion to their shares — that is to say, the capital they have furnished.   It is true that the use of share-capital, like that of borrowed capital, is generally paid for, but only by a moderate interest, and never by a dividend: and there are even some societies which pay no interest at all.   If we remember that in joint-stock companies — the system that is extending so rapidly nowadays — it is capital that takes all the profits as well as the directorship of the business, reducing labour to the position of a wage-earner, we shall understand what a social revolution has been brought about by the co-operative system, which reverses the situation, making capital in its turn play the part of wage-earner.

So long, of course, as co-operative societies cover only a very small area of trade and production, this new system will be valuable merely as pointing out the path of progress.   But if we imagine the co-operative society enlarged so as to embrace the whole nation, then the abolition of profit would effect a radical alteration in the distribution of wealth.   For profit, under the existing system, is the sole means of enrichment, and if it disappears the spring of all great fortunes will be dried up.[1]

(2) All co-operative societies are socialistic in the sense that their object is the *economic emancipation* of certain classes of persons, and their liberation from being exploited.   The consumers' society enables consumers to dispense with bakers, grocers, and other mer-

---

[1] Apart from certain cases of extraordinary gains made by doctors, barristers, artists, actors, and singers, it is a matter of common knowledge that fortunes are only made in business, which means out of profits.   At the same time it is open to question whether a nation in which the stimulus of profit had disappeared would not find its productive activity slackening, and run the risk of sinking into the stationary state.   This is indeed a serious objection, but we shall deal with it elsewhere (see below, Book III, Part II, Chap. IV, and also a discussion on the subject in our book *Coopératisme*).

chants, by purchasing direct from the producer, or, better still, by making everything that they require themselves. The credit society enables borrowers to avoid the clutches of the money-lender by procuring the necessary capital for them direct, or even by enabling them to create it themselves by ingenious devices for saving and mutual assistance. The co-operative society for production enables the workers to do without employers by producing on their own account and by their own means, by selling direct to the public and keeping for themselves the whole produce of their labour. This co-operative policy is generally described by saying that its object is the suppression of the middleman — meaning the intermediary who is a parasite. Of course every middleman is not necessarily a parasite — far from it, — but he becomes one as soon as it is demonstrated by co-operation that his services are needless.

This elimination of the middleman who is interposed between producer and consumer, when co-operation comes to make him unnecessary, is evidently equivalent to expropriation — and that even without indemnification. However, this expropriation is effected not by coercion but by the normal method of free competition, in accordance with the rules of fair play, and without recourse to any of those devices that are too often employed in commerce — adulteration, advertising, window-dressing, discounts and premiums, sweating of employees, and so forth. If, therefore, the co-operative societies achieve success, we may say that their success will not be due to competition in the usual form of a struggle for existence, but to the kind that works by "selection of the fittest." And if there is expropriation, it will not take the form of confiscation: co-operators do not say to the capitalist, "we are going to take your capital from you"; what they say is, "keep your capital; we shall not need it, because we are going to make it for ourselves."

But if co-operation resembles socialism in the features we have just indicated, it has other features which mark it off from socialism and give it a distinctive appearance.

(3) To begin with, it does not look at things from the producer's point of view, like socialists in general and Marxians and syndicalists in particular, but from the consumer's standpoint. The profit that it seeks to abolish is not the tribute levied by the employer on the workman, but that levied by the merchant or manufacturer on the purchaser. It is true, of course, that it is the workers who make up the bulk of the consumers, and therefore their interests are the same; but these interests are regarded under a different aspect — as consuming power instead of labour power.

Further, and owing to this last feature, co-operation is not concerned with class warfare: it ignores it, because the consumer represents no special class, but everyone, without distinction of profession, age, or sex: his interests, therefore, are simply the interests of the public.   It is true that all co-operative societies do not make selling their object: production, credit, building, and so forth are the aims of some of them.   But it is the consumers' society that is becoming more and more predominant, and tending to absorb the others, or at least to lay down the lines on which the movement shall progress.

Co-operation goes farther than not encouraging strife: it may even be said that a characteristic of every great form of co-operative association is the abolition of all conflict — of any struggle between rival interests.   Thus consumers' societies do away with the conflict between seller and buyer; building societies abolish the strife between owner and tenant; credit societies, the conflict between debtor and creditor; and societies for production, the conflict between employer and wage-earner.

(4) Finally, co-operation in all its forms — consumption, credit, or production — claims to exert a moral as well as an economic influence.   In fact, it makes no appeal to revolution or even to coercive legislation to accomplish its work of emancipation; it relies on the moral forces of individual energy and the spirit of solidarity — forces that are generally opposed to each other, but are reconciled by co-operation — and therein lies its educational value.[1]   Its motto is a twofold one: *self help* — the proud boast of providing for its needs by its own means, being its own merchant, its own banker, its own lender, its own employer; — and *each for all* — the desire to seek freedom not only for oneself but for others and by others, and not to wish for salvation alone.

It is to this moral inspiration that co-operation owes its progress, as much as, and perhaps more than to its practical advantages.   It was that which attracted the "Christian socialists" of England in the middle of last century; it was that which inspired the rural credit societies founded by Raiffeisen and his imitators; and it is that mystic element which is causing the co-operative movement to extend to-day, like a new religion, among the vast populations of Russia.

---

[1] One of the earliest co-operative societies founded at Lyons in 1835 took for its motto, *Honest trade* — meaning that its aim was to inaugurate the reign of truth and honesty in commercial relations.   This in itself would be a great moral revolution.

PART II

THE VARIOUS CLASSES OF RECIPIENTS

We have just considered the *principles* that determine the distribution of wealth, both those that apply at the present day and those that have been proposed as substitutes. We must now turn to the *persons* who appear as claimants, and consider who they are and what share is demanded by each of them. It goes without saying that we have not to examine individual claims, but only those formulated by important groups or classes of the population, consisting of all who are connected by community of interests and therefore have the same claim to participate. As the claims of the various recipients are mutually antagonistic we must expect to find them creating a permanent state of warfare between these classes.

We shall take only the four typical classes of those who thus demand a share in the distribution: the landowner, who receives *rent;* the capitalist, who receives *interest;* the workman, who receives *wages;* and the *entrepreneur*, who receives *profit*.[1]

What is known as "the middle class" is not, economically speaking, a class at all, and does not require a separate chapter in the book of Distribution, since it has no claim to a share for itself: each member simply retains the ownership of what he produces.

[1] Two other recipients ought also to be considered — namely, paupers and the State; for they both receive an appreciable share of the general income, the former in the shape of *poor relief*, and the latter in that of *taxes*. But these incomes are received at second hand. We have no space to deal with them here; see my *Political Economy*.

367

CHAPTER I — THE OWNERS OF LAND[1]

I. THE EVOLUTION OF LANDED PROPERTY

Not only is property in land sanctioned by all modern systems of legislation, but it is regarded as the typical form of property. When we speak of "property," without any qualification, we are understood to mean landed property. Yet landed property is of comparatively recent date, and its establishment was even a matter of considerable difficulty.

We may distinguish, in the development of landed property, six successive stages which we will briefly describe.

(1) It will easily be understood that there is no reason for the existence of landed property among tribes that live by hunting, or even among pastoral peoples leading a nomadic life: it can arise only with the birth of agriculture. And even in the earliest stages of agricultural life it is not yet established, first, because land at this period is superabundant, and so no one feels the need of marking off his share; secondly, because agricultural methods are still in a rudimentary state and the farmer leaves one field as soon as it is exhausted, and takes another. At the beginning, land is cultivated in common, or at least with little distinction between individual shares: it belongs to society as a whole, or rather to the tribe; only the fruits of the soil belong to the man who has produced them.

(2) Population, however, becomes by degrees more settled and more fixed upon the soil. It also becomes more dense, and feels the need of adopting a more productive mode of cultivation. Thus the first stage is succeeded by a second — that of temporary possession along with *periodical division*. Though the land is always regarded as belonging to society, it is equally divided among all the heads of families, not yet in a definite and permanent manner, but only for a certain time. The period is at first only a year, since that is the or-

---

[1] The class of owners of land comprises three categories: (*a*) owners who make their land productive by employing wage-paid labour; (*b*) owners who let their land; (*c*) owners who cultivate their land themselves. These correspond in the industrial world to active capitalists (*entrepreneurs*), passive capitalists (*rentiers*), and independent workers, or craftsmen. But the distinction is not a very rigid one, for an owner may often cultivate some of his land directly and let other portions of it, or he may be a tenant farmer and yet own some land himself.

dinary cycle of agricultural operations. But then, as agricultural methods improve and require a longer time, the period for which the land is divided grows correspondingly longer and longer. This system of periodical division obtained not long ago in Russia, in the shape of the famous *mir*.

(3) But there comes a time when these periodical divisions fall into disuse, for those who have improved their land are not readily disposed to be robbed periodically, for the benefit of the community, of the increased value due to their labours. Thus arises the institution of *family ownership*, each family remaining in permanent possession of its share of land. But this is not yet individual ownership, for the right of disposal does not exist. The head of the family can neither sell the land, nor give it away, nor dispose of it after his death, simply because it is regarded as a collective heritage and not as individual property. This system is still to be found in the family communities of Eastern Europe, and notably in the *Zadrugas* of Bulgaria and Croatia, which comprise some fifty or sixty persons; but they are tending quickly to disappear before the modern spirit of independence manifested by the members of the family.

(4) The evolution of landed property passes through a stage which, though accidental in its nature, has unfortunately never been wanting in the history of human societies — I mean *conquest*. There is not a single territory on the surface of the earth that has not been taken by force at some time or other from the people who occupied it, to be appropriated by the conquering race. Yet the victors, simply because they were victors and masters, took no care to cultivate the land, but merely assumed the legal ownership of it — the "eminent domain," as it used to be called — leaving the subject race in possession of the soil by feudal tenure. This tenure, which was at first for life, and inalienable, ended by becoming an actual form of ownership, though limited by the conditions of the grant made to the tenant, by the services imposed upon him, by the dues that he was compelled to pay to his superior lord, and by the impossibility of alienating the land without the lord's permission. This feudal system was for many centuries the basis of the social and political constitution of Europe, and it has left traces in many countries. In England particularly almost all landed property has retained the form of tenure, in the eyes of the law, and is still encumbered by a multitude of restrictions very difficult to remove.[1]

---

[1] "It became a fundamental maxim and necessary principle (though in reality a mere fiction) of our English tenures, 'that the king is the universal landlord and original proprietor of all the lands in his kingdom.'" (Blackstone, *Commentaries on the Laws of England*, Book II, Chapter IV.)

(5) The growth of individualism and civil equality and the abolition of the feudal system, especially in countries which felt the influence of the French Revolution of 1789, brought about a fifth phase — the one that has marked our own epoch. This is the definite establishment of *free property in land*, with all the attributes involved in the right of ownership.[1] Yet even to-day landed property is still not entirely on the same footing as personal or movable property: it differs from it in many ways that are familiar to lawyers, and especially in the difficulties by which its sale is surrounded.

(6) One step remained for the complete assimilation of landed property to personal property, and thus to mark the last stage of development. This was to make landed property mobile or transferable, so that every individual might not only possess land but dispose of it as easily as any movable object whatever. This last step has been taken in a new country, Australia, by the celebrated Torrens system, by which the right of property in land is transformed into a simple entry in a register, so that the owner is enabled, as it were, to put his land into his pocket-book, in the shape of a piece of paper, and to transfer it to someone else almost as easily as a bill of exchange. Efforts have been made for some time to introduce this system into our old European countries, and it will probably end by becoming universal, through the natural evolution that we have been tracing.[2]

The conclusion that emerges from this rapid sketch is, therefore, that landed property has evolved progressively and continually from the collective to the individual form, and tends more and more to resemble personal property and capital, to the point of becoming indistinguishable from them.

It would seem as if there were yet one more stage to be looked for, when landed property would be represented by a document — a registered or even a "bearer" bond — and when agricultural business would be undertaken by joint-stock companies, as is the tendency in industry at present. But this logical end of the process of development does not look like being realized in the case of landed property; at all events, the experiments so far made have not been very successful.

---

[1] There still remain certain services which are, as it were, a reminder of the days of the primitive community — as, for instance, the obligation to permit gleaning after the harvest, and the corresponding grape-gleaning in vine-growing countries. Curiously enough, the owner of the vineyard is even forbidden to glean his own grapes! Legal proceedings have been taken on several occasions for this offence.

[2] The object of this system, as Torrens himself declared, is to rid landed property of all the barriers that prevented free access to it, "like the portcullis, drawbridge and moats which prevented access to the castles of our ancestors."

II. INCOME FROM LAND. THE LAW OF RENT

The earlier economists — the physiocrats, Adam Smith, and J. B. Say — taught that land *produced rent* in virtue of an inherent faculty, in the same way that it produces crops.[1] But such a doctrine was very dangerous for the defence of landed property, for it gave an opening for the question, If rent is a free gift of nature, why is it not common to all? By what right is it intercepted by the landowner, who receives it freely from nature and makes his fellows pay dearly for it?

To this question these fathers of political economy gave various replies. The physiocrats said that the owner of the soil was endowed with the function of a distributor of wealth, and that the rent he received was only a sort of fee for the discharge of this high duty. But it was already plain to Turgot, and after him to J. B. Say in particular, that property in land was simply a *monopoly* resulting from the taking possession of it. There would be no rent, in fact, if land were as unlimited in quantity as water, air, or light; and such is the case in new countries where land is to be had without stint. But in old countries the land has been occupied and made private property, with the result that those who hold it can draw an income from it by selling these gifts of nature at a high price — that is to say, by letting it at a money rent. It must be said, however, that these economists were concerned only with *explaining*, not *justifying*, the existence of rent, and this attitude was most in accordance with scientific method. But this explanation evidently could not please the defenders of landed property, and we shall see further on how they tried to refute it.

Nor could such an explanation satisfy the acute mind of Ricardo, for this great economist, as we know, was the principal author of the doctrine that bases value upon the labour and cost of production. He could not therefore admit, on the one hand, that the value of land or its produce was created by nature, either directly or even in collaboration. On the other hand, he was yet obliged to admit that income from land represents something more than the labour of cultivating it, since he saw every piece of land in England finding a tenant. Now a man could only be a tenant farmer if, after obtaining a living and paying all the expenses involved in cultivation, there was still a sufficient surplus out of the produce of the land with

[1] Here are the words of Adam Smith: "In agriculture too, nature labours along with man," and her share "is seldom less than a fourth, and frequently more than a third of the whole produce." "This rent may be considered as the produce of those powers of nature." (*Wealth of Nations*, Book II, Chapter V.)

which to pay his rent. It was to explain this awkward dilemma that he devised his theory of rent, the most famous theory in political economy, and the theme of discussion among economists for more than a hundred years.

It is important to distinguish between the two aspects of this theory: in what may be called its *static* form it explains rent by the way in which the price of agricultural produce is determined on the market; in its *dynamic* form it shows the gradual emergence of rent in the course of economic history. It is in this second form that the theory of rent has most impressed people, but it is the first that has been the most valuable contribution to economic science. We will start, then, with that one.

Suppose that several hundred sacks of wheat are sold in the market. It is obvious that they have not all been produced under the same conditions: some have been obtained by the aid of much labour and manuring; others have grown, as it were, by themselves, on a fertile plot of land; some have come from the other end of the world, and some from a farm close by. If each sack, then, were to bear a label showing its cost of production, no two of them, perhaps, would show the same figure. Thus the cost of production of sack A might have been 10s., sack B might have cost 11s., sack C 12s., and so on, down to sack Z, which cost 20s.

But we know, on the other hand, that there can never be more than one and the same price in the same market for similar products (p. 190). So the selling price of all these sacks of wheat will be the same. How, then, is the agreement between selling price and cost price to be established, if all the cost prices are different and all the selling prices the same?

The answer is this: agreement will be established simply between the selling price and the cost price of the sack that cost most to produce — say, sack Z, which cost 20s., in the example we have been imagining. The reason is very simple: the selling price must be at least enough to repay the expenses of the unfortunate seller who produced his wheat under the most unfavourable conditions, for otherwise he would give up bringing it to market. Now we are assuming that the quantity of wheat is not greater than is required and that the last sack, Z, cannot be dispensed with, so that the competition of this last producer is also indispensable.

We reach this conclusion, then: that whenever similar products are sold in the same market, the value of all of them tends to coincide with the maximum cost of production.

Now it is evident that this price, 20s., will give a differential profit to all the more favoured producers of wheat, whose cost of production is lower.   There will be a profit of 10s. for the man whose sack cost 10s., a profit of 8s. for the one whose sack cost 12s., of 5s. for him whose sack cost 15s., and so on.   It is the income proceeding from these regular profits that, strictly speaking, is called *rent*.

This is a particularly neat kind of demonstration, because it solves what looked like an insoluble contradiction.   While it satisfies the law that value = cost of production, as Ricardo conceived it, it yet shows that there is something in price *more* than cost of production.   The solution of the riddle is that the price of the wheat in all the sacks is indeed determined by cost of production, but by the cost of only one among the various sacks — the one *that was produced under the most unfavourable conditions*.   It is this single unfortunate sack that fixes the market price — assuming, of course, that it is indispensable, — and all the other sacks thus benefit by the difference, larger or smaller, between this single price, which is the same for all, and their respective costs of production, which are different in each case.

This theory implies that there is always at least one piece of land — the piece that produced sack Z — which yields no rent — nothing beyond a return for the capital and labour expended on it; and that piece plays the decisive part, as it serves as a standard for all the rest.   As for the return to all the other pieces of land, we must not say that it is due to their fertility (for if they were all equally fertile the price of wheat would be determined for them all by the same cost of production and there would therefore be no rent), but to the infertility of competing lands: it is not due to nature's generosity, but to her parsimony.

The position of the owner of a fertile piece of land is indeed a privilege — a monopoly, if you like, but a monopoly of a very special kind, for it consists not in being able to sell at a higher price, but in being able to produce more cheaply.   This, it will be said, is merely a question of terms.   But no! for whereas the monopolist injures the public by raising prices, the rent-receiving landowner merely submits to the price fixed in the market by the law of prices, or, in other words, by necessity.   And even if all owners of wheat land, in a fit of generosity, were to remit their rents, the market price of wheat would not be a halfpenny lower: they would merely be making a present to their tenants or their immediate purchasers.[1]

---

[1] Ricardo said: "Corn is not high because a rent is paid, but a rent is paid because corn is high."

This celebrated formula may also be expressed thus: *Rent does not enter into the ex-*

It will be seen that on this theory there are only *differential* rents which means that there would be no rent at all if all pieces of land were of the same quality. Now that is where Ricardo's theory seems to be, if not incorrect, yet at any rate incomplete as an explanation of rent. Can we believe, indeed, that if all the land in England became identical in quality, this equalization would cause rent to disappear, and with it the market value of all the land? Rent would undoubtedly remain just the same, although, by hypothesis, it would be the same for every piece of land.[1] It must, therefore, have some other basis that is absolute and not merely relative, which leads us back to the explanation that bases it upon the fact that land is a monopoly.

But Ricardo's theory has none the less an incomparable doctrinal value, so much so that it has been continually extended until its scope now spreads far beyond the range of landed property. The law of rent is apparent in every branch of economic science — everywhere where there are inequalities of situation in regard to production. In fact Ricardo himself stated this very clearly. Wherever similar products are sold at the same price, although produced under very unequal conditions, the phenomenon of rent, resulting from the excess of the selling price over the cost of production, appears for the benefit of those producers who are most favoured by circumstances. And we shall see later that "profit" itself is only a kind of rent.

Nevertheless it must not be said that Ricardo's doctrine has committed suicide, as it were, by extending itself. We must not make this an argument for denying it, for it is almost exclusively as an attribute of landed property that the law of rent appears with the force of a "law" — that is to say, as a permanent and necessary phenomenon, so long, at least, as there is no change in the general economic conditions (progress of cultivation, density of population, etc.) of which we are about to speak. Everywhere else, indeed, this phenomenon appears only temporarily, because the most favoured producers are generally sufficient by themselves to supply the market by indefinitely increasing their production. Instead of taking ad-

---

penses of production. Wages and interest alone constitute the expenses of production, and therefore, under the pressure of competition, the value of the product. This question, however, is one of the hardest and most disputed in theoretical political economy. We shall have to return to it in connexion with profit. From the practical point of view the interesting conclusion has been drawn from it that all rent could be confiscated by taxation without affecting the price of wheat — a conclusion that has been made use of by John Stuart Mill and Henry George (see below, § VII).

[1] Supposing, at least, that the superabundance of produce did not cause rent to disappear.

vantage of their privileged position by continuing to sell at the old prices, it is to their interest to lower prices so as to undersell their rivals and drive them from the market by degrees. They gain less on each article, but they make up for it in quantity.

For this reason, in the case of industry, although there also the general market price at any given moment and for each particular day is determined by the maximum cost of production, yet *in the long run* it is determined, on the contrary, by the *minimum cost of production*. This is a great advantage to society; it shows itself in practice in the shape of a gradual fall in the prices of industrial products and in the rate of profit. It is quite otherwise with agricultural production, for there it is to be feared that prices will be determined by a continually increasing cost of production, which will mean a progressive rise in the rent of land.

But that brings us to the second aspect of Ricardo's law.

III. THE RISE OF RENT AND SURPLUS VALUE

In the beginning, says Ricardo, men had no need to cultivate more than a small amount of land, and so they chose the best. Yet in spite of the fertility of this land its earliest occupants drew no larger income from it than they could have drawn from any other employment of their labour and capital. In fact, as there was enough land and to spare, they were subject to the law of competition which brought down the value of their products to the level of the cost of production. They therefore received no rent, in the proper sense of the term.

But there came a time when the increase of population demanded an increase in production. Then, since lands of the first class were all appropriated, *it became necessary to cultivate the less fertile plots*, which means those on which the cost of production was greater. Supposing that the first class plots yielded thirty bushels of wheat per acre, with an expenditure of £6, this means that the cost of production was 4s. a bushel. But with plots of land of the second class it would be different: these, with the same expenditure, might produce only twenty bushels, bringing the cost of production up to 6s. a bushel. It is plain that the owners of these second class plots could not sell their wheat below this price, for this would mean selling at a loss, and they would give up producing it; but we are assuming that their wheat cannot be dispensed with. It is equally plain that the owners of the lands first occupied would not dream of selling their wheat at a lower price than their neighbours. so they too would sell it at 6s. a bushel. But since this wheat still cost them only 4s., they would thenceforth realise a profit of 2s. a bushel, or £3 an acre. Here again, therefore, we find that margin between *different* costs of production and a *uniform* selling price, which we found by a different route in the previous section. In the recognized vocabulary of political economy this margin has been given the celebrated name of *rent*.[1]

Later on, the never-ending increase of population calls for a further increase in the means of subsistence, and obliges men to cultivate lands of still more inferior quality, which will produce, say, only fifteen bushels of wheat per acre. Then the cost price on this land will rise to 8s. a bushel, and the result will be an equal rise in the selling price of all the wheat in the market, for the reasons just given. Henceforth the owners of the land first occupied will see their rent rise to 4s. a bushel, and even the owners of the second class lands will in their turn see a rent of 2s. emerging to their advantage.

But why, it will be said, should we assume that men will be obliged to extend cultivation to new plots of land in order to increase production? Could they not increase production by cultivating the good plots better? — They certainly could; but it must be remembered that owing to the law of diminishing return every increase in the yield means a more than proportional increase in the expenditure, and consequently entails a rise in the cost of production. If we tried to obtain sixty bushels of wheat per acre from the land that yielded thirty bushels with an expenditure of £6, we might perhaps succeed, but we should have to expend, say, £18, and the cost price of each bushel would thus be raised to 6s. The ultimate result would therefore be exactly the same as in the preceding case, when second class lands were taken into cultivation. (At this point the student should read again the section on the Law of Diminishing Return, p. 70, with which Ricardo's law is closely connected.)

This "order of cultivation," as Ricardo called it, may go on indefinitely, resulting always in *a rise in the price of food, to the detriment of consumers, and an increase in rent, to the benefit of landowners*, who see their incomes increasing without any effort on their part, by what John Stuart Mill called an "unearned increment."

The increase of rent, therefore, does not correspond to any real increase in wealth for society, but rather to a decrease, for one must

---

[1] It is unfortunate that no special term has been adopted to describe this class of income, for the word *rent* lends itself to misinterpretation: it must never be confused with the actual payment made by the tenant for the hire of land. [The term *economic rent* is often used in English to distinguish rent in the Ricardian sense from the everyday use of the word.]

be poorer than before if one is under the painful necessity of resorting to poorer lands in order to live.

The opposition between the interests of the landowner and those of society is still more plainly shown by the fact that all agricultural progress must cause a fall in rent. This result, paradoxical as it appears, is a feature of Ricardo's theory. But why is this? At first sight we should be tempted to think — and such would certainly be the opinion of the landowner himself — that all agricultural progress ought to be reflected in an increase of rent. Yet this, says Ricardo, is by no means the case; for this progress, by enabling the yield of the good plots to be increased, will result of necessity in *rendering unnecessary the cultivation of the bad plots.* These will then be abandoned, or turned into pasture or woodland, and since it is these very lands that kept the price of wheat at its highest level, when their influence is removed the price level will fall to the point determined by the cost of production on the good lands, cultivated by the new methods; and the rent, which is only the result of the price of wheat, will fall along with that price. Consequently it is greatly to the *individual* interest of the landowner to apply any improved methods of agriculture, but it is contrary to his interests that such progress should become *general.*

Such is Ricardo's theory. It has been said that it does not in any way correspond to historical reality, and was merely an *a priori* notion conceived by Ricardo to support his labour theory of value. An American economist, Carey, has even undertaken to prove, not without some good reason, that the order of cultivation has in actual fact been exactly in the opposite direction — that is to say, that cultivation began with the least fertile land — the lightest soil — because this was the easiest to cultivate, or else with high-lying land, because this was the easiest to defend, and that agriculture only slowly and gradually became able, as it became better equipped and more skilful, to clear the rich and heavy lands that were protected even by the superabundance of their vegetation.[1]

But there is no real contradiction between these two theories. To begin with, we may say that both economists were right in respect of the environment in which they dwelt. Ricardo lived in England — in an island country, where the land had been appropriated for centuries and the value of the soil was increasing as the population increased. Carey looked out upon a New World where land was superabundant and where none was utilized but that which was easiest of access and easiest to cultivate.

[1] See Carey's *Social Science.*

Furthermore, everything depends on what we are to understand by *the best lands*. If we mean those that are shown by chemical analysis to be richest in nitrogen, phosphates, and potash, then Ricardo's theory may be wrong, for primitive agriculture knows nothing of these things. But Ricardo meant simply those lands which yield the maximum of produce with the minimum of labour; he was not reasoning as a chemist, nor even as a scientific agriculturist, but as an economist of the hedonistic school.

However, the interest of the controversy lies here: if it is true, as Carey thinks, that in every country and in the world in general it is the richest lands, in the physical sense of the word, that are still remaining in reserve, only the poorest having yet been cultivated, then in that case there is reason to foresee in the future an increasing output from the land, a cheap and plentiful supply of food, and consequently a gradual fall in rent, to the very great advantage of consumers and of society as a whole. Rent would thus be robbed of the ugly character it possesses in the Ricardian theory.

But here we meet with Ricardo's thesis under another form — that of the *law of the increasing surplus value* of land — which confirms his conclusions although it is based upon a different and rather opposite kind of reasoning. This law has found its most eloquent exponent in Henry George.[1] Instead of regarding rent as being due to a kind of niggardliness on the part of nature, to the increasing difficulty of cultivation and the rise of the price of wheat, it considers it to be the result of all the causes of social progress — increase of population in the first place, but also increase of wealth, order, and security, scientific progress, development of means of transport, and so forth — which all tend to raise the value of land, and that independently of all labour on the part of the owner, who, in Henry George's picturesque phrase, has only to sit and smoke his pipe while waiting for the inevitable surplus value.

On this theory, unlike Ricardo's, there is no longer any hope that the progress of agricultural knowledge will lower rent; its effect would of course be to increase the quantity of the produce and thereby lower its price, but this would only be for a short time, because this increase in agricultural produce would bring about an increase in population and wealth which would raise the value of land. It is not like industry, where an increase in supply causes depreciation, because land, which supplies man with food, itself creates the demand for its produce.

[1] See his celebrated book, *Progress and Poverty*. For the solution proposed by Henry George, see below.

And now, what have the facts to say? Do they confirm these theories as to the progressive rise in the value of land and rent, or do they contradict them?

They confirm them in a striking manner in the case of two kinds of landed property: for all land in new countries, and also for plots of land in towns, at any rate in growing towns, which is the usual case.

As regards new countries, if we take as an example the United States — the country that led Henry George to formulate his theory, — the statistics are striking. Between 1850 and 1900 the value of agricultural property rose from 800 million pounds to 3,400 millions, and in 1916 to 6,920 millions (or 8,200 millions including the buildings). It may be said, of course, that this enormous increase is largely due to an extension of the area under cultivation; but this would not be a sufficient explanation, especially of the doubling of the value in the last period of sixteen years alone.[1]

But for the old countries of Europe the statistics are less confirmatory and even seem to lend support to the opposite theory — the theory of economists of the optimist school who are unwilling to regard as a law an increase of rent independent of all individual labour. Thus the statistics for France, after showing, it is true, a continual rise in the value of land up to 1880, have shown since then a considerable fall, to the extent of about one-third. And it is the same in England.

Thus the official estimate of the value of the land in France for the years 1851–53 was 61,189 million francs, for 1879–81 it was 91,184 million francs, and for 1908–12 it was 61,757 million francs. The total income from land for the same three periods was (in millions of francs) 1,824, 2,646, and 2,057 respectively. The value of the land, after increasing nearly 50% between 1851 and 1881, fell again in the first year of this century to the same figure as in 1851. If, however, we take the income value instead of the capital value, there was a slight increase of 7% or 8% in sixty years, which is not much.[2]

---

[1] As M. d'Avenel says, "Every time the sun sets, rural property registers a rise of 17 million francs" (15, to be precise).

Henry George himself reckoned that every emigrant added about 400 dollars (£80) to the value of United States territory. As about 20,000,000 emigrants have landed there since the beginning of last century, this would mean that by their presence alone they have conferred upon American soil a surplus value of 1600 million pounds. It is very ungrateful of the Americans, therefore. to set up so many obstacles in the way of immigration nowadays, and to describe so many immigrants as "undesirables."

[2] [These statistics, taken from the *Annuaire Statistique* for 1917, have been slightly abridged.]

But this retrograde movement in the value of land, or its ceasing to advance, is due to the competition of new lands,[1] coming into play as the result of great colonizing undertakings and such great improvements in the means of transport as those that have appeared so strikingly during the last forty years, opening wide the door to the wheat of America, India, and Australia, and even to meat, both alive and frozen. This fact, therefore, does not contradict Ricardo's theory at all, although many economists use it as an argument to prove the absurdity of that so-called law, any more than the actual stationary state of population proves the absurdity of the laws of Malthus; and it is quite possible that it may be merely an accident in economic history — if we may venture to call it so. In the second half of the nineteenth century so much unoccupied land was brought under cultivation that the supply of agricultural produce exceeded the existing capacity for absorption; but this state of affairs will not continue, and when these new lands are populated the rent of land will resume its temporarily interrupted progress. Already in the last few years before the war the value of land had begun to rise appreciably with the enormous increase in agricultural produce. What will now happen after the war? Given on the one hand the rise in prices, which will continue for a long time yet, and on the other hand the determination of each country to make sure henceforth of its means of subsistence by producing them itself, it looks as if the value of land and rent would resume their upward movement.

To sum up, we must bear in mind the fact that land combines, if not exclusively, yet to a greater extent than any other kind of wealth, these three characteristics:

(a) It meets the most essential need of the human race — the need of food.

(b) It lasts for ever — or at any rate longer than humanity.

(c) It is limited in quantity, for each particular kind of cultivation, for each nation, and for the whole population of the world.

In view of these facts a continuous and indefinite rise in the value of land appears to be predestined and unavoidable.

---

[1] This applies principally to England. In the case of France it may be partly due to the fact that the population is not increasing, but, as far as the country districts are concerned, shows a marked decrease. In Germany there is no sign of a fall in rent and land values: on the contrary, the value of the land increased threefold between 1850 and 1900, and between 1900 and 1913 it again increased by 25%. This is because landed property is more protected in Germany against foreign competition than in England, and because Germany benefits by an increase of population which does not exist in France.

IV. THE LEGITIMACY OF PROPERTY IN LAND

It must be owned that the explanations just given of property in land and of rent seem very damaging from the point of view of the legitimacy of these institutions and the commonly expressed opinion that landed property is the foundation of the social order.   Indeed, if landed property is, as was taught by the physiocrats, Adam Smith, J. B. Say, etc., a monopoly arising from the appropriation of the natural powers of the land, it seems difficult to answer the charge of Proudhon: "Who made the land? God? Then, in that case — landowner, clear out!"

If we choose to believe, with Henry George, that the value of land and the inevitable rise of rent are due to social causes — increase of population, progress of civilization, and so forth, — then it seems as if this value ought to belong to society, which created it, and not to the landowner who did not.

If we prefer Ricardo's theory, by which rent is due to the general law that determines prices, then the position of the landowner is a little better, because he might say: "I have taken nothing from anyone, and even if I gave up my rents to my tenants or to the consumer, they would still remain in existence." Nevertheless this income, due to circumstances, is still an unearned increment — an income that is entirely independent of labour.

The classical economists paid little attention to trying to establish the legitimacy of landed property: they merely sought to establish its origin and its nature. And in that respect their attitude was perfectly scientific, for science should undertake to explain facts and not to justify them. It belongs rather to the lawyer or the moralist than to the economist, therefore, to answer the question whether landed property is legitimate.

We have already discussed the legitimacy of private property in general (p. 338), and we tried to discover whether its foundation was labour or social utility. It might be thought that we need only refer back to that discussion, landed property being only a particular case of property in general. This is true; but none the less land has certain unique characteristics, of such a kind that many economists who accept private property in general, who deny that they are socialists, and who even claim to be individualists, are yet unable to admit that land can be an object of individual appropriation. Why is this, then?

The reason is that both the arguments employed to justify ordinary property seem in this case to be particularly weak.

If we admit, with most economists, as well as socialists, that labour ought to be the basis of the right of property, then, since land is obviously not created by man, it must logically follow that land ought not to be individually appropriated.

It is true that the optimist school absolutely denies this distinction between land and movable wealth. It declares that land is the product of the labour of the cultivator just as much as the vessel of clay fashioned by the hand of the potter. Of course man did not create the land, but neither did he create the clay. Labour never creates anything; all it does is to modify the materials that nature supplies. Now this operation on the part of labour is no less real and no less effective when applied to the soil itself than when applied to materials drawn from its bosom. We are referred for examples to such pieces of land as those which peasants of Valais or the Pyrenees have entirely constructed on the slopes of their mountains by carrying the earth in baskets on their backs. An ancient author tells us how a peasant, accused of sorcery because of the abundant crops that he obtained from his land while the neighbouring fields were merely barren wastes, was summoned to appear before the Roman prætor, and there, holding up his two arms as the only defence he had to offer, exclaimed: "These are my sole magic!" Landed property has only to repeat to-day the same proud answer, to defend itself against the attacks that are made upon it.[1]

And even if the land were not a direct product of labour, it is at least (they say) the product of capital. The value of land and its time-honoured surplus value are sufficiently explained by the improvements made in it and the expenditure incurred by its owners. It is even asserted that if we were to reckon up all the expenditure incurred by the successive owners of the land, we should reach the conclusion that there is no land *which is worth what it has cost.*

Despite the element of truth that this argument undoubtedly contains, it does not seem to us conclusive. No doubt man and land have at all times been bound together by the tie of daily labour, and even by labour of the hardest kind — the kind that gave rise to the expression about labouring "in the sweat of one's brow." The Latin word *labor*, indeed, from which "labour" is derived, originally referred to the tilling of the soil, as the French word *labourer* does to-day. But if land is the *instrument* of labour it is not the *product* of labour. It existed before there was any human labour. No

---

[1] The historian Michelet said: "Man has the best of claims to the land — that of having made it." The physiocrats also based the right of property on the expenditure incurred to create an estate, and called it "advances on the land."

doubt man is always improving and modifying this wonderful in-
instrument with which nature has provided him, by his labour and
his expenditure, so as to adapt it better to his purposes, and in this
case he obviously confers upon it new utility and new value. We
can even admit that as the art of agriculture progresses, land tends
to become more and more the product of labour. In market-garden-
ing, for instance, the mould that is employed is an artificial compound
prepared entirely by the gardener. Yet it is always possible, in
theory, if not in practice, to discover the primitive value of the soil
beneath the layers accumulated by human capital and labour.

This original value appears plainly enough in the forest or the
natural grass-land that have never been cleared or cultivated, and
that may yet be sold or rented at a high price. It appears in those
sandy beaches in the French departments of Gard and Hérault that
have never been tilled except by the sea winds and that none the less
made the fortunes of their lucky owners as soon as it was discovered
by chance that they would grow vines immune from the phylloxera.
And it appears, too, in the building sites of large cities, where the
plough has never passed and which have still a value infinitely higher
than that of the best cultivated soil.

Even in the case of cultivated land this natural value of the soil
is still quite appreciably apparent in the *unequal fertility* of plots of
land, for of two plots on which the same expenditure is made, the
one may yield a fortune every year while the other will barely repay
its expenses.

As for the argument that no land is worth what it has cost to
cultivate, this rests upon an error in calculation.[1] We certainly do
not dispute the fact that if we add up all the expenditure incurred
on a piece of English land ever since the day when the Ancient Britons
came to clear it for cultivation, the total would be infinitely greater
than the present value of the land. But to make the calculation
right we must also add up all the receipts from the land from the same
date. When the account had been thus corrected it would certainly
show that the land has yielded a permanent and regularly increasing
revenue.[2]

---

[1] Moreover, this argument has no meaning in the case of building sites, for these
are always uncultivated land.

[2] Still less can landed property and the income arising from it be justified by the
argument that all land has been *bought by money*, and that therefore the income it
yields is only the interest on the money thus invested. This argument looks convincing at first sight, but it really involves reasoning in a circle. As a matter of fact,
it is not because a piece of land is sold for £5000 that it brings in £150 in rent: it is
because it naturally produced £150 in rent, without any labour on the part of the

To establish the legitimacy of landed property must we, then, fall back on the other basis of property — social utility? That seems, indeed, a more solid foundation.

Given the more or less rapid but general increase of the population on the earth, a choice must be made of that mode of exploiting the soil which will allow the greatest number of persons to be fed on a given area. Consequently it has always been thought necessary, in order to encourage labour, to assure to the cultivator a right not only to the produce of his land but to the land itself as the instrument of his labour. This right was at first temporary, but was extended for longer and longer periods, as progress in cultivation came to require longer processes, until it ended by becoming permanent.

A right to the fruits implies a right to the soil, at any rate for a certain time. The man who has sown must certainly be allowed time to reap. Five or six years must elapse before the man who has planted a vine can gather his first crop of grapes, and half a century is needed before the man who has sown an acorn can cut down the oak. It should be noticed, too, that even in annual cultivation, however imperfect, there are some kinds of labour (such as dressing and manuring, drainage, irrigation, building and setting up of plant) which can only be paid for by the successive crops of ten, twenty, or perhaps fifty years. Yet it is essential that the man who performs this labour should have the chance of recouping himself: otherwise it can be taken as certain that he will not perform it.

That is why, even if society claimed for itself the right of eminent domain over the land, it could do no better in the general interest than to delegate its right to those who can make the best use of it. Now so far it is individual owners who have succeeded best in this task, and until the contrary is proved there is reason to believe that they are the most suitable for the performance of this social function.[1]

owner, that it was able to be sold for £5000. The question is simply to find out why it produced this rent. It is as if one tried to silence those who criticize the monopoly enjoyed by notaries or stock-brokers and demand its abolition, by saying that the tenure of these offices is legitimate and indisputable because the present holders have bought and paid for them.

The only conclusion that can be drawn from this argument is that the landowner (like the holder of any office that is bought for money) has a claim to the repayment of the price if he is expropriated. But that is a different question altogether.

[1] Collectivists assure us, it is true, that the collective exploitation of the soil will yield results far superior, even from the technical point of view, to those that individual ownership can give, because it alone will enable the processes of large-scale production to be employed and their advantages to be realized   But that is purely a conjecture that is incapable of proof, whereas the institution of landed property, even of small-scale property, can show splendid results; and they will be more splendid still when small-scale property is supplemented by co-operation.

For this reason colonization in all new lands — America, Australia, Algeria, etc. — has been carried on under the system of individual property.

But while acknowledging the services rendered to civilization by the institution and extension of landed property (see above, pp. 64–69), we must not shut our eyes to the conflict between social interest and private interest to which it very often gives rise.   This conflict may be summed up as follows: in exploiting his land the owner does not necessarily aim at making it produce the utmost possible, whether in quantity or quality, but at obtaining the maximum profit. As economists put it, he aims at "*rentability*" rather than at *productivity*.   He will not hesitate, for instance, to turn arable land into pasture, or even, if he is a rich English peer, into a hunting or shooting ground, without any anxiety as to whether it would not be better that the land should support men rather than bullocks or pheasants. Or, conversely, he will cut down a forest to realize the value of it, because he reckons that the capitalized price will bring him in more than the income derived from it.

In any case, if the basis of property is no other than public utility, then it seems as if it ought not to possess the absolute character that the law confers upon it.

(1) In the first place, it seems useless, and even contrary to the object aimed at, to extend the right of property to land on which *no effective labour is employed*.   In this respect Moslem legislation is more true to the principles of political economy than ours — who would have thought it? — for it only admits the right of individual ownership in the case of lands on which labour has effectually been employed.   These lands are called "living," in distinction to uncultivated land, which is called "dead," and which has to remain in collective ownership.

(2) Even if we do not go back to the past to discover whether landed property originated in cultivation, and if we look only at the present, it seems that landed property ought to submit to the condition that the land is to be made use of.   For if ownership is a social function, the recognition of the right of property ought to be accompanied by the obligation to perform this function effectively. That very rule is generally followed nowadays in all grants or sales of land in the colonies: residence and effective cultivation are stipulated for.   It is difficult to see why a condition that is considered necessary in establishing the right of property in new countries should be thought superfluous in old ones; and if this were done we should avoid the scandal of seeing in many countries, as in Eastern

Europe and Italy, vast stretches of land held by owners who do nothing at all, while the agricultural workers either emigrate or die of poverty for lack of land.

In the case of mines, French law has provided for the forfeiture of property rights in the event of non-exploitation.

During the war a special law compelled landowners to cultivate their land. If they defaulted, the cultivation was to be undertaken by other owners or by the parish. And although this law was only rarely put into force, it is of value as showing what the post-war system of property ought to be.[1]

V. SYSTEMS OF LAND SOCIALIZATION

The criticisms and complaints that we have been describing in connexion with the institution of landed property were bound to give rise to programmes of agrarian reform. These are of all kinds, ranging from a return to agrarian communism to a mere extension of land taxation.

1. *Agrarian Communism*

This system rarely appears in the shape of complete community of ownership. More often it takes the form of exploitation in separate shares, with periodic division of the land, simply in order to prevent individual possession from becoming transformed eventually into a right of ownership. This system is well known, because it was formerly applied on a vast scale in Russia, where the *mir* was a community consisting of the inhabitants of a village, owning the land and sharing its produce among its members by the process of drawing lots. The *mir* system was in process of dissolution, but it was not abandoned by the peasants without regret or without resistance, as is proved by the fact that in many cases community of ownership remained in actual practice after it had legally come to an end.

The Russian revolution, while decreeing communism, confined itself in fact to the confiscation of large estates without touching peasant properties. It even looks as if the latter would be greatly multiplied, so that it is the communist system of the *mir* that will really be abolished!

2. *State Purchase of the Land*

In other systems individual property in land would be retained, but under certain restrictions: it would be subjected to State control

[1] [English legislation, by the Defence of the Realm Act, was somewhat similar. See Gide's *First Principles of Political Economy* (English translation) p. 93.]

and would lose its permanent character and become a sort of grant or concession. The State, as owner of the soil, would grant it to individuals for exploitation for long periods of 50 or even 99 years, as in the case of railway concessions. When the time had elapsed the State would resume possession of the land (as it will resume possession of the railways in France in 1950), and would then grant it for a fresh period, making the new grantees pay the equivalent of the surplus value by which they would benefit, either in a lump sum or by an annual rent. In this manner the State as representing the community would benefit by the whole surplus value, which would ultimately provide an enormous revenue.

Such a system as this does not appear to be incompatible with a good utilization of the soil, especially if the precaution were taken of renewing the concessions some time before the expiry of the term. It even seems unquestionable that such a state of things would be more favourable to good cultivation than the present situation in many countries, where almost all the land is cultivated by tenant farmers who can be turned out at will. Man is a short-lived creature, and does not need an eternity in front of him to make him undertake even the greatest works: this is proved by the fact that such undertakings as railways and the Suez and Panama Canals are based only on concessions for 99 years.

This system merely involves the abandonment of the principle of perpetuity, by which the right of property lasts as long as its object, which in this case is eternal. Time, which destroys all else, has no other effect upon land than to confer new youth upon it with each returning spring. But we must not forget that what lasts for ever is only the soil itself and its natural powers: the changes effected by labour, and even incorporated in the land, endure but for a time.

Here again we may learn from the constitution of property in the colonies. In the Dutch colonies, and until recently in Australia, land is only granted for a limited time. It is true that the period of the concession amounts to 99 or even 999 years. But although such a period is equivalent to perpetuity, yet this clause suffices to safeguard the State's eminent domain and to enable the State to exercise control over the landowner. The owner, in fact, being only a grantee, a kind of tenant on a quasi-perpetual lease, has no longer the characteristic right that attaches to ownership — the *jus abutendi*, the right to do what he pleases with his property.

In all new countries and in the colonies half a century ago there still remained an immense public domain, which has unfortunately

almost entirely disappeared through the grant of immoderate concessions at a low price to individuals or to companies. If these
grants had been made only temporary, the States would have had
valuable resources in reserve for the future, and would perhaps have
facilitated the solution of the social problem for future generations.
Only it is just where it would be easiest to prevent the abuses of
landed property that there is least need to do so! In fact, landed
property has no drawbacks but is purely advantageous in the case
of new and rising countries, as can be seen, for instance, in the
pampas of the Argentine Republic or in Australia. On the one hand,
it applies only to lands cleared by pioneers, and is only extended as
cultivation extends; so that it is consecrated, as it were, by labour.
On the other hand, it still occupies only a small part of the soil, and
land is superabundant in quantity; so that it does not in the least
constitute a monopoly, but remains in humble subjection to the law
of competition, like any other form of business.

It is only as society develops and as population grows more dense
that the nature of landed property begins to change and to assume
by degrees the character of a monopoly that may go on growing
indefinitely — and then it is too late to buy it back. For to put such
a plan into operation would involve repurchase as a preliminary, if
it was wished to act justly, as it should be. But State purchase
would be absolutely ruinous: the value of the land in France is
estimated at some three thousand million pounds,[1] so that the
State would have to borrow that sum to compensate the landowners.

Certain financial arrangements might, however, be devised which
would make this plan less burdensome. We ourself, a long time back,[2]
suggested a system of purchase which would be far less burdensome.
The State might purchase the lands by *paying for them immediately,
but not requiring delivery for 99 years.* Under such conditions it is
certain that the State could get them at a very low price; for the
owner would compare, on the one hand, dispossession at such a distant date that neither he nor even his grandchildren would suffer by
it, and, on the other hand, the sum of money that he might obtain
immediately; and he would scarcely hesitate to accept the price,
however low it might be. We even made a mathematical calculation
of this price by means of annuity tables: £1000 to be received in 100
years, at the rate of 5%, would be worth to-day £7 19s. 7d.; there-

---

[1] [The corresponding figure for Great Britain is about 5¼ million pounds.]
[2] *De quelques doctrines nouvelles sur la propriété foncière*, in the *Journal des Économistes*, May, 1883.

fore £3,000,000,000 — assuming that to be the value of the land in France — deliverable in 100 years, is worth at the present time just under £24,000,000, paid in cash, which would not be a very high price to pay.

3. *Confiscation of Rent by Taxation*

This is the system made famous by Henry George,[1] though it was suggested to him, as he himself acknowledged, by the physiocrats. It consists in imposing upon landed property a progressively increasing tax, calculated in such a way as to absorb, as it arises, all the income due to causes that are external and independent of the activity of the owner — the unearned increment.[2]

It was thought by Henry George that in consequence of the continuous increase of rent, this tax would suffice to cover all the expenses of the State, so that all other taxes could be abolished, to the great benefit of producers and consumers. For this reason the system is usually known as the *Single Tax System*. Various leagues and societies have been formed to advocate it, in America, in Australia, and even in England. But the system is open to serious objections.

To begin with, the confiscation of rent by taxation would be bound to result in a considerable reduction in the value of the land, exactly as the confiscation of the land itself would: only the shell of the nut would be left for the landowner, as Henry George himself has said. Consequently the payment of compensation would be imperatively necessary, as a matter of equity; and then the financial difficulties would be very much the same as those we have just described. Henry George replies, of course, that it is rather society that would have to claim compensation from the landowner, to make up for the income he had enjoyed for so long without any right to it; but it must be remembered that this landowner had bought and paid for the land, together with the rent proceeding from it, in reliance on the laws, and that the laws are a pledge of the liability of the society which has voted them.

Moreover, there is this practical objection: that there are two elements to be distinguished in the surplus value of the soil. One is due, certainly, to various social and impersonal causes, but the other

---

[1] An American author whose chief book, *Progress and Poverty*, has had remarkable success. George died in 1897.

[2] "We would simply take for the community what belongs to the community — the value that attaches to land by the growth of the community; leave sacredly to the individual all that belongs to the individual." — *Henry George.*

proceeds from the labour of the owner, or at least from the capital that he has advanced. Now it was admitted by Henry George himself, in the words just quoted, that we should have to be careful not to touch this second element, not only for fear of violating the principles of equity, but also for fear of discouraging all initiative and all progress in agriculture, which is already only too fond of the beaten track. But such separation is very difficult in practice: the owner himself would not succeed in making it correctly, much less any government official.[1]

Finally, the idea that a single tax on rent would enable all other taxes to be abolished, was very much too optimistic even at the time it was mooted; and it is still more so in the present post-war period.

VI. THE DEMOCRATIZATION OF LANDED PROPERTY

The democratization of property is not the same thing as its socialization: it does not mean abolishing or even restricting individual ownership, but, on the contrary, making it accessible to all. Nevertheless the two systems have this in common: that they both aim at abolishing or mitigating the evils of landed property by wedding it to labour.

What is to be done, then, to create small properties, or to make them universal? There are three methods:

(1) The most direct method is for *the State to lend the agricultural worker the requisite money for the purchase of the land* — a moderate amount of land, of course. This is the system adopted in very many countries. It satisfies the desire of the peasant who would like eventually to become the owner of the land he has long been cultivating as a labourer, tenant, or *métayer*, but who is unable to do so for want of money. There are land banks already that meet this need, but they are too expensive and too dangerous, owing to the risk of expropriation, for anyone to advise the peasant to make use of them. The State can offer more favourable terms.

The need for such a measure was first experienced in England, since in that country there are only 60,000 small peasant proprietors cul-

---

[1] Another objection to be raised is that if society confiscates for its own benefit all favourable chances, on the ground that they are not the act of the landowner, it would be only fair that it should make itself responsible for all unfavourable ones, for the very same reason — not only losses due to inclement seasons, but such depreciation of value as may result from industrial changes, importation, emigration from the country districts, depopulation, and all other causes that may produce a *deficit value* in the land. In short, the logical consequence of this system would be to guarantee a fixed income to the owner, if all his profit were abolished.

tivating their land themselves, as against three or four millions in France. In fact many laws have been passed in recent years to enable the agricultural proletariat to buy or rent land, and to procure it for them if it is not on the market, by having recourse to expropriation in the interests of public utility.

This democratization of property has nowhere been practised with more rigour, or, it may be said, with more generosity on the part of the State, than in Ireland. It is true that there were great historic sins to be atoned for; but they have been atoned for. Already two-thirds of the land of Ireland has become the property of the former tenants, thanks to the money advanced by the State. These advances will soon reach the sum of £120,000,000, to be repaid in small annual instalments, spread over about sixty years. Owing to this peaceful agrarian revolution and also to the development of agricultural co-operative associations, the social condition of the population has been transformed.

But it is particularly since the war that the conversion of great estates into peasant properties has been effected by new legislation in almost all the countries of Eastern Europe — Roumania, Greece, Hungary, etc.

Even in France, although small properties are already numerous, there are several laws for putting land at the disposal of those who wish to acquire it, or for enabling those who need capital for the utilization of the land they possess, to obtain it.

(2) The second system is the *compulsory equal division of the land* at every succession, imposed by law. This is what was done by the Napoleonic Code, thus accentuating the development of property in the individualist and equalitarian direction. The famous Article 826 is not content with mere *equivalence* when it imposes an equal division between all the children: it gives to each of them the right to claim his share *in kind*, which means that in the case of the smallest field each heir can demand his third, or his quarter, or his tenth; and if division is impossible there must be a judicial sale, involving enormous expense. A father can scarcely avoid this result, since he may only bequeath a "disposable portion," which is of very limited extent.

There is no doubt that such a system, though crude, is effectual; and if England, for instance, were to adopt it, many of the vast estates of the English landowners would be cut up into small pieces in the course of a few generations.[1]

---

[1] [We omit the author's statistical details concerning the present state of peasant proprietorship in France.]

(3) **A third method** — less direct but more efficacious — is to *make land a commercial commodity*,[1] by making it as easily transferable as any other kind of goods. This is an excellent way to remedy the evils that are charged against landed property, for it matters not that land is a natural monopoly if anyone can acquire it. Nor does it matter that it is eternal if it only remains for a short time in the hands of each owner. By this means, the law of surplus value, if it comes into force, will no longer serve to enrich a single family: each will have his share, since property is at the same time scattered and transferable. It is also the best way to attract the necessary capital to the land, for capital will not willingly seek the land if it has to be buried there for ever.

What measures must be taken to bring land into the stream of circulation?

To begin with, it goes without saying that the causes of inalienability must be abolished — such as the system of entail in England, and the dower system in France. Secondly, the formalities and expense of alienation must be reduced to a minimum: at present they are relatively heavier when the value of the land is small than when it is great, so that they are more burdensome on small estates than on large ones. Finally, the man who acquires land must be given complete security, so that he need fear neither eviction nor annoyance. The system of land-ownership in most countries is very far from satisfying this requirement, for the new possessor is never perfectly sure that the seller was the rightful owner, and yet he cannot have any greater right than the former owner has transferred to him.

In Australia a system has been devised, called the Torrens system from the name of the statesman who invented it (in South Australia, in 1858), which has since been adopted in other countries, and especially in new countries, such as Tunis, for instance. To put it shortly, we might describe it as the application to land of the registration system that applies to persons — the system by which births, marriages, and deaths are entered in a register, of which copies are handed to the interested parties by way of evidence. In the same way each piece of land has its history and description entered in a register, and a copy of the page is delivered to the person concerned. This certificate enables him, as it were, to carry the land in his pocket. If he wants to sell it, he takes the document to the registrar, who

---

[1] This is also called the *mobilization* of land; but this term is liable to confusion, because it also means something quite different — namely, the credit methods used to facilitate borrowing on land.

enters the transfer in the register and hands the new owner a fresh certificate, without the need of any intervention on the part of a lawyer.

VII. SYSTEMS FOR THE PRESERVATION OF LANDED PROPERTY

The agrarian policy described in the last section, that aims at making landed property accessible to all either by subdivision or by facilities for transfer, is not favoured by all economists. Those, for instance, who belong to the catholic social school or to the Le Play school, believe that the system of turning land into money and making a commodity of it, is contrary alike to the interests of cultivation and to those of the family. It deprives the land of the twofold attribute of immobility and perpetuity that nature has conferred upon it, and owing to which it can best maintain the permanence of the family, the stability of business undertakings, and the carrying-out of far-reaching plans.

The fatal consequences of this "mobilization" of land would be, in particular, the following:

(1) The *subdivision* of property. The division of property by equal partition seems to its opponents to be inspired not so much by a love of small properties as by a hatred of large ones; and by its crude mechanism it would often defeat the ends it aims at. It scarcely touches the great estates, because the owners of these have generally enough transferable wealth to be able to keep the estate in the hands of one of their children, while assuring to the rest an equal share in money; and they willingly agree to this arrangement, for the sake of the dignity of the family name. On the other hand, the owner whose entire fortune consists in his little bit of "property," cannot withdraw it from the partitioning knife. Thus at each death his little estate becomes further subdivided, in a geometrical progression, until nothing remains but scraps of land that are of no use, unless they are got rid of by selling them to some rich neighbour who will use them to round off his own estate.

Incredible instances are cited in many places of this chopping-up of land — of strips no broader than a scythe, or even a sickle! If equal division has not been so destructive of property in France as might have been feared, it is because it has been partly neutralized by two causes, which, however, are still more unfortunate. These are Malthusianism, which avoids the division of land by abolishing children; and emigration from the country districts, by which means, even where there are several children, only one is left on the land, if that.

A minimum point should at any rate be fixed, below which all subdivision should be prohibited, so that the heirs should merely have to choose between leaving the land in the possession of one of them, and selling it. This minimum would be, as it were, the atom of property, like the atom of the physicists, which is said to be indivisible.

(2) The subdivision of property is frequently accompanied by another evil — the possession by one owner of a large number of pieces of land. This system has no necessary connexion with small property. There may be, and there are in some countries, large estates made up of portions of land scattered sometimes far apart. In this case all the inconveniences of small and large properties are combined.

But against this evil at least one remedy is indicated: for each owner to exchange distant portions for near ones, so as to have all his property in one piece. This operation[1] has long been practised in the Germanic countries, as well as in Alsace, and since the war in the devastated areas of Northern France.

(3) Finally, if there are dangers in the excessive subdivision of land, there would be a still greater one in excessive ease of alienation: this is nothing less than the destruction of small rural property. Of what use would it be to set up a class of small landowners, at great expense, by means of advances by the State, if they were then left free to sell and to borrow? They would quickly slip back into the ranks of the proletariat. It would be necessary, therefore, to carry out the opposite process to mobilization — that is to say, to make the land inalienable and exempt from seizure — or if not all land, then at least the amount necessary for the existence and maintenance of the family.

Nevertheless, no country has dared to withdraw the right of sale, for by thus imposing a civil disability upon all small proprietors it would run the risk of displeasing them and defeating its own ends. But in some countries the small proprietor has been given the power to make his land exempt from seizure, which keeps away all lenders. This is what is called the *homestead* system, from the name given to such properties in the United States, where it has been established since 1839 (in Texas) — a system which is now becoming acclimatized in various other countries. In France, after some fifteen years of hesitation and several projected laws, the law of 1909 was eventu-

---

[1] [Called *remembrement* in French; we have no equivalent term in English.]

ally passed to sanction the homestead, or, in the French phrase, the *bien de famille*. But this legislative experiment, loudly extolled by liberal and conservative economists alike, has failed completely. At the end of 1913, after the law had been in force, therefore, for more than four years, there were only 243 homesteads, of which the rural ones — the only ones of any interest — numbered 158. French small proprietors object to inflicting disabilities upon themselves, even if it be only the inability to borrow.

CHAPTER II — NON–WORKING CAPITALISTS

I. THE POSITION OF THE *RENTIER*

Man has been defined as "an idle animal" — a definition which is unfair to him, since he is no more idle than any other animal, nor even as idle as some. But all the same he has displayed extraordinary ingenuity in evading the law of work: slavery, parasitism, begging, theft, and gambling, have all originated in this way. But the best way to avoid work, because it is at the same time the surest and the most respected, is *to have a private income.*

Although *rentiers* — persons of independent means — do not work, that does not prevent their living, and in very many cases living well. Not only are their incomes often larger than those produced by labour, but they possess the special advantage of being more regular: whether it snows or blows, whether the *rentier* be in health or confined to his bed by sickness, whether he be young or aged and infirm, a stay-at-home or a globe-trotter, still his income follows him everywhere and never fails him. Thus the fact of having a private income ensures, first of all, those two good things, security and independence, that are better than all the pleasures that other kinds of fortune can procure. That indeed is a privileged position, and we may well ask these lucky mortals what god has bestowed this leisured life upon them — *deus vobis haec otia fecit.*

They will reply that it is labour itself: that they are living upon *the produce of past labour.*

What is the worth of this reply? If this past labour is *his own* labour — if the *rentier* is a retired official in receipt of a pension, or one who has saved up for his old age, — then no one can raise any objection. Man cannot be doomed to compulsory toil for ever: if he has worked during the productive part of his life it is only fair that he should be able to rest during the unproductive part.

But if this past labour is the labour of *somebody else* — his father, grandfather, great-grandfather, or even some stranger who at some time or other made a fortune and left it to the *rentier* with the right to consume it in idleness, — then the question becomes more difficult.

Why should it be so? it will be said. We have compared pieces of money to orders or tickets conferring the right to consume a given amount of wealth at one's own choice, up to their total value (p.

212). Well, a man has earned a large number of these tickets by his labour: if he does not want to use them himself, now or later, he will hand them on to someone who will use them instead.

From the economic point of view that is all very well; but from the moral standpoint we may be more exacting. Has the idle *rentier* done his duty towards society by the mere fact that he has paid for what he receives with money that represents — even putting it at the best — only past labour — the labour of those who are now dead? Ought he not to pay in present, personal services the equivalent of the income he receives? Notice that the *rentier* does not live at all on his past labour, as he thinks he does, but on *the present labour of somebody else*. The things he consumes every day are the produce of living and not of dead labour — new bread, early vegetables, new clothes, the daily paper, and so forth. Now does not justice demand that in exchange for what his fellows produce every day for him, he should himself produce something for them? The economist Augustin Cochin — a catholic, and by no means a socialist — said, "The *rentier* is a wage-earner who has been paid in advance." If he has been paid *in advance*, there must be some labour *remaining due* from him. What he owes, in fact, is to "make himself useful," as we say. If he is of no use, he will meet the fate of parasites, and will sooner or later be abolished, and it will be in vain for economists to point out that he has provided in good money the exact equivalent of all that he has consumed.

But *idleness* must not be confounded with *leisure*. Idleness is a state of revolt against the law of work. Leisure means intermission of work in the course of a life that may otherwise be very active and laborious, and that is even more so, the more it is interspersed with periods of leisure. These periods are like infrequent clearings in a gloomy forest, where the sunlight can penetrate: there is the evening leisure after the day's work is done; the weekly day of rest; the leisure of the holidays, which will not always remain the privilege of brain-workers but will become a possibility and a right for hand-workers as well; and finally there is the leisure of retirement after a well-filled life. Leisure, in the form of recreation, is not only useful for the smooth working of labour itself; it is indispensable to the development of the internal and external life; to meditation, which should not be reserved for sages alone; and to the performance of many duties besides that of earning one's daily bread — family duties, social relations, participation in good works, committee work, trade union or co-operative society meetings, political gatherings, religious worship, and so forth.

It is true that it is not very easy to determine where leisure ends and idleness begins. It is easy, of course, to class a man who lives by begging or gambling; but the case of the *rentier* we have been discussing is more difficult. Is he an idler, or simply a man of leisure?

It must be acknowledged that from the historical point of view the *rentier* in the past performed a real social function, and even the most important of functions — that of creating the arts, letters, sciences, politics, culture, and civilization in general. We owe all these good things, in which the poorest have their share, to the idle *rentiers* of Greece, Rome, and Judæa — all those ancient societies where idleness none the less appeared in a particularly odious form, because it rested entirely upon force — upon robbery and slavery. In all civilized societies to-day the *rentier* is not necessarily a parasite, though he may happen too often to be so as a matter of fact. But generally, and to an increasing extent under the pressure of public opinion, it is upon the *rentiers* that the task devolves of performing what we might call the gratuitous functions — those which bring no reward, such as charity in its numberless forms, politics, and literature, and which can only be performed by men who have other means of subsistence. That is how things are done in democratic societies like the United States.

But must we conclude that it will always be so? For the proper conduct of great social interests, for unravelling the delicate threads of politics and diplomacy, and for worthily holding the sceptre of taste in the world of letters and of art, must we always require white hands that labour has not hardened, and leisured brains that have never been oppressed by the anxiety of performing an allotted task and earning the daily bread? Perhaps not. These lofty functions are not necessarily incompatible with labour — even manual labour. The existence of a *rentier* class would cease to be indispensable to the intellectual, artistic, and moral life of society as soon as sufficient leisure was assured to all workers.

II. HISTORY OF MONEY-LENDING: USURY AND THE REGULATION OF INTEREST

Money-lending at interest was practised throughout ancient times and in terribly harsh forms; yet it was stigmatized by many great men, like Moses, Aristotle, and Cato, who was himself a usurer, and was condemned by almost all religions. On the coming of Christianity the attack upon it was renewed with redoubled energy in the writings of the Church Fathers, and when the Church had firmly established its power it succeeded in getting loans at interest formally prohibited, in civil as well as in canon law. The law of Mahomet did the same: "God has permitted sale but forbidden usury," says the Koran. The true Moslem receives no interest for money lent, not even from the Christian banker with whom he has deposited it.[1]

Although this doctrine has been treated in more modern times with profound contempt, and regarded as a mark of ignorance of all the laws of economics, yet it admits of a very easy historical explanation.

We have already observed (p. 280) that credit in the shape of loans of money could only lead to ruin if it was not productive in character. Now in former times it could only serve, and did only serve, for consumption. So the ancients and the canonists were not so utterly wrong as they are thought to have been. On the contrary, they had a very clear idea of the economic state of the times in which they lived when they declared that lending was barren.

The borrowers were the poor plebeians of Rome, who borrowed from the patricians to obtain food, and the impecunious knights of the Middle Ages, who borrowed from the Jews and Lombards to equip themselves for the Crusades. All borrowing, therefore, was for personal and consequently unproductive consumption. Naturally, when the day for repayment arrived the borrowers could pay neither the interest nor even the capital, so they had to pay with their bodies and their labour as slaves of their creditors.[2] In these circumstances money-lending appeared to the lender as an abuse of the right of property, and to the borrower as an instrument of exploitation and destruction, which is sufficient to explain such long-standing and persistent condemnation.

In those days capital was scarcely known, even by name. Yet then as now there were many people who had great need of money, and since there was no one then, any more than now, who was inclined to lend it for nothing, some kind of compromise had to be discovered. So people set their wits to work, and the many ingenious methods devised by medieval casuistry make one of the most inter-

---

[1] The Christian bankers of Cairo know very well how to take advantage of this form of Moslem piety

[2] The houses of the Roman patricians were equipped with cellars used as prisons, *ergastula*, for insolvent debtors. In the Middle Ages debtors were less harshly treated, in spite of the example of Shylock. A powerful insolvent debtor had merely to furnish hostages to his creditors and pay for their food, which must, however, have been very burdensome. For this reason the canonists said: *Jus usurae, jus belli.*

esting chapters in the history of economic doctrines. The principal devices were these:

(1) In all cases where it was recognized that the borrower could make a profit — for instance, by commercial undertakings, and especially by maritime commerce, the most hazardous of all — it was considered that interest was no longer usurious, but became legitimate on account of the risk incurred by the lender.[1]

(2) If the lender definitely transferred to the borrower the ownership of the capital sum lent — that is to say, if he gave up all claim to repayment — then in this case also the legitimacy of interest was easily admitted; for the lender could not be asked to give up both capital and income. The loan took the form of an *income-yielding investment.*

(3) If the interest was stipulated for in the form of a penalty in case of non-payment of the capital on the appointed day, this also was valid.   And since there was nothing to prevent the fixing of the date for repayment on *the day after the loan was made*, it is obvious that the rule could be easily evaded in this manner.

The Reformation naturally caused a reaction against the canonist doctrine, not only through the spirit of opposition, but through the same foreshadowing of modern notions as was visible also in its political and democratic ideas. At the same time this is true only of Calvinism, for Luther himself continued to condemn interest. Calvin, however, showed himself disposed to tolerate money-lending under certain conditions, and in the sixteenth and seventeenth centuries the scholastic arguments against usury were refuted by two great French huguenot lawyers, Dumoulin and Saumaise,[2] the latter an exile in Holland.   It is interesting to notice, however, that the Jesuits as well as the Reformers contributed to the admission of money-lending into practice, by inventing ingenious arrangements for evading the economic law: for instance, the *contractus trinus*, or threefold contract, by which the lender was held to associate himself with the risks and profits of the undertaking, but at the same time insured himself against the risks and gave up his claim to the profits in exchange for a fixed annual sum.

But to find economic doctrine declaring itself in favour of money-lending at interest we must come to the economists — to Turgot, the author of *Mémoire sur les prêts d'argent* (1769), and Bentham,

---

[1] The Lateran Council (1515) defined the situation perfectly: "There is usury wherever there is profit which does not arise from anything productive, and which involves neither labour, nor expense, nor risk, on the part of the lender."

[2] [Better known as Salmasius, the celebrated opponent of Milton.]

who wrote *A Defence of Usury* (1787). From that time forth all economists have been agreed. And this time they are right. Why is this? Because the position of things has entirely changed.

On the one hand, the parts have been inverted. It is no longer the impecunious now who borrow from the rich — the plebeians from the patricians. On the contrary, it is generally the rich, the powerful, the speculators, the great companies, the bankers, the owners of gold-mines, and the great States in particular, who borrow from the public, from small folk — who draw upon the people's savings and the peasant's stocking. The result is this: that it is most often the lender rather than the borrower whose fate is deserving of commiseration. It is no longer the weak and defenceless borrower who must be protected by law and public opinion against the rapacity of the lender; it is the ignorant lender who must be protected by law and public opinion against the exploitation of the great borrowers of whom modern financial history offers many scandalous examples.

On the other hand — and these two changes were simultaneous — the object of the loan contract has changed. Men have almost given up borrowing for consumption; they borrow now to make their fortunes. Although loans are still described by lawyers as consumption loans, they have now assumed their true economic character as a mode of production. It is, as we have seen (p. 116), the *entrepreneur* — the actual agent of production — who hires the capital and pays interest for it, and this interest appears among his expenses of production just like the wages of labour and the rent of the factory. It would be foolish, therefore, to wish this *entrepreneur* to be exempted from paying interest, from humanitarian motives, for the only result would be to increase his profits.

Of course this process of development is not yet everywhere complete. In the agricultural parts of the East, in Russia, the Danubian countries, Italy, and Algeria, credit still retains its earlier form, and there as of old it is the borrower — the peasant — who is eventually expropriated by the lender. It is in those countries, too, that the movement known as anti-semitism has arisen. For this reason, old laws against usury may still be perfectly appropriate in some lands and in some circumstances.

Moreover, even in more advanced countries the old dislike of interest has left some traces upon legislation, if not in the form of prohibition, yet in that of *limitation* of the rate of interest.[1]

---

[1] [We omit the author's instance from French legislation. In England the legal maximum rate of interest was fixed in the sixteenth century at 10%; thence it was lowered to 8% and 6%, and in 1714 it was fixed at 5%. It was not till the nineteenth century that all restrictions were removed.]

Economists, however, protest against all limitation.   It is certain that the fixing of a maximum price for the hiring of money is an altogether exceptional measure, since it is not practised in the case of house hire or the hiring of land.   We believe, too, that it could be abolished without any inconvenience.

None the less, the act of lending *habitually* above the current rate of interest, even if there is no limit placed upon this rate, constitutes a punishable offence — the offence of usury.

There is no real contradiction, although there may appear to be, in allowing freedom in settling the rate of interest and yet punishing those who make a trade of lending at excessive rates, any more than there is in allowing consumers liberty to drink and yet punishing the publican who supplies drink to a drunken man.

III. THE CAUSE OF INTEREST

The question of the legitimacy of interest is the oldest question in political economy, having been debated more than two thousand years before that science really existed.   We have sketched its main features in the last section.   But a distinction must be drawn between two aspects of the question that are commonly confounded.

What used to be discussed was more especially the *legitimacy* of interest — that is to say, its legal cause: whether the lender has the right to receive anything beyond the capital that he has lent.

What is discussed nowadays is more particularly the *explanation* of interest: what is its economic cause?   Does it represent a real surplus value of capital, and if so, whence does this surplus value arise?

1. *The Legal Cause of Interest*

This cause is the fact that all capital is private property, for the right of property necessarily implies that no one can be compelled to hand over his goods without receiving anything in return: a gratuitous loan would be as unintelligible as a gratuitous sale.   In fact, what makes this discussion obsolete and scholastic, is that none of those who denied the legitimacy of interest — neither Aristotle nor the legists and canonists — *disputed the legitimacy of the appropriation of capital*.   They were not by any means socialists.   They never contested the right of the owner to receive rent for the hire of house or land; why, then, deny him the right to receive interest?

However, we will recall their arguments.

(1) It was said that a distinction must be made according to

whether the borrower had or had not made a *productive use* of the borrowed capital. But what does this matter? Even in cases where the capital has not been put to productive use, and where it could not be, owing to circumstances — in other words, in cases where it is not really capital, but merely an object of consumption — why should the owner of this kind of wealth be obliged to lend it for nothing? It is not his fault if the borrower squanders the capital he has received instead of making proper use of it. The command of Christ "Lend, hoping for nothing again," relates solely to the Gospel order of things and not to the economic order, exactly like the command to him that has two coats to give one of them away. From the legal point of view there is obviously sufficient justification for interest in the mere principle that no one can be robbed of his wealth, and that whoever consents to dispossess himself for the benefit of another has the right to do so only on such conditions as he chooses to lay down.

(2) It was said, in the second place, that a distinction must be made, on the side of the lender, according as he had or had not *suffered privation*. But what does this matter, either? Since when has the remuneration that I claim — whether profit or wages — been in proportion to the privations that I experience? On what principle should I be obliged to put freely at the disposal of my fellows the wealth that I cannot or do not wish to make use of myself? Must I let other people establish themselves in my house because I am compelled to be absent, or allow them to eat my dinner because I am not hungry? This thesis could only be maintained on the principle that in this world man *has a right only to the amount of wealth that is strictly necessary for his personal consumption*, and that any excess belongs rightfully to the community — which means the adoption of pure communism.

(3) Thirdly, it was said that interest on capital must not be confused with the rent of land or houses, because land yields a periodical harvest and houses, if they do not yield fruit in the literal sense, at least provide numerous utilities — such as shelter from the weather, a comfortable family home, and a legal domicile — which are all perpetual, or which at any rate last as long as the house itself. The rent paid is the price of these harvests or these amenities, and, like them, should be perpetual or at least periodical. Of course the money paid by the tenant as rent has come out of his pocket, but he has received an equal value in exchange, just as when he pays for his daily bread.

Capital that has been lent, on the other hand, and that always takes the form of circulating capital and particularly the typical form of money-capital, is not a durable kind of wealth like a house: it is destroyed by the very act of production. The coal that is cast into the furnace disappears in smoke, the raw material is transformed, the money is expended in wages. How, then, can interest pay for the use of a thing whose very nature it is *to be consumed by its first employment?*

Besides, houses and lands, simply because they are durable, remain the property of the lessor, even when they are let, whereas borrowed money is necessarily consumed, because it is what the lawyers call "fungible." That is the very meaning of the words used to denote loans of money in legal language: in Roman law the word is *mutuum* (*ex meo tuum*, mine becomes thine), and in French law, *consumption* loan — the lender definitely alienates his money and the borrower becomes the definite owner thereof. Would it not, then, be contradictory to admit that the borrower may become at once the owner and the hirer of the same thing?

This last objection is no better founded than the rest. For if house-rent or land-rent is legitimate, how can the rent of capital not be so, since capital can always be used to purchase a house or land? Calvin himself remarked on this. When two kinds of wealth are interchangeable, one cannot be worth less than the other.

As for the legal argument that rent cannot be received for goods that one no longer owns, it is easy to reply that the capital lent is neither coal nor money but capital in the abstract — pure value. Now that is a permanent form of wealth, that retains its identity as well as, and even much better than, a house which sooner or later perishes and falls into ruin. Capital value remains for ever, like the Proteus of mythology in all his transformations. As for the borrower, too, he becomes the owner of the *coins*, certainly, and will definitely keep them; but he does not become the owner of the *value:* that is why he will have to return them, in the shape of other coins. The conception of hire is therefore quite applicable to the case of loans of money.[1]

The question is quite different, however, if we consider the legitimacy of the private appropriation of capital, as is done by socialists

---

[1] Another argument that we do not include here, though it has held an important place in the history of this question, is the one that justifies interest by the *abstinence* required for the creation of capital. We have already rejected the notion of abstinence as a factor in the formation of capital (see p. 113); still more do we set it aside as a justification of interest. Even if we admit that saving involves sacrifice, this sacrifice is sufficiently rewarded by the acquisition of the capital itself, without any necessity for adding a premium in the shape of interest.

to-day, instead of the legitimacy of interest. It is obvious, indeed, that if the appropriation of capital is robbery, the levying of interest must be so too. But this is quite a different matter.

We have seen (p. 23) that capitalist appropriation has been vigorously attacked by socialists. The precise aim of Karl Marx's famous book on *Capital* was to prove that this appropriation was the result of a historic process of spoliation, and that it remains the means of continuing this spoliation and indefinitely increasing it. Collectivists, it is true, admit that capital may be the object of a legitimate property right when it takes the humble form that economists like to give it — the canoe dug out by Robinson Crusoe, the plane that Bastiat's carpenter made, or the coins packed away in an old stocking or placed in the savings-bank by the peasant. But the real capital, they say — the capital that brings riches and power — is not that. It is never the produce of personal labour, or savings effected out of the product of personal labour. On the contrary, it consists of *savings effected out of the produce of the labour of someone else* — the labour of wage-earning workers, — savings which can only increase in so far as they are used to set other workers to work, so as to draw fresh profits from their labour. No great fortune, they say, has been created in any other way than this.

We should have to conclude from this argument, then, that there are two kinds of capital: the small, whose appropriation is legitimate because it is the fruit of honest and individual labour; and the great — a kind of vampire capital — whose appropriation is illegitimate because it involves the appropriation of the produce of other people's labour. Now since all great capital obviously began by being small, it must follow that the appropriation of capital is legitimate at its birth and up to a certain stage of development, after which it becomes improper. Capital, on this theory, is like those animals that are good when they are young, but become wicked when they grow up. But where is the critical point to be placed? It will be the point where capital has become too large to serve simply as an instrument for its owner's labour, and is used by him to set others to work in sufficient numbers to enable him and his heirs for ever to live on their income. Here we get back to the collectivist doctrine, and must refer ther eader to our previous discussion (pp. 355–361).

We need only recall this point: that we cannot lay it down as a principle that all capital, even on a very large scale, is necessarily and by its very nature an instrument of exploitation, and that it can only increase by draining the life-blood of labour. Vampire capital is by no means the normal form: on the contrary, it is a

monstrous perversion of true capital, whose real function is to serve
as the instrument and the handmaid of labour. We can say of
capital what has been said of money: that it is a bad master, but a
good servant; it is merely a matter of keeping it in its right place.
That is what co-operative societies do: they know quite well that
they cannot do without it, but they do not allow it to rule, or to
take possession of the profit.

We must remember also that if we admit the existence of much
capital to be an indispensable condition of economic progress — a
postulate that no socialist disputes, — and if we believe that the
development of production imperatively demands a stock of accumulated wealth, then we ought to regard the function of those who
accumulate this wealth and put it on the market as a very important
one. And the most effective way of encouraging these makers of
new capital — these social treasurers — certainly seems to be to
assign to them the ownership of the wealth that they have capitalized, with the right to make a profit on it. If private property in
capital were abolished, and a collectivist system established in its
place, it would certainly be necessary to establish and remunerate a
personnel for the performance of this service.

Nevertheless we have the right to ask whether these "treasurers"
are not paid too highly for the function they perform, and whether
their services could not be obtained at a cheaper rate. That is
another question. We are assured by economists that competition
keeps their remuneration down by means of the unavoidable fall of
the rate of interest. That seems to us very doubtful (see below);
but more confidence can be placed in the good organization of credit,
and especially of mutual credit.

2. The Economic Cause of Interest.

Having done with the justification of interest, it remains for us
to explain its nature and its origin. This is no longer a legal question
— whether the lender has the right to demand interest — but an
economic question — whether capital really yields a surplus value,
which is interest. The question goes beyond that of loans, or even
the appropriation of capital. For instance, we may discuss whether
the rent paid for land is really due to the landowner or whether it
ought not rather to be nationalized; but in any case there is no doubt
that it represents a real value, and a new one — the harvest yielded
by the earth. Is it the same with interest? Does it represent an

equal value received by the borrower, as in all cases of exchange?[1] Or is it merely a kind of tax that the borrower has to deduct from his own income, making himself by so much the poorer?

This question is not out-of-date, like the one we have just dealt with: it is of the greatest present interest, and a question that is very far from being settled. For the last thirty years it has been the subject of huge books and innumerable articles in journals. The explanations that have been proposed may be reduced to two typical ones, as follows.

(1) The oldest explanation is that of the *productiveness* of capital: interest exists because it is the nature of capital to produce a value greater than its own; and interest is precisely this increase or surplus value.

We are not dealing here with productiveness in the material sense of the term — productiveness by way of generation, as when a cow produces calves; nor even by way of fructification, as the *rentier* thinks when he tears off his dividend coupons as they fall due, just as he gathers his fruit when it is ripe. It is understood (see above, p. 62) that capital acts in production only as an assistant to labour; but by the productiveness of capital is meant the extra produce due to labour when it is assisted by capital. Thanks to his net, the fisherman will catch ten times as many fish; thanks to his saw and his plane, the carpenter will make ten times as many boards. It is in this sense that the term was understood by Bastiat, and that is the argument that he repeated with such wearisome iteration in his controversy with Proudhon. Economists have long been satisfied with this explanation, and it will no doubt seem an adequate one to the reader: it is clear and simple. But the more modern economists describe it as "naïve," and have subjected it to a pitiless analysis.[2] It has suffered the same fate as the law of supply and demand (p. 193) and the quantity theory of money (p. 212).

To begin with, it is remarked that if interest is due to the productiveness of capital, this explanation fails utterly in the case of loans for consumption. In this case, then, it must be inferred that interest has no cause, which means that it is merely a tax levied on the

[1] There certainly seems to be something fictitious about interest, to judge from the fantastic results that may accrue from compound interest, and which obviously cannot correspond to anything in actual existence.

[2] In the front rank must be placed the Austrian economist Boehm-Bawerk, who criticized the theory of productiveness, as well as all the other explanations of interest that had been proposed, in a book that marks an epoch in the history of economic doctrines (1884). In a second volume (1889) he expounded his own theory, of which we are about to speak.

borrower's purse — a legitimate one, if you like, since it results from
a contract, but one which corresponds to no value that has been
exchanged.

Even in the case of capital employed productively (*e.g.* a plane)
the notion of productiveness is said to be equivocal, for it implies
material productiveness (*e.g.* boards). Now though it is obvious
that the employment of capital enables labour to produce more,
both in quantity and in utility, it is by no means proved that it
enables it to produce more in *value*. To create abundance is not to
create value (p. 42). *Technical* productiveness must not be confounded with *economic* productiveness. Does machinery confer upon
the products it makes a greater value than that of hand-made products? Yes, if there is a monopoly; no, if there is competition.
In-the latter case the products whose price is reduced to the cost of
production acquire no extra value beyond that represented by the
cost and depreciation of the machinery. It is intelligible that the
price of boards must include the value necessary to repair the machine or the plane — the allowance for depreciation; — but it is
impossible to understand by what natural law it ought to include an
extra value that would be the *income* of the machine or the plane.

Finally, if productiveness were the actual, or at least the sole
cause of interest, then the rate of interest ought to be determined by
the degree of productiveness of the capital. How then should we
explain the general tendency of interest to fall, when capital continues to grow more and more powerful and productive?

(2) A more modern explanation is this: that interest is *the price of
time*, or in the ingenious phrase of the American economist Irving
Fisher, its cause and its measure is *impatience* to enjoy. Strictly
speaking this explanation is not a new one, for the idea that interest
is the price of time did not escape the canonists,[1] and was forcibly
expressed by Turgot in his defence of interest. But only with Boehm-
Bawerk and the psychological school did the notion find scientific
expression, thanks to their admirable ingenuity of analysis. This
very abstract theory has filled volumes and could not be described
here in any detail.

This explanation has the very great advantage of being just as
applicable (and perhaps even better applicable) to consumption
loans as to production loans. Indeed the man who borrows for

---

[1] But the canonists, while aware of the argument that *interest is the price of time*,
refuted it nobly by saying that time cannot be sold and has no price because it belongs
only to God. That is a very different conception from the American one, that *time
is money*.

consumption is generally more "impatient" to receive the money than the man who borrows with a view to production.

It has also this further superiority: that it does not apply only to loans, but has a far wider sphere of application. It applies even when capital remains in the hands of its owner instead of being lent. If I own a thousand pounds and prefer to make use of it myself, by putting it into the ground or into the furnace of an engine, in the shape of seed, fertilizer, or coal, or if I have it consumed by workmen in the shape of a food allowance or money wages — in all these cases I sacrifice a present good to obtain a future good in the form of crops or manufactured articles. I lend the money to myself, as it were. So there is always an exchange of the present against the future, and I should not make it if I were not to get back at the end of the year the money I had spent *plus something more*. That is what the capitalist unconsciously means when he says that his capital *ought* to bring him interest.

If this surplus value is not realized, he will say rightly that he has incurred a loss. If his accounts are properly kept he will only count as net profit the excess over the interest on the capital employed.

In short, as it is well expressed in everyday speech, every loan is an *advance;* and what does "advance" mean, if not the gaining of *time?*

Yet this theory, after a period of striking success, is beginning nowadays to be somewhat discredited.

Indeed, we may well ask ourselves on reflexion whether it is quite certain that man always prefers a present good to a future good. It is indisputable whenever we are dealing with a present want, but it is not the same in the case of *a future want:* here, on the contrary, the situation may be reversed. A sack of seed wheat will be worth far more to me at sowing time, nine months hence, than to-day in January, since I shall only have the trouble of keeping it from now till then. If a man insures his life or his children's education, paying a single or a graduated premium, is he not sacrificing a present good to one that is to come? And why does he do this, if not because he thinks the future good preferable? But we may go still further. Whoever lends his money, surely does so precisely because he has no use for it at present, and because he thinks it will be more useful to him at the time of repayment than now. Now since there are necessarily as many lenders as borrowers, it cannot be said that there are always more people who prefer a present good than there are who prefer a future good.

A future good, though identical with a present good, has always a lower value: that is a psychological law, confirmed by everyday experience. To have something for dinner to-day is a very different thing from having something for dinner in a year's time, or ten or a hundred years'! The value of a good thing diminishes in proportion to its distance from us in time, exactly as the size of an object diminishes when it is far away; and just as an object getting more and more distant becomes finally invisible, so value ends by becoming negligible or even disappearing altogether if the time is very far off.[1] If it were not so — if a future good had the same value as a present one — the most astonishing results would follow. For instance, the value of any piece of land, even the smallest, would be infinite, or at any rate would amount to millions of pounds; for its value would be the sum of all the crops expected from it as long as the earth endures, or at least as long as there are men to cultivate it! Now we know quite well that it is nothing of the kind: the value of a piece of land is not more than twenty or thirty times the value of its present crop, because the value of each future crop is only reckoned at a figure that diminishes rapidly until it reaches zero.[2]

This being admitted, let us consider what happens in the case of lending. The lending of money is not a hiring contract, as in the case of a house or land: it is an exchange contract. But an exchange of what, since all capitals in the form of money are identical? It is an exchange of a present good for a future good. I hand you a present good in the shape of a bag of money containing £100, or a bank-note of the same value, and I receive in exchange a future good in the shape of a promise to pay £100 in a year's time. But if the exchange were made on these terms the values would not be equal, for £100 payable in a year is not worth £100 to-day. If I put the present £100 in one scale of the exchange balance and the future £100 in the other, the latter will be the lighter: so a little extra weight must be added to the scale containing the future value — say £5 — in order to restore the balance. This supplementary amount is precisely interest. Or else, what comes to the same thing, we must remove a portion from the heavier scale — say £5, leaving only £95 — and this deduction is what is called discount.

---

[1] This law seems merely a scientific translation of such popular sayings as, "A bird in the hand is worth two in the bush." But all that these proverbs convey is the fact that every future satisfaction is always uncertain, whereas the theory described in the text has a deeper signification, namely, that the future satisfaction, even when certain, *is not worth as much as* the present satisfaction.

[2] Thus the public has learned, not without surprise, from the discussions about German reparations, that the present value of 8,000 million pounds to be paid in 42 annual instalments is only about 2,400 or 3,200 millions.

The only difference between a loan in the strict sense of the word and discount, is of course that in one case the interest is added to the capital when it is repaid, while in the other case it is deducted from the capital at the time of borrowing.

Is there not a vicious circle in this explanation also? If present capital is generally preferred to future capital, is it not simply because the possession of present capital enables us to invest it at interest? Is not the preference for present money determined by the existence of interest, and not the other way about?

Between these two explanations one may make one's choice. Yet they are not incompatible: they may even be presented as complementary to each other — and that not by a convenient process of eclecticism but for the same reason as we gave in dealing with value. Just as value seems to be determined not by a single force but by two opposing forces, one on the seller's side, and one on the buyer's — the two propping each other up, like the two sides of an arch, — so, in the case of interest, we must look at both the lender's and the borrower's side of the transaction. On the borrower's side, in the case of a production loan, it is the degree of productiveness of the capital to be borrowed; on the lender's side, it is his degree of preference for the anticipated future good over the present good that he gives up. And it is the rate of interest that reconciles these opposing claims, by its rise or fall, assuming, of course, that there is competition between borrowers on the one hand and lenders on the other.

IV. THE DETERMINATION OF THE RATE OF INTEREST

We have seen that the rate of interest[1] was for a long time settled by law, and was so in France for non-commercial loans until quite recently. But such legislative limitation can only give legal sanction to what is approximately the current rate; otherwise it would be useless. What matters, then, is to ascertain the economic and natural laws that determine the rate of interest, like those which determine the rate of wages or the prices of goods.

If capital were borrowed in kind, in the shape of factories, ma-

---

[1] The *rate* of interest is the ratio between the amount of the income and that of the capital. To express it most conveniently, the capital is represented by the conventional figure 100, and the rate of interest as a percentage — 3%, 4%, 5% etc. It used to be calculated differently: the interest was expressed as a fraction of the capital. Thus money lent at 5% was said to be a loan of *the twentieth penny*, because the interest was one-twentieth of the capital; 4% was called the twenty-fifth penny, and so forth.

chinery, or any sort of instruments of production, there would be set up for each of these a *different hiring price*, according to their respective qualities, durability, and productiveness, just as the rent of houses varies according to their degree of comfortableness and their situation, and as the rent of land varies according to its fertility.

But capital always takes the shape of money (or its equivalent in credit instruments). This is, first, because the borrower always prefers to receive money rather than capital in kind, having thus more liberty to adapt the loan to the purposes he has in view; and, secondly, because it is necessarily in this form that capital is put on the market by all those who have saved and are seeking to invest their savings. In fact, capital in kind could not be created by saving, but only money capital.

Now this substitution, which transforms a hire into a loan, has certain remarkable results.

On the one hand it tends to eliminate all causes of variation and to *equalize* the hiring price of all capital; for all capital must be of the same value if it is lent and borrowed in the same form, as money. Henceforth it has differences of quantity only, and not of quality. Moreover, capital in this form is essentially mobile, and therefore moves almost instantaneously to any point where it is attracted by a higher rate of interest; and the result of this is that any differences are rapidly smoothed out. Therefore at any given moment there is only one rate of interest in the national, and even in the international market.

But, on the other hand, this substitution of money introduces into the determination of the hiring price of capital a differentiating cause which assumes very great importance: the degree of *solvency* of the borrower. In fact, as we have already observed, the borrower is not really a hirer: he acquires the definite ownership of the money, and can do what he pleases with it. It is possible, therefore, that he may be unable to return it; thence arises a risk for the lender, which will cause him to demand higher interest as *compensation for the possible loss* of his capital. The high interest is a premium of insurance, which the lender naturally requires the borrower to pay.

Interest should therefore be divided into two parts: (1) *Interest properly so called*, representing the price paid for the right of disposing of the capital. This is the same for all loans (on the same market and at the same time); (2) An *insurance premium* against the risk of loss. This varies for each loan, and it is this which determines almost entirely the differences between the rates of interest of all investments in public funds or Stock Exchange securities.[1]

What, then, are the causes determining this general rate of interest, or, in other words, the price of hiring money capital? We must not imagine that we can discover a single cause, any more than we can in the case of the value of commodities or the price of labour. There are many causes, but they may be summed up under the old formula of supply and demand.

The supply of capital in the shape of money or credit instruments depends in the first place (1) upon the *saving power* of the country, aided by good credit and savings institutions to facilitate this saving and provide outlets for it. But (2) it is not enough for capital to be abundant in the country: it must also be abundant in the market, and must be offered for loan. This implies the existence of a numerous class of persons *unable or unwilling to utilize their capital by their own personal industry*, for in a society where everyone made use of his own capital, it is plain that, however abundant it might be, it would not be offered. Lastly, (3) the supply of capital depends on the *security* of the investments. Without this, as has happened in the past and as still happens in countries exposed to the inroads of enemies or of their own governments, capital will be uselessly hoarded instead of being offered on loan.

The demand for capital is determined by its *productiveness* — not exactly the average productiveness of the business undertakings in a given country at a given moment, but more precisely the productiveness of the *least productive* businesses among those to which capital is offered; for it is they that command the market for capital, simply because they cannot give more. If these businesses can only give 3% interest, more remunerative ones, which could pay more if necessary, will be careful not to do so.

In a new country, endowed with all manner of natural resources — virgin land to be cleared, mines to be exploited, and roads to be made — the rate of interest will be very high: firstly, because capital is scarce, and the more so since those who possess it are keeping it to make use of it and not putting it on the market; and also because in such a country there are no undertakings bringing in small returns — they are despised.

---

[1] To these two elements we ought to add a third: the *premium for depreciation*, representing the annual payment necessary to repair the capital that has been used once, in the case of capital in kind, or to reconstitute the money capital after it has been spent. But this is not really interest: it is a portion of the future capital coming to replace past capital.

In an old country, on the other hand, the converse causes will operate: capital accumulated by long saving will be offered in abundance; and as modes of employment with a high degree of productiveness will all be already supplied, this capital will be driven into less productive businesses, thus keeping down the general rate of interest.

Loans at interest, like wages and rent, are speculative contracts — that is to say, the lender forgoes all claim to the profits of the undertaking in return for a fixed annual payment. We have seen, however (p. 412), that when lenders prefer the chances of gain or loss to the security of a fixed income, the borrower promises them only a share of the profits if there are any, and nothing if there are none; and if there is a loss, it is on the capital provided by the shareholders that it falls first. But then this is not, legally speaking, a loan at all, but a *partnership:* the credit instruments of these lenders are called *shares* instead of *bonds*, and their income, instead of being called *interest*, is called a *dividend*. The rate of dividend must naturally be higher than the rate of interest, as it represents a more uncertain income: it must include a premium of insurance against the risk of bad years. Generally, too, the dividend also includes, besides interest and insurance premium, what is called profit. But we shall recur to this question when we come to deal with profits.

V. WHETHER THE RATE OF INTEREST TENDS TO FALL

If we must desire a rise in wages from the social point of view, we must conversely desire a fall in the case of interest.

It must be desired in the first place from the point of view of distributive justice; for by the very fact of reducing the share deducted from the total production by the capitalist, a fall in the rate of interest must (other things being equal) increase by so much the share available for labour; and the more so because the rate of interest determines not only the income of the capitalist, but also, indirectly, the rate of profits and of rent, and consequently of the whole income of the possessing classes.

It must be desired also as a stimulus to production; for by continually lowering the hiring price of capital, and consequently the expenses of production, it must facilitate the execution of undertakings that were formerly impossible. Here are lands to be cleared, and houses that one would like to build to house the workmen, but it is well known that land and houses will not bring in more than 3%. If, then, the current rate of interest is 5% it will be impossible

to get capital for these undertakings, for they could only be undertaken at a loss. So they will be left alone. But suppose that the
rate of interest falls to 2%: there will immediately be a rush to execute
them. Turgot compared a fall in the rate of interest, in a celebrated
simile, to the gradual fall of waters that allows cultivation to extend
over new lands.

But it is not enough that this fall should be desirable. Is it probable? Has it a permanent character? Is it to be regarded as a true
economic and natural law, like that of the increasing value of land
or the fall in the value of money?

The law has always been affirmed by political economy, and especially by the French optimist school, from Turgot to Paul Leroy-
Beaulieu; and Bastiat included it among his most beautiful "harmonies."

The theory rests both on reasoning and on facts.

As far as facts are concerned, the great fall of the rate of interest
is one of the most characteristic economic phenomena of the second
half of the nineteenth century: from 5% in the middle of the century
it fell to 3% in 1897, the year that marked the lowest point.

As a matter of theory, most of the causes already enumerated as
determining the rate of interest seem bound to operate in the direction
of a fall. It seems reasonable to think that in every progressive society capital must become more and more *abundant*, like all wealth
that is produced, and that consequently its final utility and its value
must go on diminishing. *Security*, also, ought to go on increasing,
at any rate if we admit that civilization implies more fidelity to their
engagements on the part of individuals and States, or more effective
means of control on the part of creditors. And alongside of these
optimistic forecasts we can even place a pessimistic one, which nevertheless will operate in the same direction — namely, that capital
will in future become *less productive*, and that profits will diminish,
alike in agriculture, owing to the law of diminishing return, and even
in industry and transport, because opportunities for employment
in these directions are limited. It seems indisputable, for instance,
that the railways which may yet be constructed in France will be
far less productive than the great lines already built.

It even seems that there is scarcely any assignable limit to this
decrease, for here there is no limit set by the cost of production, as
in the case of commodities, or by the cost of subsistence, as in the
case of the wages of the workman. The only limit is the point
below which the capitalist will give up lending and prefer to hoard
or to consume his capital. But what is the rate below which he will

rather spend or lock up his money than lend it? Will it be 1% — or 1 per thousand?

Bastiat declared that interest might fall below any assignable figure, yet without ever reaching zero, like those well-known curves in mathematics which approach nearer and nearer to a straight line called an *asymptote*, without ever touching it, except at infinity. Some economists would go further still and believe that the rate of interest may fall to zero, which would mean the disappearance of interest and free credit.

Those are the arguments for the indefinite diminution of the rate of interest. None of them, however, seems to us decisive.

In economic history, in fact, the fall of the rate of interest never appears as a regularly descending line — like the fall in the value of money which has continued almost without intermission for more than a thousand years — but as a broken line without any well-marked direction, either upward or downward. The fall during the second half of the nineteenth century was very striking; but what are fifty years in the whole course of history? Under the Roman Empire the rate of interest was no higher than it is to-day, and in Holland in the eighteenth century it had already fallen as low as at the end of last century. It is quite possible, therefore, that in the future the rate of interest may rise; and a very marked rise was indeed observed, even before the war, in the rate of interest for public funds and the chief Stock Exchange securities.

It was in 1897 that the fall in the rate ceased and a period of rise began, showing itself in the form of a fall in the price of all fixed-income securities. Thus the price of $2\frac{1}{2}\%$ Consols, which in 1898 was nearly 111, had fallen by 1913 to below 74, which represented a rate of interest of nearly $3\frac{1}{2}\%$.

But since the war it has been a very different matter. The upward movement of interest and the fall in the price of securities have been greatly accelerated, so that the rate has risen above 6%. This rise is only too easily explained by the enormous need of the belligerent States for money, and the immeasurable destruction of capital. The rise in interest would have been greater still if the belligerent States had not resorted to the issue of paper money on a large scale, with the double result, on the one hand, of reducing to that extent the issue of government loans, and on the other hand, of providing the public with the funds necessary for subscribing to these loans.

There is every reason to believe that the rise in interest will definitely continue long after the war, since the same causes will remain

in operation.[1] Given the urgent necessity for reconstruction everywhere, the world will experience a veritable famine of capital; and
if, as Mr. Irving Fisher says, the real cause of interest is "impatience,"
it will surely never have operated with such intensity as now! Moreover, since the supply of capital will be at a minimum, owing to the
terrible extent to which it has been consumed, and since the productiveness of businesses after the war will undoubtedly be greater
than it has ever been before, on account of the rise of prices, we certainly cannot see a single reason for believing that the rate of interest
will fall for some time yet.

But this time, too, will pass, and if we look beyond it and try to
forecast the fluctuations of the various factors that influence the rate
of interest, we can but find them quite uncertain. The increasing
abundance of capital is indeed probable; but it may very well be
counterbalanced by an increasing demand. Does not every business undertaking require a greater and greater amount of capital?
And so far as risk is concerned, does anyone imagine that there
are fewer insolvent debtors now than there used to be, or fewer
bankruptcies, fewer gigantic swindles, or less capital swallowed up
in hazardous enterprises and, above all, in the bottomless gulf of
armaments? Certainly not! Why, then, should anyone feel justified in concluding that it will be different in the future?

In the matter of productiveness, if we look only at a given industry,
such as railways or gas lighting, there is undoubtedly a limit to their
development; but if we look at production in general, we can see
that old industries are continually being replaced by new ones. Now
there is no ground for asserting that motor transport, for example,
will be less remunerative than rail transport, or electric lighting less
remunerative than gas.

In short, what seems most likely is that the rate of interest will
pass through the same long periods of alternate rise and fall in the
future as in the past.[2] It does not appear to us to be established,
therefore, that belief in an indefinite fall in the rate of interest can be
erected into a law, or that there is any foundation for regarding it

[1] For many arguments in support of this view see an article on "The Rate of Interest after the War," by Mr. Irving Fisher, in the *Annals* of the Academy of Philadelphia (November, 1916). The contrary view has also been maintained, however.

[2] This forecast, which we made in the first edition of this book in 1883, did not
agree with that of M. Paul Leroy-Beaulieu, who, like almost all economists of the
liberal school, has always predicted a fall. This prediction was fulfilled down to 1897,
when the fall was succeeded by a rise.

as one of the factors tending to bring about the equalization of human conditions.

This is not to say, however, that we may not be right in expecting the share of wealth accruing to capital to be reduced in the future; but this reduction will take place in profits rather than in interest (see below, Chapter IV). Nor would such a result be due to the operation of some natural law, but to purposive and persevering human action, operating probably through co-operative credit associations and similar consumers' societies.

With regard to the hypothesis that the rate of interest might fall to zero, or even lower, this is by no means such an absurdity as it would be to see all wealth becoming free on account of its superabundance. For the production of wealth necessarily involves labour, and is therefore burdensome, whereas the transformation of wealth into capital is only a change of destination, not necessarily involving labour, or even hardship. Of course purely gratuitous lending will always be an act of generosity and, as such, outside the sphere of political economy. But it is conceivable that, in cases of abundance of capital, the lender might be satisfied with the certainty of re-covering his capital at the right time, and with being exempted meanwhile from the trouble of looking after it. That is exactly what sometimes takes place in the case of loans in the shape of deposits.

CHAPTER III — WAGE–EARNERS

I. WHO ARE THE WAGE–EARNERS?

Wages, as defined by many economists, are "any kind of income received by a worker in exchange for his labour." But this definition, which lumps together with the workman the peasant, the craftsman, the shopkeeper, the official, and the employer himself in so far as he takes an active part in the business, is somewhat tendencious in the wideness of its scope. It is inspired by the desire to refute the attacks of socialism by denying all difference between the claims of the various recipients of shares in the distribution of wealth, and including all incomes under a single heading: it makes capitalists and landowners "comrades" of the wage-earners.[1] The term "wages," in economics as in everyday speech, should be used to describe not just any kind of income, nor even every kind of remuneration of labour, but simply a very special kind, namely, *the price of labour hired and employed by an entrepreneur.*

We have seen, indeed, on many occasions, that the *entrepreneur* system is the characteristic feature of modern economic organization. Now the wage system is inseparable from the *entrepreneur* system: the two are like the two sides of a medal, or rather like the sale and purchase of a single commodity. The commodity in this case is labour; the wage-earner is the vendor, and the *entrepreneur* is the purchaser.

Defined thus, the wage system is merely one mode of remuneration, in no wise necessary or unique, but comparatively recent in economic history — a system which has only become general as a result of the modern capitalist and labour-employing organization of industry, and which might very well disappear along with that organization. That will become more apparent in the course of the following section.

Our definition of the wage system obviously includes all who work under the orders of a master, in agriculture, industry, transport, or commerce, whether they are manual workers, clerks, engineers, or even managers, and even if they have a salary of £20,000 a year.

[1] This was what Mirabeau, the orator of the French Revolution, meant when he said: "I know only three ways of living in society: one must be either a beggar, a thief, or a wage-earner. A landowner himself is only the first among wage-earners."

But, conversely, it excludes all producers who work on their own account — that is to say, (a) *independent producers:* peasants, retail dealers, and craftsmen, though they are often poorer than wage-earners; (b) those who practise a *liberal profession:* doctors, lawyers, artists, etc. For both these classes work not for a *master*, but for the public — for a *client*.

II. HISTORY OF THE WAGE SYSTEM

The wage system was still unknown during that long period that we have called the period of family industry when the master of the house procured all he required by the labour of his servants, slaves, or serfs. It is true that in every age, even in ancient times and under the slavery system, there have been poor but free men who hired out their arms to a rich man in exchange for a certain price in money or in kind. But these free workers of antiquity were rather what we should nowadays call craftsmen — independent producers making a living out of some trade, who were sometimes hired as extra hands when the number of slaves or servants was insufficient.

There was scarcely more room for the wage-earner, properly so called, under the second system — the corporative or guild system. No doubt the journeymen were paid by the master, but their relation to him was not that of a wage-earner to his employer. Their very name, "companions" (from *cum pane*, denoting a "messmate") shows plainly the nature of the relation between them, at any rate at the beginning. Nor was it only the relation of a common life and mutual assistance: there was also the bond of reciprocal obligations of a somewhat crude kind. Journeymen could not be dismissed at their master's pleasure, but they might not leave him; their wages were fixed by the guild statutes and sometimes by the local authorities, but they could not get them increased. But they all hoped one day to set up for themselves as masters, and for many of them this hope was realized.

But when at the end of the Middle Ages the small town markets ceased to be the centre of economic life, and the way was prepared by the setting up of the great modern States and the opening up of new routes for the creation of national and even international markets, the small masters of former days were not rich enough to produce sufficiently. They were gradually replaced by capitalists — great merchants, who were later on to become the captains of industry; and thus little by little was developed the typical master or employer. At the same time the guild companions saw the path to mastership barred to them. They began to form a separate class; they were excluded from the corporations, and consequently from all participation in the fixing of their own wages; and in opposition to the masters' associations they set up associations of workmen — the earliest form of trade unions. Henceforth capital and labour were to walk apart.

One further step was necessary to create the type of wage-earner that exists to-day. This was the abolition of all the restrictions and regulations that caused the inferiority of the guild system and that bound the workman while they protected him. Labour had to be made absolutely mobile, so that it could be organized at pleasure. This was first accomplished by the *manufacturing* system, which was created with various privileges conferred by the State, outside the guild organization, and was thereby exempted even from the guild regulations. The manufacturers were thus enabled to apply the division of labour freely, and to produce on a large scale. In this way the edicts of Turgot and of the French Revolution, decreeing the complete freedom of labour, were realized in a more general manner.

Thenceforth the workers were indeed free — free to sell their labour at the price determined by the law of supply and demand, free to refuse it, and free to depart when they pleased. But naturally the masters were also free under the same conditions — free to pay the minimum price at which workers could be procured, whether men, women, or children, and free to discharge them at their pleasure. The wage contract was henceforth as free as a contract of sale, and, in a sense, even more so, because the law did not condescend to have anything to do with it. So labour became a commodity whose value was determined by the same laws as any other commodity. The wage system was thus actually established.

No one, not even among socialists, dreams of denying that this system gave a great impetus to production and provided industry with a powerful tool. But neither will any impartial observer deny that this reciprocal freedom benefited the employers more than the workers at the beginning. The workers were isolated, unorganized, the victims of legislation which refused them the right to combine, and in the worst possible position for making use of the commodity they possessed — namely, their labour — which they could only sell at a low price, the more so because the disintegration of the guild system coincided with and facilitated the introduction of machinery. It is generally agreed that from the end of the eighteenth century to about the middle of the nineteenth, the condition of the wage-earning workers of Europe was very hard — far more degraded than that of the poorest peasants — and that the system of liberty was less beneficial to them than the previous systems.

III. THE INCREASE OF WAGES

Even in our own day it must be admitted that the share of wealth allotted to wage-paid labour, whether manual or even intellectual, has always been very moderate in comparison with that received by the other agents of production. The average rate of wages before the war was 5s. 9½d. a day in Paris and 3s. 4d. in provincial towns. If we reckon 300 working days in a year, though the average is really a good deal less than this, we get an annual income of £86 11s. 3d. in. Paris and £50 in the provinces. But those are the wages paid in industry. For agricultural workers the average was not more than 2s. 5d. a day, or say £36 a year. Moreover, those are men's wages: women's were only half these amounts; the average was not more than 2s. 5d. in Paris and 1s. 8d. in the provinces.[1]

When the workman has a family and can add to his own wages those of his wife and such of his children as are over school age and have not yet left home, then the total income of the family may be sufficient. But this accumulation of wages is only possible for a short part of his life, since he must wait till the children are old enough to leave school, and since they very often leave home as soon as they are 18 or 20. The workman, moreover, is compelled to retire much sooner than the *bourgeois* or the official, and his wages, instead of increasing like theirs, tend to fall rapidly as he grows older.

It is true that however low wages may be, they are yet considerable compared with what they were only half a century ago. The gradual rise of wages is a fact that cannot be disputed. From the thousands of statistics drawn up by all countries, we are enabled to draw the conclusion that wages, both agricultural and industrial, were far more than doubled during the course of the nineteenth century.[2]

---

[1] [The following are examples of English pre-war average weekly wages, drawn from the *Labour Gazette*, the official organ of the Ministry of Labour: Building trades (excluding labourers), 39s. 5d.; Engineering (excluding labourers), 40s. 11d.; Shipbuilding (excluding labourers), 39s. 10d.; Labourers in the above trades, 24s. 2d.; Printing and Bookbinding, 34s. 10d.; Furniture making, 38s. 6d. The wages of dock labourers ranged from 4s. 6d. to 6s. 8d. per day of about 10 hours. Agricultural wages were about 15s. to 22s. per week.]

[2] In the case of France the wages index number rose between 1810 and 1910 from 100 to 275, so that wages increased nearly threefold, whereas the index number for the cost of living only rose from 100 to 140.

Since the war we may say that the rate of wages has been about trebled[1] — call it about 16s. to 20s. a day in industrial employments, and 9s. 6d. to 12s. in the country.

But if it is borne in mind that the index number for prices rose from 100 in 1914 to over 400 in 1920, and is still over 300, it will be realized that though *nominal* wages have risen enormously, *real* wages have rather fallen.[2] For the distinction must never be lost sight of between nominal wages, which are merely the sum of money (paper or metal) received by the wage-earner, and real wages, which are the total satisfaction, the quantity of goods, that he can procure with this money.

Moreover, there is every reason to believe that this is only a temporary inflation that will collapse as soon as prices themselves fall; in fact, the fall in prices that began in 1920 was immediately followed by a fall of wages in many industries.

Even supposing that a rise in real wages could be predicated, the problem must not be regarded as solved, for we should have to recognize that it has been far exceeded by the *increase in wants*. And since the feeling of comfort or poverty depends far less on the absolute amount of the income and the standard of consumption than on the relation between income and wants, it follows that even with an increased wage the working classes may feel themselves worse off; for human nature is such that even comfort seems like wretchedness if it is contrasted with the opulence of its neighbours. Nor must it be said that this increase of wants is attributable to the working classes themselves, for it is quite obvious that most of it is due to imitation of the wealthy classes.

This is not simply a question of unsatisfied appetites: it is also a matter of justice. The workers consider that they have a right not only to such an improvement in their position as their employers

---

[1] [The rise has not been quite so great as this in England. "It is estimated that at the end of February, 1922, *weekly full-time rates of wages* of adult workpeople, in the industries for which particulars are available, were approximately 100 per cent. above the pre-war rates. As the length of the normal working week had been considerably reduced in the same period . . . the percentage increase in hourly rates of wages would be substantially greater. At the end of 1920, shortly before the decline in wages began, the increase on pre-war rates in the same industries is estimated to have been about 170 or 180 per cent." (*Labour Gazette*, March 1922, p. 109.) The article goes on to give certain reasons for thinking that this figure of 100 per cent. may possibly be somewhat in excess of the true average for *all industries*.]

[2] [The English price index number only reached 276 in 1920 (see the table on p. 61) and has since fallen to 179. So real wages as well as nominal wages would appear to have risen in England since 1914.]

may think sufficient, but to an increase of income at least proportional to that of other classes of society. Now is this the case? Has the increase of wages been *proportional to the general increase of wealth?* All economists of the liberal school answer in the affirmative, and try to prove that the share received by labour has increased more in proportion than the share received by capital.

But this proof was not very convincing as regards the past, and the war will not have brought any fresh arguments to its support; for though it is true that wages have benefited to an enormous extent, it is easy to see that their increased value is still below that of profits. No doubt the workers may think themselves lucky compared with the capitalist *rentiers* who have suffered all the evils arising from the depreciation of money, with hardly any compensation. But all the same the real war profiteers are not the wage-earners but the manufacturers, the merchants, and, above all, the farmers.

IV. THE LAWS OF WAGES

To define the laws of wages is to try to formulate their action — to seek to discover the general causes that determine the rate of wages and make it rise and fall. It is one of the great problems of political economy, and has provided matter for controversy that has lasted for a hundred years and more, like the problems of rent and interest (see above, pp. 337–375, 398–418).

One might be inclined at the outset to ask oneself whether there are really any natural laws determining the rate of wages. Is it not a vain enquiry, since the rate varies from trade to trade and from place to place, and is determined in each particular case by free discussion — or what is presumed to be free — between employer and workman?

This would be a fallacious argument. For the price of goods also varies according to their nature, the place, and the time; and of them, too, it may be said that the price is the outcome of free discussion between seller and purchaser. Yet that does not prevent our seeking for the laws that determine prices. There is no contradiction in this. Prices and wages are undoubtedly determined by agreements between men,[1] but these agreements are themselves conditioned

---

[1] Yet it is not really correct to say of wages, any more than of prices, that they are settled by particular agreements: everyone knows, on the contrary, that just as there is a current price for every commodity — a price which can only be modified to a very slight extent by individual bargaining, — so, too, there is a current rate of wages for each kind of labour which is obligatory alike upon employers and workmen.

by general causes which it is our business to discover. To believe in the existence of natural laws in political economy is simply to believe that when men make agreements, they are swayed by certain psychological motives or certain external circumstances which are of a general character and may be picked out from the confused mass of particular wage contracts.

Now since labour, under the existing economic organization, is only a commodity like any other, and is sold and bought (or hired) on the market, it seems evident that its price must be determined by the same laws as those which settle the prices of other commodities. These laws we have already studied in connexion with value, and they are summed up in the common formula of supply and demand, or in the vivid and picturesque version of it given by Cobden: "Whenever two workmen run after one master, wages fall; whenever two masters run after one workman, wages rise."

But this is rather a mere statement of fact than an explanation. The real problem is to ascertain *why* it should sometimes be the workmen who run after the master, and sometimes the other way about.

A satisfactory law of wages ought to explain all variations in wages: (1) why wages are higher in one country than in another; (2) why they are higher at one time than at another; (3) why they are higher in one trade than in another.

In the history of economic doctrines we must distinguish three main theories on this subject. The first two, however, after having shone in the front rank, are now eclipsed.

1. *The Wages Fund Theory*

This was for a long time the classical theory in England, and one which held an important place in the history of economic doctrines. It is the one which approaches most closely to the formula of supply and demand, of which, in fact, it is merely a more precise statement.

The supply, according to this theory, consists of the workers — the proletarians — who are in search of work and who offer their services in order to earn a living. The demand, on the other hand, consists of the capital that seeks investment. We have already seen (pp. 105–108) that there is no other way of giving productive employment to capital than by using it to set workmen to work. *The rate of wages will be determined by the ratio between these two factors.*

Take the circulating capital of a country, which economists used to call the *wages fund* because in their view its function was to support the workers while they were at work; and then take the number of workers. Divide the first figure by the second, and the quotient will give you the amount of wages. Thus if the circulating capital amounts to five hundred million pounds, and the number of workers is ten millions, the average annual wage will be exactly fifty pounds.

It is obvious that on this theory wages can only vary according as one of the two factors varies. So a rise of wages is only possible in the two following cases:

(*a*) If there is an increase in the wages fund — the total to be divided; and this can only increase through saving;

(*b*) If the working population — the number of participators — diminishes; and this can only happen if the workers put into practice the principles of Malthus and either abstain from marriage or limit the number of their children.

But this theory, though still upheld by some economists, is greatly discredited at the present day.

To begin with, the fact on which it is based — namely, that a certain amount of working capital is needed for setting the workers to work — is of interest only from the point of view of production and has nothing to do with distribution. It is indisputable that wages are paid out of capital, since the money that the *entrepreneur* uses to pay his workmen is certainly capital; but it by no means follows that the rate of these wages is determined by the amount of this capital. The question whether an *entrepreneur* will have the wherewithal to set his workmen to work — enough raw materials or tools — is one thing: the question of what share in the income from the business he will be able to allow them, is quite another. The answer to the first question depends on what he possesses: the answer to the second depends on what he will produce. The demand for labour depends on industrial activity, but this activity depends in its turn far more on the expectations of the *entrepreneurs* than on the amount of money that they have in their cash boxes or that their credit enables them to obtain from their bankers.

Furthermore, the apparent precision of this theory is a mere illusion. After all, when we examine it closely, it resolves itself into this: that the rate of wages is found by dividing the total sum paid in wages by the number of wage-earners — which is mere tautology. Or, if we choose to take it in the broadest sense, it means that the greater the wealth of a country the higher are wages in it — a proposition that is too trivial to possess any scientific interest.

2. *The Iron Law of Wages*

This second theory also starts from the fact that manual skill, or labour power, under the existing organization of society is only a commodity that is bought and sold on the market. The workers are the sellers, and the employers the purchasers. Now wherever competition can have free play, is it not a law common to all kinds of goods that their value is determined by their cost of production? That is what economists call *natural price,* or *normal value.* It must therefore be the same with this commodity called labour or manual skill. Its price also, which is wages, must be determined by its cost of production. It only remains to find out what the term "cost of production" means when applied to the person of the worker.

Let us take a machine as an example. Its cost of production is represented by: (1) the value of the coal it consumes; (2) the amount that must be set aside every year for depreciation — that is, to replace it by a new one when it is worn out. In the same way the cost of production of labour will consist of: (1) the value of the food that the workman must consume to keep himself in a fit state to produce; (2) the depreciation fund necessary to replace him when he is past work — that is to say, to bring up his child to manhood.

For this reason *wages must fall to the minimum strictly necessary to enable a worker and his family to live,* or, to put it more generally, to enable the working population to live and to perpetuate itself.

Such is the theory generally known as the *brazen* or *iron law.* This high-sounding name, invented by Lassalle, captured the imagination from the outset: for thirty years it made the refrain of a socialist war-song and served to inflame the passions of social hatred by proving to the workers that the economic organization left them no chance of improving their position.

The theory is both true and false. It is true in so far as it means that normal wages tend to be determined by the cost of living, increasing when that increases, and diminishing when it falls.[1] In fact, the workman must find means to live, even if he is only a slave — at any rate so long as he cannot be dispensed with. Moreover, besides the economic necessity there is also a moral one, acting either by free concessions on the part of employers, or by pressure in the shape of a strike. This fact could not be more clearly demonstrated than it has been in our own time, when six years ago we saw the cost

---

[1] We say *normal* wages, because in exceptional circumstances *current* wages may fall below this point — as, for instance, when there is a superabundant supply of female labour or immigrant labour.

of living and the rate of wages rising in parallel lines, and then quite recently the falling curve of prices bringing about a fall in wages.

But the theory is false if we mean by it, as its inventors did, that wages can never rise above what is strictly necessary to existence — that is to say, that the minimum is also the maximum. We have only to look around us to see that the workman's wages are never subject to any maximum — except the maximum that results, for him as for each of his fellow sharers, from the limitation of production. And to recognize that wages are a function of the cost of living, as we have just said, is by no means to imply that they are invariable, for this cost of living is itself capable of increasing indefinitely, even in proportion to the increase in the workers' wants. Instead of speaking of an "iron wage," we speak nowadays of a "living wage" — meaning thereby a wage that enables the worker to live in conformity with the habits and customs of the social environment in which he is called upon to live.

3. *The Productiveness of Labour Theory*

The third theory, while seeking like the others to deduce the law of wages from the law of value, yet reaches entirely opposite conclusions. The value of labour, it is said, cannot be assimilated to the value of a commodity that is subject only to the law of supply and demand under the influence of competition, for the worker is not a product but the very agent of all production. Consequently, his value must be determined by the same causes as those which determine the value of the instruments of production — land and capital. That is to say it is determined especially by the productiveness of the instrument. When an *entrepreneur* hires a piece of land, the rate of rent that he pays is calculated by the productiveness of the land. And we have seen (p. 413) that it is the same in the case of capital. Why then, when it comes to the hire of labour, should not the rate of wages be proportional to the productiveness — the efficiency — of labour?

However, the productiveness theory has been expressed in different ways. The older form is very optimistic. According to this, the worker would receive in theory, obviously not the whole value produced by the business, in which case the employer, obtaining nothing, would give up working, but at least *all that remains* of the total produce, after the shares of the other collaborators — interest, profit, and rent — had been deducted. These latter shares would be strictly determined, whereas labour's share would possess the advantage of being indefinite.

If this theory were well founded it would be as encouraging as the other two theories are the reverse. If, in fact, the rate of wages depends solely on the productiveness of the workman's labour, then his fate rests in his own hands: the more he produces, the more he earns; everything that is of a kind to increase and improve his productive power — such as physical development, moral virtues, vocational instruction, inventions and machinery — must infallibly increase his wages.

This theory agrees well with certain facts. To begin with, it is plain that the productiveness of labour exerts a general influence on the rate of wages in the sense that an increase in the wealth of a country increases the total national dividend, and thereby ultimately increases of necessity the share of all the recipients, including the workers. Moreover, it succeeds better than the other theories in explaining the inequalities of wages. For if the engraver receives more than the labourer, the American more than the Frenchman, the twentieth century workman more than his predecessor in earlier centuries, is not this because the labour of the former is more productive than that of the latter? And if we believe apprenticeship to be useful to a workman, is not this because we consider that a workman who knows his trade produces more than an unskilled one, and that, producing more, he will be better paid?

But, on the other hand, if this theory offers a satisfactory explanation of *differences* in wages, it gives none at all of *variations* in wages. Why do they rise or fall at certain times? Why, for instance, have they doubled since the war? Why are the workers o all countries so much afraid of the competition of those who are precisely *the least productive:* women, unskilled workmen, colonial natives, and home workers? This explanation obviously leaves out of sight one of the essential factors in the rate of wages, namely, the abundance or scarcity of labour.

Nowadays this theory of the determination of wages by the productiveness of labour takes a form that is more scientific and free from all optimist or finalist prejudices. All it does is to extend to wages, regarded as the price of labour, the same explanation as that adopted to explain the value of everything — the doctrine of final utility. Just as each new unit of any kind of wealth whatever, when added to what is already possessed, brings only a diminishing amount of utility, which falls ultimately to zero (see the example given on p. 46 of the buckets of water), so, it is said, each new dose of labour, the assistance brought by each new workman engaged for the performance of a given piece of work — digging potatoes, sewing or reaping corn, mining, manufacturing, shop-keeping, etc. — is of decreasing utility and productiveness. Now it is the productiveness of the last workman that will determine the rate of wages for all the workmen engaged in the business. So it is certainly the productiveness of labour that determines the rate of wages, but only the lowest grade of productiveness — the *marginal productiveness* — just as it is the value of the least useful unit of a product that determines the value of the whole, and just as it is the cost of the wheat grown on the least productive soil that determines the price and the rent for all the rest of the soil. Suppose there are ten workmen, engaged successively: the first will produce 10 units, the second 9, the third 8, and so on, down to the tenth, who will produce only 1. Then the wages of this last man, and also of all his fellows, will be 1 unit.

But why, it will undoubtedly be asked, should the workmen who have produced most be reduced to the wages of that one among them who has produced least? Why should not the wages of *all* be equal to the maximum produce, or at any rate to the average produce? — Because in that case the last, or marginal, workman would receive a wage higher than the produce of his labour, and the employer would consequently hasten to dismiss him, because he would cost more than he produced. — Why not suppose, then, that each workman will receive in wages just what he has produced — the first 10, the second 9, and so forth? — This would be fair, but impossible, because all these workmen are by hypothesis equal in capacity and freely interchangeable, and it is an axiom in political economy that in the same market there can only be one price for the same objects. The ten workmen receive the same wages because they are worth as much as each other.

It will be seen that this new theory of productiveness, unlike the first one, takes account of the abundance or scarcity of labour, for it is precisely upon the number of workers employed that the final productiveness depends. It therefore lends itself better to the explanation of facts, and especially of the depressing influence exerted upon the rate of wages by the introduction of new workers, such as women, or foreign or native immigrants: these may be said to act as marginal workers.

In conclusion, it seems that we must give up looking for a simple explanation — that is to say, for a single cause of the rate of wages — just as we had to in the case of the value of products. It is even less possible, indeed, in the case of labour. For the employer, labour is a commodity, and its price will be determined mainly by the economic factors that can be summed up in the popular formula of supply and demand, or in the doctrine of final productiveness which is really only its scientific expression. But for the worker there are other factors that also affect the rate of wages: economic factors, of which the most important is the level of his wants, or his standard of life; and moral factors also, the most important of which is his realization of his social value and of such methods as he may discover of enforcing his rights by trade union or political methods.

V. THE FAIR WAGE

To explain the laws that determine wages, as we have just been doing, is to enquire what wages *are* in actual fact. But there is another question that may be asked: we may enquire what wages *should be*, either from the point of view of justice, or from that of a national economy.

From the economic point of view the theoretical problem of the fair wage may be stated in these terms — almost, we might say, in mathematical terms: given the two factors, manual labour and capital, co-operating in any business, what share of the produce ought each one to receive? Of course in proportion to the share of productiveness of each factor. But by what standard can we establish a common measure for the two? Here is Robinson Crusoe providing a boat and a fishing-net, and Friday providing only his bodily strength. At the end of the day Friday brings along ten baskets of fish: how many should be given to Crusoe, who represents capital, and how many to Friday, who represents labour?

Thus stated, the problem unfortunately seems as insoluble as the one ironically propounded by John Stuart Mill: if both blades of a pair of scissors are used to cut a piece of cloth, which blade has a right to the largest share? — or as this one, reported by the correspondent of a French newspaper from the Congo: the owner of a canoe was disputing about the fare with the paddlers, and asking them what the paddlers could do without the canoe; to which they replied, "What could the canoe do without the paddlers?"[1]

---

[1] A German economist managed to obtain a solution to the problem, however. This was von Thünen, who tried in his book *Natural Wages* (which is really only a portion of his book on *The Isolated State*) to determine the natural rate of wages by mathematical methods. By "natural wages" he meant wages as they ought to be, and so it would have been better to call them reasonable or ideal wages, for nature has nothing to do with these laborious calculations. Through a string of equations he finally reached the simple formula $W = \sqrt{ap}$, which means that the natural or fair wage (W) is the geometric mean between the worker's cost of living (a), and the value of the total produce (p). All that is required is to multiply these two factors and extract the square root of the product. To make the formula clearer

From the moral point of view the question is rather different: what wage will satisfy the just claims of the worker?   Productiveness is no longer the sole cause here: there are many other factors, such as the wants of the workers, their personal dignity, their consciousness of their rights, and so forth.

This question of the *fair wage* has had a long and splendid history, beginning long before there was any science of economics.   It was the subject of ingenious enquiries on the part of all the canonists of the Middle Ages.   For them, a fair wage was the one that gave the worker the exact equivalent of the labour he supplied, but, as their economic knowledge was not sufficiently advanced to enable them to define this "exact equivalent," this notion remained in the air, or, to tell the truth, resolved itself into a tautology.[1]   So their conception of a fair wage resulted in practice in a much simpler definition — the very one that was consecrated by Pope Leo XIII[2] in his famous encyclical on the condition of the working classes, called *Rerum Novarum:* "It is a law of natural justice that wages should not be insufficient to provide subsistence for the sober and honest workman."   But it not easy to see why justice should demand for the worker only what is sufficient for a modest living for a "sober" workman, while no such limitation is suggested for other classes of society, including employers. This definition applies well enough to a minimum wage, but not to a fair wage.

The tendency nowadays is to extend this conception of a fair wage, taking the requirements of a working-class family as the standard, rather than those of an individual worker.   This means that the fair wage would have to be higher for a man with many children than for one with few or none.   From the economic point of view this doctrine is untenable: why not apply the same rule to a fair price, and say that there should be different prices in shops for different customers according to the number of their children?   But from the standpoint of humanity, of social peace, and especially in the interests of the birth-rate,[3] this differentiation of wages according to number of

we can express it in figures: if the worker's cost of maintenance is 2 and the value of his produce is 4.5, then the natural wage will be 3, which is the square root of 9, the product of 2 and 4.5.

[1] The conception of a fair wage was also mixed up by the canonists with that of a fair price, for the very simple reason that the wage-earner, properly speaking, was hardly in existence in their time: the worker was rather a craftsman whose labour was remunerated by the sale of his produce.

[2] [1810–1903.]

[3] [This argument applies particularly to countries, like France, where the falling birth-rate constitutes a serious problem.   The words used by Professor Gide are "the French birth-rate."]

children has much to justify it.   Moreover, the *family wage*, as it is called, is already in existence in France.   Many industrial undertakings and railway and mining companies, etc., have adopted this method.[1]

For the majority of economists, however, the question of a fair wage does not arise, for wages are what they are, and cannot be otherwise. They are fair, just as a price is fair, in so far as they result from the law of supply and demand, on condition, however, that this law has free play.   And if it is wished to make them fairer still, the only thing to be done is to try to remove the causes of pressure or oppression that put obstacles in the way of free competition.

Of course it is not disputed by the members of this school that wages may often be insufficient and that it may be desirable to see them increased.   But, they say, the only way to improve them is to put workman and employer on the same footing as the seller and buyer of any other commodity.   With this object they make various suggestions. They either propose, like M. de Molinari, to set up Labour Exchanges (*Bourses du Travail*) in which the price of manual skill would be quoted as the prices of stocks and shares are quoted on the Stock Exchange; or else, like M. Yves Guyot, they advocate the formation of "commercial labour associations," which would sell the labour of their members on more advantageous terms than it could be sold by individual workers.   But the word "fair" is here used in the sense of "correct," as when we speak of "a correct account"; and this is to confuse what *is* with what *should be*.   Since the law of supply and demand is offered to us as a natural law, it cannot for that very reason create justice or fairness, any more than the law of gravitation can.

For socialists the question of a fair wage does not arise either, any more than for economists, but for an opposite reason.   What the worker ought to receive, according to them, is nothing less than the entire value of the product.   And this demand is logical, if we agree with Karl Marx that all value is only crystallized labour (p. 50). But we have seen that this theory is no longer accepted as an adequate explanation of value, and consequently the simple solution by which wages are equal to the entire value of the product falls to the ground along with it.

[1] The objection to making family wages universal is the risk of unmarried men being preferred to fathers of families when employers are engaging workmen.   To meet this difficulty, Associations (*Caisses de Compensation*) have been formed among the employers, to receive the contributions of the employers collectively and distribute them in the shape of supplementary wages to the workers concerned.

VI. THE VARIOUS KINDS OF WAGES

(1) The simplest kind of wage, and for a long time the only one in use, is the *time* wage — either a daily wage, or, as is common nowadays, an hourly one. The disadvantages of this form of payment are great: it supplies no stimulus to production, it is a premium on laziness, and it is unfair to the good workman. Nevertheless it is the method preferred by the workers' associations because it is absolutely equalitarian and involves no risk of overtasking the workman or driving him to produce too much.

(2) By the *piece-work* or *task-work* method, wages are paid not by time but by the amount of work actually performed. This mode of remuneration greatly stimulates the worker's activity, and it also seems the fairest method, in the economic sense of the word. But it involves a somewhat serious risk to the employer and even to the consumer — the risk of sacrificing quality to quantity, especially in cases where the work cannot be directly supervised.[1]

But workers, and their unions in particular, are generally opposed to piece wages, for many reasons: (a) because the price per piece can always be altered, and the employer does not fail to reduce it when he finds that a good workman can make high wages out of it; and the more he tries to produce the more is the piece price lowered, so that by this means the maximum of labour may be extorted from the worker for the minimum of wages; (b) because piece-work gives the more efficient or more energetic workman a superiority which is repugnant to the equalitarian feelings of his less gifted comrades; (c) because it leads to overproduction, and consequently to a fall of prices and even of wages; (d) because it increases unemployment by encouraging one workman to do the work of two; (e) because it impels a workman to overwork himself through a desire for a higher rate of pay, and leads him to use up his strength and sacrifice the present to the future.

(3) These drawbacks may be mitigated by substituting *collective* piece wages (not to be confused with the collective contract already referred to) for individual piece wages. The employer deals with a group or gang of workmen who undertake to perform a certain piece

[1] The productive inferiority of piece-work is less marked in manufacturing industry, because here the work can be closely watched and its results are under direct control. But in agriculture the method of *task-work* is more dangerous, (a) because in this case supervision is much more difficult than in a factory, and the larger the estate the more difficult it is; (b) because the results of agricultural work cannot generally be estimated till a very long time after, and then only in a very uncertain fashion: if the harvest fails, who can tell whether it is the fault of the sower? (c) because in agriculture good work is far more important than quick work.

of work for a price which they divide among themselves as they please. From the point of view of productiveness, this system gives the same results as piece-work, but it is generally better received by the workers on account of the independence that it gives them. It is, as it were, a little co-operative association formed in the heart of the employer's factory and selling the produce of its labour to the employer.

(4) The *premium* system of wages consists in the payment of a fixed minimum, together with a supplementary sum calculated according to the excess of production above a certain minimum — either according to the saving effected in raw material or coal, or according to the saving of time effected in a given piece of work. But this system lends itself to an infinite variety of arrangements: the premiums may be simple, or progressive, and so forth. Thus in the Taylor system they are combined with a minimum wage that is assured to the workman, so that the premium serves to increase the remuneration of those who exceed this level. This is the method that approaches nearest to the theoretical wage as determined by productiveness.

VII.   PROFIT–SHARING AND COPARTNERSHIP

Profit-sharing is only a form of payment of wages, even according to those who advocate it; but it deserves a section to itself because it may be regarded as a method of changing the wage system into a contract of association between master and man.

The system of rewarding labour by a share in the profits of the enterprise seems to have been practised from times immemorial among fishermen and in agriculture. *Métayage* may be regarded as a form of profit-sharing between landowner and cultivator. But in the realm of industry the first experiment that met with any considerable success was the one made in Paris in 1842 by a house-painter named Leclaire.[1]

[1] The share allotted to the workers may either be paid to them in money or placed to their account in a savings-bank or superannuation fund. This latter plan is the one most commonly employed in France: it has the advantage of ensuring the wise use of the supplementary allowance; but, on the other hand, by postponing the enjoyment of it to a distant date it diminishes to that extent the stimulating effect that is looked for from the method of profit-sharing.

["Profit-sharing has been carried on with a fair measure of success by many other houses in France, particularly since 1870, as well as in Switzerland and in Germany. In England and in the United States the results have not been so good . . . The most noted experiment in profit-sharing in England was that of the Briggs collieries, near Leeds . . . But in 1875, under the stress of hard times, the whole scheme was wrecked." (Hadley, *Economics*, p. 374.)]

Profit-sharing has had its enthusiastic advocates and apostles, who expect many advantages from it, both moral and economic. It is expected to accomplish the following things:

(1) To reconcile labour and capital and raise the standing of the workman by transforming him from a mere instrument of production into a partner;

(2) To increase the productiveness of labour by stimulating the workman's activity and interesting him in the success of the business;

(3) To increase his income by adding to his ordinary weekly wage, which is still devoted to his current expenses, a dividend at the end of the year which he can either save or use to meet extraordinary expenses;

(4) To avert unemployment by establishing permanent ties between the employer and his workmen.

But the method has also many opponents, among economists and employers on the one hand, and among socialists and workers on the other.

The economists, while admitting that it has some merits, agree with M. Leroy-Beaulieu in regarding it at the best as merely a "condiment" to the wage system, and refusing to find in it a transformation of that system. They raise against it, as a general solution of the problem, the grave objection that the workers cannot, strictly speaking, claim their share of the profits as a right, since these profits are in no wise their concern but exclusively their employer's. In fact, they say, profits are not the result of the technical and material manufacturing process, but of a sale made at the right moment and in the right place. This is entirely a commercial art, and one to which the workers are complete strangers. This is proved by the fact that there are businesses to be seen everywhere of which some make large profits and others losses, though they employ an absolutely identical staff of workmen — in mines, railways, and so forth.

If this objection means that all the value produced by a business is solely due to the work of management and the special art of getting customers, then the assertion certainly seems very much exaggerated: the quality of the manual skill employed must count for something. If it is meant that profits are due as a rule to circumstances independent of the workman's labour, we shall not contradict it, but we would observe that it is a dangerous assertion to make, because it may just as easily lead to a refusal of any share in the profits — to the employer! But since no one denies him the right to benefit by good fortune in the shape of profits or dividends, then why should not the workers themselves have the right to profit by these same lucky chances, which could not be exploited without their assistance? Remember that this is regarded as quite natural in the case of mere shareholders, although profits are certainly even less their concern than the workers'.

The employers raise two objections: one is a matter of principle — that a system of sharing profits without a corresponding sharing of losses is unfair; the other is of the practical order — that they do not like being compelled to make known to their workers, and thereby to the public, the amount of their profits, and still less the absence of any profit.

But this last objection does not apply in the case of joint-stock companies, for their balance sheets have to be published.

The first objection is more apparent than real, for profit-sharing applies only to *net* profits. Now net profits are obviously calculated after losses have been deducted, or, to put it more accurately, after the deduction of the annual payments to a reserve fund to cover possible losses. Do the shareholders share the losses — otherwise than by the reduction or suspension of their dividends? Yes, it will be said: they are liable to suffer loss up to the amount of their shares. — Well, the workers are also liable to suffer loss in the shape of losing the employment by which they earn their living.

As regards socialists, their dislike to profit-sharing is very logical: if profit is a theft committed by employers against workmen, then a proposed reform to legalize it by making the robbed themselves share in the proceeds of the robbery seems the height of impertinence.

The workers themselves are afraid that the method will be employed as a bait, with the sole object of making them produce by extra work a greater value than they will receive in their increased income; or else that it is meant to detach them from their unions and cheat them of the right to strike. They regard it also as having the somewhat humiliating character of an act of generosity — a sort of gratuity or tip.

The reason why profit-sharing does not make progress is chiefly that it suffers under the disfavour that attaches nowadays to every kind of patronage, and even to everything that has a tendency to tighten the bond between employer and workman: what they both demand is to be as *independent* of each other as possible.[1]

Another reason is that the shares distributed to the workers have generally been very small, representing on an average only 5% or 6% of their wages, which is less than they could obtain by a successful

[1] [For the objections of the English trade unions to profit-sharing, see **Webb**, *Industrial Democracy* (1902) pp. 551-2.]

strike.   But this moderate result is not to be wondered at, for we are prone to overestimate the real amount of profits.   As the profits of any business are accumulated in the hands of one man, whereas wages are dispersed among hundreds or thousands, one gets a false idea of their respective importance.   But if all employers were abolished and their profits divided among all the workers, the latter would be very disagreeably surprised to find in how small a degree each one's share was increased by this expropriation.

However, this institution has not said its last word.   To begin with, there are some important branches of production in which profit-sharing has not yet been seriously tried, although they are the ones in which it seems as if it should give the best results, and the ones, too, in which the system first started: we refer to agriculture and sea fishing.

It is possible, moreover, that it may be made compulsory in a certain number of businesses — those that are managed by the State or the municipalities, such as mines, railways, trams, lighting, etc.

Profit-sharing can scarcely be regarded as a real transformation of the wage system, because it does not change the actual character of that system: it has the semblance and not the reality of a form of association.   But might we not go a step further and turn the wage contract into a real contract of partnership, so that it should involve a sharing not only in profits but also in management and responsibility, including losses?   Yes, if the workman had shares in the business in which he is engaged.   In this case he would share in the management and in the losses to the same extent as any other shareholder. This is what is called *copartnership.*

The practical difficulty, as may well be imagined, lies in providing the worker with the means of acquiring shares.   Profit-sharing is the simplest way, for all that is needed is to convert the portions of profit into portions of shares in the business; but the same end can be attained without the aid of profit-sharing, as, for instance, by facilitating the acquisition of shares by small payments that the workman can make out of his savings.

In France a law was passed in 1917 to give legal form to this system by the creation of a new form of joint-stock company with power to issue *labour shares* as well as ordinary shares.   These will be allotted free to workers employed in the business, and will confer the same rights as ordinary shares in the matter of dividends and attendance at shareholders' meetings.   But instead of being the individual property of the workers, they will be allotted to the whole of the workers in the factory, organized as a co-operative society, and this society will do as it pleases with the dividends it receives.

It would be good to see this system become general, but it must be admitted that it has been somewhat coldly received by employers, as might have been expected. They are not likely to show much eagerness to use this power of granting freely to their workmen a share of their capital and diminishing to that extent the profits of the business. And what they will like still less is the prospect of seeing their workers exercising their right of control in the management of the company in their capacity of shareholders.

On the other hand, contrary to expectation, the law has not received any warmer welcome from the workers. It is harder than it was imagined to persuade the workman to become a shareholder in the business in which he works. He has for the most part shown very little eagerness to make use of the power that has been conceded to him, so much so that it has often been necessary to change this permission into an obligation. But this plan gives rise to some doubt as to the moral and social efficacy of a system that creates partnership by force.

VIII. TRADE UNIONS

In ordinary circumstances the workman who deals *individually* with the employer is placed in a position of necessary inferiority: he cannot stand out for, or even discuss, his wage — he must take it or leave it. And if he is starving he gives in. The reasons for this are as follows:

(1) Because the capitalist can wait, while the worker cannot. The latter is in the position of a merchant who finds it imperatively necessary to sell his merchandise: the merchandise in this case being labour.

(2) Because the *entrepreneur* can easily do without the workman when the latter is by himself, whereas the workman cannot do without the employer. The master can always find another man: if necessary he can import one from abroad, or even replace him by a machine. But the workman cannot so easily find another master: he cannot import one by railway or by sea, nor has anyone discovered the secret of replacing him by a machine.

(3) Because the *entrepreneur* is better acquainted with the state of the market. He sees farther, and, above all, it is quite easy for him to act in concert with his fellow employers, or at any rate to know what they are doing.

But the whole situation is changed as soon as the workman can form an association with his comrades in the same trade, for then the two parties are on an equal footing up to a certain point:

(1) Because association gives the workman the means of refusing his labour and supporting himself meanwhile by the help of the subscriptions of his fellow members. If the resources of the society are sufficient, they form an unemployment fund to prevent the capitulation to hunger that we have just mentioned.

(2) Because it binds together all the workers in a given industry, so that the employer has to deal with them all instead of with individuals.

A *collective wage contract* takes the place of an individual one, which is a contract only in appearance.

(3) Because it provides the workers with an information bureau, and with competent and experienced leaders who are capable of judging the state of affairs as well as the employers themselves, and who prevent the workers from taking unwise steps.

So when economists declare that it is not in the power of workmen's associations to fix the rate of wages, we must reply that they do not claim to do this, but that they merely wish to obtain such a wage as the general state of the market permits, instead of one that is forced upon them by accidental disturbing circumstances, such as the fact of having had no dinner, or having a large family to bring up.

It is only recently, however, that the workers have won this right to combine and form associations. Of course, professional associations of workers date from a long way back — not from the medieval guilds, which were generally composed of masters and whose successors must rather be looked for in the employers' associations of to-day, but from the journeymen's associations, and, even further back than the Middle Ages, the workmen's associations in Rome and other ancient societies. But this venerable institution was abolished, at least in France, by the Revolution, suffering the same fate as the masters' guilds as a remnant of the old régime. It was not till a century later that the famous law of the 21st March, 1884, for which Waldeck-Rousseau was responsible, restored to workmen and employers alike the right of forming associations.

[In England, as we have seen, trade unions obtained legal recognition in 1871. The rise of Marxian socialism in the next few years had less influence here than on the continent, and the "syndicalism" of the French has also met with little favour, though the modern movement called *guild socialism* is somewhat similar in its aims.

English trade unionism has been on the whole less political and more purely economic in its functions and ideals than the correspond-

ing movements on the continent.   Its main objects may be summarized as follows:

(1) To substitute collective for individual bargaining in the settlement of th⌐ wage contract;

(2) To insist on the payment of a standard (minimum) rate of
wages and the adoption of a uniform (maximum) working day;

(3) To encourage the employment of conciliation and arbitration
(see below, section x) in the settlement of disputes;

(4) To demand "safe, healthy, and comfortable conditions of
work";

(5) To provide mutual insurance against sickness, accident, old
age, unemployment, and so forth;

(6) To promote legislation for the attainment of trade union ends.][1]

IX. STRIKES

A *strike* — that is to say, a refusal to work — is generally regarded
as the sole object and essential function of a trade union;[2] but this is
a grave mistake.   A well-organized union can win victories without
promoting strikes, just as a general can be victorious without fighting
battles; and it is even the case that the best organized and most powerful unions are the ones that declare the fewest strikes.[3]   None the
less, the strike is certainly the *ultima ratio*, though only after all other
methods have failed.   What, indeed, is a strike?   It is not simply the
act of refusing to work, for that has never been a punishable offence.
Nor is it the act of abandoning work that has been begun, for the
cancelling of a labour contract, like that of any other contract with
no definite time limit, is quite legal.   It is a *means of constraint* exercised by the wage-earners on the employer, to force him to alter
certain conditions of work, as, for instance, to raise the agreed rate
of wages or to reduce the hours of labour.   It is not the only means
of constraint: there may be others, such as *sabotage* — but here the
coercion consists in the sudden interruption of labour and the injury

---

[1] [The latter part of this section has been substituted for the author's account of
the French trade unions.   For further information see Sidney and Beatrice Webb's
Industrial Democracy (Longmans), or George Howell's *Trade Unionism, New and Old*
(Methuen).]

[2] [This is scarcely true, perhaps, of English opinion at the present day.]

[3] ["It is a matter of simple history that strikes have been far more numerous in
industries which have practised Collective Bargaining without Trade Unionism,
than in those in which durable combinations have existed."   (Webb, *Industrial
Democracy*, 1902 edn., p. 220, where the authors also refer to "the ignorant assumption
that there is some necessary connection between strikes and Trade Unions.")]

that results to the employer. Moreover, this method is only effective in so far as it is employed collectively by a large number of workers — all those in the factory, without exception — and even, if possible, by all workers in the same industry, so that the masters cannot assist each other, or even — and in this case it attains its maximum effectiveness — by all workers in all industries — what is called a general strike. The characteristic of a strike, therefore, is *combination:* in fact that is its legal name.

The strike, then, should be regarded as a form of warfare, since its object is to obtain by force what cannot be obtained by good will. Strike tactics, also, tend more and more to be modelled on those of warfare — for instance, the opening of hostilities without a previous declaration of war, so as to take the enemy unawares; the organization of a staff supplied by the union or federation: the setting up of a headquarters with a commissariat service of "soup kitchens" to feed the strikers and their families; the evacuation of the children into other towns from motives of economy; the posting of sentinels and pickets at the factory gates to prevent non-strikers from entering, or even at the railway stations to prevent them from arriving; and finally, too often, an armed struggle, either against blacklegs, who are compared to traitors who go over to the enemy in time of war, or else against the troops sent to protect the non-strikers. Sometimes there is even the burning down of factories, the blocking of railways, or the plunging of towns into darkness, according to the nature of the strike — in which things it is easy to recognize all the aspects of warfare. Moreover, this is precisely what the syndicalist understands by a strike: he regards it as the typical form of class warfare. Finally, the strike is used nowadays not only in conflicts between employers and workmen but also in political contests: thus on several occasions already in Sweden and Belgium the working classes have decreed a general strike in order to obtain universal suffrage.

It is not to be wondered at, therefore, that striking — or more usually any form of combination — has everywhere been specially made a punishable offence until quite recently. In France, however, the right to strike was recognized before the right of association, for the law abolishing penalties for striking was passed in 1864, whereas the right of association was not recognized until 1884. No one to-day disputes the legitimacy of strikes, and we must do the economists of the liberal school the justice of acknowledging that they were the first to declare it, long before it was legally recognized. The reason is this: that even if the strike is regarded as an attack on social solidarity, the working class must certainly be allowed the right to defend its interests by its own strength, in the absence of any tribunals that can settle conflicts between capital and labour, just as in cases of international conflicts, in the absence of a supreme court to settle them, the nations must be allowed the right of making war in defence of their independence or their honour. Moreover, it would be the more unjust to refuse the right of combination to the workers, as it is impossible to refuse it to the employers: in fact, any law that punishes the crime of combination really only punishes the workers. For if the law can effectively prevent the workers from taking the necessary measures for organizing a strike — such as meetings and demonstrations of various kinds — it is altogether powerless to prevent a few employers from meeting in a private house and arranging to reduce wages.[1] Adam Smith himself observed that there is always a tacit combination among employers, and the fewer they are the easier it is to form it. If there is no counterbalancing agreement among the workers, they are bound to be oppressed.

There are certain cases, however, in which a strike seems to involve so much danger to public security that the question arises whether it should not still be regarded, exceptionally, as a crime and be punished accordingly. This danger arises not only in the case of public functions in the sense of State services, but in that of all "public services" in the wider sense of the term — services whose interruption is far more prejudicial to public safety than that of such and such a class of administrative officials: for instance, water supply, or town lighting, or the railways, even when the latter are in the hands of private companies. A stoppage of the railway service is no less serious than a post office strike, for the post office cannot carry on without the railways.[2]

It is a question still very much debated whether strikes can have any effective influence in the direction of raising wages. Economists of the liberal school are not disposed to admit it, for they believe that

---

[1] The *lock-out*, which was often employed in England, was introduced into France only recently and in a somewhat timid fashion — in 1906 in the Fougères boot-making trade. Its particular object is to meet that particular manœuvre which consists in declaring a strike first in one factory, and then, when that has capitulated, in another, and so forth, the strikers being in turn supported by their comrades who remain at work. The lock-out defeats these tactics by cutting off the wages of all the workers in the affected industry in the same district at a single blow.

[2] In many countries there are laws against strikes in public services — in Holland, Italy, and Russia in the case of railways, and in England in the case of water and lighting and any strike that may affect life or property. In France there have been many projects of the same kind, but they have always been checked by the protests of the trade unions.

the rate of wages, like the price of goods, is determined by natural laws that govern all the haggling and disputes of the parties concerned. Yet we think it cannot be disputed that this violent method has helped to raise the rate of wages, and especially to reduce the length of the working day; for in this case the action of what are called natural laws would be quite unintelligible. The effectiveness of strikes must not be judged solely by the number that have succeeded or failed, as given in statistics. A single successful strike may raise wages in a multitude of trades. Moreover, it is the ever threatening fear of a strike that makes wages rise, rather than a strike itself.

Those who deny the efficacy of strikes in raising wages call attention to the fact that the rise has been equal, if not greater, for wage-earners who have never struck and who may even be without any organized union: for agricultural workers and domestic servants, for example. Why is this? Because these workers have benefited indirectly by the rise of wages in other industries where the workers are organized. If wages have risen in the country districts it is because the workers there have left the country to seek higher wages in the towns. Similarly, the wages of domestic servants follow the rate of industrial wages. So it is ultimately the organized trades that regulate the labour market, whereas hitherto, on the contrary, it has been the crowd of poverty-stricken wretches that has weighed the market down. And that means immense progress, both economic and moral.

It is also said that the workers lose more than they gain by a strike, even when the strike is successful. What is meant by this is that the wages they lose in consequence of unemployment, the little economies they are obliged to make in order to live, or the debts they incur to their tradespeople, more than outweigh the increase of wages that they may obtain. But it has been proved mathematically by calculations made by the Labour Ministries of France and Italy that this argument is incorrect, and that the increases of wages obtained by the strikers, even supposing they only lasted for a year — certainly a very unfavourable supposition for the workers, for the increases once made are generally permanent — leave a fairly considerable profit, even after deducting the wages they have lost.[1]

It may be said, it is true, that there is nothing to prove that the workers might not gain as much or more, and without any loss, by amicable negotiations; and the example of England might be cited, where the majority of wage increases — nine-tenths of them — are

[1] See Gide's *Institutions de Progrès Social.*

obtained by friendly negotiations between workers and employers. But those who use this argument forget that the reason these negotiations are successful is generally that English workmen are powerfully organized and that their strikes are formidable affairs!

The wretched wages of women workers appear to be due, at any rate in part, to the fact that they have never struck, and that it is known that they will not do so.

Another difficult question is that of ascertaining what influence strikes may have upon the prices of products, and consequently how they react upon consumers. There is a wide-spread opinion that this influence is a real one, and a large part of the rise in prices before the war was even attributed to it. But this is by no means proved. No doubt a certain amount of correlation can often be observed between strike movements and price movements, but it is quite possible that in such cases, contrary to the general opinion, it is the second that causes the first. A rise in prices, in fact, acts as a promoter of strikes in two ways at once: by raising the cost of living and by increasing profits; the result of which is that the workers are more eager to demand an increase of wages and have more chance of obtaining it. It cannot be denied that there are some industries in which a rise of wages in consequence of a strike does involve a rise of prices — notably in house-building during the last few years, because that is a case of monopoly. But there is no reason to think that strikes can cause a *general rise of prices*. In fact, no cause except an alteration in the value of money can have a general influence upon prices (p. 217).

Yet, it may be said, whenever a strike ends in a rise of wages, which very frequently happens, must not the increase be taken from somewhere? Certainly not; it may be made up for by a diminution of profits or by a reduction of the cost of production: nothing has done more than strikes to promote the progress of machinery.

X. CONCILIATION AND ARBITRATION

Since international conflicts, which used to produce incessant warfare, are tending nowadays to be settled by conciliation and arbitration, as has already happened in many cases, why should not an attempt be made to apply the same method to conflicts between capital and labour, instead of settling them by the clumsy weapon of the strike — the appeal to the law of force? In every land, indeed, that attempt is being made.

Conciliation and *arbitration* must be carefully distinguished from each other: these two institutions, though working often through the same organs, nevertheless differ from each other in certain essential features:

(a) They differ in regard to the time at which they operate. Conciliation acts before the conflict breaks out, in order to prevent it. Arbitration generally only intervenes after it has lasted some time, in order to settle it.

(b) They differ in procedure. In conciliation the two parties meet to talk things over and try to convince each other. In arbitration there is always a third party taken from outside: he is the arbitrator, whom each party tries to convince, like advocates before a judge.

(c) They differ above all in their results. In conciliation the two parties pledge themselves to nothing: if they do not succeed in convincing each other they withdraw without result. In arbitration a solution is necessarily reached and is necessarily accepted in advance by both parties — so much so that it is the rule, at any rate where the workers understand the meaning of the method, for the strikers to resume work immediately arbitration is agreed to, without waiting for the decision.

From these differences it results that arbitration is a far more serious matter than conciliation, and one that is far less readily accepted by the disputants, for it means putting themselves entirely into the hands of a third party. But for the same reason it is also far more effective. One is naturally led to ask, therefore, whether it could not be made compulsory upon employers and workers.

Compulsory arbitration courts have been established in several countries;[1] but between the office of a judge in civil cases and that of a judge in conflicts between capital and labour there will always be this important difference: that the former must judge according to a written law, or at any rate according to principles of law that are generally admitted, whereas in economic conflicts the judge has no criterion. Here is a workman demanding a wage of 5s., and an employer declaring that he cannot pay more than 4s. What is —

---

[1] Such a court exists in New Zealand. It is a real tribunal, from whose jurisdiction no one can be withdrawn. It was instituted by a law of the 21st December, 1894, and the example was followed in turn by the various Australian States. For a long time it yielded good results, and was expected to bring about the reign of social peace. But it is beginning now to provoke keen hostility not only from employers, who find an official rate of wages imposed upon them by the court, but from the workers themselves, who object to being deprived of the right to strike and have several times already refused to obey the arbitrator's ruling.

I will not say the written law — but what is even the economic or moral law on which the arbitrator is to base his verdict? A fair wage? But what is that? We have seen already (see above, p. 431) what difficulties such a problem presents. Should the workman's needs be taken as the standard? Or the *entrepreneur's* profits? Or simply custom? For centuries economists have struggled in vain over these problems. Then what is the arbitrator to do? He will split the difference, as we say. And that is why arbitration is generally demanded more insistently by the party which has less right on its side, for it has everything to gain and nothing to lose. Arbitration almost always benefits the worse side: if both parties accept it, then it is a good method; but not if it is compulsory.[1]

In default of compulsory arbitration it has been suggested that the first step towards conciliation might at least be made obligatory — that is to say, the appearance of the parties before an elected council, — and that an enquiry also might be enforced. The parties would remain free not to agree, but the mere fact of their coming face to face, and the publicity of the enquiry, might be productive of good results.

But the establishment of conciliation boards will not suffice to avert conflicts. There must be permanent organs for bringing employers and workmen together and enabling the latter to exercise that share of control over the industry which they value more highly even than a rise of wages, and which they will demand more peremptorily than ever in these post-war days. That is what has been attempted in France by the institution of labour councils, though they have not managed to acquire a sufficiently definite sphere of action. And that is what the English have undertaken, in establishing permanent *industrial councils* (of two grades, regional and national), composed of delegates elected in equal numbers by the employers and the workers, and assisted by a representative of the State with purely consultative functions. They would constitute a sort of parliamentary government in industry. Yet the Whitley

---

[1] Arbitration and conciliation were established in France by a law of the 27th December, 1893, but only as a permissive measure, and in a somewhat cautious form. The duty of inviting the parties to come to an agreement falls upon the local magistrate (*juge de paix*). He can only intervene officially if a strike has been declared, except on the demand of one of the parties. If both parties consent, they appoint delegates to discuss the matter before the magistrate. If the discussion fails, the magistrate suggests appointing an arbitrator (never himself, in any case: he would be technically incompetent). This proposal the parties are free to accept or refuse. But this law has given only moderately good results — in fact it would be no exaggeration to say that it has failed.

Councils, as they are named from the originator of the law, have not yielded the results that were expected. The most ingenious mechanism will not produce social peace if it is not inspired by a new spirit — by a feeling of solidarity of interest between the opposing groups.

XI. LEGISLATIVE PROTECTION OF WAGE–EARNERS

The regulation of labour constitutes the proper function of what is called *labour legislation*. During the last fifty years or so, legislative intervention, with the object of protecting the wage-earners, has increased enormously in every country.[1] The principal methods adopted are as follows.

1. *Limitation of the hours of labour*

The shortening of the working day is one of the reforms to which most importance is attached nowadays, and before the war it was celebrated by a great international demonstration every First of May. It is regarded by socialists as a means of freeing the worker from exploitation at the hands of his employer, and enabling him to prepare for the social and political struggle. The workers regard it as a method of working less without any reduction of their wages, but, on the contrary, with a chance of a rise owing to the scarcity of labour caused by the reduction of the number of hours worked. But it should be looked upon particularly as a means of raising the intellectual, moral, and even physical level of the workman, by allowing him the requisite leisure for *recreation*, in the full sense of the word — that is to say, for ceasing to be a producing machine and becoming a man for a certain number of hours a day. A man's working life is not everything: family life, civic life, and intellectual life have claims upon his time as well. A long working day, even if it be only ten hours, means starting work too early. If the workman lives far away from the factory, as he very often does, and as it is very desirable that he should do, he has to get up before daybreak and leave his house without having time for breakfast. Still less does a woman worker get time for her household duties. Such a system is very unhygienic and very conducive to drink. The same thing applies to the return home in the evening. One reason for the failure of the movement for popular universities was certainly the

---

[1] It is well known that the Treaty of Versailles established an International Labour Office, alongside of the League of Nations, and having its headquarters also at Geneva. Its function is to control and extend labour legislation everywhere.

excessive length of the working day, which made the workers too late and too tired to listen.[1]

The question must be considered separately, according as we are concerned with *children, women,* or *men.*

(*a*) As regards children, all civilized countries, with a few rare and shameful exceptions, are in agreement nowadays in prohibiting child labour in factories. The age-limit alone varies. In England it is 12[2]. In France it is 13, because that is the age at which compulsory education ends and the child must have obtained his certificate.

It is very desirable that the legal age for labour — the industrial majority, as it is called — should be raised to 14, as it is in Switzerland and Austria, because 13 is too early not only to begin industrial work but to finish primary education. Unfortunately, on the other hand, the deplorable condition of the birth-rate in France would make it highly dangerous to adopt a reform that would increase the expenses of parents by prolonging the period during which the child remains dependent upon them. Between these two equally serious national perils — the risk of seeing the present generation degenerate, and the risk of losing the generations to come — a compromise might be tried: between the ages of 13 and 16, or even 18, there might be a period of apprenticeship in which *paid* factory labour and vocational instruction might go on simultaneously, a certain number of hours per week being compulsorily reserved for this instruction.

(*b*) As regards women the question is more difficult. There are some "whole-hoggers" who would like them to be excluded from the factories, like the children. Nor are they without good arguments for this course — the destruction of the family home, the terrible mortality among neglected infants, the perils to the morality and health of girls and women engaged in factories, and in the case of expectant mothers the risk even of miscarriage and still births. But on the other hand it must be said that at a time when the emancipation of women and the equality of the sexes is talked of more than ever, it would be monstrous indeed to inflict upon all women a sort of incapacity for earning their living by labour: it is hard enough already for them to obtain a living honestly, without having the

---

[1] One great improvement would be the introduction of "the English day" — the abolition of the midday meal, involving a break of nearly two hours. This would enable the workman to start for the factory two hours later or else to leave it two hours earlier. Except in this way, the utilization of leisure time, which is the principal advantage of the short working day, is scarcely possible.

[2] [This is no longer the case; the age was raised to 14 by the Education Act of 1918, and may even be 15 if the Local Education Authority so decrees.]

factory gates closed against them. And if the law were unwise enough to confine this disability to married women or mothers, leaving the others free to work, it would be worse still, for it is certain that such a plan would deal a fatal blow at marriage and motherhood — which would be more dangerous in France than anywhere else.

But if the right of women to work is admitted, there remain the various measures that were instituted before the war for the protection of female labour. The chief of these is the prohibition of work during a period of some weeks before and after confinement. Factory labour in the case of expectant mothers frequently causes miscarriage, and even a full-time child is often born rickety. Moreover, during the infancy of the children the mother's work in the factory necessarily involves artificial feeding, and consequently an extraordinary infant mortality among the working population — as many as 30% of the infants die in the first year after birth in certain working class districts, as against 11% for the whole of France. As regards the woman herself, the resumption of work immediately after confinement may cause serious disorders. Yet the law would do more harm than good, and the woman herself would try to evade it, if it were to involve the loss of her wages during this period, at the very time when the mother has most need of good feeding. The obligation to pay these wages cannot be imposed upon the employer, for in that case married women would be in danger of not finding work. There remains only one solution, therefore: this is to make the State responsible for the woman's wages during this critical period.[1]

(c) For adult men the principle of legal compulsory limitation has had far more trouble in overcoming the arguments of the liberal school. What is the good, it was said, of making the law intervene in the case of grown men who are the best judges of their own interests and of the use of their time, and who, moreover, when they are organized in unions, are possessed of sufficient means to get the working day shortened? The proof of this is that in countries where the working day is shortest — England, the United States, and Australia — there is no general law imposing a limit. — This is true; but not all countries have reached this degree of organization, and this very organization into unions cannot be accomplished unless the working classes have sufficient leisure at their disposal. So instead of saying that the trade union organization makes legal limitation unnecessary, it would be more true to say that legal limitation of labour is often the indispensable preliminary condition of that organization.

[1] [We omit a foot-note relating to maternity benefit societies in France.]

As for the argument about free choice, it is enough to reply that, given the system of large-scale industry, such freedom does not exist. The workman must enter and leave the factory when the bell rings; whatever his personal wishes, he is obliged to put in the number of hours of labour that is fixed not only by the rules of the factory but by custom or competition no less tyrannical than law. Hence the question of freedom is put out of court, and we have merely to consider whether the shortening of the working day is conducive to the welfare of the working classes, and even indispensable to the progress of the nation. Now the experience of countries where it is already practised seems decisive on this point.

After the objection on the ground of principle comes the practical one — that this shortening will necessarily result in diminished production and lower wages. To this it may be replied that workers will be able to produce more if they are less driven and have more leisure for their intellectual, moral, and physical development. And if they produce more there is no reason why their wages should diminish.

At the same time we must not push this doctrine to an absurd extreme and claim, as the syndicalists are too much inclined to do, that the less a man works the more he will produce! We must be careful, above all, not to make use of contradictory arguments, as they frequently do — asserting on the one hand that short working days will make labour more productive, and on the other that they will give more work to everybody and eliminate unemployment. For it is quite obvious that if the workers, though working less, produce as much, there will be no need to employ a larger number of them. A choice must be made between these two arguments.

In practice we see that the countries where the shortest days are worked — Australia, the United States, and England — are at the same time the countries where wages are highest and production greatest. Only, if the shortening of the hours of labour is to give these excellent results, there are certain necessary conditions that are not fulfilled everywhere:[1] (a) To begin with, the workers must agree to *intensify* their labour so as to make up for the shortening of time. Now workers do not wish to do this — in France, for instance — for they maintain that if they do they will get just as tired and the employer will gain by it. They want the reduction in the hours of labour to compel him to engage more workmen, which they believe will do away with unemployment and make wages rise.

---

[1] See a remarkable article that is still apposite though already old, by **Professor** Brentano, in the *Revue d'Économie Politique* for April 1893, on *Les rapports entre le salaire, la durée du travail et sa productivité.*

(b) Even if the workers are willing to put in more work in less time, they must also be capable of doing so, for this intensification presupposes an amount of endurance and energy with which not every race is gifted. Thus the French workman does not seem able to run as many looms at once as the American workman. (c) Finally, the equipment and plant must be improved sufficiently to allow of this intensification of labour, and even to enforce it: the machinery must be able not only to follow the workman, but to outstrip him. Now that is the employer's business: the workman can do nothing in regard to it.

In this matter the example was set by France, more than half a century ago, when the law of 1848 fixed the limit at 12 hours; but in practice this law was in advance of economic evolution and remained for a long time a dead letter. However, in large factories the working day before the war was reduced to 9 or 10 hours.

It is well known that the workers used to demand the "three eights" — eight hours' work, eight hours' leisure, and eight hours' sleep. The old English rhyme included also a fourth "eight":

> "Eight hours to work, eight hours to play,
> Eight hours to sleep, eight shillings a day."

And it is well known that great demonstrations were tumultuously organized every First of May in every country to demand this reform. But it seemed altogether premature. And there was every reason to believe that the result of the war would be to postpone it for a long time; for the working day was extended without limit during the war in-the interests of national defence, and after the war the needs of national reconstruction, it was thought, would be no less urgent. But, contrary to these anticipations, the war has resulted in France in the establishment (by a law of April 1919) of an eight-hour day — and that with such suddenness as to upset the whole national economy, and especially the exploitation of railways. But the claims of the workers became so threatening after the end of the war that the government could no longer postpone the reform.

However, the same measure has been general throughout Europe, under the same pressure. Between the signing of the armistice in November 1918, and the end of 1919 — in one year alone — thirteen European countries, including all the new republics, established an eight-hour day; and others are preparing to do the same.

Indeed, eight hours is even coming to be regarded as a maximum that will soon have to be reduced to seven, or even six. Unfortunately it does not seem, at any rate at present, as if this shortening of the working day had been made up for by an increased production per hour. The workers have not even admitted the necessity for such compensation. They throw the responsibility for diminished output upon defective organization and inadequate plant.

2. *A guaranteed legal minimum wage*

This is a measure insistently demanded not only by socialists but even by many of the catholic social party.

It might indeed be said that it is no more outrageous to fix a minimum rate of wages than a maximum rate of interest. But the danger of a minimum wage is that if it is fixed too low it may bring the average wage down to its level, and if it is fixed too high it will make employers engage only workmen whose labour is worth more than this minimum and refuse all the rest. The result would be that all inefficient workers, whether they are novices, or old, or disabled, or unskilful, who earn their living to-day none the less by receiving a moderate wage for moderate work, would find employment no longer and would come upon the rates. So true is this that the Australian legislatures have had to authorize the payment of wages below the legal rate, for "half-workers." Nevertheless, it may be said in answer to this objection that a social system under which the efficient receive good wages and the inefficient are merely assisted, would perhaps be an improvement on the present system, under which the competition of the bad workmen too often brings down to their level the wages of the good ones.

Notwithstanding these difficulties, several countries, such as Australia and England, have taken a step in this direction. It is not a case, however, of a general minimum wage established by legislation, but of the fixing of wages in certain industries — those that are specially addicted to the sweating system[1] — by the interested parties themselves; to this fixed rate legislation simply gives legal sanction. It is rather a kind of compulsory collective contract.

In France a minimum wage has been established by law for women engaged in home industry in the clothing trades. The practical difficulty lies in enforcing the law, for the women workers generally prefer not to lodge complaints, in the fear of being deprived of work by the employers whom they denounce. So to avoid this difficulty there have been established benevolent leagues for female protection,

---

[1] This is the system by which work is done at home, on the piece-work plan, for an employer who is usually only a subcontractor, and who distributes the work and makes his profit by cutting down the price.

to look after the enforcement of the law by lodging complaints directly.

3. *Substitution of collective agreements for individual labour contracts*

This reform is the great question of the day, and has already been formulated in legislative proposals in several countries — France, Italy, etc. It has long been remarked that the abuses of labour contracts are due especially to the extreme inequality of the contracting parties:[1] the workman offers a commodity which cannot wait, for it is nothing but his very person, and he must at the same time work to eat and eat to work, whereas the employer loses nothing by waiting except his profit and the interest on his capital — a very small matter — which lies idle while the workman is absent. But the situation changes completely if all the workmen are drawn up in a solid mass before the capitalist who employs them, and if, moreover, they are supported by funds that enable them to wait and to bargain also. In this case the operation of the law of supply and demand is not perverted: on the contrary it acts under the same conditions as in all other contracts. That is what is called the collective labour contract. Hitherto it has arisen only in the form of peace treaties on the conclusion of strikes. But why should it not become the normal method of establishing wage contracts, instead of being an accidental affair resulting from a conflict?

The difficulty is that every contract involves an exchange of wishes, and therefore the existence of real persons. But how is a group of workers to be given a legal personality and legal representatives? Who is to sign the agreement? And who will be pledged by the signatures affixed? To-morrow, perhaps, or soon after, these particular workers will be replaced by different ones: they will be no longer the same. Are we to say that they are represented collectively by their trade union? Yes: that is the very solution that is adopted. But the unions comprise only a small fraction of the working population. It may be that none of the workers in the factory where this collective agreement is to be negotiated is a member of one. Will not the employer then have the right to make the stereotyped reply: "I am willing to treat with my own workmen, but not with strangers"? And even if this difficulty can be surmounted, will the union itself offer more guarantees? What will be its liability in case of non-performance of the contract? Will it pay damages? And if so how, if it has no funds?

---

[1] Twenty-three centuries ago Thucydides said: "There can be no justice among men unless they treat with each other on an equal footing." (Book V, Chap. 89.)

What makes employers object so much to the collective agreement is their feeling that in this new kind of contract they will themselves be morally and financially pledged, but that the workers will not. It must be admitted that though experiments in the method of collective agreement have so far yielded good results in England and even in Germany, it has not been the same in France. The contracts have very often been broken, the two parties throwing the responsibility for the breach upon each other. The method can scarcely be efficacious except where the working classes are almost completely organized and have acquired a sense of responsibility, or where the leaders at any rate have sufficient authority to sign on behalf of all and to make the workers keep the engagements entered into in their name.

Strictly speaking, the collective agreement — which is a better term than "contract" — is not a true labour contract, for it does not compel Peter to work for Paul, nor fix the price that Paul must pay Peter. All it does is to lay down certain general rules to which employers and workers will have to conform in future, such as the scale of wages, the maximum number of working hours, the obligation to employ only unionists, and so forth; and since these conditions cannot be fixed for a future of unlimited duration, a term of three or four years is generally adopted. It is like a frame in which must be placed all the individual contracts connected with the same firm, or even with all firms in the same industry or district. Thus the collective agreement may grow into a kind of local legislative enactment, except that instead of being voted by parliament, this law would be made by the common consent of the workers' and employers' unions. This would be a step towards the system described as *compulsory trade unionism* — meaning not exactly that all workers would be obliged to join the union, but that they would be bound to conform to its decisions.

Such agreements are obviously opposed to individualism, owing to the solidarity that is their distinguishing feature: they tend to stereotype wages without respect of persons.[1] But the sacrifice thus made by the pick of the workers to the majority is not without moral value.

[1] Economists of the liberal school, too, have sometimes expressed themselves strongly on the subject. M. d'Eichthal wrote in the *Journal des Économistes* (1907): "The collective agreement tends to make mediocrity the rule and the limit for everyone."

XII. SECURITY AGAINST RISKS

For the workman to receive an adequate wage and not to be sub-jected to too oppressive labour is not everything. There is yet a third condition without which his life is full of anxiety. This is *security*. The man who has to live from day to day must have security against the risks that threaten every moment to deprive him of his work, and consequently of his bread. There are three of these risks that are common to him and to all men — *sickness, old age,* and *death* — or even four if we count *disablement* separately; and two that are peculiar to his calling — namely, *accidents arising from his work*, and *unemployment*. That makes five or six, which is a great many. And they all have the common characteristic of de-priving him temporarily or permanently of his wages, and conse-quently of reducing him and his family to poverty. Now what can he do by himself against so many enemies? Very little.

We must distinguish between *preventive* measures, whose object is to prevent risks from occurring, and *remedial* measures, whose aim is to make good the pecuniary damage at any rate, when it has been impossible to avoid the evil. It is the latter kind alone that are in-cluded under the heading of insurance.

From the *preventive* standpoint, the worker can to some extent avoid sickness and put off the coming of old age and even of death, by prac-tising temperance and conforming to the rules of hygiene, in so far as his modest income permits. But it is scarcely within his power to avoid the other two risks — accident and unemployment — for it is obvious that both of these depend on technical or social causes to which he is subjected, but which he cannot alter.

From the *remedial* point of view the worker can at the utmost obtain, by saving, some resources to provide for a rainy day or to live on in his old age. But if he has nothing but the savings-bank for this purpose, who can imagine that that will suffice to ensure to him or his family the equivalent of the wages lost by all the fatalities we have just mentioned, or even by a single one of them, such as prolonged illness, disablement resulting from an accident, or old age?

There are capitalist insurance companies, it is true, which insure against all imaginable risks; but their rates are totally impossible to the working man's pocket — and besides, they scarcely want small working-class clients.

If therefore the worker is powerless by himself, must he not ask help from others? These others must be the employer, and the State.

(1) Help must be sought from the employer, at least so far as

concerns the risks of accident and unemployment. For as regards accidents, it may be said that since the workman under the existing wage system is merely a tool employed in his master's service, the master ought to stand the expense of breakage and wear and tear, just as he does in the case of his machinery. And as regards unemployment, we may say that it rests to some extent with the employer to avoid it, by regulating his production better, as he well knows how to do by means of agreements and trusts when it is a question of avoiding a bad market.

Even in the matter of risks that are common to all men — sickness, old age, and death — a certain amount of responsibility may fall on the employer, in so far as the first may have been aggravated, and the two others hastened, by the unhealthy nature of the work; for it is only too certain that for the worker, occupational diseases are more frequent, and old age and death come much sooner to him than to the members of other classes. There would be no injustice, therefore, in making the employers share in the insurance against these latter risks.

(2) Help must also be sought from the State, as representing the nation and in virtue of the law of social solidarity which requires that since all members of society share the fruits of production, they should all share also in its necessary cost. That is especially the case with unemployment, because this scourge is always due to social causes (see below, p. 460).

Only, when the State undertakes to guarantee the worker against the consequences of the risks of life, has it not, in return, the right to compel him to co-operate himself in this insurance as far as his resources permit? — and if this obligation be imposed on the worker, must it not be imposed, in fairness, on the employer too? In this way, State intervention in insurance leads logically to compulsory insurance.

These two points — *compulsory insurance for those concerned*, and the *collaboration of the wage-earner, the employer, and the State* (in varying proportions, according to the nature of the risk) — characterize the system called "German" because it was started in Germany by a series of famous laws commencing in 1883.

After these general considerations on the subject of workers' insurance, we go on to some brief details concerning each kind.

1. *Sickness*

This is the only one of the five risks that private initiative has succeeded in meeting, though to a scarcely sufficient extent, by means of association. In fact, though sickness, however little prolonged, makes a terrible hole in the income of the workman whom it strikes individually, and is even one of the most frequent causes of pauperism, it is none the less true that if we take a large enough number of men of average age and health, the number of days of sickness does not exceed seven or eight per year. Consequently, the expenses of sickness strictly speaking — that is to say, doctors' fees and cost of medicine — which would be an intolerable burden upon a normal workman's pocket, fall but lightly upon the resources of a society. Hence the success of sickness insurance societies, which, in return for a very moderate payment, guarantee to their members in case of sickness: (1) the cost of treatment, by doctor and chemist; (2) a payment equal to half the patient's wages; (3) generally some other benefits, such as funeral expenses and some moderate assistance to the widow and orphans; (4) besides this, some societies give also a small old age pension.

But these societies do not as a rule insure the members of the workman's family, nor do they, even for the men, provide for a long illness.

Private association, therefore, does not seem adequate to guarantee the working population against this risk. For this reason the German law[1] has made sickness insurance compulsory on all wage-earners, and has mitigated the hardship of it by making the employers pay a third of the premiums. It has also extended the system to include maternity benefits.

2. Accidents arising from employment

Accidents occurring during work are different from sickness in their causes but not in their results — namely, unemployment, more or less prolonged, and perhaps permanent, if the accident involves mutilation. They differ from sickness above all in the fact that here the responsibility of the employer is much more closely implicated. In fact, if he cannot be held responsible for the sickness of a worker, except in cases of occupational disease, it is difficult for him to evade liability for an accident, even when it occurs by chance. For the fact that it has happened in a factory or during work is sufficient to implicate the man in whose factory and for whom the work was being done. That is the doctrine now generally admitted, and known as *business risk* — which means that accidents incurred by employees during their work should count among the general

[1] [On which the English system of National Health Insurance is modelled.]

expenses of the business, just like accidents happening to the plant
and materials, and that they should therefore fall entirely upon the
head of the business, the worker being exempted from all share in
the insurance against this risk. — Even when the accident is his
own fault? Yes, because the negligence and imprudence of the
workman, and even his disobedience to orders, are themselves business
risks that ought to enter into the normal calculations of the *entrepreneur* and be reckoned among his general expenses.

But since it is the employer who will have to pay the indemnity, it
is for him, and not the workman, to insure against this risk. Ought
he to be compelled by law to insure against it? The German law
compels him, but not the French: the latter leaves him free to insure
or not as he pleases.

3. *Old age*

It may seem absurd to class old age among risks, since it is expected
and even hoped for by everyone: the risk is rather that of dying
before old age. But none the less — and therein perhaps the inequality of social conditions is most cruelly felt — old age without
money saved, old age with no prospect but the workhouse or dependence upon one's children — which is in some respects harder
still — is the nightmare of all wage-earners. It is true that old age
can be foreseen a long time in advance and can be prepared for all
through life, so that anyone who is overtaken by it without having
made proper preparation incurs the reproach of improvidence.
But besides the wish there must also be the power to save for one's
old age; and are there so many of the middle classes who save,
even if they are able to do so without trouble?

To procure a retiring pension by individual saving would lay a
heavy burden upon the worker — a deduction of at least 15% of
his wages continuously from his earliest days — a deduction that is
generally impossible and even selfish, since it would have to be paid
at the cost of his children's bread.

That is why the French law of 1910, passed after endless discussion,
reproduces in its essential features the German law, as follows: —
(1) compulsory insurance for all wage-earners by means of a deduction
from wages made by the employer; (2) an equal contribution from
workers and employers;[1] (3) a State grant in the shape of an addition to the pension, of a very moderate amount (100 francs);

[1] Fixed at a uniform rate (9 francs for men and 6 francs for women, and the same
for employers), whereas in Germany there is a scale of payments graduated according
to the wages.

(4) the right to a pension on retirement at the age of 60, the amount varying according to the number of payments made.

This system of compulsory insurance has not been as successful in France as in Germany. It may even be said to have failed. The premium is paid by scarcely more than half those who should be included, and these, moreover, are the oldest. The law has been up against the resistance of four kinds of opponents at once: economists of the liberal school, who object to compulsion;[1] socialists, who object to any contribution being imposed on the worker; mutual benefit societies, who are afraid that the subscriptions of their members will be absorbed by the compulsory payments to the State scheme; and lastly, and above all, the workers themselves who refuse to pay for an insignificant pension which most of them will never get.

Now that the war has upset both the value of money and the rate of interest, all calculations will have to be worked out afresh and the law will have to be completely refashioned.[2]

4. *Unemployment*

By unemployment is meant the interruption of work consequent upon the discharge of the worker and his difficulty in obtaining employment elsewhere. This discharge may be due either to dullness of trade, to an economic crisis involving a stoppage or slackening of production, or to the closing of a factory in consequence of such circumstances as a fire, bankruptcy, death of the employer, and so forth. Unemployment is the most frequent and, we might also say, the most incomprehensible of all the risks incurred by the wage-earner.

[1] M. Colson, one of the chief representatives of the liberal school, said in 1916, at the Congress of the "Société d'Économie Sociale": "It can be asserted without hesitation that the institution of workmen's pensions is a bad thing . . . . and leads to social disorganization."

[2] Disablement constitutes a special risk, distinct alike from old age, since it may exist from birth, and from sickness, since it is permanent. It would be the most terrible of all risks if it were not that it is, fortunately, exceptional. The German law, which is generally spoken of as a law of insurance against old age, is really entitled a disablement law, and it is disablement that it has particularly in view. It may be admitted, indeed, that insurance against disablement covers insurance against old age, for of two things one: either the old worker is disabled, and eligible for the disablement allowance; or else he is fit and able to work, in which case it seems scarcely necessary to pay him any indemnity.

The projected French law, on the other hand, pays little attention to anything but old age, and in this it corresponds to the feeling of the public. For while everybody wants to be insured against old age, because everybody expects to grow old, no one is concerned about insurance against disablement, because no one expects to become disabled.

In fact, it is a terrible mystery in our economic organization that a man who wants to earn his living by his labour so often finds it impossible to do so, for it is incomprehensible that a man's labour should be useless, unless everyone were sufficiently provided not only with necessaries but with luxuries as well. Now the very fact that the unemployed worker is deprived of everything and oppressed by want, is sufficient proof that this state of abundance is far from being realized.

The socialism that preceded the French Revolution of 1848 demanded that the State should ensure to every man the *Right to Work*, and even went so far as to regard the legal recognition of this right as the solution of the social problem. The deplorable experiment in national workshops during that revolution was connected with the same idea. We do not talk about the Right to Work nowadays. We see, indeed, how absolutely impossible it is for the State to provide useful work — work that is really productive of value — for anyone at all. And what matters to the workman is not the right to work but the right to live, so that the demands of modern socialism are rather for the guarantee of a minimum wage, while waiting for the socialization of the instruments of production, which might perhaps eliminate all stoppage of work but which even in that case would transform unemployment into holidays, the workman receiving the equivalent of his wages.

Against this terrible evil of unemployment there are two remedies — the one preventive, and the other remedial — but both of them inadequate.

(*a*) The first is that of setting up special institutions for obtaining some other employment for the worker. The workers' unions would like to have the monopoly of finding employment, because this would be a sure means of enabling them to enlist all workers and exercise control over them by placing only their own members in employment. It would also enable them to support their members on strike by keeping out "blacklegs." But it goes without saying that employers on their side resist this claim and try to keep the placing of workmen in their own hands — which is an easy matter for them since it is they who have the jobs at their disposal.

Between these two extremes lies the best system, which combines the three elements by making the employment bureau to consist half of employers and half of workmen, with an independent chairman: the bureau to operate at the cost and under the control of the municipal authority. This plan is practised in Germany and has been introduced into France since the war.

Well-organized employment bureaux might go beyond the mere struggle against unemployment, and carry out in particular the important task of guiding young workers in their choice of a pro, fession.

But this method is an insufficient remedy for unemployment, for all statistics show that except for uncommon trades the demand for places is always greater than the number of vacancies. What can be the cause of this mysterious phenomenon? For with so many people in want of necessaries it seems simple enough to employ the spare labour in producing just these necessaries that are lacking. It is no doubt due to the cause already indicated (p. 79) — that machinery and everything that is included under the head of industrial progress tends to reduce the amount of labour requisite to produce a given result. That is why the method of employment bureaux has to be supplemented by insurance.

(b) Insurance is the method of compensating the unemployed worker for his losses by paying him the whole or part of his lost wages, as in the case of the other risks we have been considering. It must be observed, however, that insurance is much more difficult here, not only on account of the extent and frequency of the risk, but especially because it is almost impossible to distinguish true unemployment, due to lack of work, from the false variety which is due to laziness.

Hence arose the idea of collaboration between the trade unions and the municipalities, the latter providing the necessary funds and the former organizing the scheme of insurance and paying the benefits to those concerned.

In what is called the Ghent system, dating from 1901, a grant is made by the municipality and distributed by an independent organization. In practice the Ghent system generally employs the trade union as this intermediary, but the members of any association formed to combat unemployment have a right to a share in the grant, without necessarily belonging to a trade union. And even individual saving, in the shape of savings-bank deposits, is assimilated to unemployment insurance, and benefits by grants proportional to the amounts withdrawn from the savings-bank.

France is very backward in the matter of unemployment insurance. Although unemployment has assumed formidable proportions since the universal slump that followed the war at the end of 1920, she is still using the palliative method of distributing alms, under the name of unemployment grants — a method that is at once humiliating,

ineffective, and terribly burdensome to the State and the municipalities.[1]

XIII. THE FUTURE OF THE WAGE SYSTEM

The abolition of the wage system, more even than the abolition
of property, which is rather the means than the end, stands in the
front rank among the demands of the working classes — or, more
strictly speaking, it includes all their demands.

This expectation does not necessarily give rise to a feeling of class
hatred, but rather to grievances that are very justifiable, as well
from the moral and social as from the purely economic point of view.
These complaints are not so much against the inadequate share
that the wage system allocates to the worker (see above, p. 427)
in the process of distribution, for this inequality might be diminished
sooner than is expected.   There are more serious grievances than
this.   While recognizing that the wage system has perhaps been
the indispensable instrument by which industry and the general
wealth have made such enormous progress during the past century,
we must admit that it has not brought lasting social peace, and that
it even seems now to be hindering the increase of production.   The
reasons for this are as follows:

(a) From the social point of view the wage system creates an
inevitable *conflict of interests* between employer and worker — the
same conflict, in fact, as that which exists between the seller and the
purchaser of any other commodity — the one trying to pay the
lowest wage possible in exchange for the greatest amount of work,
and the other trying to put in the least possible amount of work in
return for his wages; and in this way the strife of classes is embittered.

The more wages are raised, in fact, the more profits are reduced,
and conversely, *other things being equal*.   We have added and itali-
cized this last phrase because it is obvious that if the conditions of
productiveness change — if, for instance, the total produce of all
businesses were to be doubled — then wages and profits might be
doubled *simultaneously*.   This is even a common case in new countries, where productiveness is great: there high wages and large
profits can be seen at the same time.   But the conflict of interests
is there just the same, even when this happens.   Moreover, it is
made plain by incessant strikes.   Thus, then, the employer and the
worker appear to us in the existing economic order of things as two

---

[1] [A few sentences dealing with French institutions have been omitted from this
section.]

figures standing up against each other in an attitude of mutual defiance, though they are unable to do without each other and are bound together, as it were, by an iron chain.

(b) From the economic standpoint the result of the wage system is to *deprive the worker of all interest in doing well*, and thereby to do serious injury to production. For the worker, having no claim on the profits of the business, and having sold in advance for a fixed sum his eventual share in the produce of his labour, has no further inducement to work except the fear of dismissal.[1] But if such a motive may determine a workman to put in the minimum amount of work it is quite inadequate to cause him to make the best use of his productive capacity, for it makes work into positive drudgery. Of course we have seen various methods devised for remedying this defect in wage-paid labour by stimulating the workman's activity by piece-work, by the payment of bonuses (see p. 434), or by the Taylor system;[2] but these are only palliatives. The nature of the contract reduces the worker to a purely passive part, and robs him of all interest, if not in the immediate result of his work, yet at all events in the success or failure of the business. It is hard to persuade men that they ought to work their best when they have no claim upon the wealth that issues from their hands.

(c) From the moral point of view the wage system makes man an *instrument for enriching* another man. Undoubtedly every man is called upon to work for another, by the system of division of labour, and instead of protesting against this state of things we must regard it as a manifestation of the moral law of solidarity. But the relation of the wage-earner to his master is not one of interdependence but of dependence, pure and simple. The workers are known by the cruelly realistic name of "hands," and that, indeed, is just what they are; but they cannot be prevented from bitterly seeing generations of employers and shareholders succeeding each other and growing rich from such and such a factory or mine in which they, too, have worked from one generation to another, and have yet remained poor. It is true that one might prove to them that this fortune is not their doing, economically speaking; but it would not be easy to prove that this state of things conforms to Kant's principle of morality which he called the "supreme practical

---

[1] "The good shepherd giveth his life for the sheep. But he that is an hireling, and not the shepherd, whose own the sheep are not, seeth the wolf coming, and leaveth the sheep, and fleeth. . . . The hireling fleeth, because he is an hireling, and careth not for the sheep." (S. John x, 11–13.)

[2] See my *Political Economy*, (D. C. Heath & Company, publisher).

principle ": to remember always that we ought to regard the person of our neighbour as an end and not as a means.

But when men talk of abolishing the wage system, what is it exactly that is meant?

The only clear way to abolish the wage system would be to make every wage-earner an independent producer, producing by his own means and on his own account, like the craftsman or the peasant. But such a system would be incompatible with large-scale industry and would hinder the advance of economic evolution. Nor is it demanded by anyone, no more by socialists than by the liberal school of economists. Now as soon as ever the necessity for the collective organization of labour is admitted, it will be useless to replace the capitalist joint-stock company system by any system of socialization whatever — whether syndicalist, co-operative, or nationalized — for the worker will inevitably be employed in the service of the undertaking, which will command him and pay him for his work: and then will he not still be a wage-earner?

But at any rate, it will be said, the workers will no longer work for a master, but for an association of which they will themselves be members — either a commune, a co-operative society, or a nation. Very well; but then the appropriate formula would be "abolition of the employing system," rather than "abolition of the wage system." And are we to believe that the worker would be very conscious of this change? It is by no means certain, to judge from the state of mind of workers who are already in this position — in the service of the State, or of municipalities, or of co-operative societies. They are not the last to go on strike!

Yet all the same there would be something different in these new forms of business: profit would have been eliminated, and so the worker would no longer be tormented by the feeling which, rightly or wrongly, preys upon him to-day, that his labour serves to enrich his employer. Consequently the famous formula, "abolition of the wage system," seems as if it should be changed into "abolition of profit." And that brings us to the subject of the next chapter.

CHAPTER IV — THE *ENTREPRENEURS*

I. HISTORICAL EVOLUTION OF THE EMPLOYING SYSTEM

We have already made the acquaintance of the important person who is known in economics as the *entrepreneur* (see p. 116). We have seen that it is he who takes the initiative and assumes the direction of every productive operation when it gets beyond the range of individual action. But he occupies a no less important place in distribution as well, for it is he who is *the great distributor*. It is he who pays his collaborators for their assistance, and the share that he gives to each of them is precisely what constitutes their income. To the worker he pays *wages*, to the capitalist *interest*, to the landowner *rent*. Then he keeps the remainder — if there is any remainder — for himself; and this makes his income, under the name of *profit*.

In everyday speech the *entrepreneur* is called the *master*, but if we look more closely we shall see that this is not exactly the same thing, for there may be a business without a master, such as a co-operative society. Moreover the term "master" refers particularly to his relations with his wage-earners: it implies a certain moral idea of protection, patronage, or mastership, and a certain conception of the rights and duties of a leader towards his subordinates, which is foreign to the strictly economic definition of the *entrepreneur*, or, as he is also called, the employer.

This notion of the duties of an industrial leader towards his workers has undergone various interesting changes during the last century, without going back as far as the days of the guild system. Three periods may be briefly distinguished:

(1) At the beginning of the industrial era and down to about the middle of the nineteenth century, the idea of the employing system in the sense just indicated did not exist. There were only *entrepreneurs* confining themselves to their economic function and concerning themselves simply with producing as much as possible, at the lowest cost, and with making the best use of the available labour power — the best, that is to say, in their own interests. And they utilized not only the labour of men, but also that of women and children, which was more profitable because it was less expensive. This was

466

the system of *laisser faire*, as typified by the famous phrase of an English employer who, when asked what would happen to the workers he dismissed, replied: "I trust to the laws of nature."

From the economic standpoint, however, it must be acknowledged that the capitalist employers of that heroic age were the creators of modern large-scale industry. It is from the moral point of view that their history is not pleasant — except, of course, for certain individuals, among whom we must remember particularly the great Scottish manufacturer, Robert Owen, who is more worthy of recollection for having been the first to set up a model factory than for his communist theories.

(2) About 1850 there emerged a new conception. We can point even to its birthplace and its authors — a group of protestant manufacturers in the town of Mulhouse in Alsace. This was the conception of the *good master:* it was formulated in the famous saying of another employer, Dollfus of Mulhouse: "The master *owes* the workman *more than his wages.*" What does this mean? That the payment for labour, determined according to the current price of manual skill by the law of supply and demand, does not meet all the demands of justice: something yet remains due; that the worker ought not to be regarded as a mere tool, but as a collaborator with the employer; and that the latter ought to investigate his needs and attempt to provide for them.

Thus was inaugurated the great movement in the direction of institutions set up by employers — working class houses and cities, savings organizations, benefit and retirement funds, profit-sharing sometimes, schools for children, and so forth — which occupied the places of honour in all exhibitions of social economy and carried off all the awards. We must do the masters the justice of acknowledging that most of the reforms introduced by labour legislation or in answer to the demands of the trade unions had been first started by the initiative of the employers. This confirms the oft-proved law of sociology that reforms are most often due to the action of those who are not directly interested in them.[1]

Unfortunately this generous movement frequently degenerated into a species of control over the private life of the worker, which he found intolerable.[2] It was natural enough that the good employer who real-

---

[1] See our book, *Institutions de Progrès Social.*

[2] In one of the great American businesses — The Pullman car company — in which these institutions had grown into a veritable workmen's city, the workers used to say: "We were born in a Pullman house, fed from a Pullman shop, taught in a Pullman school, catechised in a Pullman church, and when we die we shall be buried

ized the duties he owed to his workers should also attribute paternal rights to himself, and if he agreed to make sacrifices he wished only to make them in good earnest, by making sure that the worker would show himself worthy of them.   But it might have been expected that the worker would show himself ungrateful, and that is just what happened.   Considering especially the mentality of the modern workman, urged into class warfare, it is obvious that he would think it a grotesque and hateful idea to regard his employer as a father.   He does not believe in the so-called sacrifices of his master, and even if they are real he scorns them as alms.   He demands them in the shape of increased wages — nothing more and nothing less.

We believe that the rôle of the modern employer may be defined by saying that he should stick to his industrial function: he should abstain from all interference with the life of the worker outside the factory, even to "do him good," but should do everything possible to provide him *inside the factory* with the most perfect conditions in the matter of safety, hygiene, and comfort — which things are also conducive to the maximum productiveness.   An example of this kind is being set already by certain large employers in England and the United States.

(3)   A third period began recently when the employers, finding themselves faced by workers organized in unions and declaring that they wanted no relations with their masters except on the basis of class warfare, had to defend themselves instead of trying to protect their workers.   This spirit of hostility seems to grow in proportion even to the improvements that are made in the workers' condition.   This fact, which is disconcerting at first sight, is regarded by the employers as a sign of a discouraging ingratitude; but it is the manifestation of a well-known psychological law.   New wants only begin to be felt when the earlier ones are satisfied: the workman who is stupefied by fifteen hours of labour wants only to eat and sleep, but the one who has obtained the benefit of a shorter working day and the leisure that results from it, feels a thousand new wants arising within him.   They seem excessive in comparison with his earlier wants, but as a rule they are not so, if they are looked at by themselves.[1]

So employers' institutions have given place to what might be called

in a Pullman cemetery and go to a Pullman hell."   It has even happened that some of these employers' institutions have degenerated into instruments of scandalous exploitation, so that the legislator has had to intervene to suppress them.

[1] Vinet of Lausanne, a Christian moralist, but poles apart from working class socialism, has written these remarkably revolutionary words: "A people never demands anything but what it actually needs."

militant ones, for their aim is to meet the workers' organizations with employers' organizations more powerfully armed and able to give blow for blow, to meet a strike by a lock-out and the enrolment of strike-breakers, to answer the workers' black list by black-listing the labour leaders, to create insurance funds against strikes to meet the unions' strike funds, and so forth. The employer's lot is going to be a very hard one: it will no longer be a hereditary business, handed down from father to son like a lawyer's practice. Many of them will give up the struggle, and a kind of natural selection will take place, which, however, will increase the strength of the employing class.

(4) Must we not look forward to a last phase: the permanent elimination of the employer? That, indeed, is the view of the syndicalist and the socialist. They claim to prove that the employer is no longer of any use, but a mere parasite. The increasing prevalence of the joint-stock company in business — what the French call the *anonymous* society — shows clearly enough, they say, that there is no employer here in the sense in which the word is used by economists — that is to say, an individual who is at the same time the owner of the business and the manager who receives the profits in return for his daily labour. The employer has been eliminated, or rather, has been split up into managers and salaried officials on the one hand, and on the other a crowd of idle shareholders who do not know each other and sometimes know nothing about the business with which they are connected, beyond the name of the company appearing on their shares. If these parasites were abolished, the business would go on just as before. Now in consequence of the present line of development which substitutes large-scale for small-scale production and the joint-stock company for the individual business, all employers will soon be reduced to the rôle of shareholders with nothing to do but to tear off dividend coupons. Then their uselessness will be proved by facts and their social rôle will be ended.

This argument is not conclusive, however, for in joint-stock companies there are employers all the same. The employers are assuredly not the shareholders — mere money-lenders, called by the appropriate name of "sleeping partners"; it is the members of the board of directors, and most frequently only some among them, such as the chairman or the secretary, who keep everything going. It is no longer, it is true, the hereditary monarchical government of the individual employing system: it is an oligarchy, elected by a small number of capitalists and invested with full powers — a republic on the model of that of Venice.

If, then, we can look in the future for a form of business in which the employing system has disappeared in the shape of a capitalist monarchy, it does not seem possible to abolish it in the democratic shape of government by elected leaders. Whether it be a co-operative, a syndicalist, or even a communist form of business, direction and management will always be required. But it may be admitted that the leadership will no longer be connected, as it is to-day, with the possession of capital, and that it will no longer carry the privilege of receiving the profits. Thus extended, the abolition of the employing system is part and parcel of the abolition of the wage system: they are the two sides of a single demand, and we can only refer back to the preceding chapter.

Meanwhile the employer's authority will probably have to resign itself more and more to a threefold control that will go on increasing:

(1) Control by the State, which will not entirely withdraw the hold over industry that the war conferred upon it, for it will argue that the needs of national reconstruction are no less urgent than those of national defence.

(2) Control by the workers, who set more store by a recognition of their claim to share in the government of industry than by a rise of wages.

(3) Control by the consumers themselves, which has already been started, though in a timid fashion as yet, by the admission of representatives of consumers' co-operative societies to some official boards.

II. WHAT IS PROFIT?

At first sight this is a very simple question, which any small grocer can answer: it is the *excess of selling price over cost price*.

But this simplicity is more apparent than real, for the exact determination of the specific income called "profit," which appears as the normal result of every industrial, agricultural, and commercial undertaking, is none the less one of the most difficult and still one of the most discussed questions in economic science.

Let us question the grocer or, better still, the peasant. At the end of the year he makes up his accounts and says, "I have spent so much and received so much: I have therefore gained the difference." Is that profit in the economic sense of the word? Not at all. On the one hand, this surplus which he has gained includes payment for his labour, interest on the capital he has employed, and the rent of his shop or land, whether he has hired it or whether he owns it; and all these are the kinds of income we have already met with — wages, interest, and rent. We see nothing different here that requires a new name. The peasant or grocer makes no distinction in this mixture of incomes between its constituent elements, nor does he need to do so.

At the other end of the scale let us take a big business, such as a mining company. Here the different kinds of income will appear more clearly because they are separated. The company pays wages for labour, including the highest salaries paid to its engineers and directors; it pays interest for the capital it has borrowed in the form of shares or bonds; and though it does not as a rule pay rent, properly speaking, for its land, because it owns it, yet it has to pay a royalty to the State for the subsoil, of which it obtains only a grant. There you have the cost of production clearly determined in its threefold shape: wages, interest, and rent; and what remains is the *net product*, or profit, which will be either distributed in dividends, or paid into a reserve fund, or employed to pay for the depreciation of the fixed capital. In this case, therefore, profit appears plainly as a form of income entirely distinct from the other three.

The *entrepreneur* has to deduct from the value of the produce the shares of all his fellow-workers: nothing can be simpler than that preliminary operation. But how is his own share to be explained, and by what right does he receive it? Observe, to begin with, that he has generally provided the land and buildings, and probably the whole or part of the capital also, as well as, in every case, some labour of organization and management. Now in all these cases he obviously has the right to receive a share in the same way as his collaborators. It makes no difference that these elements represent the personal contribution of the *entrepreneur* and that he has not had to obtain them from others. If he had not employed them in this business he would have been able to make use of them otherwise — he could have let his building site, invested his capital, and made use of his own labour and intelligence elsewhere. Consequently he must assuredly receive from the business at least the equivalent of what he would have obtained in other ways from the value he owns: otherwise he will not undertake the business.

As regards rent, nothing is simpler: it will be estimated at the same rate as the *entrepreneur* would have to pay to obtain a similar site.

It is the same with his capital: interest will be reckoned at the current rate, at which he has to pay for the capital he borrows. And in practice, in every proper system of book-keeping, the *entrepreneur* sets down in his account book the interest on the capital he has provided.

It is only in the case of the personal labour of the *entrepreneur* that the calculation becomes more difficult. What wage should be allotted to him? The same salary, we must reply, as he would have to pay to a man who had the requisite qualifications to replace him — to a good manager — or the same as he could demand himself if he wished to sell his services.   No doubt this valuation is somewhat arbitrary; yet there are some *entrepreneurs* who count among their expenses and enter in their books a certain salary which they allot to themselves. Presumably this salary will be higher than the *entrepreneur* would pay to an equally deserving employee, and higher even than he would demand himself if he were seeking for a manager's post.   But that is understandable, because he must take into account the responsibilities, the anxieties, and the risks of his job — not only the risk to his capital, which is already allowed for, but the risk to his position and commercial standing.   And if he were not to earn more as an employer than as a paid employee, it would be better for him to become an employee: he would at least earn a peaceful life.   There are only too many people, in France especially, who argue precisely like that.

If therefore the *entrepreneur* keeps his accounts properly he will be sure to keep them on this basis: he will work out the amount of interest on his own capital, the wages due for his own work, and, lastly, the rent of the house or land that he owns.   But these are not what is called profit, for they will all be entered among the costs of production of the business, and the *entrepreneur* will not consider that he has made a net profit unless there remains a *surplus* after all these have been allowed for.

But why should there be a surplus?   And if there is, by what right will the *entrepreneur* receive it, when he seems to have satisfied all his claims already?   He has been paid as a worker, as a capitalist, and as an owner: what more is he to have?   If it is this surplus or residue alone that constitutes true profit, then profit remains in the air, without any foundation: how is it to be justified, or even explained economically?

This is a very big problem, and many very divergent solutions have been offered.

1. Here, to begin with, is the ordinary explanation of "the man in the street," and also of economists of the old school.

This surplus represents a real creation of value, which is due to the *entrepreneur* in virtue of the following claims:

(*a*) *Invention*, which is the most important act in all production, as we have seen (p. 88). — The conclusion is drawn that the great fortunes made in industry — Bessemer steel, the Singer sewing-machine, and so forth — are the result of inventions.   We have seen already that the really productive act is an idea. Now, it is said, the rôle of the *entrepreneur* is simply to have ideas — not necessarily inspirations of genius, but commercial ideas, and particularly the power of discovering what will please the public. It is not enough for him to invent new models: he must invent new wants.

(*b*) The *direction*, or better still the *co-ordination*, of the factors of production. — Collective labour is more productive than isolated labour — this is one of the fundamental laws of political economy — but only on condition that it is organized, disciplined, and commanded. Someone, therefore, must distribute tasks and assign to every man his place: that is the duty of the *entrepreneur*, and for that reason he is called a "captain of industry." In fact, industry is like war. Who is it wins the battle? The general. Of course good soldiers contribute to the victory, just as good weapons do, but these are only the conditions of success, and not its efficient cause. This is proved by the fact that the same troops, with the same weapons, will be beaten if they are badly led. Similarly in business it is the leading that does everything, as is proved by the fact that of two businesses employing workers of equal efficiency, we constantly see one succeeding and the other failing miserably.

(*c*) *Commercial speculation.* — To produce is nothing: the important thing is to sell — to find outlets. So business is tending more and more nowadays to take on a commercial character. That again is one of the characteristic features of the work of the *entrepreneur*, and a matter of the highest social importance, because it results, though unconsciously, in a tendency continually to restore the equilibrium between production and consumption.

(*d*) *Insurance against risk.* — It is natural for all business to involve a certain amount of risk, since by its very definition it means making advances without knowing when they will be repaid, and undertaking tasks without knowing whether they will succeed. Now no one will be inclined to take these risks unless he is attracted by the prospect of a certain profit — that is to say, by the prospect of getting out of the business more than he has put into it. In industrial undertakings we cannot accept the famous maxim of William of Orange: "There is no need of hope to make us undertake a task, nor is success necessary to make us persevere."

But these explanations, although perfectly reasonable, do not give us the answer to the riddle, whether and in what way profit constitutes a kind of income *specifically distinct from other incomes*. In fact, all that we call invention, direction, and speculation, are only forms of labour, and as such they yield wages and nothing else. We do not make a separate category for intellectual work as opposed to manual work, or for the labour of the merchant as distinct from that of the manufacturer.   Then why make a separate category for the labour of invention, direction, or speculation?   What the *entrepreneur* receives under these various heads will have to be set down as the remuneration of his labour — there is no getting away from it.   And the proof is this: that of all these kinds of work described as characteristic of the *entrepreneur* — invention, direction, and even the work of seeking for markets — there is not one which cannot be entrusted, and which is not as a matter of fact entrusted in all great company businesses, to salaried managers, engineers, chemists, commercial travellers, and so forth.   If the *entrepreneur* undertakes this work himself he allots a salary to himself under this heading, as we have already observed, which certainly means that he regards this remuneration as belonging to cost of production and not to profit.

The question of insurance against risk is another matter: we have nothing to do here with payment for work.   But to tell the truth we cannot understand how risk can be regarded as an explanation of profit.   No doubt in every business which has good years and bad years something must be deducted from the gains of the good years to make up for the losses of the bad ones, which is the same as saying that we must base our calculations on the average of, say, five or ten years instead of one year.   So also in every business that is liable to permanent losses, like mining businesses, supposing that only one out of two is successful, then those that succeed must produce enough to make up for the losses of those that fail, for otherwise no *entrepreneurs* would be prepared to try their luck.   But why is it that the gains of the good businesses *must* yield *more* than enough to compensate for the losses of the bad ones?   This necessity is what we do not see.

2. By socialists profit is explained in the simplest fashion: it is a *deduction from the produce of the labour of the worker.*

It is particularly since the appearance of Karl Marx's book on Capital that the attack has taken definite form.   The following is a brief account of the way in which this doughty champion demolishes the income of the *entrepreneur* — the employer.

The comparison that has been drawn by economists between the rôle of the *entrepreneur* and that of the worker, he says, is absurd, or at all events out of date.   In former times the master who worked with his workmen — *primus inter pares* — might have been regarded as a worker and producer.   The same case may still occur occasionally in small-scale industry; but in large-scale industry, which for

Marx will be the only form in the future, the master is only the master because he is a rich man and a capitalist, just as in former days a man was an officer because he was a noble. And the master makes his capital yield a profit simply by the method of sale, like a trader: he buys in order to sell again. What does he buy? The workman's labour power, in the shape of work. What does he sell? That same labour power in the concrete form of goods. And the surplus price is what constitutes his profit.

The only question is how to explain this surplus that constitutes profit. Whence does it come? The Marxian theory of value simply consists in the assertion that things have no other value than that which is conferred upon them by labour, and that their value is measured by the amount of this labour (p. 52). It seems therefore that the employer cannot sell the produce of the worker's labour for a greater value than he has paid for that labour. That is the very crux of the problem — the "mystery of iniquity," whose discovery has brought glory upon Karl Marx. Let us listen to the argument.

The product placed upon the market by the *entrepreneur* has, indeed, a value determined by the labour it has cost. Suppose that the workman has spent ten hours in making it: then the value of the product will be measured by ten hours of labour — *the product will be worth ten hours.*

But what will be the value of the workman's labour? It is determined, like that of the product itself, and like that of every commodity, such as a machine, for example, by its cost of production. Now in the case of this human machine called labour or skill, the cost of production is no other than the expense that is requisite to produce a workman — that is to say, to bring him up and keep him alive. Supposing that the necessary expense of maintaining this workman and redeeming this human capital is represented by five hours' labour a day — why then *labour will be worth five hours of work*, no more and no less. Therefore, by paying the workman, in the form of wages, a value equivalent to five hours' labour, the employer is paying labour precisely what it is worth according to the laws of value and exchange. But as the produce of the labour of this same workman is worth ten hours, there is a difference between the buying price and the selling price — a surplus value of five hours. This is what Marx calls *Mehrwerth*, which is translated into French as *plus-value*, and into English as *surplus value*. It is the keystone of his doctrine.

To put it briefly, there is a certain number of hours' labour by which the employer profits without having to pay for them, and during which the workman works for nothing. *Profit is a certain quan-*

tity of unpaid labour: there lies the whole secret of capitalist exploitation.[1] And it goes without saying that these hours that are not paid for are multiplied by the number of workmen employed, so that the more workmen there are the greater will be the profit.

This demonstration can be put into a clearer but less accurate form by starting from the fact that *the value produced by a man's labour is generally greater than the value required to support him.* This is the case even with the isolated and primitive worker (as is proved by the fact that but for this surplus value civilization could never have arisen nor could population even have increased), and still more with the civilized worker whose power is multiplied by the division of labour and collective organization. Now when the employer has become the possessor of this labour power by purchasing it, he devises a thousand ingenious ways of increasing this surplus value — by prolonging the length of the working day as much as possible, by stimulating the workman with the deceptive bait of piece wages, and by working women and children to exhaustion with the help of machinery that enables him to utilize their slender strength. And, on the other hand, technical progress, by enabling everything that is indispensable to the material existence and maintenance of the worker to be produced at a lower cost, reduces the value of labour to that extent, because this value cannot exceed the cost of maintenance. If we were to imagine that the productiveness of labour could be increased to such an extent that five minutes would be sufficient to produce food for a man working ten hours a day, then the value of a workman's day would only be equivalent to that of five minutes' labour: that is the wage that the employer would pay, and he would keep the surplus — that is to say, the whole of the value produced during the remaining 9 hours 55 minutes.

All this ingenious dialectic, designed to prove that profit, by its very nature, constitutes a spoliation of labour and consists of a certain quantity of unpaid labour, is impressive and even incontrovertible if we admit the postulate that every commodity is worth only the amount of labour incorporated in it, and that labour power in the existing economic system, being a commodity like any other, cannot likewise be worth more than the amount of labour that has gone to produce it. But if we believe, on the contrary (see pp. 44–49), that value is determined by other factors than the labour of the workman

---

[1] Marx's demonstration is more complicated than we can make it here. To reproduce it exactly, we should have to distinguish between *profit* and *surplus value.* See Gide and Rist's *History of Economic Doctrines* (English translation published by D. C. Heath and Company).

— and by other factors, also, than the labour of the *entrepreneur* — that it is determined by the play of those complex causes that are summed up in the everyday formula of the law of supply and demand or in the more learned form of the doctrine of final utility — then the explanation of profit by the exploitation of labour disappears, at any rate as a theoretical explanation.

3. Here, lastly, is the explanation adopted by economists of the more modern schools. Profit properly so called is a special kind of income due to certain favourable circumstances, personal or real, which enable the *entrepreneur* either to *sell above* the normal cost of production, because he enjoys an actual monopoly; or else to *produce below* the normal cost of production, and thus to benefit by a *differential rent*, similar to that which we have already described in connexion with the landowner.

This state of monopoly is far commoner than is often thought. To begin with, it may be a legal monopoly, resulting from a patent or a protective tariff. But it may arise also from many other circumstances, such as the possession of a more or less considerable capital, which in a poor or new country always constitutes a certain monopoly; or the fact of bearing a name already well known in the industry; or the occupation of a good site — for instance, in the case of a public house, a situation at the entrance to a factory or even a cemetery. Who is there who does not enjoy some little monopoly? It is this extra profit that creates great fortunes, when exceptionally favourable circumstances offer themselves. It seems as if Shakespeare must have had this in his mind when he wrote of the

> " tide in the affairs of men,
> Which, taken at the flood, leads on to fortune;
> Omitted, all the voyage of their life
> Is bound in shallows and in miseries."

Never has this flood reached such proportions as during the late war. Never, in any age, has man seen arise more enormous and more rapid fortunes, side by side with equally terrible ruin.

But if this be so, then profit looks like an occasional and accidental income, that is bound to disappear with the disappearance of the circumstances that gave it birth. And such is indeed the case: the profit derived from any invention diminishes and may disappear as soon as it becomes public property — as soon, that is, as the monopoly disappears. It is one of the classical laws of political economy that competition exerts continuous pressure on prices until it has brought them down to the level of the cost of production — that is to say, until profit has disappeared.

However, in every progressive and dynamic society (as Clark says), every outworn invention is replaced by another; to every de-throned monopoly another one succeeds. Profit is only a passing wave, but wave follows wave unceasingly. None the less, if we can imagine a society in the stationary state and under a system of un-restricted competition, then profit would indeed have disappeared as a distinct kind of income (see below), just as the waves and the tide of which Shakespeare spoke would come to an end in a world with-out wind and without a moon.[1]

III. THE RATE OF PROFIT

The working classes are prone, as a rule, to exaggerate the rate of profit, by making a violent contrast between the employer's gain and their own meagre wages. No doubt by taking only isolated cases one could cite numerous and amusing examples of enormous profits and of millions gained by inventions which after all are nothing less than strokes of genius, such as shoe-laces, safety pins, lever-topped collar studs, steel pens, roller skates, pencil-cases with an erasing rubber at one end, various children's toys, and so forth. What a fortune the inventor of the picture postcard would have made if he had been able to patent it!

We could certainly even give examples of profits due to spoliation — either of the workers or of the consumers, — and it was not only socialists but a preacher, Bourdaloue, who referred to fortunes "at the base of which there are things that make one shudder."

Yet why should we be astonished? Do we not know that the value of things is determined by causes that are independent of all moral considerations? And this is true of every producer.

But there are many other cases where, on the other hand, the profit received by the *entrepreneur* represents only a very small portion of the wealth he has bestowed upon society. Moreover, wherever profit arises from a saving effected in the cost of production, then instead of involving a parasitic levy on consumers or workmen, it results in a much greater profit for the nation than even for the *entrepreneur*. In this case he generally keeps in the shape of profit only a small part of the saving that has been effected; and even this fair remuneration is

---

[1] That is what Léon Walras means by that striking formula that is so astonishing at first sight: *the normal rate of profit is zero.* He means that under the hypothetical régime of free competition that serves as a base for his system of mathematical equa-tions, the price at which the *entrepreneur* buys productive services (including those that he provides himself), and the price at which he sells the produce when made, must of necessity be equal. This obviously reduces his profit to zero.

quickly snatched from his hands by the action of competition, so that what was at first a minimum cost of production for him alone, soon becomes the normal cost of production.

If, instead of confining ourselves to isolated cases, we consider the sum total of profits in any society, or even in any single industry, we cease to obtain the impression that they are excessive. They represent quite a small deduction from the total value of the produce.[1]

In order to effect a considerable change in the actual position of the wage-earner by eliminating profit, we should have to assume much more than a mere transfer of profit from the employer to the workman, which would only be a slight change: we should have to assume that the abolition of the wage system, of which the abolition of profit is only the reflection, would result in such a transformation of the mentality and activity of the workers that the wealth created by each of them would be greatly increased. We are not one of those who regard this hope as chimerical; but it is a matter of social education rather than of distribution.[2]

It is generally taught that the rate of profits is governed by the same causes as the rate of interest, and for the majority of economists the fall in that rate is no less certain a law than that of the gradual fall of the rate of interest (above, p. 415). However, the one seems hardly more certain than the other. It may be admitted, to be sure, that as businesses grow, the rate of profit, which is merely the ratio between the amount of gain and the amount of capital employed, goes on diminishing, because the *entrepreneur* can gain more with a smaller profit per unit of capital. It may also be owned that since profit, as we have shown, is only the outcome of a monopoly, it must diminish and

---

[1] An enquiry was made in England in 1907 into the balance-sheets of the great mining and railway industries. It gave the following figures:

	Million Pounds	Percentage of the Total
Wages	446	66
Rent	31	4.5
Interest	104	15
Profits	97	14.5
	678	100.0

If the £97,000,000 of profits, therefore, were handed over entirely to the wage-earners, the increase in wages would amount to less than a quarter — just under 22%.

[2] For instance, does anyone imagine it would be sufficient to say, in reply to the arithmetical argument in the preceding footnote, that if the mine belonged to the miners, they would extract more coal from it? It is true in the case of the peasant who tills his own field, but this is because the latter is engaged in an individual enterprise — it is the same man who sows, ploughs, and reaps. It is not necessarily the same in businesses that involve collective labour.

even disappear in each business, by the very fact of competition. But as each monopoly, when it disappears, is replaced by a new one — as one wave is succeeded by another — it does not look as if this conclusion could rightly be extended to cover industry as a whole.

IV. THE ELIMINATION OF PROFIT

We have just given the explanation of profit, but does this imply the legitimacy of profit?

Of all the kinds of income there is not one that has been more hotly contested than profit.   This is not only because the *entrepreneur*, as we have many times pointed out, is the hero who plays the leading part on the economic stage, and it is naturally around him that the fight is thickest.   It is not only because profit is almost the sole source of great fortunes, for money is only made "in business."   Nor is it only because profit is regarded as the cause of every rise of prices, and the profiteer, in every period of turmoil such as the world is now passing through, is accused of speculation and branded as a monopolist.   It is, above all, because profit is a form of income whose nature is doubtful, for which it is difficult to discover any solid foundation, and which seems to be not so much the necessary remuneration of services rendered, as the result of fortuitous circumstances — a stroke of good fortune — just like rent or the earnings of a monopoly. Consequently it is felt that it might disappear like these other kinds of income without any injury to production.

Nor must it be thought that this is the opinion of socialists alone. It is also the view of economists of the neo-classical school, for, as we have just seen, they declare that under a system of absolutely free competition the rate of profit would be zero.   It is the opinion, too, of co-operators, for they are not content to show that the abolition of profit is theoretically possible: they actually accomplish it in the working of their consumers' societies.[1]   So these opposing schools agree in admitting, at any rate in theory, that profit can disappear, in the one case by the suppression of all monopoly, and in the others by some kind of mechanism, like collectivism or co-operation, which restores it to the community.

But we must make a distinction.   The profit whose abolition is foretold or even already accomplished, is pure profit, residual profit,

[1] This is just what we see realized already in consumers' co-operative societies, and it is precisely this that makes them so interesting as heralds of a new economic order.   They do not abolish profit in so far as it consists of wages of management and interest on capital, and it is entered among the expenses of production.   But the extra profit, consisting of an addition to the selling price, is abolished, for even if it

or "extra" profit; but it is not profit as the term is understood in everyday speech — profit in the sense of remuneration for the actual assistance rendered to production by the *entrepreneur*, and for the risks that he incurs. To abolish this remuneration would be to abolish all business, and thereby to do away with production itself. Profit in this sense could only be abolished if it were proved that the *entrepreneur* is merely a parasite, whose functions are obsolete, and who can perfectly well be dispensed with. But this point does not yet seem to have been reached.

Even as regards pure profit — that which results from monopoly or chance — there is some ground for asking whether its disappearance would not strike a blow at production. Those economists who teach the law of the diminution of profits foresee as a consequence " the stationary state," by which they mean that the progress of industry would come to an end as soon as men were deprived of the chance of profiting by strokes of good fortune.

This is probable; but then no doubt other motives of human activity would arise, more noble than the desire for gain, and even if we had to end in a stationary state, industrially speaking, the prospect would not seem very alarming: John Stuart Mill himself regarded it with tranquillity.

remains in the shape of a distribution of bonuses, it is restored to the purchasers, on whom it was levied. It is no longer profit, therefore, but what the French call a *ristourne* — resembling the repayment of insurance premiums. (See, below, the section on Consumers' Co-operative Societies.)

BOOK IV — CONSUMPTION

CHAPTER I — SPENDING

I. THE MEANING OF THE WORD "CONSUMPTION"

This last Book is absent from most treatises on political economy, and there is no lack of economists who assert that consumption has nothing to do with economics but belongs to the sphere of ethics or hygiene. Consumption, according to one of them, is only an essentially individualist matter. But it is difficult to see why consumption should be a more individualist action than production, for the ideas it calls up are rather those of conviviality — the family table, the feast at which men meet in friendship, or even the Lord's Supper, the symbol of Christian communion.

Consumption is not merely the act of eating: the word must be taken in a wide sense to cover the best possible use of the wealth that is available. It is the final cause and the "consummation" of the whole economic process of production, circulation, and distribution.

The term "consumption" is liable to certain misinterpretations that must be guarded against.

(1) It must not be thought that consumption is synonymous with *destruction*. It is true — and it is this that leads to confusion — that there are some wants, such as food, for example, and lighting, which can only be satisfied by the transformation of the objects that serve for food or fuel. To make use of bread and wine — that is, to change them into flesh and blood — we are obliged to eat and drink them; and to warm ourselves we are obliged to burn coal or wood — that is, to reduce them to smoke and ashes; and that is an unfortunate necessity.[1] But there are many other kinds of wealth which can be utilized without being destroyed: houses, gardens, money, furniture, and works of art. It is true that such things are not everlasting and generally perish sooner or later, either by accident or by the mere process of time — *tempus edax rerum*. But this destruction

---

[1] We need hardly say that by "destruction" is only meant the destruction of utility and value, not the annihilation of matter; for it is quite obvious that just as man can create nothing by production, so by consumption he can destroy nothing.

should certainly not be attributed to consumption. This is proved by the fact that we try to make things last as long as possible, and if we could make everything incapable of wearing out — clothes, linen, furniture, houses, and so forth — they would answer their economic purpose much better instead of worse; for they could then be utilized for ever, which would be the ideal form of consumption. Progress in consumption consists simply in consuming as much as possible while destroying as little as possible. The consumption of art is typical, by its immaterial character, of the kind of consumption that is to be desired: the enjoyment of the object causes it no damage. If the Venus of Milo is mutilated, the fault lies with the barbarians, and not with the admiring contemplation of those who look upon her.

Even in cases where consumption results in the destruction of utility, a wise economy will find means to make use even of dead utilities by causing some new utility to arise from their ashes. In industrial production the utilization of residues or by-products is already practised, and is, as we have seen, one of the causes of the superiority of large-scale production. Thus paper is made from rags; the refuse of food-stuffs and the slag of the furnace are converted into fertilizers; from coal tar is derived a complete series of perfumes and of colours; and soap and light are obtained from household refuse. But it was the great war that brought into the front rank this science of economical consumption, which until then had been somewhat despised. It was carried out to an incredible extent in that one of the belligerent countries which had to suffer most from the shortage of commodities — that is to say, in Germany. It is to be hoped that this teaching will not be thrown away, and that it will put an end to the terrible waste of wealth that was practised before the war. What is economic science if it is not the science of economy? In a perfect economy no unit would perish, but all would be transformed; and consumption would only be the story of the metamorphoses of wealth.[1]

(2) If consumption is not to be confounded with destruction, neither is it to be confounded with *production*. It might be thought that this confusion is much less likely to be made than the other; but none the less it is frequent and easy.

In fact, all production of wealth necessitates the continual consumption of raw materials, coal, provisions, and everything that goes by the name of circulating capital (p. 109). The economic process makes a closed circuit: man produces in order to eat, and he also has to eat in order to produce. But all the same, if we wish to understand

---

[1] Thus, thanks to the shortage of paper, it has just been discovered that even the dead leaves that autumn strews upon the ground can be used for making paper.

the matter, we must mark the beginning and end of the circuit at some point or other. Now the end of the whole economic process is the satisfaction of man's wants. It is at that point alone that wealth is permanently consumed. Up to that point and throughout all its transformations it is simply in course of production. The "splendid gesture of the sower" must remain above all others the symbol of the act of production: to call it an act of consumption, thereby assimilating two things as opposite to each other as sowing the corn and eating it, would create utter confusion.[1]

(3) Although consumption is the sole end of production it is a mistake to think that the best means of increasing production is to increase consumption. That, however, is a common view, and it is that which makes public opinion so indulgent and even sympathetic towards all acts of extravagance.

It may be admitted, to be sure, that very great consumption, after the American fashion, is a powerful stimulus to production, as it is in the United States. It is evident that consumption is the object of all production and the sole reason for its existence. It is plain that if men were to eat no more bread they would sow no more wheat. But because consumption appears as the *final* cause of production, it by no means follows that it is also the *efficient* cause. It must be borne in mind that the only agents of production are those we have already described — labour, land, and capital — and consumption cannot create or increase any one of them. On the contrary, consumption is incessantly undoing their work and emptying the reservoir that they are labouring to fill. If this reservoir were fed by a continuous stream, in such a way that the more one drew from it the more came into it, then there might be some excuse for the mistaken idea that the more wealth is consumed the more it will be produced. But such is not the case. No one would venture to maintain that the more fruit one gathered the more would the orchard yield, that the more fish one caught the more would the ocean bring forth, or that the more wood one burned the higher and thicker would the forest grow.

What favours this confusion is the fact that consumption in actual practice means *spending*: it is the price that must be paid to obtain what we want. Spending is consumption expressed in terms of money. Now money that is spent is never consumed: it is only

---

[1] To avoid this confusion, economists generally describe the consumption of wealth whose object is production as "reproductive" consumption, while they call that which aims at the immediate satisfaction of our wants "unproductive" consumption. But this latter term is an unfortunate one, for it seems to imply a measure of blame: what is called "unproductive" consumption is precisely the true and only consumption.

transferred from the buyer to the seller.   That is why in the eyes of the public all expenditure, even the most foolish, appears inoffensive since it merely transfers money from Peter to Paul — in fact, it is even regarded as praiseworthy because it "helps trade."   But to judge aright about spending we must look not at the money but at the wealth that the money buys, and see whether or not this has been usefully consumed.

II.   RIGHTS AND DUTIES OF THE CONSUMER

One of the last words of Bastiat on his death-bed was this: "We must learn to look at everything from the point of view of the consumer."   And therein he was only giving utterance to the spirit of the classical political economy.   But liberal economists, faithful to the spirit of their school, think it unnecessary to take any special measures to establish the rule of the consumer: they believe that free competition will take care of that.   In fact, under the system of free competition, they say, every producer must strive to do his best for his customer, the consumer — to give him the best he can at the lowest price.   So the consumer, like a king, would only have to let himself be served.

This optimistic picture is not borne out by facts.   No doubt it is to the interest of the producer to satisfy his customers, since that is generally his surest way of increasing their numbers and therefore his profits, but that is only his indirect or ultimate object: his immediate object is profit, and not the service of anybody else.   And if he can manage to increase his profit more by raising his prices or selling adulterated goods, experience shows that he will not fail to do so.   It is notorious that in recent years and in every country the raising of prices and the adulteration of goods have assumed disquieting proportions.   No doubt the consumer has some safeguards in professional spirit and commercial honour, but there we are on moral and not economic ground.

The consumer will do well therefore not to trust to *laisser faire* and not to play the idle part of a sluggard.   He needs to put up an energetic defence of his interests, which — and herein lies their superiority — are bound up with the more general interests of society.

But this power of the consumer has remained until recently a purely theoretical one, for want of organization.   Consumption does not create among men the same community of interests, the same permanent concentration of effort, as does the exercise of the same profession, in spite of competition.   For this reason professional organization has far outstripped the organization of consumers. But the latter has recently begun to be effected, in very varying forms of association.

Some of these associations are ambitious of bringing about a revolution to transfer economic government from the producer to the consumer: these are the consumers' co-operative societies. We shall deal with them separately in the next section.

But there are other associations, far more numerous than is often imagined, which have more specialized aims. These consumers' associations are of two different types: those which aim at instructing consumers as to their *rights* and their interests and the means of satisfying them; and those whose object is to teach them their *duties* and the means of performing them.

(1) As regards consumers' associations which aim at defending their rights we must mention the following: first of all, the leagues formed to combat high prices, which were very numerous during the war; leagues formed for defence against protection, like the Anti-Corn Law League that played so prominent a part in English economic history between 1839 and 1846; associations against the adulteration of goods; and those whose aim is to look after the interests of the consumers of certain public services, such as the telephone service and the railways.

Nor is it only in the formation of associations or unions that the consumers have taken a leaf out of the workers' book: like them they have not hesitated of late years to resort to the strike weapon — known rather, though incorrectly, by the name of *boycott*. And this weapon has proved as effective in their hands as in that of the workers. Thus there has been a strike of consumers against the Meat Trust in the United States; a strike of beer-drinkers against the brewers in Germany; a strike of gas consumers against the gas companies in various towns in France; and in 1910 there was even a strike at Roubaix of the consumers of alcoholic drinks — but this one, alas, did not become general and was short-lived. For the most part these strikes succeeded in making the producers give in.

To put it shortly, the consumer is no longer willing simply to play the part of a *client*, in the historical and humiliating sense of the word: he claims the right to take his part in the government of economic affairs.

(2) The object of associations of the second class is to preach and practise the duties of the consumer; for if the latter is king in the economic realm, his kingship obviously involves some responsibilities— the one cannot exist without the other. It rests with the consumer, by

changing the character of his expenditure — that is to say, by employing his money differently — to divert capital and labour from those branches of production in which they are employed, and turn them in any direction he pleases.   In this way the consumer exerts a decisive influence over the three agents of production — land, labour, and capital — even if he lives merely as a *rentier*.   He commands these three agents; and, like the centurion in the Gospel, he says "unto one, Go, and he goeth: and to another, Come, and he cometh."   And it is precisely this power of command that imposes special duties upon the rich, however little this fact has been realized hitherto.

These associations can be further subdivided into two classes:

(*a*) The first are those which set out to fight against consumption that is harmful, immoral, and destructive, and to teach by way of example.   In the front rank of these are the temperance societies; then come the vegetarian societies, and such others as those that combat the use of tobacco or opium, or the wearing of birds' feathers in ladies' hats.

(*b*) The second kind are those that aim at putting a stop to all the requirements of consumers that are of a kind to impose a useless burden upon labour: for instance, orders given to dressmakers at the last moment, so that if they are to be executed in time, the work must be done at night; the delivery of goods on Sunday; the sending of trunks too heavy for the porters to carry; and the letting of houses in which the kitchens and the servants' rooms are unsatisfactory. These societies — called *purchasers' social leagues* — publish *white lists*, on which are entered only those shops that undertake to conform to certain conditions in the matter of wages, time for rest, and so forth, for their workpeople; or else they distribute labels to be affixed to goods to certify that the industry is properly conducted.   It will easily be understood that if these leagues contained a large number of rich consumers, the tradesmen would be very anxious to appear on the white lists or to obtain the labels, and would therefore be encouraged to treat their employees well.

Yet these purchasers' leagues, whose object is beyond all praise and which even mark a new era in economic organization, have recently called forth somewhat keen criticism, and that from unexpected quarters, for it proceeds from economists of the liberal school.   They think that the consumer is totally unfitted to meddle with the technical organization of labour, and to allot good or bad marks to producers.

Moreover, socialists are even less favourably disposed than individualist economists towards this question of the functions of the consumer. They consider that attention should be directed to the producer, and that he alone should lay down the laws of production. They think that the society of the future must be based on professional association and not on combinations of consumers. And they even hold that it is in the former alone, and not in the latter, that the moral ideals of the future will be worked out. The idea of the kingship of the consumer would be a mere *bourgeois* notion.[1] It is easy, indeed, to understand that the supremacy of the consumer is incompatible with the essential doctrines of Marxian socialism — class warfare and the victory of the working classes — for the very nature of the consumer excludes all class division. Production necessarily divides men, by creating an opposition of interests, of groups, and of classes. Consumption is no respecter of persons or of classes: and therein, as it seems to us, lies its superiority.

III. THE CONSUMERS' CO–OPERATIVE SOCIETY

We have already had to concern ourselves with consumers' societies (p. 364) when dealing with socialist doctrines, and we saw that they brought forward a new programme. This programme was clearly formulated in the Declaration of that band of weavers who have become famous as the Rochdale Pioneers, in 1844. What they said was that as soon as possible the society would proceed to the organization of production, distribution, and education, within its own borders and by its own means. This means that the society was not concerned with remodelling the nation: it was intent on creating a new economy within each society, and thus making of it a microcosm that would spread and multiply by a process of imitation. Although economists have always laughed at this programme as ridiculously pretentious, yet it is beginning to be realized.

In fact, these consumers' societies in England already contain four million members, which, counting in the members of their families, represents some twenty million persons, or nearly half the population of Great Britain — there are very few members in Ireland. The amount of their business reaches 160 million pounds, on which they realize profits of over 20 million pounds, which they divide almost in their entirety among their members. Almost all the societies are federated and combined, not only under a central government — the Co-operative Union — and in annual conferences, but in two powerful Wholesale Societies, the English and the Scottish, with headquarters at Manchester and Glasgow respectively.[2]

[1] For arguments to the contrary, see our book, *Le Coopératisme*, and especially the discussion therein under the heading, *Le règne du consommateur*.

[2] For fuller information see our book, *Les sociétés coopératives de consommation*.

These societies are numerous also in Denmark, Finland, and Russia, and they are extending all over the world, from Iceland to the Caucasus. In France there are more than 4,000 societies, but most of them unfortunately are very small and unorganized. It took twenty-six years to arrive at a great federation of these societies (1913).

The war, in spite of the destruction that it wrought, has given the co-operative movement an impetus that has surpassed all the expectations of its warmest adherents — and that, too, in every country. In Russia to-day, co-operation in its various forms covers the whole vast country as far as Siberia, with 50,000 societies. It is the only institution that has remained standing amidst the general ruin, and the only one that has been respected by the Soviet government, and it is due to it that economic life has been able, after a fashion, to continue.

In England, in Germany, in Italy, in Switzerland, everywhere the amount of sales has enormously increased, and sometimes more than doubled.[1] It is true that the increase is partly only nominal, so far as it is due to the rise of prices; but, on the other hand, the reduction of consumption caused by this rise must also be taken into account. Moreover, the number of members has notably increased also,[2] and, above all, co-operation has improved its standing in public opinion. These societies have become one of the indispensable organs of social life, in the proper sense of the term. There will soon be scarcely a town or village that has not its co-operative society, just as it has its school and its church.

As a rule these societies are everywhere constituted after what is called the Rochdale type, which is characterized by these four features:

(1) Selling at ordinary *retail prices* and not at cost price, so as to realize a surplus;

(2) The distribution of this surplus among the members *in proportion to their purchases*, and not in proportion to their shares, which only yield them a moderate rate of interest;[3]

[1] [The net sales of the English Co-operative Wholesale Society rose from 35 millions in 1914 to 105 millions in 1920, though falling to just under 81 millions in 1921.]

[2] [The membership of societies affiliated to the English C. W. S. rose from 2.3 millions in 1914 to 3.4 millions in 1921.]

[3] This distribution seems opposed to the character of the co-operative business, as we have defined it, which is to make no profit. But this is not really so. It is true that the English call these surpluses "dividends" (or, familiarly, "divies"); but the name given to them in France (*ristournes*, or *trop perçus*) clearly indicates that they are simply the repayment to the purchaser of the amount he has been called upon to pay in excess of the cost price. They are not profit, therefore; and this is proved by

(3) The appropriation of a certain portion of these bonuses to works of *social solidarity*, such as the education of the members, benevolent funds, propaganda, festivities and excursions, etc.;

(4) The principle of *one vote per member* in the meetings of the society, without regard to the number of his shares. This is a principle of democratic equality which makes it impossible for capital to obtain possession.

The immediate advantages of these associations, both economic and moral, are as follows:

(a) The establishment of a *fair price* — that is to say, a price that is sufficient to cover all the expenses of production and even to satisfy all the economic necessities that are summed up in the law of supply and demand, but a price that is free from all the usurious additions that are due only to combination among producers and to the ignorance of consumers.

(b) The fixing of an *honest price*,[1] by doing away with the adulteration of goods, dishonesty in the matter of weight and quality, and lying advertisements. The reign of honesty in trade would mean no slight revolution!

This salutary influence exerted upon prices by co-operative societies appeared so plainly during the war that it opened everybody's eyes — not only the eyes of the public, who hurried to these places of refuge, but even those of governments, who had hitherto been somewhat hostile to them on electoral grounds. Where administrative regulation of prices had shown itself powerless and even harmful, the action of the co-operative societies was perfectly effectual. The municipalities had to have recourse to their services, or, where they were lacking, to try to find substitutes for them by establishing municipal shops — butchers' shops in particular.

(c) The *education of the consumer* — teaching him what goods he ought to prefer, and which of them are least costly in proportion to their feeding properties. In Belgium these societies have been the most powerful agent of the anti-alcohol movement. In all countries during the war they mitigated the terrible effects of the food shortage by averting panic, controlling their members, and teaching them not to rush to the shops and not to hoard food at

the fact that the State, which is not easily imposed upon, has given up levying income tax upon them.

It must be owned, however, that the members themselves take little account of this difference, and await their bonuses as eagerly as ordinary capitalist shareholders their dividends.

[1] See footnote to p. 193.

home like the majority of consumers. And when one commodity ran short they were able to ration their members before the governments had invented food cards.

As for the more distant results, which can only be realized by the progressive absorption of industrial undertakings in proportion as the co-operative societies come to produce themselves all that they require, we have already mentioned these in describing the co-operative programme (pp. 363–366).

As regards the last items on this programme, of course the consumer's societies are still far from attaining their end: maybe they will never reach it. But at least it is not rash to assert that they are called upon to take an increasingly large place in the new economy, particularly in the lands that have to be reconstituted since the war. In fact, if it is true that the speeding-up of production is the urgent need of these countries that have been drained to the last drop, then no less urgent will be the need for a wise economy in consumption.

IV. HOUSING

Among all the kinds of expenditure, house-rent merits special study for two reasons: first, because of all private wants housing is the one of greatest *social* importance — greater even, from the social standpoint, than that of food; — and, secondly, because of all expenses this is the one that has increased most rapidly and that weighs most heavily on the pockets of the working classes and even of families in comfortable circumstances.

In ancient times the house was not only the home of the family but the altar of the household gods: so every man, rich or poor, had his own. Nowadays, when the exigencies of modern life have driven men back into a kind of nomadic existence, and they are no longer allowed to take root where they were born, the great majority of men live in hired houses. And the tendency of all the causes — social, economic, and political — that impel people to concentrate in the large towns — administrative centralization, large-scale production, railway development, and the growth of amusements — is constantly to increase rents, greatly to the profit of the urban landowner, but greatly to the injury of the public.

Most of the evils that afflict the working population — the loosening of the family tie, the public house habit, the early initiation into vice, the transmission of contagious diseases and epidemics — are the result for the most part of the shortage of house accommodation. Moreover, the dignity of life for man, and still more for woman, is closely dependent upon a certain measure of home comfort.

Why, then, is it not the same with houses as with all other products, for which the supply generally follows the demand and sometimes even outstrips it? For is not a house simply a product of human industry — unlike land, streams of water, or mines? In a sense, yes; but yet there are two essential differences between the production of houses and that of other kinds of goods. These are as follows:

(1) A house can only be built on a particular plot of ground: now, building sites are so limited in number that the construction of a new house generally means pulling down an old one. That is why house-rent remains a monopoly price, limited only by the tenant's means.

The only effectual remedy would be a movement in the opposite direction to what has hitherto been the progress of development — that is to say, a stoppage of the growth of large towns, a return to the country districts of the people who have left them, and the restoration, as M. Luzzatti has said, of the worship of the household gods. In fact a certain amount of centrifugal movement is already to be observed in our large towns. This movement is accelerated by the development of cheap means of transport — motor buses, trams, and underground railways — which enable workers and employees to find healthier and less expensive accommodation far away from the middle of great cities. But the workers are not very fond of getting too far away from the urban centres — the land of public houses and the pictures.

(2) The production of houses, by which we mean the building industry, has not benefited by mechanical progress to the same extent as other kinds of industry. The methods of building are hardly any different or better to-day than they were in the time of the Romans.[1]

It must be noticed also that all the regulations imposed upon builders in the interests of public health and sanitation — going so far even as the expropriation and demolition of insanitary dwellings — only increase the evil, however excellent they may be in themselves. In fact the severe conditions imposed upon builders are bound to have the effect of increasing the cost of new houses and thereby making them still more inaccessible to the poor. And of

[1] The housing problem has been intensified by the war in two ways: (1) by increasing the cost of construction very considerably; (2) by doubling the rate of interest, which reacts upon the rate of rent.

course if we go to the extreme of pulling down old houses, that means diminishing their number as well.

Can a solution be found in fixing rents, as food prices were fixed during the war, and for the same reason, namely, that it is a question of satisfying an indispensable need? But between the case of bread and that of houses there is this essential difference: that the baker is a merchant, who makes bread only to sell it, whereas the owner of a house can always refuse to let it. No doubt if we assume the letting to be already accomplished and the tenant in possession, the law can reduce the rent or even abolish it entirely; something of this sort has already been done during the war. But the problem is to find houses for those who are without them; and such a remedy as this is bound to diminish the supply for the future, for if rent were abolished it is obvious that no one would any longer build houses to let: the rich alone would have houses built to live in themselves.

There seems nothing for it, then, but to appeal to the collaboration of all the factors of social progress — employers, philanthropists, institutions of public utility, mutual aid societies, municipalities, the State, and the interested parties themselves, organized in co-operative societies. From them must be demanded the requisite capital for the erection of as many houses as possible, in the most economical manner; they must relinquish all profit, and be content with a moderate rate of interest, so as to reduce rents to the actual cost price of the houses.

All these methods have, in fact, been already employed, as follows:

(1) Very many houses have been built for their workpeople by employers or companies, in the form of *workmen's towns*. This has not been done entirely from philanthropic motives, but because factories and mines situated at a distance from large centres of population are unable to obtain workers unless they can be assured of accommodation.

Some of these towns in England and the United States are marvels of comfort, hygiene, and even artistic arrangement.

But this method only touches the fringe of the housing problem, for it is in cities and not in the country that the problem is most acute.

(2) *Co-operative building societies* have been formed by the workers themselves, generally with the aid of philanthropic capitalists. They buy the land themselves, have the houses built, and sell or let them at cost price to such of their members as want them. But in America and England the majority of these societies do not themselves undertake the building: they simply lend money for the pur-

pose, in very ingenious and very economical ways. These loans, being perfectly secured, serve as investments for the savings of those members who are compelled to wait a long time for their turn to be housed, or of those — and they are the largest number — who have no intention of becoming owners; so that these societies act as savings-banks even more than as building societies.[1]

(3) Philanthropic capitalists can also assist in the construction of houses, either in their lifetime, by lending capital without interest or at a small interest, to *building societies;* or else after their death, in the form of *foundations.* This is perhaps the most useful way in which a man can employ his wealth, from the social point of view, and it imposes only the minimum of sacrifice upon him. But unfortunately it is only too uncommon.

(4) Lastly, the solution of the housing problem can be aided by the *municipalities* and the *State*, either directly, by the actual building of houses, or indirectly, by giving assistance to building societies. Given the seriousness of the situation of the tenant — a situation that contains, maybe, the seeds of revolution — it certainly seems that from the public authorities alone can the necessary effort be forthcoming.

Many towns in England, Germany, and Switzerland have already adopted this method. They have been driven to do so by the circumstances just described: they have shut up insanitary houses, and have therefore found it necessary to replace them. In England, when the death rate in any area exceeds a certain figure, the municipal authority pulls down the houses and replaces them by new ones which it lets at cost price. Now that the war is over, England is intending to make an extraordinary effort to ensure proper housing accommodation for the families of the hundreds of thousands of men who fought or died for their country.[2]

[1] In France in 1912 there were only 400 or 500 co-operative or philanthropic building societies. They were all very small, and in some twenty years had built, at the outside, only £6,000,000-worth of houses (say, enough to accommodate about 20,000 families).

[2] All this can only yield results in the distant future: so those who are impatient — and there are many who have every right to be — are demanding that the municipal authorities should take immediate possession of all houses. This revolutionary solution would obviously not increase the number of houses. But it would enable a larger number of people to find accommodation, by rationing the number of rooms occupied by each household. It would also lower rents, whether the expropriation was carried out without compensation to the owners, or whether it was done at the expense of the ratepayers.

V. LUXURY EXPENDITURE

The word *luxury* in its ordinary acceptation means *anything that satisfies a superfluous want*. But this definition, though in common use, cannot provide us with any element of moral or economic valuation, for, as Voltaire said, the superfluous is a very necessary thing. We must desire that there should be a little superfluity — and therefore a little luxury — for everybody, even for the poorest. On the other hand, economic history teaches us that there is no want, not even among those that seem to us nowadays to be most urgent, that was not originally regarded as superfluous. It cannot be otherwise; first, because when a want is new, it follows from this very fact that no one else has yet experienced it; and, secondly, because its satisfaction necessarily requires a considerable amount of labour, owing to lack of experience of the industry and the inevitable uncertainty of the first attempts. If there is one thing that seems indispensable nowadays, it is undoubtedly underclothing: "to be reduced to one's last shirt" is a proverbial expression for the utmost degree of poverty. Yet at some periods a shirt was regarded as an article of extreme luxury and as a gift for a king. It is the same with hundreds of other things. So if asceticism had prevailed and aimed at repressing all luxury wants, it would have nipped in the bud all wants which make man civilized, and we should to-day be still in the position of our ancestors of the stone age. Luxury is the flower that contains the fruit; and to destroy all the flowers is to destroy also all the fruit.

This is by no means to say that we could not at any given moment establish a hierarchy of wants, so long as we remember that in this hierarchy there is a gradual rise, or rather a continual transformation of wants, those that are called superfluous becoming gradually crystallized or solidified into necessary ones. And this transformation could not be checked without putting an end to the progress of civilization. That is why laws for repressing luxury — sumptuary laws, as they are called — which have so often been enacted in the past, would have had fatal results if they had not, fortunately, remained inoperative.

Expenditure is not, therefore, to be condemned, either from the moral or even from the economic standpoint, simply because it satisfies a superfluous want; for if the want is regarded now as superfluous, we cannot foresee the future. To judge rightly, we must adopt a different point of view: we must consider what are the *means* employed, at the time and in the country in question, to satisfy the luxury want, and ask whether the amount of wealth and labour that is devoted to it is not likely to reduce the amount that should be reserved for other more immediate wants. It is a question of proportion.

But it remains to discover how the want of proportion is to be measured.

In the case of private luxury it can only be done by comparing the amount of money expended with the individual income from which it is drawn. But from the social point of view the true criterion is not the amount of money expended, but the amount of wealth or labour consumed in providing satisfaction for a given want. Now we must always bear in mind these two facts: that the amount of wealth in existence is insufficient at the present time to satisfy the primary needs of the great majority of our fellow men (see p. 352); and that the productive forces — land, labour, and capital — which feed and renew this store of wealth, are all three limited in quantity. Hence it will appear as a very definite duty not to divert to the satisfaction of a superfluous want too large a portion of the productive power and wealth that are available for meeting the necessities of existence of everyone.

Take, for example, the taste for flowers, which was absolutely unknown to our forefathers. This is undoubtedly a luxury in the ordinary sense of the word, as it meets a superfluous want. The pot of flowers that the workman places in his window is undeniably a luxury, but a luxury that is as harmless as it is charming. But if at a banquet (or a funeral) the table (or the coffin) is covered with flowers that represent the entire output of a whole garden and a year's labour; if to decorate a drawing-room we must have orchids brought from Borneo or Madagascar by expeditions that have cost thousands of pounds and perhaps even human lives, or blue dahlias that have been grown under glass with the consumption of more coal than would have kept ten families warm throughout a whole winter — then in these cases we must no longer call it luxury, but extravagance, display, or ostentation.

If a wealthy spendthrift gives his friends a dinner costing £50 a head, morality may grieve, and his family will do well to get a guardian appointed for him; but political economy is not concerned about the matter, because the money that leaves the spendthrift's pocket will be better in the caterer's hands. And as for the dishes that have been consumed — the oysters and soups and truffles and famous wines — they will have taken nothing from the tables of the poor. Can it be possible for one person to consume £50-worth of food?

No; it is not in the power of a spendthrift to make an ogre of himself: the national food supply is no more depleted by this dinner than by one that cost half a crown a head, or even less. But if after dinner the guests begin to smash the glasses, as seems to have been the fashion at banquets given by Russian officers, then that is the point at which luxury becomes socially injurious.

If a fashionable lady wears a dress that cost £100 at the dressmaker's, society loses nothing by it if the price is paid solely for the novelty of the cut or the reputation of the dressmaker, for it is not likely that it has used up more material or more labour than an ordinary dress. But if this same lady has sewn to her ball dress a few yards of lace that has taken several years to make, then the nation will suffer, though no doubt the workwoman will not complain.

If an English peer spends thousands on a picture gallery, it is well — though it would be better still if he endowed a public picture gallery with the money. But if for the pleasure of giving his friends some grouse-shooting he makes moors out of land which could have produced food for hundreds of his fellow-countrymen, and thereby drives them into exile; if he maintains an army of gamekeepers who would be more usefully employed in tilling his land than in preserving his game, especially in a country that has to import three-quarters of its bread from abroad — that is luxury of an anti-economic kind.

People are scandalized at the fantastic prices paid for works of art, even in the midst of the distresses of war-time. But what does it matter if a picture has been sold for thousands of pounds, since the money has passed from the hands of a millionaire collector into those of a dealer? It is only the artist's labour that we must consider, and in this case the economist has no reason to protest, for true art does not generally require an amount of labour disproportionate to the result. Quite the contrary: a block of marble and a chisel, or a square yard of canvas and a few tubes of paint, together with some days of labour, are sufficient to provide all human generations with exquisite and continually renewed enjoyment. It is a characteristic of art to produce great enjoyment by very simple means.

There is also such a thing as public luxury, indulged in by States or cities. This meets, as a rule, with more indulgence, and rightly so, because being a collective affair it benefits everybody and may even to some extent give a share in the enjoyments of luxury to that part of the population which could never obtain them by its own resources. Moreover, public luxury generally takes the form of monuments of a durable and sometimes almost everlasting character, so that they may be considered sooner or later to liquidate their cost, and bear no resemblance to fleeting forms of consumption. Yet here also the question of proportion arises: the magnificence of the palace of Versailles cannot make the economist forget that the millions it cost were paid out of the people's bread.

However, public opinion, and even some economists, are far from thinking that luxury involves a waste of labour: they regard it as a stimulus to labour in so far as it quickens men's desires, if only by the envy it arouses. But if the labour called forth by luxury is employed in its turn to produce articles of luxury, is not this like the labour of the daughters of Danaus?

There are others who admit that luxury dissipates productive power, but who consider that it exerts a good influence in the matter of distribution, because it brings about a sort of restitution of the superfluous wealth of the rich, in the shape of wages for the poor. But this restitution could be accomplished exactly the same, and far more usefully, in the shape of investments in productive undertakings (see, below, the section on Investment).

VI. STATE CONTROL OF CONSUMPTION

Governments in every age have considered it one of their functions and duties to see that their people did not suffer from famine, or excessive high prices, or bad quality of manufactured products, and also, on the other hand, to restrict or prohibit consumption that they regarded as contrary to the public well-being.

But economists, as soon as there were any, have never ceased to protest against this legislative interference. It seemed to them more intolerable in matters of consumption— that is to say, in the sphere of private life — than in the domain of production or transport, which is more or less a public matter.

The forms of State intervention in the matter of consumption can be classed under five heads:

(1) To make sure that consumers have a *sufficient quantity*. We need only recall what the Bible says of the granaries established by Pharaoh's minister to ensure a supply of corn during seven years of famine; the distributions of corn to the Romans, which were started in the days of the Gracchi and continued down to the time of the Empire; and the measures taken by the French government at various periods before the Revolution to make sure that the markets were supplied with corn. Since that time, men have been obsessed by the fear of overproduction rather than of famine. So this early form of intervention seemed to be definitely abandoned when the Great

War came and turned it into a terrible reality. The mobilization of almost the whole adult male population on the one hand, and on the other hand the enormous increase in the cost of transport, due to the blockades imposed by the belligerents on each other, resulted in such a shortage of all food-stuffs that the governments of almost every country in Europe had to resort to the most stringent measures — the system of compulsory and equal *rationing* — in order to assure a minimum of food to the civil population.

(2) To protect consumers against a *raising of the prices* of prime necessaries which might make their consumption impossible for the poor. This case is not the same as the preceding one, as it does not always imply a shortage.

In France a law of 1791 gave the municipalities the right to fix the prices of bread and meat.[1] And it is interesting to observe that this law is still in force 130 years later, despite the vigorous criticisms of the economists! It is the most venerable of all the laws that exist in the legislative arsenal.

During the war the regulation of prices developed to such an extent in some of the belligerent countries as to become almost the regular thing. It was applied in France from the beginning to such prime necessaries as bread, sugar, and frozen meat, and then later on to milk, butter, potatoes, and so forth. But the results were on the whole discouraging, for either the law was not kept, and the tradesman sold above the regulation price, with the connivance of the buyer, or else, when it was kept, the seller gave up bringing his produce to the market. It became necessary, therefore, to supplement price regulation by a more stringent measure — that of *requisitioning* goods from the producer.

The establishment of municipal shops proved much more satisfactory, for the municipal selling price became the rule of the market through the action of competition.

(3) To protect consumers against the *adulteration of goods*. While the two preceding forms of State intervention are exceptional in their character, this one, on the contrary, is becoming more widespread. The reason for this is twofold: on the one hand, the truly marvellous progress that has taken place in the art of adulteration; and, on the other hand, the parallel progress that has been made in the knowledge of the laws of health — that is to say, of the properties of food-stuffs and the best methods of utilizing them for the maintenance of our functions and strength. Many laws have

---

[1] [Many similar measures were enacted in England during the Middle Ages.]

been enacted in all countries against the adulteration of wine, butter, milk, sugar, meat, and so forth.

Of all forms of State interference this is the one that economists of the liberal school regard as the most improper. In the case of consumption, this meddling with the affairs of the kitchen on the part of the legislator, who puts on the doctor's robes for the occasion, seems to them as ridiculous as that of the doctor on the island of Barataria who pointed out with his imperious wand the dishes that poor Sancho might and might not eat.

Yet to affirm, as these economists do, that the consumer is competent to know what he is consuming, and to look after his own interests, is to fail to recognize that even if he were to have a complete knowledge of hygiene he generally has no choice in the matter, especially if he is one of the poor. Does anyone imagine that the babies who are poisoned by adulterated milk are "the best judges of their own interests"?

It is true that protection might be accorded to consumers by the numerous private associations, leagues of consumers or purchasers, anti-adulteration societies, agricultural unions, and consumers' co-operative societies of which we have already spoken, especially if they were given the right to prosecute — a right which French law refuses to private societies but which English law confers upon them. But these societies must have the law to fall back upon, and the law, in its turn, needs private assistance, for otherwise it is to be feared that it would remain of no effect.

(4) To prevent the consumption of *harmful commodities*, if not by prohibiting the consumption itself, which would in practice be difficult, then at least by prohibiting the manufacture and sale of such things.

The sale of alcohol is prohibited in several countries. It is well known that the prohibition of all fermented drinks (and not only distilled liquors) has been extended to the whole area of the great American republic, after being first localized in certain States. Prohibition exists also, though in a less absolute form, in Finland and in Norway. China, by a decree of the 22nd November, 1906, has prohibited the consumption of opium under severe penalties, and this campaign was strongly supported by the "Young China" movement. It is the same in Japan. In France the campaign against alcohol has gone no farther at present than the prohibition of absinthe.[1]

---

[1] The sale of opium is forbidden in France, but in French Indo-China it is the subject of a profitable monopoly!

(5) Lastly, the law might have to intervene not to protect the interests of the consumer but to *impose certain duties* upon him — duties that are required by his social function — and notably to prevent certain kinds of waste of natural wealth. As examples we may cite the prohibition of shooting and fishing during several months of the year. There are other products whose sale will no doubt sooner or later be forbidden, because their consumption involves acts of stupid or fierce destruction — as, for instance, the feathers that are worn on ladies' hats. But so far it is only a few private societies that endeavour to make war — not very successfully — against this Red Indian fashion.

It is under this heading that we must place laws against luxury — what are called *sumptuary* laws. Though very numerous in the past, they have been given up, not only because they were usually ineffective and vexatious, but also because, as we have seen (p. 495), it is difficult and dangerous to draw the line above which luxury begins. None the less, there are certain taxes on articles or services of luxury — on motor-cars and carriages, on servants, on gambling, and on tourists — which may to some extent act as sumptuary laws.

CHAPTER II — SAVING

I. THE TWO ASPECTS OF SAVING

The word *saving* stands for two very different kinds of acts which are not even related to each other, though in everyday speech and even in books on political economy they are generally confused. There should be two different words for them, but as economic science does not yet possess a terminology of its own, we are obliged to use the same term with different epithets to qualify it.

1. *Economy saving*

This is the art of satisfying one's wants by consuming as little wealth as possible — of making the best use of the goods and money at one's disposal — of *economizing*, in the proper sense of the term. It is an application of the hedonistic principle, which consists, as we know, in obtaining the maximum of satisfaction with the minimum of sacrifice.

We have already seen, in connexion with the integration of industry, the increasing importance that is attached to economy of raw materials and of power, either by the utilization of industrial waste or *by-products*, as in gas-works, oil refineries, and wool-combing, or by the recovery of the heat that is lost in the gases that issue from blast furnaces, or in the combustion of incandescent coke.

But this science of economy is as important in consumption as in production. It is well known in domestic life in the humble shape of household economy. A clever housewife can cook and prepare a dinner with half as much coal and half as much butter as another who wastes them; and, what is better still, she can provide more nourishing food for her husband and children with less money. The virtues of the "Norwegian cooking-pot" in economizing fuel have been much extolled since the war. Nor is it only in the matter of food, but in wants of all kinds, that economy finds a place: a careful man will make his coat look like new for three times as long as another who wears his out immediately. And one man with a slender income will manage to obtain as much satisfaction and even to live as full a life as another who lets money run through his fingers.

Economy is indeed an art, and one which, like all arts, needs to be learned. It would be a great advantage and a great source of wealth if it were taught at any rate to those whose special task it is to practise it — namely, to women.[1]

Furthermore, there is not only the question of household economy: there is also to be considered the question of economy in national consumption in the widest sense of the term. This can be effected in infinitely various ways, the study of which has hitherto been entirely neglected, though their importance has been revealed by the war. We will only cite a few examples:

(a) The application of the law of substitution — the replacing of expensive commodities by others that are more useful: for instance, the use of more nutritious food-stuffs. Tables of alimentary equivalence have been published, showing the cost of a gramme of nitrogen or carbon in different kinds of food. The war led to the discovery of a surprising number of substitutes, not only in foods but in textiles and other kinds of goods, and no doubt many of these will remain permanently in use. People have hitherto utilized the resources of their countries very badly, and perhaps the best argument for protection would be that if rationally established it would educate nations in this respect.

(b) A more rational use of waste products in consumption as in production: for instance, household refuse, which has hitherto given much trouble and caused great expense to local authorities, can be used either as manure, or as fuel, providing a serviceable supply of heat when it is burnt.

(c) The preservation of perishable commodities, particularly by using methods of cold storage in transporting and keeping meat, fish, fruit, milk, and so forth. An enormous quantity of wealth that used to be lost is now saved by all these inventions.

(d) The more economical employment of such natural wealth as water, peat, and especially sunlight. Some years before the war the strange idea of daylight saving was conceived in England, where the difference between the solar day and the civil day caused more trouble than in other countries. The civil day, by which the business of life is regulated, fits in badly with the solar day: it begins too late and ends too late, and thus involves a consumption of artificial light

---

[1] Domestic instruction is being much extended nowadays, especially in Germany. In Berlin and other towns there are schools that give theoretical and practical training, with kitchens instead of laboratories. In Germany and Switzerland there are even *travelling* schools, with movable kitchens, which journey from village to village like caravans.

which represents a very considerable expense when the whole of the British Isles is taken into consideration. But all that is needed is to put the legal time an hour in advance of the sun, to make everybody start work an hour sooner and end the day an hour sooner.[1]

2. *Prudential Saving*

The word "saving" is used also in another sense. Here it applies not to economical consumption, as before, but to *deferred* consumption. Instead of satisfying his present wants, man thinks of his future wants: he feels them as intensely as if they were present ones, and so he "puts something by," as we say, for the morrow, or for his old age, or for his children, or "for a rainy day." This is not simply economy: it is something quite different — foresight, or prudence.

Saving has long been extolled by economists as the only source of riches, and, for the working classes, as the only means of bettering their condition. But public opinion, on the other hand, has always shown scant sympathy for saving, and great men like Montesquieu have even said: "If the rich do not spend freely, the poor die of hunger."

These two views are generally reconciled by saying that the poor should save and the rich should spend. But this twofold advice — making privation a duty for the worker, and enjoyment a duty for the capitalist — very naturally annoys the former. Nor does it seem to us well founded, even on economic grounds alone, and we should be inclined rather to reverse it.

As regards the classes that are advised to save, we are not going to say that saving is impossible for them, for it is always possible, even for the poor. The elasticity of human wants is marvellous, and as they are capable of indefinite extension, so also they are capable of indefinite compression. Moreover, since the working classes find means to spend millions on drink and tobacco — a deplorable fact — it is obvious that they could save if they wished, and would be much better for so doing.

Yet if the advice to save that is so arrogantly given to the poor seems to us not always justified, it is because saving that is effected out of necessaries, or even out of legitimate wants, is more disastrous than useful. It is absurd to sacrifice the present to the future when-

---

[1] But though this reform has yielded good results in towns it is different in the country districts, where hardly any artificial light is used and where labour is necessarily regulated by the sun.

ever the sacrifice of the present is *of such a kind as to compromise the future*. Every public or private expenditure that conduces to a man's physical or intellectual development should receive unhesitating approval, not only as being good in itself, but as preferable even to saving. Strengthening food, good clothes, a healthy house, comfortable furniture, more frequent medical and sanitary attention, instructive books, some such recreations as walks, travelling, games, and concerts, and, above all, the education of the children — all these must be looked upon as *investments* rather than expenses, and as the best of all investments, since they increase a man's value and productiveness.

As regards the rich, is the opposite advice any better justified — the advice given them by Montesquieu and so many others, to spend freely? If the duty of spending is imposed upon the rich, whose duty is it to save? Would it not be a monstrous thing to throw it upon the poor?

The social utility of saving lies in the formation, by the accumulation of private savings, of a mass of available capital on which new enterprises can draw according to their needs. If France has been enabled honourably to retain her rank as an industrial power, alongside of countries that are superior to her in population, in activity, and in equipment, it is due above all to her power of saving.

Since saving is useful to the country, it is therefore a duty, but only for those who can perform it without leaving any legitimate want unsatisfied. It is they who are, or should be, the stewards or treasurers of society.

The rich man who saves, therefore, should be praised and not blamed. Even if instead of using his money productively he *hoards* it, in the narrowest sense of the word — though there is little fear of that nowadays — he will still be doing no harm to anyone. What, in fact, are those coins that he buries in the ground or locks up in his safe? Each of them, as we know, is to be looked upon as a ticket that gives its owner the right to withdraw a certain portion from the sum total of existing wealth (see p. 238). Now the man who saves is merely declaring that he gives up this right for the time being. Very well; he can do as he pleases; he is hurting nobody; the share that he might have consumed will be consumed by others, and there is an end of it.[1]

---

[1] Those who hoarded gold or bank-notes during the war were constantly being branded by the newspapers as evil-doers. As far as gold is concerned, it is true that it would have been better to send it to the Bank to help strengthen its reserve or to facilitate gold payments abroad. And it is true also that the hoarders of notes would

It is only from the moral standpoint that we are right in condemning avarice, because it makes the love of riches take a grossly
materialist form, and especially because the miser generally divests
himself of all his social functions and lives a selfish life. But from
the purely economic standpoint, Harpagon[1] is an entirely inoffensive
character.

There is only one case in which hoarding might cause some injury
to society. This is when it is applied to objects that are not capable
of being preserved, and may therefore result in a real destruction of
wealth — as in the case of the miser in Florian's fable, who hoarded
apples until they were rotten:

> "And when one went completely bad,
> He ate it, though his heart was sad!"

And yet, it is said, if the rich were to begin to save all their income,
if in a fit of penitence they were to force themselves to live on bread
and water, what would become of industry and commerce?

In this case, no doubt, the production of articles intended for the
consumption of the rich would cease through lack of demand; but
the production of necessary commodities for the consumption of the
people in general would continue. And as this production would
thenceforth provide the only outlet for all the investments of the
rich, it would receive a powerful stimulus on this account. It is
probable therefore that such commodities would become more
abundant and that their price would fall.

II. THE CONDITIONS OF SAVING

Saving in the shape of hoarding is known and practised even by
animals — or at least by some of them — and notably by the ant.
Apart from work and an occasional rough attempt at division of
labour, this is the only economic act which is common to animals
and men and which can therefore be described as "natural" in the
fullest sense. And even in the vegetable world saving is a very
frequent phenomenon, in the form of reserves accumulated to meet
the needs of the future.

Yet it must not be thought that saving accomplishes itself spontaneously. On the contrary, it requires for its accomplishment a set
of conditions that are hard indeed to fulfil.

have done better to exchange them for war loan. Yet by hoarding these notes they
were doing their country a very great service in withdrawing the excess of paper money
from circulation and preventing it from increasing the demand for goods and aggravating the rise of prices.

[1] [The miser who plays the title-rôle in Moliére's comedy, *L'Avare*.]

(1) In the first place, labour must be sufficiently productive to leave a *surplus beyond the necessaries of life*, for if it is unwise to sacrifice future wants to present well-being, it would be madness, on the other hand, to sacrifice the present to the future.

Saving should only be effected, therefore, on consumption which is not necessary to the needs of physical and mental life — in other words, on luxury wants: so that, however paradoxical it may sound to couple these two words together, saving itself may be said to be a luxury which is only obtainable and commendable in wealthy societies and among those who are rich.[1]

For this reason also it cannot be laid down as a general principle that saving necessarily involves privation or abstinence. This *ex parte* notion was inspired, consciously or unconsciously, by the desire to furnish an argument for the payment of interest on capital, which was then regarded as the reward for a long fast. That is no doubt true of the saving of the poor: for them it is a very painful and even perilous operation, for it involves the amputation of an essential want. We have just said that in this case it is not to be commended. But for the man who has a quantity of surplus wealth at his disposal, saving ceases to be a meritorious sacrifice, and may even become a necessity. For after all, every man's power to consume is limited, even if he were another Gargantua.[2] There is a limit to our needs and even to our desires, and nature has marked it out herself in the form of satiety (see p. 35).

(2) In the second place, a subjective condition on the part of the man who saves is a certain amount of foresight — that particular faculty that consists in feeling a future want as if it were present. The man who wishes to save puts two wants in the scales — a *present* want that he must refuse to satisfy, as, for instance, the hunger that afflicts him now, and a *future* want that he would like to make sure of satisfying, such as the desire to have food for his old age. On the one hand he is restrained by the thought of the more or less considerable sacrifice that he must impose upon himself, but he is impelled on the other hand by the more or less considerable advantage that he expects from the saving. His will oscillates between these two opposing forces, and the one that proves itself most powerful will determine

---

[1] In wealthy countries, saving seems to fluctuate between 10% and 20% of the total income. Thus the annual saving in France is estimated at some 160 to 200 million pounds out of a total income of 1200 to 1400 millions.

[Sir Robert Giffen estimated the annual savings of the English also at 200 millions, or about 13% of their total income.]

[2] [A man of insatiable appetites, the hero of Rabelais' book of that name.]

him in one direction or the other[1]. It should be observed that the
present want is a reality, of which we are physically conscious: the
future want is a pure abstraction, felt only by the imagination. It
needs such habits of mind and moral dispositions, therefore, as have
familiarized us with abstract images, and these imply an advanced
stage of civilization.

Our occupations, especially in modern societies, and our education
compel us to concern ourselves continually with the future. Whether
we are learned men seeking to penetrate the secrets of the future,
politicians taking thought for the morrow, business men immersed
in speculation, or simple traders concerned with monthly bills and
the yearly stock-taking, we are all unconsciously familiarized to a
greater or less extent with this unknown quantity, and take it into
account. But that involves a mental effort of which the savage is
incapable, for he is conscious only of the want that he actually feels,
and, in Montesquieu's famous phrase, cuts down the tree to get the
fruit. The effort is a difficult one even for those of our fellow-
countrymen whose social condition and habits of mind resemble those
of primitive man, and who live, like him, from day to day. Savages,
children, paupers, vagrants are all alike and for the same reason improvident.

(3) Thirdly, there is required, as an objective condition in the
thing saved, a physical attribute: *the power of being preserved.* That
quality, in a state of nature, is somewhat rare. There are not many
objects whose consumption can be postponed without inconvenience
and without involving deterioration or even total loss. Things often
perish as quickly when they are put aside and not used as when they
are made use of. Furniture and textiles decay; linen becomes worn
and discoloured in the linen chest; iron grows rusty; food-stuffs go
bad or are eaten by insects; wine itself, though at first it improves,
eventually perishes. Even wheat requires great care if it is to be kept
for several years, although it is one of the kinds of wealth that keep
best, and certainly owes its important position to this fact.

Owing to the want of this "keeping" property, saving was restricted
in practice to a very narrow field before men discovered the use of
money, or at any rate of the precious metals as accumulators of value.
Only then was saving really created, with its potentiality for all the
marvellous developments it has undergone in later times. Gold and
silver, as we have seen, are almost the only unchangeable substances.
So whoever wishes to save, instead of trying to preserve perishable

---

[1] We have already described a similar psychological conflict in connexion with
labour (see p. 96). See also, in connexion with interest, p. 412.

objects, exchanges them for money, puts this in a safe place, and after as long a time as he likes, he or his great-grandchildren will merely have to exchange it again into any form of wealth that they choose. When some treasure is discovered to-day that has lain buried for hundreds of years, what the lucky discoverer benefits by is consumption that has been *deferred* for all that period of time.

And since credit instruments were invented, saving has found in them a more marvellous instrument even than money. Here is a man with £50 in his possession in any form you please: he might consume it, but he decides not to use his right of consumption at present, and he exchanges it for a kind of draft on society at large to the amount of £50. After any length of time he or his descendants will have the right to draw from the mass of wealth then in existence, not indeed the actual wealth that they had relinquished, and which has long since been consumed by others, but its equivalent.

(4) Lastly, there must be *instruments* or institutions for effecting and facilitating saving, even if it be only a granary to keep corn in, a cellar for wine, or a money-box for money. These institutions will make the subject of the next section.

III. INSTITUTIONS FOR FACILITATING SAVING

In all civilized countries there exist institutions of various and ingenious kinds intended to facilitate saving.

(1) The best known of these are *savings banks* in the proper sense of the term. They are establishments that are designed to facilitate saving by undertaking the care of the sums saved. They render the depositor the service of keeping his savings safe from robbers — and even more perhaps from himself.

Indeed, the best way to safeguard savings is to take them out of their owner's hands, so as to prevent his yielding too easily to the temptation to spend them. The money-box, so well known to children, with a small slit for the insertion of the coins, is an ingenious application of this idea. The box has, in fact, to be broken in order to regain possession of the money, and though this is not a difficult matter, this slight obstacle is regarded as sufficient to give time for reflexion and for the child to overcome the temptation.[1]

The savings bank is only an improved money-box. The small sums deposited in it remain, of course, at the disposal of the depositor:

---

[1] This method is still in use in some countries. Thus ever since 1906 the Paris Savings Bank, to encourage saving, has lent to every depositor of ten francs (8s.) a little money-box that can only be opened by the officials of the Savings Bank. Several thousands of them have already been asked for.

but they are no longer in his hands or in his pocket, and certain formalities are always required before he can recover them, which take rather longer than the breaking of a money-box.

Moreover, the savings bank is a money-box in which the money multiplies. For, to encourage saving, these banks pay a small interest to the depositor. This interest should only be regarded, however, as a kind of premium or reward — a stimulus to saving — and it should not be too high. The function of a savings bank, in fact, is not to serve as an institution for investing money.[1] Its business is to enable people to put money aside and even to build up a little capital. But when this capital has been formed, if the depositors wish to invest it — that is to say, to make a profitable use of it — they have merely to withdraw it: the rôle of the savings bank is ended, and it rests with other institutions such as we have already studied in dealing with banks and credit establishments, to take charge of it.[2]

(2) *Mutual provident societies* consist of persons who pay a monthly contribution towards the formation of capital; after a certain time, say twenty years, they divide amongst themselves the capital thus accumulated, or else, more usually, merely the income that has accrued.

How is it that men manage to save more when they combine than they can do in isolation? First, because the rule of the monthly contribution makes saving a habit and an obligation. Secondly, because a society can make better use than an individual of the remarkable power of compound interest. Lastly, because in the majority of these societies the survivors benefit by the contributions of those who have died, which is really a method of exploiting another man's death, or at least of speculating on it: it is very much the same as what used to be called the *tontine* system. When these three causes operate together with cumulative effect, the results in the matter of the fruitfulness of saving are surprising.

(3) Popular banks, or *mutual credit societies*, although they are actually banks of deposit and discount, making loans to artisans and shopkeepers, act also as savings banks: they have even been described as "perfected savings banks." Such in particular is the char-

---

[1] For this reason the amount of the deposits allowed to each depositor is very wisely limited.

[2] Savings banks were at one time private institutions or municipal foundations, as they still are in most cases. But in most countries nowadays there is a State savings bank, with branches at every post office.

[We omit the rest of this footnote, which deals with the organization of French savings banks.]

acter of the German popular banks of the Schulze Delitzsch type (see my *Political Economy*.)

(4) *Consumers' co-operative societies* also act as instruments of saving by doing away with that privation or abstinence which makes saving so painful and which yet seems inherent in it. They have managed to solve this apparently insoluble problem and to create what has been admirably described as "automatic saving," by means of a plan as simple as it is ingenious, which should be added to the advantages already enumerated (p. 363). Goods purchased wholesale are sold by the society to its members at retail prices, and the profit on each member's purchases is carried to his account, either to be paid back to him at the end of the year or to be kept on deposit in his name.

If, therefore, a working class family makes all its purchases, say to the value of £50, at a co-operative store, and if the store makes a profit of 10%, the family will find at the end of the year that it has saved £5, and *the saving has cost it nothing* — what I mean is that the family has not been obliged to reduce its consumption in any way whatever: it has even had goods of the best quality; it has not paid any more for them; and yet it has saved — in fact the more it has bought the more it has saved!

(5) *Insurance* may be regarded as a method of saving. Here the saving takes the form of a small *premium* paid by each insured person. The virtues of this method must not be exaggerated, however. Unlike saving, which implies an increase of wealth, insurance merely prevents impoverishment, and that only for the individual, for it is clear that it cannot prevent the destruction of wealth. The house that takes fire is burned down; the ship that founders is lost; the head of the family dies; therefore, *for society* the loss is definite and permanent, but *for the individual* this loss may be reduced to an insignificant sacrifice and thus rendered harmless by insurance.

IV. INVESTMENT

A better place for this section might seem to be in that part of political economy which treats of production, for does not investing money mean withdrawing it from consumption to make use of it in some productive undertaking?

Yes, so far as the investor is concerned; but it is important to notice that money invested is consumed just the same. Instead of employing his money in satisfying his present or future wants, the capitalist hands it to others for them to consume it reproductively. Of course he does so only from self-interest, but from the social standpoint his action is none the less very beneficial.   As John Stuart Mill said in a suggestive phrase: "A person does good to labourers, not by what he consumes on himself, but solely by what he does not so consume."[1]

It is obvious that all investment means some consumption, either unproductive or reproductive.   What can the borrower do with the borrowed money — whether it be the State, a company, or a private individual — except spend it?   The money would certainly not be borrowed merely to be shut up in a safe.

Yet the strong prejudice that we have already noticed as existing against those who hoard, exists also against those who invest.   It is thought that the man who locks up his securities in his portfolio is really hoarding them — that is to say, is withdrawing money from circulation.   People do not see that this money is spent just as much and just as quickly in this case as if it were spent by the capitalist himself.   It is true that money spent directly is generally spent on the spot and for the benefit of a man's immediate neighbours, whereas money that is invested may travel round the world, setting workmen to work in other lands and under other skies — Chinese labourers, perhaps, building railways in Asia, or Kaffirs toiling in the gold mines of the Transvaal.   In a word, investment may become a form of absenteeism of capital, and then arises the great question of investments abroad, which provokes such keen controversy (see my *Political Economy*).

At one time there was hardly any other way of investing money than buying land or lending the money on mortgage.   Investment in any other form was difficult and well nigh impossible, for want of *means of investment*.   At a time when loans at interest were forbidden, or at any rate could only be made in a roundabout fashion; when the chief borrowers — the great joint-stock companies and the modern governments — were not yet in existence; when even houses were scarcely ever let, but each man owned his own — no one could know how to invest his money, and there was nothing for it but to hoard it. Such is still the case to-day in Eastern lands, because there the same two causes are in operation which used to put obstacles in the way of investment here — namely, the prohibition of interest as usurious, and, above all, the fear of robbery.[2]

---

[1] [*Principles of Political Economy*, Book I, Chapter V, § 9.]

[2] Lord Cromer related in a report from Egypt in 1907 how a village sheik who had bought a piece of land for £25,000, came back half an hour after signing the agreement, followed by a string of mules bearing on their backs this sum of money, which he had dug up from his garden.

Nowadays this obstacle has been removed. Our age offers to would-be investors a thousand openings that were unknown to our fathers. In 1815 there were only *five* securities quoted on the Paris stock exchange; in 1869 there were 402; to-day there are more than 1200, not counting the hundreds of others that are quoted in the provinces or on foreign stock exchanges.

Hence arises the extraordinary multiplication of small capitalists. Even where the earth is most completely subdivided it does not admit of so much subdivision as the investment of capital does. To take French government stock alone, it was estimated before the war that there were more than two million holders of this stock. What must the number be now, when the amount of stock has increased sixfold?

It may be thought, perhaps, that these investments are too attractive, for they make it too easy to adopt the manner of life of the *rentier*. If people had fewer opportunities of investing their money they would be obliged, or at any rate encouraged, to employ it themselves, by becoming manufacturers, merchants, or farmers.

A second cause is generally pointed out in explanation of the ease and multiplicity of investments at the present day: this is *security*. But this is more questionable, for if it is true that the capitalist lender is no longer exposed to the rude perils of private or public brigandage as he was in former days, owing to legislative progress and increased refinement of manners, yet it may be said, on the other hand, that risks have increased in proportion as capital is employed at a greater distance, the borrower is more unknown, and the business itself is more hazardous. In the matter of security the investments that our fathers made in their neighbours' land, guaranteed by a good mortgage, cannot certainly be compared with a modern investment in, say, the manufacture of cigarettes or liquid air, and that, too, in countries which the capitalist would often find it very hard to locate upon the map. Nor is there any reason to affirm that respect for engagements, whether private or public, is more sacred now than it used to be; and in the case of agreements with foreign nations, the failure of international law to ensure their observance is becoming increasingly common.

But if it is not true that there is more security now for the *rentier* in the matter of revolution, war, or even fiscal attacks, yet it is true that he enjoys a measure of *independence* hitherto unknown, on account of the mobility and almost ubiquity of invested capital, the facilities for drawing an income anywhere, and the speed with which capital can be realized in case of need. This is why investments in land have been abandoned in favour of "portfolio" investments.[1]

[1] This has become less true since the war, for investment in land has come into favour again with capitalists who are fearful of a fall in the value of money and think it safer to turn their money into land — or even into unproductive forms of wealth, such as works of art or precious stones.

CHAPTER III — POPULATION

I. THE LAWS OF MALTHUS

Questions relating to population form a science distinct from political economy, called *demography*. Yet this science touches political economy at so many points, and all the great classical laws of political economy, such as the laws of rent and wages, are so closely connected with the laws of population, that the latter can hardly be refused a place in a course on economic science. This place may be assigned to it in any department of political economy — in production, in distribution, or in consumption — at the author's pleasure.

All questions relating to population resolve themselves ultimately into this one: Will the earth suffice to feed its inhabitants?

Every man on entering the world brings with him a mouth. He brings two arms as well, to be sure, but the mouth begins to function at once, whereas the arms have to wait some fifteen or twenty years. Therefore, in the natural order of things, consumption far outstrips production. Nor is this all, for, as we have seen, economists are afraid that production — at any rate of food — will be limited in the future by the law of diminishing return (see pp.69–72). Hence arises the question we have just asked.

These fears were admirably expressed rather more than a century ago by the English economist, Malthus. He declared, in a formula that has become extremely famous, that *population has always tended to increase in a geometrical progression, whereas the means of subsistence can only increase in an arithmetical progression.* He expressed the increase of population as a geometrical progression whose common ratio is 2 — that is to say, whose terms go on doubling, — and the increase of subsistence as the simplest kind of arithmetical progression, whose common difference is 1, so that the series is merely that of all the whole numbers. He thus obtained the following series:

Progress of population: 1: 2: 4: 8: 16: 32: 64: 128: 256....
Progress of production: 1: 2: 3: 4: 5: 6: 7: 8: 9....

Malthus estimated the average time between two consecutive terms of the series at 25 years. The result is, therefore, that after 200 years the population, if allowed free play, would be to the means of subsistence in the ratio of 256 to 9; after three centuries it would be as 4096 to 13; and after some thousands of years the difference would be infinitely great.

But since it is impossible, in actual fact, for the number of persons to exceed the amount of food necessary to support them, it follows that at each stage of this double series the term in the top line is forcibly kept down or limited by the one in the bottom line — which means that all the surplus population is eliminated by want of food.

It should be observed that Malthus was not giving utterance to these fears for a more or less distant future: according to him, this formidable pressure of population is being exerted now, at every moment, as it was in the past. And the purpose of his book is to prove that the balance has only been maintained by a kind of periodical thinning-out of the human race by means of war, epidemics, famine, poverty, prostitution, and other dreadful scourges, which he regards, however, from this new standpoint, as really providential laws.

At the same time, he said, the outlook for the future might be less gloomy if men had the wisdom to substitute *preventive* obstacles for *repressive* ones, by voluntarily setting a limit to the increase of population. With this object Malthus counselled them not to marry until they were in a position to maintain their children. He called this moral restraint — "moral," in the sense that he did not admit of recourse to illicit unions or prostitution as a means of mitigating this prolonged period of celibacy.

A century has elapsed since the publication of this celebrated doctrine,[1] and it seems at first sight as if experience has completely given the lie to both these famous progressions.

So far, indeed, as the progress of food production is concerned, we see everywhere a greater increase of wealth than of population, both in new countries like the United States and in old ones like France. Before the war the markets were crowded with industrial and agricultural products, to such a degree that the various States erected customs barriers to protect themselves against what they called the flood of foreign goods, so that the problem of Malthus was reversed and the question was, how to find sufficient outlets for production.

As regards the too rapid increase of population, this seems to have been still more strikingly contradicted by experience. For it is the decrease of the birth rate that is rapid, not only in France but in all countries which are following the same path, so that it has become a source of anxiety to all who care for their country's future. We are concerned to-day with the opposite problem: what is to be done to restore the falling birth rate?

[1] [*An Essay on the Principle of Population,* first published anonymously in 1798; second edition, considerably altered, 1803; by the Rev. T. R. Malthus (1766–1834).]

Yet it by no means follows from these facts, as it is continually declared, that the laws of Malthus are wrong. Which of the two is wrong? Is it the one that expresses the growth of population as a geometrical progression? This might rather be accused of being a mere truism. It is obvious that reproduction, by its very definition, means multiplication, and that, if left to itself, it would infinitely exceed the possibilities of agricultural and even industrial production. And facts confirm this instead of contradicting it. Europe just before the war had reached a total of 460 million inhabitants, and had seen her population treble itself in the course of a hundred years; and despite the enormous diminution in the birth rate her population was continuing to increase at the rate of five or six millions a year, which would suffice to double it in 60 years — say 900 million inhabitants in the year 1980, and 1800 millions in the year 2040!

Is it the second law, then, that is wrong — the one that expresses the increase in the food supply? But this might rather be accused of optimism, for this rate of progress is beyond the bounds of possibility. If we look at that branch of production which Malthus and Ricardo had specially in view — the production of bread — it looks as if it were already approaching its highest limit. In fact, the white population of the world, which is the bread-eating population, and which in Malthus' time, just over a century ago, was not more than 200 millions, is today in excess of 650 millions: it has therefore more than trebled itself, while during the same period the production of wheat has been hardly more than doubled. No doubt there still remain vast areas suitable for the cultivation of wheat, and moreover, the yield of lands already cultivated may still be largely increased in new countries and even in old ones, like France. But it does not look as if either of these modes of increase could keep pace with the growth of the white population, notwithstanding the universal fall in the birth rate. And what would it be like if the birth rate had remained at its old level? It is true that "man shall not live by bread alone," and that he even eats less and less of it and substitutes a hundred other kinds of food as production grows more varied, so that if the limit is soon reached for each kind of food considered separately, it looks as if it could be made continually to recede by adding new dishes to our bill of fare. But even with these substitutions the limit cannot recede indefinitely, for all known and imaginable foods are made of the same materials — a small number of elementary substances which exist only in a limited quantity.

II. THE FALLING BIRTH RATE — CAUSES
AND REMEDIES

We have no right, then, to say that Malthus' laws are wrong, for they will be eternally true. The mistake lies in believing that reproduction is necessarily bound up with the sex instinct, when it depends in reality upon quite different causes, and in not seeing that the causes which used to encourage reproduction have all grown weaker at the same time.

(1) First there are the *economic* causes. In former times children added to the family income by their labour from a very early age, and for a long time thereafter while they remained living at home. Nowadays, all profitable employment of children is prohibited by education acts and factory legislation. Moreover, children are now in a hurry to leave home as soon as they are able to earn their own living. The middle classes have to educate and find professions for their children, which is an expensive matter. So the result is that for everyone, workers and middle classes alike, it is a very bad business to have children.

(2) Then there are *social* and *moral* causes. In former times there was a desire to perpetuate one's family, to increase the power of one's city or country, to establish the worship of one's ancestor, to create immortal souls, or at least to hand on the torch of life that one had received. To-day the family is scattered, not only by the abandonment of traditions, but especially by professional needs; patriotism glories in quality more than in number; the commands of the churches, which condemn neo-malthusian practices, are scarcely any longer obeyed.

The general increase of comfort itself acts as a check to the birth rate. This is proved by the fact that the birth rate is lower among the rich than among the poor. It is quite understandable, indeed, that in the case of the rich the reproductive instinct should be checked by the competition of a multitude of luxury wants, whereas among the poor it is almost the sole desire, apart from the desire for food. It is justifiable to conclude, therefore, that births will be restricted in each class in proportion as it reaches a condition of comfort, and in each nation as its well-being advances. And this conclusion is fully borne out by facts; for precisely in proportion as wages increase, do the working classes begin, in their turn, to become neo-malthusian. The law is verified in the case of nations as well: the countries that have the highest birth rates are the Balkan countries and the semi-Asiatic parts of Europe.[1]

(3) Lastly we came to the *political* causes. The development of democracy operates in the same direction, for, other things being equal, the birth rate appears to decline more rapidly in the most completely democratic countries. The United States and Australia are the countries in which the birth rate is the next lowest to that of France. An attempt has been made to explain this by the possibilities of advancement that are held out to each individual by such a régime but which would be hindered by the cost of a family: this is what Dumont called by the picturesque name of *the law of capillarity*. The fact can be explained more clearly by saying that the democratic system creates a set of conditions unfavourable to the formation of large families, both by its virtues and by its defects — by the spread of education and comfort, by the increase of officialism and feminism, and by the growth of the proletariat (a word which means etymologically "the class that produces children").

We may therefore conclude that the human race to-day is more than secured against excessive multiplication: on the contrary, we are seeking nowadays to raise the birth rate.

Why should we do so? say the malthusians. Why wish to strive against a favourable and unexpected current that is carrying the nations away from the abyss into which they were being dragged?

If the decline in the birth rate were the same in all countries, or at any rate in all European countries, there would indeed be no economic, political, or even military reason for anxiety about the situation, for the balance of power would remain unchanged: the problem would only arise from the point of view of the destiny of the human race. But such is not the case: the birth rate in one country may be double what it is in another,[2] and these differences give rise to increasing inequalities in density of population. The consequences of this may be formidable. That is why not only in France, which is the most threatened country, but also in the most prolific countries which are

[1] That is why Paul Leroy-Beaulieu taught that the birth rate *varies in inverse proportion to the degree of civilization*, meaning by "civilization" "the development of well-being, of education, and of new and democratic ideas." But this is too sweeping a generalization, for there are countries no less advanced than France in general education and well-being, where yet the birth rate is fairly high (the Scandinavian countries, Germany, Holland, etc.).

[2] The birth rate is lower in France than in any other known country — 19 per 1000, whereas in other countries it varies between 25 and 35 per 1000. But the decline in the birth rate is universal, and even more rapid in several countries than in France.

afraid of losing their lead, means are being sought after to stimulate the growth of population or at least to remove the obstacles that hinder that growth.

The remedies proposed are innumerable: premiums upon births; the payment of extra salaries to officials and of increased wages to workers in proportion to the number of their children; the reduction of the cost of living by the abolition of protective duties; increased housing facilities; reform of the succession laws; simplification of marriage formalities; taxes on bachelors; exemptions from military service or, conversely, its greater stringency. But of all these remedies there is hardly one that is likely to be effective except the first — high premiums for each child after the second: this might perhaps be sufficient to reconcile the individual with the national interest, which are here in conflict with each other. For there is no doubt that if a child were a source of income instead of an expense, he would generally be welcome.

What will be the effects of the war in the matter of population? So long as it lasted it caused a tremendous decline in the birth rate in all the belligerent countries and even in neutral ones. Since it ended, on the other hand, there has been a decided rise, even in France. But will it last? Statistics of former wars certainly do not justify such an expectation, whatever may be said to the contrary. Supposing, on the other hand, that all the factors that operate in the direction of restriction are intensified, then the upsetting of the balance of the sexes and the consequent enormous increase in the number of widows and women condemned to celibacy; the development of feminine professionalism by the entry of women into all kinds of work, even those which were thought before the war to be barred to them; the incredible rise in the cost of living and in taxation, resulting probably in an increased amount of emigration; not forgetting the spread of venereal diseases — it is to be feared that all these causes, operating cumulatively in the direction of lowering the birth rate, will weigh far more heavily in the balance than the patriotic desire to fill the places of the dead, and that consequently the decline in the birth rate, which was so marked before the war, will continue even more rapidly after it. It is true that if it is more or less the same in all the ex-belligerent countries, the balance in Europe will no doubt not be very much altered; but it may be altered, and to a serious extent, to the advantage of the new countries of America and the old races of Asia.

APPENDIX

I. METALLIC MONEY IN THE UNITED STATES

In 1792 our statesmen, following the example of the countries of Europe, adopted the double standard of gold and silver. At Hamilton's instance the legal ratio was fifteen grains of silver for one grain of gold. Soon afterward, silver cheapened so that 15.61 grains were required in the bullion market to purchase one grain of gold. As a result, gold went out of circulation, and the country was thrown practically upon a silver basis. Gold, which had begun to grow scarce in 1810, entirely disappeared in 1817. In 1822 Mr. Raguet, an economist of the period, wrote to the *National Gazette* that "although the coinage of gold continues to be large ($1,319,030 in 1820), not a gold coin is anywhere to be seen in circulation." The facilities of the Mint were simply used by merchants to certify the weight and fineness of gold for export.

In view of these facts, various projects for a change were brought forward in Congress, and in 1834 the so-called Gold Bill provided for a ratio of 1 to 15.60; but when it came up for discussion an amendment was moved making the ratio 1 to 16, and this amendment was adopted without a division. Then another amendment was offered making the ratio 1 to 15.625, and was supported on the ground that it was the true market ratio, and that it would keep gold and silver in concurrent circulation. The adoption of the ratio 1 to 16, it was contended, would drive silver out of circulation. Yet this ratio was finally adopted, making the United States a gold-standard nation in practice, although the double standard was retained in theory. Since 1837, when other changes were made, the weights of the coins and their legal ratio have remained unchanged. The silver dollar was given 371.25 grains of pure metal, and the gold eagle 232.2 grains; this is a legal ratio of 15.988 to 1. This ratio of practically 16 to 1 — almost as celebrated a formula in economics as the formula for π in geometry — then overvalued gold so decidedly that silver coins began to disappear from circulation. In 1850 the silver dollar was worth $1.02 in gold and had entirely disappeared from use. In the early fifties the discovery of gold in California and in Australia caused the annual output of gold to increase fourfold.[1] Silver, on the other hand, became still more scarce in consequence of the development of trade in India, which absorbed vast quantities of this metal. The result was that gold continued to cheapen so that Congress in 1853 had to reduce the silver content of the fractional silver coins in order to prevent them from being melted and sold for bullion. The legislation of 1834 and 1837 had thrown the United States upon a gold basis, for while the legal ratio was 16 to 1, the commercial ratio until 1873 was about $15\frac{1}{3}$ to 1.

In 1870 Congress again began to consider the question of revising the coinage laws. The silver dollar had then been out of circulation for more than a generation, and was worth $1.027 in gold. By the act of 1873 the silver dollar was dropped from the list of authorized coins, and the gold dollar was definitely named as the unit of value.

At about the same time, however, another great change took place in the production of precious metals. The output of gold decreased with the gradual exhaustion of the gold mines of Australia and California. The discovery of the "bonanza" silver mines in the West greatly increased the production of silver; the world's annual output of this metal was increased by about half. Then Germany adopted the gold standard, demonetized her silver money, and cast upon the market the silver thalers which she no longer wanted. Once again the relative value of the two metals was changed, but this time in the opposite direction. In the market for precious metals one could purchase, for a pound of gold, not merely 15 or 16 pounds of silver, but 17, then 18, then 19, and in 1876 nearly 21 pounds of silver. In other words, silver had lost a fourth of its value compared with gold. It was henceforth evident that every ingot of silver which constituted a silver coin underwent a proportionate depreciation. In 1876 the gold value of 371.25 grains of fine silver (the amount contained in a silver dollar) was only 89 cents.

Now people saw that if the coinage of the silver dollar had not been stopped by the law of 1873, the cheapened dollar might have come back into circulation and driven out gold. There arose a demand for the free and unlimited coinage of the silver dollar, and, yielding to the subsequent agitation, Congress in 1878 passed the Bland-Allison Act. This act provided that the United States should purchase monthly not more than $4,000,000 and not less

[1] The average annual world's production of gold from 1841 to 1850 was valued at about $37,000,000; from 1851 to 1860 the annual output averaged nearly $135,000,000.

than $2,000,000 worth of silver bullion, to be coined into silver dollars of the previously customary weight. These silver dollars were made full legal tender. Under this Act the Treasury always purchased the minimum amount, and placed $378,166,793 in circulation between 1878 and 1890. Yet this law failed to raise the value of silver, for in 1889 the silver dollar was worth only 72 cents. In 1890 the Bland-Allison Act was repealed and the Sherman Act passed. The new law required the Secretary of the Treasury to purchase monthly 4,500,000 ounces of fine silver bullion at the market price, which was not to exceed $1 for 371.25 grains. Treasury notes were issued in payments for this metal; they were to be redeemable on demand in coin, and to be a legal tender in payment of all debts, except where otherwise expressly stipulated in the contract. But even these increased purchases of silver failed to sustain its price, which, after a brief rise, fell to 60 cents in 1893. Between 1890 and 1893 the net exports of gold exceeded $150,000,000, in spite of the fact that our exports of merchandise greatly exceeded imports. The banks began to hoard gold and to pay their obligations in paper or in silver. The government was compelled to pay out large quantities of gold, while its revenues were composed chiefly of paper and silver. In 1893 the Sherman Act was repealed.

In 1893 the United States suffered a severe panic, followed by a depression and a loss of gold reserves through export abroad, so that President Cleveland was obliged to make a contract with a private syndicate for the purpose of restoring the gold necessary to the Treasury for the redemption of currency. In the presidential campaign of 1896 the silver question was the principal issue, the democratic party, led by W. J. Bryan, advocating the free coinage of silver, on the ground chiefly that the decline in commodity prices caused by the enhancement of the purchasing power of gold had increased the burden of debtors to the benefit of creditors, with the consequent impoverishment of the masses of the population and the enrichment of the few who were at that time derisively known as "bloated bond holders." The republican party, which had endorsed the gold standard, won a decisive victory at the polls, however, and in 1900 the Gold Standard Act was passed, by the terms of which the dollar consisting of 25.8 grains of gold nine-tenths fine was made the standard unit of value, and the Secretary of the Treasury was charged with the duty of maintaining all forms of money issued or coined by the United States at parity with the gold dollar. No legislation fundamentally affecting the gold standard has been passed since 1900, though the Pittman Act, enacted during the World War in 1918, provided for the melting of a large amount of silver in the vaults of the Treasury and its sale to Great Britain at one dollar (and costs) an ounce. This act was a war measure passed for the purpose of supplying England with silver with which to maintain the redemption of rupees in India. The Pittman Act provided for the repurchase of the silver thus disposed of whenever the silver could be obtained at one dollar an ounce. Accordingly in 1920, when the price of silver, which had been for a time so high as to make it profitable to melt silver dollars, had declined to below one dollar an ounce, the Treasury began to purchase silver and by the summer of 1923 the supply of silver in the vaults of the Treasury was restored to the original amount.

II. BANKING DEVELOPMENT IN THE UNITED STATES

Early American Banks. At the present time the issuing of notes is not regarded as a necessary function of banks, nor is it the chief part of their business. But in the early history of our country the main business of a bank was to issue "circulating notes." In New England the commonest conception of a private bank was that of a company or partnership formed to supply circulating notes as a medium of exchange in addition to the "bills of credit" issued by the colonial governments. In the charters of the earliest banks, such as the Bank of North America, there is no mention of circulating notes, since the right to issue them existed without legislative authorization. It was generally believed, moreover, that if these circulating notes were based on landed security, current redemption would not be necessary. According to this view, no capital was needed to start a bank, but merely confidence.

The first bank in the modern sense of the term appears to have been the Bank of North America, conceived by Robert Morris, the financier of the Revolution, and chartered by the United States government and the state of Pennsylvania in 1781. It was closely followed by the Bank of Massachusetts, chartered in 1784, and the Bank of New York, which began business in the same year. The last-named institution owes its foundation to Alexander Hamilton, who counselled the New York merchants against the "land bank" which they were about to found, and who drew up articles for a "money bank" in its stead.

The two United States Banks. Hamilton was also responsible for the conception of the first Bank of the United States, chartered by Congress in 1791. The capital was $10,000,000, of which $8,000,000 was open to public subscription, and the remainder subscribed by the United States government. It was provided that payment should be made one-fourth in specie and three-fourths in government obligations bearing 6 per cent interest. This provision naturally strengthened the credit of the government by creating a demand for its obligations. At the same time the government pledged itself to grant no other charter for a bank during the continuance of this one, which was limited to twenty years. The bank could not be indebted for a greater amount than its capital stock, over and above the amount of its deposits; that is, the deposits were not to be counted as liabilities, in estimating its right to contract debts. This meant substantially that the notes issued by the bank might be equal in amount to the capital stock. The notes of the bank were made receivable for all public dues so long as they were redeemable in gold and silver coin.

The consensus of opinion with regard to this bank is strongly in its favor. It served as a regulator of the currency and maintained a high standard of commercial honor. Unfortunately, the renewal of the charter was made a political issue. The weakness of the Federalist party, which had been favorable to the bank, and the opposition of the state banks, who wished to get rid of a superior rival, resulted in a refusal to renew the bank's charter.

The state banks now held the field alone. Almost all of them were of the joint-stock type, based on the principle of limited liability.[1] In 1812, a year after the charter of the Bank of the United States had expired, the second war with Great Britain began. A short time afterward nearly all the banks of the country except those of New England suspended specie payments. This was followed by an enormous increase of issues, so that the outstanding notes, which had been estimated at $20,000,000 in 1811, rose to somewhere between $62,000,000 and $70,000,000 in 1813, and to somewhere between $99,000,000 and $110,000,000 in 1815. The circulating paper was of every degree of value, down to utter worthlessness.[2] These flagrant evils of the financial system called for reform, and as a result the second Bank of the United States was chartered in 1816, on a similar plan and with the same general objects as the first bank of the same name. The capital was $35,000,000, of which the government subscribed one-fifth. During its early history the bank was shamefully mismanaged, but it was later restored to a sounder position. The notes of this bank, too, which were required to be paid in specie, were receivable for all

---

[1] Concerning these banks Mr. J. R. McCulloch wrote as follows: "Had a committee of clever men been selected to devise means by which the public might be tempted to engage in all manner of absurd projects, and be most easily duped and swindled, we do not know that they could have hit upon anything half so likely to effect their object as the existing American banking system. It has no redeeming quality about it, but is, from beginning to end, a compound of quackery and imposture."

[2] Professor W. G. Sumner, in his *History of American Currency*, tells of one bank in Massachusetts with a nominal capital of $1,000,000. Only $19,141.46 was ever paid in; and of this the directors subsequently withdrew their own subscriptions, leaving $3,081.11. One man bought out eleven directors for $1300 and then loaned himself $760,265. When the bank failed, it had $86.46 in specie, whereas the notes outstanding were estimated at $580,000.

public dues. It brought about the resumption of specie payments and put an end to the disorders and fluctuations which had previously prevailed.

This bank, like its predecessor of the same name, was drawn into politics when the question of a renewal of its charter arose during Jackson's first administration. The recharter of the bank was made the main political issue of 1832, and Jackson's opponents, who defended the bank, were defeated. Thus, in 1836, the charter expired and Congress refused to grant a new one.

The State Banks up to 1863. There seems no doubt that the evils of this period were due chiefly to vices of banking. The facility of local issue, without the reality or scarcely the pretence of redemption, made the banks reckless as to the character of the enterprises to which they gave assistance; while the money thus put into circulation enhanced prices and still further stimulated both speculative investments and speculative trading. The retribution came in the panics of 1837 and 1839, during which the United States lost the deposits it had placed in the private banks, and in the long and dreary prostration of industry which followed.[1]

The first improvement in the state-bank system originated in Massachusetts, where the Suffolk Bank in Boston, chartered as an ordinary bank of issue and deposit in 1818, offered to redeem country bank notes at par if the issuing banks would provide funds for that purpose and would also make permanent deposits in the Suffolk Bank (which regarded the use of these deposits as a compensation for its services). At first only a few of the country banks acceded to this proposal, whereupon the Suffolk Bank made it a point to send home for redemption all the notes of the non-assenting banks which it could find. Eventually all the country banks were forced into the arrangement, because it was found that under the new system their credit was so much improved that their notes acquired circulation in all parts of the United States and Canada.[2]

Two important banking experiments were tried in New York by the legislature of that state, known respectively as the *safety-fund* system and the *free-bank* or *bond-deposit* system, both of which found imitators. The first of these, introduced by the law of 1829, was practically a mutual insurance of the banks for the protection of their creditors. It provided that every bank chartered under it should pay into a "bank fund" one-half of one per cent of its capital each year, until the fund should be equal to three per cent of

[1] See Francis Walker, *Political Economy*, page 441.

[2] See Horace White, *Money and Banking*, second edition, page 325.

its capital stock. This fund was to be applied solely to the payment of the debts of insolvent banks after their assets were exhausted. Whenever the fund should be reduced, the banks were called upon for fresh contributions at the same rate as the original ones. The law also provided for the appointment of three commissioners to examine all the banks three times a year, or oftener if required to do so. Any three banks might call for a special examination of any bank in the system.

It is probable that the safety-fund would have proved ample indemnity to the holders of bank notes if it had not unfortunately been applied to the payment of other debts than those due for circulation; but the numerous bank failures of 1840-1842 exhausted the fund. Many banks, moreover, fraudulently issued more notes than the law allowed. This was made possible by the absence of anything like a proper system of public registration or supervision of issues. By the time that the system had been brought nearer perfection by amendments of various kinds, the charters of the "safety banks" expired, and the national bank system was established.

The second New York experiment, — more radical than the first, — was begun in 1838. Before that year no one could get a banking charter in the state of New York without a special act of the legislature, and no one could invest money in a new bank without the consent of the bank commissioners of the state. The right to start a bank was made a part of the spoils of the triumphant political party, and this corrupt state of affairs led to a popular reaction and to the passage of a law enabling any person or association of persons to engage in the business of banking and to circulate notes on condition that these notes be secured by deposits of such public stocks, bonds, mortgages, etc., as were approved by the state comptroller. Later the law was amended so that only the stocks of the United States and of the state of New York should be accepted as security for the note issues of the free banks.[1]

In several of the states which followed the example of New York, the free-bank and bond-deposit system proved a failure because bad securities were not infrequently taken for the note issues. Be-

---

[1] The National banking system was to some extent modelled upon this New York bond-deposit system.

Besides the banks of Massachusetts and New York, to which we have had occasion to refer because of the experiments which they tried, important progress was made by the banks of some other states. A Louisiana law of 1842 required the banks of that state to keep a cash reserve in a definite proportion to their deposits and circulation. This appears to be the first law of its kind in America.

fore these states had time to perfect their system, the Civil War broke out, and the National Bank Act soon afterward superseded all other systems.

The National Banking System. The financial necessities of the Civil War made it desirable to place large government loans upon the market. Accordingly, Mr. Chase, Secretary of the Treasury, advocated a system of "national banks" whose note issues should be secured by an abundant deposit, at the Treasury department, of United States bonds. In order that these banks should have a practical monopoly of the right of issue, the state banks were to be obliged to pay a virtually prohibitive tax of 10 per cent on their notes. These suggestions were not all carried out until 1865, and although their adoption came too late to be of any help in the financial difficulties of the war, they resulted in placing the bank currency of the country on a more secure and convenient basis. Before this time, the innumerable state banks, under special charters, and practically subject to no real regulation or supervision, had put into circulation the most heterogeneous bank money conceivable. Part of this money was subject to a discount of as much as 25 per cent when offered for acceptance far away from the place of issue, or when issued by a bank whose name was not familiar. This unwillingness to accept some of the bank money is perfectly comprehensible when we recall that banks were constantly failing, that there was an abundance of notes issued by banks which had no real existence save in the minds of the rogues who manufactured the notes, and that professional sharpers made it a business to alter or counterfeit bank notes.[1] Under the new system all these evils disappeared, and now a national bank note issued in one state will circulate all over the Union as readily as at home.

The principal features of the national banking system, as at present organized, are as follows: —

There is a bureau of the Treasury Department, the chief officer of which is the Comptroller of the Currency, having the duty of

---

[1] Those who were in the habit of receiving bank notes found it necessary to study carefully the "Counterfeit Detectors" and other publications whose purpose it was to inform their readers what notes to accept and what notes to refuse. One of these detectors (Bicknall's *Counterfeit Detector and Bank Note List* of January 1, 1839) contained the names of 54 banks which had failed; of 20 fictitious banks, the pretended notes of which were in circulation; of 43 other banks for the notes of which there was no sale; of 254 banks the notes of which had been altered or counterfeited; and enumerated 1395 descriptions of counterfeited or altered notes then supposed to be in circulation, of denominations from $1 to $500. In 1859, Nicholas' *Bank Note Reporter* had 5400 separate descriptions of counterfeit, altered, and spurious notes. (See Horace White, *Money and Banking*, second edition, page 352.)

taking charge of all matters relating to the "national banks." A national bank is organized in much the same way as any other corporation, by any number of persons not less than five. Upon application to the Comptroller the corporation will be granted or refused a charter, according to the decision of the Comptroller. When granted, the charter continues for ninety-nine years. Each bank is required to report its condition not less than three times a year.

The minimum amount of capital which a national bank must have depends on the population of the place in which it is located, but can never be less than $25,000, and in cities having a population of 50,000 it must be at least $200,000.[1]   Each national bank, beside being allowed to carry on the ordinary business of a bank (making loans, discounting notes, buying and selling exchange) is allowed to issue "national bank notes" for circulation as money of the United States.   The stockholders are liable for the debts of the bank up to the par value of their stock in addition to the funds invested in that stock.

National banks have authority to issue bank notes, which must be secured by United States government bonds of a par value equal to the volume of notes issued.   The bonds must be deposited with the Treasury of the United States, and in addition the banks must maintain a redemption fund amounting to 5 per cent of the notes in circulation.   The notes pay a tax of between one-half and one per cent, depending somewhat on the rate of interest borne by the bonds deposited as collateral.

The national bank notes are not legal tender, although the government will receive them for all taxes except duties on imports.   Each national bank is required to receive the notes of every other bank at par value, and to redeem its own notes on demand in legal-tender money.   If it cannot do this, the Comptroller will sell the bank's bonds and thus obtain money to redeem them.

Each bank was required to keep a reserve of lawful money.   In the so-called "reserve cities" designated by Congress[2] the amount was 25 per cent of their deposits.   Banks outside these cities needed to keep a reserve of only 15 per cent of their deposits, and were

---

[1] The minimum capital required for the organization of a national bank was reduced from $100,000 to $25,000 in 1900, and this reduction resulted in a rapid increase of the number of banks, especially in agricultural districts, and in the general growth of the banking habit among the people of the United States.

[2] The Federal Reserve Act passed in 1913 provides that designations of cities as reserve cities and changes in the existing cities so classed shall be made by the Federal Reserve Board.

permitted, moreover, to deposit 60 per cent of their reserves with an approved depositary in the reserve city. The banks in the reserve city in turn could keep one-half of their reserves in a bank in one of the central reserve cities, *i.e.*, in New York, Chicago, and St. Louis.[1] The banks in these three cities were required to keep a 25 per cent reserve in actual cash.

It is evident that one great merit of this system was the unification of banking in all the states and territories. In fact, all the national bank notes of similar denomination, — the smallest denomination is $5, — present a similar appearance, being manufactured by the United States government on a uniform plan. Inasmuch, furthermore, as the government bonds have always commanded a premium, there has never been any doubt as to the soundness of the currency issued under this system. "With regard to its volume," says President Hadley, "there have been many complaints. For some years the banks were anxious to increase their circulation, and a limitation on the total amount which they were allowed to keep outstanding was considered a hardship. After 1880, on the other hand, the price of the United States bonds became so high as to render the maintenance of the circulation unprofitable, and a large amount was surrendered, reducing the total volume of the bank-note issues to a figure less than half of that which the law would have allowed."[2] At the present time, however, the circulation of national bank notes is at its highest figure, largely because the higher price level caused by the war has increased the demand for all classes of currency.

Defects of the National Banking System. While the National Bank Act had served to make our banking system more uniform and more dependable, experience soon demonstrated that there were many undesirable features in the credit and currency conditions as they developed under the Act. Among these defects the most important were the concentration of a large part of bank reserves in the financial centers, on the one hand, and the scattered condition of the remainder in the vaults of innumerable small banks, on the other. At times when the demand for credit and currency was heavy, as is the case every autumn when crops begin to move to market, the banks throughout the country would jealously guard their vault

[1] St. Louis was a central reserve city until July 1, 1922, when the Federal Reserve Board changed its status to that of a reserve ctiy.

[2] Hadley, *Economics*, page 256. On September 1, 1902, there were 4269 national banks, with a total capital of $673,763,767, and the amount of national bank notes in circulation was about $350,000,000.

reserves for fear of not being able to meet their customers' requirements and would begin to withdraw from their city correspondents that portion of the reserves which was kept there in accordance with the provisions of the law. The city banks, which were obliged to keep 25 per cent of their deposits as reserves, generally had the bulk of the funds held for country banks invested in demand loans secured by stock exchange collateral. When large numbers of these country correspondents attempted to withdraw parts of their deposits, the city bank would call their loans, cause the borrowers to sell the collateral in order to repay the loans, and would thus bring about a price decline in the stock market. This decline would necessitate the calling of more loans as the collateral became inadequate, and the movement would thus feed upon itself and grow like an avalanche, increasing all the time in scope and severity. At times, when the banks of the country were in a strong position, the critical autumn season would pass with only a flurry in the market, but at a time following a boom period, when loans at the banks were at a high level, when much speculation was in evidence, and when many new enterprises were being launched, the defects of our banking system would result in a financial panic, such as the one which occurred in 1907. Not only were the reserve provisions of the Bank Act faulty, but the national bank note currency was highly inelastic, since it was secured by government obligations, of which the supply was limited and which were hard to obtain at short notice. Consequently, when the country needed currency to pay the harvest hands, there would be a money stringency which in years of particularly heavy demand would contribute to the development of a panic.

The Panic of 1907. In 1907 conditions were like those described in the preceding paragraph. The country was prosperous, many new enterprises were under way, a large volume of securities was being floated, and the banks were called upon to finance an exceptionally heavy volume of production and trade. Out of this prosperous condition, which had given rise to much speculation and to the launching of many unsound undertakings, arose the panic of 1907. One of the most important New York trust companies was obliged to close its doors, many other banks were forced to suspend payment, cash money was so scarce that it commanded a premium of 2 per cent, and the country was facing disaster, which was averted only through the coöperation of the bankers, who issued clearing house certificates to take the place of money and joined together in a pool to prevent a further spread of the panic, and through the intervention of the United States Treasury, which deposited $35,000,000 of its funds with the New York banks in order to save the situation. The panic subsided, but many banks were able to pay off their depositors only very gradually, and a year and a half elapsed before the financial machinery of the country had fully regained its normal condition. In the meantime many persons had suffered severe losses, the panic had been followed by business depression, and it became apparent that a thorough overhauling of our banking system was urgent.

The National Monetary Commission. As a temporary measure of relief, Congress passed a law in 1908, which expired by limitation on June 30, 1914, but was later extended for another year. This law, known as the Aldrich-Vreeland Emergency Currency Act, authorized the formation of currency associations throughout the country and empowered them to issue emergency currency subject to a heavy tax and secured by their joint assets. The same law provided for the creation of a National Monetary Commission, consisting of Senators and Representatives, to study the problem presented by our banking system and to propose a permanent remedy for its defects. The Commission, under the chairmanship of Senator Nelson W. Aldrich of Rhode Island, employed many experts, including some of the best financial economists of the United States, to investigate conditions and banking methods here and abroad, and collected material which was published in twenty-three volumes containing about 26,000 pages. At the same time the Commission proposed for the reorganization of the American banking system a plan which was widely discussed and was in many respects the basis of the law that a few years later established the Federal Reserve System.

The Federal Reserve Act. — Woodrow Wilson, who was elected President of the United States in 1912, considered the reorganization of the banking system as the most pressing duty of his administration and called an extra session of Congress early in 1913 to pass a law for this purpose. After the holding of public hearings and the study of all existing proposals, including that sponsored by the National Monetary Commission, Congress passed the Federal Reserve Act, which was signed by the President on December 23, 1913. This Act provided for the division of the country into not less than eight and not more than twelve Federal Reserve Districts.[1] In

[1] The provisions of the Federal Reserve Act as here summarized include all the amendments passed on or before March 4, 1923. Twelve districts were actually established, with headquarters in Boston, New York, Philadelphia, Cleveland, Rich-

each district there was to be established a Federal Reserve Bank, with a capital of not less than $4,000,000 to be subscribed by the member banks.[1] All the national banks must be members of the Federal Reserve System, and state banks and trust companies may join if the amount of their capital and the character of their business meet certain definite requirements. Each member bank must subscribe as its share of the stock of the Federal Reserve Bank of its district 6 per cent of its capital and surplus — one-half to be paid in. Member banks must keep on deposit with the reserve banks without interest their entire lawful reserves against deposits. The Act reduced the legal reserve requirement on demand deposits from 15, 20, and 25 per cent to 7, 10, and 13 per cent for banks in country districts, in reserve cities, and in central reserve cities, respectively, and fixed the minimum reserves on time deposits at 3 per cent for all classes of banks. The reserve banks are administered by boards of nine directors, three of whom are appointed by the Government and six elected by the member banks. Of these six, three must represent the banks, and three the industrial, commercial, or agricultural interests of the district. Of the elected directors, one-third are selected by large banks, one-third by medium size banks, and one-third by small banks.

The reserve banks have authority to rediscount for their members notes, drafts, and bills of exchange arising out of actual commercial, agricultural, or industrial transactions, but are prohibited from supplying funds for investment purposes, for speculation, or for dealing in securities, except those of the United States government. The banks may also issue Federal Reserve notes in denominations of $5 and more, the notes to be obtained from the Federal Reserve Agent, who is one of the Government directors and acts as chairman of the board of the reserve bank. The notes, which are not legal tender, though they are obligations of the United States government, must be secured by collateral consisting of gold or eligible paper, the collateral to be deposited with the Federal Reserve Agent. The reserve banks must maintain a reserve of 35 per cent against their deposits and of 40 per cent against their notes. A 5 per cent redemption fund must also be maintained with the Treasurer of the United States against Federal reserve notes in circulation. In addition to the discounting of bills for member banks,

mond, Atlanta, Chicago, St. Louis, Minneapolis, Kansas City, Dallas, and San Francisco.

[1] In case a sufficient amount was not subscribed by the members, the Government was to provide the balance, but this contingency did not arise.

the reserve banks have authority to purchase and sell in the open market cable transfers, bankers' acceptances, bills of exchange, and Government securities. The maturities of paper discounted by Federal reserve banks must not exceed 90 days, except in the case of agricultural or livestock paper, which may have a maturity up to nine months. Similar maturities are fixed for bills purchased in the open market. The rates of discount to be charged by the reserve bank are fixed by the boards of directors, subject to the approval of the Federal Reserve Board.

This board consists of the Secretary of the Treasury, the Comptroller of the Currency, and six members appointed by the President, no two of whom may be from the same Federal Reserve District. The members of the board, whose salary is $12,000 per annum, hold office for ten years, must devote their entire time to their duties as members, and must hold no bank stock. The board has general supervision over the operations of the reserve banks, has authority to pass upon the discount rates charged by these banks, must define the general character of paper that is eligible for discount or purchase under the Act, must pass upon all appointments made by the reserve banks and upon salaries paid to their officers and employees, and has a special responsibility for the supervision and control of Federal Reserve Notes issued by the Federal Reserve Agent to the reserve banks and for the collateral back of these Federal Reserve Notes.

The Federal Reserve System in Operation. The principal features of the Federal Reserve System may be summarized as follows:

1. There are twelve autonomous regional banks, owned by the member banks, and managed by mixed governmental and private boards subject to the supervision of the Federal Reserve Board, a governmental body located in Washington. Each regional bank is expected to conduct its business out of its own resources, but in case of strain it may, with the permission of the Federal Reserve Board, obtain accommodation from another reserve bank, so that the principle of regional self-sufficiency is modified by an emergency proviso for mutual assistance.

2. Centralized reserves of all the member banks. This pooling of reserves resulting in the creation of additional lending power to be used for the benefit of all the member banks having need of credit in excess of their own lending power. This reserve bank credit, arising as it does out of coöperation between the banks, must be used with consideration for the claims of all member banks, must be utilized only to supply funds for current production and

trade, and must not be used for speculation or for investment purposes. The authority to discount paper secured by Government obligations, of which an enormous volume was created during the War, has, however, tended to weaken the direct connection between reserve bank credit and current production and trade.

3. Elastic currency, in the form of Federal Reserve Notes issued against commercial paper and backed by a 40 per cent reserve in gold.

4. Intra- and interdistrict clearings. The reserve banks act as clearing houses between nearly all the banks, member and nonmember, within their districts, and interdistrict claims are settled through book entries in the gold settlement fund held in custody of the Federal Reserve Board. By this arrangement the system has greatly reduced the cost of settlements between different parts of the country, as well as the time required for such settlements.

5. Encouragement of foreign trade through authority granted to member banks to create acceptances, to Federal Reserve Banks to purchase or discount them, and through the permission to member banks to establish branches abroad. The Act also provides for the establishment of foreign trade financing corporations, known as Edge law banks from the author of the amendment to the Federal Reserve Act which authorized them. Member banks are permitted to invest a certain proportion of their capital in stock of these foreign trade corporations.

6. Fiscal agency functions. The reserve banks act as fiscal agents of the Government in receiving tax payments, in redeeming United States currency and other obligations, in cashing coupons, etc. The Government continues to keep the bulk of its funds with commercial banks, but transfers these funds to the reserve banks when it requires them for disbursement. The reserve banks have superseded the United States subtreasuries, which have been abolished.

Of the total banks in the United States, numbering about 30,000, about 9,900 are members of the Federal Reserve System, and these members represent about 70 per cent of the country's banking resources.

As the result of the Federal Reserve Act two new kinds of currency were added to the money in circulation: Federal Reserve Notes, which have already been described, and Federal Reserve Bank Notes, which may be issued in smaller denominations, are secured by Government obligations, and were intended gradually to supplant the national bank notes. The following table shows the different kinds of money in circulation in the United States on August 1, 1923:

	Money in circulation	
	Amount	Per capita
Gold coin and bullion...............	$403,217,779	$3.62
Gold certificates...................	411,937,589	3.70
Standard silver dollars.............	56,999,291	.51
Silver certificates.................	368,928,481	3.31
Treasury Notes of 1890............	1,458,123	.01
Subsidiary silver..................	247,869,821	2.23
United States Notes...............	300,010,892	2.69
Federal Reserve Notes.............	2,160,449,086	19.40
Federal Reserve Bank Notes........	18,900,554	.17
National Bank Notes..............	725,987,506	6.52
Total.....................	4,695,769,125	42.16

From the beginning of their operation, the Federal Reserve Banks, which opened their doors for business on November 16, 1914, were affected by conditions arising out of the World War. Prior to the entry of the United States into the War, the effect of the European struggle was chiefly felt through the purchase of war supplies by the belligerents, which resulted in a movement of gold to the United States, an abundance of funds in this country, with a consequent lack of demand for credit at the reserve banks. During our participation in the War, the energies of the reserve system were devoted mainly to assisting the Government in meeting its fiscal needs. The reserve banks at that time discounted freely and at preferential rates paper secured by Government obligations, and thus enabled the member banks to finance purchases of Liberty bonds by their customers on the deferred payment plan. By strengthening the financial power of the United States government during the War, the reserve system was a real factor in the final outcome of the struggle. During the period of post-war expansion, which occurred in 1919 and 1920, as a reaction against wartime controls, the reserve banks exerted their power to curb inflation, but were only partially successful in this effort. When, however, the reaction came in the spring of 1920, when prices, which had increased $2\frac{1}{2}$ fold over the pre-war level, began to fall rapidly, and general liquidation set in, the Federal Reserve Banks were able to protect the financial structure from panic and collapse; they acted as buffers, delayed and moderated the shock, and gave business an opportunity to adjust itself more gradually to the changed conditions.

Nevertheless, the reserve banks were severely criticized by those who, not understanding the situation, accused the system of having brought about the collapse which it had helped to moderate, and particularly of having caused severe losses to the farmers, whose products had declined in price more radically than most other commodities. The system was thus made to bear the odium of developments which were entirely outside of its control, were world-wide in scope, and whose effects in the United States the reserve banks had been instrumental in alleviating.

During the past two years conditions have been more stable in this country and the reserve system has begun to assume its normal peace-time functions. In their adjustment to stable conditions the reserve banks and the Federal Reserve Board are called upon to develop new standards of credit administration in order to establish themselves as an integral part of the country's credit structure. In this work they are handicapped by the disappearance of an effective international gold standard and the abnormal movement of gold to the United States. This has the effect of depriving the reserve position of the banks, which has been the customary index of credit conditions, of its significance as an indicator of domestic develop-ments, and makes it necessary for the reserve banks to turn to other indices, such as the volume of production and trade, the price and money rate level, and the volume of bank credit in use, for guidance in the administration of credit. In recent years considerable prog-ress in this direction has been made by the reserve banks and the Federal Reserve Board, but much work still remains to be done. It is safe to say, however, that the advantages of the Federal Reserve System, which is finding many imitators throughout the world, are so great that not even its severest critics would be willing to return to conditions that prevailed before its establishment.

Agricultural Credit. — Credit for the use of agriculture may be divided into three distinct classes in accordance with the needs that it is intended to serve. (1) Long-term credit, required for the purchase of land and permanent improvements. This class of credit is in the United States provided in part by retired farmers and other private investors, and in part by mortgage and insurance companies, as well as to some extent by state banks, trust conpanies, and national banks, which by the Federal Reserve Act were granted authority to make loans on real estate under certain restrictions. In addition, the Government has created a special system of Federal Land Banks which confine their activities, under Government supervision, to the granting of mortgage credit to farmers; and the

Government also issues charters to private joint-stock land banks serving the same general purpose. The farmer's long-term credit needs are, therefore, fairly well taken care of.

(2) Short-term credit needed for the purpose of financing the production and marketing of livestock. For this purpose the entire commercial banking machinery is available, and the Agricultural Credit Act of 1923 has amended the Federal Reserve Act so as to enable the reserve banks to discount agricultural and livestock paper with a maturity up to nine months. This act also liberalizes the definition of agricultural paper so as to encourage the formation of coöperative marketing organizations, which are expected to improve the terms to farmers for credit to supply their current needs. While the cost of credit to farmers is still relatively high, any solvent farmer can now obtain all the credit he needs for the production and orderly marketing of his crops.

(3) Intermediate credit for periods from 9 months to 3 years, required by farmers for the raising of cattle and horses, and for the purchase of equipment, has been until recently the least satisfactorily provided for. But by the terms of the Agricultural Credits Act of 1923, which was passed after a joint Congressional committee had made a careful study of the farmer's credit needs, machinery was set up to make available to farmers credit to finance their longer term current operations. The Act provides for the establishment of Federal intermediate credit banks with authority to discount for banks serving agricultural communities paper having a maturity up to three years. The intermediate banks in turn may rediscount this paper, when it is within 9 months of maturity, with the Federal Reserve Bank. The Government provided the capital of the intermediate banks, which are operated in connection with the Federal farm loan banks. The Government also issues charters to private national agricultural credit corporations organized to supply the farmer's intermediate credit requirements.

It is too early to judge definitely to what extent the new banks will fill the gap in the facilities for the accommodation of farmers that existed prior to 1923 and which was brought forcibly to the attention of the country during the great decline in agricultural prices in 1920 and 1921, but the new institutions have begun operations, and it is believed that the farmer's credit needs are now taken care of in as satisfactory a manner as those of persons engaged in other industries.

Other Recent Banking Developments. Among other recent banking developments should be mentioned the guaranty of bank deposits, which has been adopted in several Middle Western and Western states, and the growth of branch and chain banking.

Guaranteeing bank deposits was tried in earlier days in several states, as has been already mentioned. Oklahoma, by passing a law in 1907, was the first state in recent years to adopt a system of deposit guarantees. This law provided for an assessment of 1 per cent on the capital of all state banks, to be used for the paying of depositors of banks that had failed. It was later amended by making the assessment bear a relationship to the volume of deposits rather than to capital. The system suffered hardships from poor management and many heavy bank failures, and the law was finally repealed after fifteen years of operation. Laws providing for the guarantee of bank deposits have been adopted in other states, including Kansas, Nebraska, Texas, North and South Dakota, Mississippi, and Washington. The principal difficulty against which the system has to contend is that it tends to encourage speculation on the part of bankers and to penalize conservative bank managers for the benefit of less careful members of the fraternity. The system is in the experimental stage, and its ultimate fate is still undetermined. It attempts to apply the principle of coöperative insurance to banking, and it may be that ultimately a properly worked out guarantee law conscientiously administered and safeguarded against abuse will represent a step in the direction of providing greater safety for those who entrust their deposits to the custody of banks.

In most industrial countries of the world bank consolidation has proceeded so far that most of the banking power is in the hands of a small number of powerful banks. This is true of England, France, Germany, and even of Canada. In the United States, on the other hand, there are over 30,000 banks, which are, in spite of occasional interlocking directorates and overlapping interests, in the main independent business units. This system of independent banking is in fact often considered as characteristically American and democratic. Nevertheless, in recent years there has been a considerable development of branch banking, so that it has been estimated that in July, 1923, nearly one-fourth of the total volume of bank loans in 29 states where branch banking is permitted by law was made by banks having branches. Among the Eastern states branch banking is most widespread in New York and Rhode Island, in the South it is most important in Louisiana, and in the West in California. National banks are not permitted to have branches, except such as have been acquired prior to the issuance of the national bank charter or through consolidation with a state bank having branches. It has been held, however, that branches in the same city as the home office, established purely for the accommodation of customers in the paying in and withdrawal of deposits are not strictly branches, but are merely distant "tellers' windows," and as such are permissible. As a matter of fact, the great majority of branches in this country are of this character. In California, however, with its great diversity of agricultural production, there have developed several powerful groups of banks having branches scattered all over the state and used largely for the purpose of distributing the risk of banking among many industries and of eliminating seasonal peaks and troughs of credit demand by having banks in many localities where the seasons of the heaviest demand for credit come at different times of the year.

Chain banking has developed in part as the result of the legal difficulties in the way of branch banking, and ranges in character all the way from a common directorship on the boards of two or more banks to an outright ownership or control of chains of banks by the same interests. It is difficult because of its very nature to determine the extent of chain banking, but it is well known that some widespread chains of banks are in operation in several states.

There is a great deal of hostility on the part of many bankers to the growth of bank consolidations and the centralization of the control over bank funds. In fact, this is one of the issues upon which the banking world at the present time is most sharply divided. The main ground of opposition is that the managers of banks with branches will not have the same community of interest with their customers as have the directors and officers of locally controlled banks. The fear of competition from powerful organized banks is also a factor in the hostility of the smaller banks to the spread of branch banking. On the other hand, the advocates of branch banking stress the increased safety arising from the distribution of risk, the economies of large scale operation, and the possibility of reducing interest rates through the practice of these economies. The contest is not unlike that which has raged in the industrial field between individual producers and large corporate enterprises. In banking, centralization has begun considerably later than in industry in this country, and it is as yet impossible to determine whether branch banking is destined ultimately to have a growth in the United States similar to that in Canada, or whether the American independent banking system will withstand the tendency toward centralization and consolidation and will remain the prevailing plan of banking in the United States.

Growth of Banking Habit.   The twentieth century has seen a
rapid development of the banking habit in the United States, and
the custom of using checks, in the place of cash, in the settlement
of money obligations has become widespread.   It is estimated that
at the present time eleven-twelfths of all payments are made by
check, and checks are, therefore, a far more important circulating
medium in the United States than is currency or specie.   This
development has enhanced the importance of bank deposits and of
bank credit as a factor in our national economy and has made the
administration of our banking machinery a matter of the greatest
consequence to the welfare of the people.

III. THE TARIFF POLICY OF THE UNITED STATES

In the United States there has been from the beginning a strong movement for the protection of home industries through the imposition of tariff duties on imported commodities. This attitude, voiced by Alexander Hamilton in his celebrated Report on Manufactures, arose largely from the fact that the United States entered upon its development at a time when the countries of Europe had had centuries in which to organize their industries and to foster their foreign trade. It was for the purpose of protecting America's infant industries as well as to raise revenue that the first tariff measure was passed by Congress on July 4, 1789, the same year during which the Constitution of the United States was framed. The duties imposed by this Act were not high, averaging about 5 per cent *ad valorem* and reaching 15 per cent only on certain articles of luxury, such as high grade carriages. The revenue produced by this Act was not sufficient for the needs of the Government, however, and between 1789 and 1812 thirteen tariff laws were enacted by Congress for the purpose primarily of raising funds with which to meet the expenses of the Government, but also in order to protect American industries.

It is clear from the reports made by committees of Congress and the debates upon the tariff bills that the necessity of protecting American industries against foreign competition was generally recognized by the lawmakers. During the period of the embargo on foreign trade imposed in 1807 and during the War of 1812 American industry was protected more effectively than by a tariff, and manufacturing, especially of textiles, made decided progress in the country. With the return of peace, however, the newly established American mills were obliged to compete once more with European, and especially British factories, and the cotton, woolen, and iron manufacturers turned again to Congress with appeals for additional protection. The Tariff Act passed in 1816 in response to this appeal was of a definitely protective character and imposed duties of 20 per cent on all cotton and woolen goods imported from abroad, and specific duties on salt and iron.

By 1820 it became evident that the Southern states, which raised cotton by slave labor and were not afraid of foreign competition, were in favor of free trade. Furthermore, these states desired to broaden their foreign markets by affording to foreign countries the opportunity to pay for American cotton by exporting manufactured goods to America. The Middle West was in favor of protection for its agricultural products, while New England, from a half-hearted attitude arising from the dual capacity of its people as both foreign traders and manufacturers, gradually developed a strong sentiment in favor of protection. This change of heart was due mainly to the fact that industry rapidly overshadowed the carrying trade in importance for the New England states. The tariffs of 1828 and 1832, therefore, in spite of southern opposition, were more strongly protective than their predecessors.

Between 1832 and 1860 there was considerable vacillation in the tariff policy of the United States, largely as a result of the conflicting interests of the various sections of the country. The tariff during this period shared with slavery the distinction of being the principal issue before the American people and aroused nearly as much animosity and heated debate as the problem of slavery itself. In 1833 a compromise Tariff Act was passed, by the terms of which considerable protective duties were to remain in force for nine years, but were to be reduced after that period. In 1842, however, a new law prevented the promised decline in tariff rates from becoming operative. Between 1846 and 1857 tariff rates were relatively low and were still further reduced in that year, partly because Government revenues at that time exceeded requirements. Throughout this period of changing tariff policy the industries of the United States continued to grow, and by the beginning of the Civil War in 1860 this country had a well developed production of manufactures.

During the Civil War the necessities of the Government for revenue caused the enactment of a series of tariff acts imposing increasingly high duties on imported commodities, especially wool and iron, and with the return of peace there appeared to be no disposition to reduce the war-time tariff rates. In fact, rates were gradually advanced by the Acts of 1867 and 1869. The desire to foster the growth of the iron and steel industry caused the enactment of particularly heavy duties on iron and steel products. During this period the policy developed of allowing compensatory duties to manufacturers when the raw materials for their products were protected by heavy rates, and in this manner a tariff structure affecting commodities in all phases of manufacture was gradually erected. In 1883 a half-hearted attempt to reduce duties was made, but the general effect of the Act passed in that year did not materially alter the character of the existing tariff.   In 1890 a decided step in the direction of further protection was taken by the enactment of the McKinley Tariff Bill, which was more squarely and frankly protective than any of its predecessors and raised the level of duties upon articles competing with domestic production to unprecedented heights.

The tariff was a leading issue in the elections of 1890 and 1892, and in November of the latter year Grover Cleveland was elected to the presidency on a platform favoring a lowering of customs duties. The Tariff of 1894 consequently provided many reductions of rates, the duty on wool being entirely removed, while those on coal and iron represented compromises.   During the following years the country went through a severe depression for which the reduction of duties was in part held responsible, and in 1897, after a defeat of the democratic party, the highly protective Dingley tariff was passed and remained on the statute books for twelve years.

In 1909 the tariff question once more became prominent.   There was much feeling on the subject of large industrial corporations having grown rich upon a tariff policy originally intended to protect infant industries.   The high tariff advocates, on the other hand, maintained that the tariff was necessary to equalize the cost of production here and abroad and to protect the high standard of living of American labor against the competition of the pauper labor of Europe.   The law as finally passed raised the general level of rates, though it removed the duty on hides and left the rates on wool and sugar unchanged.   During the debate on the law much was said about the interests of the ultimate consumer who had to bear the burden of the protection granted to industry, and there was talk of "legitimate" industries, i.e., industries for the growth of which this country is well adapted, as contrasted with industries that could never find solid root in the United States without the sheltering protection of a tariff wall.   The law also created a Tariff Board commissioned to work out and recommend rates of duty based on scientific principles.   Thus the Act of 1909, though it actually raised tariff rates, represented in some ways a departure from a purely protective policy and made a first halting step in in the direction of removing the tariff from politics and placing it on the basis of impartial economic investigation.

With the advent of the democratic party in 1912 it was evident that the tariff would be revised and revised unmistakably downward, and in 1913 this was actually done, the law passed during that year placing sugar and wool on the free list, adding many other articles to this list, and making serious reductions in the duties on almost all manufactures. While this Act did not have much effect on industry, because soon after its enactment the outbreak of the World War prevented the countries of Europe from shipping goods to the United States, yet it was regarded as the most important departure in a half century from the principle of protection.[1] Much sentiment in favor of free trade developed during the debate, though the desire of the representatives of the different regions to maintain the duties on their home products, no matter how much they might be lowered on the products of other parts of the country, prevented a downward revision as radical as might otherwise have been adopted. The tariff, to quote a famous saying, remained "a local issue."

After the War a strong sentiment for protection became apparent, and since the republican party, the traditional sponsor of protection, came into power in 1921, it was inevitable that a tariff law of a distinctly protective character would be enacted, and this was done in 1922. The strengthening of nationalistic feeling engendered by the War, together with the fear that Germany, where the level of prices was extremely low, would dump her products, especially dye stuffs, into the United States, and the demand of agricultural interests for protection of their products were among the principal factors responsible for raising the duties in the Tariff Act of 1922 to the highest level recorded in American tariff history. At the same time this Act contains provisions which have greatly improved the administration of the law, and by bestowing upon the President the power, after investigation by the Tariff Commission, to change rates of duty that have proved to be unsatisfactory, it has made the tariff potentially more flexible. Thus the latest Tariff Act marks a further step in the direction of scientific, rather than political, determination of tariff schedules.

[1] See Taussig, *The Tariff History of the United States*, sixth edition, page 448.

IV. INCOME SURTAXES

NUMBER OF PERSONS PAYING SURTAX AND AMOUNT OF SURTAX
PAID BY INCOME CLASSES

Income Class	Number paying surtax			Amount of surtax		
	1919	1920	1921	1919	1920	1921
$5,000 to $6,000	167,005	177,147	137,191	$806,926	$692,383	$641,560
6,000 to 7,000	109,674	112,444	86,030	2,006,798	2,023,158	1,653,406
7,000 to 8,000	73,719	74,511	58,760	2,777,662	2,886,839	2,309,002
8,000 to 9,000	50,486	51,211	40,156	3,171,449	3,274,111	2,583,540
9,000 to 10,000	37,967	40,129	31,110	3,581,610	3,784,466	2,942,716
10,000 to 11,000	28,499	29,984	23,416	3,693,637	3,872,596	3,025,012
11,000 to 12,000	22,841	24,370	18,743	3,857,490	4,119,372	3,170,251
12,000 to 13,000	18,423	19,388	14,887	3,940,208	4,168,823	3,184,311
13,000 to 14,000	15,248	16,089	12,575	4,017,757	4,244,561	3,267,923
14,000 to 15,000	12,841	13,739	10,393	4,100,174	4,376,737	3,314,781
15,000 to 20,000	42,028	44,531	34,230	20,918,502	22,013,101	17,024,571
20,000 to 25,000	22,605	23,729	18,100	20,879,536	21,872,136	16,731,959
25,000 to 30,000	13,769	14,471	10,848	20,271,767	21,310,372	15,936,763
30,000 to 40,000	15,410	15,808	12,047	38,081,884	38,911,865	29,727,607
40,000 to 50,000	8,298	8,269	6,051	35,875,777	35,641,581	26,097,698
50,000 to 60,000	5,213	4,785	3,431	34,864,546	31,875,512	22,878,025
60,000 to 70,000	3,196	3,006	2,240	30,326,310	28,589,460	21,171,964
70,000 to 80,000	2,237	1,969	1,423	28,644,868	25,269,888	18,321,435
80,000 to 90,000	1,561	1,356	957	26,120,745	22,607,109	15,913,503
90,000 to 100,000	1,113	977	666	23,414,934	20,580,671	13,959,294
100,000 to 150,000	2,983	2,191	1,367	101,303,450	75,636,928	46,061,722
150,000 to 200,000	1,092	590	450	68,081,248	36,137,724	27,625,002
200,000 to 250,000	522	307	205	47,071,736	27,930,180	18,670,116
250,000 to 300,000	250	166	84	30,114,879	20,275,032	10,318,179
300,000 to 400,000	285	169	98	46,209,076	27,875,298	15,998,752
400,000 to 500,000	140	70	64	32,141,569	15,709,136	14,256,917
500,000 to 750,000	129	98	46	41,861,914	31,267,938	15,589,532
750,000 to 1,000,000	60	25	17	29,571,872	12,073,878	8,231,070
1,000,000 to 1,500,000	34	19	12	23,739,007	13,030,056	7,550,836
1,500,000 to 2,000,000	13	3	....	13,506,533	3,046,350	....
2,000,000 to 3,000,000	7	4	3	10,960,546	6,732,213	3,992,977
3,000,000 to 4,000,000	6	3	5	13,037,159	5,792,268	1
4,000,000 to 5,000,000	....	....	....	....	....	....
5,000,000 and over	5	4	1	32,573,734	19,182,025	1
Classes grouped[1]						19,177,260
Total number of all incomes reporting....	5,332,760	7,259,944	6,662,176			
Total surtax reported.				801,525,303	596,803,767	411,327,684

[1] Classes grouped to conceal net income and identity of taxpayer.

INDEX